OXFORD MODERN LANGUAGES AND LITERATURE MONOGRAPHS

Marquard von Lindau and the Challenges of Religious Life in Late Medieval Germany

The Passion, the Eucharist, the Virgin Mary

STEPHEN MOSSMAN

OXFORD
UNIVERSITY PRESS

OXFORD
UNIVERSITY PRESS

Great Clarendon Street, Oxford OX2 6DP

Oxford University Press is a department of the University of Oxford.
It furthers the University's objective of excellence in research, scholarship,
and education by publishing worldwide in

Oxford New York

Auckland Cape Town Dar es Salaam Hong Kong Karachi
Kuala Lumpur Madrid Melbourne Mexico City Nairobi
New Delhi Shanghai Taipei Toronto

With offices in

Argentina Austria Brazil Chile Czech Republic France Greece
Guatemala Hungary Italy Japan Poland Portugal Singapore
South Korea Switzerland Thailand Turkey Ukraine Vietnam

Oxford is a registered trade mark of Oxford University Press
in the UK and in certain other countries

Published in the United States
by Oxford University Press Inc., New York

British Library Cataloguing in Publication Data

Data available

Library of Congress Cataloging in Publication Data

Data available

Typeset by SPI Publisher Services, Pondicherry, India
Printed in Great Britain
on acid-free paper by the
MPG Books Group, Bodmin and King's Lynn

ISBN 978-0-19-957554-1

3 5 7 9 10 8 6 4 2

Preface

This book is a substantially rewritten and expanded version of an Oxford DPhil thesis, originally written during the academic years 2003–7 and revised in 2008. It should be noted that there is no material included in that thesis, a copy of which has been made available for consultation in the Bodleian Library, which is not included in the present publication (with the exception of that which, on careful reflection, proved to be ill-judged). That thesis may thus now be safely ignored.

Some conventions. All German personal names are given in their German form. All other personal names are given either in their local form or in an English form, as modern convention demands. It proves less problematic to fully anglicize certain names, like Matthaeus of Cracow, than to decide which local form to use for a Polish-born, German-speaking, Latin-writing resident of Czech-speaking Bohemia. I use Latin forms only in those cases which are so conventional that the insistence on any other form would introduce an unnecessary novelty: thus Johannes de Caulibus, not James of the Cauli or Giovanni da San Gimignano. Place names are given in local form except in those cases where a markedly different and current English form exists: thus Munich and Prague (not München or Praha), but not Ratisbon or Leghorn (Regensburg and Livorno). In those cases where the difference between English and local forms is trivial, the local form is uniformly preferred: thus Basel and Konstanz (not Basle or Constance). A modern punctuation has been silently interposed on all quotations from manuscripts, incunables, and early printed books. If the punctuation of quotations from modern editions has been altered, the change has been marked in square brackets. Finally, the name 'Marquard von Lindau' has been excised from all footnote references, to avoid the tedium of interminable repetition; the Bibliography includes a conspectus of his works cited in this book. All other works are cited by a short-title system, with full publication details given in the Bibliography.

The genesis of the present book is complex. The idea to work on the vernacular religious literature of late medieval Germany was the product of an undergraduate seminar offered by Professor Rudolf Simek at the Rhein-ische Friedrich-Wilhelms-Universität Bonn during the summer semester of 2000. The idea to work on the history of the Franciscan order was the product of the Oxford History Special Subject on St Francis and St Clare in the autumn term of the same year. This book is as much as anything an attempt to negotiate between two disciplines and two academic cultures; to bind German systematic rigour with the broad perspectives of anglophone scholarship. I have Alexander Murray to thank for his agreement that Marquard von Lindau would make a suitable centrepiece for a research project, and for his sound advice to seek out Professor Nigel Palmer as a potential supervisor, who (then rather stupidly unbeknownst to me) was not only an Oxford academic, but the world expert on Marquard. Without Nigel's constant and unwavering support, advice, and friendship the present book would be much the poorer.

The work for this book was undertaken as a student of Oriel College, Oxford and of the Albert-Ludwigs-Universität, Freiburg, and as a Junior Research Fellow at St John's College, Oxford, my present home. Scholarships from the Arts and Humanities Research Council, Oriel College and the Landesstiftung Baden-Württemberg, and a fellowship at St John's have facilitated its production, as have travel grants to consult manuscript material from the Modern Languages and History Faculties in Oxford, and Oriel and St John's Colleges. The libraries in Freiburg and Oxford have provided excellent research environments. Particular thanks are due to David d'Avray and Annette Volfing, who examined the thesis; earlier drafts of individual chapters have been kindly read by Jeremy Catto, Henrietta Leyser, and Hans-Jochen Schiewer; and Burkhard Hasebrink and Almut Suerbaum have given advice and support well beyond reasonable expectation. An enormous debt of scholarly gratitude is due to Jeffrey Cronheim for his invaluable and hugely generous assistance in elucidating intractable Latin texts as I prepared the translations for publication. The infelicities that will inevitably remain are, of course, my own.

My friends and family should consider themselves collectively thanked for their love, friendship, and support. I would like to name a great many people here; but amongst all my friends an honourable mention is due, on account of their patient endurance of myself and Marquard over very many years, to Undine Brückner, Jeff Cronheim, Steffan Davies, Guy Geltner, Alex Hampton, Nigel Palmer, Caro Schuchert, and Nick Simons; and last, but scarcely least, to Maddy Morgan. This book, as the thesis which preceded it, is dedicated to the memory of T. J. Thorne (1912–2000).

Stephen Mossman

St John's College
Oxford

Contents

Ich was nye also fro, uncz pis ich schreib finito libro! Seyt gedechtig mein, durch Got und seiner pein, di er geliden hat—durch unser missetat. explicit hoc per totum: infunde, da michi potum!

(MS Bodl. 969, fol. 377va)

Introduction

The intellectual history of the fourteenth century is not characterized by a long and venerable historiographical tradition that bears comparison with that, say, of the twelfth or thirteenth centuries. The rather pessimistic evaluations of Johan Huizinga and Étienne Gilson bear only some of the blame; a more general benign neglect bears rather more. The tendency of intellectual histories of the later Middle Ages to leap from the early fourteenth-century figures of Scotus and Ockham to the early fifteenth-century figure of Jean Gerson is of long standing, creating a lacuna that has begun to be redressed only in very recent years. The intellectual history of the German-speaking world in this period was for a long time a terra incognita of particular opacity, and not just to English-language historiography. The last thirty years has seen new, seminal work on individual German intellectuals predominantly of the earlier and mid-fourteenth century, which has begun to uncover the luminaries of the period; names such as Johannes Tauler, Jan van Ruusbroec, and Johannes Hiltalingen von Basel. But the name of Marquard von Lindau does not spring readily to anyone's lips, neither to the historian nor to the literary scholar, and the same is true of many of the other intellectuals whom we shall encounter; men like Matthaeus of Cracow, Engelbert von Admont, and Johannes von Zazenhausen.

In Marquard's own time the situation was very different. Without doubt he was the most productive German Franciscan writer of the Middle Ages. He was also the most widely transmitted: a fair estimate would place the number of extant manuscripts containing his works at around 450, a level of very select competition. He appears to have become active around 1370, and died in 1392. He belonged thus to the generation after the more familiar figures of Tauler, Ruusbroec, and Heinrich Seuse, but before the era of the Observant reforms, and in this period—the final third of the fourteenth century—it is only the much longer-lived Matthaeus of Cracow who offers him any real competition on the German stage. On the European scene, he was an approximate contemporary of John Wyclif and

Catherine of Siena. He was neither as controversial nor as prominent as either of them, but we shall see that it is not beyond (all) reason to mention the more subtle Marquard, in terms of his contribution to the intellectual history of the later Middle Ages, in the same breath. Given that Marquard is quite so unfamiliar, we ought to begin with a comprehensive survey of the historical information on his life, provide an overview of his works, and attempt an initial location of Marquard's impact in the historical *longue durée*, a statement which the successive chapters will serve to elucidate.

Marquard does not appear in the historical record until 1373.[1] He is named in a Strasbourg charter of 3 October that settles a long-standing dispute over the rights and privileges of the mendicant orders, initiated by the secular clergy in 1365.[2] The acquiescence of the secular clerics is witnessed by members of all four principal mendicant orders in Strasbourg, including four Franciscans: by 'Jacobi custodis, Markwardi lectoris, Nicolai dicti Vŏltzsche et Hugonis dicti Kleinherre conventualium ordinis fratrum minorum domorum Argentinensium'[3] ('Jacobus, the *custos*; Marquard, the lector; and Nikolaus Vŏltzsche and Hugo Kleinherre, brethren of the Order of Friars Minor of the Strasbourg house'). Marquard is a sufficiently uncommon name to allow us to assume this lector to be Marquard von Lindau. The 'Jacobus' must be the *custos* of the Alsatian custody within the South German (Strasbourg) province. Nikolaus Vŏltzsche appears as warden of the Strasbourg convent in two charters of 1367,[4] and subsequently as visitor of the numerous Franciscan tertiary houses in the city in 1376.[5]

---

[1]   The following presentation draws on and augments with new material the seminal studies by Bonmann, 'Marquard von Lindau', pp. 315–25, and Gebele, 'Markwart von Lindau', pp. 89–95.

[2]   The document of 21 June 1365 that opened the dispute is edited by Schmidt, *Histoire du chapitre de Saint-Thomas*, pp. 377–9. On the relationship of the secular clergy to the mendicants in Strasbourg during the Middle Ages see Rapp, *Réformes et Réformation*, pp. 92–5, esp. pp. 94–5 on 1365–73; Rüther, *Bettelorden in Stadt und Land*, pp. 258–80, esp. p. 260 on 1365–73, and Turck, *Les Dominicains à Strasbourg*, p. 51.

[3]   Strasbourg, Archives de la Ville, AST HE I 215, printed in Witte and Wolfram (eds.), *Urkundenbuch der Stadt Strassburg*, vol. 5/2, no. 1091 (pp. 827–8). Two identical copies of the same episcopal charter are contained under the shelfmark AST HE I 215. Given the different archival marks on the reverse, they are most likely from two separate archives: probably (to judge from the other charters in the collection) the Dominican and Augustinian convents.

[4]   [1] Witte (ed.), *Urkundenbuch der Stadt Strassburg*, vol. 7, no. 1270 (p. 373); see also Strasbourg, Archives de la Ville, AST 1066, fols. 125ᵛ–126ᵛ; [2] Strasbourg, Archives de la Ville, AST 1066, fol. 369ʳ⁻ᵛ.

[5]   Witte (ed.), *Urkundenbuch der Stadt Strassburg*, vol. 7, no. 1697 (pp. 494–5).

Hugo Kleinherre is named in a letter dating to the period 1359–66, sent from the then Franciscan provincial minister of Southern Germany, Albert von Marbach, to the city council in Strasbourg, responding positively to the council's request that Hugo be allowed to return to the city from his current position as convent lector in Freiburg.[6] In a testament of 1371 in which Hugo is both legatee and executor, he is named as confessor of the Strasbourg convent,[7] and appears subsequently as warden in a charter of 1372.[8] The order of names in such lists is not random, and indicates relative seniority. Marquard is placed here behind the *custos* of Alsatia, but above two friars who had been (and in Hugo's case, probably still was) warden of the Strasbourg convent. As lector at the Strasbourg *studium generale*, Marquard is likely to have been the successor to Hesso von Lampertheim, whom the chronicler Nikolaus Glaßberger records as having been *lector Argentinensis* prior to his appointment as provincial minister on 25 November 1372.[9]

There exists no further direct evidence for Marquard's presence in Strasbourg at this time.[10] There is, however, some indirect evidence. A compilation of extracts from the Sentences of Peter Lombard, *compilate a fratre Marquardo lectore Argentinensi* ('compiled by brother Marquard, lector in Strasbourg') is preserved in a manuscript from the Franciscan

---

[6] Letter edited by Schmitt, 'Documents sur la Province franciscaine', no. 64 (pp. 267–8).

[7] Witte (ed.), *Urkundenbuch der Stadt Strassburg*, vol. 7, no. 1465 (p. 426); testament of Hugo Schaller von Mellisheim, 28 August 1371.

[8] Strasbourg, Archives de la Ville, AST 1066, fols. 362ᵛ–363ʳ.

[9] Nikolaus Glaßberger, *Chronica*, p. 209.

[10] [1] The extant collection of charters from the Franciscan convent in Strasbourg (now in Strasbourg, Archives de la Ville) contains no references to Marquard. My thanks to Bernhard Metz for this information, drawn from his index of this collection. [2] A set of cartularies and account books for the Franciscan properties is extant from the archive of the collegiate church of St Thomas, to which the property of the convent was transferred during the Reformation (Strasbourg, Archives de la Ville, AST 1066–9, 15th-cent. cartularies produced in the Franciscan convent; AST 1070 and 1071, 16th-cent. continuations written after the transfer to St Thomas; and AST 1073–90, 18th-cent. account books). AST 1068, 1069, and 1071 have been seriously damaged by fire and could not be consulted. No reference to Marquard was revealed by a thorough search of the remaining cartularies. References to individual friars are generally rare; it is clear that the convent conducted its temporal business through a series of secular procurators. [3] The 'collection Oberlin' (Paris, Bibliothèque nationale de la France, Ms. lat. 9074–83 and Ms. all. 214–18) comprises an often overlooked set of several hundred medieval charters relating primarily to Alsatian religious institutions, but again reveals no information concerning Marquard; for an outline description of the collection see Hessel, *Elsässische Urkunden*, pp. 64–5.

convent in Regensburg.[11] The completion of one of Marquard's longest Latin works, the *De reparatione hominis*, can be dated on the basis of an internal reference with relative certainty to 1374.[12] The scholastic form of the work and its subject matter point to the kind of scholarly audience associated with a *studium generale*. A stronger argument arises from the particular constellation of very narrowly transmitted texts Marquard used in *De reparatione*: notably the Latin commentaries of Meister Eckhart; the commentary on Matthew by the Spiritual Franciscan Petrus Johannis Olivi, which we shall presently examine; and the Dominican Ramon Martí's *Pugio fidei*, an anti-Jewish tract written in Latin and Hebrew, whose transmission remained almost entirely confined to Spain and is not otherwise attested in the German regions until the seventeenth century.[13] It is hard to conceive of a location other than Strasbourg in the South German province in which Marquard could have gained access to such texts at the same time.[14] It is fair to suppose that Marquard did spend a reasonable period at the Strasbourg convent in the early 1370s.[15]

It is difficult to say anything about Marquard's career prior to 1373, or to establish his approximate date of birth. A friar could enter the order at 14 and would be required to complete a one-year novitiate at his home convent—in Marquard's case, presumably Lindau. A friar then chosen to undertake a programme of advanced study culminating in attendance at a *studium generale* would have taken a two- or three-year course at a *studium artium*, of which there was probably one in each of the six custodies of the South German province.[16] After this, the friar was eligible for a two- or three-year course at a custodial *studium physicae* or *philosophiae*, reading advanced logic, natural and moral philosophy, and metaphysics. Parallel to this level of education were *studia theologiae*; they were often in the same

[11] Now Munich, Bayerische Staatsbibliothek, Clm 26870, 1ʳ–88ᵛ; see Palmer, 'Marquard von Lindau', cols. 122–3.

[12] See May (ed.), *Marquard von Lindau OFM. De reparatione hominis*, pp. 105–8.

[13] See Mossman, 'The Western Understanding', pp. 170–87.

[14] Only four manuscripts survive from the Franciscan convent in Strasbourg (see Krämer, *Handschriftenerbe*, vol. 2, p. 748). It is entirely plausible that Marquard would also have had access to the libraries of other convents in the city, notably that of the Dominicans.

[15] I have discussed the evidence that allows Marquard's relationship to the Knights Hospitaller in Strasbourg to be more precisely defined elsewhere: see Mossman, 'Zu Marquard von Lindau', pp. 247–56. As that argument relies partially on the evidence used here, its conclusions cannot be adduced to support this present argument.

[16] Roest, *A History of Franciscan Education*, pp. 65–9 and 76. Only the South German province appears to have had these unified custodial *studia artium*; other provinces had separate *studia logicalia* and *grammaticalia*.

convents, and so a friar might read courses in both philosophy and theology simultaneously.[17] The friar, by now at least 20 years old, could then be selected by the provincial chapter to attend the lectorate programme at a *studium generale*, after having been examined by four *magistri promotores.* Here he would have heard lecture courses on the Bible and the Sentences, and read canon law and moral philosophy. He would also have learned theological material by heart in recitation lessons, and received training in disputation and sermon production. This programme had been reduced to two years' duration in 1325, though it may have taken three years in some *studia.* Friars were not permitted to enter *studia generalia* if they were over 40, and would normally have been in their mid-twenties on completion of the lectorate programme. They would leave with testimonials on their academic performance and their personal qualities from the convent warden and the *studium* lector. On the basis of this documentation, the provincial chapter would allocate the friar as a convent lector or as lector at a custodial *studium artium.* The next chapter, usually one year later, would evaluate his performance and could then appoint him as lector at a *studium theologiae* or a *studium generale.*[18] We cannot know the precise length of Marquard's career prior to 1373, but he could not have been much less than 30 years old at this point. It is feasible to suggest that he was born around 1340, which would mean that he died in middle age, not much more than 50 years old.

The level of philosophical and theological instruction at *studia generalia* that were not attached to universities (like Strasbourg) was similar to that at those which were (principally Paris, Oxford, and Cambridge). This was particularly true of Germany, where the absence of universities until the end of the fourteenth century enhanced the prestige of the mendicant *studia.* It is telling that Heidelberg university was founded actually inside the Franciscan *studium philosophiae* in 1386.[19] Only rarely did friars in the South German province further their studies at Paris; they were usually sent instead to Bologna, even before the creation of a theology faculty at the university in 1364.[20] It is very hard to find evidence for friars attending these universities for relatively short periods of time, as most would not have matriculated on an official degree programme. It is neither impossible nor especially likely that Marquard would have spent a period outside the province. Albert von Marbach, provincial minister 1359–72, had studied

[17] Ibid. 69–76.
[18] Ibid. 87–97.
[19] Ibid. 28–42.
[20] Courtenay, 'The Franciscan Studia', pp. 88–90.

for three years at Strasbourg and then lectured as *baccalaureus* at Bologna.[21] Albert did send friars from Strasbourg to study at Paris, and there is some evidence that Hesso von Lampertheim may have been among them.[22] Letters produced by Hesso himself, provincial minister 1372–86, sending friars to the *studia generalia* at Erfurt and Bologna survive in a later formulary.[23] As lector in Strasbourg, Marquard would at least have had close associates with experience of educational centres outside his own province.

A charter of 11 April 1377, issued by Marquard himself, records the donation of his silver cross, studded with jewels and pearls, to the Franciscan convent of Lindau and names Marquard as *custos Lacus*.[24] The custody of Lake Constance was one of six in the South German province, and its *custos* was usually resident in Konstanz. The particular importance of the Konstanz convent was the presence there of the centralized archive and administration for the entire South German province, established there in 1265 following the division of Germany into two provinces; at the Reformation it was Konstanz that took over from Strasbourg as the residence of the provincial minister.[25] By then, Marquard was long dead; but he did live through much of a similarly major ecclesiastical crisis, namely the Great Schism. In order to locate him accurately in the political history of the period, it is necessary now to evaluate the evidence for his involvement in the Schism in detail.

---

[21] Rüther, *Bettelorden in Stadt und Land*, pp. 162–3.

[22] Ibid. 249–50.

[23] Edited by Schmitt, 'Documents sur la Province franciscaine', nos. 88 and 89 (pp. 283–4).

[24] Augsburg, Staatsarchiv (formerly Munich, Bayerisches Hauptstaatsarchiv), Reichsstadt Lindau Urkunden 147/1. My thanks to Dr Claudia Kalesse for providing a copy of this charter. Eduard Gebele asserted that Marquard had included a stipulation that the cross could only be sold if the convent encountered financial difficulty, and even then only to the parish church of St Stephen; see Gebele, 'Markwart von Lindau', p. 91. In fact, the stipulation affirms that the cross could never be mortgaged or otherwise alienated, not even in times of difficulty. Should this have happened, the cross would become the property of the parish church and the friars would lose all rights over it.

[25] Gössi, *Das Archiv der oberdeutschen Minoritenprovinz*, pp. 19–25; see pp. 17–19 and 25–30 on the survival and dissipation of the archive in the modern period. The Konstanz archive served as the material basis for Berard Müller's important chronicle in the 17th cent., which we shall encounter presently; see Sehi (ed.), *P. Berardus Müller (d. 1704) und P. Victor Tschan (d. 1754), Chronica*, pp. 6–7. To the two manuscripts of this chronicle known to Sehi must be added Überlingen, Leopold-Sophien-Bibliothek, Ms. 9; see Semler, 'Die historischen Handschriften der Leopold-Sophien-Bibliothek', pp. 121–2.

It is not clear whether Marquard was still *custos Lacus* when, on 26 October 1379, a papal letter was issued by the Avignonese antipope Clement VII to one Johannes Hiltalingen von Basel, prior of the order of Augustinian friars (OESA) in the Avignonese obedience and a significant intellectual figure in the south-west German region in his own right.[26] He was commissioned to offer the academic degree of master of theology to Marquard and to the Basel Dominican Theobald von Altkirch, both described in the text of the bull as having spent time in various *studia*: 'qui in pluribus et diversis studiis generalibus in theologia longis temporibus studuerunt et legerunt'[27] ('who have studied and lectured theology in several and various *studia generalia* for a long time'). The truth of this statement is, of course, open to question, as the offer is clearly that of a 'political promotion'—the attempt to secure leading ecclesiastical figures for the Avignonese obedience by offering academic titles for which the individual concerned had not fulfilled the formal criteria. These offers—of which that to Marquard was only the second—had particular pregnancy in south-west Germany. The German Empire followed the Roman obedience; but Leopold III, Duke of Austria had declared for Clement VII, and Alsace, the Breisgau, and much of the region eastwards towards Lake Constance fell under his jurisdiction. This whole area was thus deeply divided—even to the level of divisions within individual convents—and this bull represents an attempt to secure the allegiance of a senior Franciscan in the region, the province previously remaining uniformly obedient to Rome.[28] As will become clear, Marquard cannot have accepted this offer. It is perhaps as a consequence of his refusal that a similar commission was entrusted to Johannes Hiltalingen by a letter of 4 March 1380, to examine another Franciscan, Liephard von Regensburg, and to offer him not only the *licentia docendi* (the qualification secured on completing the lectorate course at a *studium generale*), but also the degree of master of theology.[29] Liephard evidently did accept, and was further appointed provincial minister for the Avignonese obedience of the South German Franciscan province, becoming a rival to the pro-Roman provincial, Hesso von Lampertheim.

[26] For an excellent biographical survey on Johannes Hiltalingen, see Tönsing, *Johannes Malkaw*, pp. 397–9; on his philosophical and theological writing, see most recently Witte, 'Der 'Traktat von der Minne'', and id., 'Die Rezeption der Lehre Meister Eckharts', with all further references.
[27] *Bullarium franciscanum*, vol. 7, no. 589 (p. 219).
[28] For a clear survey of the shifting allegiances during the Schism in the south-west German region prior to 1400, see Tönsing, *Johannes Malkaw*, pp. 125–42; on the Franciscan province specifically, see Schmitt, 'Le Parti clémentiste', pp. 83–8.
[29] *Bullarium franciscanum*, vol. 7, no. 597 (pp. 221–2).

A papal letter of Clement VII from 13 June 1385, which settled a dispute between the Franciscan convents of Susa and Chambre at the appeal of Angelus of Spoleto, the minister general in the Avignonese obedience, records Angelus' original petition; therein it is noted that the case had been heard in various chapters general, most recently in Geneva *per auditores causarum*, amongst whom Liephard von Regensburg is named and styled both master of theology and provincial minister.[30]

The defections from the Roman obedience in the South German Franciscan province during the initial years of the Schism constitute the background to two letters from the beginning of 1383 in which the next trace of Marquard is found. They were sent, as Clément Schmitt has established, from the minister provincial Hesso von Lampertheim to the minister general Peter of Canzano and the procurator of the Franciscan Order in Rome respectively, and are preserved in the same formulary to which we have earlier referred.[31] Schmitt has used them to reconstruct the history of the Schism for the South German province at this time.[32] We must examine the content regarding Marquard in more detail. The shorter letter, sent to the minister general Peter of Canzano on 10 February 1383, is of little import in this respect. Hesso notes his appointment of Marquard as *custos Lacus*—clearly now for the second time—on 21 December 1382, stating that Marquard had been bitterly opposed by Liephard von Regensburg:

Fratrum Marquardum, cuius acerrimus invasor et infector quondam fuit Liephardus, in festo S. Thomae Apostoli feci custodem Laci, ipsum ad fidelitatem Domini nostri sincerius exhortando. Spero quod faciat, et sic in optima stamus pace.[33]

(On the feast of St Thomas the Apostle I appointed brother Marquard, whose most bitter assailant and corrupter Liephard once was, as *custos Lacus*, exhorting him more candidly to be faithful to our lord. I trust that he may do this, and thus we remain in the best of peace.)

---

[30] *Bullarium franciscanum*, no. 716 (pp. 255–6); on Liephard see Schmitt, 'Le Parti clémentiste', pp. 85–6.
[31] See Schmitt, 'Le Parti clémentiste', pp. 88–90; on the formulary (Luzern, Zentral- und Hochschulbibliothek, BB Ms. 129. 4°), see id., 'Documents sur la Province franciscaine', pp. 213–24. It is likely that the formulary was produced using material in the archive at Konstanz, though it belonged to the chained library of the Franciscan convent in Luzern; see Schmid, 'Kettenbücher', at p. 64.
[32] See Schmitt, 'Le Parti clémentiste', pp. 93–5.
[33] Hesso von Lampertheim, letter of 10 Feb. 1383 to Peter of Canzano, §5, in Schmitt, 'Le Parti clémentiste', pp. 100–2, here p. 101.

The other letter, sent to the order's procurator in Rome in January or early February 1383,[34] is more informative. Hesso records that he appointed Marquard to be *custos Lacus* at the request of three very senior members of the Strasbourg city council, in whose judgement he trusted implicitly, and that Marquard had promised his full allegiance to the Roman obedience:

Noveritis quod in crastino S. Thomae Apostoli, ad reverendam, gratiosam ac amicabilem instantiam dominorum scilicet Ioannis Kanzler, qui nunc est magister scabinorum, Ioannis Philippi et Waltheri Wassicher, necnon ad humilem recogitationem Fr. Marquardi, ipsum Marquardum institui custodem Laci, et sic in optima stamus pace et omnia sunt sopita. Noveritis, quidquid in hoc mundo pro me dicti tres, cum tota Argentina civitate, facere possent, utique toto conamine facerent, prout quotidie quasi experior. Noveritis quod dictus fr. Marquardus promisit in praesentia patrum ac trium dictorum magistrorum scabinorum, quod usque ad finem vitae suae vellet de cetero stare et facere ad meam voluntatem; secundo promisit quod nulli vellet auxilio vel consilio adstare, qui esset contra me vel contra provinciam, et spero indubitanter quod faciet.[35]

(You should know that on the day after the feast of St Thomas the Apostle, at the respectful, gracious, and amicable request of lords Johannes Kanzler (who is now chief juror [*Schöffenmeister*]), Johannes Philipps, and Walther Wassicher, and further in view of brother Marquard's humble reconsideration, I appointed this Marquard as *custos Lacus*, and thus we remain in the best of peace, and everything is becalmed. You should know that whatever in the world these three, with the whole city of Strasbourg, could do on my behalf, they would do with wholehearted support, just as I experience it on what feels like a daily basis. You should know that in the presence of the fathers and of the aforesaid three chief jurors, the aforesaid brother Marquard promised that he intended to depart from the other one and act according to my will until the end of his life; and promised secondly that he would not assist anyone with material help or advice who would oppose me or the province, and I trust without a doubt that he will do this.)

In 1382 Marquard was thus already back in Strasbourg, though it is not clear in what capacity. His three backers were, as Schmitt has noted, exceptionally powerful individuals.[36] The chronicle of Jakob Twinger von Königshofen (d. 1420) describes them at the height of their power, and notes their particular aptitude in settling disputes among both laity and clergy in the city:

---

[34] On the dating, see Schmitt, 'Le Parti clémentiste', pp. 89–90.
[35] Hesso von Lampertheim, letter of Jan.–Feb. 1383 to the Franciscan procurator in Rome, §7–9, in Schmitt, 'Le Parti clémentiste', pp. 96–100, here p. 97.
[36] Schmitt, 'Le Parti clémentiste', pp. 90–1.

Do men zalte noch gotz geburte 1385 jor, do worent drige gewaltige manne zů Strosburg, genant her Johans Kantzeler, her Philippes Hans und her Walther Wassicher. dise drige worent vor antwerglüte und ammeistere gewesen, und worent gar wise und löuffig noch der welte louf; und brohtent zů mit iren listen und mit iren nuwen fünden, wan sü ouch gewaltig worent, das alle grosse sachen in der stat und in dem bistum under pfaffen und under leygen und under den herren in dem lande gůter mossen wurdent durch sü usgetragen. und noment gůt und můte underwilent von beden parten, und ouch so sü ammeister oder in dem rote worent, das sü ouch versworn hettent, und hettent sich des gewaltes der stette also gar underzogen, das meniger zů Strosburg in den rot oder an ambaht gesetzet wart noch irme willen. dovon brohtent sü in dem rote durch was sü woltent, und darumb so houbete menglich an sü.[37]

(In the year 1385 there were three powerful men in Strasbourg, called Johannes Kanzler, Johannes Philipps, and Walther Wassicher. These three had previously been guildsmen and had held the office of mayor, and were very clever in the ways of the world. With their intrigues and new tricks, because they were also powerful, they brought it about that all the important affairs in the city and in the diocese— amongst the clergy, the laity, and the landed nobility—were arranged for the best part through them. Meanwhile they accepted gifts and bribes from both parties, even when they held the mayoral office or sat on the council and had sworn not to do so. They had taken control of the civic powers so completely that many in Strasbourg were accorded offices, or positions on the council at their behest. As a result they got whatever they wanted through the council, and so everyone was bound to them.)

Their influence, however, did not last—Twinger continues by recounting what amounts to a failed coup attempt in 1385 that concluded in their trial and exile.[38]

Hesso's letter to the minister general is not as straightforward as it may seem thus far. He says next that Marquard had shown him appreciative letters that he (Marquard) had received from the minister general—whether Peter of Canzano or his predecessor Ludovico Donati (d. 1382) is not clear. He then makes a strange and ironically formulated declaration, namely that Marquard should beware lest the ready availability of absolution should encourage him in disobedience:

Noveritis quod mihi ostendit scripta multum amica sibi per patrem directa, quomodo eum toto corde diligeret etc. O felix culpa! etc. Caveatur, consulo, ne facilitas veniae incentivum praebeat delinquendi.[39]

---

[37] Jakob Twinger von Königshofen, *Chronik*, c. 5 (pp. 782–3).
[38] See ibid. (pp. 783–4).
[39] Hesso von Lampertheim, letter of Jan.–Feb. 1381, §10, in Schmitt, 'Le Parti clémentiste', p. 97.

(You should know that he showed me very friendly letters sent to him by our father, saying how he loved him with all his heart, and so forth. O happy fault! Care must be taken, I consider, that the ease of pardon should not give him the incentive to transgress.)

Subsequently Hesso speaks of letters sent to the procurator by Marquard and to himself by Liephard von Regensburg. He states that, had he responded positively to their letters, all would have turned out as they intended; but he doubted Liephard's intentions and recognized that he was up to no good (though it is unclear in what):

Nostis litteram per Fr. Marquardum vobis scriptam et mihi per Liephardum, cui et bene, meo ac aliorum iudicio, respondi. Si eorum scripta effectui fuissent mancipata, omnia ad ipsorum intentum fuissent conclusa; sed, ut ex quibusdam Liephardi dictis conicio, fraudulenter et dolose mihi litteram illam scripsit, videlicet, ut eo minus in practica profanandi, quemadmodum facere proposuerat, observaretur.[40]

(You are aware of the letter written to you by brother Marquard, and to me by Liephard, to which I, in my opinion and that of others, replied properly. If their letters had been carried into effect, everything would have been concluded to their intention; but, as I infer from certain things that Liephard said, he wrote his letter to me fraudulently and deceitfully; namely, in order that he might be less observed in the practice of acting falsely, as he had intended to do.)

It is not clear exactly what Marquard's role in all this had been. Schmitt regarded Marquard as a decided opponent of the Avignonese obedience, and rejected Bonmann's position that the 'political promotion' offered to Marquard in 1379 could not have been made without a certain openness to Avignon on Marquard's part previously.[41] Bonmann, one should note, published his article in 1934 and did not know of these letters, which Schmitt discovered in the early 1960s. Even so it is hard to follow Schmitt's position entirely. Hesso's letters are not simply reports to superior officials, but perorations on the subject of bringing lost sheep back to the Roman fold. His aim in this was to gain permission to readmit friars who had belonged to the Avignonese obedience (and who were thus excommunicate) to the Roman convents. This, argued Hesso, would enable him to reunite the province more successfully than anything else. In a letter of 29 April 1383 (a letter unknown to Schmitt), Urban VI permitted Hesso to absolve forty friars who had expressed their intent to return to the Roman obedience, and provided the form of the oath of abjuration they would be required to swear.[42] We can rule out Marquard having ever declared

[40] Ibid., §16, in Schmitt, 'Le Parti clémentiste', p. 99.
[41] Schmitt, 'Le Parti clémentiste', p. 85; see Bonmann, 'Marquard von Lindau', p. 320.
[42] *Supplementum ad bullarium franciscanum*, vol. 1, no. 40 (pp. 85–7).

formally for the Avignon papacy—Hesso could not have absolved him, let alone appointed him *custos Lacus* again at the end of 1382. But nor is it clear that Marquard had consistently supported the Roman cause. We do not know what was contained in the letter that Marquard had sent to the procurator in Rome in conjunction with Liephard's letter to Hesso, though this incident does not of itself demonstrate an earlier friendship between Marquard and his opponent Liephard. Yet Hesso's ironic exclamation, 'O felix culpa', and the statement in the letter that Marquard had relied upon easy access to absolution, indicate that Marquard's past was not unchequered. It is curious that Marquard should have required such important backers on the Strasbourg city council to regain his post as *custos Lacus*—and we should not overlook the reference in that letter to a *humilis recogitatio* on Marquard's part in securing that appointment. There is, finally, something to Bonmann's point concerning the 'political promotion' of 1379—it is hard to imagine that Clement VII would have made an entirely speculative offer, or to someone who was known as a firm Roman supporter. We cannot insist on a particular reconstruction of events from such limited evidence. Nonetheless it is plausible to suggest that Marquard had taken a long time to declare finally for the Roman obedience, or to dissociate himself from individuals known to support the Avignonese cause like Liephard. This might indeed explain Liephard's fierce enmity to Marquard. Michael Tönsing has uncovered important new evidence for the existence of a sizeable 'neutral' party in Strasbourg and the upper Rhine during the earlier years of the Schism.[43] Now Marquard may not have declared openly that no choice was necessary, or refused to declare for either party, but the neutrals' very existence demonstrates that there were not just two possible positions in the Schism. It is thus plausible that Marquard did not formally declare for the Roman obedience until becoming engaged in a dispute with Liephard around 1380–2, perhaps linked to the latter's acceptance of the kind of 'political promotion' that Marquard had refused.

There is no further documentation for Marquard's career until 1389, with the exception of a Lindau charter mentioned by Eduard Gebele, dated to 25 September 1383, in which Marquard is titled *custos Lacus*. The charter is apparently lost and its contents unknown.[44] He reappears back

---

[43] See Tönsing, *Johannes Malkaw*, pp. 25–7.

[44] Gebele, 'Markwart von Lindau', pp. 91–2. Gebele does not indicate his source, but it is probably an annotation by Karl Wolfart to Stettner, 'Marquard von Lindau', at p. 233 n. 119. The registers of the Lindau charters (now in the Staatsarchiv Augsburg), in which collection Marquard's charter of 11 Apr. 1377 is found, contain no further reference to Marquard. My thanks again to Dr Claudia Kalesse for this information.

in Strasbourg on 19 November 1389, at an extraordinary provincial chapter to elect a new provincial minister in succession to Johannes von Heilbronn, who had died on 17 September. Marquard himself was elected. Our source here is the Franciscan chronicle of Nikolaus Glaßberger (d. 1508), who records that Marquard held provincial chapters at Nuremberg in 1390, at Esslingen in 1391, and at Basel on 24 June 1392.[45] The eighteenth-century chronicle of Malachias Tschamser indicates that Marquard issued statutes at Nuremberg, which proved moderately successful in correcting problems within the province:

Den 22. Mayen [1390] halten unsere Mindere Brüder Conventualen oder Baarfüßer zu Nürnberg ihr Provincial Capitul under dem Praesidio und Vorsitz A. R. P. M. Fr. Marquardi von Lindaw, allwo bey 225 Brüder zusammen kommen, und weil underschiedliche Gravamina, Klagen und Beschwärnußen vorgetragen wurden, theils gegen den armen Zeiten und beschwärlichen bürgerlichen Kriegen, theils wegen Beschwärlichkeit der zerfallenen Studien und Zerrüttung der klösterlichen Observantz etc., als hat gemelter P. Minister Provincial sehr heilsame und nützliche Constitutionen und Satzungen zum Flor, Zier und Aufnahm der Provintz geordnet, wodurch allen obigen Beschwärden, wo nit gäntzlich abgeholffen, doch bestentheils vorgebogen wurde.[46]

(On 22 May 1390 our conventual Friars Minor held their provincial chapter at Nuremberg under the presidency and chairmanship of the most reverend father, master Marquard von Lindau, where around 225 brethren assembled together. On account of various grievances, plaints, and hardships that were presented—partly because of the poverty of the time and the burdensome civil wars, partly because of the exigencies of the derelict *studia* and the breakdown of monastic observance, and so forth—the aforementioned father and provincial minister issued highly restorative and helpful constitutions and statutes to the flourishment, embellishment, and improvement of the province. Through these, all the above complaints were, where not totally resolved, nonetheless ameliorated for the most part.)

At Esslingen in 1391, Marquard then issued certain new statutes 'pro renovatione morum', in addition to renewing the statutes issued at Nuremberg.[47] It is not clear on what source Tschamser drew or how reliable it was, particularly where the judgement of the statutes' efficacy is concerned. Nor is it clear that Tschamser had the actual texts before him, as he does not give the incipits for the statutes, in contrast to those issued by Hesso von Lampertheim.[48]

---

[45] Nikolaus Glaßberger, *Chronica*, pp. 218–20.
[46] Malachias Tschamser, *Annales oder Jahrs-Geschichten*, vol. 1, p. 447.
[47] Ibid. 449.
[48] See ibid. 419 (Strasbourg, 1374), 426 (Colmar, 1377), and 435 (Mainz, 1383).

There is further evidence for Marquard's activity as provincial minister relating to two ongoing issues: the foundation of the Poor Clare convent at Valduna in Vorarlberg, and the trial of Johannes Malkaw. Anton Ludewig's careful history of Valduna has established Marquard's role there. The Austrian count Rudolf von Montfort had assisted the foundation of a hermitage by a former merchant from Brixen, one Marquard von Tegernsee, in a Vorarlberg forest in 1388. The hermits, however, left for reasons unknown in 1391, and at this point Marquard (von Lindau) became involved. The principal sources agree on the course of events: a convent chronicle (the *Valduna-Chronik*), written by Klara von Embs in 1602; a now-lost collection of historical notices known as the *Diarium* of Valduna; and the late seventeenth-century chronicle of Berard Müller, mentioned earlier. Rudolf approached Marquard with the intention of founding a Poor Clare convent at Valduna. They were probably personally acquainted, for Rudolf had founded the Franciscan convent of Viktorsberg in 1383 whilst Marquard was *custos Lacus*, and the Viktorsberg lay within the custody. Rudolf died in 1390, but Marquard continued with the project and summoned three women from an isolated tertiary house at Äschach in the Grimmenstein forest (near Walzenhausen in Appenzell) to inhabit Valduna, receiving them into obedience—as tertiaries—on 14 August 1391. When Marquard died, the *Valduna-Chronik* relates that the women considered leaving Valduna, but were provided with alms and other support locally that enabled them to stay.[49] Bonmann, Gebele, and Gatz have all expressed a certain surprise that Marquard called tertiaries to Valduna, when there were twenty-two convents of Poor Clares in the South German province and three alone in the custody of Lake Constance.[50] The explanation is probably quite simple. On a practical level, Valduna consisted of a few half-constructed buildings in the middle of a mountainous forest. It would have made sense to introduce sisters used to living in similar conditions. Moreover, the foundation of a full convent required a papal permission that the establishment of a tertiary house did not. Marquard had evidently applied for such permission, which was not granted by

---

[49] See Ludewig, *Das ehemalige Klarissenkloster*, pp. 1–17; see pp. x–xii for a detailed survey of the extant source material. For a more readily available summary, see Gatz, 'Valduna/Vorarlberg', pp. 48–53. The *Valduna-Chronik* is not edited; for Müller's chronicle, see Berard Müller, *Chronica* [ed. 1964], pp. 222–3. Müller and Klara von Embs were probably using copies of the same source material to produce their respective chronicles. Klara would have had access to the Valduna records, whilst Müller may have found copies of the same charters in the central archive at Konstanz.

[50] Bonmann, 'Marquard von Lindau', p. 325; Gebele, 'Markwart von Lindau', p. 95; Gatz, 'Valduna/Vorarlberg', p. 51.

Boniface IX (Urban VI's successor) until 16 August 1391.[51] He would not have known how long this decision would take, or whether the petition would be successful. The status of Valduna as a de facto Poor Clare convent was finally confirmed by Marquard von Randegg, bishop of Konstanz, on 10 April 1403, at which point the institution already housed around fifty professed and twelve lay sisters.[52]

Marquard also had a minor role to play, as Michael Tönsing has shown, in the continuing saga surrounding Johannes Malkaw, a priest from north-eastern Germany who had arrived in Strasbourg in 1390. Having already been expelled, for various reasons, from the dioceses of Cologne and Trier, he began to preach vituperatively against the Avignonese party and 'neutrals' in the Schism, and against the mendicant orders and the civic elite in Strasbourg in general. By this time, the Avignonese party was very weak in the city, but Malkaw's activities threatened to reinvigorate old grievances and stirred popular unrest. He began to destabilize the uneasy, but more or less stable peace that existed between clergy in the region loyal to the different popes. In a final attempt to control his activity, the Dominican inquisitor Nikolaus Böckler and the episcopal commissar Reinbold Schlecht had Malkaw arrested and charged him with heresy.[53] His trial included two public interrogations, the second—for which a set of extracts from the official transcripts survives—held on 10 March 1391. A very large number of witnesses, representatives of most of the religious institutions and the city council, were assembled. Their function was not that of jurors, but of advisers, present to establish the juridical competence of the inquisition and produce a set of opinions (recorded in a document known as a *consilium*) on the guilt, or otherwise, of the accused, to be submitted to the bishop for a decision. The witness list survives in the aforementioned set of extracts from the transcripts, and attests to the presence of the Franciscan provincial minister—Marquard.[54] The text has a certain importance in establishing Marquard's relationship with persons known to be associated with Rulman Merswin's foundation at the Grüner Wörth, incorporated into the Order of St John since 1371, which I have discussed elsewhere.[55] The extant material provides no insight into Marquard's actual role in the

[51] *Bullarium franciscanum*, vol. 7, no. 72 (p. 23).
[52] See Ludewig, *Das ehemalige Klarissenkloster*, pp. 17–21; and Gatz, 'Valduna/Vorarlberg', pp. 53–8.
[53] See Tönsing, *Johannes Malkaw*, pp. 10–34.
[54] See ibid. 34–50; esp. pp. 38–9 for the identification of the witnesses, with the text edited pp. 225–7; on the manuscript preserving the text (Stuttgart, Württembergische Landesbibliothek, HB I 83, fol. 128ʳ), see p. 382.
[55] Mossman, 'Zu Marquard von Lindau', pp. 249–50.

process, which may not have extended beyond his presence as one among many at Malkaw's second public interrogation. A *consilium* is known to have been produced at a meeting of the witnesses held on 28–30 March 1391, but does not survive.[56]

One final piece of evidence indicates that Marquard, whilst provincial minister, was at least in contact with senior Jews, and possibly engaged in disputations against them. The source for this evidence is a Hebrew text: the famous *Sefer ha-Nizzahon* ('Book of Contention' or 'Book of Victory') of rabbi Yom-Tov Lipmann Mühlhausen (d. 1421), one of the foremost Jewish intellectuals of his generation. The *Sefer ha-Nizzahon* is directed towards Jews considering conversion to Christianity, and seeks to prevent their conversion by challenging the interpretation of almost every Old Testament verse that been understood in a Christological sense. In so doing it covered almost every topic in the inter-religious debate, which gave it a particular prominence in the polemical tradition. Lipmann was the first Jewish writer systematically to deploy contemporary philosophical and logical techniques in polemical argumentation, and the *Sefer ha-Nizzahon* is extant in forty-four manuscripts—more than any other surviving Ashkenazi Jewish work. It was written in or shortly after 1400, as it contains an appendix that refers to an execution of a large number of Jews in 1399/1400 at an unspecified place, and there is some evidence that points to Prague as the location of its composition.[57]

Lipmann provides no information in the *Sefer ha-Nizzahon* that would allow the circumstances of its production to be more closely ascertained, with one exception: three separate references to an unnamed Christian interlocutor from Lindau with whom he engaged in disputation. The identification of this figure as Marquard has been proposed by Ora Limor and Israel Yuval. They note that the figure is referred to as 'head of the clergy in Lindau', 'priest in Lindau', and 'leader of the priests'—Sebald Snelle's Latin translation of 1643–5 refers to him as the 'primarius sacrificulorum Lindavii'—and summarize that he 'was clearly a churchman with a fairly high position in the local church hierarchy; he was not a bishop, for otherwise Lipmann would surely have referred to him not as *komer* or *kohen* but as *hegmon*, the equivalent Hebrew term for bishop'.[58]

---

[56] Tönsing, *Johannes Malkaw*, pp. 40 and 48–50.
[57] See Limor and Yuval, 'Skepticism and Conversion', pp. 160–74; for a bio-bibliographical survey of Lipmann see Breuer et al., *Germania Judaica*, art. 'Prag', 1116–51, at pp. 1129–31.
[58] Limor and Yuval, 'Skepticism and Conversion', p. 175; see below for the references to Snelle's translation.

But at the same time, Marquard had been dead for at least eight years by the time the work was composed, and their geographical spheres of activity— Lipmann was active above all in Thuringia and Bohemia—are not known to have overlapped. Close examination of the three passages in which the priest from Lindau is mentioned reveals, surprisingly, that the proposed identification must be correct, despite the temporal and geographical problems. Two of these passages fail to provide information sufficiently tangible to permit an identification. One concerns the interpretation of the Hebrew word *'almāh* (young woman) in Isaiah 7: 14 ('ecce virgo concipiet, et pariet filium': 'behold, a virgin will conceive, and bear a son').[59] This, however, is a very well-known issue. The interlocutor brings no more information to the discussion than he could have gained from the standard biblical commentaries, and shows evidence of knowing just a couple of basic Hebrew nouns. A second passage is similarly uninstructive. Here, the Christian interlocutor enquires as to why song and music did not play a part in the Jewish rituals that he observed, despite the practices described in the Old Testament, and states that he knows that the Jews mock the Christians because they sing in their religious celebrations.[60] The third, however, provides the clinching evidence. It concerns the understanding of Psalm 103: 26, on the creation of Leviathan. The interlocutor adduces a long aggadic statement on the interpretation of this text which is taken from the Avodah Zarah, a section of the Talmud, and which he regards as patently erroneous. Lipmann explains that this aggadah must be understood as a parable, and not as literally true.[61] The specific content of this discussion is not relevant here. What is significant is that the Christian interlocutor is able to cite, accurately and at length, an obscure interpretation about Leviathan from a work only available in Hebrew. Now there is no evidence from his works that Marquard had any such facility in Hebrew, which at first sight appears to exclude him entirely. However, Marquard did know the *Pugio fidei* by the Spanish Dominican Ramon Martí. This, as I have identified elsewhere, was the source of his knowledge of the Qur'ān and the ḥadīth collection of Muhammad ibn Ismail al-Bukhārī, from which he quoted variously in the *Dekalogerklärung* and in *De reparatione*

---

[59] Lipmann Mühlhausen, *Sefer ha-Nizzahon*, trans. Snellius, *R. Lipmanni Disputatio Adversus Christianos ad Esaiae* [...], no. 225, pp. a3ʳ–a4ᵛ.

[60] Ibid., *R. Lipmanni Disputatio Adversus Christianos ad Josuae* [...], no. 179, p. b1ʳ⁻ᵛ.

[61] Ibid., *R. Lipmanni Disputatio Adversus Christianos ad Jeremiae* [...], no. 290, pp. d4ᵛ–e1ʳ.

hominis.[62] An examination of the *Pugio fidei*—primarily an anti-Jewish work—reveals that it contains, in Latin translation, exactly the same aggadah as the interlocutor cites, to precisely the same extent, attached to the same scriptural verse, and which it regards equally negatively.[63] In addition, it contains a discussion of the meaning of the word *'almāh* in Isaiah 7: 14.[64] As the transmission of the *Pugio fidei,* as mentioned earlier, was so limited and not otherwise attested in the German-speaking regions in the Middle Ages, this must be regarded as conclusive proof that the anonymous interlocutor from Lindau in the *Sefer ha-Nizzahon* was Marquard, presumably—given the appellation of this figure in the Hebrew text—during his term in office as provincial minister. Where they met remains unknown.

Marquard died on 15 August 1392. Berard Müller's entry for him in his catalogue of South German provincial ministers notes that he died unusually young—confirming the overall picture of his biography as suggested previously—and states that he was buried in the choir of the Franciscan church in Konstanz:

1389. In Capitulo Argentinae ad fest. S. Elisabethae celebrato in Ministrum electus fuit fr. Marquardus de Lindavia Custos Lacus vir ad omne officiorum genus dexterrimus sed praemature nimis Constantiae 1392 ipso festo assumptionis B. Mariae V. cum tribus annis solumodo praefuisset vita defungitur ibidem a facie altaris in choro humatus.[65]

(1389. In the chapter at Strasbourg, celebrated on the feast of St Elizabeth [19 November], brother Marquard von Lindau, the *custos Lacus,* was elected to be minister. He was a man most skilful in every kind of office, but in Konstanz on the feast of the Assumption of the blessed Virgin Mary [15 August] in the year 1392, he departed this life excessively prematurely. He had governed for only three years, and was buried in that place [i.e. Konstanz] in the choir opposite the altar.)

Marquard does not figure frequently in subsequent Franciscan historiography, a result of the more general lack of chronicles for the South German province in the later fourteenth century. Perhaps, as Bonmann suggests, this indicates an attempt to airbrush out the paralysing divisions of the Schism.[66] A very important conspectus of Marquard's works was produced

---

[62] Mossman, 'The Western Understanding', pp. 170–87.
[63] Martí, *Pugio fidei,* pars 3, d. 3, c. 22, §12; ed. 1651, p. 723; ed. 1687, pp. 930–1.
[64] Ibid., c. 7, §1; ed. 1651, pp. 578–9; ed. 1687, pp. 737–8.
[65] Berard Müller, *Chronica* [ed. 1957], p. 62. Only the second part of Müller's chronicle was published in 1964; the first, unpublished part is edited in typescript. Copy consulted: Würzburg, Universitätsbibliothek, 30/Hbh XIII 363(38).
[66] Bonmann, 'Marquard von Lindau', pp. 315–16.

soon after his death. This is extant in a manuscript dating to 1434, belonging to one Hermann Sakch, at that time confessor of the Poor Clare convent in Regensburg, and independently in the chronicle of Nikolaus Glaßberger.[67] Sakch's manuscript also contains a catalogue of around fifty significant Franciscans, purely a list of names with just four exceptions:

[35] Magister franciscus de marronis, qui terna vice scripsit super sententias et sermones famosos de tempore et de sanctis fecit. [36] Fr. Bertholdus de Ratispona praedicator gentium, qui facit sermones Rusticani. [37] Fr. David de augusta, doctor theologiae, qui scripsit formam noviciorum et tractatus de exteriore et interiori homine et super regulam sancti francisci. [38] Fr. Marquardus de lindaw doctissimus, qui multos pu[l]cherrimos tractatus compilavit provincialis.[68]

([35] Master Francis of Meyronnes, who wrote three commentaries on the Sentences and produced a renowned set of sermons for the *temporale* and the *sanctorale*. [36] Brother Berthold von Regensburg, preacher to the people, who produced the *sermones Rusticani*. [37] Brother David von Augsburg, doctor of theology, who wrote the *Forma novitiorum*, the treatise *De exterioris et interioris hominis compositione*, and a commentary on the Franciscan Rule. [38] The most learned brother Marquard von Lindau, who was provincial minister and composed many most beautiful treatises.)

At least one Franciscan of the subsequent generation, then, considered Marquard not only worthy of inclusion in a list of Franciscan *magnae personae*, but—in drawing out four names worthy of particular comment for their literary achievement—placed Marquard in the august company of Francis of Meyronnes, Berthold von Regensburg, and David von Augsburg, each of them a personage of European significance.[69]

Aside from Nikolaus Glaßberger, the later chroniclers who do mention Marquard add little else. Fortunatus Hueber's chronicle of 1686 draws exclusively on Glaßberger, with the exception of the statement—presumably pious invention—that Marquard died of exhaustion from good

---

[67] Palmer, 'Marquard von Lindau', cols. 83–5. See Nikolaus Glaßberger, *Chronica*, pp. 218–19; Hermann Sakch's text survives in Munich, Bayerische Staatsbibliothek, Cgm 2928, fol. 45ᵛ, edited by Bonmann, 'Marquard von Lindau', pp. 328–33; on the manuscript, see Schneider, *Die deutschen Handschriften*, pp. 364–79.

[68] Cited from the extract in Bonmann, 'Marquard von Lindau', pp. 327–8 n. 52; text in Cgm 2928, fols. 36ᵛ–37ʳ; see Schneider, *Die deutschen Handschriften*, p. 368.

[69] For another 15th-cent. Franciscan *Literarkatalog* to include Marquard (in Würzburg, Franziskanerkloster, Cod. I 111, fols. 93ʳ–95ᵛ), see Bonmann, 'Ein franziskanischer Literarkatalog', pp. 125–33 and 139–49.

works.[70] We have already seen all Berard Müller and the *Valduna-Chronik* had to say. Malachias Tschamser, as we have seen, appears to have had information on the provincial chapters Marquard held. He relates the same information as Müller on Marquard's place of burial, which suggests they had a common source.[71] He adds that Marquard was *lector theologiae* at Würzburg; but he says the same of Johannes von Heilbronn and Johannes Löw von Thann, Marquard's predecessor and successor respectively. As Müller accords this title to them, but not to Marquard in his catalogue of provincials, we might suspect that the frequently inaccurate Tschamser has transposed this title onto Marquard erroneously.[72]

The aspect of Marquard's activity that is least evident from the extant documentation of his life is probably that in which he was most involved: the *cura animarum*, the cure of souls, inside and outside the vast network of religious and semi-religious institutions in south-west Germany. In Strasbourg alone there were two convents of Poor Clares, about a dozen official Franciscan tertiary institutions, and probably around twice that number of beguinages operating in the period—statutes for twenty-five such houses are extant, and it appears to have been the Franciscans who provided most of their pastoral care.[73] Smaller towns would naturally have had fewer or smaller institutions, but Strasbourg was not exceptional, and roughly comparable to the other larger towns like Basel, Freiburg, Konstanz, Würzburg, and Munich. One need only look at the list of attested institutions generated in the final volume of the *Alemania Franciscana Antiqua* to see quite how dense the network of Franciscan *loci* in the South German province actually was.[74] We can be confident that there were about sixty male convents and twenty-three Poor Clare convents in the province at this time; the number of tertiary houses was certainly into three figures, and

---

[70] See Fortunatus Hueber, *Dreyfache Cronickh*, cols. 102 and 154–6. Copy consulted: London, British Library, 502 h. 10. There are very minor differences to Glaßberger in some of the incipits given in the catalogue of Marquard's works. Hueber wrongly states that Marquard died in Basel, evidently by overlooking 'ipso anno' in the following sentence in Glaßberger's chronicle: 'Eodem anno [1392] fuit convocatio Basileae in festo Iohannis Baptistae, et ipso anno obiit frater Marquardus Minister in festo Assumptionis beatae Mariae' ('In that year [1392] there was a chapter in Basel on the feast of John the Baptist [24 June], and in the same year brother Marquard, the minister, died on the feast of the assumption of the blessed Mary'); see Glaßberger, *Chronica*, p. 220.
[71] Malachias Tschamser, *Annales oder Jahrs-Geschichten*, vol. 1, p. 451.
[72] See ibid. 440 (Johannes von Heilbronn), 445–6 (Marquard), and 451–2 (Johannes Löw von Thann); cf. Berard Müller, *Chronica* [ed. 1957], p. 62.
[73] See Rüther, *Bettelorden in Stadt und Land*, pp. 291–303.
[74] *Alemania Franciscana Antiqua* 18 (Landshut, 1973), pp. 368–79.

probably well so, given that there were undoubtedly more such houses than those for which concrete evidence survives. It is hard to know how large these institutions were. In 1362 there were sixty professed Franciscans in the Strasbourg convent;[75] we have already seen that the Poor Clare house at Valduna was of similar size in 1403. These are probably a little above average, but still reasonably representative figures. Tertiary houses would have been considerably smaller.

It is difficult to assess the relative influence of the Franciscan Order in the urban centres of late medieval Germany. Andreas Rüther has provided a comprehensive survey of all individual studies of particular towns and their mendicant convents, and there is no need to repeat that work here.[76] What is clear is that the Franciscans and Dominicans dominated the ecclesiastical landscape of the German towns, with the smaller mendicant orders having a more patchy coverage. They enjoyed intimate relationships with the civic elites, relationships that were not always cosy—it is a sign of their influence that councils sought to restrain the growth in mendicants' properties as early as the later thirteenth century, to control the development of burgeoning economic powers in the cities.[77] Most recently, Thomas Ertl has discussed the relationship between mendicants and the German towns in the thirteenth century, representing the coming of the friars as a Christianizing process: a 'Verchristlichung der Stadt'. He argues that the mendicants engaged with the civic world in a new and sophisticated manner, developing a social ethics connected to contemporary realities and the social structure of the towns. In their preaching, the town became an idealized locus for the practice of Christian virtue, and in this idealized form, a model of perfection for cooperation in a Christian life. All of this was far removed from the conception of the town as a sinful environment to be fled for the security of the desert—that is, the isolated monasteries of the older orders. The new valorization not only of manual work, but also of mercantile activity, dismissed not the activity itself as sinful, but the excessive greed in its conduct. *Avaritia* replaced *superbia* as the principal vice in the mendicants' conception of the urban world. The towns had grown, and the mendicants had fulfilled the inhabitants' spiritual needs in an innovative and profoundly urban manner.[78]

[75] Rüther, *Bettelorden in Stadt und Land*, p. 162.
[76] See ibid. 9–29 and 101–4.
[77] See ibid. 223–51; for a good general survey of the German friars in this period see Freed, *The Friars and German Society*, pp. 21–53.
[78] Ertl, *Religion und Disziplin*, pp. 197–252 and 367–88.

The sophistication of Ertl's presentation is not belittled by stating that, in outline, the contours of this development in the context of thirteenth-century urban growth are well established, not least by David d'Avray.[79] A new set of questions arise for the fourteenth century with particular reference to Germany. Urban expansion took place later in Germany than in other European countries (notably Italy and France), and the German towns became tremendously wealthy—far more so, indeed, than one might expect. As Alexander Murray writes,

A lot is heard about Renaissance Florence and its great bankers, the Medici, whose banking services to the papacy included the supply of two popes, Leo X and Clement VII. A lot was meant to be heard: rhetoric and civic pride were of the essence of that culture. So we forget the north, and that the Medici were only Europe's second biggest bankers, far behind the Fuggers of Augsburg[80]

The German cities became loci of mercantile and artisanal wealth creation independent of the countryside around them, and so resistant in their economic vigour to the repeated exigencies of agricultural depressions.[81] How this affected the mendicant orders, and in particular the more widespread Franciscans, is essentially unknown. Further issues follow: whether, for instance, the mendicants held a more dominant position relative to the secular clergy in German towns than elsewhere, given that they were already installed in the towns during the main period of urban expansion, and so did not have to find a niche around the edges of an established urban ecclesiastical geography. Questions of this kind could only be addressed by drawing on all the numerous individual case-studies referred to above, a task of sufficient magnitude to lie outside the bounds of this study. Ertl restricts his study to the period before 1350 (and in practice to the thirteenth century), on the grounds that the social significance of the mendicant orders in the later Middle Ages declined, marked by the end of new foundations. He holds this position on the basis of four principal tenets: that the attraction of novelty was gone; the assimilation to the condition of the older orders proceeded apace; the criticism of mendicancy increased; and the educational advantage over the secular clerics decreased with the spread of literacy and higher education.[82]

---

[79] See d'Avray, *The Preaching of the Friars*, pp. 204–25.
[80] Murray, 'The Later Middle Ages', pp. 125–6.
[81] With further references, see Isenmann, *Die deutsche Stadt*, pp. 400–2; a comprehensive survey of the German towns (with maps) in the later Middle Ages is given by Scott and Scribner, 'Urban Networks'.
[82] Ertl, *Religion und Disziplin*, pp. 16–17.

To argue conclusively for this one way or another would require a different kind of study. The argumentation is nonetheless open to challenge. If the Franciscan Order had lost some of its distinctiveness by the time Marquard entered its ranks, and did not project a collective 'Franciscan ethos', then neither was it on the decline. Its network of convents, libraries, and other concrete manifestations like tertiary houses and confraternities was firmly established. Indeed, its network was so firmly entrenched that an individual friar, or a group of friars, now occupied a position within a set of institutionalized mechanisms that would allow the rapid dissemination of writings, and thus the concomitant effecting of intellectual change, through their reception not just within the Franciscan Order itself, but in all the religious orders, the secular clergy, and the urban laity. We cannot speak of a 'Franciscan ethos' in Germany after 1350, either because it did not exist as a distinctive mentality or because the evidence for it has not been gathered. But we can speak, at least in theory, of a 'Marquard ethos' within German intellectual culture at large, not just within the Franciscan Order. As we shall see, there are compelling reasons to take exactly this line.

It is then necessary to ask from what, and to whom, this 'Marquard ethos' could have been projected. Nigel Palmer has produced a comprehensive catalogue of Marquard's works that does not require detailed reproduction here.[83] But it is worth considering the variety of his oeuvre, which can be divided by genre into five broad categories. As the dating of individual works with any degree of certainty is only possible in isolated cases, a further differentiation according to sequence of composition cannot be attempted.

The first category is that of a dozen or so treatises in Latin, mostly of short or medium length and scholastic in form, which deal with specific theological issues and were almost certainly written for the Franciscan *studia*: texts such as *De penis inferni* and *De paupertate*. Amongst these one work stands out on account of its considerably greater length and more extensive transmission: *De reparatione hominis*, the completion of which is to be located with some certainty in 1374. In theme, extent, and depth it can be compared to Anselm's *Cur Deus homo*: a Franciscan attempt to produce an encompassing theological exposition of man's creation, fall, and salvation. The second category comprises a set of four lengthy allegorical treatises, all written in the Victorine style, on the contemplative ascent to union with God. Three of these are in German: the *Auszug der Kinder*

---

[83] Palmer, 'Marquard von Lindau', cols. 85–124.

Israel, of which about eighty manuscripts are extant, *De Nabuchodonosor* and the *Hiob-Traktat*. Just one, *De arca Noe*, is in Latin. The third category encompasses Marquard's vernacular German treatises on pragmatic issues of the Christian life. This category includes some genuine bestsellers in late medieval Germany, like the *Dekalogerklärung* (*c.*140 manuscripts) and the *Eucharistietraktat* (*c.*75 manuscripts), together with shorter and less widely read German works like *De anima Christi* and *De fide*. The fourth category is not really a category at all, but a single work: Marquard's immense Latin treatise of philosophical theology written as a commentary on John 1: 1–14. This work deals with a whole range of issues and incorporates a very sophisticated treatment of certain aspects of Eckhart's philosophical theology, based on a reading of Eckhart's extremely rare Latin oeuvre. Remarkably, it was translated into German (on which more below) and circulated in female convents in Southern Germany. The fifth and final category is a collection of forty-one sermons in German, dealing extensively with the contemplative life and mystical union. Although completed in 1389, much earlier versions of individual sermons can be identified, a circumstance which points to a work that emerged from a lengthy preaching career. Some of the collected sermons contain an original and distinctive philosophical understanding of the soul's union with God, developed through a careful reading of the entire pseudo-Dionysian corpus and Thomas Gallus' Latin commentaries on Dionysius, and at least in part written in direct response to Eckhart's writings on the subject.[84]

A number of further observations are required. First: the boundaries between the works are not strict, especially where the longer and more wide-ranging works are concerned. For example, some of the more technical issues in the German sermon collection are closely related to formal disquisitions on the same material in the commentary on John, being given a pragmatic cast as they are applied to contemplative practice when placed in the context of a sermon. The situation is similar with the *Dekalogerklärung*, which is only partially concerned with the ethical and catechetical issues with which a commentary on the Ten Commandments might be expected to deal. Instead it is principally concerned with the same kind of contemplative and even mystical topics which are treated by the sermon collection, whilst presenting a different approach to these topics in keeping

---

[84] See principally Blumrich, 'Feuer der Liebe'; id. (ed.), *Marquard von Lindau. Deutsche Predigten*, pp. 54*–80*; id., 'Die deutschen Predigten Marquards von Lindau'; Löser, 'Rezeption als Revision'; id., 'Jan Milíč in europäischer Tradition', pp. 232–4; Largier, 'Das Glück des Menschen', pp. 851–4; and Störmer-Caysa, *Gewissen und Buch*, pp. 156–60.

with its structure. Second: the intellectual *niveau* of the most sophisticated works—notably the commentary on John—is very high indeed, quite in line with the writings that emanated from the universities. Other, less obviously sophisticated works are written in the light of this distinguished theological background. Even a very short and uniquely transmitted work like *De horto paradisi*, written in German with Latin components, reflects a substantive knowledge of contemporary theological issues, without in itself constituting a novel contribution to the intellectual debate on those issues themselves.[85] The breadth of Marquard's output is significant in itself, and no one work, taken alone, can be considered representative of the rest. Third: the boundary between the different languages, Latin and German, is fluid. Marquard wrote works of a similar nature in both languages, as is most obvious with the allegorical treatises on contemplation. It is a remarkable feature of many of his works that they were translated into the 'other' language very soon after, and possibly even before, his death: this includes German translations of *De reparatione hominis* and the commentary on John. Many of the works incorporate elements from the 'other' language within them—and not, as one might initially expect, Latin technical terms appearing untranslated in German works. Rather, the opposite is true: *De paupertate*, for example, is a complex Latin work that incorporates a series of words, including the Eckhartian *abegescheidenheit*, consistently as untranslated German technical terms.[86] Nigel Palmer has undertaken a thorough study of these phenomena in Marquard's works,[87] and the further illumination of this issue would require the systematic editorial work that, for most of the relevant works, has not been undertaken. The important conclusion that must be drawn is not the obvious point that Marquard reached a wider audience by writing in German. Rather, the near-interchangeability of the languages themselves in his works illustrates the elevation of the status of German as an intellectual language in the cultural milieu to which Marquard belonged. It is obvious that earlier writers made significant contributions in this direction, notably Meister Eckhart. But the period from around 1330 is characterized by a growing productivity of German-language works in scholastic form, and as Georg Steer has proven, the development of a German vocabulary sufficient for the translation of Latin scholastic writing.[88] An equivalent status in the two languages is reached towards the end of the century, evident in Marquard's works, their

[85] See Mossman, 'Die Konzeptualisierung des inneren Menschen'.
[86] See Hartinger (ed.), *Der Traktat De paupertate*, pp. 125–35.
[87] See Palmer, 'Latein, Volkssprache, Mischsprache', pp. 70–101.
[88] See Steer, *Hugo Ripelin von Straßburg*, pp. 18–31 and 433–9.

early translations, and above all in the narrowly transmitted works of the 'Meister des Lehrgesprächs', whom Karl Heinz Witte identifies as Johannes Hiltalingen von Basel.[89] Whether Marquard's works should be seen as representatives of a more general phenomenon, rather than texts that gave the decisive impetus to that phenomenon, is a question that could only be approached on a much broader textual basis. The most recent history of fourteenth-century German literature proves singularly unhelpful in this respect. It excludes Marquard on the grounds that his work was particularly influential in the fifteenth century; he becomes thus a man 'ahead of his time', divorced from his historical context.[90] In truth, Marquard's achievements form a major part of the development of German and Latin prose-writing in the period immediately after Eckhart, Tauler, and Seuse. He constructed a scholastic tradition and made new use of the vernacular and Latin in other literary forms, in a period in which the number of notable writings in German is otherwise somewhat limited: and unlike his significant predecessors, Marquard was not a Dominican, but a Franciscan.

Only in certain cases is the implicit audience of Marquard's works obvious. The Latin scholastic works on specific theological issues are clearly aimed at other friars. The transmission of the German sermon collection makes it almost certain that it was produced for an audience of religious women.[91] Some works provide intimations of their implicit audience. The allegorical treatises deal so comprehensively with the mental suffering and other difficulties associated with the intensive practice of contemplation that it is unlikely they were written for an audience that was not at least semi-enclosed. For other works, notably the *Dekalogerklärung*, the *Eucharistietraktat*, and *De anima Christi*, there is no single obvious implicit audience. Either they offer guidance on such a wide range of topics (the *Dekalogerklärung*) as to be applicable to many different audiences, or their material concerns pragmatic issues, like the manner in which Christ's Passion should be considered or the eucharistic sacrament received, that is just as applicable within as without an enclosed or semi-enclosed context.

This question of ambiguous implicit audience brings us to the important issue of the relationship between the traditional dichotomy of lay and religious in the new context of the towns of late medieval Germany. We

---

[89] On Hiltalingen and the 'Deutsche Scholastik', see summatively Witte, *Der Meister des Lehrgesprächs*, pp. 3–5; further Steer, *Scholastische Gnadenlehre*, pp. 35–6 and 178–94; and Ruh, *Geschichte der abendländischen Mystik*, vol. 3, pp. 354–88, esp. pp. 354–5, 361–2, and 384–6.

[90] Janota, *Orientierung durch volkssprachige Schriftlichkeit*, pp. 140–1.

[91] See Blumrich (ed.), *Marquard von Lindau. Deutsche Predigten*, pp. 14*–26*.

are faced with an urban milieu in which enclosed and semi-enclosed convents, tertiary houses, beguinages, confraternities, and other forms of religious affiliation were integral and widespread, and in which an expanding network of mendicant *studia* taught novices. Large numbers of friars preached here to an increasingly well-educated, German-literate, and numerous mercantile and artisan population. In such a world the traditional dichotomy of lay and religious breaks down. This issue has been widely discussed in recent historiography, principally by Christoph Burger. He has argued in favour of retaining the term 'laity', but as a wide term to encompass all those who were not either ordained, capable of sophisticated Latin, or educated at university. These, the 'religious', stand then at one end of a broad and diffuse spectrum. The classification of this spectrum should not, argues Burger, be attempted by trying to evaluate the relative level of religious devotion associated with particular forms of life—an essentially impossible task—or by dividing those who followed a formal rule from those who did not. There is no practical difference between the devout layperson with no formal religious affiliation, the beguine, the member of a tertiary order, or a brother or sister of the Common Life, in terms of the quality of their religious experience. The key distinction is not the adoption of a particular rule, but the level of theological knowledge approximately common to all town dwellers with a religious interest who were not ordained or university-educated.[92] Other scholars, recently including Berndt Hamm and Mathilde van Dijk, have taken a similar line in characterizing the 'wide audience' for works such as Marquard's in late medieval Germany and the Netherlands, ranging from priests and confessors through enclosed religious women to the educated laity without formal religious affiliation.[93]

This core argument is convincing. It is supported by the absence of an explicit or otherwise obvious audience in Marquard's works that deal with pragmatic issues of the Christian life. This phenomenon is not confined to Marquard. Georg Steer has demonstrated that the writings of Rulman Merswin and his largely non-ordained circle in Strasbourg show absolutely no traces of a specifically 'lay' piety, but instead seek to establish a practicable spiritual form of life, equally applicable to all varieties of Christian, with 'der Mensch'—the person, defined no further—as the addressee.[94] If we

---

[92] See Burger, 'Direkte Zuwendung', pp. 87–91; and id., 'Transformation theologischer Ergebnisse', pp. 53–6.
[93] See Hamm, 'Was ist Frömmigkeitstheologie?', pp. 13–14; and van Dijk, 'De wil op God afstemmen', pp. 84–6.
[94] Steer, 'Die Stellung des >Laien<', pp. 643–8.

wish to set aside a closely defined category of religious, then it cannot be in direct opposition to 'laity', but at one end of a spectrum that proceeds through a series of interrelated and fluid gradations towards the individual without religious interest at all, who, logically, must occupy the opposite pole. It is only in this sense that we can say that Marquard's works were predominantly written for 'the laity'.

Marquard's works, then, may express a 'lay piety' thus broadly conceived; but not a 'popular' piety. The fashionable dichotomy of 'elite' and 'popular' religion is even less helpful than that of 'religious' and 'lay', because it relies—as Klaus Schreiner has argued—on a set of distinctions based on categories that do not, in reality, apply to the characterization of the differing nature of religious experience. 'Popular' religion has come to be associated with the superstitious and the irrational, with the lower social classes, and with the mass experience; 'elite' religion, by contrast, is associated with the logical and rational, the higher social *niveau*, and individual, personal and private experience. Schreiner has argued at considerable length that there is no real evidence for these distinctions—certainly not for the association of a particular kind of religious experience with a particular social class. There are clearly important differences of the level of theological knowledge between the clergy and the laity and in their respective functions; but these are distinctions which do not bear upon piety. The clerical—lay distinction served to define the position of the clergy and safeguard their authority conservatively; it does not function well as a hermeneutic tool to assess comparative levels of religious knowledge, and certainly not levels of religious experience. Vernacular works like Marquard's, produced for 'the laity' writ large, conceive of their audiences as divided up in terms of the stage of their spiritual development, not of their belonging to a particular social group. This does not, of course, mean that all religious experience was the same and cannot be categorized at all. We require instead a more contingent model; one which recognizes that there existed forms of piety common to all Christians—pilgrimage, eucharistic communion, devotion to Mary and the saints, and so on—which were approached and functionalized in different ways by different social groups at different times; and one which recognizes that the *laicus* in a prosperous late medieval German town was a very different creature to his illiterate counterpart in a twelfth-century English village.[95] We are required to adopt a more fluid and more subtly differentiated model of religious experience and piety to characterize the late medieval German laity, far

---

[95] See Schreiner, 'Laienfrömmigkeit', esp. pp. 1–41, 57–63, and 75–8.

removed from the set of associations the concept of 'popular piety' commonly evokes, and one which assesses the implications of the way in which the devotional works of the period divide their audience themselves, rather than seeking to interpose a heuristic model upon them.

If we reject the associations of 'popular piety' as invalid, then we must also reject the term 'popularization' as a generally applicable term to describe the transfer of theological knowledge by late medieval clerics. Undoubtedly, some works—though not Marquard's—represent a simplifying popularization of theological information, and these works are principally catechetical in nature. Yet we also have a large body of material that engages in a much more sophisticated way with the pragmatic issues of the Christian life, such as might best be called 'applied theology', and which is increasingly written in the vernacular. Burger has termed this process of communicating information the 'transformation' of theological knowledge: the adaptation of theology at (near-)university standard into a literary form and structure accessible to a readership without a university education, with only a limited, or no consequent, substantive reduction in the intellectual level of the material transmitted. Importantly, Burger argues against the perception of a dichotomy between conservative-minded clerics, concerned to preserve theological knowledge as the domain of an intellectual elite, and reform-minded individuals who 'transformed' such knowledge into new and accessible forms to educate and instruct 'the laity'. The intention of those who produced this kind of material was moral, and not intellectual education, which led in turn to the acquisition of spiritual control over their audience. This was achieved by setting the direction of thought in that audience, through the propagation of particular models of, and approaches to features of, the Christian religion in their sermons and treatises.[96] Together with Burger's valuable concept of 'transformation', we must also recognize the increasing status of German as an intellectual language, which made possible the composition of extremely sophisticated theological works in more or less scholastic form directly in German: a phenomenon which, as mentioned earlier, is in full fruition from around 1370 and ought inextricably to be linked to Marquard and Johannes Hiltalingen.

The end product of these processes forms a literary and theological genre of its own, occupying a position between Latin scholasticism and vernacular catechesis at a lower level. To characterize this new genre of the later

---

[96] See Burger, 'Transformation theologischer Ergebnisse', pp. 47–53 and 57–62; id., 'Direkte Zuwendung', pp. 91–109; and Hamm, 'Was ist Frömmigkeitstheologie?', pp. 15–17.

Middle Ages, Berndt Hamm offers the term 'Frömmigkeitstheologie'—
approximately translated, 'theology of piety', but perhaps better left as a
terminus technicus in German. Hamm provides a useful definition of piety,
regarding it as the realization of aspects of religion either at the more
theoretical level of systematic reflection on the conduct of an individual's
own life, or at the more practical level of adjusting that conduct in order to
incorporate new approaches, or to change existing approaches, towards
particular elements of religious belief. 'Frömmigkeitstheologie' is then a
form of late medieval theological literature that, in various ways, seeks to
guide the individual to shape the conduct of his life externally and of his
thought internally in a particular way. This literature addresses pragmatic
issues and does so using forms and structures different to those of the purely
academic world, increasingly distancing itself from the abstract theology
and philosophy of the schools, and from the exclusivity of speculative
mysticism. Hamm argues persuasively that the later Middle Ages, seen
thus, was not a period of intellectual stagnation, but of the redirection of
intellectual energies into the production of new forms of theology; new
forms that—crucially—did not merely repackage the conclusions of twelfth-
and thirteenth-century scholastic theology, but were innovative and dynamic in their generation of new ideas, new insights and new approaches.
The intellectuals writing 'Frömmigkeitstheologie' were responsive to the
incorporation of new elements into their theology from pastoral experience
and the *cura animarum*, both within and without the convent context,
giving the literary product new levels of practical relevance and intimacy
that were alien to the more abstract writing of the schools. Particularly
important is the absence of institutional barriers in 'Frömmigkeitstheologie'—the authors do not present themselves primarily as representatives of
a particular order, theological school, or narrow academic tradition in their
works, thus seeking to effect intellectual change on a wide scale with their
works across the entire spectrum of the lay world, as we have earlier defined
it. This is not to say that all 'Frömmigkeitstheologie' was the same. We find
marked tensions between, for example, those who sought security from
human weakness in the institutional forms, manifestations, and practices of
the church, and those who emphasized the inner, immediate encounter of
the soul with Christ's mercy at the other side of the spectrum.[97]

The background to the production of 'Frömmigkeitstheologie' was formed, argues Hamm, by a climate of an intensified fear of divine judgement and of diabolical assault, with a concomitant search for certainties in the receipt of grace and, ultimately, salvation.[98] Sven Grosse has discussed whether this mentality, and in particular *scrupulositas*, was prevalent with an especial intensity in the later Middle Ages. Cautiously, and almost certainly correctly, he concludes in the affirmative. Wars, plagues, and even schisms were not novel elements—even if they were of exceptional severity in the fourteenth and fifteenth centuries. Urban growth, combined with the new attention to pastoral care from the mendicant orders, was novel, and produced a concomitant and equally novel increase in the desire to conduct a lay life in more strict accordance with religious forms, together with a more intensive attention to the reform of convent life in the monastic context. Associated with the contemporary theological conception of grace and salvation as uncertain (not as capricious or random, that is, but as essentially unknowable to the individual in this life), this may have lain behind the profound insecurities that generated the need satisfied by 'Frömmigkeitstheologie'. Fear, moreover, was only negative when excessive or disordered; the correctly adjusted *timor filialis* drew the individual to humility, and towards a balanced state between hope of salvation and fear of distancing the self from God through sin.[99] Grosse's work focuses on the fear of insufficient confession in the fifteenth century; we will return directly to this issue of fear, in relation to eucharistic communion, in Chapter 2. Hamm states the underlying assumption summatively:

Angst verursachend war ein durch Vorgänge der Verinnerlichung und Intensivierung der Frömmigkeitsmaßstäbe verstärktes Gefühl des geistigen Ungenügens, der Unfähigkeit, Gottes Gebote zu erfüllen, Todsünden zu vermeiden und eine ausreichende Reue, Beichte und Genugtuung zu haben.[100]

(Fear was caused by a feeling of intellectual inadequacy; of the inability to fulfil God's commandments, to avoid mortal sin, and to have a sufficient repentance, confession, and satisfaction—a feeling that had been strengthened by processes of the interiorization and intensification of the norms of piety.)

It was against the background of these concerns that 'Frömmigkeitstheologie' was written, and to these concerns that it addressed itself directly. Different methods were applied, and different traditions developed. It will

---

[98] See id., 'Was ist Frömmigkeitstheologie?', pp. 29–31; and id., 'Normative Zentrierung', pp. 165–7.
[99] See Grosse, *Heilsungewißheit und Scrupulositas*, pp. 31–4; on the theology of uncertain grace and salvation, see pp. 35–42; on the useful and harmful kinds of fear, pp. 42–4.
[100] Hamm, 'Die „nahe Gnade"', p. 544.

be our task to elucidate those traditions and define the trajectory of
late medieval thought on the most central issues. 'Frömmigkeitstheologie',
then, provides a useful term to characterize much of Marquard's oeuvre.
There are a number of ways in which we might further approach the
historical contextualization of his writings. One of these would be to
argue that Marquard occupies a special position in the theses concerning
the broad sweep of the intellectual and cultural history of late medieval
Germany that Hamm has developed, to which we should now briefly turn.

'Frömmigkeitstheologie' was a concrete manifestation in written form of
what Hamm has termed 'normative Zentrierung'; another term best left in
German, in translation 'centripetal normativization'. Hamm uses it to
describe the processes in religion and society of intensifying the concentration upon a guiding, orientating, and regulating normative centre. In
theology, this took the form of a focus on what was most useful and
necessary to the individual, leaving behind the abstract speculations and
exploration of new territories of earlier periods. Hamm sees 'normative
Zentrierung' as a response to the increasing complexity of late medieval
urban life—expanding literacy, manuscript and book production, 'lay'
education, bureaucratization, and rationalization. In this world, guidance
and direction, security and order were sought in a complex and moderniz-
ing environment seen as beset by the temporal and spiritual insecurities that
created a climate of fear. The focus on the essential is paradigmatic for
'Frömmigkeitstheologie', conceived as an attempt to provide a normative
answer to complex issues and to the very complication of society itself. The
monastic reform movements of the fifteenth century represent an important strand of 'normative Zentrierung': the desire to regulate and order
convent life to form a uniform, secure basis that could function as the
spiritual bedrock of a well-ordered society. The explosion in what one
might loosely term 'cultural production' and the concomitant, superficial
appearance of multiplicity—most obvious in the growth of the cult of
saints—veils an underlying 'normative Zentrierung': the lives (and often
martyrdoms) of the saints guide the individual to the indirect imitation of
Christ as the central, normative figure, and the cumulative impression of
multiplicity in the cult of saints as a whole obscures the reality of personal
devotion to individual saints as intercessors and guides.[101] Further, Hamm
argues, 'normative Zentrierung' was not a phenomenon confined to religion. Rather, it can be identified in contemporary developments in state

---

[101] See id., 'Das Gewicht von Religion', pp. 163–70 and 172–3; and id., 'Normative
Zentrierung', pp. 163–7, 174–6, and 191–9.

formation, political organization, law, humanist thought, and so on. All of these developments shared a common origin in a changed *mentalité*, and remained interrelated without being interdependent. He concludes:

Es zeigt sich gegen Ende des Mittelalters durchaus die Parallelität unterschiedlicher Primärinteressen, die in den Grundlagen von Lebensorientierung und Mentalität verwurzelt sind. Aus diesen Wurzeln ergibt sich die Mehrgleisigkeit voneinander unableitbarer Verdichtungsvorgänge, die jeweils ihre spezifische Eigendynamik haben.[102]

(Towards the end of the Middle Ages the parallelism of different primary interests becomes clearly visible; interests that are rooted in the foundations of mentality and the orientation of the lived life. From these roots the multiple paths of mutually independent processes of intensification are derived, each of which has its own particular dynamic.)

We have briefly mentioned the tension between the focus on the exterior and the interior. Hamm views this tension as characteristic of 'normative Zentrierung', as it is found in devotional literature. Where one intellectual advocated the security inherent in the adherence to the institutional forms and manifestations of the church (notably indulgences) in the sphere of the objectifiable and quantifiable, another would insist on the search for truth and certainty through an intensification of inner religious experience and the immediate personal experience of the divine.[103] This second possibility, constituting a shift towards the interiorization of devotion and religious experience, is understood as a distinctive feature of late medieval spirituality and, as we will see, is particularly important for understanding Marquard. Klaus Schreiner has noted the increased concern for 'lay' education in the later Middle Ages as a feature that marks the placing of greater responsibility on the individual for their own salvation, a salvation that now required personal understanding.[104] Thomas Lentes has developed these ideas further. He has argued that understanding—*cognitio*—came to be seen as contributing an enhanced value to devotional practice, and even as a prerequisite for its efficacy, in the later Middle Ages. The balance between the exterior and the interior of the earlier period, in which exterior forms of devotion were held to reflect the inner state, whether those forms (notably Latin prayers) were understood or not, and so to be efficacious in God's sight regardless of the level at which they were understood, was swept away. This was not, Lentes holds, an overnight break, but a gradual process of

---

[102] Id., 'Das Gewicht von Religion', pp. 173–81, here p. 180.
[103] See ibid. 170–2; and id., 'Was ist Frömmigkeitstheologie?', pp. 33–4.
[104] Schreiner, 'Laienfrömmigkeit', pp. 51–6.

transition across a broad spectrum of intermediary positions, a process that he has traced with particular reference to the attitudes towards prayer and towards relics. At one end of this spectrum was the explicit rejection of the possibility of the external, manifested for instance in the ascetic discipline of the body, having any role to play in the constitution of an ordered internal disposition.[105]

Lentes perceives this process of transition as a gradual shift from the mimetic power of the body to the mimetic power of text: 'An die Stelle des Körpergedächtnisses als Form der Erinnerung, Vergegenwärtigung und Einübung des Heils trat nun das Schriftgedächtnis'[106] ('Written memory now took the place of bodily memory as the form of the remembrance, the actualization, and the practice of salvation'). He concludes that this shift to the definite superiority of the interior person over the exterior, aside from all the theological-dogmatic controversies, must be seen as one of the defining aspects of the Reformation movement. The Reformation, approached from this perspective, represents the dogmatic insistence on one extreme position of the late medieval spectrum; the continuation of a particular and pre-existent tendency that, through the exclusion of all else, was simultaneously a comprehensive break with late medieval thought.[107] Berndt Hamm has proposed this independently as a more general model for understanding the relationship of the Reformation to the patterns of thought in the later fifteenth century. Thus the famous *sola*-formulae of the sixteenth century—*sola scriptura, sola fide*, and so on—are the ultimate apogee of 'normative Zentrierung'; the radicalization of the focus on the necessary to exclude the remaining multiplicities of the Catholic past, and to exclude the intermediaries by which the relationship between man and Christ was negotiated.[108] Martin Luther, Hamm notes, was a passionate Observant partisan who drove the Observant insistence on the strict regulation of the conduct of life to its radical extreme, thereby simultaneously extending and breaking with the Observant tradition in his stringent focus on that which he considered truly necessary in man's relationship to God.[109] This is obviously not the only historiographical model by which the Reformation can be understood, but it has found favour amongst historians of the sixteenth century. Heinz

---

[105] See Lentes, '>Andacht< und >Gebärde<', pp. 29–63.

[106] Ibid. 63.

[107] Ibid. 64–7.

[108] See Hamm, 'Normative Zentrierung', pp. 169–73 and 200–2; and id., 'Das Gewicht von Religion', pp. 193–6.

[109] Id., 'Das Gewicht von Religion', pp. 172–3.

Schilling, indeed, views the Reformation as part of an ongoing process, midway between the *reformatio* of the fifteenth century and the emergence of Protestantism—the 'Konfessionalisierung'—in the later sixteenth century. He emphasizes, however, that the Reformation ought not to be seen as the fulfilment of late medieval reforms left incomplete or otherwise stymied in the fifteenth century. Rather, *reformatio* and Reformation should be seen as adequate responses to the particular constellations of issues faced in their own times.[110] This model of the transition of late medieval thought in Germany towards and into the Reformation remains, as its proponents acknowledge, just that—a conceptual model. There is very little available groundwork, the results of which can be used to test its validity, or to illustrate how these intellectual developments took place across the late Middle Ages. The intellectuals and texts on whom its proponents have worked are almost universally very late; Hamm himself draws principally on the works of Johannes von Paltz (d. 1511) and Johannes von Staupitz (d. 1524). If we ask where the beginning of 'Frömmigkeitstheologie' and 'normative Zentrierung' is to be located, then we find no definite answer, though Jean Gerson seems to be regarded as the principal intellectual impetus in the earlier fifteenth century.[111] It is self-evident that the temporal boundaries are extremely hard to define. Yet we must proceed now by making some claims for the significance of Marquard von Lindau: the first of which being to regard him as the first 'Frömmigkeitstheologe'.

We can, of course, trace individual elements back ad infinitum; but ultimately a point must be set at which all the elements in the particular matrix of features that we associate with 'Frömmigkeitstheologie' and the related model of late medieval intellectual history are present for the first time. We find this point with, and not prior to, Marquard. He is an intellectual whose literary productivity was so extensive that it bears comparison to Gerson's. Not one, but several of his works became bestsellers of the first rank, and came to be the standard texts *sine qua non* circulated by Observants of all orders in the fifteenth century. It is not without reason that the most recent literary history of fourteenth-century Germany, as we mentioned earlier, excludes Marquard to save him for the fifteenth-century volume. He was responsible for a set of works addressing pragmatic issues of the Christian life that offer not a multiplicity of approaches, but one,

[110] See Schilling, 'Die Reformation'; and id., 'Reformation—Umbruch oder Gipfelpunkt', esp. pp. 28–9.
[111] See e.g. Hamm, 'Das Gewicht von Religion', pp. 163–70; and id., 'Was ist Frömmigkeitstheologie?', pp. 21–4.

correct form of conduct: the beginnings of 'normative Zentrierung'. These approaches to the central features of the Christian religion—the crucified Christ, the eucharist, and so on—differ markedly from those of his contemporaries. We can go further in our claims. Marquard did not merely alter the approach offered, but the presentation of those very features themselves. He recast such central devotional foci as Mary and the Passion of Christ in a radically divergent manner, changing the terms in which it was possible to think about them in a manner that pointed forwards to the fifteenth and sixteenth centuries. Not all of Marquard's writing is so innovative, of course, but much of it is; and it will be our task to establish his relationship to the existing intellectual traditions on particular issues in order to ascertain the nature of his modification of earlier sources and preexistent ideas. The 'long fifteenth century', culminating with Martin Luther, can be seen as beginning with Marquard around 1370. We must avoid overstated claims that would link Marquard directly with the Reformation, see him as solely responsible for intellectual change across too many areas, or exaggerate the novelty of his thought. On many issues, he was conservative enough. Yet his works on the most important features of experienced religion—of piety—were so widely read that we can legitimately view them not just as representative, but as actively constitutive of a marked shift in the trajectory of German thought and religious writing at the beginning of the long fifteenth century.

We will deal, then, with three key issues—Christ's Passion, and the manner of its contemplation and imitation; the cult of the eucharist; and the devotion to Mary. The implications of Marquard's remarkable deployment of Islamic theological material for the history of the Western European intellectual engagement with Islam in the later Middle Ages has been addressed elsewhere. On all these issues, Marquard must be examined both horizontally and vertically: horizontally, to establish his position amongst his contemporaries, and vertically, to establish his relationship to those writing on the same topics before and after him. He can thereby form a fixed point in the definition of particular intellectual traditions across wider periods than his own lifetime. And this can only be done on a pan-European basis, for whilst Marquard was German and the Reformation was—initially at least—a German phenomenon at the other end of the long fifteenth century, he was not just a member of an international religious order, but also drew on an enormous wealth of Latin material that reflected the much wider currents of thought in which he is to be located.

1

The Passion

The crucifixion of Christ stands at the very centre of the Christian religion as a moment of profound theological and devotional significance. Its position in the theological economy of salvation was cast in the new light of the theory of satisfaction, and thereby elevated to a new level of importance for the entirety of the Middle Ages, by Anselm's *Cur Deus homo*. In the devotional framework of the later Middle Ages, meanwhile, its position went beyond that of *primus inter pares* alongside other elements of central soteriological significance: specifically the incarnation and the resurrection. Instead the Passion formed the central apex of the faith. Richard Kieckhefer has observed this focus on the Passion in the devotional *mentalité* of the fourteenth century to be so exclusive as to eliminate almost entirely the significance of the resurrection, with which one would otherwise, on theological grounds, expect the Passion to be intimately associated.[1] Marquard's elder contemporary Ludolf von Sachsen (d. 1378) described the cross as the culmination of Scripture, the Passion as the epitome of perfection, and Christ's death as consummation of all Christian teaching. Knowledge of the Passion enables the individual to know everything necessary for salvation:

[I]n cruce Domini, est finis Legis et Scripturae, in Passione ejus, summa omnis perfectionis, in morte ipsius, est consummatio omnis sermonis. Unde Apostulus dicebat: 'Non judicavi me aliquid scire inter vos, nisi Jesum Christum, et hunc crucifixum' [1 Cor. 2: 2], nempe quia hoc scire, est omnia scire quae ad salutem spectant.[2]

---

[1] Kieckhefer, *Unquiet Souls*, pp. 91–8.
[2] Ludolf von Sachsen, *Vita Christi*, pars 2, c. 51 (ed. 1865, p. 571ª; ed. 1870, vol. 3, pp. 375ᵇ–376ª). References to Ludolf's *Vita Christi* are given first to the 1865 folio edition, and then to the 1870 4-vol. octavo reprint. A reduced-size facsimile of the 1865 edition, with unchanged pagination, is now available, published as Ludolphus the Carthusian, *Vita Christi*, 5 vols, Analecta Cartusiana 241 (Salzburg, 2006–7).

(In the cross of the Lord is the culmination of the law and of Scripture; in his Passion is the apogee of every perfection; and in his death is the consummation of all his teaching. Wherefore the Apostle said, 'I resolved not to know anything amongst you, except for Jesus Christ, and him crucified', because to know this is indeed to know everything that pertains to salvation.)

The growing theological and devotional focus more broadly on the humanity of Christ in the eleventh and twelfth centuries had, as Giles Constable has demonstrated, made Christ's life on earth into the supreme exemplar for imitation. The apostles, saints, and church fathers came to be seen as those who had already followed in his footsteps: edifying examples, perhaps, but only models for imitation insofar as they had imitated Christ. This literal imitation of Christ found its greatest and most obvious exponent in Francis of Assisi (d. 1227) and became a normative feature of late medieval piety.[3] Simultaneously a shift of emphasis in the image of the crucified Christ had taken place. Christ was no longer *Christus triumphator*, but *Christus patiens*, the innocent man suffering and nailed to the cross: a transition newly explored by Rachel Fulton.[4] Christ crucified became, to use Eric Saak's phrase, the source of identity for the late medieval believer.[5] In terms of religious literature, Berndt Hamm has pointed repeatedly to the Passion as the ultimate focus of the process of 'normative Zentrierung', and which occupied a position of unparalleled significance within the late medieval 'Frömmigkeitstheologie'.[6] The construction of the image of the Passion is thus the ideal place to begin an analysis of Marquard's works.

From the late twelfth century, the well-known developments in medieval devotion to the Passion were accompanied by a massive expansion in the production of new literature of all genres on the subject, an expansion that continued into the early modern period and beyond. The fourteenth century witnessed the production of compendious narrative treatises on the life and Passion of Christ, of which Ludolf's *Vita Christi*, from which the quotation above was drawn, is distinguished by its particular enormity. In the mid-fourteenth century the first Passion narratives in the German vernacular began to emerge. Recent work by Thomas Bestul, Eric Saak, and in particular Tobias Kemper has given new attention to the identification,

---

[3] Constable, *Three Studies*, pp. 169–93.
[4] Fulton, *From Judgment to Passion*, pp. 9–192.
[5] Saak, *High Way to Heaven*, p. 469.
[6] Hamm, 'Normative Zentrierung', pp. 191–9; id., 'Das Gewicht von Religion', pp. 169–70.

categorization, and analysis of this literature.[7] The expansion in the quantity of literature produced was matched by a corresponding expansion in the narrative content on the Passion. Kemper's study draws on and advances older work by Kurt Ruh, F. P. Pickering, and James Marrow in demonstrating precisely how the processes of narrative elaboration operated. He shows that the exegetical and typological principles by which the New Testament accounts of the Passion were amplified and expanded were present, *in nuce*, in the relationship between the Gospels themselves and Old Testament material. The legitimating principle of the *concordantia Veteris et Novi Testamenti* underpinned the mapping of Old Testament passages in various ways onto elements of the Passion narrative.[8] Alongside these central processes by which parts of the Old Testament (in particular Psalm 21), understood as *evangelica narratio*, were transposed onto the figure of Christ and integrated into the Passion narrative, Kemper identifies a series of other sources for the elaboration and extension of that narrative. Of these, the most important are the New Testament apocrypha, in particular the *Evangelium Nicodemi*; the consideration of Passion relics, especially after the translation of the Byzantine collection to Paris in 1238–42; and the introduction of 'factual' material: natural scientific, medical, geographical, and topographical information together with rationalizing explanations of inconsistencies in the evangelical accounts.[9]

The extensive elaboration of the account in narrative texts was not a purely literary phenomenon, but reflected a deepening interest in the events of the Passion and the increased desire to know those events more intimately. Saak explains this in terms of a wider cultural shift, on the basis of his examination of Jordan von Quedlinburg's *Meditationes de passione Christi*. He argues that the elaboration of the Passion story in the Middle Ages both reflected and served to constitute the broader process of the self-definition of Christian society. This is to be seen specifically in the emphasis on the Jewish role in and responsibility for the crucifixion, which Saak interprets (in conscious accordance with the theories of R. I. Moore) in terms of the definition of a Christian society against outsiders. The demonization of the Jews in Passion texts, he argues further, was not so much a 'racial' demonization of the Jews qua Jews, but a demonization of Jews as

[7] The central developments are surveyed by Bestul, *Texts of the Passion*, pp. 34–68. A comprehensive handbook of the medieval Passion narratives in Latin and German is provided by Kemper, *Die Kreuzigung Christi*, pp. 52–169.

[8] Kemper, *Die Kreuzigung Christi*, pp. 4–8 and 12–37. For a convenient summary of the earlier studies in English see Bestul, *Texts of the Passion*, pp. 26–33.

[9] Kemper, *Die Kreuzigung Christi*, pp. 44–51.

representatives of negative human traits that medieval writers sought to target and exclude. This 'demonisation of human sin', to use Saak's phrase, forms the anti-Semitic tone of the medieval texts that elaborated the various corporeal sufferings of Christ, the better to show the different ways in which Christ was assaulted by the Jews of his time—and thus to admonish contemporary individuals against taking similar underlying attitudes.[10] There is certainly something to this argument, and we will return to Saak's position later, once we have considered Marquard himself. But even if we accept it at this stage, it does not explain the whole interest in elaborating the Passion narrative, much of which elaboration had nothing to do with the Jews.

Kemper has shown that the intention of medieval writers in using the Old Testament exegetically and typologically to write the history of the Passion differed markedly from that of the Gospel authors themselves. The evangelists were concerned to use Scripture to show Christ as the innocent man suffering and the just man condemned, and to support the faith in Christ as the awaited Messiah and son of God. None of this was doubted in the Middle Ages: whilst the exegetical and typological methods of utilizing Scripture to construct a narrative of the Passion may have been similar, the purpose could not be. This purpose was more simple: to know the history of the Passion and the life of Christ more intimately. Kemper roots the origins of this desire in the new reception of apocryphal texts from the twelfth century onwards, and the contemporaneous and similarly novel interest, stimulated by the Crusades, in the relics of the Passion. The medieval texts themselves justify their enterprise with reference to the incomplete and inconsistent status of the evangelical accounts. The continuation of the narrative elaboration in the later Middle Ages was a feature of contemporary contemplative practice: the requirement to meditate in prayer on every detail of the Passion and each individual suffering of Christ.[11] This might be regarded simply as a feature of 'gezählte Frömmigkeit': the well-known late medieval phenomenon in which merit was conceived in quantitative terms and the maximum possible merit achieved by the accumulation of, for instance, prayers or indulgences. Perhaps more accurately, we might regard the desire to know every detail of the Passion as a reflection of the desire to conform every aspect of an individual's life as closely as possible to the life of Christ, and in particular to the consummation of that life (remembering Ludolf's terminology) in the Passion. This

[10] Saak, *High Way to Heaven*, pp. 544–58.
[11] Kemper, *Die Kreuzigung Christi*, pp. 37–44.

might be regarded as the 'positive' side of the coin, in contrast to (but not incompatible with) the 'negative' side: namely Saak's interpretation of the elaborated Passion narratives as a sequence of admonitions, of things not to do and attitudes not to hold.

Much of the elaboration of the Passion story consisted of an increasingly graphic and ultimately gruesome focus on the bodily sufferings of Christ. The earliest Passion narrative to be written originally in German, the well-known *Christi Leiden in einer Vision geschaut*, was produced most likely in the second quarter of the fourteenth century, and is already at this early stage a particularly noteworthy representative of the exceptionally graphic depictive tradition. It survives in three different recensions and purports to contain a nun's vision of the Passion, from the arrest of Christ to the resurrection. All versions consist almost entirely of narrative, with very little additional commentary or guidance in contemplative practice.[12] Marrow says of this work that its purpose was not to instruct the reader or engage him in deeper meditation on the topic, but simply to move him by graphic depiction of Christ's sufferings.[13] Pickering was less cautious. 'Taken out of its context, it must appear the work of a sadistic maniac; even in its context (sensational devotional literature) it is still the most extravagant representative of its kind I have so far been able to discover.'[14] Saak regards *Christi Leiden* as 'graphic simply for the sake of impression'.[15] The prologue, which Pickering considered to be an integral component of the original version, describes how the nun desired that Christ's Passion simply be more intimately known to her. Her thoughts switched from the incarnation to Christ's deeds and to his suffering, as she sought that which would stimulate her desire for the Passion:

Nu begerde sy dat ir dat lyden Christi vns heren gruntlich zo hertzen gienge vnd arbeite sich darna mit vil begerden. Nu gedechte sy an syn komen in menscheliche nature, Nu an manche wunnencliche doegende die he dem menschen gedaen hatte, Nu an syn demoedich lyden dat he vmb syne doegent geleden hait, vnd gedechte hyn vnd her, so wat sy vant dat ir begerde reitzen solde zo Christus lyden.[16]

(Now she desired that the Passion of Christ our Lord would enter her heart of hearts, and applied herself to this end with great desire. Now she thought about his advent in human nature; now about the many delightful virtues that he had manifested to mankind; now about his humble Passion, which he suffered for his

---

[12] On the different redactions of this work and their dating see, with all further references, ibid. 147–50, and now Bacher, 'Mgf 1030 Berlin', pp. 84–5.

[13] Marrow, *Passion Iconography*, pp. 18–19.

[14] Pickering (ed.), *Christi Leiden*, p. 4.

[15] Saak, *High Way to Heaven*, p. 518.

[16] *Christi Leiden*, 62. 20–7.

virtue; and she thought about this and about that, about whatever she found that should stimulate her desire for Christ's Passion.)

Her vision is received in response to her inability to focus on the Passion. The divine voice that then speaks to her maintains simply that God desires 'that the Passion of his child is perceived and known' ('dat man syns kindes lyden bevyndet vnd bekennet').[17] There is little more in any recension of the entire work on how or why the subject matter is to be approached.[18] On one level, one might argue that the ways and purposes of considering the Passion were too self-evident and manifold to require explanation. Yet the guidance that *Christi Leiden* provides is so brief and so sparsely distributed in the work that it is hard not to concur with the common view, that the work itself was intended simply to move the individual to shock and sympathy—even if it would be complemented in practice by other material in the Passion devotion of those who read it.

Similar in its almost exclusively narrative approach, and in its graphic emphasis on bodily suffering, is the *Extendit manum* Passion treatise attributed to Heinrich von St Gallen, a master of the university of Prague. Much longer than *Christi Leiden*, it is another of the earlier Passion narratives written originally in German, and is distinguished by its enormous transmission. With more than 180 extant manuscripts, it is one of the most widely circulated medieval German texts of all. The earliest known manuscript dates approximately to 1400 and a securely datable manuscript survives from 1416; its composition, regardless of the problematic attribution of its authorship, is generally placed in the last quarter of the fourteenth century.[19] It is thus exactly contemporary with Marquard's works. Aside from the narrative, it contains just two short passages on the manner of contemplation: a statement regarding disciplines that foster conformity to Christ,[20] and a brief section translated from the *Stimulus amoris* added at the very end.[21]

---

[17] *Christi Leiden*, 62. 32–3.

[18] The preface compiled from Seuse's *Vita* that is added to the second recension refers to a Dominican friar who sought to suffer and be crucified with Christ, and introduces the motif that considering the Passion by reading the work provided consolation; see *Christi Leiden*, 60. 12–14. Further elements that direct the reader to meditate on the subject matter are found in the body of the common text at 65. 25–30, and in one of the lengthy interpolations in the third recension, edited pp. 38–41, ll. 59–68.

[19] On these issues see, with all further references, Kemper, *Die Kreuzigung Christi*, pp. 154–6. For a full discussion of Heinrich von St Gallen and the works attributed to him see Hilg (ed.), *Das >Marienleben<*, pp. 373–88.

[20] Heinrich von St Gallen, Passionstraktat *Extendit manum*, 61. 17–29.

[21] Ibid. 74. 7–76. 8; cf. Eisermann, *>Stimulus amoris<*, pp. 527–9.

Not all late medieval works on the Passion took an exclusively narrative approach, of course. The long and widely circulated Latin treatises all combined narration with instruction and guidance in the meditation and contemplation of the Passion, beginning with the preface to Bonaventura's *Lignum vitae* (*c.*1260), the seminal *Meditationes vitae Christi*, written around 1300,[22] and Ubertino da Casale's *Arbor vitae crucifixae*, the first recension of which was written in 1305—all incidentally Franciscan texts. The longest of all, the Carthusian Ludolf's *Vita Christi*, combines material from a wide range of existing works with particular focus on the manner in which the historical events (though no less graphically described) were to be contemplated.[23] The *Vita Christi* is slightly earlier than Marquard's writings, being written at some point in the period 1348–68, and probably prior to 1360 in the Charterhouse at Mainz.[24] It was especially popular in Germany. Strasbourg, where Ludolf is believed to have spent his latter years, became the epicentre of its transmission. A copy of the first part of the work was donated to the Franciscan convent there in 1375, at which time Marquard may have been a resident.[25]

With this broad background in mind we must now turn to Marquard. We will look first at his presentation of the Passion, and then at the response that his works on the subject require and encourage of their readers. As with any late medieval author, all his works contain occasional references to the Passion. But three in particular adopt the Passion as their central focus: the third part of his (German) treatise *De anima Christi*, and his sermons on Good Friday (no. 10) and on Christ's suffering (no. 14). In addition, we can draw as necessary on the theological background to these German works presented in his Latin treatises *De reparatione hominis* and *De perfectione humanitatis Christi*.

The sequential depiction of the Passion receives limited attention in these works. The introduction to the Good Friday sermon briefly describes the innocent suffering of Christ on the cross. The crucified Christ is compared to the needy poor, who place themselves on the path in front of churches so as to evoke compassion:

---

[22] For this 'early' dating of the *Meditationes vitae Christi* see Geith, 'Lateinische und deutschsprachige Leben Jesu-Texte', pp. 274–80, and Kemper, *Die Kreuzigung Christi*, pp. 98–107.

[23] See Kemper, *Die Kreuzigung Christi*, pp. 124–33 and 136–40; on Ludolf's sources see further Baier, *Untersuchungen zu den Passionsbetrachtungen*, pp. 197–389.

[24] Kemper, *Die Kreuzigung Christi*, pp. 136–40, with all further references.

[25] Baier, *Untersuchungen zu den Passionsbetrachtungen*, p. 135.

>Respice in faciem Christi tui<, inquit psalmista. [Ps. 83: 10] Also schribet der kûng Dauid: >Sich an das antlit dines Cristus.< Es ist sitt, das arm dûrftigen, die krank vnd siech sind, sich seczend fûr die kilchen an den weg vnd den lúten zôgend ir krankhait vnd ir siechtagen, dår vmb daz si erbårmd mit in habend. Suss håt hût getån der hôh wirdig gottes sun, vnd ist hûtt gegangen an das crûcz arm vnd blôss, daz er nit hett, dår vff er sin hôbt genaigen môht [Matt. 8. 20], vnd håt erzôiget allen menschen sin armût, sin liden vnd sinen verwunten lip, sin hend, sin fûss durch negelt, sini ôgen rôt von wainen, sin siten offen, sinen blaichen mund getrenket mit essich vnd mit gallen, sin hôbt gecrônet von den dornen, sin antlit verspûwen von den juden, vnd håt gesprochen durch den propheten Jeremiam: >O uos omnes qui transitis etc. O ir all, die da gånd durch den weg, nemend war vnd sehend, ob kain schmerz gelich si minem schmerczen.< [Lam. 1: 12] Hånd erbårmd mit mir, vnd sehend min antlit an, wan ich es alles vnschuldeklich lid durch ŵwern willen.[26]

('Respice in faciem Christi tui', said the Psalmist. Thus writes King David, 'Look upon the face of your Christ.' It is customary that the needy poor, who are ill and sick, sit down on the road in front of churches, showing their illnesses and ailments to the people, so that they may take pity upon them. The exalted son of God has acted thus today, and today he has gone to the cross poor and naked, 'such that he had nothing upon which he could rest his head'. To all mankind he has shown his poverty, his suffering, and his wounded body; his hands and his feet pierced with nails; his eyes red with tears; his side opened; his blanched mouth quenched with vinegar and gall; his head crowned with thorns, and his face spat upon by the Jews; and he has spoken through the prophet Jeremiah, 'O vos omnes qui transitis, etc. O you all, who pass by along the road, behold; and consider if there is any pain equal to my pain.' Take pity upon me, and look upon my face; because I am suffering it all innocently for your sake.)

The focus of this passage, however, is on the appropriate response to the image of Christ's suffering, rather than on the sequential presentation of that suffering itself. The individual is exhorted to gaze on Christ's face (following Psalm 83: 10), to consider the extent of his suffering (following Lamentations 1: 12), and to have pity and compassion with Christ because he suffered innocently for mankind's sake. The direct address to the reader in the second person, the focus on Christ's face (which evokes the Veronica imagery associated with the cult of the Holy Face), and the comparison with an instance of contemporary reality in the form of the needy poor combine to create a sense of immediacy and an intimacy between the crucified Christ and the individual. It is then the appropriate response to the crucified Christ that forms the substance of the sermon itself. Similarly in the *Eucharistietraktat*, a short sequence of the principal points of the Passion forms the basis of a prayer to be said following sacramental

---

[26] *Predigt* 10, ll. 2–15 (p. 87).

reception, structured to impress upon the individual the fact that it was for his sake that Christ suffered, and in supplication to seek participation in Christ's eternal reward.[27]

The primary textual basis for a consideration of Marquard's presentation of the Passion is therefore his German treatise *De anima Christi*. This mediates into German and extends ideas incipient in his long Latin work *De reparatione hominis*. It is a tripartite treatise on the imitation of Christ, dealing successively with his poverty, humility, and suffering, beginning with the injunction of Exodus 25: 40: 'Inspice et fac secundum exemplar' ('Look carefully, and act according to the exemplar').[28] The third section, on suffering, is divided into six subsections. The second part of the first of these deals with the multiplicity of Christ's corporeal sufferings. In this we find a very short narrative of the Passion, attributed to Bernard of Clairvaux. This switches midway to present a list of the injuries inflicted upon the organs of Christ's five senses, and the wounds received by the parts of his body:

Von diessem manigfeldigen lyden redet sant Bernhart, spricht eynen suberlichen spruch vnd ludet also: Vnßer herre vnd vnser erloser wirt durch lieden mit allerleÿ pÿne in allen deÿlen der sÿnne vnd von allen menschen: Die konige, die spotten. Die richter vrteylten. Der iunger verkaufft ÿne. Die zwolffboden flohen. Die bischoff[,] schriber vnd glissener clageten. Die heyden geysselten. Die schare verdumete. Die ritter creucigeten[. D]az heubt, do von erziederten die engelischen geiste, wart von dicken dorne durch stecket. Das schone antlitze uber alle menschen kynden wirt entstellet von dem verspeyen der Iuden. Die liechten augen uber die sonne, die werdent in den dot verfinstert. Die oren enhorent nit den sang der engele,

[27] See *Eucharistietraktat*, 292. 15–293. 5; for a discussion of eucharistic prayers on the Passion see Schuppisser, 'Schauen mit den Augen des Herzens', pp. 171–2 n. 14.

[28] On *De anima Christi*, see Palmer, 'Marquard von Lindau', cols. 96–7. To the manuscripts listed there can be added Einsiedeln, Stiftsbibliothek, cod. 283 (1105), 491–7 (section IV; c.1483); New York, Jewish Theological Seminary of America, MS NH 108, 70^r–80^r (section I, incomplete; second half of 15th cent.); and Trier, Stadtbibliothek, Hs 627/1525 oct., 13^r–23^r (sections I–III; c.1500). The additional sections IV–VII, which are transmitted after the treatise proper in certain manuscripts, are unrelated to the theme of the core treatise of sections I–III. Marquard's authorship of texts IV–V is probable, as indicated by Blumrich (ed.), *Marquard von Lindau. Deutsche Predigten*, pp. 43*–44*, on the basis of textual comparisons with the sermon collection; his authorship is similarly probable for section VI, a eucharistic tract in four parts, on account of its very close relationship to the authentic *De corpore Christi*. The authorship of section VII, a short text on the discretion of spirits, remains doubtful. A close comparison of the German and Latin versions of section III reveals that the Latin text (Munich, Bayerische Staatsbibliothek, Cgm 661, 269^v–272^v) is a secondary translation and that *De anima Christi* is, in correction to Nigel Palmer's earlier statement, an original composition in German.

mer das spotten der sunder. Der munt, der do leret die chore der engele, der wirt
getru[n]cket mit eßige vnd mit gallen. Die hende, die die hymmel schuffen, die
werdent gestrecket an das crutze, der gantze lÿp wirt durchslagen. Die fuße, der
schemel angebedet wirt, die werdent an das crutze, der gantz lip wir[t] durchslagen.
Die sÿtte mit eÿme spere [wirt] durchstochen. Vnd nicht bleip an ÿme, dan
die zunge alleÿne, das er vor die sunder beden mochte vnd sin mutter dem iungern
beuelhen.[29]

(St Bernard talks of this manifold suffering. He makes a seemly statement that is as
follows: Our Lord and our saviour is pierced through with every kind of pain, in
every portion of his senses, and by every estate of mankind. The kings scorned him.
The judges condemned him. The disciple sold him. The apostles fled. The prelates,
scribes, and Pharisees accused him. The pagans whipped him. The crowd damned
him. The soldiers crucified him. His head, which the angelic spirits adorned, was
gored by fat thorns. His face, more beautiful than that of any child of man, is
disfigured by the Jews' spittle. His eyes, brighter than the sun, are dimmed in death.
His ears hear not the angels' song, but the scorn of sinners. His mouth, which taught
the choirs of angels, is quenched with vinegar and gall. His hands, which created the
heavens, are stretched out on the cross; his whole body is beaten through and
through. His feet, whose resting place is adored, are beaten through and through
with his whole body. His side is pierced by a spear. And nothing remained in him,
save his tongue alone, so that he could pray for the sinners and commend his mother
to his disciple.)

After this passage, Marquard asks which of Christ's corporeal sufferings was
the greatest. He identifies four possibilities. In each case the content is
unexceptional in the context of contemporary literature on the Passion,
established using conventional strategies, and the item concerned is stated
briefly, without an especially graphic accentuation. In all cases, parallels can
easily be found in the standard contemporary works.

---

[29] *De anima Christi*, 201. 14–37. This passage is cited in the original Latin in the
same context in *De reparatione hominis*, a. 23 (120. 29–121. 1); the source is not
identified there by the editor. In fact, the entire passage is taken from Bonaventura's
Soliloquium, c. 1, §4, 33 (vol. 8, pp. 28–67), here pp. 39[b]–40[a]. The initial section 'Vnßer
herre … creucigeten' is from Bonaventura's own pen; the subsequent section, 'Daz heubt
… beuelhen' is then introduced in the *Soliloquium* as a quotation attributed to Bernard
of Clairvaux. This quotation is not found in Bernard's authentic works, but it can be
identified in the *Manipulus florum* of Thomas of Ireland, a florilegium written at Paris in
or shortly before 1306. There it is attributed to 'Bernardus, in quodam sermone'; see
Manipulus florum, q3[rb–va] ('Passio', entry z); and for a conspectus of Bernard quotations
in the *Manipulus florum* see Rouse and Rouse, *Preachers, Florilegia and Sermons*, pp. 420–
1. The switch in the character of the corresponding section in Marquard's works, from
the narration of the Passion to the description of Christ crucified, is thus explained. The
whole passage is excerpted from the *Soliloquium*, but the distinction between Bonaventura's initial words on the Passion and the embedded quotation from a pseudo-
Bernardine text has been erased.

First, Marquard considers the flagellation. An Old Testament verse (Ps. 128: 3) ultimately underpins his statement. Initially, however, he quotes from an unspecified chancellor of Paris, who maintains that the whips were equipped with knife-points that removed a piece of flesh each time they pierced Christ's body:

Doch zum ersten mogte geantwort werden, das er das groste lÿden enphing, do er gegeÿsselt wart. Wann iß schriben ein kentzeler von Pariß, das er gegeÿsselt worde mit ysern messern, die forne heubter hatten, also das sie mit dem slahen in den edeln lÿp dieff gingen vnd ÿn dem wieder uß ziehende ÿe eÿn deÿl synes zarten lybes heruß rissen. Darumb sprach er auch durch den wÿsensagen: Vff mÿme rucke hant gesmÿdet die súnder [Ps. 128: 3]. Diß enist zwiuel nit, iß were eÿn große bitterkeÿt vnd eyn große bitter martel, wann sie in [an] alle erbermde an allem deÿle sÿnes edeln lybes geÿsselten.[30]

(But first one might answer that he received the greatest suffering when he was whipped. For a chancellor of Paris writes that he was whipped with iron knives that bore barbs at the front, so that they went deep into his noble body when the whip was cracked, and each tore out a piece of his tender body as they were pulled out. Thus he spoke also through the prophet: 'The sinners have hammered upon my back.' There is no doubt that this would be tremendously severe and a great and bitter torture, because they whipped him mercilessly in every part of his noble body.)

The second possibility for Christ's greatest corporeal suffering is the crown of thorns. The thorns were pushed through Christ's skull into his brain, causing internal as well as external trauma. In the contemporary tradition, this idea rested on a typological association with the blinding of Samson; an association so long-standing that Marquard does not even have to adduce it directly.[31] The third possibility is his capture, beating, and being spat upon

---

[30] *De anima Christi*, 202. 5–16. The same discussion is found in *De reparatione hominis*, a. 23 (121. 21–122. 9); with the flagellation considered at 121. 23–5. The chancellor is not further specified; Marquard simply begins 'nam ait quidem cancellarius in suis sermonibus' ('for a certain chancellor said in his sermons') (121. 23–4). On the narrative elaboration of the flagellation see Marrow, *Passion Iconography*, pp. 134–41; see further p. 80 and n. 329 for the use of Ps. 128: 3 in this context. For parallels, see Johannes de Caulibus, *Meditationes vitae Christi*, c. 76, ll. 36–50 (p. 265); Michael de Massa, *Vita Ihesu Christi*, p. 46[rb]; Ludolf von Sachsen, *Vita Christi*, pars 2, c. 62 (ed. 1865, pp. 638[a–b]; ed. 1870, vol. 4, pp. 536[b]–538[a]); and Heinrich von St Gallen, Passionstraktat *Extendit manum*, 50. 15–26.

[31] *De anima Christi*, 202. 16–23; cf. *De reparatione hominis*, a. 23 (121. 35–41), with a long exposition, and attribution of the statement on the piercing of the brain to Bernard. On the crown of thorns in medieval texts see Kemper, *Die Kreuzigung Christi*, pp. 199–207; on the typological association with the blinding of Samson, see Marrow, *Passion Iconography*, pp. 141–2. Marquard's quotation from Bernard in *De reparatione*

by the Jews. This spitting on his face was such that, according to an unnamed teacher, Christ would have suffocated had he not been sustained by divine assistance. The underlying typological association here, which Marquard again does not directly adduce, is to the legend of the martyrdom of Hur, Moses' brother-in-law, through suffocation by being spat upon in the face.[32]

The fourth possibility, and that which Marquard concludes constituted Christ's severest corporeal suffering, was the second unclothing of Christ, after the flagellation and prior to the crucifixion itself. The clothes replaced on his whipped body stuck to the wounds, and caused greater pain when the clothes were removed again. Of all Christ's wounds, all but five were inflicted prior to the nailing to the cross, and those inflicted by the second unclothing were, supported by a physiological justification, the most severe:

Zúm vierden schriben etzliche, das er das groste lÿden vber alle lÿpliche lÿden enphyng in dem, do sie ÿme sÿn gewant uß zogen vnd ÿne crutzigen wolden. Das halden auch ich vnd bewÿset also: Wann der erwirdige sanctus Anßhelmús sprichet, das Cristus enphing sehß dusent sehß hundert vnd sehße vnd sechtzig wunden. Wann er die an funff enden enphing in der stat vnd da ÿme die bosen Iudden ÿn der wirßheit vnd in dem fließenden der wonden sÿn eÿgen gewant hant an gethan, daz sich da druckente vnd want von der wÿde wegen in die wonden vnd darinne verhartete. Vnd auch von dem dragene des sweren crutzes das gewant in die wonden gedrúcket vnd verbacken deste me vnd ÿme da darnach vnder dem crutze, da alsus syn gewant in den verserten lip verhartet was, vnd do so gar vnmÿldeclichen vnd mit grymmer boßheit vnd großer hertigkeit das gewant abe gezogen wart. Von dem abe ziehen sÿne dieffe[n] verserúnge vnd syne wonden wiedder ernúwet vnd widder fliessende worden. Das schetze ich, das das sÿn groste, bitterste lyden were, als eyn

appears in the same context in Ubertino da Casale, *Arbor vitae crucifixae*, lib. 4, c. 11 (p. 313[b]). For further parallels, see Johannes de Caulibus, *Meditationes vitae Christi*, c. 76, ll. 63–74 (p. 266); Michael de Massa, *Vita Ihesu Christi*, p. 46[va–b]; Ludolf von Sachsen, pars 2, c. 62 (ed. 1865, p. 640[a–b]; ed. 1870, vol. 4, pp. 540[b]–1[a]), with a discussion of the thorns' sharpness but not the piercing of the brain; and Heinrich von St Gallen, Passionstraktat *Extendit manum*, 52. 19–22.

[32] *De anima Christi*, 202. 23–34 (no parallel in *De reparatione hominis*). On the typological association with the martyrdom of Hur, together with a parallel from a 15th-cent. Dutch life of Christ for the statement that Christ required divine assistance to avoid suffocation by spitting, see Marrow, *Passion Iconography*, pp. 132–4. For further parallels, see Johannes de Caulibus, *Meditationes vitae Christi*, c. 75, ll. 163–8 (p. 262); Michael de Massa, *Vita Ihesu Christi*, p. 46[vb]; Ludolf von Sachsen, *Vita Christi*, pars 2, c. 60 (ed. 1865, p. 621[b]; ed. 1870, vol. 4, p. 502[a–b]), with the idea that such spitting was a standard Jewish custom, occasionally resulting in suffocation; and Heinrich von St Gallen, Passionstraktat *Extendit manum*, 57. 10–21, with further instances of spitting at 42. 27–43. 6 and 44. 13–18.

igliche mensche selber wol befindet vnd werck ader duch daruff leget, Wer ẏme des uß zucket, als iß darinne verhartet ist, iß geet ẏme durch alle synen lẏp vnd dut yme vil weherser wann das erste snẏden an ẏme selber.[33]

(Fourth, some write that he received the greatest suffering beyond any other bodily suffering when they took off his clothes and wanted to crucify him. I hold this position too, and it is proven as follows. For the venerable St Anselm says that Christ received six thousand, six hundred, and sixty-six wounds. He received these in five places in the city, and then, his wounds flowing, the evil Jews in their wickedness replaced his clothes, which pressed upon him, adhered to his wounds on account of their breadth, and dried in them. His clothes were pressed into his wounds even more by his bearing of the heavy cross. After this, as he stood beneath the cross, when his clothes had hardened in his lacerated body, his clothes were taken off again with the utmost cruelty, fierce wickedness, and great severity. From this unclothing his deep lacerations and his wounds were reopened and flowed with blood again. In my estimation that was his greatest, and most bitter suffering. Each and every person can sense this for themselves, [if they cut themselves] and place a woven cloth or bandage on the wound: as the bandage is pulled away when it has dried in the wound, the pain shoots through the entire body and hurts much more than the initial cut.)

The painful reopening of Christ's wounds in this way is founded on Old Testament parallels, to which Marquard again does not allude here. It was another standard feature of the contemporary narrative texts on the Passion, first introduced in the *Meditatio passionis Christi*, a thirteenth-century work commonly attributed to Bede.[34] Marquard's rationalization of the painfulness of this unclothing, given at the conclusion to the quotation above, is very distinctive. The painfulness is evident, says Marquard, because anyone who has bandaged a wound and allowed the cloth to harden with blood therein will know that the removal of the bandage causes more pain than the initial injury. This is not a stock feature of the contemporary narrative texts. Significantly, however, the motif of the clothes hardened with blood is found in the German Passion treatise of the Franciscan Johannes von Zazenhausen († *c.*1380). Written in the period between 1360 and 1371, this work achieved a moderate circulation,

[33] *De anima Christi*, 202. 35–203. 21; cf. *De reparatione hominis*, a. 23 (121. 41–122. 9), with ascription of the physiological justification to Bonaventura.

[34] See Kemper, *Die Kreuzigung Christi*, pp. 179–88; on the Old Testament parallels, see Ruh, 'Zur Theologie des mittelalterlichen Passionstraktats', p. 24. For parallels in the contemporary literature, see Johannes de Caulibus, *Meditationes vitae Christi*, c. 78, ll. 10–12 (p. 270); Michael de Massa, *Vita Ihesu Christi*, pp. 47vb–48ra; Ludolf von Sachsen, *Vita Christi*, pars 2, c. 63 (ed. 1865, p. 652^a–b; ed. 1870, vol. 4, p. 565^b–566^b); and Heinrich von St Gallen, Passionstraktat *Extendit manum*, 58. 5–22, with a second such painful unclothing at 61. 30–62. 11.

being extant in twelve manuscripts.[35] Alongside *Christi Leiden in einer Vision geschaut* and the *Goldene Muskate*, neither of which was widely circulated, this was one of only three (four if one accepts a very early dating for Heinrich von St Gallen's *Extendit manum* Passion treatise) narrative works on the Passion to be written originally in German prior to Marquard's death in 1392. The relevant passage on the painful unclothing reads thus:

> Merck, do si vnserm hern vör dem crewtz nackent auszugen, do waz der vnder rock vast in sein frisch wunden verpachen; vnd do man in auz zöch, do prachen die wunden all wider auf. Die marter tet im vil wirs, wann do er mit den gayseln verwunt wörd; noch entet im vör kain marter nie so we. Daz mag ain ieglich mensch wol versten, der ez reht betraht, wie we es tüt, dem man auzz einer wunden ain werck czerret oder ain tůch daz dor inn verpachen ist.[36]

(Note that when they undressed our Lord naked in front of the cross, his undergarment was firmly dried into his fresh wounds. When he was undressed, the wounds were reopened anew. This torture hurt him much more than when he was wounded by the whips; nor had any earlier torture hurt him so much. This can be easily understood by anyone who properly considers how much it hurts when a woven cloth or a bandage is pulled out of a wound into which it has dried.)

The textual parallel of the concluding statement to the corresponding passage in *De anima Christi* is very close indeed. It is probable, though not certain, that Johannes von Zazenhausen's treatise was the earlier of the two works. It would be difficult to argue for a direct relationship on the basis of such a short parallel passage. If one is not based on the other, then both drew on a common source.

Marquard's treatment of the corporeal Passion of Christ in *De anima Christi* is not at all extensive. The four instances of bodily suffering to which he pays particular attention represent a very small selection from the countless sufferings described at tremendous length in the contemporary Passion literature from which he could have chosen. All four—the flagellation, the crown of thorns, the defilement by the Jewish onlookers, and the unclothing prior to the crucifixion—have their origins in the New Testament accounts, even if they have been elaborated in the medieval tradition. Marquard is, moreover, considerably less graphic than the gruesome and gory descriptions of the same events produced at about the same time by Heinrich von St Gallen. Marquard pays surprisingly little attention to matters of the body at all: and unlike the sermons, this is not because *De anima Christi* is preoccupied with the response

[35] See Kemper, *Die Kreuzigung Christi*, pp. 151–3.
[36] Johannes von Zazenhausen, *Deutscher Passionstraktat*, cited from Nuremberg, Stadtbibliothek, Cent. VI, 54, fols. 211ʳ–302ᵛ, at fols. 257ᵛ–258ʳ. My thanks to Tobias A. Kemper for access to copies of this work.

on the reader's part. Rather, Marquard's focus is far more strongly on the interior, mental sufferings of Christ, which becomes clear from this overview of the structure of the third section of the work:

Introduction (200. 1–7)

1. Manifold nature of Christ's sufferings (200. 8–201. 38)
    1. in the soul
    2. in the body
    Question: Which was the worst of the corporeal sufferings? (202. 1–203. 21).

2. How suffering (formulated generally) was perceived so profoundly by Christ's soul (203. 22–204. 15)
    Question: What mental issues caused Christ to sweat blood in the garden of Gethsemane? (204. 16–38)

3. The particular receptivity of Christ's body for suffering, corporeal, and mental (205. 1–32)
    Question: Was Christ's suffering moderated by his participation in the hypostatic union of the Trinity, thus constantly perceiving the joy of divinity? (205. 33–206. 31)

4. The temporal extent of Christ's interior sufferings (206. 32–207. 21)
    Question: Which was the worst of the interior sufferings? (207. 22–9)

5. Christ's (interior) suffering was never ameliorated and never stopped (207. 30–208. 32)
    Question: Did Christ suffer in his soul whilst he was asleep? (208. 33–209. 6)

6. Christ needed supernatural assistance to survive, because his interior sufferings were so grave and unceasing (209. 7–29)
    Question: Why did Christ choose to die by crucifixion?—with an appended discussion of the principles of satisfaction (209. 30–212. 7)

Marquard does not just relativize the corporeal Passion by treating it with much greater brevity than the interior sufferings, which we shall examine presently. In two other works, he makes decisive statements— unusual in his oeuvre—against the contemporary elaboration of the bodily sufferings of Christ. The first of these is found in the Good Friday sermon. He concludes a discussion of the appropriate response to the crucified Christ's face, which forms the first of three sections to the sermon, with a question. In this he attacks the invention of 'secret sufferings'—that is, sufferings of Christ that are not based upon scriptural authority:

Die fråg: Weles sind die haimlichen liden, die v̊nser herr laid, als ettlich lût haltend? Die antwûrt: Sant Dyonisius sprichet >De diuinis nominibus<, capitulo primo: >De hac occulta deitate non est audendum aliquid dicere uel cogitare etc.< Das sprichet, das man von got nichtes nit sol sagen noch gedenken, denn als vil v̊ns die hailig geschrift ze bekennend git. Vnd bi disem spruch merkest du wol, das man kain haimlich liden fûr die wårhait halten sol, daz nit in der hailgen geschrift begriffen ist. Vnd hier vmb sol man sich vff daz sicher keren vnd daz vnsicher låssen.[37]

(Question: What are the secret sufferings that our Lord underwent, as some people think? Answer: St Dionysius says in the first chapter of *De divinis nominibus*, 'De hac occulta deitate non est audendum aliquid dicere uel cogitare, etc.'. This states that one should not say or think anything at all about God, except insofar as Holy Scripture gives us to understand. From this saying you should note clearly that one should not believe any secret suffering to be true that is not encompassed by Holy Scripture. Therefore one should turn towards the safe ground, and leave the unsafe.)

Marquard makes an even more categorical rejection of the contemporary trend of inventing new sufferings of Christ without scriptural authority in his Latin commentary on John 1: 1–14. This rebuttal forms one of a short series of statements that condemn various errors of heretics, ancient philosophers, and others:

[. . .] vnde et multi deuoti aliqua ex se ipsis addunt et meditantur de passione Domini vel de operibus Christi, que nullus ewangelistarum scribit nec sanctus aliquis posuit; et plerumque talia super falso sunt fundata ex adinvencione propria. Idcirco inquit beatus Dyonisius in *De angelica ierarchia*, capitulo primo, quod de Deo nostro nihil est dicendum aut cogitandum, nisi quod scriptura sacra exprimit.[38]

(Wherefore many devout people add something from their own pen concerning the Passion of the Lord or the works of Christ, and meditate upon it; something that none of the evangelists wrote nor any saint maintained to be true. For the most part such things are grounded on error and derive from personal invention. Therefore

---

[37] *Predigt* 10, ll. 115–24 (p. 90). The context of the question within the sermon removes any suspicion that the Dionysius quotation might continue to pertain to its original context of the hidden aspects of God. Marquard uses it as a suitably authoritative statement on the general principle of not inventing things about God that cannot be supported by Scripture.

[38] *Johannes-Auslegung*, art. 8, §3, cited from Konstanz, Heinrich-Suso-Gymnasium, cod. 36, 8ʳ–42ᵛ, at fol. 31ʳ (Ko), collated with Manchester, John Rylands University Library, cod. lat. 70, 141ʳ–184ᵛ, at fol. 170ʳ (Ma). Variant readings, with the preferred reading first: de passione Domini (Ko)] de passione Christi (Ma); falso (Ma)] ecclesiam (Ko); in De angelica ierarchia (Ko)] De angelica ierarchia (Ma); nisi quod (Ko)] nisi quam (Ma). On the relationship of these two manuscripts, see Sturlese, 'Über Marquard von Lindau', pp. 280–1.

the blessed Dionysius says in the first chapter of *De angelica hierarchia* [actually *De divinis nominibus*], that nothing is to be said or thought about our Lord unless it is something that Holy Scripture articulates.)

The 'haimlich liden' ('secret sufferings'), the focus of Marquard's criticism, refers to a series of invented incidents ascribed to Christ during the day and night immediately prior to his crucifixion, and which are without scriptural foundation. There has been little modern research into the secret sufferings, and there is no precise definition as to exactly what does (or does not) constitute a secret suffering. Ulrich Köpf, who has most recently given attention to the issue, identifies three broad groups of secret sufferings: the sequence of Christ's repeated falling down; the sufferings experienced during the night Christ spent imprisoned in Caiaphas' house; and a small group of motifs associated with the flagellation, including Christ searching in the dust for his clothes and acquiring his 'secret shoulder wound'.[39] It is the second of these groups—Christ's sufferings in the dungeon—that became most prominent, and gave rise to a rich iconographical tradition in the early modern period (notably 'Christus auf dem Dreikant', 'Christus im Kerker', and 'Christus mit der Zungenwunde').[40] The early modern texts listing a sequence of fifteen secret sufferings ascribe their revelation to Margareta von Freiburg (also known as Margareta Beutlerin, or Margareta von Kenzingen; d. 1458), although Friedrich Zoepfl, in his seminal study of the secret sufferings in 1937, regarded the establishment of precisely fifteen secret sufferings as an early modern development.[41] The texts associated with Margareta do, however, provide evidence alongside other fifteenth-century texts of the late medieval origins of the secret sufferings, and James Marrow argued that all the principal iconographical components were present in the Netherlands by the second quarter of the fifteenth century at the very latest. These included a specifically Dutch 'secret suffering', the 'spikeblock': a wooden board studded with nails and attached to Christ's waist by a cord, lacerating his legs and ankles as he bore the cross to Calvary.[42] In fact, one member of an interrelated group of

[39] Köpf, 'Passionsfrömmigkeit', pp. 745–6.
[40] Köpf, 'Produktive Christusfrömmigkeit', esp. pp. 832–8, 850–1, 856–61, and 868–73, with comprehensive art historical references; on the iconographical and literary tradition in the modern period (to at least 1989) see in addition Moser, 'Die fünfzehn geheimen Leiden'.
[41] Zoepfl, 'Das unbekannte Leiden', pp. 320–9, augmented by Schmidt, 'Das geheime Leiden'; on Margareta von Freiburg in this context see now Köpf, 'Produktive Christusfrömmigkeit', pp. 862–8, and on Margareta in general Dinzelbacher and Ruh, 'Magdalena von Freiburg'.
[42] Marrow, *Passion Iconography*, pp. 196–8; on the spikeblock see pp. 170–89.

Dutch texts on the Passion, all produced in the later fifteenth and early sixteenth centuries, actually bears the title *De heimelike passie*.[43] D. A. Stracke, who edited this particular text, indicated that the term 'heimelike passie' referred to all elements of the Passion narrative not attested in the Gospels, and certainly *De heimelike passie* itself has a much broader remit than the 'secret sufferings' as defined by Köpf alone. But Stracke was writing a generation before the studies by Pickering and Ruh that laid the foundations for the understanding of the narrative elaboration of the Passion by the exegetical interpretation of Old Testament texts.[44] And even though Marrow himself used the English term 'Secret Passion' to refer 'to the entire class of literature, or to extra-Gospel elaborations of the passion in general',[45] nonetheless a distinction must be drawn between the narrative elements derived exegetically from Scripture, and entirely invented elements without scriptural basis. Such a distinction is recognized by Kemper,[46] who does not otherwise treat the secret sufferings, and also—despite his very general use of the term 'Secret Passion'—by Marrow, concerning the spikeblock.[47] The distinction is also clear from Marquard's critique. For Marquard distinguishes not between the Gospel accounts and all other material, but between the narrative elements that can be legitimately established from Scripture—that which is 'in der hailgen geschrift begriffen', perhaps best translated as 'encompassed by Scripture'—and that which is pure invention and stems 'ex adinvencione propria'.

Marquard is not alone in the Middle Ages in his rejection of the unconstrained elaboration of the Passion narrative. Kemper discusses similar statements in the *Coelifodina* of Johannes von Paltz (d. 1511). In the prologue to this work, five typical errors of Passion preaching are discussed, amongst which is found a condemnation of the introduction of *figmenta* without a basis in Scripture, the works of established ecclesiastical authorities or even reason. Kemper notes that this condemnation does not include such material as is derived from exegetical and typological interpretation of the Old Testament, of which the *Coelifodina*—no less reticent than any other late medieval text on the Passion—contains plenty of

[43] See Ruh, 'De Heimelike Passie'; the version bearing *De heimelike passie* as its title edited by Stracke, 'Een brokstuk', at pp. 136–88; further Marrow, *Passion Iconography*, p. 218.
[44] Stracke, 'Een brokstuk', pp. 188–90.
[45] Marrow, *Passion Iconography*, p. 259 n. 100.
[46] Kemper, *Die Kreuzigung Christi*, p. 37.
[47] Marrow, *Passion Iconography*, pp. 183–4.

examples.[48] This same distinction is also true of a Dutch treatise on the Passion from the second half of the fifteenth century, discussed by Marrow, in which the invention of the spikeblock is criticized for its lack of any foundation in Scripture, authoritative tradition, or even in truth. Significantly, this unidentified author cites a little book called 'die verholen passie' ('the concealed Passion') as the only source transmitting knowledge about the spikeblock.[49] And ultimately the same distinction holds true for Marquard, whose statements on Christ's bodily suffering ultimately depend, in certain part, on the established exegetical-interpretative principles.

Marquard, however, was writing at least a century before either Johannes von Paltz or the anonymous Dutch critic of the spikeblock, which Marrow regards as a 'notably early' reaction to the excessive elaboration of the Passion narrative.[50] The criticism of the inventive elaboration of the bodily sufferings of Christ with which these authors are associated is present, fully formed, in the later fourteenth century in Marquard's works. Placed together, these three authors are potentially indicative of a current of opposition to the fictive elaboration of the Passion well before the Reformation, with Marquard as the earliest figure by far. Perhaps more significant, however, is the contrast between Marquard's position and that formulated in contemporary fourteenth-century works, in which the elaboration of Christ's life with extra-scriptural detail is not criticized, but justified. Thomas Bestul discusses such a passage in the prologue to the *Meditationes vitae Christi*,[51] a justification which, more precisely contemporary to Marquard, is incorporated and extended in the prologue to Ludolf von Sachsen's *Vita Christi*:

Nec credas quod omnia quae Christum dixisse vel fecisse meditari possumus scripta sunt, sed ad majorem impressionem ea tibi sic narrabo prout contigerunt, vel contigisse pie credi possunt, secundum quasdam imaginativas repraesentationes, quas animus diversimode percipit. Nam circa divinam Scripturam meditari, intelli-

---

[48] Kemper, *Die Kreuzigung Christi*, pp. 37–8; cf. Johannes von Paltz, *Coelifodina*, 9. 1–6.

[49] Marrow, *Passion Iconography*, pp. 184–6, with a discussion of what 'die verholen passie' might be at n. 786; on the treatise itself see pp. 207–8. It is known in just two manuscripts, both of which are more recently described: Brussels, Koninklijke Bibliotheek van België, Hs. 2694, on which see Deschamps and Mulder, *Inventaris van de Middelnederlandse handschriften*, vol. 8, pp. 10–11; and Ghent, Bibliotheek der Rijksuniversiteit, Hs. 1016, on which see Reynaert, *Catalogus van de Middelnederlandse handschriften*, pp. 86–9.

[50] Marrow, *Passion Iconography*, p. 185.

[51] See Bestul, *Texts of the Passion*, pp. 17–18; cf. Johannes de Caulibus, *Meditationes vitae Christi*, prologus, 90–103 (p. 10).

gere, et exponere, multifarie possumus prout credimus expedire, dummodo non sit contra veritatem vitae, vel justitiae, aut doctrinae, id est, non sit contra fidem, vel bonos mores. Quicumque vero asserit de Deo aliquid quod non est tibi certum, vel per naturalem rationem, vel synderesim, vel per fidem, vel per sacram scripturam, praesumit et peccat. Cum ergo me narrantem invenies, ita dixit vel fecit Dominus Jesus, seu alii qui introducuntur; si id per Scripturam probari non possit, non aliter accipias quam devota meditatio exigit: hoc est, perinde accipe ac si dicerem: meditor quod ita dixerit vel fecerit bonus Jesus: et sic de similibus.[52]

(You should not believe that everything that we may consider Christ to have said or to have done has been written down. But to give you a better impression I will relate those [unwritten] things just as they happened, or can piously be believed to have happened, according to certain imaginary representations that the mind grasps in different ways. For we can meditate on Holy Scripture, understand it, and expound it in different ways, as we believe it to be useful—providing that it is not against the truth of [his] life, justice, or doctrine: that is, that it is not against faith, or good morals. Indeed whoever claims something about God that does not seem certain to you—either by natural reason, conscience, faith, or Holy Scripture—is presumptive, and commits a sin. When therefore you find me relating that the Lord Jesus, or others who are introduced, acted or spoke in a particular way, then even if it cannot be proven by Scripture, you should take it exactly as devout meditation requires. That is, take it as if I were to say, 'I consider that the good Jesus acted or spoke in such a manner', and thus of similar instances.)

The position shared by the *Meditationes vitae Christi* and Ludolf von Sachsen is diametrically opposed to that taken by Marquard. For these works, narrative elements need not be justified from Scripture—they must simply not contradict it.

Marquard's rejection of excesses in the contemporary approach to the narrative elaboration of the Passion is not the end of the story. Nor is he simply content in *De anima Christi* to present Christ's bodily sufferings in a comparatively very mild and restrained manner. Rather, he reformulates the terms in which the Passion itself is presented by shifting the focus completely away from Christ's bodily suffering and onto his interior suffering. This shift is accomplished in two ways: by the interiorization of Christ's bodily suffering, and by the creation of a new category of purely interior, mental sufferings.

Marquard interiorizes Christ's bodily suffering in the second part of the Passion section of *De anima Christi*. The bitterness of Christ's suffering, says Marquard, may be seen in that it was perceived so inwardly and profoundly by his soul. This interiorization of (exterior) sufferings occurred

---

[52] Ludolf von Sachsen, *Vita Christi*, prooemium (ed. 1865, p. 4[b]; ed. 1870, vol. 1, pp. 8[b]–9[a]).

as a result of the sharp perceptivity of Christ's faculties of memory and reason: his soul had 'so clare spitze gehugniße vnd auch vernufft' ('such a clear, focused memory and reason too').[53] His reason grasped even the slightest suffering to the deepest possible extent, so that his whole self was moved to the utmost and placed in the most terrible suffering.[54] Simultaneously, Christ's desire—'begierde'—was located in the faculty of the will. As his desire was always for justice (a statement of his desire to redeem mankind by satisfaction), and he understood that so much injustice would be inflicted upon him and his friends, an especially inner suffering and unspeakable pain was present in his will. With all the other powers of his soul conformed to his will, all his suffering was perceived by his entire soul in the most interiorized and profound way possible: 'alle sȳn lȳden off den ynnigsten vnd gruntlichsten wart in sȳner selen entphangen von ynnigem begriffen'[55] ('all of his suffering was received in his soul in the most interiorized and profound way, as it was grasped inwardly'). Thus Marquard establishes the interiorization of Christ's exterior suffering, and introduces the idea of interior suffering independent of bodily pain. The especially just soul of Christ suffered not because of the corporeal afflictions per se, but because they were acts of injustice which offended his overwhelming desire for justice.

Marquard then asks whether Christ's sweating of blood as he prayed in the garden at Gethsemane derived solely from the profound realization and perception of his coming Passion. In the *Eucharistietraktat*, this sweating of blood is briefly mentioned, with two causes given, fear and burning love: 'ṽnser herr bettet vor siner marter vff dem berg, da er von angsten vnd jnbrúnstiger minne blůt schwitzte'[56] ('before his martyrdom our Lord prayed upon the mountain, where he sweated blood as a consequence of his fears and his burning love'). Here in *De anima Christi*, Marquard offers an excursus on this subject, determining which of these was the primary cause. On the one hand stands the opinion that fear was the cause, as

---

[53] *De anima Christi*, 203. 22–31, here ll. 30–1.

[54] The background to this statement on the perception of pain by Christ's soul is Bonaventura's discussion on the same subject: see Bonaventura, *In II Sent.*, d. 16, a. 2, 'De passibilitate et dolore animae Christi specialiter' (vol. 3, pp. 352^a–359^b): notably q. 3, in corp., 'Dolor vero compassionis primo erat in ratione et ex ratione redundabat in sensualitatem' ('The pain of compassion was in fact first in the faculty of reason, and from reason resonated into the part of the mind that received sensory stimuli') (p. 358^b); see further Strack, 'Das Leiden Christi', pp. 135–6.

[55] *De anima Christi*, 203. 31–204. 14, here 204. 12–14; cf. *De reparatione hominis*, a. 23 (122. 10–27), with a slightly different argumentation.

[56] *Eucharistietraktat*, 274. 29–31.

Christ's humanity was overcome by it. On the other, the opinion that fear drives blood inwards—not outwards—and so the sweating of blood was rather a consequence of Christ's love and the earnestness of his prayer. Marquard decides upon a middle path: fear drove the blood inwards, but Christ set himself against this fear, and his burning love drove the collected blood through the body and out of it. The earnestness of prayer and love was the primary cause, but fear played its part: 'Suß was des ußdringens alleÿne eÿn sache der große ernst vnd die mÿnne. Aber fo[r]chte halff auch etwas dartzu, als ich gesprachen han'[57] ('Thus one cause on its own of the emanation was the great earnestness and love. But to a certain extent fear contributed to it as well, as I have said'). Marquard makes the same point in *De reparatione hominis*, with additional discussion of the reasons why fear was not the primary cause. In his conclusion there, he adds further that the sweating of blood was not miraculous—'non fuit miraculosa'—and so, as we have seen, can be explained in physiological terms.[58] Without denying Christ's fear, Marquard downplays its primacy within his soul. This downplays the emphasis which that primacy places on the significance of his forthcoming corporeal sufferings. This is the opposite approach to that taken by the treatise *Christi Leiden in einer Vision geschaut*, in which the significance of the forthcoming corporeal sufferings is heightened by emphasizing Christ's fear of his approaching Passion as the ultimate cause for the sweating of blood.[59] Both Heinrich von St Gallen and Ludolf von Sachsen offer (different) explanations that also suggest a cooperation between love and fear, but eventually have recourse to the supernatural and rely upon the assertion of a miraculous event having taken place to explain the sweating of blood.[60]

---

[57] *De anima Christi*, 204. 16–38, here ll. 35–8.

[58] See *De reparatione hominis*, a. 23 (122. 28–123. 3).

[59] *Christi Leiden*, 63. 34–64. 17. Bonaventura makes a similar statement in his *Lignum Vitae*, c. 5, §18 (vol. 8, pp. 68–87), here pp. 75ᵇ–76ᵃ. In his commentary on Luke, he explores the significance of the sweating of blood, not its causes. It demonstrated the intensity of Christ's prayer to his father, and his desire to shed his blood for mankind: 'Ideo autem sanguis decurrebat in terram, ad ostendendum, quod pro Ecclesia orabat et pro illa effundere sanguinem suum cupiebat' ('Thus however blood flowed onto the earth, to demonstrate that he was praying for the church, and that he desired to pour out his blood for the church'); see Bonaventura, *Commentarius in Evangelium Lucam*, c. 22, §51–8 [vv. 39–46] (vol. 7, pp. 555ᵇ–558ᵇ), here p. 557ᵇ; see further Poppi, 'La passione di Gesù', pp. 77–80.

[60] See Heinrich von St Gallen, Passionstraktat *Extendit manum*, 35. 19–36. 2; and Ludolf von Sachsen, *Vita Christi*, pars 2, c. 59 (ed. 1865, p. 609ᵇ; ed. 1870, vol. 4, p. 476ᵇ).

The issue of Christ's emotions at Gethsemane and the related issue of his sweating blood has a long theological tradition, which has recently been discussed by Simo Knuuttila and (independently) Kevin Madigan. The issue is constitutive for Marquard's understanding of Christ's interior suffering beyond the issue of the sweating of blood. The background is formed by the more general issue of whether an initial thought itself constituted a sin, or whether sin was first present only in the deliberation on an initial thought. Medieval theologians differed on the issue, but all held this same underlying distinction between initial thoughts, termed 'first movements' or 'pre-passions' (*propassiones*), and the deliberation upon them, the resultant emotions or 'passions'. The distinction was derived from Jerome, who had distinguished 'between a pre-passion as a non-deliberated emotional reaction and a passion as an affection with consent'. He had first made this distinction in his commentary on Christ's suffering in the garden of Gethsemane, and his elaborations on the issue were incorporated into all the early and high medieval commentaries on the relevant scriptural passages.[61]

The issue was this. Matthew's Gospel states that Christ had become sorrowful in Gethsemane, and had declared that his soul was pained even unto death. He prayed to God to remove the burden that he faced, but then declared that God's will, and not his, should be done:

Tunc venit Iesus cum illis in villam quae dicitur Gethsemani. Et dixit discipulus suis: 'Sedete hic donec vadam illuc et orem.' Et adsumpto Petro et duobus filiis Zebedaei, coepit contristari et maestus esse. Tunc ait illis: 'Tristis est anima mea usque ad mortem. Sustinete hic et vigilate mecum.' Et progressus pusillum procidit in faciem suam orans et dicens, 'Mi Pater, si possibile est, transeat a me calix iste. Verumtamen non sicut ego volo, sed sicut tu.' [Matt. 26: 36–9]

(Then Jesus came with his followers into the place called Gethsemane. And he said to his disciples, 'Sit here while I go to that place and pray.' And after he had taken Peter and the two sons of Zebedee to himself, he began to be sad and sorrowful. Then he said to them, 'My soul is sorrowful unto death. Wait here and keep watch with me.' And having walked a short way forwards, he fell down on his face, praying and saying, 'O my Father, if it be possible, let this cup pass from me. But yet not as I will, but as you will.')

Christ then repeated a similar prayer twice (Matt. 26: 40–5). Mark's Gospel contains the same narrative of the threefold prayer (Mk. 14: 32–42), stating that Christ began to fear and become weary ('coepit pavere et taedere' (Mk. 14: 33)) in place of Matthew's statement that Christ began

---

[61] Knuuttila, *Emotions*, pp. 179–80, with all further references.

to be sad and sorrowful ('coepit contristari et maestus esse' (Matt. 26: 37)).
Luke's Gospel omits the significant statement that Christ's soul was pained
unto death, but describes Christ as suffering in agony ('factus in agonia'
(Lk. 22: 43)). He adds that an angel descended to comfort him, and that his
sweat was as drops of blood falling to the ground:

[. . .] et positis genibus orabat, dicens: 'Pater, si vis, transfer calicem istum a me.
Verumtamen non mea voluntas, sed tua fiat.' Apparuit autem illi angelus de caelo
confortans eum, et factus in agonia prolixius orabat; et factus est sudor eius sicut
guttae sanguinis decurrentis in terram. [Lk. 22: 41–4]

(Having knelt down he prayed, saying, 'Father, if you will, take this cup away from
me. But yet let not my will be done, but yours.' And now an angel appeared to him
from heaven, comforting him, and suffering in agony he prayed more extensively;
and his sweat became like drops of blood falling on the earth.)

Gethsemane thus represents something of a hornet's nest of Christological
problems—most crucially, how Christ (who is God, and so impassible)
could experience fear.[62]

Jerome reasoned thus. Christ, like all humans, had a natural will and a
rational will, except that in Christ's case his rational will always conformed
to his divine will and so always submitted to the will of the father. Christ,
being omnicognizant, knew of his impending crucifixion. The natural will
tends, quite literally by nature, towards good things and away from bad
things without deliberation; the rational will makes decisions on the basis
of deliberated evaluations. If Christ's sorrow in Gethsemane had been a
passion (i.e. an emotion), it would have been a deliberated evaluation of the
rational will. This would have meant that Christ knew that something bad
was going to happen to him *against his will*—that is, against his rational
will, and consequently against the divine will of God. That would have
been logically impossible, because it was God's will that Christ should be
crucified. His natural will, however, would have reacted negatively to the
prospect of crucifixion, in itself a bad thing, as it naturally tended away
from the bad. Christ's sorrow in Gethsemane had, therefore, to be an
unreflected 'first movement'—to use Jerome's term, a pre-passion—of his
natural will (assuming, like Jerome, that such unreflected 'first movements'
were sinless), which his rational will, following the divine will, then
opposed.[63] If we look at Jerome's actual statement, we see that he intro-

---

[62] For a full discussion of the Christological issues associated with Gethsemane, see
Madigan, *The Passions of Christ*, pp. 63–6.
[63] Knuuttila, *Emotions*, pp. 193–5.

duces the further idea that Christ did not begin to be sorrowful out of fear of (bodily) suffering, but because of the rejection and betrayal by his people that he would face:

'Et adsumpto Petro et duobus filiis Zebedaei coepit contristari et maestus esse' [Matt. 26: 37]. Illud quod supra diximus de passione et propassione etiam in praesenti capitulo ostenditur, quod Dominus, ut ueritatem adsumpti probaret hominis, uere quidem contristatus sit sed, ne passio in animo illius dominaretur, per propassionem coeperit contristari. Aliud est enim contristari et aliud incipere contristari. Contristabatur autem non timore patiendi qui ad hoc uenerat ut pateretur et Petrum timiditatis arguerat, sed propter infelicissimum Iudam et scandalum omnium apostolorum et reiectionem populi Iudaeorum et euersionem miserae Hierusalem.[64]

('And after he had taken Peter and the two sons of Zebedee to himself, he began to be sad and sorrowful.' What we have said above of the passions and pre-passions is again demonstrated in the present chapter: because the Lord, so that he might show the truth of the humanity he had assumed, was truly in fact sorrowful; but so that a passion would not dominate in his soul, began to be sorrowful by way of a pre-passion. For it is one thing to be sorrowful, and another to begin to be sorrowful. He, who had come so that he would suffer and had accused Peter of fearfulness, was sorrowful however not from the fear of suffering, but because of the most wretched Judas, the scandalization of all the apostles, the rejection of the Jewish people, and the destruction of the lamentable Jerusalem.)

Jerome's distinctions formed a standard part of almost all the medieval commentaries that tackled the issue, and so constituted a generally known understanding of Christ's sorrow in Gethsemane. Disconsonant patristic positions (notably those of Ambrose and Hilary of Poitiers) were reconciled by the scholastic theologians, as Madigan has shown, to Jerome's explanation of this very difficult biblical scene.[65] Knuuttila provides a comprehensive conspectus of references that we need not repeat here;[66] the *Glossa ordinaria* forms a reasonably representative example:

'Coepit contristari' [Matt. 26: 37] non timore passionis qui ad hoc venerat, sed pro scandalo apostolorum et perditione impiorum. Hieronymus: 'Coepit contristari vt veritatem assumpti hominis probaret. Vere contristatus est, sed non passio eius animo dominatur. Verum propassio est, vnde ait, "coepit contristari". Contristatur autem non timore patiendi qui ad hoc venerat, sed propter infoelicem Iudam et scandalum apostolorum et eiectionem iudaeorum et euersionem hierusalem.' 'Tristis' [Matt. 26: 38] anima est quae timet et tristatur. Petrus inferior non timet dicens

---

[64] Jerome, *Commentarius in Matheum*, lib. 4, ll. 1213–24 (pp. 253–4).
[65] Madigan, *The Passions of Christ*, pp. 66–71.
[66] See Knuuttila, *Emotions*, pp. 180 n. 5 and 194 n. 47.

'animam meam ponam pro te' [John 13: 37], quia vt homo vim mortis ignorat. Christus timet, quia vt deus in corpore constitutus fragilitatem carnis exponit; qui corpus suscepit omnia debuit subire quae corporis sunt.[67]

('He began to be sorrowful', not from the fear of suffering, as he had come for this purpose; but because of the scandalization of the apostles and the perdition of the ungodly. Jerome: 'He began to be sorrowful so that he might show the truth of the humanity he had assumed. Truly he was sorrowful, but a passion does not rule in his soul. It is rather a pre-passion, wherefore it says, "he began to be sorrowful". He, who had come for this purpose, was sorrowful however not from the fear of suffering, but because of the wretched Judas, the scandalization of the apostles, the exile of the Jews and the destruction of Jerusalem.' 'Sorrowful' is the soul which is sad and afraid. Peter subsequently is unafraid when he says 'I will lay down my life for you', because he, being a man, does not know the power of death. Christ is afraid, because he, being God incarnate, displays the frailty of the flesh; for he who has received a body, has had to take upon himself everything that pertains to the body.)

The patristic and scholastic tradition thus saw Christ's sorrow on Gethsemane as a (sinless) pre-passion, a manifestation of his natural will and thus an indication of his human nature. The sweating of blood was an extension of this sorrow, dependent on Luke; in late antiquity the information concerning the angelic visitation and the intensity of Christ's sweat was evidently felt to point too strongly in the direction of a passion rather than a pre-passion, and the pertinent passage (Lk. 22: 43–4) was struck out of the *Codex Siniaticus* and omitted from a number of very important early manuscripts.[68]

Marquard's position on the sweating of blood is compatible with this earlier tradition. Fear (the pre-passion) drove the blood inwards; but Christ set himself against this fear—that is, he engaged his rational will—with burning love, i.e. the love for mankind that motivated his desire to seek crucifixion and redeem mankind, driving the blood outwards. Marquard's physiological explanation as to how the sweating of blood actually occurred is very distinctive, and permits the identification of his very surprising source: Petrus Johannis Olivi's *Lectura super Matthaeum*. In commenting on Christ's prayer in Gethsemane, Olivi addresses two issues: the *actus orandi* (the question as to why and how Christ, who was God, prayed to the Father, who was God—a problem with a long intellectual history of its own)[69] and then the *forma orandi*, the nature of

---

[67] *Glossa ordinaria*, to Matt. 26: 37–8 (vol. 4, p. 81ᵃ).

[68] Köpf, 'Produktive Christusfrömmigkeit', p. 825.

[69] See Madigan, *The Passions of Christ*, pp. 73–90.

that prayer and Christ's experience in Gethsemane. Here he asks six questions, of which the fifth asks why Christ sweated blood as he prayed.[70] Marquard reproduces an abbreviated form of Olivi's answer.

It is easiest to demonstrate the textual dependence by placing Olivi's (Latin) commentary alongside the Latin text of Marquard's *De reparatione hominis*, rather than by comparing it to the German text of *De anima Christi*. I provide a subsequent translation of Marquard's text alone.

Marquard von Lindau
De reparatione hominis, a. 23
(122. 28–123. 3)

Petrus Johannis Olivi
Lectura super Matthaeum 26. 36, et seq.
(fols. 147vb–148ra)

(147vb) Ad quintum dicendum quod quidam dicunt quod ille sudor fuit ex multo horrore mortis, quod probant ex tribus.

Primo quia ipsa oratio erat pro euasione mortis, tanquam timens eam.

Secundo quia angelus confortans eum tunc apparuit. Confortatio autem ut videtur est contra timorem.

Tertio quia in agonia et in laborioso certamine mortis dicitur tunc fuisse.

Quapropter et sanguinem sudavit ex intimo fervore. Non enim aestimo, quod sudavit ex timore sanguinem, iuxta quod autumant plurimi, quia timoris est sanguinem ad interiora revocare, non ad exteriora diffundere. Et etiam timoris est infrigidare et non calefacere. Et quamvis ex luctu sensualitatis et horrore seu timore per accidens sanguis effluxit, non tamen dolor per se hoc fecit.

Alii dicunt quod fuit ex multo feruore, quod duppliciter [sic] probant.

Primo quia ut dicunt ex timore hoc esse non potuit, quia timoris est sanguinem ad inte (148ra)riora reuocare, non ad exteriora diffundere. Eius et est infrigidare, non calefacere.

Secundo ex proprietate fortis orationis, cuius est feruere, et ebullire, ac inflammare. Et Luce .xxii°. videtur hoc attribui prolixitati orationis. Dicto enim quod 'prolixius orabat' [Lk. 22: 43] subditur 'et factus est sudor eius,' et cetera [Lk. 22: 44].

Timor enim potuit ad hoc cooperari recolligendo totum calorem ad intima et sic per consequens per accidens calefacere.

Michi videtur quod ex vtroque simul hoc esse potuerit, et ita esse congruerit. Timor enim ad hoc potuit cooperari tribus modis.

---

[70] Olivi's *Lectura super Matthaeum* is unedited. I quote from Oxford, New College Library, MS 49, fols. 147ra–148vb; on this manuscript see Douie, 'Olivi's "Postilla super Matthaeum"', pp. 67–8.

Secundo quia excessivus timor habet
fortissime dissolvere omnes humores et
concutere totum corpus, et sic per viam huius
validissimae dissolutionis potuit fieri fluxus
sanguinei sudoris.

Tertio quia timor iste naturalis viriliter
resistebat fervori urgenti, occasione autem
huius resistentiae maior accessio fiebat in
corpore. Intimus autem fervor rationis, quo
Christus se totum eviscerabat et offerebat
patri et se totum modo ineffabili exponebat
morti, timori resistebat. Et sic ex ista mutua
resistentia linguor iste sanguineus
exprimebatur et emanabat.

Ex his igitur patet, quod ista sudatio
sanguinea non fuit miraculosa nec etiam per
se ex timore causata, sed ex concurrente
timore et fervore intimo, sanguis iste
benedictus sic emanabat.

Primo recolligendo totum calorem ad
intima, et sic tandem per accidens
calefaciendo; quia recollectio caloris ad
interiora reddit ipsum calorem magis in se
mutuum, ac per consequens et in intimis
magis accensum.
Secundo quia excessiuus timor habet
fortissime dissoluere omnes humores et
concutere totum corpus. Vnde etiam in
Ezechiele dicitur quod 'propter nimium
timorem cuncta genua fluent aquis dissoluta'
[cf. Ez. 7: 17] scilicet humore ruine. Per viam
ergo dissolutionis potuit fieri fluxus sudoris
sanguinei.
Tertio quia terror ille naturalis naturaliter
resistebat feruori orantis. Et loquor de
resistentia nichil habente de vicio occisione
autem huius resistentie maior accensio fiebat
in corpore. Feruor autem orationis quo
Christus se totum euiscerabat patri, et se
totum modo ineffabili exponebat morti,
causam priorem superangebat.

(Therefore he sweated blood on account of his innermost ardour. I do not think that he sweated blood out of fear, as most assert, because it is in the nature of fear to draw blood inwards, and not to impel it outwards. And it is also in the nature of fear to cool something down, and not to heat it up. And so although the blood flowed out because of the anguish of the sensory power of the soul (the *sensualitas*), and so contingently because of terror or fear, nevertheless suffering did not cause this in itself. But fear was able to contribute to this [first] by drawing all the heat together in the innermost part of the body, and thus contingently heat up the body in consequence. Second, because excessive fear has the property to liquefy all the humours most aggressively and weaken the entire body; and thus by means of this most vigorous liquefaction a flow of bloody sweat is possible. Third, because this natural fear strongly opposed the driving force of his ardour; by reason of which opposition a greater intensity [of ardour] arose in his body. The innermost ardour of his reason, moreover, by which Christ totally emptied himself, offered himself to the Father and abandoned himself to an unspeakable death, opposed the fear. Thus I state that this bloodiness was forced out and emanated as a result of this mutual opposition. From this it is therefore clear that this bloody sweat was neither miraculous nor, in fact, caused by fear in itself; but rather this blessed blood emanated on account of the conflict between fear and innermost ardour.)

This is not the only excerpt from Olivi's commentary on Matthew that Marquard adapts. Indeed, the section of text in *De reparatione* immediately prior to the quotation presented above is itself extracted from a slightly later passage in Olivi's commentary to Matthew 26: 36.[71] A much more significant borrowing concerns the issue of Christ's interior suffering, which Olivi addresses after concluding his six questions noted above, and which we shall consider presently.

Before Marquard continues in *De anima Christi* with that theme, however, he offers a short excursus on how Christ's physical sufferings were felt especially profoundly by his body.[72] This functions as the companion piece to his discussion of the profound perception of suffering by Christ's soul. He begins by asserting that Christ had an especially tender body, 'der nit von harter naturen eÿnes mannes, mer von dem reÿnsten, luttersten blut, so in der wirdigen meÿde lyp was geformiret, also gar zartiglichen vnd meysterlichen'[73] ('which was not of the tough nature of a man, but rather of the purest and most spotless blood that was formed in the noble Virgin's body, and was thus most tender and exquisite'). Caroline Bynum has shown that the feminization of Christ's body in this way was an uncontroversial and widespread tenet of later medieval considerations of Christ's physiology.[74] Marquard's source was probably Bonaventura, who makes exactly the same point in his treatise *De perfectione vitae*.[75] At the same time as Marquard feminizes Christ, so too he asserts that his body was

---

[71] Compare *De reparatione hominis*, a. 23 (122. 21–7) with Olivi, *Lectura super Matthaeum*, fol. 148^{rb–va}.

[72] *De anima Christi*, 205. 1–32.

[73] Ibid. 6–9. The point on the formation of Christ's body from the purest blood in Mary recurs frequently in Marquard's oeuvre: see *Predigt* 5, ll. 97–101 (p. 44); *Predigt* 21, ll. 109–12 (p. 140); *De reparatione hominis*, a. 23 (123. 14–16); and *De perfectione humanitatis Christi*, 156. 27–9.

[74] See Bynum, *Fragmentation and Redemption*, pp. 98–101.

[75] Bonaventura, *De perfectione vitae*, c. 6, §5 (vol. 8, pp. 107–27), at pp. 121^b–122^a. The same idea on the tenderness of Christ's body, without the explanation of Christ's flesh deriving wholly from Mary, is in the *Sermo de dominica in Quinquagesima* (p. 203^b); see further Strack, 'Das Leiden Christi', pp. 134–5.

so noble and royal that it was more receptive to pain,[76] and that Christ's limbs were so sensitive that they felt all things most deeply, another standard point of Bonaventuran derivation.[77] Finally, he adds a peculiar physiological statement about Nazarenes, of which Christ was one. Nazarenes, says Marquard, are so full of blood that it is even in their hair and nails, which they consequently do not cut. When a person is full of blood that is integral, and not superfluous, that person has greater love, liveliness, and receptivity to suffering. On this occasion, even Marquard is aware of the peculiarity of the point, conceding that he had not read it 'in bewerter schrifft'[78] ('in an authoritative work').

After this, Marquard turns to Christ's interior sufferings proper. He does not confine Christ's suffering to the immediate circumstances of the crucifixion. Rather, it began at the moment of his conception. Suffering, as Marquard says in a sermon on the holy martyrs, was 'daz edel klaid dez geminten gottes sun, daz er an leit in der mûter lib vnd trûg schlåffend vnd wachend bis in den tǒd'[79] ('the noble clothing of the beloved Son of God, which he put on in his mother's body, and bore day and night unto his death'). It was, as he says at the beginning of the third section of *De anima Christi*, the third foundation (along with poverty and humility) upon which Christ's life rested: 'bitter lÿden, in dem Cristus stǔnt an underlaß in alle sÿme leben'[80] ('bitter suffering, in which Christ remained for his entire life, without any remission'). The temporal extent of Christ's suffering is a prominent theme of the third section of *De anima Christi*. Marquard begins the fourth subsection with an opening statement on its continual quality:

---

[76] *De anima Christi*, 205. 9–14; cf. *De reparatione hominis*, a. 23 (123. 17–21).

[77] *De anima Christi*, 205. 12–14; cf. *De reparatione hominis*, a. 23 (123. 22–5), which offers a slightly different point: that Christ suffered particularly in the most sensitive parts of his body. See Bonaventura, *In III Sent.*, d. 16, a. 1, q. 2, fund. 4 (vol. 3, p. 348ᵃ): 'Item, quanto sensus tactus est vivacior, tanto dolor, qui est secundum sensum, est acutior, unde in illis membris, in quibus viget sensus tactus, est dolor acutissimus; sed in Christo fuit sensus tactus vivacissimus; «prudentissimum enim animalium est homo», ut dicit Philosophus, et inter omnes Christus, cum fuerit optime dispositus: ergo dolor, quem sensit, super omnes dolores fuit acutissimus' ('The livelier the sense of touch is, the more acute the pain felt by that sense is. Thus the most acute pain is in those limbs in which the sense of touch is strong. But Christ had the liveliest sense of touch of all; "for man is the most knowledgeable of the animals", as the philosopher says, and Christ above all, since he had been made in the finest order. Therefore the pain that he felt was the acutest of all pain').

[78] *De anima Christi*, 205. 14–24, here ll. 23–4; cf. *De perfectione humanitatis Christi*, 156. 30–3.

[79] *Predigt* 18, ll. 18–20 (p. 126).

[80] *De anima Christi*, 200. 4–5.

Zum vierden wirt gepruffet bitterkeÿt des lÿdens, das iß so lange werende was. Wann der susse Cristus eyn stunde nach eyn nŭwe in der zÿt an bitter lyden nÿe enwas, wanne in dem ersten nuwe der gescheppede syner selen entphing vnd weret in alle syme leben biß in den dot.[81]

(The bitterness of his suffering is seen fourthly in its extremely long duration. For the sweet Christ was not without bitter suffering even for an instant after his first moment in the temporal world, because he felt it in the first moment of the creation of his soul, and it lasted for his entire life until his death.)

He then outlines five objects that Christ's soul perceived without intermission across his entire life, which caused this unceasing interior suffering. The parallel section of *De reparatione hominis* likewise pays attention to this theme, and uses very distinctive terminology in order to identify the incipient point of Christ's suffering: 'Nam ab instanti suae conceptionis numquam fuit sine intensione doloris usque ad obitum mortis amarissimae'[82] ('For he was never without the intensity of suffering from the moment of his conception until the final moment of his most bitter death'). Marquard repeats the statement that Christ suffered 'ab instanti suae conceptionis', which corresponds to the German 'in dem ersten nuwe der gescheppede syner selen', in the following exposition no less than four times.[83] His source, as indicated above, is not Bonaventura or a more conventional source, but again Olivi's *Lectura super Matthaeum*. The precise interrelationship will be examined shortly, after the broader issue is addressed: namely, what it means to relocate the origin of Christ's suffering in the moment of his conception.

The relocation of the origin of Christ's Passion is a striking and persistent theme in late medieval devotion. It took two principal forms, both of which can be conveniently identified in Ludolf's *Vita Christi*. The first involved setting the beginning of Christ's corporeal sufferings at some early point in his earthly life. This served to encourage imitative suffering as a general virtue and principle of the Christian life, by extending Christ's sufferings across his whole life. This is an extension of the notion whose origins are conventionally associated with Bernard of Clairvaux, namely that Christ was born, grew up, and went through all the stages of human life in order to provide a complete, lifelong model for man to follow.[84] Ludolf draws our attention to the origins of Christ's sufferings in his childhood, and sets the

---

[81] Ibid. 206. 32–7.
[82] *De reparatione hominis*, a. 23 (124. 10–11).
[83] Ibid. (124. 9–35).
[84] Constable, *Three Studies*, pp. 188–90, and Köpf, 'Die Passion Christi', pp. 27–31.

beginning of Christ's suffering in the hardship he faced in the stable at Bethlehem. This is all then placed in the context of a discussion of Christ's lifelong poverty, humility, and suffering, so that man might more closely imitate the entire life of Christ:

Potuisti etiam attendere in utroque [ie. in the birth of Christ, and in the Christ-child himself], et maxime in puero Jesu, non parvam corporis afflictionem. Inter ceteras autem, haec una fuit, quod quando mater sua in praesepio eum locavit, et pulvinar vel alius hujusmodi non haberet, ad caput ejus quemdam lapidem, non sine grandi cordis amaritudine posuit, interposito forte feno, quod ab animalibus mutuo accepit. Et, ut dicitur, adhuc ille lapis, ibidem ad memoriam reservatus, videtur. Paupertatem igitur et humilitatem, afflictionemque corporis studeas et tu pro posse amplecti, et in his Christum pro modulo tuo imitari.[85]

(You have been able to take note in both [the birth of Christ, and the Christ-child himself], and most of all in the Christ-child, of the not insignificant affliction of the body. Amongst the others, moreover, one was that when his mother placed him in the crib, she did not have a cushion or anything similar of that kind. Under his head she placed a certain stone, not without a bitter unhappiness in her heart, although she had put some hay in between which she had borrowed from the animals. It is said that this stone, kept in remembrance in the same place down to the present day, is still to be seen. You should consider therefore his poverty, his humility, and the affliction of his body, to embrace Christ as best you can, and to imitate him in these things as far as you are able.)

In Ludolf's scheme, we can see a clear link between this and his incipient injunctions to contemplate all of Christ's life, identifying with each of those who saw or were with Christ at all the stages of his life.[86] In a later passage in which Ludolf enumerates all the *afflictiones* of Christ's life, he elaborates on the idea taken from a text commonly attributed to Augustine that the life of a Christian was a bearing of the cross unto death, as it had been for Christ. It is very important to note that Ludolf places the incipient point of these afflictions at Christ's birth, not—unlike Marquard—at his conception:

[S]ciendum est, quod si nos omnia quae Christus in mundo passus est, vellemus enarrare, innumerabilia utique essent, praesertim cum tota vita Christi in terris quaedam passio fuerit. Nimirum, cum etiam tota vita cujuslibet Christiani, si secundum Evangelium vivat, quaedam crux atque martyrium sit, ut Augustinus

---

[85] Ludolf von Sachsen, *Vita Christi*, pars 1, c. 9 (ed. 1865, p. 40^b; ed. 1870, vol. 1, p. 82^b).
[86] See ibid. prooemium (ed. 1865, pp. 1^b–2^b; ed. 1870, vol. 1, pp. 2^b–4^b). Ludolf's strategy here is adopted from Jordan von Quedlinburg; see Elze, 'Das Verständnis der Passion Jesu', pp. 128–30.

dicit, quanto magis hoc indubitabile est de ipso Domino Christo, qui Evangelium condidit, et in seipso perfectissime adimplevit? Exordiendo enim a primordio Nativitatis suae, inspice quam pauper natus fuit, qui nec domicilium neque vestes habuit, sed in vili diversorio natus, in praesepi super feno exiguo ante bruta animalia reclinatus, pannis vilibus involutus fuit[87]

(It should be known that if we wanted to relate all the things that Christ suffered in the world in full, they would simply be innumerable—principally because Christ's entire life on earth was truly a Passion. Surely, since the entire life of every Christian is verily a cross or a martyrdom, if he lives according to the Gospel, as Augustine says; then how much more undeniable is this of the Lord Christ himself, who established the Gospel and fulfilled it in himself most perfectly of all? Commencing at the beginning of his nativity, observe how he was born poor, and had neither dwelling place nor clothes; but was born in a cheap inn, laid in a crib upon some meagre hay in front of the brute animals, and swaddled in shabby rags)

The second form of the relocation of the origin of Christ's sufferings is more complex. It involves the relocation not of the beginning of Christ's bodily afflictions, but of the Passion itself as a soteriologically efficacious event. It is mutually compatible with the first form of relocation, and it is likewise to be found in Ludolf's *Vita Christi*. By associating the soteriological value of the Passion with the letting of blood, the beginning of the Passion as a soteriologically efficacious event is relocated to the moment of circumcision:

[C]oepit hodie Dominus Jesus suum sacratissimum sanguinem pro nobis fundere, cum ipsius caro cultello incideretur lapideo. Tempestive coepit pati pro nobis, et qui peccatum non fecit, poenam hodie portare incepit pro peccatis nostris. Non solum enim in virili, sed etiam in infantili aetate sanguinem suum pro nobis voluit fundere.[88]

(The Lord Jesus began today to shed his most blessed blood for us, when his flesh was cut with a small stone knife. He began to suffer for us early on; and so he who committed no sin today began to bear the punishment for our sins. For he wanted to shed his blood for us not just as an adult, but even in his childhood years.)

---

[87] Ludolf von Sachsen, *Vita Christi*, pars 2, c. 51 (ed. 1865, p. 570b; ed. 1870, vol. 3, p. 375a); see further Baier, *Untersuchungen zu den Passionsbetrachtungen*, pp. 534–7, with identification of the (pseudo-)Augustine quotation at p. 537 n. 36. This quotation derives (see p. 233 and n. 5) from a sermon compiled from various patristic sources, possibly put together by Ambrosius Autpertus (d. 784), and commonly attributed in the Middle Ages to Augustine. For the original text see Augustine, *Sermo* 207 [In natali sancti Laurentii 2], in J.-P. Migne (ed.), *Patrologia latina*, vol. 39 (Paris, 1865), 2128–9.

[88] Ludolf von Sachsen, *Vita Christi*, pars 1, c. 10 (ed. 1865, p. 47a; ed. 1870, vol. 1, p. 96b).

The circumcision is then regarded as the first of six such bloodlettings that structure Christ's life as a redemptive work.[89]

This extension of Christ's sufferings across his life by associating the six (or seven) bloodlettings has been discussed, with a number of late medieval English examples, by R. N. Swanson. He suggests that it presents suffering as a lifelong component of Christ's life, in order to encourage corporeal suffering as an enduring component of the imitation of Christ.[90] But it also needs to be distinguished from the first process of extension, namely the location of the start of Christ's sufferings in the harsh circumstances of his birth. The temporal extension of the Passion as a soteriologically efficacious event across Christ's life, linked by the six (or seven) bloodlettings, is a separate process of extension to the invention of ever more corporeal afflictions for Christ to have suffered, none of which (unlike the bloodlettings) has any significance for the theology of redemption. One form of extension extends Christ's sufferings, whilst another extends his redemptive Passion.

For Caroline Bynum this second form of extending the Passion, namely to relocate its origin as a soteriologically efficacious event in the circumcision, is an assimilation, explicable with reference to medieval attitudes to blood: 'Since medieval physiological theory saw all bodily fluids as reducible to blood and saw bleeding basically as purging, bleeding was an obvious symbol for cleansing or expiation, and all Christ's bleedings were assimilated.'[91] The definitive medieval work on the subject—Bonaventura's *Vitis mystica*, whose structure is formed around the seven bloodlettings[92]—reveals that the connection drawn between them is not just an assimilation, but a typological prefiguration. Bonaventura begins his discussion of the circumcision with a reminder to his audience of the association between the circumcision and the naming of Christ (both of which took place on the same day, the feast being celebrated on 1 January). Christ's name, 'Jesus', means 'saviour'; giving Christ this name at the time of his first bloodletting signifies his later shedding of blood for the salvation of mankind:

Primam igitur sanguinis effusionem legimus in circumcisione, quando fuit nomen eius vocatum Iesus, iam tunc mystice significando, quod effusione sanguinis sui nobis futurus erat verus Iesus, id est salvator.[93]

---

[89] Ludolf von Sachsen *Vita Christi*, pars 1 c. 10 (ed. 1865, p. 47[a–b]; ed. 1870, vol. 1, pp. 96[b]–97[a]).

[90] Swanson, 'Passion and Practice', p. 17.

[91] Bynum, *Fragmentation and Redemption*, p. 87.

[92] On the seven bloodlettings in Bonaventura's oeuvre, see Strack, 'Das Leiden Christi', p. 146.

[93] Bonaventura, *Vitis mystica*, c. 18 (vol. 8, pp. 159–229), here p. 183[a].

(We read thus of the first shedding of blood in the circumcision, when he was called by the name 'Jesus', to signify mystically at that point that with the shedding of his blood the true Jesus, which means the saviour, was going to be present with us.)

The circumcision, Bonaventura continues, prefigures the crucifixion in an efficacious, typological sense as the moment at which Christ began to shed his blood for mankind:

Bene igitur in prima sanguinis Agni purissimi effusione aptatum est hoc nomen Iesus, quoniam pro nostra salvatione sanguis fundi coepit, qui in completione salutis totus fuerat effundendus.[94]

(This name 'Jesus' was rightly given in the first shedding of the lamb's purest blood; because for our salvation his blood, which was to be entirely poured out in the fulfilment of salvation, began to be shed.)

Marquard does not use either of these more conventional possibilities to extend the compass of Christ's bodily suffering across his entire life. In *De anima Christi* Christ's life on earth is neither presented as a life of bodily suffering that began in the harsh conditions of the stable in Bethlehem; nor is the beginning of the Passion located typologically in the circumcision. In contrast to Ludolf's *Vita Christi*, Marquard's *De anima Christi* represents the Passion as a soteriologically efficacious event as the single event of the crucifixion. Yet if Christ's corporeal sufferings are not extended in any temporal way, then Marquard must extend something else to make his statement that Christ suffered 'ab instanti conceptionis' hold true. Marquard (and Olivi) can be located more firmly in the tradition, and the concept of Christ's suffering 'ab instanti conceptionis' better understood, by beginning with a fuller consideration of Bonaventura's position on the suffering of Christ.

Bonaventura held that Christ's entire life was worthy of reward—that is, it was efficacious in the context of the satisfaction of God—'ab instanti conceptionis'. He explains this in two *quaestiones* in his commentary on the Sentences, concerning the precise moment at which Christ began to gain reward ('meruit').[95] But suffering is not included in the reasons why Christ gained reward from the moment of his conception. Instead he argues that Christ gained reward through his desire to save mankind, his humiliation in the incarnation, and so forth. A useful summary of this position is found in the *Breviloquium*. Here he sets out a number of reasons as to why Christ

---

[94] Ibid. (vol. 8, p. 183[b]).
[95] Bonaventura, *In III Sent.*, d. 18, a. 1, q. 1 and q. 2 (vol. 3, pp. 380[a]–384[b]).

must be considered to have had the plenitude and perfection of every reward.[96] The second of these reasons is the lifelong duration of his acquisition of reward, 'ab instanti conceptionis usque ad horam mortis' ('from the moment of his conception until the hour of his death'). He argues this as follows:

> Ratio autem ad intelligentiam praedictorum haec est: quia, cum in principio reparativo, Christo scilicet Domino nostro, necessario fuerit plenitudo gratiae et sapientiae, quae sunt nobis origo recte et sancte vivendi; necesse est, quod in Christo fuerit plenitudo et perfectio omnis meriti secundum omnem modum plenitudinis. Quia enim in Christo fuit plenitudo gratiae unionis, per quam erat Deus ab instanti conceptionis, habens gloriam comprehensionis et motum liberi arbitrii; hinc est, quod necessario fuit in Christo perfectio meriti et quantum ad excellentissimam dignitatem merentis et quantum ad celerrimam opportunitatem temporis.[97]

(The argument furthermore to understand the aforesaid is this: since at the very beginning of his redemptive work the plenitude of grace and wisdom was necessarily in Christ our Lord, grace and wisdom being for us the source of living an upright and holy life; so it is necessary that the plenitude and perfection of every reward according to every measure of plenitude was in Christ. For because the plenitude of the grace of union, by which he was God, was in Christ from the moment of his conception, whereby he had the glory of heavenly understanding [i.e. the beatific vision] and the movement of free will; so it was that the perfection of reward was necessarily in Christ—both with regard to the most excellent worthiness of acquiring reward, and with regard to the earliest appropriate time [of doing so].)

Marquard, incidentally, knew this doctrine as well: he repeats it in *De perfectione humanitatis Christi* as the fourth and final *privilegium* of Christ's soul, with a discussion that follows Bonaventura of the precise moment at which Christ began to gain reward ('in primo instanti' or just 'ab instanti conceptionis').[98]

It is not merely an argument *ex silentio* that Bonaventura omits the idea that Christ suffered 'ab instanti conceptionis' from his discussion on Christ's meritorious existence from that point. For Bonaventura (as later for Ludolf), Christ's sufferings began with his birth, with the soterio-

---

[96] Bonaventura, *Breviloquium*, c. 4, §7 (vol. 5, pp. 199–291), here pp. 247[a]–248[b].

[97] Ibid. (vol. 5, pp. 247[b]–248[a]); on the nature of Christ's merit 'ab instanti conceptionis' (reliant on the presence of habitual (as distinct from actual) merit in him from this point, a consequence of his possession of the plenitude of grace)), see Gonzalez, 'The Work of Christ', p. 377.

[98] *De perfectione humanitatis Christi*, 160. 30–9.

logically efficacious Passion commencing at the circumcision.[99] This is confirmed in the *Vitis mystica*, where we should note the clear statement that Christ suffered 'a principio ortus sui'—from the beginning of his birth, not his conception:

O suavissime universorum Domine et Salvator, bone Iesu, quas tibi dignas referam gratiarum actiones, qui a principio ortus tui usque ad mortem durissimam, immo et post mortem pro me tantum tui sanguinis effundisti, qui ardorem excellentissimae caritatis tuae tam crebris sanguinis tui effusionibus manifestare curasti![100]

(O sweetest Lord and saviour of all, kind Jesus, what worthy deeds of thanks may I offer in return to you, who shed so much of your blood for me from the dawn of your birth until your harshest death—nay, even after your death; you, who thought to manifest the ardour of your all-excelling love with such frequent outpourings of your blood!)

Similarly in *De perfectione vitae*, Bonaventura gives the nativity as the point at which Christ's corporeal afflictions began:

A prima enim die nativitatis suae usque ad ultimum diem mortis semper fuit in passionibus et doloribus, sicut ipse testatur per Prophetam dicens: 'Pauper sum ego et in laboribus a iuventute mea' [Ps. 87: 16]; et alibi dicit: 'Fui flagellatus tota die['], id est [']toto tempore vitae meae' [Ps. 72: 14].[101]

(For he was continually in suffering and sorrows from the first day of his birth until his last day of death, just as he himself attests through the prophet when he says 'I am poor, and in travails from my youth'; and in another place he says 'I was scourged all day long'—that is, 'for the entire duration of my life'.)

The distinction between those states of mind that could have existed in Christ before the nativity, like humility or poverty (understood by Bonaventura as poverty of spirit, conceived as Christ's submission to the will of the Father in the incarnation), and that aspect of Christ's life which could only affect him after his birth—namely suffering—can be seen most clearly in the *Sermo* 1 *de sabbato sancto*. Bonaventura adapts Psalm 87: 16, 'pauper sum ego et in laboribus a iuventute mea' ('I am poor, and in travails from my youth'), and defines poverty (implicitly of spirit) as an enduring condition existent in Christ 'a principio incarnationis' ('from the start of his incarnation'), whereas his sufferings began only 'a iuventute sua' ('from his youth').

---

[99] Strack, 'Das Leiden Christi', pp. 133–4.
[100] Bonaventura, *Vitis mystica*, c. 23 (vol. 8, p. 187[b]); cf. c. 17 (pp. 182[b]–183[a]).
[101] Id., *De perfectione vitae*, c. 6, §5 (vol. 8, pp. 121[b]–122[a]).

Quamquam verum sit, quod sex diebus operatus est Dominus et die septimo requievit, veriori tamen modo habet veritatem in operibus recreationis, quia per sex lustra temporum operatus est Dominus et septimo requievit; quia a principio incarnationis Christus pauper fuit et in laboribus a iuventute sua, sed potissime fuit in laboribus per dies ante passionem[102]

(Although it may be true that the Lord worked for six days and rested on the seventh day, this holds true nevertheless in a truer way in the works of re-creation [i.e. of salvation]: because the Lord worked for six periods of five years [i.e., until Christ was 30] and rested in the seventh; because Christ was poor from the start of his incarnation and in travails from his youth, but was in the greatest travails in the days before his Passion)

The corporeal sufferings of Christ cannot be extended backwards beyond the point of the nativity, whereas his states of mind and his capacity to merit can be. To attribute suffering to Christ 'ab instanti conceptionis', a non-corporeal concept of Christ's sufferings must *ex necessitate* be employed. Otherwise, it would be necessary to suggest that Christ suffered physically by being in Mary's womb.

Bonaventura does touch on Christ's interior sufferings, without either presenting them as a coherent category or considering them as present 'ab instanti conceptionis'. As we have mentioned earlier, he does present an influential consideration in his commentary on the Sentences of how Christ's soul perceived exterior pain.[103] Additional considerations on Christ's interior sufferings are not, however, dealt with in this systematic way, but—to use Bonifatius Strack's phrase—'durch alle Werke hindurch zerstreut' ('strewn throughout all his works'). Thus he treats the various ignominies associated with the shameful manner of Christ's death: but presented as signs of Christ's humility and humiliation, not as ways in which Christ suffered inwardly. Naturally, he presents certain instances that caused Christ sadness and inner pain—the absence of his disciples at the crucifixion, or his sight of Mary's sorrow under the cross—but these are presented as individual moments, and are not extended as underlying and enduring features of Christ's life.[104] Christ's inner suffering, as he approached death, at the forthcoming separation of soul from body is likewise not a concept that Bonaventura extends across his entire life. Indeed, Bonaventura notes (following Bernard of Clairvaux) that the *passio* that Christ felt both by the prospect of death and by the pain of the crucifixion

---

[102] Id., *Sermo I de sabbato sancto* (vol. 9, pp. 267ᵃ–270ᵃ), here p. 267ᵃ.
[103] See id., *In III Sent.*, d. 16, a. 2 (vol. 3, pp. 352ᵃ–359ᵇ); and Strack, 'Das Leiden Christi', pp. 135–6.
[104] Strack, 'Das Leiden Christi', pp. 136–7, with the quotation p. 136.

itself was exceeded by his *compassio* for mankind. Had this not been so, Christ would not have sacrificed himself upon the cross.[105] Marquard too held this unexceptional position.[106] Strack has shown at length how Bonaventura understood this compassion as a manifestation of his *caritas*, his love for mankind;[107] and this love was something that Bonaventura did consider as an enduring inner feature of Christ's life 'ab instanti conceptionis'. Suffering was not such a feature. We see this clearly, and finally, when Bonaventura considers in his commentary on the Sentences whether external works add anything to good intention (they do). In favour, he states that Christ's suffering was an external work added later to the good intention that was present in Christ from his conception:

Christus nobis aliquid meruit per passionem, quod ante non meruerat nobis, utpote apertionem ianuae et multorum charismatum diffusionem: si ergo caritas Christi fuit eminentissima ab instanti conceptionis et maioris fuit efficaciae cum passione quam sine; videtur ergo, quod in quolibet alio excellentia operis exterioris addat ad meritum bonae voluntatis sive intentionis.[108]

(Christ acquired something for us through his Passion that he had not acquired for us beforehand, namely the opening of the entrance [to heaven] and the disbursement of the many gifts of the spirit. If therefore Christ's love was of the most all-excelling kind from the moment of his conception, and was of greater efficacy with his Passion than without; then it is clear that in everything else the merit of the exterior work adds to the merit of the good intention or will.)

Marquard's position represents a significant development from this. Otherwise heavily influenced by Bonaventura's theology, Marquard has a very different understanding of Christ's sufferings. He presents a coherent category of specifically interior sufferings of Christ, which began 'ab instanti conceptionis' and which endured for his entire life. Five items constitute this category. First, all the dishonour ever done to God by people, and the gulf between God's goodness and sinners' failings. Second, that his suffering would be lost on so many for whose sake he would be dying. Third, all the scorn, poverty, and suffering he would face. Fourth, all the suffering that would be inflicted upon his mother and his especial friends. Fifth, all the prayers and immeasurable humility he would have to offer to his father, and the thanklessness of mankind:

---

[105] Ibid. 136; id., *Christusleid im Christenleben*, pp. 47–8; cf. Bonaventura, *In III Sent.*, d. 16, a. 2, q. 3, in corp. (vol. 3, pp. 358^b–359^b).
[106] See *De reparatione hominis*, a. 23 (121. 5–20).
[107] Strack, 'Das Leiden Christi', p. 139; id., *Christusleid im Christenleben*, pp. 40–6.
[108] Bonaventura, *In II Sent.*, d. 40, a. 2, q. 1, fund. 3 (vol. 2, p. 926$^{a–b}$).

[D]er susse Cristus eyn stunde nach eyn núwe in der zỹt an bitter lyden nỹe enwas, wanne in dem ersten nuwe der gescheppede syner selen entphing vnd weret in alle syme leben biß in den dot. Vnd diß qwam do von, wann sỹne sele sach ane vnderlaß die funff gegenworff. Zum ersten, das sie clerlichen sach alles das vneren an, das got vmmer von keynem menschen solde gescheen. Vnd wanne die sele got so gút bekante vnd gebreche der sunder so dieff ane sach, herumb hatte er do von súnderlichen stedigen smertzen. Zum andern male, das syne sele sach, das syn manigfeldige, große lyden verlorn solde werde[n] an so viel menschen, durch der willen eß alles doch leỹt. Zum dritten male, das sie sach alle smacheit, armud vnd lyden, das sie vnd den edeln lỹp anfallen solde. Zum vierden, das sie sach alles das drucken vnd harte lyden, das syne wirdige mutter vnd alle syne lieben frunde vmmer biß an den iungsten tag solden lyden, das yme doch sunderlichen von syner wirdigen mútter wegen durch sele vnd hertze drang. Zum funfften male, das sỹne sele ane sach alle bede vnd vnsegeliche demud, die er von den menschen [wegen] dem ewigen vatter vmmer thún solde vnd darbỹ erkante die große vndanckbarkeit des menschen. Diese funff gegenworffe machten ỹme lyden vnd vnsegeliche pỹne in alle syme leben.[109]

(The sweet Christ was never without bitter suffering even for an instant after his first moment in the temporal world, because he felt it in the first moment of the creation of his soul, and it lasted for his entire life until his death. And this was so because his soul perceived these five objects without intermission. First, his soul clearly perceived all of the injustice that would be done to God by mankind. His soul knew God to be so good, and saw the sinners' failings to be so deep; and so he had continual, especial pain from this. Second, his soul perceived that his great and manifold suffering would be lost on so many people, for whose sakes he suffered it all. Third, his soul perceived all the scorn, poverty, and suffering that would befall his soul and his noble body. Fourth, his soul perceived all of the oppression and harsh suffering that his noble mother and all his beloved friends would suffer for all time until the Last Judgement. This pierced his heart and soul especially on account of his noble mother. Fifth, his soul perceived all the intercessions and inconceivable humility that he would have to manifest to his Father for man's sake for all time; and with this realized the great thanklessness of mankind. These five objects gave him suffering and inconceivable pain for his entire life.)

In the parallel passage in *De reparatione hominis*, Marquard cannot repeat often enough how each of these were present in Christ 'ab instanti conceptionis'.[110] He then appends (in both works, but in more length in *De*

---

[109] *De anima Christi*, 206. 37–207. 21; cf. *Eucharistietraktat*, 273. 32–274. 3.
[110] *De reparatione hominis*, a. 23 (124. 9–35). *De reparatione* gives six, not five points, dividing the final point of the sequence in *De anima* into two without any material alteration.

anima Christi) a question that asks which of Christ's interior sufferings was the greatest. He concludes that this was the dishonour done to God—the dishonour of mankind's ongoing sin:

Die frage: Von welchen hatte nǔ die sele Cristi das groste lyden? Die antwort: Von dem vneren des vatters, wann die ere des vatters mÿnnet er uber alle ding. Vnd wann syn sele sach, das der vatter solde so manigfeldig enteret werden, sunderlichen ÿn ÿme vnd yn synen lieben frunden, das betrachte ÿme das groste lyden, das sÿn sele in allem lÿden hatte.[111]

(Question: From which of these now did Christ's soul have the greatest suffering? Answer: From the dishonour done to the Father, because he loved the honour of the Father above all else. And when his soul perceived that such manifold dishonour should be done to the Father, especially in him and in his beloved friends, this constituted the greatest suffering for him that his soul felt in all his sufferings.)

The idea of Christ's desire for the restoration of *iustitia*, for the redemption of mankind by satisfaction, has been transposed into a new context. Its logical consequence, Christ's hatred of all which damaged that *iustitia*—namely the continual sin of mankind—is understood as his greatest interior suffering.

Marquard relegates the corporeal aspects of Christ's suffering into second place in the remainder of the third section of *De anima Christi* by using a series of devices to enhance the reader's sense of the gravity of the interior sufferings. The fifth part of the treatise establishes that Christ's lifelong sufferings 'ab instanti conceptionis', which he has just defined in the fourth part as interior, were entirely without any temporary amelioration: Christ is said to have wept, but not to have laughed.[112] Marquard makes the causes of Christ's interior suffering directly responsible for this absence of any amelioration, and expresses this even more clearly in the (nonetheless much shorter) corresponding passage in *De reparatione*:

Quinto eius passio magna, immo permaxima fuisse convincitur, quia erat sine omni interpolatione. Solent enim, qui amaro sunt corde, habere sublevamina et in cibi vel potus sumptione suarum miseriarum oblivisci. Ipse autem dei filius continue et incessanter obiecta predicta [i.e. the causes of interior suffering] inspexit et comedendo et bibendo et loquendo continue sine interpolatione crucem, quam passurus erat, vidit, et praedicta sex obiecta.[113]

---

[111] *De anima Christi*, 207. 24–8; cf. *De reparatione hominis*, a. 23 (124. 36–9). In his sermon on Mary's sorrow under the cross, he says the same of her greatest spiritual suffering: see *Predigt* 21, ll. 89–97 (pp. 139–40).

[112] *De anima Christi*, 207. 30–208. 32.

[113] *De reparatione hominis*, a. 23 (124. 40–125. 4).

(Fifth, his suffering is clearly proven to have been great—indeed, the greatest of all—because it was without any intermission. For those who are bitterly unhappy in their hearts are accustomed to experience relief and to forget their miseries in the consumption of food or drink. The Son of God, however, perceived the aforesaid objects [of his interior suffering] continually and incessantly: and even when he ate, drank, and spoke, he saw the cross that he was about to suffer and the aforesaid six objects continually and without intermission.)

Christ's suffering did not even cease whilst he slept. His soul continued to suffer, and the pain radiated from the soul into his body. It was only with supernatural assistance that Christ was able to withstand his unimaginable interior suffering and sleep:

Die frage: Sint Cristus slieff vnd ruwete als eyn ander mensche, enhatte er do in dem slaffe nit vnderblibúnge sÿnes lÿdens? Die antwort: Als Cristus slieff vnd ußerlich liplich ruwete, so enruwete doch die sele nit, mer ir was alle ir lyden also geÿnwortig, als abe sie wechte. Vnd das lÿden der selen drang dann uß yn den lip, das der lip an lÿden nit enwas yn dem slaffe. Darumb was der slaff des lybes von sunderlicher ordenunge gottes vnd auch die nature ÿe etwas suchens vnd eyn deÿl wirckens yres gelaßens in dem slaff hatte.[114]

(Question: Given that Christ rested and slept like any other human, did he not have any respite from his suffering in his sleep? Answer: When Christ slept and rested his exterior body, his soul was not at rest. Rather, all the sufferings of his soul were as present to it as if it had been awake. The soul's suffering then penetrated outwards into the body, so that the sleeping body was not without suffering either. Consequently the body's sleep came from an especial divine ordinance, also so that his nature had a certain level of exertion and was partly active in its bearing during sleep.)

The sixth and final part of the Passion section of *De anima Christi* extends the argument of the magnitude of Christ's suffering, stating that it was so great that Christ's soul required constant supernatural assistance to remain alive at all.[115] Nor, as Marquard had earlier established (in a question appended to the third part of the section), was the great joy that Christ experienced through his participation in God either diminished or ameliorated by his continual suffering. This was no natural state, but ordained—following Henry of Ghent in particular, and the *communis opinio* in general—'von sunderlicher ordenunge gottes' ('by an especial divine ordinance').[116]

---

[114] *De anima Christi*, 208. 33–209. 6; cf. *De reparatione hominis*, a. 23 (125. 8–12), which offers a shorter, but more technical explanation.

[115] *De anima Christi*, 209. 7–29.

[116] Ibid. 205. 33–206. 31; cf. *De reparatione hominis*, a. 23 (123. 26–37).

The creation of a coherent category of interior sufferings, borne by Christ throughout his entire life and present from the moment of his conception, has not been previously identified by modern scholarship. Its origins lie not with Bonaventura, as we have seen, but in the unlikely milieu of the Spiritual Franciscans, and Marquard's direct source in the even unlikelier location of Olivi's *Lectura super Matthaeum*. The context is again Christ's sorrow and sweating of blood in Gethsemane.[117] Earlier we examined the fifth of six questions that Olivi poses with regard to this episode, namely the question as to how Christ sweated blood. After these questions, Olivi presents a long consideration on how the zenith of possible sorrow was present in Christ, partly because of the disposition of Christ's mental powers to be particularly receptive to all objects of (interior) sorrow, and partly because of seven lethal sorrows:

> Ut autem plenius *advertas* causas tante tristicie eius, nota quod in ipso fuit summus dolor, tam ex parte rationum obitinarum seu mortinarum, quam ex parte dispositionis potentiarum suarum. Ex parte quidem rationum obitinarum fuit in eo dolor septiformis.[118]

> (In order that you may perceive the causes of his great sorrow more fully, note that the most extreme suffering was in him; both on account of the lethal or fatal reasons, and on account of the disposition of his mental faculties. On account of the lethal reasons, indeed, there was a sevenfold suffering in him.)

Both parts of the following consideration are excerpted by Marquard. The much shorter part concerning the particular receptivity of Christ's mental powers to sorrow is incorporated, as mentioned earlier, in *De reparatione hominis* immediately prior to Marquard's disquisition on the physiological causes of Christ's sweating of blood. The seven interior sorrows that Olivi lists are adapted more freely by Marquard, and elevated to a new status both in *De reparatione* and, in German, in *De anima Christi*.[119] We will use *De reparatione* as our point of comparison here, as it is easier to compare Latin with Latin. The adaptation is complex. Most obviously, Marquard loses one point from Olivi's list entirely: the seventh sorrow, and the most 'corporeal' of the causes—Christ's sorrow over his present bodily suffering:

---

[117] On Olivi's understanding of the Passion in general in the *Lectura super Matthaeum* see Madigan, *Olivi and the Interpretation of Matthew*, pp. 122–3, and Douie, 'Olivi's "Postilla super Matthaeum"', pp. 82–7.

[118] Olivi, *Lectura in Matthaeum*, fol. 148rb, which gives 'adictas causas', corrected here to 'advertas causas'.

[119] *De reparatione hominis*, a. 23 (124. 9–39); *De anima Christi*, 206. 32–207. 29.

Septimo de actuali sufferentia mortis et tormentorum corporalium, que vtique non solum ferebantur ab extra, sed a predictis internis doloribus in eius corpore multipliciter redundabant.[120]

(The seventh came from the actual endurance of bodily torments and death, which certainly were not just borne by the external body, but resonated variously from the aforesaid internal sufferings into his body.)

The order of the remaining points is slightly adjusted, with no major effect: Olivi's sequence of 1–6 is presented in the order 1, 2, 6, 3, 4, 5. Marquard is in full agreement over the principal cause of Christ's interior suffering: the dishonour done to God as a result of the sins of mankind, past, present, and future; 'hic dolor', says Olivi, 'ut credo fuit, in Christo omnium summus' ('this suffering, as I believe, was the most extreme of all in Christ').[121] The most striking feature of the adaptation, however, is Marquard's accentuation of the character of these sorrows 'ab instanti conceptionis'. Olivi does not make this point very strongly at all. In fact, he only uses the phrase once, in the third sorrow. It is evidently not the sorrow itself, but the supplications, humiliations, laments, and tearful intercessions on mankind's behalf with the Father that Christ had 'ab instanti conceptionis':

Tertio de impetranda venia ac gratia et gloria nobis, per ineffabiles supplicationes et humiliationes sui ad patrem, et per ineffabiles lamentationes et lacrimabiles intercessiones pro nobis ad Deum, quas habuit ab instanti conceptionis tempore, sed circa crucem magis ostendit.[122]

(Third, from the pardons, gifts, and glories to be procured for us through his incalculable supplications and humiliations to the Father, and through incalculable lamentations and tearful intercessions for us with God, which he delivered from the first moment of his conception, but displayed more during the crucifixion.)

Whilst Olivi does place much stronger emphasis on Christ's interior sufferings in Gethsemane than Bonaventura, the position he formulates in this third sorrow is basically compatible with Bonaventura's understanding of what Christ had, and did not have, 'ab instanti conceptionis'. Marquard, by contrast, extends all of these causes of interior suffering back to the point of Christ's conception, and is thus rather more radical than Olivi. He states the point of origin twice in introducing the corresponding passage in *De reparatione*:

---

[120] Olivi, *Lectura super Matthaeum*, fol. 148rb.

[121] Ibid.; cf. *De reparatione hominis*, a. 23 (124. 36–9) and *De anima Christi*, 207. 22–9.

[122] Olivi, *Lectura super Matthaeum*, fol. 148rb.

Quarto eius passio permaxima fuisse convincitur ex sua divinitate. Nam ab instanti suae conceptionis numquam fuit sine intensione doloris usque ad obitum mortis amarissimae. Nam ab instanti conceptionis sex obiecta habuit in anima generantia passionem.[123]

(Fourth, his suffering is clearly proven to have been the greatest of all on account of his divinity. For from the moment of his conception he was never without intense suffering until the final moment of his most bitter death, because from the moment of conception he had six objects in his soul that caused suffering.)

The point is restated firmly at the conclusion to the passage: 'Haec igitur sex obiecta habuit ab instanti suae conceptionis usque ad mortem crucis'[124] ('He had these six objects, therefore, from the moment of his conception until his death on the cross'): and in three of the six individual causes of the interior suffering, Marquard introduces the phrase over and above Olivi. Let us take, for example, their statement concerning Christ's perception of the suffering that would be inflicted on the elect (and above all on Mary) in the entirety of the future. Marquard's addition is most clearly visible here, as there is less ancillary adaptation and abbreviation occurring. First, Olivi:

Quinto de omnibus passionibus et tormentis electorum suorum, et maxime sue piissime matris, quos omnis et singulis eorumque passiones ac temptationes et pericula, ipse incomparabiliter visceralius in suo corde portauit et sensit, quam ab aliquo ipse et eius passio portari potuit vel sentiri.[125]

(Fifth, from all the sufferings and torments of his elect, and most of all of his most holy mother. He bore those sufferings, temptations, and trials of each and every one of them himself, and felt them more incomparably intimately in his heart than his own suffering could ever be borne or felt by someone else.)

The corresponding point in *De reparatione* is the fourth in Marquard's sequence:

Quarto tormenta futura omnium electorum et maxime matris suae benedictae, quas omnes et singulas eorumque passiones, temptationes, pericula et tormenta visceraliter in suo corde ab instanti suae conceptionis portavit et sensit plus quam ab aliquo sua propria passio portari potuerit vel sentiri.[126]

(Fourth, the torments that were to befall all the elect and most of all his blessed mother. He bore and felt each and every one of their sufferings, temptations, trials, and torments intimately in his heart from the moment of his conception, more than his own suffering could have been borne or felt by anyone else.)

[123] *De reparatione hominis*, a. 23 (124. 9–13).
[124] Ibid. (124. 34–5).
[125] Olivi, *Lectura super Matthaeum*, fol. 148[rb].
[126] *De reparatione hominis*, a. 23 (124. 23–7).

Marquard's use of Olivi raises many questions: not least, exactly how Marquard could draw on the works of an individual whose oeuvre had been subject to two papal examinations that culminated in the condemnation of his *Lectura super Apocalypsim* by John XXII in 1326. At least one member of the second investigatory commission found the same faults in Olivi's Matthew commentary that he located in the Apocalypse commentary, and although there is no contemporary evidence that the *Lectura super Matthaeum* was condemned, the Dominican inquisitor Nicolas Eymeric recorded in 1376 that John XXII had indeed condemned it because it contained 'haereses aliquae consimiles' ('some similar heresies') to those located in the *Lectura super Apocalypsim*.[127] Perhaps, though, the issue is not as problematic as it may seem. First, there is evidence that some of the manuscripts of Olivi's *Lectura super Matthaeum* circulated anonymously. At least one copy travelled under the far more reputable name of Nicholas of Lyra, and of the nineteen manuscripts examined by Marie-Thérèse d'Alverny, the only complete copy from Germany (Klosterneuburg, Stiftsbibliothek, Cod. 769), a fourteenth-century parchment manuscript, was marked by a late fourteenth-century hand as a work of Alexander of Hales.[128] Second, Marquard was well acquainted with the oeuvre of another speculative theologian to have attracted the critical attention of John XXII, namely Meister Eckhart, and displays no reticence in adducing such 'radical' works in support of his arguments. Third, Olivi's works held a certain appeal to the Franciscan Observants of the fifteenth century, not least Bernardino of Siena, whom Decima Douie describes as 'particularly fond' of the *Lectura super Matthaeum*.[129]

With Olivi and Marquard, directly dependent upon each other, as fixed points in place, we can begin to define the intellectual tradition of understanding Christ's interior sufferings in this way around them. It can, in fact, be identified more widely amongst the milieu of the Spiritual Franciscans, reaching different audiences through different works. Ubertino da Casale emerges as a key figure in this tradition. In 1305, some twenty-five years after Olivi had written his *Lectura in Matthaeum* (probably produced in the

---

[127] Madigan, *Olivi and the Interpretation of Matthew*, pp. 130–2; d'Alverny, 'Un adversaire de Saint Thomas', pp. 186–92.

[128] D'Alverny, 'Un adversaire de Saint Thomas', pp. 192–206, here pp. 203–4. Ciceri's more recent conspectus counts a total of 21 manuscripts of the complete text; 5 more with miscellaneous extracts; 19 with just the commentary on ch. 18; and 10 with just the commentary on the Lord's Prayer: see Ciceri, *Petri Iohannis Olivi*, pp. 41–9. Aside from the Klosterneuburg copy noted above, no other manuscript of the complete work is securely of German provenance, although all but 2 of the 19 manuscripts containing the commentary to ch. 18 are from Germany.

[129] Douie, 'Olivi's "Postilla super Matthaeum"', pp. 91–2, here p. 91.

academic year 1279–80 or 1280–1),[130] Ubertino undertook the first recension of the *Arbor vitae crucifixae*. At this point, Ubertino had withdrawn
to the Italian mountain friary of La Verna, the site of Francis's stigmatization. The first of the two prologues to the *Arbor vitae* includes a detailed
account of his literary activity there, which enables the different stages of
the work's production to be reconstructed.[131] It is this version that was
printed in 1485, on which text modern scholarship has relied. Carlos
Mateo Martínez Ruiz has proven that Ubertino would subsequently produce a second, heavily revised recension of the work prior to his death
around 1330; a discovery that has major implications both for the interpretation of the *Arbor vitae* itself, and above all for the understanding of the
subsequent transmission and reception of the work, but which need not
concern us immediately here.[132]

Ubertino's first prologue incorporates considerable autobiographical
material. He tells us that, at a certain point in his life as a friar, he came
to study in the province of Tuscany, and found people in whom the spirit
of Christ was very strong. One of these was Petrus Johannis Olivi, under
whom he studied at Florence for two years between 1287 and 1289.[133] He
introduced Ubertino to the knowledge, amongst other things, of the most
profound perfections of Christ's soul, and his study with Olivi clearly
represented a turning point in his spiritual progress. Olivi taught Ubertino,
with the spirit of Christ working inside him, to consider his beloved
(Christ) in all things, and to feel himself always crucified together with
him, in mind and in body. This experience is at the root of Ubertino's
doctrine of the mystical transformation into the crucified Christ that the
Arbor vitae sets out. Ubertino points to a central aspect of this experience in
stating that he frequently felt almost submerged in the deepest sorrows of
Christ's heart ('inter abyssales cordis sui dolores')—that is, his interior
suffering.[134] Later on in the prologue, Ubertino describes how he came
to write the *Arbor vitae* in 1305. The beginning of this process involved
writing commentaries on a series of short verses (the *versiculi* that ultimately serve as the chapter headings in the *Arbor vitae*). This was all Ubertino

[130] On the date of the *Lectura in Matthaeum* see Madigan, *Olivi and the Interpretation of Matthew*, pp. 72–3; Burr, *Olivi and Franciscan Poverty*, pp. 47–8 and 54–5 n. 36.

[131] See Martínez Ruiz, *De la dramatizacion*, pp. 31–63 and 233–7; note that pp. 40–5 correct and replace the earlier account in id., 'Il processo redazionale'.

[132] See Martínez Ruiz, *De la dramatizacion*, pp. 63–75, 271–7, and 310–18; and id., 'Ubertino da Casale'.

[133] Burr, *The Spiritual Franciscans*, pp. 47–8, and Martínez Ruiz, *De la dramatizacion*, pp. 171–7.

[134] Ubertino da Casale, *Arbor vitae crucifixae*, prol. 1, p. 4[b].

intended to produce, but when he arrived at a certain *versiculus*, he felt strongly moved by the spirit of Christ to expound at length there on his *dolores cordiales*. This done, it served as the catalyst for the production of an entire life of Christ:

Cum uenissem autem ad illum[135] uersiculum 'Iesus futura preuidens', fortissime fuit mihi immissum a spiritu Iesu ut cordiales dolores Iesu exponerem [. . .], pro omnibus uolentibus in Christi passionibus exerceri. Quo facto, instigabar a Iesu quod sue passionis describerem totum cursum; et dum in his procederem, immissum est mihi quod totam uitam Iesu transcurrerem, et paruulum libellum ex euangelica silua transcriberem, quem dilecti Iesu myrrhe fasciculum appellarem.[136]

(When, however, I had reached that versicle 'Jesus, foreseeing what was to come', it had been communicated to me most strongly by the spirit of Jesus that I was to set forth the heartfelt sorrows of Jesus [. . .], for all those who wanted to be schooled in Christ's sufferings. With that done, I was instructed by Jesus that I was to narrate the whole sequence of his Passion. While I was making progress in this, it was communicated to me that I was to cover the entire life of Jesus and to transcribe a small booklet from the Gospels' groves, which I was to call a bundle of myrrh of the beloved Jesus.)

Ubertino then mentions other things about which he was moved to write, notably the deplorable state of the church and laxity in the Franciscan order. But as far as the life of Christ is concerned, it is Christ's *dolores cordiales* that he singles out, pointing to the centrality of this concept to his own contemplative experience and to the production of the treatise. He guides the reader explicitly to the chapter with the *versiculus* 'Iesus futura preuidens'. This is book 4, chapter 9 in the first recension, which was divided into two chapters (8 and 9) in the second—though without, states Martínez Ruiz, making much perceptible change to the content.[137]

This chapter is naturally that which considers Christ in Gethsemane. Ubertino begins with a discussion on the technical nature of the emotions Christ displayed there. He then explains that Christ was not subject to the same mental vicissitudes as other humans. By implication, the sorrow that was revealed in Gethsemane was not a temporally limited expression of his natural will. Nevertheless, it was fitting (*conueniens*) that he should choose this moment to reveal to the faithful by these perceptible signs something

---

[135] The incunable text here offers 'primum', which I correct to 'illum', as Martínez Ruiz has shown 'primum' to be an error in a subarchetype to which the incunable text is related: see Martínez Ruiz, *De la dramatizacion*, p. 43.

[136] Ubertino da Casale, *Arbor vitae crucifixae*, prol. 1, p. 6ᵃ.

[137] Martínez Ruiz, *De la dramatizacion*, pp. 69–71 and 347.

that he had kept hidden since he was in Mary's womb, and which was beyond the comprehension of any created being—the 'agonia dolorum cordis' ('agony of the sufferings of his heart').[138]

He proceeds to a technical discussion of the physiological causes of the sweating of blood, and concludes with exactly the same distinctive, non-miraculous explanation that Olivi and Marquard share:

> Timor concussit suum sensitiuum, ex quo humor sanguineus fuit ad interiora reductus. Super quem timorem reiiciendum fortissimus et inestimabilis amor, tanquam mire immensitatis malleus repercutiens et ipsum excludens. Omnes poros corporis Iesu et uenas relaxasse uidetur, ut sic toto corpore flueret guttis sanguinis decurrentis in terram.[139]
>
> (Fear struck his sensory appetite, by which the sanguine humour was drawn into his innermost parts. Above the fear that had to be expelled was an exceedingly strong and inestimable love, like a hammer of wondrous size, striking back and driving it out. It seems that every pore and vein of Jesus' body opened, so that he flowed in his whole body with droplets of blood falling onto the ground.)

Next, he explains the meaning of the sign that Christ gave by sweating blood. First, it was a manifestation of the sorrows Christ had felt for his entire life, from the moment of his conception ('ab instanti conceptionis sue') and which he had kept hidden. Second, it represented the sorrows he was experiencing at the present time. Third, it was a prefiguration of the sorrows he was about to suffer, in his corporeal body and in his mystical body (i.e. the elect).[140] Ubertino then describes how each part of Christ's body had suffered during his life, or would come to suffer in the Passion. It is no wonder, he concludes, if such a burden were to be expressed by sweating blood—but he does not think that this is the case. Rather, the sign of sweating blood expressed Christ's continual interior suffering; a suffering that had been present 'ab instanti conceptionis sue':

> Quid ergo mirum, si pondus tantarum passionum attendens, sustinens, et exprimere uolens, sic uoluit in sudore membrorum relaxare uenas. Sed magis credo internorum dolorum et anxietatum cordis sui immensitatem hoc signo uoluisse exprimere; licet multe rationes sint in hoc signo uoluisse exprimere; licet multe rationes sint in hoc signo contente. Vt autem modicum de his doloribus disseramus, cum reuerentia aliquid incipio balbutire[.][141]

---

[138] Ubertino da Casale, *Arbor vitae crucifixae*, lib. 4, c. 9, pp. 307[b]–308[a].
[139] Ibid., p. 308[a].
[140] Ibid.
[141] Ibid., pp. 308[b]–309[a].

(What wonder then, if, as he gave his whole attention to, endured, and wanted to express the burden of such suffering, he wanted to open his veins in the sweat of his limbs. But I believe rather that he wanted to express the immensity of his internal sufferings and the anxiety of his heart by this sign. It may be that there are many reasons in this sign that he wanted to express; it may be that many reasons were contained in this sign. So that we may, however, discuss his sorrows a little, I begin, with reverence, to stammer a bit.)

Ubertino's 'modicum' is (unsurprisingly) a great deal, despite his subsequent asseverations that he is only providing his reader with a small taste of the infinite sea of the sorrows of Christ's heart. His focus lies above all else on the entirety of human sin, and he explains the complex mechanisms in detail by which Christ's perception of all sin, past, present, and future, was the principal cause of his sorrow. He goes beyond the standard understanding of Christ's sacrifice as formal satisfaction for the sin of mankind, to view Christ as personally and directly afflicted in his mind by the totality of human sin: his love (*amor*) for man impelling him to bear this inconceivable weight of suffering (*dolor*).[142] Christ did not just know of man's sin, but suffered from that knowledge. Sin was the principal cause of Christ's sorrow for several reasons, but chief amongst them—like Olivi, and Marquard—is the injustice that sin inflicts upon God. Ubertino makes this point repeatedly. In this passage, the relationship between individual sins as acts of injustice and the necessity for Christ to bear inner sorrow in reparation for each single act of injustice is made clear:

Et quia naturalis est filius Dei patris tantum aggrauauit istam iniuriam quantum ipsum dilexit, et inquantum istas iniurias ad satisfaciendum accepit, tantum dolorem assumpsit pro qualibet singulari iniuria omnis peccati quantum erat grauitas iniurie et requirebat emendam. Et si unius iniurie tanta est grauitas: quanta est simul omnium?[143]

(And because he is the natural son of the Father, he made that injustice greater the more he loved him; insofar as he took up those acts of injustice to make satisfaction for them, he received as much suffering for any single act of injustice as the weight of the injustice of every sin for which he needed to make amends. And if the weight of one act of injustice is as great as this, how great is that of them all together?)

The burden of responsibility for Christ's suffering lies squarely on the shoulders of contemporary individuals—Ubertino's addressees—whose sin causes Christ inexpressible sorrow:

---

[142] The full implications of the reciprocity of *amor* and *dolor* in this passage are discussed by Martínez Ruiz, *De la dramatizacion*, p. 346; see pp. 520–30 on this dichotomy in the *Arbor vitae* as a whole.

[143] Ubertino da Casale, *Arbor vitae crucifixae*, lib. 4, c. 9, p. 309[b].

Sic laborare eum fecimus in peccatis nostris, quia flexit rigorem diuine iustitie et eleuauit grauissimum pondus nostre culpe; quia uenit ut sponsus perfectissime diligens sponsarum decorem in doloribus et angustiis totum se reliquauit, et totum se per cineres malitiarum nostrarum infudit ut faceret de se lauacrum, ut posset delere et lauare tantam turpitudinem et maculam peccatorum. Et istam rationem doloris quam habebat illa dulcissima anima in horrore aspectus macularum nostrarum, quis enarrare sufficiat?[144]

(And thus we made him toil in our sins, because he turned aside the inflexibility of divine justice and raised up the heaviest burden of our guilt; because he came as the bridegroom who most perfectly loves the beauty of the bride, and forsook himself totally in sufferings and distress; he covered himself totally with the ashes of our acts of malice in order that he might make a ewer of himself, so that he might be able to expunge and wash away the great ugliness and stain of the sinners. And who could suffice to explain fully that reason of sorrow which this sweetest soul had in horror at the sight of our blemishes [i.e. our sins]?)

The examples Ubertino uses to illustrate his points are graphic and shocking, his intention being to confront the reader with horrible situations that are nonetheless far less awful than what Christ has to suffer in bearing each individual's sin.[145] The ingratitude of man for Christ's sacrifice, manifest in man's continuing to commit new sins, constitutes an additional reason for Christ's inner suffering (a *noua ratio doloris*). Ubertino concludes his chapter with a concatenation of further reasons for this interior suffering, stretching over nearly three columns, and which expand at length on Olivi's list of seven items.[146] The close parallel to Olivi's text here has already been noted by Martínez Ruiz, who has briefly made mention Ubertino's distinctive presentation of Christ's *dolores cordiales* (and it is this note that made possible the identification of Olivi's *Lectura in Matthaeum* as Marquard's source).[147]

Ubertino was also acquainted with another prominent Spiritual Franciscan, namely Angela da Foligno (d. 1309). We can identify a very similar conception of Christ's interior suffering in her *Liber*; notably in the second part, a series of texts offering guidance on various aspects of religious devotion known as the *Instructiones*. *Instructio* 3 provides a consideration of Christ using the common motif of the 'liber vitae', and examines his sorrow, prayer, and poverty in turn.[148] His sorrow—that is, his interior

---

[144] Ibid., p. 310ª.
[145] Ibid., pp. 309ᵇ–310ª.
[146] Ibid., pp. 310ᵇ–311ᵇ.
[147] Martínez Ruiz, *De la dramatizacion*, pp. 342–7, here pp. 344–5 n. 44.
[148] Angela da Foligno, *Liber*, Instructio 3 (pp. 442–83).

suffering—was so acute, Angela explains, for six reasons.[149] The first of these was the 'divina dispensatio': the continual influx of divine wisdom to Christ's soul, which meant that he saw the ineffable measure of such excessive suffering apportioned to him from the moment of his creation to the end of his life: and not only saw it, but suffered by this foreknowledge. We can leave aside three further reasons as uncontroversial, reasonably standard ideas: Christ's compassion with Mary, his compassion with the apostles over the sorrow they would feel on his departure from earthly existence, and the particular tenderness and receptivity to pain of his soul. The most significant reason from our perspective, however, is Christ's compassion with mankind. He saw the sins committed and punishments received by mankind, past, present, and future, and had compassion with suffering man. His compassion manifested itself in bearing the sins of mankind, and it is from this that he incurred suffering:

Fuit etiam in Christo dolor intensissimus et acutus ex compassione supermirabili quam habuit humano generi quod diligebat tam summe. Compatiebatur enim unicuique cum summo dolore secundum mensuram uniuscuiusque quantitatis delicti et poenae, quam eos incurrere et incurrisse sciebat certissime. Quia enim Christus quemlibet electorum suorum ineffabiliter diligebat et hoc amore devisceraato in eos, secundum mensuram cuiuslibet, continue praesentialiter sentiendo eorum offensam commissam et commissuram et poenam et poenas quas ex tanta offensa sustinere debebant, compatiebatur eisdem tollerando eorum poenas cum summo dolore.[150]

(An acute suffering of the most intense kind was also in Christ from the compassion, transcending all admiration, which he had for the human race that he loved in the highest. For he was compassionate with the greatest suffering to each and every one of them, in proportion to their crimes and the punishments which he knew most certainly that they were incurring and had incurred. For because Christ loved every single one of his elect ineffably, and by this love that he had emptied into them, he felt—continually, and as if present to him—the offences they had committed or were going to commit, and the punishment and pains that they must bear on account of such offences, according to the measure of each and every one of them; and he had compassion with them by bearing their punishments with the greatest suffering.)

Angela deepens the intensity of this suffering by introducing a new idea: that Christ suffered from the compassion he had with himself, on seeing the burden of sins, suffering, and punishment that he would be required to bear as a consequence of his compassion with mankind:

[149] Angela da Foligno, *Liber*, Instructio 3, 7–75 (pp. 442–9).
[150] Ibid., Instructio 3, 26–35 (p. 444).

Fuit etiam dolor in Christo compassionis proprie suimet. Compatiebatur enim Christus sibi ipsi de dolorosa poena et ineffabili quam super se infallibiliter venire videbat. Videns enim Christus se ad hoc missum a Patre ut omnium electorum suorum dolores et poenas in seipso portaret, nec posse falli, quod tam acutissimum et ineffabilem non sustineret dolorem, et se ad hoc totaliter datum, compatiebatur sibi ipsi cum summo dolore.[151]

(The suffering of his own compassion with himself was also in Christ. For Christ had compassion for himself from the grievous and inconceivable punishment that he saw inexorably coming upon him. For Christ, because he saw himself sent by the Father in order that he might bear in himself the pains and sufferings of all of his elect, could not be mistaken that he might not have to bear such inconceivable suffering of the acutest kind; and so having been given totally for this purpose, he had compassion for himself with the greatest suffering.)

Subsequently, Angela explains how Christ made known his great interior suffering through the cry of dereliction. She establishes that this suffering began at the moment of his conception—'in ipso creationis suae instanti'—and says that the cry of dereliction serves to admonish the individual to imitate Christ by suffering internally in like manner, a recurrent theme of this third *Instructio*:

[S]olum pro nobis clamavit verbum illud, ut superacutissimum dolorem et continuum, quem non pro se sed pro nobis protulerat, nobis indicaret, et etiam ut moneret nos semper esse dolendos. Quia enim creatio corporis et eius organizatio et animae infusio et Verbi unio simul et semel fuerunt—ex qua supermirabili unione anima illa repleta fuit summa sapientia et ineffabili, omnia sibi praesentialiter praesentia ineffabili et infallibili repraesentans—ideo superacutissimum et omnino ineffabilem dolorem quem se videbat infallibiliter sustinere in ipso creationis suae instanti—divina haec sapientia dispensabiliter dispensante—totum et totaliter sustinuit et portavit continue usque ad animae separationem et carnis.[152]

(He cried that word out for us alone, in order that he might signal to us the continual suffering of the most intensely acute kind that he had carried not for himself but for us, and also that he might admonish us always to be in suffering. For because the creation and composition of his body, the infusion of his soul and the union with the Word all took place together at the same time—from which union, transcending all admiration, his soul was filled with the highest and infallible wisdom, and was thus able to make everything infallibly present to itself in an ineffable way. Thus he bore and carried the completely ineffable sorrow of the most intensely acute kind, which he saw himself infallibly to be sustaining in the moment of his creation itself—with divine wisdom ordering this appropriately—wholly, totally, and continually until the separation of his body and soul.)

---

[151] Ibid., Instructio 3, 38–47 (pp. 444–6).
[152] Ibid., Instructio 3, 112–22 (p. 452).

Instructio 28 returns to the same theme in shorter form. Christ is to be imitated in the three principal aspects of interior suffering, poverty, and being despised. In explaining how interior suffering is to be understood, Angela refers again to its incipience 'ab instanti conceptionis suae', uses Christ's words in the garden of Gethsemane as the concrete evidence that this suffering existed, and alludes to contemporary man as its cause:

Vult anima etiam transformari in dolores quos ipse sustinuit. Fecit enim eum Deus Pater Filium doloris, et semper fuit in dolore. Nam ab instanti conceptionis fuit in summa tristitia, quia divina sapientia tunc ostendit ei omnia quae debebat pati; et iste dolor tunc incoepit et duravit usque ad separationem animae a corpore. Et hoc manifestavit oratio, quam fecit cum dixit: Tristis est anima mea usque ad mortem; nam quia dixit mortem esse finem istius doloris, datur intelligi principium quod fuit tempus conceptionis. Et quia istorum dolorum fuimus causa, debemus in istos dolores transformari, quod facimus secundum mensuram amoris.[153]

(The soul also wants to be transformed into the sufferings that he himself bore. For God the Father made him the Son of suffering, and he was always in suffering. For he was in extreme sorrow from the moment of his conception, because at that point divine wisdom showed him everything that he had to suffer. And at that point this suffering began, and it endured until the separation of his soul from his body. And the prayer that he made when he said 'My soul is sorrowful unto death' demonstrated this: for because he said that death was the end of this suffering, it is given to be understood that the beginning was the time of his conception. And because we were the cause of those sufferings, we ought to be transformed into those sufferings, which we effect according to the measure of our love.)

In Angela's *Instructiones* we find essentially the same perspective on the relationship between the sin of contemporary mankind and the suffering of Christ, together with a similar understanding of the nature of that interior suffering itself—not least, the idea that it began 'ab instanti conceptionis suae'—that we encounter in Ubertino's *Arbor vitae*. This should not surprise us. Angela and Ubertino were acquainted from around 1298.[154] Most of the scholarly interest in their relationship has concentrated on its personal aspect; in particular, the question of their respective involvement with individuals or small groups associated with the Spiritual Franciscans. The separate issue of the relationship between their works is less well studied. Alfonso Marini has provided a recent conspectus of all existing research, and has discussed the potential parallels between the works that have been postulated. Few of these have any particular solidity. It is even

[153] Angela da Foligno, *Liber*, Instructio 28 (pp. 638–49), here 62–71 (p. 644).
[154] For a recent survey of Angela's life and extant works, see Ruh, *Geschichte der abendländischen Mystik*, vol. 2, pp. 509–15.

less clear what direction the textual influence, if there was any, took. Ubertino wrote the *Arbor vitae* in 1305, before Angela's death, but the dating of her *Liber* is controversial. It is clear that it is the product of a long process of writing and revision, and that it was a collaborative work: Angela dictated in Italian to a series of scribes, principally a somewhat mysterious 'frater A.' ('brother A.'), who wrote the text down in Latin.[155] As a consequence, if the *Arbor vitae* were the prior text, then we would be very unlikely to find direct textual parallels anyway. Regardless, this distinctive conceptualization of the interior sufferings of Christ is probably the clearest indication of an intellectual community between the two works identified thus far.

The origins of the elaboration of Christ's lifelong, interior suffering are clearly to be sought broadly in the milieu of the Spiritual Franciscans, developed in the decades after Bonaventura's death in 1274, and functionalized differently by its various exponents. Olivi is responsible for the creation of a coherent category of interior sufferings and for the theological foundations of the idea. He is the first thirteenth-century intellectual to offer an original theological treatment of Christ's sorrow in Gethsemane, a theme that had been treated with great caution by earlier scholars, but which offered (or rather, *because* it offered) the only extensive insight into Christ's mind during the Passion to be found in the evangelical accounts. Ubertino is responsible for the elaboration of Olivi's insights within the context of writing the life of Christ, for accentuating the emphasis on the lifelong aspect of Christ's interior suffering, and for placing the burden of responsibility for causing this suffering squarely and directly on the shoulders of contemporary man. Angela, finally, presents the tenor of Ubertino's teaching distilled into components of a guide to perfected spiritual life. Whatever the literary genesis of Angela's *Liber*, her work is significant above all in its demonstration that the new conceptualization of Christ's interior suffering was not merely an abstruse theological issue debated between two trained intellectuals (Olivi and Ubertino), but was more widely received and discussed amongst the set of named individuals held to constitute the Spiritual Franciscans in the years around 1300. Marquard's *De reparatione* offers testimony to the theological development of these ideas, inherited here from Olivi, in a Latin scholastic context about seventy-five years after Olivi's death, and about forty-five years after that of

---

[155] See Marini, 'Ubertino e Angela', pp. 319–25; possible parallels between the works are discussed pp. 325–33, with some examples for comparison pp. 334–44; on Ubertino's relationship with Angela see additionally Burr, *The Spiritual Franciscans*, pp. 334–44, and Martínez Ruiz, *De la dramatizacion*, pp. 208–10.

Ubertino. *De anima Christi* is considerably more significant. Not only does it attest to the reception and further development of these ideas in the German vernacular, but it elevates this conceptualization of Christ's suffering to a new status within the work that treats the issue. For despite the importance and originality of these ideas, proportionally they constitute just a fraction in each case of the total extent of Olivi's *Lectura in Matthaeum*, Ubertino's *Arbor vitae*, Angela's *Liber*, and Marquard's *De reparatione*. In *De anima Christi*, however, these ideas form the principal theme of one-third of the whole work—and a very different kind of work at that, namely a vernacular treatise on the imitation of Christ.

Having sketched the intellectual genesis of these ideas, let us turn to the question of their reception beyond Marquard. The later Middle Ages is conventionally and rightly understood to have witnessed an explosion of literature that focused on the corporeal sufferings of Christ in ever more gruesome and manifold ways. Amongst the important fourteenth-century Latin works that we have mentioned so far, there is no discussion of interior suffering in the *Meditationes vitae Christi* or in Michael de Massa's *Vita Christi*. In Ludolf von Sachsen's compendious *Vita Christi* there is just one tiny fragment on the issue. It is found in an epilogue to the narrative of the crucifixion, not in the presentation of Gethsemane, which is treated with much more conventional brevity. Ludolf states that the pain of Christ's suffering had not been confined to the events of the Passion itself. Rather, Christ's foreknowledge of his coming corporeal suffering was present, causing him pain, from the moment of his conception until the hour of his death:

Non est autem aestimandum quod Passionis suae poena, in ejus solum captione et traditione fuerit inchoata; sed potius ab instanti suae conceptionis usque ad mortem ejus duravit. Cum enim mortem suam acerbissimam, quam pro salute nostra pati voluit firmissime praesciret, et eam futuram infallibiliter cognosceret, oportuit quod in qualibet hora pro ea naturaliter doleret, praesertim cum cogitaret tantam mortis acerbitatem, et tantam doloris generalitatem, quae per totum corpus et omnia membra corporis, et per omnes vires inferiores animae diffundi debebat.[156]

(It is not, however, to be reckoned that the pain of his Passion began only when he was captured and turned over [to the authorities]; but rather, it lasted from the moment of his conception until his death. For when he foresaw his bitterest death, which he wanted most steadfastly to suffer for our salvation, and knew infallibly what was to befall him, it was fitting that he should suffer in his nature in accordance with that [i.e. the knowledge of his death] in each and every hour—especially when

---

[156] Ludolf von Sachsen, *Vita Christi*, pars 2, c. 67 (ed. 1865, p. 687ᵃ; ed. 1870, vol. 4, p. 639ᵃ).

he thought of such a great bitterness of death and such an all-encompassing kind of suffering that was to penetrate both through his whole body and its every limb, and through all of the lower powers of his soul.)

This passage would appear to be Ludolf's own. The section continues with a long text on Christ's Passion ostensibly drawn 'ex verbis Augustini' ('from the words of Augustine'; an undoubtedly spurious attribution).[157] This focuses on Christ's lifelong bodily suffering, beginning with the cold and difficult conditions he faced in the stable. Nothing more is made of his mental suffering 'ab instanti conceptionis'. None of these three Latin works, crucial to the development of the Passion narrative in the fourteenth century, goes much beyond Jerome or the *Glossa ordinaria* in their presentation of the sweating of blood in the garden of Gethsemane.[158]

Amongst German works of the fourteenth century, it goes almost without saying that the graphic *Christi Leiden in einer Vision geschaut* contains nothing on the issue. There is scarcely anything more in the Passion narrative of Heinrich von St Gallen. The sole instance in which anything relevant is mentioned is in a quotation attributed to Bernard, in which three causes of Christ's tears upon the cross are set out:

Bernhardus spricht, das der herre weinte an dem crucze durch drierleie sache wille: Die erste sache dorumme, das her sach an alle der werlde nimant, der im siner marter danckte, dan der schecher alleine. Czum andren male dorumme, das der herre sach sine liben iungere so iemerlichen czustreuwit. Czum dritten male dorumme, daz her sach sine lipe muter sten vor sinen ougen und erkante das, das sie liber were tot gewest danne lebendic; daz liden tet dem herren wirs dan alle wunden, die her hatte an sime lichnam.[159]

(Bernard says that the Lord had three causes to weep on the cross. The first cause was that he saw no one in the whole world who thanked him for his martyrdom, save the thief alone. The second was that he saw his beloved disciples sundered so pitifully. The third was that he saw his beloved mother standing before his eyes, and recognized that she would rather have been dead than alive. This suffering hurt the Lord worse than all the wounds that he had on his body.)

It is evident that these are not lifelong interior sufferings: they are specifically tied to Christ being crucified. Christ's compassion with Mary is an ancient and long-standing theme, as is the idea that his compassion for her

---

[157] Ibid. (ed. 1865, pp. 687ᵃ–689ᵃ; ed. 1870, vol. 4, pp. 639ᵃ–643ᵃ); cf. Baier, *Untersuchungen zu den Passionsbetrachtungen*, vol. 2, p. 234.

[158] For the Gethsemane scene see Johannes de Caulibus, *Meditationes vitae Christi*, c. 75, ll. 13–140 (pp. 256–61); Michael de Massa, *Vita Ihesu Christi*, pp. 42ᵛᵃ–43ᵛᵇ; Ludolf von Sachsen, *Vita Christi*, pars 2, c. 59 (ed. 1865, pp. 605ᵃ–611ᵃ; ed. 1870, vol. 4, pp. 468ᵃ–480ᵃ).

[159] Heinrich von St Gallen, Passionstraktat *Extendit manum*, 66. 12–21.

outweighed the physical pain of his crucifixion. That idea is associated with the standard notion that Christ's compassion for mankind, and especially for his mother, must have outweighed the pain of his Passion; had this been the other way round then he would not have sacrificed himself to redeem mankind.

Only one German work prior to 1400 other than Marquard's *De anima Christi* offers a discussion of Christ's interior suffering: the Passion treatise of the Franciscan Johannes von Zazenhausen. After narrating Christ's prayer in Gethsemane, and providing two subsequent quotations from Augustine, Johannes introduces an excursus on Christ's interior suffering that is presented as a distinction attributed to Hugh of St Victor. Johannes states that Christ's interior suffering began at the moment of his conception and endured for his entire life. It was not caused just by the knowledge of his forthcoming crucifixion, but, rather curiously, by the bearing of everything that every single person in all time would suffer in body and soul:

Hugo: Hie solt du mercken daz vnser behalter zwayerhant marter leyt. Ein leyt er an seinem leibe; die wert ie, wann er etwaz marter oder smachheit laid. Dise pein hett dick an im vnderleidung, so man im kayn laid tett. Die ander leyt er an seine[m] gaist. Die marter hüb an im an, do er enpfangen wörd vnd sein sel in seinen leib gegozzen wörd; die weret an im on vnderlaß biz das sein sel von seinem leib an dem crewtze schyed, daz er in vier vnd dreyßig jarn ainen awgenplick on ängstlich marter seines gaistes nie was. Wann alles, daz er an diser naht vnd an disem tag laid— lasters, schand, verspeyen, geyseln, krönen mit dörnen, mit pitterm tranck der gallen mirren vnd eßig, nägelen an daz crewtz—daz laid er alles zü mal sein sele mit ain ander allczeyt vör hin. Vnd nit allain alle ding, die er an sein selbes leibe laid, doch alles daz von Adam biz an den jungsten tag menschen der an der welt ende sol gepören werden, ieglicher sunder an seinem leibe oder an seiner sele ie geleyt peine, betrübt oder traurikayt oder noch leiden werdent: daz laidt Ihesus an seiner sele alles vnd allczeyt, vnd also gar peynlich daz im in iamers weyse [wirst det an siner selen ÿcliches lyden] denn es in tett oder noch tůn wurde an irm leibe so si ie mitten lyden[t].[160]

(Hugh: Here you should take note that our saviour suffered two kinds of torture. One kind he suffered in his body, and this lasted whenever he suffered any torture or ill-treatment. This pain was frequently interrupted when no one was inflicting suffering on him. The other kind he suffered in his spirit. This torture began to afflict him when he was conceived and his soul was infused into his body, and it endured without intermission until his soul departed from his body on the cross.

---

[160] Johannes von Zazenhausen, *Deutscher Passionstraktat*, fol. 225^{r-v}. All quotations from this text are given from the Nuremberg manuscript, checked against the copy in Mainz; from which, as here, the portion omitted (by homoteleuton) in the Nuremberg manuscript is given from fol. 111rb.

As a result he did not spend a moment of his thirty-four years without the terrible torture of his spirit. For everything that he suffered in this full day and night—the scorn, the shame, the spitting, the flagellation, the coronation with thorns, the bitter drink of gall, myrrh, and vinegar, the nailing upon the cross—he suffered all of this together and at the same time in his soul continually. And not just everything that he suffered in his own body, but every pain, distress, or grief that every individual human born in every corner of the world from Adam until the Last Judgement ever suffered, or would yet suffer, in body or in soul. Jesus suffered all of this continually in his soul, and so very painfully that every instance of suffering hurt him worse in his soul in the form of sorrow, than it did or would do to those who suffered it in their bodies.)

Johannes then sets out two underlying causes that made this interior suffering possible. First, Christ's divine omnicognizance. He saw everything that had happened and would happen, and so from the moment of his conception until his death he saw all the suffering that he would have to bear, and that every person had suffered and would suffer until the end of time. He suffered this in the lower powers of his soul and was more painfully tortured in his spirit than anyone who suffered bodily torture. This was because his interior suffering endured for his whole life without pause, whereas the bodily sufferings of the martyrs were inflicted over much shorter periods. Like Marquard, Johannes mentions that Christ did not laugh, though often cried. Second, Christ's great love for mankind. His compassion for mankind, and his suffering at the knowledge of the suffering that all mankind would bear caused him unspeakable pain. A series of scriptural quotations is adduced to substantiate the position that whatever harm is inflicted by one person upon another, is inflicted upon Christ. Finally, Johannes concludes his excursus with a discussion of how Christ was able to suffer internally if he was simultaneously united with God, source of the greatest joy.[161]

The ascription of this long excursus to Hugh of St Victor certainly does not imply that it is a verbatim translation from a much older Latin text. The work in question is Hugh's *De quatuor voluntatibus in Christo*, a short piece on the nature of the wills in Christ. Hugh discusses the relationship between passion and compassion, where compassion is defined as a form of mental suffering that proceeds from the emotional effect of witnessing another's suffering, and notes that Christ experienced both. He was fully human just as he was fully divine, and as compassion is the *proprium* of mankind—a feature that distinguishes man from animal—so Christ

---

[161] See Johannes von Zazenhausen, *Deutscher Passionstraktat*, fols. 225ᵛ–227ᵛ.

experienced compassion, defined in this way, as much as he suffered in body. By suffering both in body and in mind, Christ was able to heal mankind in body and mind:

Nunc [vita] infirma in utroque et passione videlicet in carne, et compassione in mente, tunc in utroque sanabitur, ut per immortalitatem carnis contra passionem, et per immutabilitatem mentis contra compassionem confirmetur. Sicut enim aegritudo carnis est pati, ita aegritudo mentis est compati. Propterea Deus homo, qui utrumque tollere venit utrumque toleravit. Suscepit passionem in carne; suscepit compassionem in mente. In utroque aegrotare voluit propter nos, ut in utroque nos aegrotantes sanaret. Infirmatus est passione in poena sua; infirmatus est compassione in miseria aliena. [. . .] In carne sua doluit pro nobis patiendo, in mente sua condoluit nobis compatiendo[162]

(Now ailing in both—in the flesh, by suffering (*passio*), and in the mind, by the experience of compassion (*compassio*)—human life will then be healed in both, so that it may be strengthened against suffering by the immortality of the flesh, and against the experience of compassion by the immutability of the mind. For just as the malady of the flesh is to suffer, so the malady of the mind is to experience compassion. Therefore the God-man, who came to take both away, endured both. He received suffering in the flesh; he received the experience of compassion in the mind. He wanted to be sick in both for our sake, so that we, who are sick, might be healed in both. He ailed with suffering in his pain; he ailed with the experience of compassion in the misery of others. [. . .] He was afflicted in his flesh by suffering on our behalf; he was afflicted in his mind by experiencing compassion for us)

Hugh then continues with his principal theme of the work, the examination of the different wills in Christ and the relationship between them.[163] It is evident that *De quatuor voluntatibus*, and in particular this passage, provides some of Johannes von Zazenhausen's working material for his excursus on the interior sufferings of Christ. There are two important differences. First, Hugh does not know the idea of Christ suffering internally 'ab instanti conceptionis suae', which Johannes introduces independently. Second, Johannes's discussion of Christ's compassion for mankind is more extensive, and relies on the underlying idea of the faithful as Christ's mystical body to support the idea that Christ felt the suffering that all mankind had suffered and would suffer. The emphasis that Johannes places on Christ's compassion for mankind does suggest the influence of Bonaventura. It was his innovation to emphasize how Christ's compassion for mankind, driven by his excessive love for mankind, actually

---

[162] Hugh of St Victor, *De quatuor voluntatibus*, cols. 844–5.
[163] On this work in the medieval understanding of Christ's prayer see Madigan, *The Passions of Christ*, p. 79.

outweighed the gravity of his corporeal passion.[164] Though not explicitly present in Johannes' excursus, the emphasis on Christ's love for mankind in the context of his crucifixion does reflect the strongly caritative charge of Bonaventuran Passion theology.

It is not clear upon which, if any, of the Spiritual Franciscan works discussed earlier Johannes von Zazenhausen's excursus on Christ's interior suffering is dependent. The Gethsemane scene is elaborated, and the distinctive idea that Christ's interior sufferings began at the moment of his conception is present. But Johannes develops his excursus in an unusual way, by reference to Christ bearing the suffering inflicted on the entirety of mankind, implicitly reliant on the doctrine of the faithful as Christ's mystical body. Nor does the list of consulted authors provided in the Latin prologue to Johannes's Passion narrative (which includes Hugh of St Victor) include Olivi, Ubertino, or Angela. That said, this list cannot be accorded too much weight as a comprehensive catalogue of source texts. Alongside the named authors, Johannes states that his narrative is written 'cum exposicionibus [. . .] aliorum[. . .] sanctorum, phylosophorum etiam non nullorum'[165] ('with the expositions of other saints, and also of several philosophers'). Livarius Oliger has already noted that Johannes names authorities in the main body of the work who do not appear in the list,[166] and it is possible that Johannes may have known a pertinent work anonymously. Finally, we do not find the crucial idea that links Olivi, Ubertino, Angela da Foligno, and Marquard: put simply, that the sin of contemporary man is responsible for Christ's interior suffering, which outweighed the corporeal pain of the Passion. At least, that is, not in this excursus. Much later in the work, Johannes sets out a series of reasons why Christ bowed his head as he gave up the spirit and died. The first of these is that Christ wished to indicate how severely he was burdened by the weight of human sin; a burden under which he had sweated blood in Gethsemane:

Zü dem ersten mal naygt er sein haubt auf sein prust das er vns zaygt wie swerlichen er mit vnscrn sünden beladen wäre. Vnder dirr pürden hett er blütfarben swaiz vergoßen. Diser last waz im so swär, vnd [er] trüg an so lang biz er dor vnder viel, vnd sein haubt an sein hercz naigt vnd starib. Do von sprichet er durch den propheten Jeremias, 'Ir sunder, ir seit swer burden.'[167]

---

[164] See Strack, 'Das Leiden Christi', pp. 138–40, and id., *Christusleid im Christen-leben*, pp. 46–8.

[165] The Latin prologue is edited by Oliger, 'Die deutsche Passion', pp. 245–8, with the list of authors at p. 246.

[166] Ibid. 248.

[167] Johannes von Zazenhausen, *Deutscher Passionstraktat*, fols. 271ᵛ–272ʳ.

(He inclined his head upon his breast first to show us how heavily he was burdened with our sins. He had shed blood-coloured sweat under this burden. This weight was so heavy for him, and he carried it for such a long time until he fell under its weight, inclined his head upon his heart and died. Thus he speaks through the prophet Jeremiah, 'You sinners, you are a heavy burden.')

Johannes was thus at least aware of this idea, although how precisely is not clear. Its presence in his German Passion narrative, however, is extremely minor. Kemper has noted that the work has a special status amongst the fourteenth-century narratives of the Passion for its general reticence towards the graphic elaboration of the crucifixion, and its preference of the *sensus historicus* over the *sensus allegoricus*.[168] It does not follow that the work discusses Christ's interior suffering instead of his corporeal torment. Rather, Johannes has what one might term an antiquarian interest in the associated details of the central narrative. He offers many excurses on such diverse themes as the different kinds of Roman soldier present at the crucifixion; the position of the wound in Christ's side; the significance of the number 40; and the different levels of faith held by Mary, the apostles, and the women in Mary Magdalene's circle immediately after Christ's death.

An emergent concern for the interior sufferings of Christ can, however, be identified in the religious literature of the Netherlands, which I have discussed at length elsewhere, and summarize here very briefly.[169] Jan van Ruusbroec's *Geestelijke brulocht*, which Marquard knew well in German translation, includes a short but significant passage that formulates a coherent category of Christ's interior sufferings.[170] On the one hand, this passage is very different to the 'Franciscan' understanding. The responsibility of mankind's sin is not mentioned, and the stubborness of the Jews is instead underlined. The interior suffering is not lifelong, but confined to the crucifixion. The context is provided not by Christ's sorrow in Gethsemane, but by the withdrawal of the Father's assistance and consolation from the Son that the cry of dereliction expresses. On the other hand, the passage does nonetheless attest to an elevation of the status of Christ's interior sufferings to equivalent weight with his bodily sufferings in an

---

[168] Kemper, 'Die Kreuzigung Christi', pp. 152–3.

[169] For all the following, see Mossman, 'Ubertino da Casale and the *Devotio Moderna*' [in press].

[170] Jan van Ruusbroec, *Geestelijke brulocht*, I: 289–301 (ed. Eichler, pp. 93–4); 305–18 (ed. Alaerts, pp. 187–9). All references to Ruusbroec's *Brulocht* are given first to Wolfgang Eichler's edition of the 14th-cent. German translation, and then to the corresponding passages in J. Alaerts's edition of the original Dutch. On Marquard's use of the *Brulocht* see Eichler (ed.), *Jan van Ruusbroecs 'Brulocht'*, pp. 41–7.

extremely influential work for the spirituality of fourteenth-century northern Europe. A concern for Christ's interior suffering is also evident in the
devotional works of Gerard Zerbolt van Zutphen (d. 1398). Zerbolt too
presents a coherent category of such interior sufferings independently of
Bonaventura, on whom he otherwise relied heavily for his material on the
Passion, and suggests cautiously that they may have outweighed Christ's
corporeal sufferings. It is only in Jan van Schoonhoven's epistolary treatise
De passione Domini, written in the period 1404–7, that the conceptualization of Christ's interior suffering takes on a markedly different character
that reflects the direct inheritance of the 'Franciscan' tradition. In Schoonhoven's case, the work in question is Ubertino's *Arbor vitae*, the second
recension of which circulated widely (and almost exclusively) amongst the
canons regular of the Windesheim Congregation, and the direct dependence extends well beyond the issue of Christ's interior suffering. In the
fifteenth century, the evidence for the reception of these ideas via the *Arbor
vitae* in the Low Countries, and specifically in the milieu of the *Devotio
Moderna*, multiplies greatly.

Marquard's *De anima Christi*, furthermore, also belonged to this widespread reception of Franciscan literature on the interior sufferings of Christ
in the fifteenth-century Netherlands. It enjoyed a substantial transmission
in Dutch translation. The context of that transmission is instructive. In one
such manuscript, the two principal texts are Marquard's *De anima Christi*
and Alijt Bake's *De vier kruiswegen*, a treatise on the contemplation of the
crucified Christ that includes a consideration of his interior sufferings
(albeit one not known to be dependent on Olivi or the *Arbor vitae*).[171] A
more interesting case is provided by a short Dutch text that I have discussed
elsewhere, which bears the rubric *Vanden inwendighen gheuoelen Christi*
and covers three leaves of a later fifteenth-century quarto manuscript that
belonged to the Franciscan female tertiaries of Sint-Catharinadal in
Hasselt.[172] This text is a compilation from a series of earlier works, including
Meister Eckhart's sermon *Beati pauperes spiritu*.[173] It deals extensively with
Christ's interior suffering by means of a very long excerpt on the topic from
Marquard's *De anima Christi* (corresponding to 206. 33–207. 29). The
compiler appended directly to this a quotation attributed to Ubertino,

---

[171] Uden, Museum voor Religieuze Kunst, no shelfmark (formerly 's-Hertogenbosch,
Bisschoppelijk Archief, no shelfmark); see Lievens, 'Alijt Bake', pp. 147–8, and
Scheepsma, *Deemoed en devotie*, pp. 254–5.

[172] Mossman, 'Ubertino da Casale and the *Devotio Moderna*'; for the text see
The Hague, Koninklijke Bibliotheek, 135 F 12, fols. 185ᵛ–187ᵛ.

[173] See Ubbink, *De receptie van Meister Eckhart*, pp. 215–16.

which states that whilst Christ was in Gethsemane, he received a pain
equivalent to a five-pronged spear being stabbed into his heart for every
mortal sin that had ever been or ever would be committed. The text is
additionally significant as it provides only the second piece of known
evidence for the direct influence of Marquard's *De anima Christi*, alongside
the works of the Franciscan (and, like Marquard, provincial minister of
Southern Germany) Konrad Bömlin (d. 1449). In almost unaltered form it
constitutes the entire middle section of his most extensive German work, *Daz
gúldin búch*, and is the principal source for two long sermons on the
Passion.[174]

De anima Christi, then, had a perceptible influence in the fifteenth
century, both in Southern Germany and the Low Countries, where it
circulated alongside works that develop similar ideas on the interior
suffering of Christ (though here Ubertino, and not Olivi, is the key figure).
The final third of this treatise is a Passion meditation, and as such is among
the oldest extant Passion meditations—as distinct from narrative works—
in German. The earliest such text listed in the conspectus compiled by
Kemper dates to *c.*1400.[175] Only this third part of the work is known to
have been subsequently translated into Latin, and to have thus awoken the
interest of a fifteenth-century recipient as a text sufficiently distinctive to
merit the effort of such an undertaking.

The treatise is also important in the context of the Passion piety of
the later fourteenth century. The emphasis on Christ's interior sufferings
'ab instanti conceptionis' has two principal purposes. First, it enables
Marquard to present suffering as a constant and enduring feature of
Christ's life, which must therefore become a constant feature of the life of
the imitator of Christ. This weakens what we might term the 'synchronic
aspect' of imitative suffering, the obvious connection that binds Christian
suffering to the Lenten and Easter period in the ecclesiastical year. Such
suffering now becomes an integral component of the *imitatio Christi*
conceived more broadly. In *De anima Christi*, it now accompanies Christ's
interior poverty (notably of will and of spirit) and humility, the lifelong
nature of which is scriptural,[176] as enduring features of the imitable model

---

[174] Völker, *Die deutschen Schriften*, pp. 174–8.

[175] See Kemper, *Die Kreuzigung Christi*, pp. 159–60.

[176] See Phil. 2: 7–8: 'sed semet ipsum exinanivit, formam servi accipiens; in simili-
tudinem hominum factus, et habitu inventus ut homo. Humiliavit semet ipsum factus
oboediens usque ad mortem, mortem autem crucis' ('but he emptied himself, taking the
form of a servant; he was made in the likeness of man and found as a man in habit. He
humbled himself, and became obedient unto death; death, even, on the cross'). On the

Christ presents. But this could have been achieved more conventionally, and equally well, by extending Christ's bodily sufferings backwards in time, beginning with the poor circumstances of his birth—the approach taken by Bonaventura and Ludolf von Sachsen, following the path set initially by Bernard of Clairvaux. Olivi was not writing a life of Christ, but a scholastic commentary on theological issues raised by Matthew's Gospel; Ubertino, who was writing a life of Christ, regarded those physical afflictions not principally as instances of suffering, but rather as instances of poverty.[177] Ubertino presents Christ's life above all as a life of poverty: in the first book of the *Arbor vitae*, for example, he asserts of Christ that 'pugil noster accinctus est pauperta[t]e. Natus est enim pauperrime in confusione mundane affluentie; hanc nascendo inchoauit, conuersando continuauit, moriendo consummauit'[178] ('our champion was girded with poverty. For he was born the poorest of all in confutation of worldly wealth; he began this in his birth, continued it in his public life, and consummated it in his death'). Marquard was not a Spiritual Franciscan, and was not obsessed by material poverty; his statements on this issue in the second section of *De anima Christi* reflect a strongly Bonaventuran, 'centrist' position.

The second purpose of emphasizing Christ's interior sufferings 'ab instanti conceptionis' is to provide a different model on which to ground the lifelong *imitatio Christi*: an interiorized model, which required not the physical perception of suffering, but a transformation of the mental state of the individual into one of continual inner suffering. The doctrine rests on an important theological shift. It was long established that Christ had foreknowledge of his passion from the moment of his conception, and that his prayer at Gethsemane expressed a temporary pre-passion, an indication to mankind that he was truly human. Now Christ not only had full foreknowledge, but suffered internally and mentally as well for the entirety of his life. The prayer and sweating of blood at Gethsemane was a manifestation of that continual interior pain, brought on by the proximity of the crucifixion. This shift serves additionally to move attention away from the quantification of the gruesomeness of Christ's corporeal sufferings; to alter the balance between the corporeal and the psychological in understanding, contemplating, and imitating the Passion; to address the

term *humilis*, divested of its pejorative import, as the most important adjective used in the early church to express the nature of Christ's life and Passion see Auerbach, *Literatursprache und Publikum*, pp. 35–6.

[177] See Damiata, *Pietà e storia nell'Arbor vitae*, pp. 87–9.

[178] Ubertino da Casale, *Arbor vitae crucifixae*, lib. 1, c. 11 (p. 63ᵃ); cf. lib. 1, c. 9 (pp. 33ᵇ–46ᵇ, at p. 43ᵇ).

question of what the individual actually saw when visualizing the crucified Christ, a question on which Valentin Groebner has written eloquently, by remodelling the image that was visualized.[179] A second theological shift is also perceptible. Anselm's *Cur Deus homo* had established the mechanics of satisfaction, the process by which mankind was redeemed. Christ's death had reversed the fall and enabled man to be saved. The actual responsibility for his death lay with the Jews and Romans who had performed the crucifixion. The doctrine of satisfaction was now no less true, but it was overlaid with a new accentuation. Christ's suffering was not principally corporeal, but mental. Christ had not only borne the burden of human sin in the technical sense of reversing the effects of the fall—of original sin— but had literally borne its burden, not just knowing the sin of all mankind but suffering from that knowledge. His death was not just because man is sinful and requires redemption, but because human sin was the direct causal agent of his suffering.

This is an approach towards the Passion which points directly towards the sixteenth century. For Ulrich Pinder's *Speculum passionis*, printed in Nuremberg in 1507, the final stage in the contemplation of the Passion was the recognition that human sin was its direct cause, and that the individual was personally responsible for Christ's death.[180] This is, of course, a far more direct and explicit formulation than we encounter in Marquard's *De anima Christi*. It is, however, essentially the same approach. *De anima Christi* may not have enjoyed the broad, influential transmission of some of Marquard's other works, but it is an originally German product, refor- mulating the conception of the Passion for the first time in Germany in a manner that marks the beginning of the trajectory of German thought on the issue that culminates in the sixteenth century.

It is worth returning briefly to Eric Saak's position, which was men- tioned at the beginning of this chapter. Saak, we will recall, maintains that the narrative elaboration of the Passion in the later Middle Ages placed the Jews in an increasingly negative light. He views the Jews as representatives of human sin, and therefore sees the increasing role accorded to the Jews in the responsibility for Christ's death as, in actual fact, the increasing role accorded to human sin. We find, says Saak, 'the tactical accentuation of the graphic representation of Christ's Passion. Such an intensification demo- nized the Jewish role, which was then equated with the continued agency of such horrific violence done to the most beautiful, loving savior by

---

[179] See Groebner, *Ungestalten*, pp. 94–136.
[180] See Saak, *High Way to Heaven*, pp. 536–7; for further information on Pinder's *Speculum passionis* see Kemper, *Die Kreuzigung Christi*, pp. 164–5.

continued human sin.'[181] We should note first that the Jews play almost no role at all in Marquard's *De anima Christi*. Marquard is able to intensify the demonization of human sin (to use Saak's phrase) without reference to the Jews at all. But a more subtle reading of Saak's evidence permits a more nuanced understanding of the situation. Saak supports his argument with an example from Jordan von Quedlinburg's *Meditationes de passione Christi*, in which the Jews' spitting on Christ's face is compared to a contemporary individual defiling his conscience (which, says Jordan, is the *imago Dei*) with impure thoughts and deeds. The difficulty is that Jordan presents these as analogous: impure thoughts and other contemporary sins may make a person *like* a Jew spitting on Christ's face, but they do not actually cause direct injury to the suffering Christ. Jordan repeatedly uses the term *quasi* to express this relationship. It is the human conscience, not Christ, that is being directly affected by the allegorical spitting. There is certainly no connection between human sin and the interior suffering of Christ. The Passion remains the responsibility of the Jews.[182] Yet at the same time it is fair to say that Jordan and Marquard used different methods to increase the individual's sense of responsibility for his own sin.

The transformation of the imitable model is only one side, albeit the more important side, to Marquard's engagement with the devotion to Christ's Passion. The other side is formed by his guidance on the appropriate response towards the Passion, and the related issue of how contemplation of the Passion is understood as part of Marquard's broader contemplative schema.

De anima Christi places suffering as one of three principles, along with humility and poverty, on which Christ grounded his life and erased the effects of mankind's fall. This is made clear in the introduction to the treatise:

Inspice et fac secundum exemplar. Exodi XXV° etc. [Ex. 25: 40] Also redet got zu Moÿsi sÿme diener vnd sprach also: Siech iß an vnd thũ nach dem bildener. Wer nũ mit dem seligen Moÿses ane sehende ist den bildener aller volkomenheit ÿn dem claren spiegel des lebens Cristi Jhesu vnd rech[t] bedencket, wie die edele wirdige

---

[181] See Saak, *High Way to Heaven*, pp. 555–8.
[182] The text (the seventeenth of the 65 *meditationes* in Jordan's treatise) is edited by Saak, *High Way to Heaven*, pp. 829–30; on the work see now Kemper, *Die Kreuzigung Christi*, pp. 141–2.

persone mit ir selbest wirckunge dem irrende[n] menschen eyn bÿlde des gewaren engen weges hatte in so großer mÿnne vor getragen, der fÿndet, das sin wirdig leben stunt uff drÿen stucken, mit dem er uß rŭtte den dieffen fal des ersten menschen.[183]

('Inspice et fac secundum exemplar'; in the twenty-fifth chapter of Exodus, etc. God spoke thus to his servant Moses, and said, 'Look at it carefully, and act according to the exemplar'. Whoever now looks with the blessed Moses at the exemplar of all perfection in the clear mirror of the life of Jesus Christ, and correctly considers how this noble, worthy person presented by his own actions a model of the true, narrow path in such great love to errant man, will find that his worthy life rested on the three foundations with which he obliterated the deep fall of the first man.)

It is a characteristic feature of *De anima Christi* that the focus remains throughout the treatise on the 'inspice' ('look!') and not on the 'fac' ('do!') of the initial quotation. The reader is repeatedly told to take note ('mer prufe', 'nu mercke', and so on) of this or that aspect of Christ's humility, poverty, and suffering, and thus implicitly to construct a particular mental conceptualization of Christ's life. The general strategy of the work in terms of directing the reader's response is thus relatively unambitious. That said, at certain points the reader is instructed to take up a more active, engaged response.

The conclusions to the first two sections of the treatise contain exactly this kind of instruction. At the end of the first section Marquard explains that Christ's poverty checked the greed of the *primi parentes*. Our own poverty is well received by the Father in Christ's poverty, and so the individual who desires to regain the prelapsarian qualities of mankind must 'press' himself into the poverty of Christ, by which the Father is superabundantly satisfied, and finds himself impelled to restore these prelapsarian qualities to the individual in Christ's reward:

Hie midte sÿe eÿn ende dieser tieffen armŭdt des richen godes sone, mÿt der er wieder druckete girikeit des ersten menschen vnd ÿn der alle vnser armudt gÿricheit vnd entphangen wirt von dem hyemelischen vatter. Gelust nŭ yemant, wiedder zu haben gewalt synes selbest an allen strÿt, der ÿn irrende sÿ ane seligkeit[, v]nd dartzu gewalt vnd richeit zu haben aller creaturen, die zwo edelkeit der menschen enphing vnd sie mit girickeit verloß, der drucke sich nŭ in diese armŭdt des richen Ihesu Cristi. Wann sieder mÿt der dem ewigen vatter gnung ist gebeßert vnd dartzu me[, s]o mag sÿn milde hertze gelaßen nit, er engebe dem menschen die zwo edelkeÿt wieder vnd fruchtberlicher ÿn dem verdienen synes gemÿnten sones, dann er sie in ÿme selber vmmer hette gehabet.[184]

---

[183] *De anima Christi*, 180. 3–12.
[184] Ibid. 191. 35– 92. 12.

(With this let there be an end to [the exposition of] this profound poverty of the rich Son of God, with which he curbed the greed of the first man, and in which all our poverty and greed is received by the heavenly Father. Should anyone now desire to regain power over himself without any internal resistance, which leads him astray from holiness, and further to have power and possession of all creatures—which two nobilities of man were received, and lost by greed—let him press himself now into this poverty of the rich Jesus Christ. For, given that the eternal Father is satisfied and more besides with this, his merciful heart cannot then rest unless he gives these two nobilities back to man in the reward of his beloved Son, in a more fruitful way than man could ever have had them in himself.)

A very similar passage is used to conclude the second section. Christ's humility, explains Marquard, is a manifest demonstration to mankind from his love, by which Christ checked the pride of the *primi parentes* and God is superabundantly satisfied. The individual who desires to regain the prelapsarian qualities of mankind associated with humility (namely justification, wisdom, and the soul's decoration with virtues) must 'press' himself into the humility of Christ, in which Christ gained gifts of grace that exceed man's prelapsarian condition:

Diß ist die verworffen demůd des hohen godes sones, die dem irrende menschen so uß großer mỹnne zu eỹme bilde vorgetragen ist vnd mit der dem ewigen vatter me dann gnung vmb alle hoffart gescheen ist. Darumb wann der mensche verloiß mit syner hoffart syn erste gerechtigkeit, in der er stunt vnd dartzu sỹne hoe wỹßheit vnd zierheit an dugenden syner edeln selen[. G]elust die zwo edelichs ỹemant wiedder zu haben, der drucke sich ỹn die dieffe demůdigkeit des edeln Ihesu Cristi, in der er wieder beholet viel adelicher gaben der gnaden, dann die erste gerechtigkeỹt des paradises was vnd hoher wỹßheit von heỹmlicheit des obersten gudes geỹn der wỹßheit alle bekennen eỹn nit wỹßen ist vnd alle befỹnden eyn irrende irren.[185]

(This is the scorned humility of the exalted Son of God, which was presented as a model to errant man out of great love, and with which the eternal Father is more than satisfied for all pride. Man, in his pride, lost the initial justification in which he stood, and further his elevated wisdom and his noble soul's decoration with virtues. Should anyone now desire to regain these two nobilities, let him press himself into the profound humility of the noble Jesus Christ. In this he recaptures gifts of grace that are far nobler than the initial justification of paradise, and elevated wisdom of the secrets of the highest good [i.e. the *summum bonum*], compared to which wisdom all knowledge is an unknowing, and all perception an erring error.)

The conclusion to the third section, and thus to the entire treatise, extends the same kind of instruction. In the question appended to the sixth and final part of this section, Marquard explains how Christ chose to be

---

[185] Ibid. 199. 21–34.

crucified in order to offer himself to the Father in a manner most commensurate with checking greed, pride, and lust, the sins by which the
Father had been dishonoured in man's fall, and by which crucifixion the
Father would be satisfied. The individual who considers this ('Vnd wer ÿme
nach byldet . . .') discovers the counteraction to each aspect of man's fall in
Christ's crucifixion, in which death Christ made all mankind alive again in
him. Christ did not leave man without first sacrificing himself for man, a
sacrifice so well received by the Father that he removed the postlapsarian
restrictions imposed on mankind, and in which thus man's every prayer was
heard and fulfilled. The *primi parentes* lost the delight of the corporeal
paradise, the heavenly paradise of the interior powers, and the tree of life
that brought immortality; but in the ordered bitterness of Christ's death,
man gained access to God in time, access to God in eternity (i.e. access to
heaven after death), and the eucharist respectively to replace those earlier
losses.[186] Next Marquard considers the ennoblement of humanity in the
incarnation and crucifixion of Christ. Christ is a noble vessel ('faß'), in
whom the human form is washed with God's blood, covered internally
with the gold of divinity and externally with the silver of Christ's humanity,
and decorated with the gemstones of Christ's reward and his gifts (i.e. of
grace).[187] This noble vessel of Christ's person is so beloved by God that the
Father cannot turn away anyone who bears it with him, who is similar to it
or who pleads to the Father through it; God sees all through Christ, and

---

[186] *De anima Christi*, 209. 30–211. 8; cf. *De reparatione hominis*, a. 22 (118. 15–33),
in which Marquard establishes a series of parallels between Adam's sin *ex fructo ligni* and
Christ's wish to die *in ligno crucis*. This parallel of woods was a common idea; see e.g.
Thomas Aquinas, *Summa theologiae*, pars 3, q. 46, a. 4, r. 2 (vol. 3, p. 287ᵃ); further
Heinrich von St Gallen, Passionstraktat *Extendit manum*, 15. 7–16. 11. The sacramental,
and specifically eucharistic, significance of the crucified Christ and the blood and water
flowing from the wound in his side, an image that Marquard deploys here, is presented
variously elsewhere in his oeuvre: see *Predigt* 23, ll. 175–9 (p. 156); *De fide*, 543–51 (pp.
312–13); *De reparatione hominis*, a. 25 (131. 27–31). On the particular Franciscan
devotion to Christ's wounds and the blood flowing from his side see Seegets, *Passionstheologie und Passionsfrömmigkeit*, p. 234; on the iconographical tradition see Satzinger and Ziegeler, 'Marienklagen und Pieta', p. 271, both with all further references. A
long discussion of the origin of the sacraments in Christ's side wound is given by Ludolf
von Sachsen, *Vita Christi*, pars 2, c. 64 (ed. 1865, p. 675ᵃ⁻ᵇ; ed. 1870, vol. 4, p. 614ᵃ⁻ᵇ).
Other texts trace the origin of this blood and water through Christ's wound to his heart;
see e.g. *Christi Leiden*, 78. 30–7, or the second prayerbook on the Passion for Elisabeth
Ebran, written 1429 by the Augustinian Johannes von Indersdorf (d. 1470), for which
see Weiske, 'Bilder und Gebete vom Leben und Leiden Christi', pp. 131 and 162.
[187] *De anima Christi*, 211. 8–28.

loves man insofar as he is in Christ. Thus the individual must 'press' himself into Christ's humanity with the gemstones of his reward, in order to access his divinity:

Herumb diß edele faß ẏme so wert vnd so liep ist, das er mynnet alle die, die ẏme helffent diß edele beslagen faß der wirdigen personen Cristi rům̆en vnd liep haben, nach nẏemant enkan von sẏnen gnaden den vertriben, der diß faß mit ẏme brenget ader sich ẏme in eẏnnichen weg glichet ader iß doch ẏne ermanende ist. Vnd wann er alle ding yn der clarheit diesses faßes schauwet vnd also vil als eẏn iglich mensche eẏn in diessem faße ist, vnd darnach er iß vil ader wenig liebet. Darům̆b drucken wir vns mit der krafft der steẏne sẏner gnaden vnd synes verdienens zu dem silber sẏner lutern menscheit, das wir da durch ẏnewendig kommen zu dem fẏnen golde der gotheit, in dem wir eẏns in ẏme blieben vnd do lost vnd wol gefallen entphahen, das er iß selber an mẏnnet.[188]

(Thus this noble vessel is so valuable and so dear to him that he loves all those who help him to praise and adore this nobly adorned vessel of the worthy person of Christ. Nor can he drive anyone away fom his grace who brings this vessel with him, or who is similar to it in any way, or who reminds him of it. He sees everything in the clarity of this vessel, and loves each individual person more or less depending on how far that person is in this vessel. Because of this therefore we must press ourselves with the power of the gemstones of his grace and his reward to the silver of his pure humanity, so that we may come inwardly through it to the fine gold of the divinity, in which we remain one in him and receive joy and delight there, wherein he loves himself.)

The mystical overtones of the penultimate sentence expressed in the idea of coming to union with Christ's divinity through his humanity—an adaptation of the patristic dictum *per Christum hominem ad Christum Deum*—should not be emphasized too strongly. This is the only sentence in the entire work in which an instruction to the reader refers in any way to a mystical ascent, which militates against a mystical interpretation of the sentence or of the work as a whole. Furthermore, the language of these three concluding passages is that of the treasury of merits. The clear message is that the individual is made welcome in the sight of God by acquiring access to Christ's superabundant reward and gifts of grace. The location of the individual within Christ's mystical body, to which Marquard refers in stating that Christ made all mankind alive in him through his death on the cross, underpins the standard theology by which the treasury of merits was understood to function.[189] In describing Christ as a vessel inlaid with gold (divinity) and coated in silver (humanity), in whom the human form is

[188] Ibid. 211. 28–212. 7.
[189] Shaffern, 'The Medieval Theology of Indulgences', p. 21.

washed and cleansed in blood, Marquard almost certainly has in mind the terminology of a passage from Clement IV's bull *Unigenitus* of 27 January 1343 (in which the theology of the indulgence was formally codified), which derives its own terminology in turn from 1 Peter:

'Non enim corruptibilibus auro et argento, sed sui ipsius agni incontaminati et immaculati pretioso sanguine nos redemit' [cf. 1 Pet. 1: 18–19], quem in ara crucis innocens immolatus non guttam sanguinis modicam, quae tamen propter unionem ad verbum pro redemptione totius humani generis suffecisset, sed copiose velut quoddam profluvium noscitur effudisse ita, 'ut a planta pedis usque ad verticem capitis nulla sanitas' [cf. Is. 1: 6] inveniretur in ipso. Quantum ergo exinde, ut nec supervacua, inanis aut superflua tantae effusionis miseratio redderetur, thesaurum militanti ecclesiae acquisivit, volens suis thesaurizare filiis pius Pater, ut sic sit infinitus thesaurus hominibus, quo qui usi sunt Dei amicitiae participes sunt effecti.[190]

('For he redeemed us not with corruptible things in silver and in gold, but with the precious blood of his own immaculate and unpolluted lamb itself', which was sacrificed, though innocent, on the altar of the cross, and is known to have shed no small drop of blood—which still would have been sufficient for the redemption of the entire race of man because of its union with the word—but did so copiously, like a certain flowing forth, so 'that from the sole of the foot to the crown of the head no soundness' might be found in him. How great then, so that no useless, worthless, or superfluous fine would be paid of such bloodshed, a treasury did he acquire thereby for the church militant; the holy Father wanting to lay up treasure for his sons, so that an infinite treasury exists for all men, in which those who made use of it were made partakers of God's friendship.)

Access to the treasury of merits, however, is by the acquisition of indulgences, as Clement's bull then makes clear. Marquard's model of access in *De anima Christi* is completely different. The access to Christ's superabundant reward and gifts of grace is instead achieved by 'pressing' oneself into Christ's humility, poverty, and suffering. This verb 'drucken' appears to signify both the constriction of the self into the model of humility, poverty, and suffering that Christ presents, and the incorporation of the individual into participation in the actual humility, poverty, and suffering of Christ, by which the individual can participate (implicitly as part of Christ's mystical body) in his supererogatory reward. In this context it is worth noting a passage in the first part of the third section of the treatise (which deals with the manifold nature of Christ's suffering), in which the relationship between an individual's suffering and Christ's suffering is explained.

---

[190] *Corpus iuris canonici*, Extravag. commun. lib. 5, titulus 9, c. 2 (vol. 2, cols. 1304–6); here col. 1304; see Shaffern, 'The Medieval Theology of Indulgences', pp. 25–8.

Though not formulated as a direct instruction, it functions as an implicit instruction to the reader to suffer for Christ's sake in order that that suffering is incorporated into Christ's redemptive suffering, and thereby made acceptable to the Father:

Vnd mercket dann do bÿ, wie das lyden, das durch synen willen wirt getragen, so gar in ÿme geedelt ist, wann er das alles knuppte an sÿn eÿgen lÿden vnd iß in dem synen opperte dem hymmelischen vatter an dem crutze, das iß von billichen genemelichen vnd uff genommen wart[. M]er so ist das zu envergeßint, das keÿn lyden yn keynem menschen nÿe gefallen enist, das ÿn vngedult vnd uß gnaden ist getragen, das das selbe lyden von vndanckbarkeÿt des menschen vnd vngeordenhafftig des lydens Cristi auch nit ensolde in synem wirdigen lÿden knuppen vnd dem vatter oppern.[191]

(Take note, then, how suffering borne for his sake is totally ennobled in him, because he bound it all to his own suffering, and in his own [suffering] offered it to the heavenly Father on the cross, so that it was pleasing and rightfully accepted. It is not to be forgotten, furthermore, that no suffering has ever befallen any individual, borne in such impatience and so far outside grace, that that same suffering, because of the thanklessness of the individual and its distance from the pattern of Christ's suffering, should not be bound into his worthy suffering and offered to the Father.)

The idea of coming to God through the imitation of Christ is hardly unconventional. Marquard's instructions to the reader in *De anima Christi* place a very distinctive cast upon this general idea, in which the theology and the language of the treasury of merits is functionalized as the framework by which God is ultimately reached and man is saved, but in which framework the means of access to that treasury is not through the acquisition of indulgences, but through a process of identification of the individual with, and incorporation of the individual into, Christ's humility, poverty, and suffering. Similar, isolated statements can be found elsewhere in Marquard's oeuvre.[192] This distinctive framework is significant, and bears resemblance to a very specific parallel: the indulgence theology of Heinrich Seuse's *Büchlein der ewigen Weisheit*. The radical nature of Seuse's theology of indulgences, by which indulgences are accessed not by juridical means, but by compassion with Christ (understood as *com-passio*, or 'suffering with' Christ, not just a weak form of sympathy), and which

---

[191] *De anima Christi*, 200. 22–32.
[192] *Predigt* 10, ll. 265–88 (pp. 94–5); *Eucharistietraktat* 271. 4–26; on the related idea of the purification of interior and exterior works in Christ's blood, accessed by contemplation of the Passion, see *Predigt* 14, ll. 58–62, and *Dekalogerklärung*, fols. 140ᵛ–141ʳ (cf. ed. 1516, p. 19ᵃ⁻ᵇ; ed. 1483, 20. 26–42) and fol. 200ʳ⁻ᵛ (cf. ed. 1516, pp. 84ᵇ–85ᵇ; ed. 1483, 103. 4–30).

establishes an alternative theological model by which the treasury of merits is accessed to that codified by Clement VI, has been uncovered and underlined by Arnold Angenendt and Alois Haas.[193]

Seuse's theology of indulgences—or rather, his theology of accessing the treasury of merits—operates on two levels: that between the individual and souls in purgatory, for whom indulgences are retrospectively sought to remit their sins; and that between the individual and Christ, where the individual seeks remission for his own sins prior to his death, and so shortens the time he shall have to spend in purgatory. It is this level with which we are principally concerned here. In the fourteenth chapter of the *Büchlein der ewigen Weisheit*, the conversation between the servant and Eternal Wisdom turns to the issue of contemplation of the Passion. Towards the end of the chapter, Eternal Wisdom explains that a sinner can shorten the time he will have to spend in purgatory very considerably by accessing his (Christ's) treasury of merits:

Wie sôlt nu ein grozer súnder, der vil licht me denn hundert totsúnde hat getan, und umb ieklich totsúnde sôlte nach der scrift siben jar bůzen, oder die ungeleisten bůsse in dem heissen eitoven dez grimmen vegfúres můste leisten, eya, wenn sôlte dú ellend sel ir bůze vol uz geleisten, wenne sôlte ir langes ach und we ein ende nemen? Wie wurd es ir so gar ze lang! Sih, daz hat si behendeklich gebůsset und gebessert mit minem unschuldigen wirdigen lidenne; si mag als wol in den edlen schatz mines verdienten lones kunnen grifen und zů ir ziehen. Und sôlte si tusent jar in dem vegfúr brinnen, si hat es in kurzer zit nah schuld und bůze ab geleit, daz si ane alles vegfúr in die ewigen vrôde vert.[194]

(How then should a great sinner, who has committed perhaps more than a hundred mortal sins, and according to the letter of the law ought to do seven years' penance for each mortal sin, or would have to do the incomplete penance in the hot oven of terrible purgatory—well, when should the piteous soul have completed its penance fully? When should its long alas and alack come to an end? How it would be far too long for it! See, the soul has swiftly done the penance and made amends with my innocent, worthy suffering; it can equally well reach into the noble treasury of my earned reward and draw it to itself. And if it ought to have burned in purgatory for a thousand years, it has now set aside its guilt and penance in a short time, so that it can journey into eternal joy without any sojourn in purgatory.)

Eternal Wisdom then sets out, at the servant's request, a quadripartite schema for an approach ('grif') of this nature. The first two stages involve the contrite consideration of the gravity of the individual's sins, and of the

---

[193] See Angenendt, 'Seuses Lehre', pp. 145–52; and Haas, 'Sinn und Tragweite', pp. 98–101; see further now McGinn, *The Harvest of Mysticism*, pp. 215–16, and Ulrich, *Imitatio et configuratio*, p. 45, identifying potential scriptural foundations.

[194] Seuse, *Büchlein der ewigen Weisheit* (ed. Bihlmeyer, pp. 196–325), c. 14 (258. 3–13).

insignificance of the individual's own works of reparation in comparison to the extent of those sins.[195] The next two are much more significant: the consideration of the immeasurable extent of Christ's superabundant reward, which is accessed insofar as the individual makes himself resemble Christ by compassion; and the humble incorporation of the individual's own works of reparation into those of Christ:

III. und denn mit einem húglichen wegenne der unmessigen grozheit miner besserunge, wan daz minste trôphli mins kostberen blûtes, daz da unmesseklich allenthalb us minem minnerichen libe vloz, daz vermôhte vúr tusent welt súnde besseren; und doch so zúhet ieder mensch der besserunge als vil zů im, als vil er sich mir mit mitlidenne gelichet. IV. Und dar nach, daz ein mensche als demûtklichen und als vlehlichen die kleinheit des sinen in die grozheit miner besserunge versenke und verhefte.[196]

(Third: and then with a joyful appraisal of the immeasurable magnitude of my reparation, because the smallest droplet of my valuable blood, which flowed boundlessly there from every part of my loving body, could have made amends for the sins of a thousand worlds; and so each individual draws this reparation to himself according to the extent that he resembles me by compassion. Fourth: and then that the individual should submerge the modicum of his reparation into the magnitude of mine and bind them together in humility and supplication.)

Seuse makes comparable statements in his Latin reworking of the *Büchlein der ewigen Weisheit*, the *Horologium sapientiae*, which he wrote in 1331–4. These passages, in chapter 14 of the first part of the *Horologium*, are subsequently adopted verbatim into Ludolf von Sachsen's *Vita Christi*.[197] The relationship between the *Horologium* and Ludolf's *Vita Christi* is direct. These passages are not held in common with Jordan von Quedlinburg's *Meditationes de passione Christi*, a work that stands in a very close textual relationship to the *Vita Christi*, not least in the chapter of the *Vita Christi* in question here.[198] We may cautiously place Marquard's *De anima Christi* in the same intellectual community, though the precise

---

[195] Ibid. (258. 14–22).

[196] Ibid. (258. 22–9); cf. c. 13 (251. 21–4).

[197] Seuse, *Horologium sapientiae*, pars 1, c. 14 (495. 25–498. 29); on the dating of Seuse's works see Ruh, *Die Mystik des deutschen Predigerordens*, p. 435. Ludolf von Sachsen, *Vita Christi*, pars 2, c. 58 (ed. 1865, pp. 601ᵇ–602ᵇ; ed. 1870, pp. 460ᵃ–462ᵃ); cf. Baier, *Untersuchungen zu den Passionsbetrachtungen*, vol. 2, p. 302.

[198] See Baier, *Untersuchungen zu den Passionsbetrachtungen*, pp. 314–25. The common source that links Jordan's *Meditationes* and Ludolf's *Vita Christi*, which Baier postulates here and terms the *Articulus-Quelle*, has never been found. Kemper thus indicates that the two works were most likely directly related, with Jordan's *Meditationes* probably the later of the two: see *Die Kreuzigung Christi*, p. 141.

relationship to these other works is not clear. If we assume that *De anima Christi* is roughly contemporary with *De reparatione hominis*, completed in 1374, then it is just about possible that Marquard knew Ludolf's *Vita Christi*, completed before 1368 and attestable in Strasbourg in 1375; but it is almost inconceivable that he did not know Seuse's works, given their massive transmission and much earlier date. But this is not an unproblematic assertion, because J. W. van Maren has shown definitively that none of the (very few) previously identified textual parallels between Marquard's works and those of Seuse stand up to close scrutiny.[199] That said, Marquard's Good Friday sermon and Seuse's *Büchlein der ewigen Weisheit* use the same, highly distinctive terminology to describe the crucified Christ as a book of life, as we shall shortly see. This presents the first evidence, albeit partial, for a direct connection between Marquard and Seuse, alongside their comparable views on the access to the treasury of merits. Haas follows Angenendt in identifying an intellectual proximity between Seuse's theology of access to the treasury of merits and that of Martin Luther, largely in terms of their common rejection (in Seuse's case, very much an implicit rejection) of the official doctrine of indulgences.[200] This is tantalizing, but not a trajectory I intend to pursue here. Instead, we can see that Seuse's theology of the treasury of merits was already gaining influence by the mid-fourteenth century, via the *Horologium sapientiae*, when we take note of its presence in Ludolf von Sachsen's *Vita Christi*. That picture is further modified if we now bring Marquard's *De anima Christi* into this intellectual community. It is less important in this case that a German text is involved (the *Büchlein der ewigen Weisheit* is also in German), but rather an issue of the prominence of the reception of Seuse's theology within the recipient work. Ludolf's *Vita Christi* is an extremely extensive compilatory work, in which this issue is but a minor component. It is further such a *sammelsurium* that Walter Baier was moved to comment on its lack of systematic clarity and theological uniformity.[201] And even though Seuse's *Büchlein der ewigen Weisheit* and *Horologium sapientiae* are both less extensive than the *Vita Christi*, they are still weighty works in which the question of access to the treasury of merits by suffering and compassion with the crucified Christ is treated very briefly. By contrast, Marquard's *De anima Christi* is a comparably short work, and one in which the entire framework of instructions to the reader as to how to respond to Christ's humility, poverty, and above all his suffering (insofar as such a framework exists) is

[199] van Maren, 'Zitate deutscher Mystiker', pp. 74–5.
[200] Angenendt, 'Seuses Lehre', pp. 152–4; Haas, 'Sinn und Tragweite', pp. 100–1.
[201] Baier, *Untersuchungen zu den Passionsbetrachtungen*, pp. 449–50.

written in the context of this distinctive theology of access to the treasury of merits. It is the relative prominence of this unusual doctrine in *De anima Christi* that accords Marquard a particular significance in the intellectual history of this idea in fourteenth-century Germany.

Let us turn now from *De anima Christi* to Marquard's Good Friday sermon. We have already seen the opening to this sermon, in which the individual is exhorted to gaze upon the face of the crucified Christ. The first of the three sections of the sermon then elaborates six different situations involving a response towards another, which provide a moral example to the individual to behave correspondingly, and thereby appropriately, towards Christ. Marquard does not make six specific and discrete points: it is instead the cumulative effect of the entire passage that builds up a general tenor of the appropriate response. By far the most important feature of this appropriate response is that of reciprocal love for Christ. This is introduced in the first example, that of the faithful doctor and his patient. Christ, says Marquard, freely gave mankind more than just costly medication, and more even than a limb of his own body; rather he gave his entire life for mankind to save man (or rather, to save you, as the sermon addresses the reader in the second person), and asks for nothing in return but that you love him in return.[202] The most extensive exposition on reciprocal love follows in the fifth example, that of the lover and the beloved. This falls into two halves. In the first, Marquard says that it is common to like to gaze upon the face of one whom we love. Great love, so Aristotle, manifests itself in weeping, involuntary sighing, and the eager casting of glances at the beloved's face. Christ loved man so immoderately that he could have saved mankind with a single drop of his blood, but chose instead to die so that man might feel his bottomless love. Thus the individual should rightfully be inflamed by reciprocal love and gaze on Christ's face with a loving, burning heart:

Ze dem fünften, so ist es gewonlich, wa ains minn vnd liebi hắt zů dem andern, das daz sin anlit gern ansiht. Vnd ist das es gröss minn vnd liebi zů im hắt, so werdent im sin ögen wắssrig vnd süfczet vnwissend, vnd emsigklich schůcz siner ögen tůt er vnder sins geminten anlit, als Aristotiles schribet. Vnd sider v̈ns gottes sun so gar vnmắssklich hắt geminnet, vnd úns wol ắn sin sterben hett erlöset oder mit dem minsten blůcz tropfen, vnd doch alles sin benedict blůt wolt verreren vnd willeklich sterben, daz wir sin grundlös minn spurtind, hier vmb solten wir mit widerminn enzündet werden von billichen vnd sin antlit mit minnendem, brinnendem herczen an sehen.[203]

[202] *Predigt* 10, ll. 22–40 (pp. 87–8).
[203] Ibid., ll. 83–92 (p. 89).

(Fifth, it is usual that where one has love and affection for another, he gazes gladly upon the other's face. If he has great love and affection for the other, then his eyes become tearful, he sighs involuntarily, and eagerly casts fleeting glances upon his beloved's face, as Aristotle writes. Given that the son of God loved us beyond all compare, and could well have redeemed us without his death, or with the smallest drop of blood—and yet wanted to pour away all his blessed blood and to die willingly, so that we might feel his bottomless love—so we should rightfully be inflamed with reciprocal love, and gaze upon his face with a loving, burning heart.)

In the second half, Marquard addresses the noble soul to gaze on the beloved's face and speak as the bride of the Song of Songs. The bride's exhortation 'Ostende michi faciem tuam' ('Show me your face'; Cant. 2: 14) is deployed as an exhortation to Christ to show the lover his tormented face, and specifically to show his face as a mirror in which to see moral virtues like patience, humility, love, and so forth. The bride-reader then implicitly becomes John the Evangelist, asking Christ to lower his head upon her breast and rest on her heart (or rather, my breast and my heart, as Marquard presents this exhortation as a first-person address by the bride to Christ). The bride finally desires to see Christ's face in order to appreciate his unspeakable pain, because her love and compassion are as strong as death (following Cant. 8: 6, 'fortis est ut mors dilectio': 'love is as strong as death'), which will separate her from all love of the worldly and the bodily:

Hier vmb edli sele, sich an das antlit dines geminnten, sprich mit der minenden sel: >Ostende michi faciem tuam etc. Zŏg mir din antlit< [Cant. 2: 14], wan es ist vol gnåden vnd gůtlichait. Zŏg mir din antlit verspŏczet vnd verspottet, erblaichet vnd durlitten. Zŏg mir din antlit als ainen spiegel, in dem ich schŏw gedult, demŭt, minn vnd grundlos erbårmd. Zŏg mir din antlit zwo stund vor dem tag, do du an ainer staininen sul gebunden stŭnd in allem spott vnd durchåhtung. Naig din hŏbt vff min brust, vnd rŭw vff minem herczen. Zŏg mir din antlit, das ich schŏw dinen vnsåglichen schmerczen, wan min liebi vnd min mitliden ist stark als der tŏd, der mich von billichen sol von allem lust der zit vnd des libes schaiden.[204]

(Thus, noble soul, gaze upon the face of your beloved and say with the loving soul, 'Ostende michi faciem tuam, etc. Show me your face', because it is full of grace and goodness. Show me your face spat upon and scorned, blanched, and tormented. Show me your face like a mirror, in which I see patience, humility, love, and bottomless mercy. Show me your face two hours before daybreak, when you stood, scorned and despised, bound to a stone column. Incline your head upon my breast, and rest upon my heart. Show me your face, so that I can see your unspeakable pain; because my love and my compassion is as strong as death, which ought rightfully sever me from all joy in the temporal world and the body.)

---

[204] *Predigt* 10, ll. 92–102 (p. 89).

This example is, first of all, demonstrative of the complexity and literary quality characteristic of Marquard's sermons. In just twenty lines of text in the modern edition, Marquard brings together a rich spectrum of imagery and scriptural reminiscences in a passage that switches cleverly from one form of address to another.

The argument for the literary quality of Marquard's oeuvre is not an argument to be pursued here. Instead the main thrust of Marquard's point should be noted: that Christ died for mankind out of his unimaginably great love for mankind, and so the individual should respond with reciprocal love ('widerminn') for Christ in an exclusive relationship focused solely on Christ, as signalled by the metaphor of the bride and bridegroom. This discourse of love met by love provides the impetus not only for this example, but for the whole sermon, and indeed more widely within the rest of the sermon collection. God's love for man, and man's love for God, are admittedly very common themes in medieval religious writing. Marquard, however, gives this discourse an especially strong prominence in his Good Friday sermon, and lends to it a distinctive cast. This reflects a similar prominence accorded to the discourse of love in Bonaventura's theological and devotional writing on the Passion. Marquard's emphasis on reciprocal love for the crucified Christ represents an important case in point of the phenomenon characterized by Kurt Ruh as 'Bonaventura deutsch', of which there has been little mention thus far (though there has been much 'Olivi deutsch').[205]

Let us begin with Christ's love for man, expressed in the Passion. We will recall that Marquard said in the passage above that Christ could have saved man with the tiniest drop of his blood, but that he wanted to expend all his blood and die so that his bottomless love for mankind might be made known. The idea that Christ did not ultimately have to die on the cross to save mankind is grounded in the conventional medieval understanding of the superabundance of Christ's satisfaction.[206] But the precise cast

[205] See Ruh, *Bonaventura deutsch*, esp. pp. 63–78.
[206] Ruh, 'Zur Theologie des mittelalterlichen Passionstraktats', pp. 33–4. Ruh notes that the doctrine of Christ's superabundant satisfaction is 'vor allem thomistisch[ ]' (p. 34). Aquinas does hold this position (see the *Summa theologiae*, pars 3, q. 46, a. 5, ad 3 (vol. 3, p. 289ᵃ)), but Anselm is its original proponent. Anselm transformed the old doxology that God had more marvellously redeemed what he had marvellously created into the idea that Christ's death far exceeded that which mankind owed, because Christ's life deserved to be loved more than sin deserved to be hated: see Pelikan, *The Growth of Medieval Theology*, pp. 142–3. The doctrine is common in 14th-cent. texts: see e.g. Ludolf von Sachsen, *Vita Christi*, pars 1, c. 10 (ed. 1865, p. 47ᵇ; ed. 1870, p. 97ᵃ); and in Marquard's oeuvre, *De reparatione hominis*, a. 24 (128. 26–36). An odd exception is presented by Heinrich von St Gallen, Passionstraktat *Extendit manum*, 13. 9–14. 5:

Marquard lends to this idea in adding that Christ went further than
necessary (and died) as a manifestation of love is found in identical
formulation in Bonaventura's *De perfectione vitae*:

Dic, quaeso, dilecte mi Domine, dic, cum unica tui sacratissimi sanguinis gutta
potuisset sufficere ad totius mundi redemptionem, cur tantum sanguinem de
corpore tuo effundo permisisti? Scio, Domine, et vere scio, quia propter aliud hoc
non fecisti, nisi ut ostenderes, quanto affectu me diligeres.[207]

(Tell me, I beseech, O my beloved Lord, tell me this; since a single drop of your
most sacred blood would have sufficed for the redemption of the whole world, why
did you allow so much blood to be poured forth from your body? I know, O Lord,
and truly I know, that you did this for no other reason except in order to show with
how much affection you loved me.)

In fact, Bonaventura was responsible beyond this for a major shift in the
medieval theology of Christ's Passion, with the development of what we
may term a caritative theology of redemption, on which Bonifatius Strack
has written extensively.[208] The medieval understanding of redemption had,
of course, long since been defined by the influential Anselm in terms of
satisfaction: not the appeasement of God's anger at the sins of mankind
(God being immutable), but the restoration of the appropriate relationship
between God and man; the *rectitudo* of the divine order according to the
iustitia Dei.[209] Bonaventura modified this theology. Satisfaction remained
the primary formal reason underlying Christ's desire to die, but the primary
actual reason was his love for mankind: his *nimietas* (or *excessus*) *amoris* (or
dilectionis). This is expressed variously in his theological writing, as for
example here in his commentary on John 3: 16, in which he discusses the
final of the three underlying principles of salvation. Having set out the
'principium salvans' and the 'modus salvandi', he turns to the 'ratio movens
ad salvandum':

Christ insists to Mary that his death is necessary, as one drop of blood would be
insufficient. But the standard doctrine is upheld in Heinrich's *Magnifikat-Auslegung*,
ll. 442–51 (pp. 42–3). On the wider issue of God's freedom to save mankind other than by
Christ's death, and thus whether Christ's will could really ever be free if the Father desired
the salvation of mankind, see Hamm, *Promissio, pactum, ordinatio*, esp. pp. 473–8.

[207] Bonaventura, *De perfectione vitae*, c. 6, §6 (vol. 8, p. 122^b).
[208] Strack, 'Das Leiden Christi', pp. 138–40; id., *Christusleid im Christenleben*,
pp. 40–51; see further Ennis, 'The Place of Love', pp. 137–40.
[209] Useful outlines are provided by Pelikan, *The Growth of Medieval Theology*,
pp. 129–44, and Bynum, *Wonderful Blood*, pp. 196–201; on Bonaventura's debt to
Anselm on this issue see Cullen, *Bonaventure*, pp. 146–8, and Gonzalez, 'The Work of
Christ', pp. 374–9.

'Sic enim Deus' etc. [John 3: 16] Tangitur hic tertium, scilicet ratio movens, ad sic salvandum; et haec fuit immensitas divini amoris ad hominem perditum. Propter quod dicit: 'Sic enim Deus dilexit mundum', id est hominem mundanum et peccatorem; 'ut Filium suum unigenitum daret'; ad Ephesios secundo: 'Deus, qui dives est in misericordia, propter nimiam caritatem suam, qua dilexit nos, cum essemus mortui peccatis, convivificavit nos Christo' [Eph. 2: 4–5].[210]

('For God so', etc. The third point is touched upon here, namely the motive reason to save [mankind] in this way; and this was the magnitude of divine love for fallen man. Because of this it says, 'For God so loved the world', i.e. the worldly man and the sinner, 'that he gave his only-begotten son'; and in the second chapter of the letter to the Ephesians, 'God, who is rich in mercy, made us alive together in Christ because of his excessive charity, with which he loved us [even] when we were dead in our sins.')

Outside the strictly scholastic context, Bonaventura was less restrained. In a sermon on the fourth Sunday after Whitsun he maintains, on the basis of 1 John 3: 16, that Christ's love for mankind was the only reason for his submission to suffering and death:

Si enim quaeratur: Quid movit Filium Dei ad patiendum pro nobis, non invenitur alia causa quam eius benevolentia et caritas misericordissima. Unde 1 Ioannis 3, 16: 'In hoc cognovimus caritatem Dei, quoniam ille pro nobis animam suam posuit.'[211]

(For if it is asked what impelled the son of God to suffer for us, no other cause is found than his benevolence and most merciful love. Wherefore 1 John 3: 16, 'In this we perceived the love of God, because he laid down his life for us.')

Inside that scholastic context, Bonaventura was compelled to explain exactly how he understood the relationship between love as the impetus of redemption, and the more traditional understanding of satisfaction, as here in his commentary on the Sentences:

Ad illud vero quod obiicitur de manifestatione benignitatis et misericordiae, dicendum, quod summa benignitas et misericordia in Deo non excludunt iustitiam, et ideo non sic debuit manifestari in opere reparationis, quod iustitia non haberet locum; sed ita debuit manifestari divina misericordia, quod simul cum hoc ostenderetur divina iustitia. Et hoc idem factum est, cum Deus reparavit genus humanum per mortem Filii sui, ubi fuit maxima aequitas in exigendo tantae satisfactionis pretium, et maxima benignitas in tradendo unigenitum Filium suum.[212]

---

[210] Bonaventura, *Commentarius in Evangelium Ioannem* (vol. 6, pp. 237–532), c. 3, §26 [v. 16], here p. 282[b].

[211] Id., *Sermones dominicales* (ed. Bougerol), sermo 31 (pp. 349–54), here §8 (p. 354).

[212] Id., *In III Sent.*, d. 20, a. u., q. 2, ad 1 (vol. 3, p. 421[a]).

(To the objection made about the manifestation of kindness and mercy it is to be said that the supreme kindness and mercy in God does not exclude justice, and therefore it should not have been manifested thus in the work of reparation, because justice had no place [there]; but divine mercy should have been manifested thus, because divine justice was shown together with this. And this was effected likewise when God restored the race of man through the death of his Son, where there was the greatest even-handedness [i.e. justice] in requiring the price of such satisfaction, and the greatest kindness in giving over his only begotten Son.)

This caritative theology of redemption has significant consequences for Bonaventura's writing on man's appropriate response to the crucified Christ. Understood as an act of love, it should appropriately be met by love, and specifically by an imitation of Christ's love for man in the individual's love for his fellow man. That is to say, Christ's love has an exemplary function, and this is a point that Bonaventura makes often.[213] In a sermon for the second Sunday after Easter that elaborates exactly these exemplary functions of the Passion, for instance, he binds the idea of Christ's (and, indeed, God's) exemplary love in the crucifixion to an exhortation to love one's fellow man likewise:

O admirabilis pietas Creatoris! ut servum redimeres, Filium tradidisti. Et hoc exemplum caritatis nobis reliquit, secundum quod dicitur primae Ioannis tertio: 'In hoc cognovimus caritatem Dei, quoniam ille animam suam pro nobis posuit'; et quia hoc exemplum est imitatione dignum, ideo subdit; 'et nos debemus pro fratribus animas ponere' [1 John 3: 16], non tantum pro honore Dei, sed etiam pro salute proximi.[214]

(O admirable devotion of the creator! In order that you might redeem your servant, you gave up your Son. And you bequeathed this example of love to us, in accordance with what is said in the third chapter of the first letter of John: 'In this we perceived the love of God, because he laid down his life for us'. Because this example is worthy of imitation, therefore it continues, 'and we should lay down our lives for our brothers', not just for the honour of God, but also for the salvation of our neighbours.)

This passage demonstrates clearly Bonaventura's adherence to the model of 1 John, which brings a 'horizontal' dimension to the appropriate response to the manifestation of Christ's love in the crucifixion—namely love for one's fellow man. The prominence and pre-eminence of love is a distinctive feature of Bonaventura's theology in general, as a number of modern

---

[213] Strack, *Christusleid im Christenleben*, pp. 45–6 and 114–20; Gonzalez, 'The Work of Christ', pp. 379–80.

[214] Bonaventura, *Sermo 2 de Dominica 2 post Pascha* (vol. 9, pp. 296ᵃ–301ᵃ), here §2, p. 298ᵃ.

scholars have noted. Love (*caritas*) is, literally and metaphorically, the principal commandment in his theology. He not only provided an original and highly influential justification of this, but also developed a sophisticated model by which different expressions of love—notably that towards one's fellow man, which binds the individual by love within Christ's mystical body—are interconnected, and ordered such that all correctly ordered love is ultimately subsumed within the overarching love of God; the *dilectio proximi* and the *dilectio Dei* are reconciled and organized towards a common head.[215] This builds on an understanding of the appropriate love of the crucified Christ present in the works of Bernard of Clairvaux, notably in his forty-third sermon on the Song of Songs.[216]

Whilst Marquard clearly and unequivocally shares with Bonaventura the understanding of love as the driving force underlying the crucifixion, and the requirement for that love to be met by love on man's part, the direction of that reciprocal love is quite different. This is not to say that Marquard would deny that Christ's love has an exemplary function, or that the *dilectio proximi* is unnecessary. But Marquard's model of reciprocal love is marked by exclusivity—the individual must direct his love exclusively 'vertically' towards Christ—and so the model lacks the 'horizontal' dimension of imitative love for one's fellow man that Bonaventura accentuates. A sense of duty towards Christ, and of the consequent requirement to gaze on the crucified Christ's face, is more generally evident in Marquard's Good Friday sermon and is the principal point of two (the third and the fourth) of the six illustrative examples of how to gaze on Christ's face that Marquard presents in the first section of the sermon.[217]

A third element to the broad response, alongside love and duty, is introduced by the second of the illustrative examples, namely sorrowful compassion. As a faithful son should follow the body of his father to the grave, if his father has died for his sake, so the individual should follow Christ's body similarly: 'so sǒllend wir hůt der lich nǎch gǎn ᴢe grab mit mitlidendem betrůbtem heiᴜᴢen'[218] ('so today we should follow the body to the grave with a compassionate, troubled heart'). This is unexceptional. More exceptional is the fourth and final element to the broad response that is introduced in the sixth and final illustrative example: the tuition in virtue

---

[215] See principally Delhaye, 'La Charité', pp. 505–15, and Schlosser, *Cognitio et amor*, pp. 147–65; further Ennis, 'The Place of Love', pp. 134–5 and 140–3, and Cullen, *Bonaventure*, pp. 149 and 163–4.

[216] See Langer, 'Passio und compassio', pp. 49–50, 54–5, and esp. 58–62.

[217] *Predigt* 10, ll. 52–82 (pp. 88–9).

[218] Ibid., ll. 41–51 (p. 88), here ll. 50–1.

and wisdom from the exemplar of the crucified Christ, understood using the motif of the book of life. In itself, this is familiar material; but the language with which it is expressed is distinctive, and repays closer examination:

Ze dem sechsten so ist es gewonlich, wå ain hôher erlûhter maister liset vnd leret, so sehend sin junger sin antlit an mit grôssem ernst vnd begirden. Nun ist hût die ewig wisshait vff dem hôhen sessel des hailgen crûczes erhebet, vnd ist vͦns lerend alle tugend vnd wisshait an sin selbes lib als an dem lebenden bûch, wan daz bûch ist hût vff getăn, vnd ain blatt von dem andern zertennet. Hier vmb rûffet er hûtt vnd sprichet: Sich mich an armer mensch als daz lebend bûch, vnd lis an mir, wie widerzăm mir hôhfart ist, wan ich hie hangen blôss vnd verschmăht enmitten vnder den schăchern. Lis an mir, wie widerzăm mir ist aller nid vnd hass, sider ich hăn gebetten den vatter fûr die, die mich hănd gecrûczget, vnd als ain lembli gedulteklich vnd schwigend bin in den tôd gefûret. Sus sôllend wir hût als die junger tůnd, vnd vͦnserm erlûhten maister vnder sin antlit sehen.[219]

(Sixth, it is usual that where an eminent and enlightened master reads and teaches, his pupils look upon his face with great earnestness and desire. Now today the eternal wisdom is raised to the high chair of the holy cross, and teaches us all virtue and wisdom upon his own body as in the book of life; for that book is opened today, and one leaf is torn asunder from another. Thus today he cries aloud and says, 'Look upon me, poor person, as the book of life, and read upon me how repellent pride is to me; for I hang here naked and scorned amidst the thieves. Read upon me how all jealousy and hatred is repellent to me; for I have prayed to the Father for those who have crucified me, and have been led to death patiently and silently like a lamb.' So we should act today like the disciples, and look upon the face of our enlightened master.)

The motif of Christ as a book—and as the book of life—is Carolingian at the latest, and depends on the interpretation of Apocalypse 20: 12 ('et alius liber apertus est, qui est vitae'; 'and another book was opened, which is [the book] of life') and Apocalypse 5: 1 ('et vidi in dextera sedentis super thronum librum scriptum intus et foris, signatum sigillis septem'; 'and I saw in the right hand of him who was sitting upon the throne a book written within and without, sealed with seven seals') with reference to Christ.[220] Bonaventura is regarded as the greatest exponent of book symbolism in relation to Christ, specifically concerning the imagery of the 'liber vitae', which he adapted, as Grover Zinn has shown, in part from Hugh of

---

[219] *Predigt* 10, ll. 103–15 (p. 90); cf. *De reparatione hominis*, a. 25 (130. 28–31), where Christ's Passion is described as a book in which to read the virtues, and which thereby opens the path to salvation.
[220] Rauch, *Das Buch Gottes*, pp. 9–10.

St Victor's *De arca Noe*.[221] The association of the 'liber vitae' imagery and Christ's Passion is repeated in Bonaventura's oeuvre, and has been subjected to close examination by Winthir Rauch.[222] Marquard would undoubtedly have been familiar with this association, which is a commonplace in fourteenth-century religious writing. The Latin preface to Johannes von Zazenhausen's German narrative on the Passion, for example, takes Christ as book (presumably in dependence on Bonaventura) for its central imagery.[223] Heinrich Seuse's *Horologium sapientiae* presents the crucified Christ as a 'liber vitae' in a manner not dissimilar to Marquard, and the relevant passage entered Ludolf's *Vita Christi*.[224]

The most important parallel to Marquard's usage in his Good Friday sermon is that in Seuse's German *Büchlein der ewigen Weisheit*, where it forms what Bernard McGinn regards as the very heart of Seuse's 'philosophia spiritualis' (on which more later).[225] In fact, the 'liber vitae' metaphor is deployed twice in this work, and it is the first usage that is of interest here. It comes at the end of the third chapter, in reply to the servant's plea to understand how he might progress in his response to the Passion from tearful plaint ('ein weinliches klagen') to loving imitation ('ein minnekliches nahvolgen').[226] Eternal Wisdom explains how he should go about pursuing this shift, and describes his instructions as a beginning in the school of wisdom, which can be read from the open book of his crucified life. The significant feature is the terminology that Seuse uses, and which is common to Marquard: not just the specific verbs 'uftûn' and 'zertennen' to describe the crucified body of Christ, but the appellation of Christ as the Eternal Wisdom—otherwise quite foreign to the Good Friday sermon, and to Marquard's oeuvre in general—and Marquard's statement that not just virtue (as is conventional), but also wisdom is learned from contemplation of the crucified Christ.

Entwúrt der Ewigen Wisheit: Brich dinen lust an verlasener gesicht und úppiger gehôrde; laze dir wol schmaken von minnen und lustig sin, daz dir vor wider waz, leg ab dur mich zartheit dins libes. Du solt alle din rûwe in mir sûchen, liplich

[221] Zinn, 'Book and Word', esp. pp. 152–4 and 163–4 on the 'liber vitae'.
[222] Rauch, *Das Buch Gottes*, pp. 181–7; for a conspectus of references to God and Christ as book in Bonaventura's oeuvre see pp. 5–12.
[223] Oliger, 'Die deutsche Passion', pp. 246–8.
[224] Seuse, *Horologium sapientiae*, pars 1, c. 14 (494. 13–21); Ludolf von Sachsen, *Vita Christi*, pars 2, c. 58 (ed. 1865, p. 601ᵃ; ed. 1870, vol. 4, p. 459ᵇ); cf. Baier, *Untersuchungen zu den Passionsbetrachtungen*, p. 302.
[225] McGinn, *The Harvest of Mysticism*, p. 212; see further Haas, 'Sinn und Tragweite', pp. 97–8, and Jaspert, 'Leid und Trost', pp. 177–8.
[226] Seuse, *Büchlein der ewigen Weisheit*, c. 3 (208. 31–209. 4).

ungemach minnen, vrômdes úbel willeklich liden, verschmeht begeren, dinen
begirden erbleichen und allen dinen gelústen ertoden. Daz ist der anevang in der
schúle der wisheit, den man liset an dem ufgetanen zertenneten bůch mines
gekrúzgeten libes.[227]

(Eternal Wisdom's answer: Abandon your delight in seeing the profane and hearing
the trivial; let what you previously found repellent now taste pleasantly of love and
be a source of delight; cast aside the frailty of your body for my sake. You should
seek all your repose in me, love bodily discomfort, willingly suffer evils from
outside, desire shame, diminish your [bodily] desires, and kill all your pleasures.
That is the beginning in the school of wisdom, which is read upon the opened book
torn asunder of my crucified body.)

Together with the parallels to Seuse's theology of access to the treasury of
merits, and in view of the very extensive transmission of his works generally,
these terminological similarities concerning the 'liber vitae' imagery indicate strongly that Marquard was familiar with the *Büchlein der ewigen
Weisheit*, though did not draw on it as extensively—or in the same way,
namely as a source of quotations—as he did on the works of Eckhart,
Tauler, and Ruusbroec.

   In the first section of the Good Friday sermon, then, Marquard develops
four broad themes in the individual's response to the crucified Christ: first,
and primarily, reciprocal love; second, a sense of duty; third, compassionate
sorrow; and fourth, learning virtue and wisdom from Christ as exemplar.
The second section of the sermon is structured around Christ's seven words
on the cross. This is a theme whose exposition had remained a predominantly Franciscan tradition well into the fourteenth century.[228] As Nigel
Palmer has recently noted, Marquard's (extensive) treatment of this theme
here constitutes one of the very earliest examples in German.[229] In view of
the amount of attention just given to the first section of the sermon, this
second section need not be examined in similar detail: it would require a
more substantive examination of the contemporary tradition on the 'seven
words', which would distract from the issue of the response to the crucified
Christ. For present purposes it suffices to examine the purpose Marquard
has in his presentation of the 'seven words'. Each word is equipped with an
interpretation, which is followed by at least one question. These questions
ask what the individual should learn from each word, according to the
interpretation that Marquard has provided. This instruction centres on

---

[227] Seuse, *Büchlein der ewigen Weisheit*, c. 3 (209. 5–12); cf. c. 14 (256. 15–23).
[228] See Kemper, *Die Kreuzigung Christi*, pp. 336–51.
[229] Palmer, *Bibelübersetzung und Heilsgeschichte*, p. 56; on the seven words in German
texts prior to 1400 (without Marquard) see Kemper, *Die Kreuzigung Christi*, pp. 356–8.

moral-ethical lessons, especially in the first three words.[230] The fourth, fifth, and seventh words focus again on the manifestation of Christ's love for mankind, and the necessity of reciprocal love on the individual's part. The exposition of the fourth word ('sitio'; 'I am thirsty', John 19: 28) is particularly interesting in this regard, as it uses the imagery of incorporation into Christ's mystical body by Christ's 'drinking' our love, and man's 'drinking' from the water of life (understood as the supernatural gifts of divine grace) in pursuit of his own salvation, to express this reciprocity of love.[231] The instruction then elicited from the fifth word includes an admonition to imitate Christ in the manner of his patient bearing of suffering, should it befall the individual, as such suffering flows ultimately from God's bottomless love.[232] This is strongly reminiscent of the approach towards suffering taken by Heinrich Seuse in the later part of his life (insofar as it is presented by the *Vita*), encouraged in the *Büchlein der ewigen Weisheit*, and which is established there in opposition to a more strongly (even violently) ascetic, corporeal castigation in the desire to inflict painful suffering on the self.[233]

The mention of Seuse in connection with what is a fairly general idea in Marquard's exposition on the fifth word is not without point, because in the sixth word Marquard expounds once more his theology of access to the treasury of merits, which we have seen from *De anima Christi*, and which bears close comparison to Seuse's understanding of the same issue. Christ's sixth word, his commendation of his spirit to the Father ('Pater, in manus tuas commendo spiritum meum'; 'Father, I commend my spirit into your hands', Lk. 23: 46), is interpreted as the demonstration of Christ's return to the Father's heart. It is also a rebirth and re-entrance of all loving, faithful souls into their eternal origin; a process of re-entry in which all virtue, suffering, and turns to God—whether internal or external—are borne upwards and made acceptable to the Father in Christ. In this process, continues Marquard, Christ made his legacy: he left his spirit to his Father, and in his spirit all creatures in a state of grace:

<hr/>

[230] *Predigt* 10, ll. 125–219 (pp. 90–3).
[231] Ibid., ll. 220–43 (p. 93); cf. ll. 289–330 (pp. 95–6), on the seventh word.
[232] Ibid., ll. 244–64 (pp. 93–4), esp. ll. 258–64 (p. 94).
[233] This aspect of Seuse's writing is treated extensively in modern scholarship. See representatively McGinn, *The Harvest of Mysticism*, pp. 203 and 213–15; Langer, 'Memoria passionis', pp. 69–73; Ulrich, *Imitatio et configuratio*, pp. 87–8 and 147–54; id., 'Zur Bedeutung des Leidens', pp. 126–9, and pp. 131–8 on the 'positive' function of ascetic suffering within a systematized version of Seuse's conception of the contemplative life.

Das sechst wort was: >Vatter in din hend bevilh ich minen gaist.< [Lk. 23: 46]. Vnd in disem wort zŏgt v̂nser herr ainen lutren widerker sin selbes in daz våtterlich hercz. Er zŏgt ŏch ain wider geburt vnd ain wider intragen aller minnenden gelŏbigen selen in iren ersten vrsprung. Er erzŏgt ŏch ain wider opfren vnd vfftragen aller tugentlicher werk, so all sin fründ v̂mmer sŏltend tûn, vnd ŏch alles liden, vnd inre vnd vsser minnrich ker, die immer von allen engeln vnd menschen soltend beschenhen, die opfret er alle in sinem lutren gaist dem ewigen vatter, in dem alle werk allain dem ewigen vatter genåm sind, vnd machet hie mit sin sel geråt, wan er besaczt dem vatter sinen gaist, vnd in sinem gaist alle begnådeten creaturen.[234]

(The sixth word was 'Father, I commend my spirit into your hands'. In this word our Lord expresses his pure return into the paternal heart. He expresses the rebirth and re-entry of all loving, faithful souls into their initial origin. He expresses further a reoffering and bearing up of all the virtuous deeds that all his friends should ever have done. All the suffering and loving turns [to God], both internal or external, that should ever be undergone by any angels and any person, he offered in his pure spirit to the eternal Father, in which alone all works are acceptable to the eternal Father. With this he made his legacy, because he left his spirit to the Father, and every creature in a state of grace in his spirit.)

After a pertinent quotation attributed to Ambrose, Marquard turns to the implication for the reader. The individual should hold suffering and oppression dear, says Marquard, as this is the surety of his soul; as the cross is established for mankind out of God's great love, so man should always love and contemplate the cross:

Die fråg: Was lernend wir bi disem wort? Die antwúrt: Wir lernend da bi, daz v̂ns sol so gar wård vnd lieb sin alles liden vnd drůk, sider es v̂nser selgeråt ist, vnd v̂ns beseczet ist das crůcz so vss grŏsser minn von v̂nserm herren, vnd daz wir alle zit sŏllend minn vnd betrahtung hån nåch dem crůcz v̂nsers herren. Vnd lernend ŏch da bi, das wir an v̂nserm end ŏch sŏllend so gar ledeklich vnd luterlich v̂nsern gaist bevelhen in die gnådrichen hend des ewigen vatters.[235]

(Question: What do we learn from this word? Answer: We learn from it that all suffering and oppression should be greatly honoured and beloved by us, because it is our legacy. The cross is left to us by our Lord out of his great love, and we should always have love and contemplation for the cross of our Lord. We also learn from it that we too, at the ends of our lives, should commend our spirits so freely and purely into the merciful hands of the eternal Father.)

---

[234] *Predigt* 10, ll. 265–75 (p. 94).
[235] Ibid., ll. 282–8 (p. 95).

Here, the accentuation on *compassio*—suffering—as the means by which the individual can associate himself with Christ's reward and participate in his 'selgerât' (meaning a legacy or gift, usually one donated to secure the salvation of an individual's soul) is much stronger and more exclusive than in *De anima Christi*, quite possibly conditioned by the liturgical feast (Good Friday) for which the sermon is intended.

The second section of the Good Friday sermon, then, provides four broad types of instruction: first, moral-ethical lessons; second, some didactic theological lessons; third, the repeated exhortation to love Christ in response to his love manifested in the Passion; and fourth, the admonition in the sixth word to imitate Christ's suffering and so participate in his reward. The third section of the sermon proceeds to elaborate six methods by which an individual whose devotion is cold might inflame himself to the contemplation of the Passion. A search for similar instruction reveals that Marquard had a direct source for this section, namely the third section of the first book of the *Stimulus amoris maior*. This is, in fact, a family of three ever-longer recensions of the *Stimulus amoris minor*, the original substrate of the work probably produced at the very end of the thirteenth century by an otherwise unknown Italian Franciscan named James of Milan. The last, and longest of these recensions was undertaken in the mid-fourteenth century, and consequently prior to Marquard's engagement with the work.[236] It is no surprise to discover that Marquard knew the *Stimulus amoris*. Its manuscript transmission runs into the several hundreds of copies, with a very strong tradition in several European vernaculars in addition. There were five separate translations into German alone, represented by thirty-three manuscripts of the complete text and a further twenty-five containing excerpts.[237] Though the Latin text was not very widely transmitted in Franciscan libraries (despite its Franciscan origin), there are several extant manuscripts from Franciscan libraries in the German-speaking region,[238] and the work was used by a number of German Franciscans in the fifteenth century.[239] Ludolf's *Vita Christi*, which incorporates a significant body of excerpts from the *Stimulus amoris*, provides an early attestation of its presence and influence in

---

[236] See Eisermann, >*Stimulus amoris*<, pp. 4–5, 10–12, and 229–50.

[237] A systematic examination of the texts in German is offered by Eisermann, ibid. 359–498; on the translations into the other European vernaculars (Dutch, English, French, Italian, Spanish, Danish, Swedish, Gaelic, and Polish) see summarily pp. 3–4, with all further references.

[238] See ibid. 256–64.

[239] Ibid. 554–5, with a survey of its influence on German writers into the 16th cent. at pp. 526–52.

fourteenth-century Germany,[240] and a short 'Adventsbetrachtung' ascribed to Marquard himself draws on a part of the work that describes the ten stages of humility.[241]

Of Marquard's six ways in which an individual whose devotion is cold might inflame himself in the contemplation of Christ's Passion, three are adopted from the corresponding section of the *Stimulus amoris*, which section bears the much more general heading (in Klapper's edition from a later fourteenth-century manuscript of Bohemian origin, at any rate) of 'Meditacio vel qualiter debet compati Christo crucifixo'[242] ('Meditation, or in what way one should experience compassion with the crucified Christ'). Marquard's first two methods are his own. He begins by counselling the individual to consider the Passion with a sense of personal unworthiness and a humble heart, in light of the great humility manifest in the crucified Christ. Next, the individual should love his fellow men: as love is the cause of Christ's Passion, and only in love can the fruits of the Passion be felt, so the love of the head (i.e. of Christ) cannot be felt if the limbs of his mystical body (i.e. the rest of the faithful) are not loved.[243] This strikes a horizontal note of the *dilectio proximi* bound to the vertical relationship of the *dilectio Dei* that is not present earlier in the sermon, and is strongly reminiscent, as is clear from the discussion above, of a more Bonaventuran conceptualization of the reciprocal love of Christ.

Marquard's third method is the first to be drawn from the *Stimulus amoris*. He instructs the individual to unify his mind with God in ardent love: the more God is loved, the more compassion the individual has with his suffering, and the more God is then loved in turn. God alone is to be held dear, so that ultimately the individual will be wounded and scorned as Christ was. Christ's unwillingness to curtail his suffering is to be recalled along with the fact that he prayed on the cross for the good thief before he spoke to his mother. He is to be asked to wound the individual's heart with his wounds, and to inflame the individual's (cold) desire, so that Christ may provide what the individual lacks. Where Marquard differs from the *Stimulus amoris*, aside from the

---

[240] Eisermann, >*Stimulus amoris*<, pp. 526–7.

[241] Ibid. 531–2; on the authorship of the 'Adventsbetrachtung' see Palmer, 'Marquard von Lindau', cols. 94–5, and Greifenstein (ed.), *Der Hiob-Traktat*, pp. 13 and 103–4.

[242] *Stimulus amoris* (ed. Klapper), lib. 1, c. 3 (pp. 20–36); (ed. Peltier) lib. 1, c. 2 (pp. 635^b–638^a). All references to the *Stimulus amoris* will be given first to Klapper's edition of 1939, and then to A. C. Peltier's edition of 1868 (a reprint of the Vatican edition of 1596). On Klapper's edition and the manuscript used (Wrocław, Biblioteka uniwersytecka, Cod. I F 569, fols. 113va–162ra), see Eisermann, >*Stimulus amoris*<, pp. 18–19 and 204.

[243] *Predigt* 10, ll. 331–48 (p. 96).

Marquard von Lindau,
Predigt 10, ll. 349–61 (pp. 96–7)

Die dritt wis ist, daz der mensch sol sin
gemůt verainen mit gott in hicziger liebi vnd
ernst sines herczen, wan so dir got ie lieber
ist, so du ie me mitlidens hắst in sinem liden,
vnd so du ie me mitlidens hắst, so din liebi
gen got ie me wachsend ist. Vnd also merret
liebi daz mitliden, vnd ŏch daz mitliden
die liebi.

Hier vmb so fliss dich, daz din hercz in in
gang, vnd daz du dich selber vsser im nihtes
nit schắczest, mer all din sorg vnd fliss sigi
vmb dinen gelitten gott, daz du mit sinen
wunden verwundet werdest, vnd mit sinem
spott vnd verschmäht begossen werdest.

Gedenk, daz sin fliss so grŏss waz vnd sin
ernst, daz er nit wolt ain wort reden vor
Pilatus, daz er ett sin liden lengerte, vnd daz
er e batt fůr den sůnder an dem crůcz, e daz
er redoti mit siner můter. Vnd also bitt in,
daz er mit sinen wunden din hercz verwundi
vnd din begird enzůnd, wa dir gebrest, das
daz durch in volbrắht werd.

Stimulus amoris (ed. Klapper),
lib. 1, c. 3 (pp. 20–2)[244]

Ad compaciendum domino Ihesu Christo
crucifixo primo studeas, quantum potes, te illi
unire per feruentem amorem. Nam quanto
feruencius diligis eum, tanto plus compacieris
sue passioni. Et quanto plus compacieris, tanto
plus erga eum accendetur tuus affectus. Unde
sic mutuo se augebunt dileccio et compassio,
donec uenias ad perfectum, nisi hoc remanserit
propter aliquam tuam miseriam. Et precipue
studeas abicere omnem presumpcionem,
diffidenciam et negligenciam. Debet enim
homo tam nobile opus aggredi humiliter,
confidenter, instanter et cum quanta potest
mundicia cordis. Et quamuis homo uideatur
sibi indignus et nequam, nichilo minus non
desistat, quia ipse pro peccatoribus crucifixus
est. Primo igitur sic uniaris amore sibi, ut cor
tuum iam sibi, non tibi, uideatur coniunctum.
Quomodo tunc non sencies eius vulnera aut
quas passiones habebit, que non perfundant
cor tuum? Studeas ergo, quantum potes, ut cor
tuum intret in ipsum totaliter, et extra ipsum
tanquam de nullo curabis. Tota cura tua
uertatur in deum dominum tuum passum.
Nam eius es, quidquid es, nec debes alteri
aliquid exhibere. Sic transformatus in ipsum
non possum credere quin eius vulneribus
vulnereris et perfundaris eius contumelijs,
illusionibus et obprobrijs.

---

[244] Cf. *Stimulus amoris* (ed. Peltier), lib. 1, c. 2 (p. 635ª).

excision of a large portion of text concerning humility and unworthiness (which Marquard has already dealt with in his first two methods), is in the omission of the idea of the *transformatio* of the individual into God. Marquard deals with the union of the mind with God, by contrast, in very general terms here. He accentuates not personal conformity through transformation into the crucified Christ, but the imitative potential of the exemplar of suffering that the crucified Christ presents to the individual. I provide a subsequent translation of Marquard's text alone.

(The third method is that the individual should unite his mind with God in the fervent love and earnestness of his heart. For the more you love God, the more compassion you have in his suffering, and the more compassion you have, the more your love for God grows. In this way love increases compassion, and compassion increases love likewise. Therefore take care that your heart enters him, and that you consider yourself outside him to be nothing. All your care and effort should instead be for your God who suffered, so that you will be wounded with his wounds, and doused with his scorn and shame. Consider that his effort and his earnestness were so great that he did not want to speak a word in front of Pilate, so that he prolonged his suffering; and that he prayed for the sinner on the cross before he spoke with his mother. So pray to him that he might wound your heart with his wounds and inflame your desire where you are deficient in something, so that it may be perfected by him.)

A similar pattern of adaptation is then evident in Marquard's fourth point. The equivalent passage in the *Stimulus amoris* instructs the individual to receive the sweetness of divine mercy. The individual is to consider how far he would suffer if he were to experience the gravity of all the saints' sufferings, and then consider how much more Christ had suffered—and beyond that, had suffered innocently for him. In further contemplation of how Christ's love led him to suffer in this way, the individual's heart is afflicted by those sorrows; as if then actually sustaining those sorrows, the individual will weep bitter tears, and this will be converted into sweetness. The conclusion of this process is most significant:

Tunc ergo rumina in corde tuo, quantam sustinuit angustiam et affliccionem, et quantus amor ipsum ad hoc induxit. Et sic meditando afficiatur cor tuum illis doloribus, quantum potest. Et quasi illos sustineres, amarissime lacrimis perfunderis, nec dubium, quod in dulcedinem conuertentur.[245]

(Then consider in your heart how much distress and affliction he bore, and how great was the love that moved him to this. In meditating in this way, let your heart be affected by those sufferings, as far as it can. Should you bear them like this, you will weep most bitterly with tears; there is no doubt that they will be converted into sweetness.)

[245] *Stimulus amoris* (ed. Klapper), lib. 1, c. 3 (p. 23); (ed. Peltier) lib. 1, c. 2 (p. 636ª).

Marquard's corresponding instruction adopts none of this complex process of engagement with Christ. Instead, the individual is simply instructed to consider how painful the sufferings of all the saints would be, and then to recognize how much greater Christ's sufferings were, innocently sustained out of love for sinful mankind. The consequence of this is purely that the individual have greater compassion with Christ and be inflamed therein: 'So solt du billich mitliden mit im hǎn vnd davon enzúndet werden in aller hertkait dines herczen'[246] ('So you should rightfully experience compassion with him, and be inflamed by this in all the hardness of your heart').

This same pattern is then adopted for Marquard's fifth method, introduced independently of the *Stimulus amoris*. The individual is told to consider how the death of a good friend would affect him, or how he would feel if a friend betrayed him. Christ was man's greatest and most faithful friend, and the individual must consider how he felt when his friends betrayed him; how Mary felt when she saw her son suffering; and how Christ felt when he saw his mother suffer. The purpose of this fifth element is again simply to melt the individual's hard heart.[247] Marquard follows the pattern again in the sixth and final method of the set, adapted from the *Stimulus amoris*, in which the individual is to chastise himself with a whip and consider how much greater Christ's sufferings were than anything is that you might inflict upon yourself.[248] Marquard omits—as we may by now expect—the portion of the *Stimulus amoris* text in which the individual is to pray to Christ that he might wound the individual's mind with his wounds, thus bringing about the *transformatio*. Less expected is Marquard's adoption of the method of self-flagellation in the first place. Bodily chastisement is otherwise an exceptionally unfamiliar element in Marquard's oeuvre. The inclusion of this instruction in the sermon in question here does, however, suggest that it was not an unknown practice amongst the audience for whom Marquard intended the work.

Next Marquard presents an instruction for the individual who has remained unaffected by the six methods outlined thus far. This additional instruction is also adopted from the same section of the *Stimulus amoris*. Both texts formulate this instruction as a plaint, in which the individual expresses disgust at his own inability to be moved by the contemplation of

---

[246] *Predigt* 10, ll. 362–76 (p. 97), here ll. 374–6.

[247] Ibid., ll. 377–90 (p. 97).

[248] Ibid., ll. 391–9 (pp. 97–8); cf. *Stimulus amoris* (ed. Klapper), lib. 1, c. 3 (pp. 24–5); (ed. Peltier) lib. 1, c. 2 (p. 636ᵃ).

130   *The Passion*

the crucified Christ. The plaint is very long, and—in Marquard's version—
draws the individual to recognize his own insignificance; to call upon Christ to
inflict him with his wounds, because he (and not Christ) was rightfully their
cause; and ultimately to recognize that this hardness of heart may remain
because he has previously received God's gifts thanklessly, which makes him
into a feral and unworthy person.[249] In this humility and cognizance of one's
own unworthiness, God often then comes with his fiery water of life to irrigate
the dry heart with grace, and enable it to weep inwardly:

So beschiht es dik, daz denn got des menschen demůtikait ansihet vnd in begnådet,
als v̊nser fröw sprach: >Respexit humilitatem ancille sue. Er hǎt angesehen die
demůtikait siner dirnen.< [Lk. 1: 48] Alsus komet denn gott dikk mit sinen richen
gåben vnd mit sinem fůrin lebenden wasser, vnd machet daz dúrr hercz nass mit der
gnåd sines regens, vnd machet es dik zerfliessend mit innigen trǎhern.[250]

(Thus it often happens that God then looks upon the individual's humility and
bestows grace upon him, just as our Lady said, 'Respexit humilitatem ancille sue. He
has looked upon the humility of his handmaiden.' In this way God then often
comes with his rich gifts and with his fiery, living water. He makes the dry heart
moist with the grace of his rain, and often makes it flow forth with inner tears.)

Marquard leaves the main body of the plaint largely unaltered, though
slightly abbreviated, and by omission toning down the focus of the *Stimulus
amoris* text on achieving a state of mystical *convulneratio*. The conclusion is
entirely different, though. Whereas the result in Marquard's sermon is that
God will come and irrigate the dry heart with grace, the corresponding
passage in the *Stimulus amoris* concludes with the divine gift of a new heart,
so that the individual might know Christ crucified:

Si hec omnia non ualerint tibi, tam nobilissimo beneficio es indignus. Et de cetero
non reputes te hominem, sed bestiam, et cum feris sit habitacio tua, quia indignus es
consorcio angelorum. Forte, si multum te humiliaueris, ille, qui respexit humilitatem ancille sue, respiciet humilitatem anime tue et dabit tibi cor nouum, ut
cognoscas eum passum.[251]

(If none of these things are effectual for you, you are unworthy for such an honour
of the most noble kind. From now on you should not consider yourself a man, but
a beast, and your dwelling place should be with the wild animals, because you
are unworthy of the company of angels. Perhaps, if you humble yourself greatly,

[249] *Predigt* 10, ll. 399–434 (pp. 98–9); cf. *Stimulus amoris* (ed. Klapper), lib. 1,
c. 3 (pp. 25–30); (ed. Peltier), lib. 1, c. 2 (pp. 636ᵃ–637ᵃ).
[250] *Predigt* 10, ll. 434–40 (p. 99).
[251] *Stimulus amoris* (ed. Klapper), lib. 1, c. 3 (pp. 29–30); (ed. Peltier) lib. 1, c. 2
(pp. 636ᵇ–637ᵃ).

then he, who looked upon the humility of his handmaiden, will look upon the
humility of your soul and will give you a new heart, that you may know him who
suffered.)

The *Stimulus amoris* then continues with a plaint that constitutes about half the
total length of the chapter. This begins with an impatient desire for that
promised new heart (a metaphor familiar from Ezekiel 36: 26–7).[252] Delay is
as death, and the speaker asks for liquefaction into Christ and stigmatization in
this liquefied state. The plaint continues, exploring such themes as the speaker's
spiritual drunkenness in divine love and the eventual entrance of the speaker
through Christ's wounds into stigmatized union with the crucified Christ, a
form of mystical death in which the speaker is finally brought to eternal life.[253]
    None of this finds any place in Marquard's Good Friday sermon. The
motif of the 'duricia cordis', hardness of heart, in contemplation of Christ's
Passion provides the common feature between the set of instructions in
Marquard's sermon and the related chapter in the *Stimulus amoris*. Individual instructions are adopted, but the emphasis that the *Stimulus amoris*
places on *convulneratio* and union with Christ—not to mention the idea of
actual *transformatio* into the crucified Christ—is either toned down, or
entirely omitted, such that these emphases are no longer prominent, and
certain particular features are no longer present at all. Instead the conclusion to Marquard's sermon is formed by a question that asks which kind of
person thanks God most explicitly ('aller aigenlichest').[254] The answer
distinguishes between two kinds of person who have received the gift of
inner tears in contemplation of the Passion. The first kind either have as yet
failed to subdue their bodily desires, or are happy to participate in worldly
frivolities. The second kind are those who approach the Passion with
proper, bottomless passivity ('mit rehter grundlöser gelässenhait'). This
passivity is expressed first in the recognition that Christ's suffering is
loved by the individual to such an extent that he desires to suffer in honour
of Christ's suffering, and second in the recognition that he would joyfully

---

[252] Ez. 36: 26–7: 'et dabo vobis cor novum, et spiritum novam ponam in medio vestri; et
auferam cor lapideum de carne vestra, et dabo vobis cor carneum; et spiritum meum ponam
in medio vestri, et faciam ut in praeceptis meis ambuletis et iudicia mea custodiatis et
operemini' ('and I will give you a new heart, and will put a new spirit into you; I will take
away the heart of stone out of your flesh, and will give you a heart of flesh; I will put my spirit
into you, and I will cause you to walk in my rules and to keep my judgements, and you will
labour [in them]').
[253] *Stimulus amoris* (ed. Klapper), lib. 1, c. 3 (pp. 30–6); (ed. Peltier) lib. 1, c. 2 (pp.
637ª–638ª). For an outline of the whole of this chapter see Eisermann, >*Stimulus
amoris*>, pp. 24–6.
[254] *Predigt* 10, ll. 441–60 (p. 99).

give his soul to suffer for all souls until the end of time to honour Christ's suffering. This is the greatest possible thanks that may be given to Christ for his suffering, and those who have this attitude desire to suffer in an attempt to achieve conformity with the crucified Christ:

Vnd sâmlichi menschen dürstet alle zit nâch liden, vnd was si stûret zů dem durlitten sterbenden bild Jesu Cristi, das minnend si vnd sůchend, dar vmb daz si dem alle zit gelich funden werdent. Si trinkend lieber wasser denn win, sterben ist ir gewin [cf. Phil. 1: 21], er ist ir scham, si wellend verworfen sin vnd vnder den vnnûczen die aller vnnûczesten sin, vnd sůchend all ir frôd in dem crůcz Jesu Christi, als sant Paulus sprach: >Michi absit gloriari nisi in cruce etc. Verr si von mir alli frôd denn in dem crůcz ŷnsers herren Jesu Cristi.< [Gal. 6: 14][255]

(All these people thirst continually for suffering. They love what guides them to the tormented, dying image of Jesus Christ; and they seek it out, so that they may always be found to be like that image. They prefer to drink water than wine. Death is their reward; honour is their shame. They wish to be cast aside and to be the most useless of all amongst the useless. They seek all their joy in the cross of Jesus Christ; as St Paul said, 'Michi absit gloriari nisi in cruce, etc. Let all joy be far from me, save in the cross of our Lord Jesus Christ.')

It is conformity with the crucified Christ in the bearing of suffering, and in the manner of bearing that suffering, that constitutes the ultimate response to the Passion in Marquard's Good Friday sermon. This goal of conformity is very different to the goal of mystical union by transformation into the crucified Christ at which the comparable passage in the *Stimulus amoris* (and, in fact, the work as a whole) aims. This difference, and its significance, becomes more clear if we now turn to Marquard's other sermon on Christ's suffering, which also draws on the *Stimulus amoris*.

This sermon, for Quinquagesima, is the fourteenth in the collection and bears the rubric 'Diss ist von dem liden ŷnsers herren' ('This is about the suffering of our Lord'). It is much shorter than the Good Friday sermon and we need not treat it in comparable length. As all the sermons, it is divided into three sections. The first outlines six characteristics of the divine light insofar as it illuminates the contemplative's mind, and thus presents important evidence by which to understand the function of divine illumination in Marquard's mystical theology.[256] The second identifies six fruits of contemplation of the Passion: not ancillary benefits to the individual that derive from his diligence and assiduity in meditating on the Passion, but concrete effects upon the mind that are worked by the power of the Passion

---

[255] *Predigt* 10, ll. 453–60 (p. 99).
[256] *Predigt* 14, ll. 9–36 (pp. 112–13).

itself.[257] The third and final section then enumerates six ways in which the Passion is fruitfully contemplated, and it is here that Marquard draws on the *Stimulus amoris*: specifically, on the sixth chapter of the first book.[258] This particular chapter of the *Stimulus amoris* represents the summation and the apex of the work's engagement with meditation on the Passion; it presents six points that are of particular significance in the contemplation of the Passion, arranged into a loosely hierarchical schema of ascent.[259] On account of its systematic framework, mnemonic potential, and particular didactic approach it was widely transmitted in excerpt, and was further incorporated into subsequent works—for our purposes notably Ludolf's *Vita Christi* and, in German translation, the *Extendit manum* Passion narrative attributed to Heinrich von St Gallen.[260]

The chapter of the *Stimulus amoris* begins with a summary of the six points:

Circa passionem domini Ihesu sic potest homo se habere et ad sex eam considerare. Primo ad imitandum, secundo ad conpaciendum, tercio ad ammirandum, quarto ad exultandum, quinto ad resoluendum, sexto ad quiescendum.[261]

(Man can thus approach the Passion of the Lord Jesus, and consider it with respect to these six ways. First, imitation; second, the experience of compassion; third, admiration; fourth, rejoicing; fifth, dissolution; sixth, rest.)

In fact, it is not much more than this sequence that Marquard adopts to structure his own six points. Each point in the *Stimulus amoris* is accompanied by a long exposition, which Marquard either does not adopt at all, replacing it with a very short exposition of his own, or from which he only draws a particular phrase or two. After dealing briefly with imitation, understood as following Christ's model of patiently bearing suffering,[262] and compassion, understood as feeling within oneself the pain that Christ felt,[263] Marquard introduces a third point that is entirely his own. This

---

[257] Ibid., ll. 37–69 (pp. 113–14); for six fruits of the Passion (as opposed to the contemplation of the Passion), see *De reparatione hominis*, a. 25 (130. 1–133. 6).

[258] *Stimulus amoris* (ed. Klapper), lib. 1, c. 6 (pp. 45–58); (ed. Peltier) lib. 1, c. 4 (pp. 639ᵇ–641ᵃ).

[259] See Eisermann, >*Stimulus amoris*<, pp. 27–9, with an outline of the content.

[260] Ibid. 526–33. Note that whilst Eisermann refers here to lib. 1, c. 4, he uses the chapter numeration of Adolphe Peltier's 1868 edition; in fact, this is lib. 1, c. 6 according to the numeration in Joseph Klapper's edition, which we follow here, and which Eisermann himself prefers in the summary of the *Stimulus amoris* that he offers at pp. 18–58.

[261] *Stimulus amoris* (ed. Klapper), lib. 1, c. 6 (p. 45); (ed. Peltier) lib. 1, c. 4 (p. 639ᵃ).

[262] *Predigt* 14, ll. 70–5 (p. 114).

[263] Ibid., ll. 76–80 (p. 114).

concerns contemplation in a state of aridity, in which the individual passively persists until he dies, considering himself to be unworthy of receiving any perceptible love or sweetness from God, and 'presses' himself in this parched state—a terminology familiar from *De anima Christi*—into the parched state of the crucified Christ:

Die dritt wis ist, so man es betrahtet mit grösser dúrri vnd lǎwekait dez herczen, vnd der mensch sich also dǎr inne gelǎssenlichen lidet vnd vollhertet, vnd sich vnwirdig dunket, daz im got kain bevintlich minn oder sǔssikait geb, vnd sich drukket in die dǔrri, in der v̂nser herr dǔrr vnd ersigen alles blǔtes an dem crǔcz hieng, vnd voll vss hertet bis in den tǒd.[264]

(The third way is when one contemplates it with a great aridity and tepidity of the heart. The individual passively suffers thus and persists in this state, and thinks himself unworthy that God should give him any perceptible love or sweetness. He presses himself into the aridity in which our Lord hung on the cross, dried out and exhausted of all his blood, and persists so even unto death.)

This, in essence, is the method of contemplating the Passion in Marquard's Good Friday sermon to which he directs the individual who has remained unmoved by Christ's suffering, despite having put into practice all the six ways that might engender such stimulation. Its presence in this sequence here in the Quinquagesima sermon is indicative of Marquard's systematic approach, not incorporating material from earlier works en bloc and unaltered, but rather modifying that existing material to accord with his own, original framework.

The fourth and fifth points in Marquard's sequence are then the third and fourth from the *Stimulus amoris*: contemplation in wonderment at the magnitude of the event, and consequently at the magnitude of God's love; and contemplation with great joy in view of the redemption of mankind in the outpouring of divine mercy.[265] Marquard omits the fifth point of the *Stimulus amoris* sequence, which addresses the dissolution of the heart in the reformation (or transformation) of the individual into the crucified Christ. This is exactly the aspect of the mystical theology of the *Stimulus amoris* that Marquard omitted in his adaptation of the text in the Good Friday sermon:

Quinto eciam consideremus sanctissimam Christi passionem ad cordium nostrorum resolucionem in Christum, et hoc per perfectam reformacionem in ipsum. Quod fit, quando non solum imitatur, conpatitur, admiratur et exultatur, sed eciam totus conuertitur in eundem dominum nostrum Ihesum Christum crucifixum, ut quasi iam ubique et semper sibi crucifixus occurrat. Ymmo, tunc uere resoluitur,

---

[264] *Predigt* 14, ll. 81–5 (p. 114).
[265] Ibid., ll. 86–98 (p. 114).

quando ex se exiens homo et suprapositus vniuerso, ymmo, totus supra se abstractus ab omnibus totusque conuersus ad dominum suum passum, nec aliud uideat aut senciat intra semetipsum nisi Christum crucifixum, illusum, exprobatum et passum pro nobis.[266]

(Fifth, let us also consider Christ's most holy Passion with respect to the dissolution of our hearts in Christ, and this through perfect reformation into him. This happens when one does not just imitate, experience compassion, admire, and rejoice, but is also wholly transformed into our Lord Jesus Christ crucified, so that it is as if he, who has been crucified, is present to you now, always, and everywhere. Then, indeed, one is truly dissolved, when man, taking leave of himself and placed above everything else—indeed, wholly abstracted above himself from everything, and wholly transformed into his Lord, who suffered—neither sees nor feels anything else within himself except Christ crucified, scorned, convicted, and made to suffer for us.)

Both texts then share the final point: coming to rest ('quies') in loving union with Christ. The *Stimulus amoris* accentuates the liquefaction of the dissolved ('resolutus') individual in unindividuated union with the crucified Christ.[267] Marquard instead proposes that the individual has first entered through Christ's wounds—a more common metaphor with Bernardine roots, that he explores more fully (and in direct dependence on Bernard) elsewhere.[268] In this way—and not by *transformatio*—the individual has sought union with Christ. In this state, he gives up all that pertains to him as a person, by which we ought probably to understand his will, and offers himself passively into God's power. With this mystical death, he gives himself into Christ's death, and there remains at peace:

Die sechst wis ist, so man es betrahtet in ainer wis aines fridlichen bi belibens oder aines lustlichen süssen frides, als der mensch ist in gegangen durh die gebenedicten wunden, vnd sich in den verainet hett mit Cristo, vnd denn also naiget daz höbt aller siner aigenhait, vnd git sich mit ainem gelässnen gaist in dez ewigen vatters hand vnd gewalt, vnd lät sich mit sterben sin selbes in das sterben Jesu Cristi vnd in sinen töd, vnd belibet denn fridlich mit lust vnd mit süsser rûwe in allem sinem tfinde. Diss menschen betrahtend wol vnd fruhtbärlich daz wirdig liden vnsers herren.[269]

---

[266] *Stimulus amoris* (ed. Klapper), lib. 1, c. 6 (pp. 55–6); (ed. Peltier) lib. 1, c. 4 (p. 641[a]). Peltier has 'transformatio' where Klapper gives 'resolucio', but it is not clear which is to be preferred (see Eisermann, >*Stimulus amoris*<, p. 28 n. 105).

[267] *Stimulus amoris* (ed. Klapper), lib. 1, c. 6 (pp. 56–7); (ed. Peltier) lib. 1, c. 4 (p. 641[a–b]).

[268] See *Predigt* 23, ll. 190–232 (pp. 156–8).

[269] *Predigt* 14, ll. 99–107 (pp. 114–15). The mystical death of the self to achieve a state of rest, albeit in analogy to Christ's death and entombment (and not in Christ himself, as here), is alternatively explored in *De fide*, pars 4, a. 4, ll. 355–68 (p. 306).

(The third way is when one contemplates it in the manner of a peaceful residence together or a delightful, sweet peace. [This happens] when the individual has entered through the blessed wounds, has united himself with Christ in them, and has bowed the head of all his individuality; he gives himself with a passive spirit into the hands of the eternal Father and into his power, gives himself up through dying to himself into the dying Jesus Christ and into his death, and then resides there peacefully, with delight and sweet repose in whatever he does. These people contemplate the worthy suffering of our Lord well and fruitfully.)

The pertinent chapter of the *Stimulus amoris* concludes with a summary of the sequence, which accentuates its nature as a cumulative progression in ascent towards the goal of union with the crucified Christ in mystical rest:

Sic circa passionem domini debet esse imitacio ad purgacionem et direccionem, conpassio ad vnionem et amorem, admiracio ad mentis eleuacionem, gaudium et exultacio ad cordis dilatacionem, resolucio ad perfectam conformacionem, quies et pausacio ad deuocionis consumacionem.[270]

(Thus in respect of the Passion of the Lord, imitation should pertain to purgation and redirection, compassion to union and love, admiration to the elevation of the mind, delight and rejoicing to the expansion of the heart, dissolution to perfect conformity, and rest and calm to the consummation of devotion.)

By contrast Marquard's sequence of six points is not structured as an ascent at all. The different ways of contemplating Christ's suffering are not ordered into a hierarchy, even if the sixth way is adjudged to be the most fruitful, and it is certainly not necessary to pass through each stage to progress to the next. This is most clear from the presence of the third point, the only one that is Marquard's own: it is clearly not possible for someone who remains spiritually arid in the contemplation of the Passion, and persists patiently in this aridity until his death, to progress to the subsequent level—let alone to contemplate Christ's suffering in the sixth, and most fruitful way.

The significance of Marquard's reformation of a progressive ascent into a static set of six different options, alongside his removal of any hint of the *transformatio* into the crucified Christ—the distinctive feature of the mystical Passion theology of the *Stimulus amoris*—in the section of the work he adopted in the Good Friday sermon, goes beyond the simple rejection of a particular variety of mystical theology. What is most striking about both of Marquard's sermons on the contemplation of the Passion (not to mention *De anima Christi*) is the lack of a mystical dimension, and

[270] *Stimulus amoris* (ed. Klapper), lib. 1, c. 6 (pp. 57–8); (ed. Peltier) lib. 1, c. 4 (p. 641[b]).

this in a sermon collection that is distinguished by its particular focus on the elaboration of a complex pseudo-Dionysian mystical theology. This is important because the path to mystical union through the contemplation of the crucified Christ—'per Christum hominem ad Christum Deum', where 'per Christum hominem' is understood as 'per Christum passum'— underpins a very substantial mystical tradition indeed, of which the *Stimulus amoris* is only a small part. Bonaventura represents a much more substantial part of this tradition, and is responsible for an insistence on the crucified Christ as the sole means of access to God in mystical union; a mystery revealed to, and literally incorporated in, Francis of Assisi in his stigmatization.[271] A similar insistence underlies Seuse's *Büchlein der ewigen Weisheit*, though with a rather different understanding of the precise mechanism of the eventual union itself, and set within the distinctive framework of obtaining what Seuse terms 'philosophia spiritualis'.[272] Bonaventura and Seuse (and the *Stimulus amoris*) together form a very substantial intellectual community on this issue. This is not to deny the complexity of the mystical theology of either, nor the substantial differences between them; rather, it is to note that both accord a central position to compassion (understood as *com-passio*) with the crucified Christ in the process of becoming one with Christ in mystical union, and that both insist on the inescapable necessity of this to the mystical ascent. The 'locus classicus' with regard to this insistence in Seuse's *Büchlein der ewigen Weisheit*, for example, comes in the second chapter. The servant seeks access to God's divinity, but is presented with the crucified humanity of Christ instead. The Eternal Wisdom then responds to this paradox:

Der diener: Owe herr, der anvang ist gar bitter, wie sol es ein ende nemen? [. . .] Aber herre, daz ist ein groz wunder in minem herzen: minneklicher herr, ich sûch alles din gotheit, so bûtest du mir din menscheit; ich sûch din sûzigkeit, so hebest du vûr din bitterkeit; ich wolt alles sugen, so lerest du mich striten. Ach herr, waz meinest du hie mitte?

---

[271] See McGinn, *The Flowering of Mysticism*, pp. 99–112; Schlosser, *Cognitio et amor*, pp. 240–6; and Strack, *Christusleid im Christenleben*, pp. 114–16.
[272] There is a substantial recent literature on the centrality of the crucified Christ in Seuse's mystical theology: see McGinn, *The Harvest of Mysticism* pp. 204–13; Ruh, *Die Mystik des deutschen Predigerordens*, pp. 437–41; Ulrich, *Imitatio et configuratio*, pp. 32–8, 56–62, 87–90, and 138–46; id., 'Zur Bedeutung des Leidens', pp. 129–31; Kaiser, 'Die Christozentrik der *philosophia spiritualis*'; Blumrich, 'Die *gemeinû leî*', pp. 53–5; Jaspert, 'Leid und Trost', pp. 173 and 176–86; and Haas, '»Trage Leiden geduldiglich«', pp. 146–51. How far Seuse was dependent on Bonaventura's theology is a controversial question: see most recently Ruh, *Die Mystik des deutschen Predigerordens*, pp. 454–60, esp. pp. 459–60 on the position of the crucified Christ in their

Entwúrt der Ewigen Wisheit: Es mag nieman komen ze gőtlicher hocheit noch ze
ungewonlicher sûzekeit, er werde denn vor gezogen dur daz bilde miner menschli-
chen bitterkeit. So man ane daz durchgan miner menscheit ie hőher uf klimmet, so
man ie tieffer vellet. Min menscheit ist der weg, den man gat, min liden ist daz tor,
durch daz man gan mûz, der zů dem wil komen, daz du da sûchest.[273]

(The servant: Alas, Lord, the beginning is so bitter—how shall it come to an end?
[. . .] But Lord, this is a great source of wonder in my heart: lovable Lord, always I
seek your divinity, and you offer me your humanity; I seek your sweetness, and you
extend to me your bitterness; always I wanted to suckle, but you teach me to do
battle. Well, Lord, what do you mean by this?
The Eternal Wisdom's answer: No one can attain the divine majesty, nor uncommon sweetness, unless he is first drawn through the image of my human bitterness.
The higher anyone climbs without passing through my humanity, the further he
falls. My humanity is the path that one takes; my suffering is the gate through which
he who wants to attain what you seek there has to pass.)

It is precisely this insistent accentuation that we do not find in Marquard's sermons on Christ's sufferings; the idea of access to the mystical
union through Christ's suffering humanity is only present as a weak echo.
For all that Marquard may insist on the necessity of reciprocal love in an
exclusive relationship with Christ, this is not functionalized—in these two
sermons, at least—as a path by which to come to loving union with Christ,
as it is for Bonaventura. This raises a very important final question, namely
the relationship between the contemplation of the Passion and literal compassion with the suffering Christ, and Marquard's mystical theology as
expressed in his German sermon collection.

The answer to this is neither clear nor evident. Rüdiger Blumrich refers
to the conceptualization of the access to God through Christ's suffering
humanity in Seuse's *Büchlein der ewigen Weisheit* as a direct parallel to the
third, and highest, of three different paths to God that Marquard sets out in
a question within the seventh sermon, on the prodigal son:

Die frǎg: Was weges sol der mensch gǎn, daz er wider zů dem himelschen vatter
kome? Die antwûrt: Es ist ain weg durch die creatur, als so der mensch sich in
gőtlich minn keret, vnd vnderwirfet allen creaturen durch gottes willen, vnd der weg
ist gar lang vnd krum vnd vol stain vnd dornen. Der ander weg ist, so der mensch ab
leit alle creatur, vnd mit abgeschaidner luter wis got sûchet ǎn sich selb vnd ǎn all
creatur. Der dritt weg der ist der nǎhst, da der mensch mit ainem frien vrlőb sin

mystical theologies; and Ulrich, *Imitatio et configuratio*, pp. 62–76. Mückshoff, 'Der
Einfluss des hl. Bonaventura', presents an extreme position in favour of Seuse's near-
slavish dependence on Bonaventura, which Ruh and Ulrich reject, but see pp. 251–6 on
the matter at issue here.

[273] Seuse, *Büchlein der ewigen Weisheit*, c. 2 (204. 23–205. 7).

selbes vnd aller geschaffner ding sich wirfet in das sterbend bild v̄nsers herren Jesu Cristi vnd durch sin blŏss armen durlittnen menschait in gǎt in die lutren gothait des ewigen vatters. Vnd das ist der kŭrczest sichrest weg, als Cristus selber gesprochen hǎt: >Ego sum via etc. Ich bin der weg, die wǎrhait vnd daz leben.< [John 14: 6][274]

(Question: What path ought the individual take so that he may return to the heavenly Father? Answer: One path is through creation, when the individual turns to divine love, and conquers all the created for God's sake. This path is very long, crooked, and full of stones and thorns. The second path is when the individual casts aside all the created, and seeks God in a pure and detached way, outwith himself and outwith all the created. The third path brings us the closest. This is when the individual takes unfettered leave of himself and of all created things, casts himself into the dying image of our Lord Jesus Christ, and through his naked, poor, and tormented humanity enters into the pure divinity of the eternal Father. This is the shortest and most secure path, as Christ himself said; 'Ego sum via, etc. I am the way, the truth, and the life.')

Marquard distinguishes here between three different philosophical-theological models of the mystical ascent to God, without defining those models so precisely that they can be associated with individual works or intellectuals. The third model is presented essentially as an augmented version of the second: the search for God not just having detached the mind from the created self and all other creation, but then having impelled the mind into the image of the crucified Christ to access God's divinity through his suffering humanity. Perhaps the most striking feature of this passage, though, is not the distinction between three different paths itself, but the fact that no one path is established exclusively as the sole possible way to God. All three, in fact, lead to God; the third is only to be preferred to the others as it is the shortest and securest path. This is quite different, in fact, to Seuse: the first two chapters of the *Büchlein der ewigen Weisheit* in general, and the quotation above from the second chapter in particular, make quite clear that there is only one possible path to God, namely through Christ's suffering humanity.

Blumrich discusses the first section of the thirtieth sermon, on Whitsun, in which Marquard presents six schools of wisdom.[275] The fourth of these is the school of Christ, with the focus very much on the crucified Christ. It is not just moral virtues that are learned from Christ's example, but also the abnegation of the world, and the cross and Passion of Christ as the sole focus of desire:

---

[274] *Predigt* 7, ll. 150–61 (p. 62); see Blumrich, 'Feuer der Liebe', p. 48.

[275] Blumrich (ed.), *Marquard von Lindau. Deutsche Predigten*, pp. 61*–64*; cf. *Predigt* 30, ll. 14–132 (pp. 202–6).

In diser schůl Jesu Cristi lernet man sich selber hassen, die welt verschmǎhen, vss gǎn allen geschaffnen dingen, senftmútikait vnd demútikait, vnd wie allain ains notdurftig ist in allen dingen. Man lernet in der schůl, wie man mit sterben lebend wirt, mit armůt rich, mit verschmǎht erwirdig, mit vndergǎn erhǒht, vnd wie man allen lust vindet in dem crůcz vnd in dem liden v̓nsers herren Jesu Christi.[276]

(In this school of Jesus Christ one learns to hate oneself, to reject the world, and to leave all created things; one learns gentleness and humility, and how one thing alone is necessary in everything. In this school one learns how one becomes alive through dying, rich through poverty, honoured through shame, elevated through submission, and how one is to find all delight in the cross and the Passion of our Lord Jesus Christ.)

The sixth school, by contrast, is the school of the Holy Spirit.[277] Or rather, it is the state of the highest possible purification of the mind, in which the individual achieves union with God. This passage provides one of the most detailed and important expositions of Marquard's pseudo-Dionysian mystical theology, notably in the following passage, in which the precise mechanics of the union in the 'apex affectionis' are described:

Du merkest hie bi wol, wie gar gelůtret edel menschen es můssend sin, die in disi schůl hǒrend, wan in der schůl ist weder lieht noch vernunft, noch gedank, noch red, noch wirt gesůchet weder gnǎd noch glory. Wan vernunft vnd all kreft sind dǎ berǒbet irs werkes vnd in ainer stilli aines vnwissends vmb sich vnd vmb ǎllú ding, als sant Dyonisius sprichet, mer allain der spicz der minnenden kraft sůchet ainikait mit got. Vnd in dem spicz der minnenden kraft wirt got gelobt v̓ber wesenlich mit der v̓ber wallenden minn, die da besǒffet wúrken aller ander kreft vnd blǒsslich in got gekeret ist, als Vercellensis der abt sprichet.[278]

(In this you can clearly see what highly purified, noble people it must be who belong to this school, because in this school there is neither light nor reason, thought or speech, and neither grace nor glory is sought. For reason and all the powers [of the soul] are robbed of their effect there, and in the silence of an unknowing of itself and everything, as St Dionysius says, it is just the apex of the affectionate power that seeks union with God. In the apex of the affectionate power God is praised superessentially by that overflowing love which drowns out the effects of all the other powers and has turned nakedly to God, as the abbot of Vercelli says.)

These six schools do not constitute separate stages through which the individual must pass to reach the highest level, but they are arranged in a loosely hierarchical manner, with each school representing a more advanced level of the spiritual life. The relative superiority of the sixth school over the

---

[276] *Predigt* 30, ll. 74–9 (p. 204).
[277] Ibid., ll. 100–32 (pp. 205–6).
[278] Ibid., ll. 119–28 (p. 206); cf. McGinn, *The Harvest of Mysticism*, pp. 336–7.

third in this way leads Blumrich to conclude that 'Höhepunkt und Ziel seiner *praedicatio* ist also nicht die *imitatio* und *compassio* Christi, sondern eine Theologia mystica im Anschluß an Dionysius.'[279]

We may broadly affirm this conclusion if we consider that neither of Marquard's two sermons that deal exclusively with the response to Christ's suffering explore a pronounced mystical aspect. But nor does Marquard exclude the possibility of mystical union through compassion with the crucified Christ at least in some way, as the three paths elaborated in the seventh sermon demonstrate. It is evident that much more work is required on the interrelationship of different approaches to the mystical union in Marquard's sermon collection. A provisional conclusion, however, can still be reached. For in the thirty-ninth sermon, on St Lawrence, Marquard deals with both principal approaches together. The second section of the sermon concerns six ways in which the divine fire operates in the individual (we will recall that Lawrence is said to have died by roasting on a gridiron). The exposition of the sixth incorporates the mystical union. The divine fire, says Marquard, becomes so strong in the individual that he turns against everything that is not pure God. He dies to all that is created. Then the love of the Holy Spirit penetrates his entire body and inflames it with fiery love. This fiery love burns away all dissimilitude to God, drives out every image and form of the created, and renders the mind naked of every mediate instance between it and God. Then a sweet fiery love is awakened in the individual, in which he experiences God's presence in a state of rest.[280] Here the soul is drawn into a union of love with God. At this point the fire of the Holy Spirit overcomes the individual's will, so that he becomes prepared to suffer anything that he may face, in order to repay Christ for his suffering. The true joy and worthiness of all people, Marquard continues, is the suffering and oppression represented by Christ's cross, because true divine love desires conformity only to the one who is beloved. It is the preparedness to live in conformity to Christ in humility, suffering, and oppression that is the sign of true love of the divine:

Vnd denn ist die sel in ainem schwigen vnd in dringen in gott, vnd gott zühet si mit im selber in sich selber vnd machet die sel ain minn mit im, als der clåren sunnen schin den morgen röt in sich zühet vnd in mit siner clårhait über glestet. Vnd beschihet denn, das

[279] Blumrich (ed.), *Marquard von Lindau. Deutsche Predigten*, pp. 63*–64*.
[280] *Predigt* 39, ll. 215–24 (p. 298); on the fire of divine love cf. i.a. *Predigten* 2, ll. 249–60 (p. 20); 5, ll. 204–7 (p. 46); 14, ll. 23–7 (p. 112); 16, ll. 83–6 (p. 121); 31, ll. 161–74 (p. 217); 38, ll. 184–94 (p. 285); 40, ll. 44–67 (pp. 302–3); and 41, ll. 107–9 (p. 313); see further Blumrich, 'Feuer der Liebe', pp. 49–53, and McGinn, *The Harvest of Mysticism*, pp. 334 and 337.

daz fúr des hailgen gaistes den willen des menschen ꝰberwindet, daz der alles das wil liden, daz im ieman an getůn mag, vmb daz, daz er sinem minner vergelte sines lidens. Vnd dãr vmb so tůt er alles daz, das er vermag, daz im liden vnd versmãht begegni. Vnd sãmlicher menschen wirdikeit vnd frŏd ist daz crúcz Jhesu Cristi, daz ist liden vnd verschmãht, wan gŏttlichi minn wil nieman gelich sinn denn dem, den si minnet. Vnd wer si von der gelichait zůhet, daz ist ir pinlich, vnd wer si stúret ze gelichait irs geminten, daz ist ir frŏd. Vnd da bi sol man bekennen reht gŏttlich minn, wan si allwend gelich wil sin irem geminten Cristo in aller demůt, liden vnd verschmãht.[281]

(Then the soul is in a state of silence and of penetration into God. God draws the soul with himself into himself and makes the soul to be one love with him, as the bright sunshine draws the roseate dawn into itself and outshines it with its brightness. At this point the fire of the Holy Spirit overcomes the individual's will, so that he wants to suffer everything that anyone may do to him, in order that he might repay his lover for his suffering. Therefore he does everything that he can so that suffering and shame may befall him. The honour and delight of all such people is the cross of Jesus Christ, which is suffering and shame, because godly love will be similar to no one, except to someone whom it loves. Someone who draws it [i.e. godly love] away from this similitude causes it pain; someone who guides it to similitude with its beloved causes it joy. From this one should recognize true godly love, for it constantly wants to be similar to its beloved Christ in all humility, suffering, and shame.)

Evidently the individual becomes more prepared to become like Christ as a result of the action of the fire of the Holy Spirit in the mystical union. But that becoming like Christ is also a general feature of the religious ('sãmlicher menschen wirdikeit vnd frŏd'; 'the honour and delight of all such people'), as the question that follows makes clear:

Die frãg: Wã bi bekennet ain mensch, wie vil er gŏttlicher minn hab? Die antwúrt: Als vil sich der mensch gelichet Cristo, als vil het er rehter gŏttlicher minn, wan Cristus leben ist die reht regel gŏttlicher minn vnd die brinnend guldin port, wer anderswa wil in gãn, der ist ain diep vnd ain morder [cf. John 10: 1].[282]

(Question: By what can an individual identify how much godly love he has? Answer: The more he is similar to Christ, the more true godly love he has, because Christ's life is the true rule of godly love and the burning, golden gate. Anyone who wishes to enter in a different way is a thief and a murderer.)

Bernard McGinn regards this section of sermon 39 as a resolution to the problem posed by the thirtieth, in which the school of Christ is located subordinate to the school of the Holy Spirit: 'the school of Christ and the school of the Holy Spirit are really the outer and inner dimensions of the

[281] *Predigt* 39, ll. 224–37 (pp. 298–9).
[282] Ibid., ll. 238–42 (p. 299).

same supreme love, as a discussion of the "divine fire" in Sermon 39 indicates.'[283] This is a reasonable assertion, but it is only a partial resolution to the overall issue. Marquard is faced with the difficulty of resolving different models of the mystical union. He rejects the purely intellective model associated with Eckhart at one end of the spectrum, and the especially 'bodily' accentuation of transformation into the crucified Christ of the *Stimulus amoris* at the other. He prioritizes a particular kind of pseudo-Dionysian union achieved through the 'apex affectionis', but at the same time does not exclude the possibility of achieving union through the crucified Christ. In this he is much less exclusive and dogmatic about the possible paths to union than his predecessors (especially Seuse), and this is probably the most significant conclusion that we can reach here regarding the mystical theology of his sermon collection. Insofar as he does consider union achieved through the crucified Christ, it does not have the character of a 'breakthrough' from the contemplation of Christ's suffering humanity into his divinity, as it does for Seuse. Instead, as the section above from sermon 39 makes clear, the love of Christ and the progress in achieving conformity to him, especially in his crucified condition, is a necessary response on the part of every individual. Achieving the mystical union does not diminish the necessity of that response; rather, it augments the individual's desire towards it.

[283] McGinn, *The Harvest of Mysticism*, p. 335.

2

The Eucharist

The sacrament of the eucharist stands at the centre of religious experience in the medieval church. In the twelfth and thirteenth centuries, the eucharist had been the subject of a series of momentous debates in which its theology had been elaborated and closely defined: partly in the refutation of heresies, partly in the scholastic attempt to describe the sacramental transformation in the language of Aristotelian categories. In the mid-thirteenth century it had acquired a religious feast day of its own, Corpus Christi, with all its attendant processions, plays, and paraphernalia. It held primary position among the Christian sacraments, which Gabriel Biel (d. 1495) would express at the end of the fifteenth century in the doctrine of the *esse permanens*: the other sacraments may confer grace, but only the eucharistic host actually contains grace.[1] Biel's doctrinal formulation may have been novel, but the sentiment was not. Earlier works on the eucharist are punctuated by statements on the primacy of the sacrament, normally on account of the real presence in the consecrated host. Marquard's *Eucharistietraktat* puts it thus:

Nu heb ich an den ersten puncten vnd wil dir ze erst sagen von edelkeit dirre spise, wie gar si vbertreffend ist alle ander kosperi vnd edelkeit. Vnd dz macht du mit sechs dingen merken. Das erst, das in diser spise beschlossen ist der brunn gôtlicher natur, der in im treit vatter, sun, heilgen geist.[2]

(Now I shall begin the first point and want to tell you first of all about this food's nobility, which far exceeds all other treasures and nobilities. You can observe this in six items. The first is that the source of the divine nature, which bears the Father, the Son, and the Holy Spirit within it, is enclosed within this food.)

---

[1] Goossens, 'Résonances eucharistiques', pp. 175–6 and 189; for Biel's theology of the eucharist see Oberman, *The Harvest of Medieval Theology*, pp. 271–80.

[2] *Eucharistietraktat*, §1 (257. 2–6). All quotations from the *Eucharistietraktat* silently incorporate the amendments to Hofmann's edition required by Ruh, 'Review of Hofmann', pp. 22–3.

This follows a statement that expresses the centrality of the eucharist to the religious experience in the most portentous tones: 'Vnd wússest, sol dir iemer gůtz von got beschechen vnd sol dir got jemer heimlich werden, dz můss durch das wirdig sacrament beschechen. Das bewiset die geschrifft'[3] ('You should know that if God is ever to grant you any good, and if he is ever to become intimate with you, this has to take place through the worthy sacrament').

The fifty-year period between 1370 and 1420 was itself a period of two momentous eucharistic controversies: of John Wyclif and the Lollards in England in the late fourteenth, and of Jan Hus and the Hussites in Bohemia in the early fifteenth century. Marquard must have been aware of the developments in England; he may well have known of the Bohemian preachers who would, in the later fourteenth century, pre-empt many of Hus's later propositions. Marquard's works on the eucharist were not written in a vacuum, nor as abstract considerations upon abstruse points of theology. Rather, they respond to particular features of contemporary eucharistic devotion and piety, which they seek to channel and redirect, just as much as Wyclif or Hus did in their works. Nor is Marquard the only intellectual to produce a substantive devotional treatise on the eucharist in this period. His near-exact contemporary Matthaeus of Cracow wrote the *Dialogus rationis et conscientiae* in 1388, and responded to the same set of issues that was exercising Marquard. A veritable plethora of material was being written in Bohemia, notably the sermon collections of Jan Milíč of Kroměříž (Johannes Milicius de Chremsir) and Matthew of Janov's *Regulae veteris et novi Testamenti*. Certainly the most important of all these Bohemian works, the work with the most enduring, pan-European significance, was Jan Hus's *De sanguine Christi*, written in 1405 when Hus still occupied a senior position in the Bohemian ecclesiastical hierarchy. The production of so many long treatises on the nature of eucharistic devotion is very much a 'sign of the times'—an indication that in the later fourteenth century, certain problematic trends in the eucharistic cult reached a cumulative tipping point. The reaction that was provoked varied geographically, from Wyclif's explosive assault on the established orthodoxy of the eucharistic doctrine to the meandering reflections of Matthaeus of Cracow, but the points of departure for the reactions, the underlying issues preoccupying each author, are very often the same. As we look closely at Marquard, we will be able to trace the development of individual reactions 'vertically'—across time—whilst comparing those reactions 'horizontally', by drawing on the other major contemporary eucharistic works.

---

[3] *Eucharistietraktat*, prologue (256. 5–8).

Marquard dealt with the eucharist first in four sermons that form a short
German treatise, now known as *De corpore Christi*. The contents of this
work were then incorporated into his main treatise on the subject, the
Eucharistietraktat, at some point in the approximate period 1370–90.[4]
Given that *De corpore Christi* was almost totally integrated into the *Eucharistietraktat*, it will not play a part in our examination, except at the very
rare points where it provides additional or divergent material from the
corresponding section of the latter work.[5] Further, two German sermons in
the collection Marquard produced in 1389 concern the eucharist.[6] In the
previous chapter, we have already dealt extensively with Marquard's sermons on the Passion from the same collection, and so we shall largely omit
consideration of these eucharistic sermons here.

The *Eucharistietraktat* (in the form edited by Hofmann) consists of
fourteen sections, structured as a master–pupil dialogue. The deficiencies
of Hofmann's edition and of her categorization and analysis of the major
recensions have been exhaustively and repeatedly noted.[7] The necessary re-
evaluation of the manuscript transmission would go beyond the remit of
this study, and Hofmann's categorization must be regarded as provisional.
She identifies four main recensions: Ia, in fourteen sections; Ib, in twelve
sections, lacking the short sections 12 and 13 and restructured as a dialogue
between a heavenly emissary (*bote*) and a bride of Christ; Ic, a heavily
extended version of Ia in twenty-four sections; and II, which lacks the
lengthy third section, a *Meßerklärung*, or exposition of the mass.[8]

It is not clear which of the extant recensions represents Marquard's
original work. Ic is almost certainly a later version. It contains a second
Meßerklärung, rather different in nature to the first[9] and drawing on Albert
the Great's bipartite treatise *Super missam* and the German sermons

[4] See Palmer, 'Marquard von Lindau', cols. 98–9, and Willing, *Literatur und Ordensreform*, pp. 176–7.
[5] *De corpore Christi* is not edited. Only three of the eight extant manuscripts contain
all four sections. Where necessary, I cite from Mainz, Stadtbibliothek, Hs. I 51, fols.
4ra–13ra, a mid-15th-cent. manuscript in a Central Rhenish dialect: see List and Powitz,
Die Handschriften der Stadtbibliothek Mainz, pp. 105–11. This may well represent a
subsequent recension of the treatise. I have been unable to secure a microfilm copy of
Dillingen, Studienbibliothek, cod. XV 125, fols. 15v–39r; Nuremberg, Stadtbibliothek,
cod. Cent. VI, 60, 79r–106v (the only other complete manuscript) certainly does contain
a divergent later recension: see Palmer, 'Marquard von Lindau', col. 99.
[6] *Predigten* 33 (pp. 231–7) and 34 (pp. 238–42).
[7] Ruh, 'Review of Hofmann'; Willing, *Literatur und Ordensreform*, pp. 166–9.
[8] Hofmann (ed.), *Der Eucharistie-Traktat*, pp. 174–225.
[9] See ibid. 247; on the nature of the first *Meßerklärung* see Willing, *Literatur und
Ordensreform*, pp. 180–1.

of Berthold von Regensburg, together with other sections that are compiled, in part, from Marquard's sermons 33 and 34.[10] The existence of the Ic recension is a testimony to the tendency of the *Eucharistietraktat* to become a compendious work of theological instruction on the sacrament in its later transmission. Of the two earlier recensions, Ia and Ib, neither is obviously prior. Kurt Ruh suspected that Ib represented the earlier form, which would imply a treatise written for an audience of religious women.[11] He was, however, unaware of the existence of what is now the earliest known manuscript—not a dialogue between a *bote* and a bride of Christ of the Ib recension, but a master–pupil dialogue of the Ia recension copied in 1391: one year before Marquard died. Nonetheless, this manuscript (Stuttgart, Württembergische Landesbibliothek, cod. theol. et philos. 4° 54) was written and owned by a Dominican nun at Reuthin in Württemberg. We cannot therefore postulate that the Ia recension did not circulate amongst religious women, whilst the Ib recension did.[12] The comprehensive analysis of the manuscript transmission that would test any such hypothesis may also help ascertain the priority of the Ia and Ib recensions: though as the earliest manuscript of the Ib recension dates from 1394 (Zurich, Zentralbibliothek, C 102 c), it is plausible that both recensions may derive from Marquard's own pen. Alongside the manuscripts of the complete work there exists a substantial transmission of individual sections of the treatise. From the 'original' form, whatever that may have been, two divergent tendencies in the transmission of the work can be detected: the expansion into a compendious handbook on eucharistic theology, represented by recension Ic; and the reverse tendency, the fragmentation of the treatise and the transmission of particular sections as guides to particular issues.

---

[10] Hofmann (ed.), *Der Eucharistie-Traktat*, pp. 195–207; Illing, *Alberts des Großen >Super Missam<-Traktat*, pp. 16–26 and 58–63; Willing, *Literatur und Ordensreform*, pp. 167–8.

[11] Ruh, 'Rezension zu Hofmann', p. 20.

[12] Stuttgart, Württembergische Landesbibliothek, cod. theol. et philos. 4° 54, also contains Marquard's *Dekalogerklärung* (B² recension) on fols. 2ʳ–125ᵛ, with the *Eucharistietraktat* following on fols. 125ᵛ–183ʳ. The scribal colophon at fol. 186ʳ reads: 'Hie ist ain end diser bûch von den gebotten vnsers herren, vnd ist geschriben worden in dem zit do man zalt von cristus geburt drúzehen hundert iăr vnd in dem ainen vnd núnczigosten iăr. Wer dis bûch hab oder vinde, der gebe es mehthilten der schenkinen, closterfrôwen ze Rúti. Gedenkent min och durch got' ('This is the end of the book of our Lord's commandments, which was copied in the year 1391. If someone should have or find this book, he should give it to Mechthild Schenkin, nun at Reuthin. Remember me too for God's sake'). 'Rúti' is the Dominican female convent of Reuthin near Wildberg on the Nagold. Despite the early date, neither of the works is attributed to Marquard in the manuscript.

The *Eucharistietraktat* was not the first treatise on the eucharist to be written in German. Already available was the *Buch von den Sechs Namen des Fronleichnams* of the Mönch von Heilsbronn: a Cistercian work heavily dependent upon Albert the Great's *De corpore Domini* (one half of the *Super missam*) and the Cistercian *Sermones Socci*, and written probably during the first quarter of the fourteenth century. By omitting much of Albert's theological instruction and interpolating three long excurses on contemplation, the *Buch von den Sechs Namen* becomes a German-language guide, rather theoretical in tone, to the role of the eucharist in the contemplative life.[13] Just over fifty manuscripts contain either the full work or excerpts from it. By contrast, the *Eucharistietraktat* survives in at least sixty-eight manuscripts with the full version in German, six manuscripts in Latin translations, and at least sixty-one manuscripts with one or more sections excerpted from the full work.[14] The only other German work to approach the *Eucharistietraktat*'s breadth of transmission is the German translation(s) of Matthaeus of Cracow's *Dialogus rationis et conscientiae*. This work, written in 1388, was translated into German even prior to 1400 in Silesian dialect—perhaps, as Beifuss suggests, by one of the substantial Silesian community resident in Prague, or as Schmidtke suggests, by one of Matthaeus' Silesian students in that city.[15] A total of twenty-eight copies, evidently several different translations, are extant.[16] The Latin version enjoyed an enormous transmission of around 250 manuscripts, with a particularly strong concentration in Germany.[17]

If the *Eucharistietraktat*, with its prologue that invites the reader to approach the sacrament as the bride of Solomon came to Jerusalem,[18] may indicate an implicit audience of religious women, the implicit audience of the *Dialogus* is clerical. This can be seen, for example, in the discussions in the work of the frequency of, and attitude towards,

---

[13] See the comprehensive analysis of the *Buch von den Sechs Namen* in Willing, *Literatur und Ordensreform*, pp. 95–131; and Steer, 'Mönch von Heilsbronn'.

[14] A conspectus is provided by Palmer, 'Marquard von Lindau', cols. 99–100. To the list of complete manuscripts can be added Berlin, SBB-PK, Hdschr. 242, fols. 82^r–209^r.

[15] See Beifuss, 'Matthäus von Krakau', pp. 990–4, and Schmidtke, 'Pastoraltheologische Texte', pp. 182–8; for Matthaeus' biography see now Nuding, *Matthäus von Krakau*.

[16] See the conspectus in Worstbrock, 'Matthäus von Krakau', cols. 180–1, and the additional manuscripts noted in Beifuss, 'Ein frühneuhochdeutsches Erbauungsbuch', p. 14 n. 21; see pp. 15–22 for an outline classification of the different translations.

[17] A conspectus is provided by Seńko and Szafrański (eds.), *Mateusza z Krakowa*, pp. 356–63; and Worstbrock, 'Matthäus von Krakau', cols. 177–8.

[18] *Eucharistietraktat*, prologue (254. 1–255. 14).

celebrating the mass.[19] It is, however, not an exclusive restriction. In the first section, to take another example, the value of the priest's celebration of the mass (and the harm that may come to a priest who does not celebrate the mass) is discussed, and Conscience, whom Reason seeks to persuade, is convinced by Reason's arguments.[20] Yet Conscience moves the dialogue onwards by stating that she is only convinced insofar as these arguments apply to priests. They have no relevance either to the laity or to priests who are personally *indispositus* to receive the sacrament because of sin they have committed, but not yet confessed.[21] The next sections then expand the framework of the dialogue to consider these groups, though by no means in a systematic manner: the content of the treatise applies generally, except where priests are specifically addressed. Matthaeus is known to have been engaged in close pastoral relationships with devout citizens of Prague, and the personal, affective tone of the work reflects this lay element alongside the explicit priestly audience.[22]

The evident difference in implicit audience between the *Eucharistietrak-tat* and the *Dialogus* must be noted, but it does not substantially restrict the opportunity to use the two works comparatively. Their authors were exact contemporaries (Matthaeus of Cracow lived a little longer, and died in 1410) and the two works written within no more than a few years of one another. Neither is intended as a reference work or a purely theological exposition, but rather as devotional, exhortatory treatises, which their dialogic forms suit. Most significantly, they both deal with the same issues: though as a general characterization, Marquard's treatise covers more ground in less depth, whilst the *Dialogus* handles a smaller set of issues in an often long-winded fashion. They thus form useful foils for one another.

We shall look first at the purpose of the *Eucharistietraktat* to gain a solid starting point. This allows us to address the key issue: the problem of 'worthy reception' and fear of the sacrament, with the related matters of spiritual communion and the frequency of reception. We will then see how Marquard's attitude to *exempla* concerning the eucharist furthers the

---

[19] See e.g. the discussion of the attitude the priest should adopt who is required to celebrate the mass repeatedly (notably ll. 904a–908): Matthaeus of Cracow, *Dialogus*, §8, ll. 900–919a (p. 397). The edition of the *Dialogus* is inaccurately numbered. Every fifth line should be numbered, but the number of lines counted as five varies: the treatise contains about one-fifth more lines than line numbers. Here the lower-case letters a, b, and c will be used to indicate the sixth, seventh, and eighth lines of what the edition presents as a five-line block.

[20] Matthaeus of Cracow, *Dialogus*, §1, ll. 81–170 (pp. 369–72).

[21] Ibid., ll. 176–93 (pp. 372–3).

[22] Marin, *L'Archevêque, le maître et le dévot*, pp. 483–5.

purpose of the work and marks a sharp break with convention. There is little purpose in setting out the eucharistic theology of the *Eucharistietraktat* (or of the *Dialogus*): it is, as we would expect, completely orthodox. We must focus instead on two significant theological issues, in which the *Eucharistietraktat* takes an aggressive stance towards the prevailing direction of contemporary piety: the perception of sweetness in the sacrament, and the interrelated complex of eucharistic visions and the cult of the holy blood. Here we will be able to draw together a much larger amount of evidence, using the *Eucharistietraktat* as a starting point: both to position this treatise historically, and to document the wider histories of these issues. Finally, we will complete the picture of Marquard's attitude to the eucharist with an examination of the incorporation of mystical thought in the *Eucharistietraktat*.

In a recent article, Miri Rubin puts forward the hypothesis that by the mid-fifteenth century, the ecclesiastical establishment sought to reclaim and relocate the eucharist from amongst its cultic trappings, 'as the church sensed that its perfect symbol of mediation became too charged and overdetermined with conflicting meanings [. . .]. The material manifestation of the divine had been exhausted through the development of edifices of images, meanings and uses which at once fragmented it as a central symbol and over-burdened it as a collective token.'[23] I shall argue that the 'tipping point' in the eucharistic cult occurred much earlier, in the last quarter of the fourteenth century, when the series of long and important treatises on eucharistic devotion mentioned above was produced almost simultaneously across northern Europe. But that a reaction took place is beyond doubt.

Certainly, the cult of the eucharist was in full swing, even if its zenith was yet to be reached—sacramental processions and confraternities, the icing on the cake for the cult, appear to be a fifteenth-century phenomenon.[24] In the fourteenth century, and especially after 1350, visions and other kinds of eucharistic miracles came to predominate in hagiographies, notably in those of religious women. They supplanted the more traditional healing miracles in the *vitae*, and so altered the paradigm of what constituted sanctity.[25] Germany in particular teemed with miraculous hosts that had either appeared to bleed or resisted fire (and sometimes both), which became—most famously at Wilsnack—enormously popular centres of

---

[23] Rubin, 'The Eucharist', here p. 59.
[24] See Sprandel, 'Der Sakramentskult', pp. 301–2.
[25] See Vauchez, *The Laity*, ch. 20 (pp. 237–42), esp. p. 242.

pilgrimage, and we will look at these later.[26] In Strasbourg, a principal site
of Marquard's activity, the feast of Corpus Christi had been introduced
gradually and rather late into its various churches—not until the 1320s is it
established in all the main institutions.[27] Even so, it had been established
there for at least two generations by Marquard's time.

Specifically important for works like the *Eucharistietraktat* and the
Dialogus, which focus on the attitude towards reception of the sacrament,
are the practices of elevation and exposition of the host. The elevation of
the host at the point of consecration had become standard practice in the
ritual conduct of the mass by around 1200. The connection between the
sacrament and the Passion of Christ became stronger in the fourteenth
century, with the relatively general recommendation of the use of the
Lord's Prayer during the elevation and communion giving way to prayers
relating to the Passion.[28] A further change was experienced in the later
fourteenth century, with the practice of exposing a consecrated host on the
altar during the celebrations of a feast day. This began, following Godefridus Snoek's conclusions, as a feature of the Corpus Christi feast, and was
a German phenomenon. It is first recorded in 1372, when it was permitted
by the bishop of Brandenburg for his diocese. It quickly expanded both
geographically and in terms of the frequency and duration of the exposition. As early as 1416 the bishop of Passau restricted the practice of
exposing the host on the altar, which had been commonly taking place
most days of the week, as he feared habitual exposition would promote
irreverence to the sacrament.[29] It was certainly a development of which
Marquard would have been aware. The first mention of the exposition
during matins is to be found in a Strasbourg *ordinarium* of 1374, for the
feast day of Corpus Christi, and the practice quickly spread. By this time,
the host was normally exposed in a monstrance: another fourteenth-century
innovation over earlier practice, when the host had been kept in a closed
pyx, and one which represents an increasing tendency to treat the host in
the same way as a relic.[30]

[26] See the useful conspectus of the sites at which miraculous hosts were kept and
venerated in Browe, *Die eucharistischen Wunder*, pp. 139–46; and now Bynum, *Wonderful Blood*, esp. pp. 49–68.
[27] Barth, 'Fronleichnamsfest', pp. 233–5.
[28] Caspers, *De eucharistische vroomheid*, pp. 187–92.
[29] Snoek, *Medieval Piety*, pp. 283–4.
[30] Ibid. 286–90.

The development of the cult of the eucharist in this way served to create a climate of awe and, indeed, fear of the sacrament. The doctrine of transubstantiation added to this climate by emphasizing the gulf between humanity and God—the natural confronted immediately by the supernatural. Awe and evident displays of devotion to the sacrament were not merely a feature of late fourteenth-century eucharistic piety, but were, in the mindset of the devout, even required. From Matthaeus' *Dialogus*, we can see that this went as far as the opinion that a person who did not make evident displays of devotion and fervour to the sacrament was less worthy to receive it. Reason rails against this, arguing angrily that a priest, carrying out his duties, is no less worthy than an enclosed contemplative to receive; that devotion is wrongly believed to consist in the manifestation of obvious, external signs of fervour; and finally, that a person's goodness (and implicitly, their worthiness to receive the sacrament) depended on the virtue of their mind, rather than on the fervent manifestation of their devotion.

Ratio: [. . .] sed quid putas esse devotionem?
Conscientia: Nihil aliud nisi, sicut describi solet, promptitudinem animi et fervorem bonae voluntatis ad Deo serviendum quam mens cohibere non valens certis manifestat indiciis.
Ratio: Putas quod illa sola habeantur et ostendantur in suspiriis et lacrimis et non etiam in praedicando, confessiones audiendo ac aliis operibus misericordiae tam corporalibus quam spiritualibus.
Conscientia: Bene credo quod etiam in istis habeantur, sed ut communiter magis ac dulcius in obsecratione quam occupatione.
Ratio: Haec consistit in gratia Dei, sed, licet ut communiter contemplativi magis devoti sint et fervidi, non tamen propter hoc activis bonis neganda est communio, cum etiam unus contemplativorum magis devotus sit alio, nec tamen propter hoc minus devotus abstinere tenetur, maxime cum bonitas hominis plus multo consistit in virtute animi quam fervore.[31]

(Reason: [. . .] But what do you think devotion is?
Conscience: Nothing other than as it is usually described: the readiness of the soul and the ardour of the good will to serve God, which the mind is unable to restrain and so manifests with evident signs.
Reason: You think that these are only to be contained and displayed in sighs and tears, but not in preaching, hearing confessions, and in other works of mercy, both corporeal and spiritual.

---

[31] Matthaeus of Cracow, *Dialogus*, §3, ll. 439–55 (pp. 381–2). See also §3, ll. 399–406 (p. 380), in which Reason objects to external manifestations of fervent devotion being used as the yardstick to judge an individual's suitability to receive the sacrament: they are, says Reason, entirely unrelated.

Conscience: I do believe that they are also contained in these things, but, as it is generally held, more so—and more sweetly—in prayers than in actions.
Reason: That depends on the grace of God; but, although contemplatives may, as it is generally held, be more fervent and devout, communion is nevertheless not to be denied because of this to those who are good and living the active life. Similarly, although one contemplative may be more devout than another, the less devout one is not bound to abstain because of this—most of all because the goodness of man depends far more on the soul's virtue than on its ardour.)

We shall look presently in closer detail at the precise reasons for fear of the sacrament, which represented the major problem in the eucharistic cult in the later fourteenth century. But first, with this background in mind, we should turn to Marquard, and to the purpose of the *Eucharistietraktat*.

In its edited and earliest extant form, this treatise contains fourteen sections that are not ordered according to a strict system. Certainly, the sections dealing with theology and doctrine come towards the beginning; those dealing with the preparation for reception of the sacrament are grouped in the middle; and those dealing with the rewards of reception are at the end. Beyond this outline, however, the structure is dependent more on association by common theme rather than on a clear and systematic progression. Yet that does not mean that the treatise is an incoherent selection of considerations upon an essentially random selection of points. Underlying the treatise is a central principle, to which all other concerns are subordinated: the stimulation of love and desire to approach and receive the sacrament. Other elements, like the transmission of information on eucharistic theology or the provision of instructions on preparing for reception, are included only insofar as they further this central aim. This is encapsulated in the prologue, in which Marquard makes a definite statement on the purpose of the work to this effect:

Vnd dar vmb das vwer minn dester fúrbas gereitzt weid zů dem sacrament vnd zů der edlen spise des himelschen Salomones, vnd ich ettwas gnůg sig vwer begird, so wil ich úch XIIII stuk sagen von diser spise. Vnd beger, dz si von dem himelschen Salomon, vwerm gemachel, in vwer hertz getruket werdent vnd mit frucht an gesechen.[32]

(So that your love is stimulated all the more towards the sacrament and towards the noble food of the heavenly Solomon, and so that I may satisfy your desire somewhat, I will tell you fourteen things about this food. Desire that they may be impressed into your heart by the heavenly Solomon, your bridegroom, and gazed upon fruitfully.)

[32] *Eucharistietraktat*, prologue (256. 9–14).

The treatise is punctuated throughout by exhortations to adopt an attitude of love towards the sacrament. The first section, for example, outlines six nobilities (*edelkeiten*) of the eucharist. *Edelkeit* is neither a precise nor an easily definable term. It signifies a distinguishing theological feature of the sacrament that demonstrates its eminence: such as the presence of the Trinity in the host by virtue of the hypostatic union, or Christ's soul radiating from the sacrament and illuminating the angels. The section concludes with a piece of exhortation, in which Marquard states clearly the primary purpose of detailing the *edelkeiten*:

Dis han ich dir geseit von der edelkeit dirre wirdigen spise, dar vmb, das du ein senden iamer nach dem herren gewinnest, den du in diser spise vindest[, v]nd mit diner begird uss Egipten land varest zů dem ewigen kúng Salomon zů der himelschen Jherusalem.[33]

(I have told you this about the nobility of this worthy food so that you will acquire a longing heartache for the Lord, whom you find in this food, and will journey through your desire out of Egypt to the eternal King Solomon, to the heavenly Jerusalem.)

The second section then sets out seven miracles (*wunder*) of the sacrament, which are further features of eucharistic theology. Unlike the nobilities, they are more closely focused on the sacramental transformation, and the section allows Marquard to transmit doctrinal information. These doctrinal points are subordinated to the underlying principle of stimulating love of and for the sacrament, as we see in Marquard's reference back to the second section as he begins the third:

Der Meister sprach: Ich beger, daz dir dise vorgeschribne puncten ein reitzen sig zů dem himelschen Salomon, won wnderlich ding sicht man gern und was seltzen ist, das hat man gerne. Vnd wan du wol brůfest, das so vil wunderlicher wisen in dem sacrament sind, das sol dir ein zeichen sin zů im, dz din hertz in begirden dar zů bewegt werde, daz es von Egipto aller zitlicheit var in begirden zů dem wnderlichen ewigen Salomon, den du in dem sacrament in so grossen wndren vindest.[34]

(The master said: My desire is that these aforesaid points may stimulate you to the heavenly Solomon; for wondrous things are eagerly seen, and rare things are coveted. As you grasp clearly that there are so many wondrous aspects to the sacrament, this should be a sign to point you towards him; so that your heart may

---

[33] *Eucharistietraktat*, §1 (261. 10–14).
[34] Ibid., §3 (267. 27–34). See also a similar passage in the conclusion, at §14 (323. 23–324. 2).

be impelled in desire to journey out of the Egypt of the temporal world to the wondrous eternal Solomon, whom you find in the sacrament in such great miracles.)

The love is reciprocal, as Marquard indicates in an important statement in the fourth section:

[. . .] soltu wússen, dz der wirdig kúng nit ist in der gesegneten ofloten in eines herren wise oder in eines richters wise, mer er ist da in eins minnriches vatters wise, als lieplich vnd als begirlich. Vnd wer es muglich, dz du in sechest, so sechest du in nit in zornlicher wise, mer du sechest in da mit zertanen armen, bereit, den menschen umb ze vachen, der in enpfachen wil. Also ist sin gestalt in aller lieplicheit vnd in minricheit.[35]

([. . .] You should know that the worthy king is not in the consecrated host in the manner of a ruler or a judge, but rather he is there in the manner of a loving father, as lovable and as desirable. If it were possible for you to see him, you would not see him in a furious state; rather, you would see him there with outstretched arms, ready to embrace the individual who wants to receive him. This is the manner of his appearance, in the fullness of love and affection.)

Many more examples could be adduced. Marquard's aim throughout is to create a correct attitude in the reader towards the eucharist. On the one hand, he provides evidence of the sacrament's distinction and preeminence, to encourage proper respect towards it and so to God. On the other, he subordinates all these considerations to an overarching discourse of the stimulation of love, not fear, for the sacrament and so promoting the love of God. Nowhere is this balancing act clearer than in a statement in the seventh section:

[D]er rich gewaltig kúng [súchte] in diser spise gerechtikeit des mentschen, so soltest du sin billich erschreken. Aber ich sag dir, das er dise spis als vss grundloser minne hatt vff gesetzt vnd als gar des menschen vnwirdikeit vergessen het, dz ich dir niemer den minsten teil kan gesagen.[36]

(The mighty and powerful king sought the justification of mankind in this food, and so you ought rightfully be afraid of it. But I tell you this, that he has established this food out of such bottomless love, and has forgotten the unworthiness of mankind so completely, that I can never tell you even the smallest part of it.)

---

[35] Ibid., §4 (281. 22–8).
[36] Ibid., §7 (299. 27–9). See also a similar statement by the pupil on what he has learnt, at §5 (284. 34–285. 10), and Marquard's subsequent statement that those who truly love God are called to receive the sacrament more truly than those who happen to fulfil the formal requirements, at §5 (285. 25–31).

The impetus of Bonaventura's caritative theology, which we have already seen with regard to the Passion, is clear—and the eucharist is, after all, the memorial of the Passion.[37] Just as love moved Christ to suffer and die, so the eucharist is established of God's bottomless love, which love is to be met by the love of man for God. The key to understanding the intention underlying Marquard's purpose in this treatise is, however, not Bonaventura. It is indicated by a phrase in the quotation cited above: God, says Marquard, has totally forgotten man's unworthiness.

This alludes to the central problem surrounding the eucharist in the late fourteenth century: fear of the sacrament, and its corollary, the individual's sense of worthiness to receive. Put simply, only a person who was worthy of reception had nothing to fear as a consequence. This is not the same issue as the more general awe of the sacrament itself that the development of its cult had provoked, though that certainly contributed to the fear of reception. It is a much more serious issue that has theological roots. The problem was not just that the eucharistic host was the body of Christ (and the doctrine of transubstantiation made that real presence more real than it had ever been before) and therefore innately to be feared, but the interpretation of a crucial passage of Scripture from Paul's first letter to the Corinthians:

[I]taque quicumque manducaverit panem vel biberit calicem Domini indigne, reus erit corporis et sanguinis Domini. Probet autem se ipsum homo, et sic de pane illo edat et de calice bibat. Qui enim manducat et bibit indigne, iudicium sibi manducat et bibit. [1 Cor. 11: 27–9]

(Therefore whoever eats the bread or drinks the cup of the Lord unworthily is guilty of the body and blood of the Lord. Let a man however inspect himself, and so let him eat of that bread and drink of that cup. For he who eats and drinks unworthily, eats and drinks judgement to himself.)

The scriptural basis for the celebration of the eucharist rested, the evangelists' descriptions of the Last Supper aside, on Paul's description of the rite in 1 Corinthians 11: 20–34. Paul requires that each person examine himself ('probet autem se ipsum homo'), and implicitly make a statement of his worthiness to receive: for the unworthy recipient brings divine judgement upon himself. The centrality of this statement in the scriptural foundations of the eucharist made it inescapable, its force amplified against the background of the highly developed late medieval art of introspective confession. In the medieval liturgy the passage was prescribed as the epistolary reading for Maundy Thursday, immediately prior to the paschal reception

[37] See esp. the relevant sections in the *Meßerklärung* of the *Eucharistietraktat*: §3 (271. 4–26 and 273. 11–277. 13).

of the sacrament required of all the faithful by the Fourth Lateran Council.[38] Sven Grosse, who mentions the fear of sacramental reception only very briefly in his study of late medieval scrupulosity, nonetheless regards it as more severe than the fear associated with confession, which forms the main basis for his own study.[39] The consequences of unworthy communion were genuinely terrifying. For Hugo Ripelin von Straßburg, author of the *Compendium theologicae veritatis*, these numerous consequences included an early death:

Sicut recte communicantibus multa bona proveniunt, ut dictum est, sic indigne sumentibus corpus Christi multa mala occurrunt. Nullius enim opus placet Deo, nisi placeat ipse prius. Indigna enim communio peccatis hominem illaqueat, damnationem praeparat, proximum scandalizat, mentem excaecat, tentationi subjugat, Deum irritat, vitam temporalem breviat, gratuitis spoliat.[40]

(Just as many benefits come to those who receive the sacrament well, as was said, so many evils befall those who consume the body of Christ unworthily. For the work of no man is pleasing to God, unless he may first himself please him. Unworthy communion in fact ensnares man in sins, prepares his damnation, gives offence to his neighbour, blinds his mind, subjugates him to temptation, angers God, shortens his temporal life, and deprives him of the gifts of grace.)

A second contributory factor within this complex was the possibility of spiritual communion: receiving the benefits of the sacrament without actually receiving the eucharistic host itself. The practice seems to have originated from a late twelfth-century development, namely refusing to administer the eucharistic host to a sick or dying person who was in danger of regurgitating the host. Instead, the host was placed on the heart or the head, to benefit the person by the presence of Christ in the sacrament.[41] In the first half of the thirteenth century, the first discussions of spiritual communion as a concept are to be found, in the works of William of Auxerre (d. 1231) and Guiard of Laon (d. 1248).[42] It comes as no surprise that both spent most of their careers at the University of Paris, and were active there at exactly the same time when the theology of reception was being elaborated. The ideal form of reception was, of course, to receive the

---

[38] Caspers, '*Meum summum desiderium*', p. 140.

[39] Grosse, *Heilsungewißheit und Scrupulositas*, pp. 201–2.

[40] Hugo Ripelin von Straßburg, *Compendium theologicae veritatis*, lib. 6, c. 16 (pp. 213b–215a), here pp. 214b–215a.

[41] See Caspers, *De eucharistische vroomheid*, pp. 95–6.

[42] On William, see Macy, *Treasures*, pp. 175–6; on Guiard, see Caspers, *De eucharistische vroomheid*, p. 96.

res et sacramentum: to receive the eucharistic host (the *sacramentum*) and to comprehend and communicate with what it actually was—the real presence of Christ, the *res* of the sacrament. Yet just as it was possible to receive the *sacramentum* without understanding what it was, so it was equally possible to receive the *res* without the *sacramentum*: to communicate with Christ, without receiving the eucharistic host itself. This idea of spiritual communion became widespread from the mid-thirteenth century, and was treated in a number of influential works. It quickly became allied to the idea of the priest as the head of the mystical body of the congregation. The priest received sacramentally, and the congregation looked on and participated spiritually.[43] Simply looking at the sacrament was not generally considered to have any particular benefit; spiritual communion was only held to be beneficial if the participant had prepared himself suitably beforehand and approached the sacrament with the required devotion and intent.[44] Given these preconditions, it was held to be just as efficacious as sacramental reception.

The popularity and growth of the practice of spiritual communion was in part related to ecclesiastical restrictions on the permissible frequency of sacramental reception, an issue we will address shortly. Primarily, though, its growth was a response to the fear of sacramental reception that derived from a new emphasis in preaching and in devotional works on 1 Corinthians 11: 29: the necessity of introspective preparation and the need to be sufficiently worthy to receive the sacrament and not bring down judgement upon oneself. This danger was not present in spiritual communion—but all the benefits of reception were.[45] That fear of sacramental reception had begun to become problematic can be seen as early as the mid-thirteenth century. The Franciscan David von Augsburg (d. 1272) considered the related issue of the proper frequency of reception in his famous treatise *De exterioris et interioris hominis compositione*. Therein he noted the existence of two kinds of person, those who would happily receive, and those who were absolutely terrified of the sacrament:

---

[43] See Macy, *Treasures*, pp. 179–80; Caspers, 'The Western Church', pp. 86–8, and id., '*Meum summum desiderium*', pp. 135–9.

[44] See Caspers, 'The Western Church', p. 90. The further development of the practice was linked to the introduction of the exposition of the consecrated host during the mass: see Snoek, *Medieval Piety*, pp. 203–5.

[45] See further Caspers, *De eucharistische vroomheid*, pp. 213–15, Browe, *Die häufige Kommunion*, pp. 147–8, and Rubin, *Corpus Christi*, pp. 148–52.

Alii etiam ardentiori desiderio trahuntur ad illius salutaris cibi perceptionem; alii vero quodammodo terrentur, cum debent accedere, et nisi conscientia urgeret, vel consuetudo Religionis indiceret, vel timor maioris a Deo elongationis impelleret; valde raro accederent ad illud terrificum Sacramentum.[46]

(Some are drawn by more fervent desire to the reception of this beneficial food. But others are, in a certain way, terrified when they ought to go to receive; and unless conscience were to drive them, the custom of the Christian religion were to enjoin it, or the fear of greater estrangement from God were to impel them, then they would only very rarely go to receive that terrifying sacrament.)

The issue is clearly in the back of David's mind, for he makes the point later that reception is not contingent on worthiness, but makes the recipient worthy:

[. . .] eum [i.e. Christ] non recipimus, quasi qui digni simus, sed ut, illo nos saepe visitante et habitaculum cordis et corporis nostri subintrante, magis ac magis digni efficiamur.[47]

(We do not receive him as if we were worthy people, but so that, with him visiting us often and entering the dwelling place of our hearts and bodies, we may be made more and more worthy.)

Whilst David does set out a series of guidelines for the appropriate frequency of sacramental reception, he does not discuss fear of the sacrament and worthy reception much further. In the mid-thirteenth century, the problem had not developed the gravity it would have in the late fourteenth.

The emergence of 'worthiness' as a criterion of judgement, and as a necessary precondition for sacramental reception, can be seen in a work by another Franciscan: this time, Nicholas of Lyra (d. 1340). Nicholas's *Dicta de sacramento* (also known as *De sacramento eucharistiae*) is a short treatise that sets out fourteen requirements that a person desiring to receive the eucharist must fulfil. Many of these are formal conditions, such as being an adult, being both baptized and confirmed, and not knowingly being in an unconfessed state of mortal sin. Amongst them, though, is the seventh criterion: that the person should be *devotus*. The sacrament, says Nicholas, is a spiritual food that ought to be consumed spiritually. A person without sufficient devotion receives unworthily: 'Sic eciam si quis deuocionis caret ardore, dignus non est ad sumendum cibum sacramentalem'[48] ('And thus

---

[46] David von Augsburg, *De compositione*, lib. 3, c. 70, §1 (pp. 374–5).

[47] Ibid., §3 (p. 377).

[48] Nicholas of Lyra, *Dicta de sacramento*, §7. I cite from the earliest incunable edition of 1473, in which Nicholas's *Dicta* were printed after (pseudo-)Aquinas' *De venerabili sacramento altaris* (Cologne: printer of Augustine, 'De fide', 8 Apr. 1473). [Copy

someone who lacks the fervour of devotion is unworthy to consume the
sacramental food'). It is precisely the usage of such an inchoate concept as
devotus as a criterion to judge the permissibility of an individual to receive
the sacrament that leads to the fear of reception. An individual can never
truly be sure that he is sufficiently devout to be a worthy recipient. It is
exactly this problem that we saw Matthaeus of Cracow complaining about
in the *Dialogus* earlier. And unworthy reception, as Nicholas makes clear
when outlining why reception is withheld from those in an unconfessed
state of mortal sin, is itself a mortal sin.[49] In comparison to others, Nicholas
is tame on this issue: the terrible consequences of unworthy reception were
generally hammered home with the most blood-curdling *exempla*, of which
we shall see some specimens later.

Worthiness for reception and fear of the sacrament emerge as a major
subject in Marquard's *Eucharistietraktat*. In the sixth section, Marquard
outlines the necessary attitude that the individual who is to receive the
sacrament should hold. He is quite firm that the prospective recipient
should be cognizant of his *un*worthiness, and is absolutely certain that a
feeling of being too sinful to receive should not hold anyone back from
sacramental reception. He concludes:

Nu merke, dz ich dir geseit han, wie du dich vor dem tisch, e du zůgangest, halten
solt. Won du solt dich in vorcht vnd in demůtikeit diner vnwirdikeit zem ersten
neigen. Vnd zů dem andren mal soltu ein gůtes getrúwen zů der erbermd gottes han.
Zů dem dritten mal soltu begern, dz du von der krafft des edelen sacramentes
gebessret werdest, also dz dich minne diner besserunge dar zů tribe. Dise drú ding
sind gar notdurfftig einem jeklichen menschen, e er zů gat, vnd sind licht an in
selber, das merkest du wol. Hier vmb etlich menschen, die da sechend in ir súnd, die
wellent dar vmb ân dz sacrament sin. Das sol nit sin. Si sond den artzat dester balder
sůchen, dz jnen ir súnd werd abgenomen, vnd sond sprechen: „Her, kum bald in
min hus, e dz min sel noch me sterb!" Vnd wússest, wenn ein mensch ein demůtig
vorcht hat, jn der er sich unwirdig bekennet, vnd er ein gůt getrúwen zů der gůti
gottes hat vnd begert, in dem sacrament gebessret werden, so mag er wol zůgan, won
es ist zů einer notdurfft gnůg hie mit.[50]

---

consulted: Oxford, Bodleian Library, Auct. 1 Q 5. 34 (12), which contains this book
bound with 13 other quarto prints, all from Cologne and mainly from the workshop of
Ulrich Zell: see *Bod-inc* T-185 (p. 2520) and A-541 (p. 312).] The date of composition
of the text is unknown. It is considered authentic on account of its uniform attribution to
Nicholas in all extant manuscripts and printed editions: see Labrosse, 'Œuvres de Nicolas
de Lyre' (1923), pp. 403–4.

[49] Nicholas of Lyra, *Dicta de sacramento*, §8.
[50] *Eucharistietraktat*, §6 (291. 15–31).

(Now take note that I have told you how you should conduct yourself in front of the altar, before you go to receive. For you should first bow yourself in fear and in the humility of your unworthiness. Second, you should have firm faith in God's mercy. Third, you should desire that you will be improved by the power of the noble sacrament, so that the love of your improvement may impel you to [receive] it. These three things are most necessary for each and every individual before he goes to receive, and are easy in themselves, as you can clearly see. There are some people who look into their sins, and as a consequence want to go without the sacrament. This ought not be so. They should seek out the doctor all the more quickly, so that their sin may be taken away, and should say, 'Lord, come quickly into my house, before my soul dies even more!' And you should know that if someone has humble fear, in which he recognizes himself to be unworthy, firm faith in God's goodness, and desires to be improved in the sacrament, then he can certainly go to receive, because these things are sufficient prerequisites.)

The seventh section is entirely dedicated to this theme. Its introduction contains the statement quoted earlier, that God 'als gar des menschen vnwirdikeit vergessen het, dz ich dir niemer den minsten teil kan gesagen'[51] ('has forgotten the unworthiness of mankind so completely, that I can never tell you even the smallest part of it'). Marquard continues his introduction with a long, poetic exhortation to recognize the love with which God instituted the sacrament, and to respond with love.[52] The meat of this very long section then deals with six reasons why a person might be totally frightened of the sacrament and consider himself unworthy to receive, each of which is rendered invalid by a lengthy refutation. Each refutation focuses exclusively on the demonstrable love of God for man in the sacrament, so as to remove the cause for fear and encourage the person to reciprocal love instead. The second will stand as an example for them all, because it is here that Marquard takes on the real heart of the matter— 1 Corinthians 11: 29. However much the person may consider himself unworthy because of his own sinfulness, he should not let this prevent him from reception. The sacrament is a vehicle of divine love, and God looks at what the person would like to be—not how they are. That, says Marquard, is the real sense of Paul's statement. Only someone with no desire at all to be a better person, who is quite happy being sinful, has anything to fear:

---

[51] Ibid., §7 (299. 28–9).
[52] Ibid. (299. 32–300. 16). For the identification of two long quotations from Johannes Tauler, *Predigt* 60c, in this passage see Willing, *Literatur und Ordensreform*, p. 211.

Zů dem ander mal hat der mensch den gebresten, dz er vermassget vnd vnluter ist, vnd weiss wol, das er den gůten got mit schwerren súnden dik hatt erzúrnet vnd ob er im ie genemen dienst hab getan, des weiss er nit. Dar vmb sol der mensch billich erschreken, sider sant Paulus sprichet: „Quicumque manducaverit": Wer da isset das brot oder trinkt den kelch des herren vnwirdenklich, der nússet im selb gericht vnd vrteil. Vnd sanctus Agustinus spricht, dz nieman, der vnluter ist, sol gan zů diser spise. Aber nim war, das da wider der milt herre alle sine milte minne doch erzöiget in dem sacrament. Won er da nit wil mit dem menschen vmb sin schuld rechnen, ob er kumet mit waren rúwen. Noch wil in nit ansechen, als er ist gewesen, mer als er gern were, ob er echt kumt mit volkomner gantzer begird. Vnd des zů einem zeichen, so hat der milt kúng in die gelicheit des brotes verborgen vnd gesicht noch gehöret da nit zů einem zeichen, das er des menschen gebresten nit wil ansechen, in dem er gewesen ist, mer er wil in ansechen mit siner vernunfft, als er gern were, ob er echt gantz begird hat. Dar vmb meint sant Paulus vnd sant Agustinus, das nieman sol zů gan, er beger denn warlich wirdikeit vnd luterkeit sines hertzen. Vnd wenn er dz tůt, so wil in ŏch der lieb Cristus in den ougen ansechen.[53]

(Second, man has the failing that he is stained and impure. He knows full well that he has often angered the good God with grave sins, but knows not whether he has ever given him pleasing service. Because of this, the individual ought rightfully take fright, given that St Paul says, 'Quicumque manducaverit'. He who eats the bread or drinks the cup of the Lord unworthily, consumes his own judgement and sentence. And St Augustine says that no one who is impure should go to receive this food. But look, and see that on the other hand, the merciful Lord expresses all his merciful love in the sacrament. For he does not want to hold the individual to account for his guilt there, if he comes with true repentance. Nor does he want to look upon him as he has been, but rather as he would like to be, if he truly comes with perfect and complete desire. As a sign of this the merciful king has hidden himself in the similitude of bread, and neither sees nor hears there as a sign that he does not want to look upon the individual's failings, in which he has been; rather, he wants to look upon him with his intellect, as he would like to be, if he truly has complete desire. It is in this way that St Paul and St Augustine mean that no one should go to receive unless he truly desires worthiness and the purity of his heart. If he does that, then the dear Christ too wants to look him in the eyes.)

The fifth concerns those who, for different reasons, feel themselves insufficient and too frightened to receive: either they feel too poor in virtue, too insufficient in their sense of repentance, or too distant from God.[54] Marquard's conclusion could hardly be more definite:

---

[53] *Eucharistietraktat*, §7 (301. 7–27).
[54] Ibid. (303. 3–304. 11).

Sich, dise lúte wússent nit, das sich der riche kúng so vss grosser minne hat gesetzet in das edel sacrament mit allem sinem schatz vnd richeit vnd begerte anders nit, denn dz der mensch sines schatzes kouffte mit minne vnd begirden. Owe dar vmb alle armen hertzen an tugenden, alle túrre hertzen an heissen trehen, alle låwe hertzen an gôtlicher minne, kerend zů dirre edelen spise, gant zů disem richen kråmer vnd begerend allein, so wirt úch geben! Minnent allein von gantzem hertzen sinen schatz, so wúrt úch nút verseit alles des, dz ir begerent![55]

(Look, these people do not know that the mighty king has placed himself out of such great love into the noble sacrament, with all his treasure and riches, and desired nothing else save that man should buy his treasure with love and desire. Alas, therefore, all poor hearts without virtues; all dry hearts without scalding tears; all tepid hearts without godly love; turn to this noble food, go to this rich merchant and simply desire, and you will be given gifts! Simply love his treasure with all your heart, and nothing that you desire will be refused you!)

God is not interested, concludes Marquard, in external works and displays of devotion, but in the *inwendig* state of the individual, and that should be characterized by love. 'Dis alles han ich dir geseit', he finishes, 'dz du widerumb zů dem wirdigen sacrament gantz minn vnd ernst habest[, s]ider sich der liebe Ihesus da vss grundloser minne in das sacrament hat gesetzet'[56] ('I have told you all this so that you, for your part, may have total love and earnestness for the worthy sacrament, given that the dear Jesus has placed himself into the sacrament out of his bottomless love').

Marquard deals with another crucial point of the theological tradition relating to this complex at the end of the eighth section. He responds to the question of whether a person is better off receiving the sacrament or abstaining from it out of a sense of humility. His answer incorporates Augustine's reflection on Zacchaeus and the Centurion: one of whom welcomed Christ into his house, whereas the other did not because he felt himself too unworthy. This had been the basis for all theological discussion of the question previously, and had frequently been adduced, since Augustine's first use of the comparison in this context, in discussions of the appropriate frequency of reception.[57] Neither the Bible nor Augustine gave preferential treatment to either party. Marquard, on the other hand, proceeds by stating that reception is superior to abstinence, because

---

[55] Ibid. (304. 3–11).
[56] Ibid. (306. 6–9).
[57] Browe, *Die häufige Kommunion*, pp. 150–2; cf. Augustine, *Epistula* 54 (pp. 226–33), §4, ll. 62–95 (pp. 228–9).

love is greater than humility.[58] In actual fact, as Antje Willing has
discovered, Thomas Aquinas already held the position that Marquard
would later take.[59]

But the context of Aquinas' discussion is that in which Augustine
originally used the comparison, a discussion of the appropriate frequency
of reception. Marquard, by contrast, is not dealing here with this question
at all, but with the question of the validity of abstention through a sense of
unworthiness. In the ninth section, Marquard refers back to Augustine's
comparison when he is considering who receives the benefits of the sacrament by purely spiritual reception. After moving through formal cases,
such as the person who is too sick to ingest the host or who has died before
the priest could come with the *viaticum*, he comes to those who are so truly
fearful that they cannot bring themselves to receive. They too receive the
benefits of the sacrament in spiritual reception, being comparable to the
Centurion. But Marquard is not totally sure about this: 'schetz ich' ('I
reckon'), he says, a rare indication of uncertainty. And even these irredeem-
ably fearful people must, he concludes, receive at least their required
paschal communion sacramentally:

Zů dem vierden alle die, die in luterkeit irs lebens got dienent, vnd si sich selb so
schnőd vnd so bős ansechend vnd fúr die vnnútzesten creaturen diser welt so mit
grosser demůtikeit, dz si nit getúrrent zů dem sacrament gan vnd da bi gantz begird
zů dem sacrament hand vnd siner frucht begerent von gantzem hertzen, dieselben,
schetz ich, dz si ouch geistlich das sacrament enpfachent. Won si sind gelich dem,
der da sprach: „Herr, ich bin nit wirdig, das du komen sőllest vnder min tach." Vnd
als dem selben gnad beschach von Cristo, also beschicht ouch disen. Doch so es ist
von der heilgen kilchen gebotten, so sol nieman, der in den gnaden gottes ist, ân das
sacrament beliben durch keiner demůtikeit willen, won es hilffet denne nit dar zů.[60]

(Fourth, all those who serve God in the purity of their lives, regard themselves to be
so contemptible, so evil, and to be the most useless creatures in the entire world, and
do so with such great humility that they do not dare to go to receive the sacrament;

---

[58] *Eucharistietraktat*, §8 (307. 29–308. 28).
[59] Willing, *Literatur und Ordensreform*, pp. 203–5; see Aquinas, *Summa theologiae*,
q. 80 a. 10 ad 3 (vol. 4, pp. 554^b–555^a); for a discussion of Aquinas' use of the
Augustinian comparison, see Browe, *Die häufige Kommunion*, pp. 151–2. Willing
holds further that the opening question to this section of the *Eucharistietraktat* (307.
29–33) is taken from Jan van Ruusbroec's *Geestelijke brulocht*, on which Marquard draws
heavily at an earlier point in the eighth section. This parallel appears to be more apparent
than real. For in the passage under comparison, Ruusbroec is dealing with the absence of
burning desire to receive the sacrament, not (like Marquard) the urge to abstain from
receiving the eucharist out of a sense of humility; cf. Ruusbroec, *Geestelijke brulocht*,
II: 1275–80 (ed. Eichler, p. 173); b1399–b1404 (ed. Alaerts, p. 447).
[60] *Eucharistietraktat*, §9 (310. 32–311. 9).

and yet at the same time have complete desire for the sacrament and desire its fruits with all their hearts: these people, I reckon, also receive the sacrament spiritually. For they are like the one who said, 'Lord, I am not worthy that you should enter under my roof.' As grace was granted to that man by Christ, so it is granted to these people. But when it is commanded by the holy church, then no one who is in a state of grace should remain without the sacrament for humility's sake, because it doesn't help at all.)

Ultimately, Marquard does associate certain negative consequences with a particular kind of unworthy reception. This occurs in the final section, after a much longer discussion of the twelve fruits of sacramental reception. He does not spend very long on the punishments for 'unworthy' reception, and there are but three.[61] Most importantly, he uses 'unworthy' to refer specifically and exclusively to those who receive the sacrament whilst knowingly in an unconfessed state of mortal sin. This is a very different category to those who simply feel themselves too unworthy to communicate; it concerns those who have not confessed, who have not satisfied the formal requirements before reception. It is only to these that Paul's dictum applies,[62] and only these that the single fear-inducing statement in the entire work concerns:

Der Junger sprach: Es ist ein sorgklich ding ob allen dingen, wan mich dunkt, das sich der mensch do müsse setzen vff die wage ewiges lebens oder aber ewiger verdampnust.
Der Meister sprach: Du seist war, es ist ein minrich werch vnd doch ein erschrokenliches werk. Dar vmb sol ouch der mensch ân ein erwirdig, kintlich vorcht für sine gebresten vnd für die verborgnen urtel gottes niemer zûgan. Vnd wenn er denn ein erwirdig vorcht vnd ein rûwig hertz vnd ein gûten willen in im hat, so mag er wol zûgan mit einem gûten getrúwen zû der milti gottes, in die wis, als ich dir vor bescheiden han.[63]

(The pupil said: It is a matter more hazardous than anything else, because it seems to me that there the individual has to put himself on the weighing scales of eternal life or eternal damnation.
The master said: You speak the truth—it is a work full of love, and yet a terrifying work. Because of this the individual should never go to receive without a reverential and filial fear of his failings and of the hidden judgement of God. If he has reverential fear, a repentant heart, and a good will within him, then he may rightly go to receive with firm faith in God's mercy, in the manner that I have explained to you earlier.)

---

[61] Ibid., §14 (321. 16–322. 11).
[62] Ibid. (322. 5–8).
[63] Ibid. (322. 12–21).

Marquard then notes, briefly, six harms that befall a person who does not communicate. These are not inflicted punishments, but are benefits that the person does not receive, or dangers to which the person exposes himself.[64] With one eye on his target audience, Marquard states explicitly that they are not incurred by those who abstain out of true humility. The generation of more fear is not his method to terrorize the fearful into reception:

Doch die, die dz sacrament von lutter demûtikeit vnd vorcht ir vnwirdikeit vnder wegen land, vnd nit dar vmb, dz si sich von den súnden nit keren wellent, die gand dise gebresten alle nit an—es wer denn, dz si nit zů giengend, so es die helig kilch gebútet.[65]

(But those who refrain from the sacrament out of pure humility and fear of their unworthiness, and not because they do not want to turn away from sin, are not subject to these deficiencies—unless, that is, they do not go to receive when holy church commands it.)

The problem of fear of reception and what constitutes unworthy reception is the principal focus of Matthaeus of Cracow's *Dialogus*. This is evident from the opening sentences themselves:

Multorum tam clericorum quam laicorum quaerela est non modica, occupatio gravis et quaestio dubiosa, quo modo se habere debeant in celebrando vel communicando, quando videlicet accedere, quo modo accendentes moti vel dispositi esse, aut quibus motivis vel indispositionibus abstinere debeant, et an melius sit continue sumere corpus Christi, frequenter aut raro.[66]

(For many, both clergy and laity, this is no trifling complaint, but rather a serious business and an uncertain question: namely, how they should conduct themselves in celebrating the mass or receiving communion; when they should go to receive; what the motivation or internal disposition should be for those going to receive, or from what motives or inadequacies they should abstain; and whether it is better to consume the body of Christ very regularly, just frequently, or rarely.)

In actual fact, the *Dialogus* spends relatively little time on the last question, the appropriate frequency of reception. It has two main concerns: the issue of perceiving sweetness in the sacrament, and above all, the correct motivation for reception and the problem of abstinence through fear. To appreciate the scale of this problem in late medieval society at large, it is worth remembering that this treatise, with its rather narrow focus, enjoyed a truly enormous manuscript circulation in Latin—not to mention its German

[64] *Eucharistietraktat*, §14 (322. 22–323. 22).
[65] Ibid. (323. 19–22).
[66] Matthaeus of Cracow, *Dialogus*, prologue, ll. 5–9 (p. 367).

(and French and Czech[67]) vernacular versions. More caution is required when making statements about Matthaeus' position than is the case with Marquard. In the *Eucharistietraktat*, the master's voice is obviously that of Marquard, and the pupil's questions serve essentially as a mechanism to shift the treatise into new territories. In the *Dialogus*, it is certainly Reason which speaks at greater length and with greater authority against the worries and objections of Conscience. In the prologue, Matthaeus indicates that Will—*voluntas*—is to sit in judgement upon the case, and decide between the two protagonists.[68] But that judgement never comes; the work has, in consequence, a certain openness of its conclusions, even as it becomes clear that Reason consistently and successfully refutes Conscience's objections throughout.

It is unsurprising that the portentous text from 1 Corinthians makes a very early appearance in the *Dialogus*. Here, at the end of the first section, Conscience addresses the fears of a priest. He may well bring benefit to the congregation by his celebration of the mass, but is in danger of bringing eternal damnation on himself—a fear clearly stimulated by Paul's statement:

Sacerdotium enim auctoritatem celebrandi tribuit non sanctitatem. Sacerdos, quia peccator, et ad celebrandum minus dignus, etsi coram hominibus celebrare permittitur, coram Deo tamen id agere districte prohibetur, et si fecerit, 'iudicium sibi manducat et bibit' [1 Cor. 11: 29]. Absit igitur, ut cum damnationis meae periculo, aliorum saluti provideam, 'cum nihil prosit mihi, si universum mundum lucretur, animae vero suae detrimentum patiatur' [cf. Matt. 16: 26]. Nisi ergo probaveris, quod mihi ut christiano communicare conveniat, celebrandum esse ratione officii, non convinces.[69]

(For priesthood confers the authority to celebrate the mass, not holiness. The priest, because he is a sinner and so less worthy to celebrate the mass—although he is permitted in the sight of men to celebrate—is nevertheless strictly prohibited to act thus in the sight of God. If he does so, 'he eats and drinks judgement to himself'. Heaven forfend, therefore, that I, with the danger of my own damnation, should provide for the salvation of others: 'since it is of no use to me if I should gain the whole world, but suffer the loss of my soul'. Therefore unless you can prove that it may be appropriate for me as an ordinary Christian to receive communion, and that the mass is to be celebrated by reason of office, you will not convince me.)

[67] See Seńko and Szafrański (eds.), *Mateusza z Krakowa*, p. 363. They list one manuscript each of a Czech and a French translation, but it is likely that there are more: they list just 3 manuscripts of a German translation, whereas 28 such manuscripts are now known.
[68] Matthaeus of Cracow, *Dialogus*, prologue, ll. 32–8 (p. 368).
[69] Ibid., §1, ll. 184–93 (p. 373).

References to 1 Corinthians 11: 27–9 then regularly punctuate Conscience's utterances throughout the *Dialogus*,[70] and serve to underline its significance in constructing fear of reception. Matthaeus' close attention to the problem of perceived unworthiness to receive the sacrament then continues to emerge in this first half of the *Dialogus*, where the stated topic under discussion is actually the sensation of sweetness in the host. This underlying concern can be seen in statements such as that concluding Reason's long discourse at the end of the second section, in which Reason maintains that the unworthier the person, the more they are benefited by reception—not the more they ought to abstain:

Propter hoc enim in nobis excitanda tanti boni praesentia indulta est, nec quantum ad hoc obstat indignitas cuiuscumque, sed quanto quis indignior est, tanto maior sit sibi gratia et tanto magis moveri debet. Ob quam enim aliam causam credendum est Deum, hominibus manifeste indignis, tantam exhibere pietatem, corporalem videlicet praesentiam Jesu Christi, nisi ad confudendum et convicendum pravitatem eorum sua tam largiflua pietate, quam advertentes erubescant, revereantur et revertantur [?][71]

(For this purpose the stimulating presence of such good in us was granted: not insofar as anyone's unworthiness restrains it; but rather the more unworthy someone is, the greater the grace may be that is given to him, and the more he should be moved [by it]. For on account of what other cause is it to be believed that God produces such a mercy, namely the bodily presence of Jesus Christ, to plainly unworthy mankind, except to confound and reproach man's wickedness by his copiously flowing mercy such that those who turn towards it may be ashamed, feel awe, and turn back [from their wickedness]?)

The first direct statement from Conscience that fear is the root cause of abstinence then comes at the end of the third section.[72] It is not, however, until the seventh that this becomes the primary subject under discussion.

This seventh section deals with the condition of those who abstain from reception. At the very beginning, Conscience has to admit that nothing is actively gained by abstinence. In the same breath, a key matter is addressed: the common idea that those who receive the sacrament infrequently enjoy a greater effect from it, and are more reverent towards it.

Conscientia: Non video, quid boni [abstinentia] conferat, nisi quod communiter reputantur rarius communicantes magis affecti et reverentius accedere; puto autem, quod ob hoc multi rarius celebrent etiam graves et magnae personae.[73]

---

[70] See e.g. Matthaeus of Cracow, *Dialogus*, §9, ll. 928–9 (p. 398) and ll. 1013–15 (p. 401).
[71] Ibid., §2, ll. 323–31 (p. 377).
[72] Ibid., §3, ll. 525–529a (p. 384).
[73] Ibid., §7, ll. 737–40 (p. 391).

(Conscience: I do not see what abstinence bestows of [any] advantage, except that those who receive communion more rarely are considered to be more affected and to go to receive more reverently. I think, furthermore, that on account of this many mighty and great persons may also celebrate the mass more rarely.)

Reason is quick to point out that these kinds of effect are not intrinsic to the sacrament, but relate only to an individual's reaction to it. In the subsequent discussion, Reason makes it clear that this reaction differs depending on the intrinsic nature of the individual concerned.[74] The responsibility lies with the individual to reform himself so that he does not become jaded by frequent attendance at the mass, or overly preoccupied with the external forms of the ritual rather than with his internal spiritual development. The easy option, simply to abstain from reception, is much less satisfactory—and the abstinent can lose his 'spiritual appetite' completely.[75] It is this underlying strategy that characterizes the succeeding sections, which cannot be set out here in full: abstinence is not condemned outright, but is argued consistently by Reason to be less satisfactory on all levels. Compared to the *Eucharistietraktat*, the abstinent comes in for some harsh criticism—as, for example, when Reason criticizes the thought process behind abstinence:

Conscientia: Credo quod multi, si hanc rationem adverterent, et quantum bonum sumere vel habere possent et quantum bonum negligunt[,] rarius abstinerent.
Ratio: Ita est, sed quia sub dissimulatione transeunt non advertentes sicut in principio dixi, quam parvae, immo nullae sunt causae, ex quibus obmittunt quasi ex quadam consuetudine pro nihilo reputant quod abstinent. Et in hoc plerique videntur habere mensuram et pondus, quae sunt abominatio apud Deum. Nam quando communicant, reputant et gaudent se bonum fecisse, sed quando abstinent pro nihilo ducunt nec dolent, se bonum obmisisse.[76]

(Conscience: I believe that many, if they were to take notice of this argument, of how much good they could receive or possess, and of how much good they ignore, would abstain more rarely.
Reason: So it is, but because they pass it by and in their disregard do not heed it, just as I said at the beginning, how trifling—nay, negligible—are the causes on account of which they refrain [from reception]; as though from some habit they don't think it to be anything that they abstain. And in this the majority appear to have a gauge and balance that is an abomination in the eyes of God. For when they receive

---

[74] As e.g. at ibid., ll. 752–759b (p. 392).
[75] See ibid., ll. 777–839 (pp. 393–5).
[76] Ibid., §8, ll. 889–899a (p. 397).

communion, they think that they have done well and rejoice. But when they abstain they think it nothing, and are not sorrowful to have held themselves back from good.)

It is in the ninth section that the core problems of fear and unworthiness are addressed. Conscience states openly that a sense of personal unworthiness lies at the root of abstinence, using an adapted citation from 1 Corinthians 11: 27: 'Indignam me iudico et horreo rea fieri corporis et sanguinis Jesu Christi'[77] ('I judge myself to be unworthy, and I am terrified to become guilty of the body and blood of Jesus Christ'). The following discussion sees Reason wrestling with the category of worthiness itself. A person who considered himself unworthy to receive, but who in actual fact was worthy, would then become unworthy if he did receive, because he would have acted against his conscience. Considering oneself worthy, on the other hand, is a statement that one is without sin: a self-deception, except in the unlikely case that one has received a divine revelation to this effect. Likewise, considering oneself unworthy is wrong, except where unworthiness is certain on account of a formal condition for reception having not been met.[78]

Marquard's solution to the problem of worthiness was to take the category out of action: to insist that God totally overlooks the individual's unworthiness, and then to reduce 'being worthy' to mean not being knowingly in a state of unconfessed mortal sin. Matthaeus' Reason tries likewise to redefine and, indeed, eliminate the category. The test for worthiness, argues Reason, lies not in being without sin, but in having the desire to repent for past sins and avoid them in future.[79] In fact, the individual who does what he can to this end should not really judge himself worthy or unworthy at all. But, on balance, to judge oneself unworthy is more dangerous. Whilst judging oneself worthy may presuppose a knowledge of the *sensum Domini*, judging oneself unworthy reeks of *desperatio*.[80] Reason nullifies another scriptural component that underpins the idea of having to be worthy to receive: the Centurion's statement of Matthew 8: 8, 'et respondens centurio ait, "Domine, non sum dignus ut intres sub tectum meum, sed tantum dic verbo et sanabitur puer meus"' ('and answering, the Centurion said, "Lord, I am not worthy that you should enter under my roof, but say the word only, and my boy [i.e. servant] will be healed"'). Whereas Marquard dealt with this by deciding against the 'Centurion'

---

[77] Matthaeus of Cracow, *Dialogus*, §9, ll. 928–9 (p. 398).
[78] Ibid., ll. 934a–948 (p. 398).
[79] Ibid., ll. 949b–953 (p. 399).
[80] Ibid., ll. 956–78 (p. 399).

position within the traditional framework of Augustine's comparison, Matthaeus' Reason argues that the example of the Centurion has nothing to do with the issue at all. Not only does it concern humility, rather than judging the self to be worthy, it actually illustrates how a person cannot possibly be worthy through his own doing. He can, in fact, only be made worthy by divine grace:

Ratio: Ista verba et similia non dicuntur temeritate iudicandi, sed reputationis humilitate, sicut etiam teste beato Bernardo in Epistola ad fratres de Monte Dei, beatus Paulus dixit: Quorum scilicet peccatorum primus sum, [cf. 1 Tim. 1: 15] non mentiendi praecipitatione, sed aestimandi affectione. Puto autem quod sic intelligi valeant et hoc communiter intendant dicentes aut intendere debeant, Domine, quantum est ex me, non sum dignus, quia peccator magnus, nec debita contritione, confessione et satisfactione purgatus, nisi misericordia tua dignetur hoc modicum quod ago acceptare et me per gratiam tuam dignificare. Et hoc est quod subditur: 'sed tantum dic verbo et sanabitur' [Matt. 8: 8].[81]

(Reason: These words and their like are not spoken with the audacity of making judgement, but with the humility of [self-]assessment: just as, by blessed Bernard's witness in the *Epistola ad fratres de Monte Dei*, blessed Paul also said: 'I am the first of them', namely of the sinners; not in a headlong fall of lying, but in the affection of [self-]appraisal. I think, however, that they may be understood in this way, and that those who say these words may, or rather should, universally mean this: 'Lord, insofar as it is of myself, I am not worthy, because I am a great sinner, whose debts are not forgiven by contrition, confession, and satisfaction; unless your mercy may condescend to accept this little that I do, and to make me worthy through your grace.' And this is what follows: 'but say the word only, and he will be healed'.)

Reason eliminates the category of unworthiness in a manner not dis-similar to Marquard. The individual ought to abstain if he is certain he is unworthy—and as we have seen, that means essentially that he is knowingly in an unconfessed state of mortal sin. Reason casts doubt on Conscience's desire to abstain when in a state of doubt about personal worthiness, because such doubt is the normal, unavoidable state of life:

Ratio: Antequam semel indigne scienter accederes, in aeternum deberes abstinere; sed si in dubio semper abstinentiam tamquam securiorem partem eligere vis, cum illud dubium in hac vita semper tibi maneat, quando unquam accedes.[82]

[81] Ibid., ll. 984a–994a (p. 400). On this issue of the individual's reliance on divine mercy and grace in preparation for sacramental reception, in the *Dialogus* and in other contemporary works, see Grosse, *Heilsungewißheit und Scrupulositas*, pp. 205–7.

[82] Matthaeus of Cracow, *Dialogus*, §9, ll. 1020–4 (p. 401).

(Reason: Before you were knowingly to go to receive unworthily once, you should abstain eternally; but if in doubt you [i.e. Conscience] wish always to choose abstinence as the safer option—although in this life that doubt always persists in you, whenever you go to receive.)

In this context, spiritual communion is simply irrelevant. As Reason stated earlier, deciding to abstain from sacramental reception without certain cause is a sign of *desperatio*, of insufficient trust in God's mercy. Matthaeus, like Marquard, has little time for spiritual communion.[83]

It is in the tenth and eleventh sections of the *Dialogus*, however, that the real difference between Marquard's approach and that of Matthaeus' Reason becomes clear. Typically for the endless *Dialogus*, the tenth section consists largely of Reason recycling all her earlier arguments. Reason locks on to the crucial point: trust in divine mercy should outweigh fear of unworthiness, which is a manifestation of *desperatio*.[84] But whereas Marquard sought to counteract fear with love, stimulating the individual's desire to receive, Matthaeus' Reason lacks the Bonaventuran (one might even say Franciscan) impulse and fights fear with fear. Aiming the accusation of *desperatio* at the abstinent, Reason fulminates:

Attende igitur, ne eam, de qua dixisti, Deo arroges iniuriam, dum propter solum illum timorem a communione te removes et gravius pecces dimittendo quam sumendo, iuxta sententiam beati Ambrosii in quadam oratione sic dicentis: Grave est quod ad mensam tuam mundo corde et innocentibus manibus non venimus, sed gravius est, si de peccatis metuimus et sacrificium non reddimus.[85]

(Mind, therefore, that you do not inflict that injustice of which you have spoken on God, when because of that fear alone you withdraw yourself from communion, and may sin more gravely in forgoing it than in consuming it, according to the blessed Ambrose's statement in a certain prayer, when he speaks thus: 'It is serious that we have not come to your table with pure hearts and innocent hands; but it is more serious if we have been afraid of our sins and do not offer up the sacrifice.')

Conscience is almost aware that Reason is not providing Marquard's solution:

Mirabiliter agis mecum, quia mihi inde causam accedendi elicis, unde ego traho abstinendi motivum et, ubi suadebam esse de accessu periculum, tu mihi de abstinendo aequalis vel maioris periculi et peccati timorem inducis. Delectabile est autem sic vinci, ubi excluditur timor, qui poenam habet et tam consolatoria fiducia ministratur.[86]

[83] Matthaeus of Cracow, *Dialogus*, §9, ll. 1033–47 (pp. 401–2).
[84] Ibid., §10, ll. 1078–97 (p. 403).
[85] Ibid., ll. 1107–14 (p. 404).
[86] Ibid., §11, ll. 1117–23 (p. 404).

(You deal with me very strangely; because you present a reason to me to go to receive, whereupon I put forth the motivation to abstain; and, where I will counsel that the danger is in going to receive, you bring forward to me an equal or greater fear of danger and sin from abstinence. It is, on the other hand, delightful to be won over in such a way that fear, which brings pain with it, is excluded, and consolatory confidence is provided.)

In response, Reason makes a half-hearted attempt at listing indications that God is pleased by sacramental reception. This is more like Marquard's strategy. The list, however, is a short one of only four points—and they are tempered by the induction of fear of abstention, as we see in the fourth:

Quartum, quia deliciae Jesu Christi sunt, esse cum filiis hominum, ut per Salomonem dicitur. Et cui dubium, quin ex deliciis essendi cum filiis hominum Deus instituerit hoc venerabile sacramentum, ut nedum spiritualem, sed etiam corporalem sui praesentiam exhiberet. Quanta autem ingratitudo, quanta perversitas, divinis deliciis non dare locum, sed miserabiliter denegare![87]

(Fourth, because the delight of Jesus Christ is to be with the sons of man, as it is said by Solomon. And who doubts that God did not institute this venerable sacrament out of delight of being with the sons of man, so that he might exhibit not just his spiritual, but even his corporeal presence. How great is the ingratitude, how great the perversity, to give no room to the divine delight, but miserably to turn it away!)

Not only is this a short list, but it is not a subject on which Reason dwells: the subject matter is quickly turned to the importance of not knowingly remaining in mortal sin. If Conscience was not now terrified enough of abstention, Reason concludes the eleventh section with an uncompromising barrage of fear-inducing material:

Igitur manifestum est, quod quandocumque huic officio vel operi commode et opportune vacare poteris nec aliquod canonicum obstat, nullam poteris dimittendi causam habere vel fingere, nisi malitiam aut negligentiam, aut pigritiam tuam, quae sunt causae irrationabiles et damnosae.[88]

(Therefore it is evident that whenever you are conveniently and opportunely able to give time to this office or to this work, and no statute of canon law stands in the way, you can neither have nor devise any reason to forgo it—save your malice, negligence, or indolence, which are irrational and damnable reasons.)

Both works, then, deal with the same core problem that the eucharistic cult had generated; both respond by attempting to eliminate the category of 'worthiness' that lay at the heart of the problem; but they take very

---

[87] Ibid., ll. 1135–42 (p. 405).
[88] Ibid., ll. 1169–73 (p. 406).

different, indeed diametrically opposed, approaches to counteract the residual fear of reception. One stimulates love for the sacrament, the other induces fear of abstinence.

This conclusion has an additional significance in relation to the argument very recently put forward by Berndt Hamm regarding the nature of the *cura animarum* in the later Middle Ages. He has challenged the *communis opinio* that the pastoral climate and preaching of the later fifteenth century was focused on the inculcation of fear—Savonarola's 'terrifica praedicatio'—onto which dark prospects the Reformation shone new light. Instead, he has argued that an equally strong opposite tradition existed, which sought to ameliorate the burden of fear and emphasize the proximity and accessibility of grace, divine consolation, and support. His examples of this are limited in number and in their individual length. They are also of the later fifteenth century, and whilst they emphasize the merciful love of God very strongly, their affective approach is strongly emotive and focused on the corporeal. Hamm concludes,

Immer wieder geht es (1) um das Moment der realen Vergegenwärtigung des Christuskörpers und damit eng verbunden (2) um Ablassbewilligungen, (3) um inneres andächtiges Beteiligtsein des Hilfe suchenden Menschen und zugleich (4) um die sinnliche Andacht des eigenen Körpers, seine äußere Fühlungsnahme zur Gnade durch Küssen, Anfassen, Anschauen, Hingehen, Niederfallen, Anreden, Abzählen usw. So wird räumlich, zeitlich oder transzendent Fernes in möglichst gesicherte, abrufbare und verfügbare Heilsnähe geholt.[89]

(Again and again the matter at issue is, first, the moment of the real visualization of the body of Christ; closely connected to which is, second, the granting of indulgences; third, the inward, devout participation of the individual seeking help; and—simultaneously—fourth, the sensory devotion of the individual's own body: its initial, exterior contacts with grace through kissing, touching, gazing, approaching, genuflecting, addressing, counting, and so forth. In this way that which is spatially, temporally, or transcendentally distant is brought, insofar as it is possible, into a secure, accessible, and available proximity of salvation.)

If we examine Hamm's argument here in the light of our new conclusions, we can make four further statements. First, that the problem of fear and its inculcation in the *cura animarum* was already serious by around 1370. Second, that the alternative, indeed opposite approach existed fully formed at the same time, with Marquard's *Eucharistietraktat* (which is much weightier than the examples Hamm has adduced thus far) at the origin of the tradition. Third, that this affective counter-tradition need not

[89] Hamm, 'Die „nahe Gnade"', pp. 545–54, here p. 554.

necessarily demonstrate an emotive, corporeal-sensual affectivity—as will soon become clearer from our further investigation of the *Eucharistietrak-tat*. Fourth, that fear was not just met with love and 'die nahe Gnade', but (as we see with Matthaeus of Cracow) with the stimulation of fear in a different direction. The preponderant climate of fear was met with a multiplicity of responses.

This does not exhaust the issue of fear of the sacrament for our study of Marquard's *Eucharistietraktat*. Whereas Matthaeus' *Dialogus* deals solely with a small group of pragmatic issues, the *Eucharistietraktat* is a more wide-ranging work, which incorporates instruction in the theology of the eucharist. Historically, this had been another area that had generated fear of the sacrament: fear deriving from the use of *exempla*. Obviously, terrifying tales of woe that had befallen unworthy communicants had generated fear,[90] and as we would expect, there are none in the *Eucharistietraktat*. More subtly, and perhaps more significantly, the essentials of eucharistic theology had traditionally been substantiated and explained by the use of powerful *exempla*. As the theological claims made for the sacrament had increased and become more complex in the thirteenth century, so the use of *exempla* had become increasingly prevalent in its explication in devotional works and in preaching. These *exempla* were designed, in the words of Eamon Duffy, 'to convict of sin and shock into faith'.[91] Their ubiquity was so astonishing that Rubin is able to write that 'every area of injunction, restriction and practice, and every custom, ritual and demand which could be mistaken, neglected, misunderstood or manipulated, was countered by an appropriate tale'.[92] Nor did these *exempla* merely serve to illustrate explanations. Not infrequently, they were the explanations. Caspers' examination of thirteenth-century episcopal statutes has revealed that some bishops of this period insisted that the priests in their dioceses avoid any explanation of transubstantiation, being far too difficult a doctrine to be commonly understood. Yet belief in transubstantiation had to be affirmed, and *exempla* were used to terrify the listener or reader into belief, rather than to convince by explanation: what Duffy means by 'shocking into

---

[90] See the representative selection of examples collected in Staber, 'Die Bildhaftig-keit', pp. 115–18.

[91] Duffy, *The Stripping of the Altars*, pp. 102–6 (here p. 104).

[92] Rubin, *Corpus Christi*, pp. 110–28 (here p. 128); Rubin, 'The Eucharist', pp. 53–7; and Caspers, *De eucharistische vroomheid*, pp. 157–8.

faith'.[93] This served to alienate the individual from the sacrament; to increase the awe, indeed the fear, of the eucharistic transformation whose explanation was too complex to be understood.

Among the greatest of all medieval collections of *exempla* was the *Dialogus miraculorum* of the Cistercian Caesarius von Heisterbach (d. 1240). The ninth *distinctio* of this work concerns the eucharist. It opens with the dialogue between a monk and a novice. The novice asks for some catechetical instruction on the theology of the sacrament before the *exempla* begin, and the monk responds with a clear statement that the sacrament was to be feared:

Novicius: Antequam visiones edisseras, peto ut breviter me expedias, quid sit hoc sacramentum, quae res sacramenti, quae causa institutionis, quae forma, quis modus conversionis, quis modus sumptionis.
Monachus: De sacramento eucharistiae tractandum est cum timore ac reverentia, quia magis in illo operatur fides quam ratio humana.[94]

(The novice: Before you relate these visions to me, I ask you to tell me briefly what this sacrament is, and what the substance of the sacrament, the reason for its institution, its form, the manner of its transformation, and the manner of its consumption all are.
The monk: The sacrament of the eucharist is to be examined with fear and reverence, because faith works in it more than human reason.)

The catechetical instruction that follows is extremely brief, and there is no explanation of any of the answers. It is clear from the novice's final statement in the opening dialogue that the *exempla* are intended to be the explanation:

Novicius: Cum iam quae dicta sunt credam, quatuor tamen mihi probari desidero non sententiis sed exemplis. Primum est quod sub specie panis sit verum corpus Christi natum ex Virgine; secundum, quod sub specie vini sit verus eius sanguis; tertium, quod digne conficientes sive communicantes mereantur gratiam, indigne autem poenam.[95]

(The novice: Although I now believe what has been said, nevertheless I ask that four things be demonstrated to me not in statements, but by examples. The first is that the true body of Christ, born of the Virgin, is under the species of bread; the second,

---

[93] See Caspers, '*Meum summum desiderium*', pp. 129–30, and indeed Browe, *Die eucharistischen Wunder*, pp. 177–84.
[94] Caesarius von Heisterbach, *Dialogus miraculorum*, d. 9, c. 1 (vol. 2, p. 166).
[95] Ibid. (vol. 2, p. 167). On Caesarius' eucharistic *exempla* themselves, see Caspers, *De eucharistische vroomheid*, pp. 141–52.

that his true blood is under the species of wine; the third, that those who actuate [i.e. consecrate] or receive the sacrament worthily merit grace, but [fourth?] that those who do so unworthily, merit punishment.)

Caesarius represents the opposite pole to Marquard's strategy on the transmission of theological information. In those sections of the *Euchar-istietraktat* concerned with eucharistic doctrine, Marquard expounds even the most difficult points fully and clearly. He uses analogy upon occasion, but never *exempla*. It is in the second section that doctrine is at the centre of attention. No miraculous *exempla* are used to substantiate doctrinal points. Instead, the doctrinal points themselves are termed *wunder*—miracles. The attention of the individual is thereby focused on the sacrament itself, without any fear-inducing stories to occlude clear understanding. Antje Willing suggests that Marquard's use of the term *wunder* to describe the tenets of eucharistic doctrine is derived from two Dominican sermons by Eckhart Rube and Florentius von Utrecht in the *Paradisus anime intelli-gentis* collection.[96] In fact the use of *miracula* or *mirabilia* to describe these tenets in thirteenth-century Latin catechetical writing is not uncommon.[97] Under the heading 'De mirabilibus, quae sunt in Eucharistia' ('On the miracles, which are in the eucharist'), nine *mirabilia*—all features of eucharistic doctrine—are elaborated in Hugo Ripelin's *Compendium theo-logicae veritatis*, a standard handbook of thirteenth-century scholastic the-ology.[98] Francis of Meyronnes presented eucharistic doctrine as a series of *mirabilia* in his commentary on the Sentences, a work that Marquard definitely knew and cited.[99] Caspers rightly notes that this tactic is itself not without danger: 'Het effect is immers dat niet de godsdienstige vorm-ing, maar de sensatiezucht van het volk wordt gestimuleerd'[100] ('The effect, after all, is that it is not the religious education of the people that is encouraged, but their desire for the sensational'). But from Marquard's strategy in setting out these doctrinal tenets in the terminology of *wunder*, we can see that he was aware of this problem and explicitly counteracted it.

---

[96] Willing, *Literatur und Ordensreform*, pp. 186–7. Willing's arguments that Marquard drew more widely on Eckhart Rube's *Paradisus* sermon on the eucharist (pp. 186–90) are liable to challenge on all points. A thorough philological investigation will resolve the question, which we cannot present here.

[97] See Caspers, *De eucharistische vroomheid*, pp. 203–5.

[98] Hugo Ripelin von Straßburg, *Compendium theologicae veritatis*, lib. 6, c. 14 (pp. 212^b–213^b), at pp. 212^b–213^a.

[99] Francis of Meyronnes, *In IV Sent.*, lib. 4, d. 8, a. 17 (fol. 186rb).

[100] Caspers, *De eucharistische vroomheid*, p. 205.

Each of the seven doctrinal tenets is set out using the same strategy. The tenet is introduced as a miracle, a *wunder*; a concise explanation of the relevant theology is provided; and, because the tenet is now within the pupil's comprehension, is no longer considered a *wunder*—sometimes with an explicit, sometimes an implicit statement. We see this strategy in the first *wunder* of the seven, which will stand as our example for the rest. Marquard's master begins by focusing attention directly on the ineffable mystery of the aspect of sacramental theology under discussion, by describing it with the term *wunder*:

Der Meister sprach: Ich wil dir von den wundren enwenig sagen, die der gewaltig kúng in dem sacrament zöigend ist. [. . .] Nu sag mir zem ersten, ob das nit ein gross wunder sig, das der rich kúng Ihesus Christus in ieklichem teil der gesegneten offloten ist als genczlich vnd als gross, als er an dem heilgen crúcz was vnd als er in dem himel liplich gross ist. Dunket dich das nit ein wunder, sider die oflat so gar klein ist?
Der Junger sprach: Ja, es dunket mich wol wunder vnd wider alle natur, vnd wusste gern, wie es gesin möcht.[101]

(The master said: I want to tell you a little of the miracles that the powerful king manifests in the sacrament. [. . .] First, tell me that it isn't a great miracle, that the mighty king Jesus Christ is as whole and as extensive in every part of the consecrated host as he was on the holy cross, and as extensive as he is bodily in heaven. Does that not seem to be a miracle to you, given that the host is so very small?
The pupil said: Yes, it seems to me full well to be a miracle and contrary to all nature, and I would like to know how it might be so.)

Having located the miraculous in the theology of the sacrament itself, rather than in any ancillary manifestation, Marquard's master then reduces the awe of the sacrament that this strategy has consequentially produced. The definition of miracles is explained; the pupil acknowledges that the doctrinal tenet may well be miraculous, but is not impossible. In this case, it is curiously the pupil who then sets out the theological explanation:

Der Meister sprach: Du solt wissen, wie das es nit sy nach gemeinem louff der natur, so ist es doch nit wider die natur, won waz der herre der natur haben wil von ieklichem ding, das ist im also ze sin natúrlich. Vnd dar vmb so spricht sanctus Agustinus, das es nit wider die natur was, dz hie vor ein rût zů einer schlangen ward und ein frow zů einer saltzsul ward, sider es gottes wille was, dz es also beschech.

<hr />

[101] *Eucharistietraktat*, §2 (262. 1–9).

Der Junger sprach: Mich dunkent die wisen wunderlich aber si dunkent mich nit vnmuglich. Wond ordnung zů einem lib der gelider mag wol gestan ăn ordnung der gelider die stat ze bekúmbrent. Dar vmb frag ich dich nit me von dem wonder.[102]

(The master said: You should know that, however much it is not according to the normal course of nature, it is still not contrary to nature—for whatever the Lord will have of nature in each and every thing, is therefore to be natural for it. Therefore St Augustine says that it was not contrary to nature that in former times a staff became a snake, and a woman became a pillar of salt, given that it was God's will that it happened like this.

The pupil said: The ways and means seem miraculous to me, but they do not seem to me to be impossible. For an order may well pertain to the parts of a body without an order of the parts to occupy a particular place. Therefore I shall not ask further of this miracle.)

The same strategy is then repeated through the rest of the section. Thus we find that in the second tenet, the master sets out the principle of ubiquity initially as a *wunder* and 'ein wunderliche ordnung gottes'[103] ('a miraculous divine order'), before explaining the principle concisely and stating just eight lines later that, as far as this matter is concerned, 'also soltu ouch kein wunder haben'[104] ('and thus you should not consider it miraculous').

The treatise does in fact contain one *exemplum* detailing a miracle. It is found in the ninth section, and provides evidence for the possibility of spiritual communion where the individual is physically incapable of sacramental reception. It is told of Bonaventura, and involves the sacrament entering his body miraculously as he lay upon his deathbed, too sick to receive the host into his mouth:

Vnd also beschach dem lieben Bona ventura, dem cardinal, do der an sinem ende lag, do getorst man im dz sacrament vor siechtagen sines magen nit geben. Do begert er, dz man im das sacrament vff sin hertz leiti. Vnd do das beschach, do tet sich sin hertz vff vnd enpfieng dz sacrament vnd do tet sich sin lib wider zů.[105]

(It so happened to the beloved Bonaventura, the cardinal, that when he lay at death's door no one dared to give him the sacrament because of his stomach illness. Then he desired that the sacrament should be placed upon his heart. When that happened, his heart opened and received the sacrament, and then his body closed up again.)

---

[102] Ibid. (262. 10–20). On the contemporary theory of miracles and the distinction between *miraculum* (a supernatural occurrence) and *mirum* (a wondrous, but not supernatural occurrence), see Paciocco, 'Miracles and Canonized Sanctity', pp. 261–2.

[103] *Eucharistietraktat*, §2 (262. 22–6).

[104] Ibid. (262. 24).

[105] Ibid., §9 (310. 5–10).

This miracle story has a complex history and was attributed to a number of individuals in the thirteenth and fourteenth centuries. The attribution of the story to Bonaventura may have taken place, Browe suggests, because of his own use of this story (attributed to an anonymous layperson) in a sermon.[106] Most importantly, it is not an *exemplum* that creates fear and distance. It shows instead that, even *in extremis*, the sacrament was not inaccessible to the individual; the individual was not alienated from sacramental reception even if its administration was refused to him, lest the host be regurgitated.

To maintain that Marquard rejected the use of miracle stories to teach eucharistic theology is not merely an argument *ex silentio*. At the end of the first section, he sets out why Christ is not visible in the host. His principal reason concerns the necessity of faith, and he adduces the only other *exemplum* in the entire work in support—not one, of course, that has anything to do with a miracle:

[. . .] dar vmb, das vnser lon von dem gelouben dester merer wurd. Won gelouben, des man nit sicht, ist ein merung des lones in ewikeit. Vnd dar vmb liset man von sant Ludwig, dz er sprach: Were, dz Cristus nach menschlicher wonung hinder im stůnd, so der priester die gesegnoten oflaten vff hůb, er wolt nit hinder sich sechen an Cristum, noch wolt sich niemer vmb kerren, dar vmb, das sin lon von des gelouben wegen nit dester minder wurde.[107]

([. . .] so that our reward from faith would be all the greater. For faith, whereby one does not see, is an augmentation of eternal reward. Thus we read that St Louis said that if Christ were standing behind him in human form when the priest elevated the consecrated host, he would neither look behind him at Christ, nor would he ever want to turn around, so that his reward from his faith would not be diminished by doing so.)

The point of this tale is that the individual, following the example of Louis IX, should have faith in the real presence of Christ in the eucharist, without requiring any physical or visual confirmation of that presence—the

[106] A conspectus of these miracles is given by Browe, *Die eucharistischen Wunder*, pp. 28–31, with further discussion in Rubin, *Corpus Christi*, p. 82. The Bonaventuran sermon in question is *Sermo 5 de feria quinta in coena Domini* (vol. 9, pp. 255ᵇ–259ᵇ), at p. 259ᵃ.
[107] *Eucharistietraktat*, §1 (260. 24–31). He also criticizes curiosity with regard to 'wunder', at §2 (267. 5–7), though this may be a warning against theological speculation about the eucharist rather than against an interest in miracles. A Latin translation of the *Eucharistietraktat* in Vienna, Schottenkloster, cod. 159 (Cat. 256) adds a similar story to the St Louis example, this time concerning Aquinas: see Hofmann (ed.), *Der Eucharistie-Traktat*, p. 233. The story originally concerned Simon IV of Montfort; it was heard and retold by Louis IX, according to Joinville, and was evidently transposed later on to Louis himself: see Browe, *Die eucharistischen Wunder*, pp. 116–17.

kind of confirmation that miracle stories provided. Caesarius also insisted on
faith in the real presence, but faith constructed through the opposite strategy.
According to him, 'Nullae etiam visiones magis fidem roborant, quam cum
eum quem sub specie panis et vini latere credimus, oculis corporeis intue-
mur'.[108] ('No visions strengthen faith more than when we gaze with our
bodily eyes upon him, whom we believe to be concealed under the species of
bread and wine'). Aquinas thought similarly, stating that visions of miraculous transformations of the eucharistic host served to strengthen the beholder's faith: they functioned 'ad instructionem fidei et devotionem
excitandam'[109] ('to encourage devotion and the instruction of the faith').
Marquard's position is, we might say, a rejection of the 'doubting Thomas'
model.

The Oxford theologian John Wyclif issued his polemical treatise *De eucharistia* in 1380, quickly followed by the shorter *Confessio* in 1381: around
seven years prior to Matthaeus of Cracow's composition of the *Dialogus*,
and broadly contemporary with Marquard's *Eucharistietraktat*.[110] With his
exposition and propagation of what was deemed in 1382 to be an ultimately heretical theology of the sacrament, Wyclif generated a massive theological controversy in a way that neither Marquard nor Matthaeus ever did.
There is naturally an extensive scholarly literature on Wyclif's theology,
and on the reasons underlying his rejection of the existing alternatives
to understanding the metaphysical nature of the consecrated sacrament,
which we need not repeat here.[111] It is clear that in part, Wyclif's objections were philosophical, and were logical consequences of philosophical

[108] Caesarius von Heisterbach, *Dialogus miraculorum*, d. 9, c. 1 (vol. 2, p. 165).
[109] Aquinas, *In IV Sent.*, lib. 4, d. 10, a. 4, q. 2 [= d. 10, §115] (vol. 4, p. 423).
[110] A tantalizing clue in the *Eucharistietraktat* suggests Marquard may have known of
the Wycliffite controversy at the time of his composition of the work (he would
undoubtedly have been aware of it before he died in 1392). He explains the principle
of multiple presence, and states 'das der einig licham vff ein zit ist in dem himel vnd vff
dem altar vnd ze Rom vnd ze Engelland vnd ze Strassburg vnd ze Lindow' ('that the one
body is simultaneously in heaven and upon the altar, in Rome and in England, in
Strasbourg and in Lindau'; *Eucharistietraktat*, §2 (262. 23–5)). It is clear why Rome,
Lindau, and Strasbourg (where Marquard had taught) should be mentioned. England is
less clear. It may simply stand for 'somewhere far away'. More suggestively, it may be
included because a serious eucharistic controversy was taking place there at the time, with
the friars leading the theological opposition to Wyclif. However, this list of places may not
necessarily be Marquard's original list, as it is frequently altered in different manuscripts.
See van Maren, 'Receptie en reductie', pp. 103–4; for variants, cf. Hofmann (ed.), *Der
Eucharistie-Traktat*, pp. 181 and 223; and Willing, *Literatur und Ordensreform*, p. 189
[111] See summatively Penn, 'Wyclif and the Sacraments', pp. 249–72; Catto, 'John
Wyclif', pp. 271–4; and Phillips, 'John Wyclif', pp. 568–9.

positions he had adopted much earlier in his academic career.[112] His complex understanding of signs and sacraments, his view of the sacrament as much more than just a sign, and his rejection of the idea that Christ was dimensionally present whilst insisting that he was figuratively (and by which he believes really) present served to underpin his own eucharistic theology.[113]

At the same time, the strictly philosophical line of argument does not sufficiently explain why Wyclif pressed such a fierce campaign in the early 1380s, at the end of his academic career, against contemporary eucharistic theology and its proponents, the pejoratively labelled 'cultores signorum'. Jeremy Catto and Heather Phillips have argued persuasively that the explanation is to be sought not principally in the philosophical debate, but in the contemporary cult of the eucharist. Wyclif's opposition was not just to existing eucharistic theology, but to the contemporary eucharistic piety that the current theology, and the method of its promulgation by the ecclesiastical establishment, served to propagate. Wyclif's doctrine of remanence in *De eucharistia* relied on a figurative conception of the presence of Christ in the consecrated host. It was thus not only a riposte to the doctrine of transubstantiation on the philosophical level, but the result of a search for the formulation of a sacramental theology that would reduce the distance between man and the sacrament: that would, in other words, locate the nature of the consecrated host on a less sublime plane, allow its supporting theology to be explained comprehensibly, and so reduce the generalized awe and fear of the sacrament.[114] Wyclif argued that the sacrament had become the focus of idolatry, because it was worshipped as if it were actually and really the body of Christ; which, he argued, clerics (and especially friars) taught that it quite literally was. In reality, Christ's body was not perceptible in the sacrament with corporeal eyes, and could not therefore be present in the host in the manner that the contemporary orthodoxy taught it to be. His fierce attack focused as much on the manner in which eucharistic theology was explained as on its doctrinal content. He held that transubstantiation was too difficult to be popularly understood and clearly explained, with oversimplifying exposition and terrifying *exempla* resulting in generalized misconception and damaging fear.[115] If Wyclif's response to the problematic issues in the eucharistic cult in the later fourteenth century was very different to that of Marquard or

---

[112] Penn, 'Wyclif and the Sacraments', pp. 253–5 and 270–2.
[113] Ibid. 245–9 and 264–70.
[114] See Catto, 'John Wyclif', pp. 273–82.
[115] See ibid. 284–6; Phillips, 'John Wyclif', pp. 561 and 568–79; and Penn, 'Wyclif and the Sacraments', pp. 248 and 255–6.

Matthaeus, the issues with which he wrestled were very similar. He was, to put it another way, essentially using different means to achieve the same fundamental ends in the alteration of the popular cult of the eucharist.

The final piece in the northern European eucharistic jigsaw of the later fourteenth century is to be found in Bohemia, where a lively and sometimes heated debate on the eucharist had broken out. Of the numerous figures who are known to have engaged in this debate before Jan Hus came to dominate the scene, two intellectuals of particular prominence command our attention: Jan Milíč of Kroměříž (Johannes Milicius de Chremsir) and Matthew of Janov. Milíč belonged to the generation immediately prior to that of Marquard and Matthaeus of Cracow. He is first attested in Prague in 1358, serving in the imperial chancery of Karl IV, and became a cathedral canon. Under the influence of the popular preacher Konrad von Waldhausen he gave up his offices to preach in the city following Konrad's death in 1369. He himself died in 1374, after having defended himself successfully in Avignon against a charge of heresy.[116] Much of his preaching was in the German vernacular.[117] More than one hundred manuscripts of his various works survive, principal amongst which is the Latin postil (sermon collection) *Gratia Dei*.[118]

In this postil, his sermon for the feast of Corpus Christi abandons his usual homiletic style in favour of the presentation of a concatenation of authoritative *sententiae* in support of his advocacy of daily sacramental reception for the laity. As often in his writing, a strong eschatological perspective is evident in this text: sacramental realities, according to Milíč, only attain their true perfection in the eternal life to come. His reinterpretation of the pertinent patristic authorities challenged the dominant, restrictive climate that discouraged sacramental reception by using those texts to substantiate the creation of a climate of fear. Instead he conceived of reception in ecclesial-communal terms, and envisaged a holy community united in Christ through frequent reception, common asceticism, and religious poverty. At the same time he did not, unlike Marquard, challenge the need to attain a suitable state of personal worthiness to receive the sacrament.[119]

[116] For Milíč's biography see Morée, *Preaching*, pp. 60–75.
[117] Ibid. 54–5 and 71.
[118] See Kadlec, 'Milíč, Jan, von Kremsier', cols. 524–7; and Löser, 'Jan Milíč', pp. 234–5.
[119] Marin, *L'Archevêque, le maître et le dévot*, pp. 469–72; and Holeton, 'The Bohemian Eucharistic Movement', pp. 28–9.

The charge of heresy against Milíč appears to have been motivated in part by his criticism of the moral standards of mendicant friars and secular clerics in Prague (for once united by their opposition to Milíč), and in part by his problematic eschatology, most notably a feature of his influential *Libellus de Antichristo*.[120] But the list of charges also touches on the eucharistic question, and includes the accusation of having taught that it was necessary for salvation for every individual to receive the sacrament at least twice a week.[121] The inclusion of this accusation was partly a result of the role the eucharist played in Milíč's eschatological vision, where it served to strengthen the bonds of the faithful community awaiting the onset of the apocalypse. But at the same time, the charge had an independent status. Its inclusion thus also reflects an opposition to the equivalent status Milíč afforded laity with ordained priests in the permissible frequency of reception.[122]

Matthew of Janov (d. 1394), also a canon of Prague cathedral, was an exact contemporary of Marquard, and knew Milíč's work well. He is the author of an immense work in five books known as the *Regulae Veteris et Novi Testamenti*, written in response to a synodal decision of 19 October 1388 that prohibited any more than monthly reception for the laity, and a series of similarly restrictive measures (some against Matthew personally) in 1388–9. Its fourth and fifth books are entirely dedicated to the justification of frequent lay communion.[123] In the sharper atmosphere, Matthew was more insistent even than Milíč on the necessity of frequent sacramental reception (and much more insistent than Hus would ever be). He stressed the communal, familial aspects of the eucharist, linking it more closely to the commemoration of the Last Supper than of Christ's Passion, and viewed the sacrament as a nourishing, strengthening force that bound the entire church together in union as part of Christ's mystical body. He argued in favour of a return to the frequent reception common in the early church, which he believed would counteract the corruption and division (he wrote, of course, at the height of the Great Schism) in the contemporary church.[124]

But Matthew reserved his fiercest criticism for the contemporary practice of eucharistic celebration, and the relationship between priest and faithful. The 'cult of respect' for the sacrament, so Matthew, was a specious

---

[120] Morée, *Preaching*, pp. 72–5; on the radical eschatology of the *Libellus de Antichristo* see pp. 145–58.
[121] Marin, *L'Archevêque, le maître et le dévot*, pp. 472–3.
[122] See Morée, *Preaching*, pp. 73–5.
[123] Marin, *L'Archevêque, le maître et le dévot*, pp. 486–90; for an overview of the contents of the *Regulae*, see Morée, *Preaching*, pp. 29–31.
[124] See Marin, *L'Archevêque, le maître et le dévot*, pp. 490–1 and 495–7.

construction. Long devotional preparations were wholly unnecessary; only mortal sin should exclude an individual from the sacrament. Purely spiritual communion served only as a device to strengthen the authority of the ordained priesthood, and was intensely damaging to the spiritual health of the individual. Matthew's overriding concern was to revalorize the status of the laity in respect of the priesthood. He was a fervent advocate of beguines and beghards, who had also attracted recent ecclesiastical censure, and stressed that the laity were equal to the priesthood in their capacity to receive the sacrament frequently (if not to consecrate), and indeed to be saintly.[125] It was these anti-establishment overtones, together with the eschatological preoccupations that Matthew shared with Milíč, which attracted opposition and some official criticism.[126]

There are obvious differences between the individuals we have mentioned: Marquard, Matthaeus of Cracow, John Wyclif, Jan Milíč, and Matthew of Janov. They all propose different solutions to essentially the same core problems in contemporary eucharistic piety—Wyclif with his novel sacramental theology; Milíč and Matthew with their advocacy of frequent lay reception; Matthaeus and Marquard using fear and love respectively to encourage sacramental reception. It is striking that a series of such heavyweight individuals from across northern Europe should produce a series of extensive, and either widely transmitted or otherwise exceptionally influential works within a twenty-year period at the end of the fourteenth century.[127] It not only provides the broader context to Marquard's treatise on the eucharist, but demonstrates that the well-known eucharistic controversies in England and in Bohemia were not independent or isolated. Rather, they were the most eye-catching manifestations of a more generalized reaction against prevailing trends in the cult of the eucharist and the methods of its instruction in the later fourteenth century.

It is difficult to make any generalizations as to how the intellectuals of the fifteenth century dealt with these issues that occupied their late fourteenth-century counterparts. This is not merely a matter of the absence of relevant modern scholarship. The weight of the Hussite controversy occludes the consideration in fifteenth-century works of the issues at which we have

---

[125] See ibid. 491–4; Browe, *Die häufige Kommunion*, pp. 33–6; Catto, 'John Wyclif', pp. 283–4; and Holeton, 'The Bohemian Eucharistic Movement', pp. 30–1.

[126] See Marin, *L'Archevêque, le maître et le dévot*, pp. 499–500; and Morée, *Preaching*, p. 29.

[127] A small group of similar works, of which Matthaeus' *Dialogus* is by far the earliest, is presented and categorized by Grosse, *Heilsungewißheit und Scrupulositas*, pp. 203–7.

looked, by imposing a new set of pressing issues: issues such as utraquism
(receiving both the bread and the wine), which were unknown to the earlier
period.[128] There are certainly some fifteenth-century works that deal with the
relationship between sacramental and spiritual reception in a similar way to
their late fourteenth-century counterparts. A good example is the *Devote
samenspraak over de veelvuldige communie*, a Dutch treatise written around
1435 and probably of Dominican origin. This treatise, a dialogue between a
confessor and his spiritual daughter, deals with the same ideas of worthy and
unworthy reception with which the fourteenth-century treatises engage. From
Caspers's descriptions, it may well be influenced by Matthaeus of Cracow's
Dialogus, whose approximate conclusion it would appear to share.[129] A key
issue of fifteenth-century discourse on the eucharist is the permissible frequency of sacramental reception, and it is to that issue that we must turn now.

In 1938 the Jesuit scholar Peter Browe published his seminal study, *Die
häufige Kommunion im Mittelalter*, until recently the only work to deal at all
with the intellectual controversies surrounding the permissible frequency of
sacramental reception. Browe's work determined the framework of the
subsequent historiography, and is probably responsible for two widespread
assumptions. First, that because all medieval eucharistic writing discusses
the proper frequency of reception, it was therefore always a controversial
issue. Second, that the issue represents a point of collision between the
desire of the recipients, whether lay or enclosed religious, to receive the
sacrament frequently, and the intention of the established ecclesiastical
hierarchy (whatever that may be) to restrict access to the eucharist and
maintain control over its reception. Both of these assumptions are correct at
certain times—not least in late medieval Bohemia. But they do not always
hold true.[130] The issue tends to be set out in medieval treatises as a series of
guidelines, rather than by insisting on the adoption of a particular position

---

[128] Marquard, for example, deals with the question of why the sacrament exists in two
kinds, body and blood, in terms of their consecration during the mass. The issue of
reception in one or both kinds simply does not arise: see the *Eucharistietraktat*, §12 (316.
10–20). On the role of the wine in the mass before the 15th cent., see Rubin, *Corpus
Christi*, p. 48.

[129] See Caspers, *De eucharistische vroomheid*, pp. 219–22; and id., '*Meum summum
desiderium*', pp. 145–6.

[130] For an example of modern scholarship following Browe's tone, see Torsy, 'Eucharistische Frömmigkeit', pp. 92–3. Caspers shows additionally that the modern, post-
Tridentine idea that sacramental reception is of a completely different order to purely
spiritual reception was not uniformly held in the later Middle Ages: see Caspers, *De
eucharistische vroomheid*, pp. 222–4.

in a controversial debate. Its widespread presence in catechetical and pragmatic works is related, more than anything else, to the general development of a science of pastoration in the twelfth and thirteenth centuries — a process not dissimilar to the development of a scholarly discussion on confessional practice. The requirement of the Fourth Lateran Council in 1215, in the canon *Omnis utriusque sexus*, that all Christians should receive the sacrament once annually at Easter was much less of a controlling restriction on existing practice, as it is sometimes interpreted, than an insistence that the sacrament *had* to be received at least once annually: an element in the wider conciliar programme of establishing a working parochial system across Christendom. Frequency of sacramental reception could become a controversial issue in individual cases, particularly from the later fourteenth century; but as Hans-Jochen Schiewer notes, there was no normative consensus on the issue, let alone dogmatic proscriptions.[131]

A representative position of the thirteenth-century reality is that with which David of Augsburg opens his discussion of the frequency of reception, in the final chapter of *De compositione*. He refuses to set firm rules:

Si vero desiderat aliquis expediri, utrum sit melius saepius, an rarius corporis Christi suscipere Sacramentum; videtur mihi, quod non possit super hoc omnibus dari regula uniformis. Varia sunt hominum merita, diversa operum studia et differentia desideria et multiplices sancti Spiritus operationes in singulis et diversi status etiam in Religione.[132]

(If someone really desires to be told whether it is better to receive the sacrament of the body of Christ more often or more rarely: well, it seems to me that a uniform rule for everyone governing this cannot be given. The merits of men vary, they engage in divergent activities, and their desires are different; the workings of the Holy Spirit are manifold in each and every one of them, and they are even of different states in the religious life.)

David continues by describing the sacrament as a spiritual medicine, which different patients require in different quantities and with different frequencies, depending on the nature of their spiritual sickness—just as a medicine for the body is administered by the supervising doctor. In the first half of the fourteenth century, Nicholas of Lyra's treatment of the issue in his *Dicta de sacramento* gives no hint that the issue was particularly controversial. He is able to summarize the teaching of earlier luminaries into a general principle:

[. . .] sed ad propositum: Circa hoc datur a doctoribus vna regula generalis, quam bonam puto et veram, et est ista: Quid si quis experiatur, quod in celebracione frequenti augeatur in ipso et timor peccati et deuocio dei et huiusmodi qui sunt

---

[131] Schiewer, 'Auditionen und Visionen', pp. 295–9.

[132] David von Augsburg, *De compositione*, lib. 3, cap. 70, §1 (p. 374); note the critical tone of Browe's discussion of David in this respect in *Die häufige Kommunion*, p. 158.

effectus sacramenti, licite ymmo laudabiliter potest omni die celebrare. Si autem in illo generetur in ipso quasi quedam familiaritas, et quod senciat se ex hoc indeuotum, et senciat se eciam ad sacramentum quasi ad mensam vel aliquid aliud officium humanum accedere; in tali casu dicunt doctores quod tunc consulendum est rarius accedere.[133]

(But regarding the proposition: A general rule is given about this by the learned doctors, which I find to be both good and true. It is this. If someone should discern, in frequent celebration of the mass, that his fear of sin, devotion to God, and everything like that which is an effect of the sacrament, were to increase in him, then he can permissibly—nay, laudably—celebrate the mass daily. If in doing so, however, a certain kind of familiarity were to be engendered in him, such that he felt himself irreverent as a result, and also felt himself going to receive the sacrament as if he were going to the dining table or some other human rite; then in that case the learned doctors assert that he is to be advised to go to receive more rarely.)

In considering the period before the Bohemian controversies introduced a new sharpness to the debate, I would argue that it is inappropriate, on the basis of such evidence as the preceding examples supply, to presume that those writers who address the issue do so with the express purpose of restricting access to the eucharist and maintaining a strict clerical control of its administration. At the same time, there is certainly something in Browe's statement that, even if weekly or daily reception was not explicitly refused, 'die Erlaubnis mit soviel ,wenn' und ,aber' umgeben [war], daß sie einer Ablehnung gleichkam'[134] ('the permission was hedged about with so many "ifs" and "buts" that it was not much different to a refusal').

In Bohemia the situation was rather different, and has recently been the subject of an illuminative study by Olivier Marin. Marin sees the first signs of the impetus towards more frequent eucharistic reception in the *Malogranatum*, a master–pupil dialogue on the three stages of spiritual perfection written around the middle of the fourteenth century in the Cistercian abbey of Aula Regia at Zbraslav, just south of Prague on the Vltava, and very widely transmitted in around 150 manuscripts. The author views sacramental reception as principal among the indispensable means towards the purification of the heart, and so dedicates four chapters to the eucharist. The *Malogranatum* seeks to encourage sacramental reception using methods rather similar to those of Marquard's *Eucharistietraktat*, placing stress

---

[133] Nicholas of Lyra, *Dicta de sacramento*, §13.
[134] Browe, *Die häufige Kommunion*, p. 22; see pp. 136–8 on practical factors that militated against more frequent lay reception, such as the required payment of monetary contributions to parochial clergy: on which see Duffy, *The Stripping of the Altars*, pp. 93–5.

on the institution of the sacrament as a medicine for the sick and the sinful, not for the perfect, and on reception out of love as preferable to abstention through fear. Unlike Marquard, the author still sees extensive devotional preparations as necessary, though views the more frequent recipient as better able to participate in the fruits of the sacrament. The author refuses to give a strict rule on the proper frequency of reception—and does so by means of what is quickly recognizable as the quotation from David von Augsburg's *De compositione* that we have just seen above. Even so, the author views weekly and even daily reception in true humility as superior to solely annual communion.[135]

The first known recipient of the *Malogranatum* outside the monastic convent was Jan Milíč, whom we have discussed earlier. Milíč was evidently the first to preach in favour of daily sacramental reception for the laity, though still with a strong emphasis on the necessity of preparations to achieve a commensurate state of personal worthiness to do so. Milíč was followed by Thomas Štitný, a married knight with five children, who in 1376 produced an extensive work in the Czech vernacular entitled the *Knížky šestery o obecných věcech křesťanských* ('six books on general matters of the Christian faith'), but which survives in only one manuscript. This includes a chapter on the eucharist that broadly follows Milíč's position, saw a weekly frequency of lay reception as ideal, and argued for a reduction in the period of abstention from sex between married couples prior to reception from three days to one.[136] The central years of the 1370s evidently saw the debate on the frequency of reception attain a level of particular intensity, marked by the trial of Milíč in 1373–4, the production of the first vernacular text in the shape of Štitný's treatise of 1376, and the first written intervention on the subject from a university academic at some point shortly thereafter in the shape of the *De frequenti communione ad plebanum Martinum* of Adalbert Raňkův of Ježov.

Adalbert attests that agitation was widespread in the city of Prague in the mid-1370s, stirred by sermons addressing the frequency debate, and with inscriptions on some church walls taking positions for and against daily lay communion. Adalbert had been an associate of Milíč, and his epistolary treatise took a broadly favourable position towards more frequent communion. At the same time he ruled out any more than a weekly frequency for reception by laity, and was considerably less radical than either Milíč or Štitný, requiring an extensive catalogue of prerequisites for personal wor-

---

[135] Marin, *L'Archevêque, le maître et le dévot*, pp. 467–9, with the quotation from the *Malogranatum* recognizably adopted from David von Augsburg located at p. 468 n. 2.
[136] Ibid. 474–6.

thiness to be met prior to sacramental reception. There is some evidence in addition that the issue was considered by further university academics in more formal theological contexts subsequently during the 1380s.[137] By the later 1380s, a climate of repression sat over Prague, with the expulsion of the beghards by royal order in spring 1388, the prohibition of any more than monthly lay reception by the episcopal synod of 19 October 1388, and further conservative moves following in 1388–9, some of which targeted Matthew of Janov (who had now become active in the debate) personally.[138] We have already discussed Matthew's response, but he was not alone. The German theologian Heinrich von Bitterfeld, having arrived in Prague in 1386, took a position broadly supportive of Matthew's in his *De institutione sacramenti Eucharistiae*, and then produced a radical polemic in favour of daily lay reception, the *De crebra communione*, in 1391.[139] The archbishop of Prague, Jan of Jenštejn, reversed the earlier prohibitions—perhaps, as Marin suggests, as a result of a personal curative experience with the sacrament in 1390; or perhaps, as Matthias Nuding suggests, as a result of the ascendancy of 'liberals' like Heinrich von Bitterfeld at the archiepiscopal court—and a synodal statute of 16 June 1391 removed all restrictions governing the permissible frequency of daily lay reception.[140]

Marquard's treatment of the issue is indirect. The sixth section of the *Eucharistietraktat* concerns the necessary attitude of those who receive the sacrament, and is divided into three parts. The first, and by far the longest part, sets out the required attitude for the annual communicant, and provides lengthy model prayers both for each of the three identified and interlinked stages of preparation (humble inspection of conscience, taking confidence in God's mercy, having desire to improve oneself), and for recitation after reception.[141] As we might expect, Marquard strikes an insistent note on God's love and mercy, manifested in the sacrament, which balances out any sense of fear that the process of preparation and prior confession may induce. Thus the first stage of preparation involves introspection of the conscience and confession, during which the individual examines his sinful life and realizes his unworthiness.[142] Immediately then

---

[137] Marin, *L'Archevêque, le maître et le dévot*, 477–83, Nuding, *Matthäus von Krakau*, pp. 38–9.
[138] Marin, *L'Archevêque, le maître et le dévot*, pp. 486–90.
[139] Ibid. 500–3.
[140] Ibid. 503–4; Nuding, *Matthäus von Krakau*, pp. 36–7.
[141] *Eucharistietraktat*, §6 (288. 20–299. 11).
[142] Ibid. (289. 16–28).

the second involves the realization that God's mercy vastly outweighs these sins, and that the sacrament was instituted to heal the unworthy rather than to reward the worthy:

Das ander stuk ist, wenn du betrachtest din vnwirdikeit, so soltu denn din hertz in zůversicht der milti gottes setzen vnd bebedenken, dz sin erbermd vnmessiger gross ist, denn din súnd vnd gebresten. Vnd solt da mit ein gůt zůversicht vnd getrúwen zů der grossen erbermde gottes haben vnd gedenken, als er sich gab in menschlich natur nicht durch der gerechten willen, mer och dur der vngerechten willen, darumb dz si in im gerecht werdin, das er ouch git sich in dem sacrament nit allein durch der gerechten willen, mer ouch durch der vngerechten willen, dar vmb dz si in im gerecht und gnadrich werdint.[143]

(The second point is that when you consider your unworthiness, you should place your heart in the confidence of God's clemency and reflect that his mercy is immeasurably greater than your sins and failings. With this you should have firm faith and confidence in God's great mercy, and reflect that as he gave himself in human nature not for the sake of the just, but rather for the sake of the unjust, so that they might become justified in him; so too he gives himself in the sacrament not merely for the sake of the just, but rather for the sake of the unjust, so that they may be justified and full of grace in him.)

None of these stages for preparation is exclusive or involve particular difficulty. In the opening to the sixth section, Marquard suggested that the sacrament should be received 'frequently':

[. . .] Won nu die natur als vast nider sinket, dar vmb bedarff si wol vfenthaltes. Hier vmb wiltu bestan in gŏtlichem leben, so ist dir notdurfftig, dz du dik dz edel sacrament enpfachest.[144]

(For human nature now falls down so easily that it is well in need of support. Consequently if you want to remain in a godly life, it is necessary for you to receive the noble sacrament frequently.)

That, however, must be understood relatively, as applying to the entire sixth section, because it is clear from the pupil's statement at the end of the first part that the previous material applied to annual communicants:

Der Junger sprach: Ich merk wol, dz dis alles einem jeklichen menschen zů gehört, der zů dem sacrament gat, ob er joch alleine ze einem mal in dem jar zů gat. Nu wússte ich ouch gern, wz sunder einem menschen zů gehŏrt, die dik in dem jar zů gand.[145]

---

[143] Ibid. (289. 29–290. 6).
[144] Ibid. (289. 9–12). This section is a paraphrase of Tauler. The idea of receiving the sacrament frequently—'dik'—is Marquard's own, though it is in keeping with Tauler's eucharistic teaching: cf. Johannes Tauler, *Predigt* 57 (266. 26–267. 2).
[145] *Eucharistietrakat*, §6 (295. 11–14).

(The pupil said: I can well see that all of this pertains to every individual who goes to receive the sacrament, should he go to receive but once a year. Now I would like to know what pertains specifically to an individual who goes to receive frequently throughout the year.)

The next two, far shorter, sections deal with the preconditions for monthly and for weekly reception. Particularly where weekly reception is concerned, the requirements do take on something of a restrictive character, that would necessitate a near-constant mental discipline and substantial interior preparation. This section is actually, as Willing has identified, adapted from Tauler.[146] But Marquard has built flexibility into the system. At the beginning of the third section, on weekly reception, he states that an individual fulfilling the requirements of the second section should, with his confessor's permission, be permitted to receive as frequently as he desires. Fulfilling the requirements of the third section then make very frequent reception certain. This, incidentally, is another adaptation from Tauler, though the mention of the confessor's permission is Marquard's own:

Du solt wússen, das ich dz schetz, wo ein mensch ist, der sich súndig in der warheit schetzet vnd er gern wolte gůt sin jn diser demůtikeit, vnd er ouch het ein erwirdig vorcht vnd wolt gern leben nach dem liebsten willen gotz vnd sich kerren von den kreaturen, als ver er mocht, ein sőlicher mensche mőchte wol wie dik er wolt zůgan—das er echt sines bichters vrlob hetti. Doch so wil ich dir fúrbas zů disem puncten antwúrten vnd sprich also: weler mensch dise vier stuk an im hat, die sant Dyonisius schribet, der mag dicke zů gan. Wand er hat denne an im, das zů einem semlichen menschen hőret.[147]

(You should know that I think that where there is an individual who honestly considers himself to be sinful, and in this humble state would like to be good; who has a reverential fear, and who would like to live according to the most beloved will of God; and who would like to turn away from the created world insofar as he could do so: such an individual could well go to receive as often as he wanted to, as long as he had his confessor's permission. But I will give you a better answer to this point, and so say this: that whichever individual has these four attributes that St Dionysius defines can go to receive frequently. For then he bears those features that pertain to such an individual.)

Finally, Marquard sets out the five signals by which an individual recognizes whether he ought to receive the sacrament frequently. These are interior signals: they include such indications as being more inclined to

---

[146] *Eucharistietrakat*, §6 (295. 15–296. 30 and 296. 31–298. 14); cf. Johannes Tauler, *Predigt* 60f. (311. 10–312. 10); and Willing, *Literatur und Ordensreform*, pp. 212–13.

[147] *Eucharistietrakat*, §6 (297. 3–12); cf. Johannes Tauler, *Predigt* 57 (267. 17–23).

performing good works, or (the same point that Nicholas of Lyra made) perceiving greater desire to receive, and not falling into lassitude and ennui.[148] In conclusion, Marquard introduces another important element of flexibility into his system, which serves to encourage a more frequent reception. He states that not all of these signals need to be present for the person to receive more frequently. The presence of one or two suffices:

Wenn nu der mentsch dise fünff zeichen in im vindet, so sol er wússen, das im gůt ist, das er dz edel sacrament dik enpfach. Vnd ob er si nicht in im alle vindet, hat er denn ettliches an im, denocht sol er dester diker zůgan, das dise fünff zeichen dester warlicher in im gewúrket werdent von des sacramentes krafft wegen.[149]

(If the individual finds these five signs in himself, then he shall know that it is good for him to receive the noble sacrament frequently. If he cannot find them all in himself, but only has some of them in him, then he should go to receive all the more frequently in any case, so that these five signs may be effected within him all the more firmly by the power of the sacrament.)

A similar flexibility is then evident in the thirteenth section, which establishes why a person should receive. Six different reasons are set out, but only one needs to be present to justify reception, and they include such general reasons as 'wenn der mentsch jnwendig ernst vnd begird enpfindet zů dem sacrament'[150] ('if the individual feels inner seriousness and desire for the sacrament'). Marquard's list of which persons should not receive, constituting the tenth section, is a short, formal list—the unbaptized, those fundamentally doubting the faith, those knowingly in a state of unconfessed mortal sin, and so forth—and provides little further insight.[151]

It is tempting to associate these three different sets of preparatory scheme, associated with three different frequencies of reception, with the three stages of the contemplative life. There is, however, no explicit indication that this should be the case. It is plausible to suggest that the *Eucharistietraktat* was written with a wide audience in mind, and was not intended to apply only to the contemplative religious living an enclosed life. Furthermore, Marquard's focus is on the preparation and accompanying prayers for those communicating annually, which provides a certain indication of the implicit audience. His tripartite division permits some flexibility, but is not explicitly

---

[148] *Eucharistietraktat*, §6 (298. 15–299. 11).
[149] Ibid. (299. 6–11).
[150] Ibid., §13 (here 316. 29–30).
[151] Ibid., §10 (311. 11–312. 7).

energetic: the reader is not exhorted to ascend from one level to the next, but is instead presented in parallel with three different schemes of preparation, respectively related to three different frequencies of reception.

Antje Willing has subjected the sixth section of Marquard's *Eucharistie-traktat* to detailed examination.[152] She maintains that the second preparatory scheme, which Marquard associates with an approximately monthly reception, was intended for those belonging to a religious order. This she argues on the basis of stipulations the scheme sets out, the absence of form prayers, and (relying on Browe), the 'normal frequency' for the religious to communicate being monthly.[153] This is not implausible, but to insist on it is too rigid. Willing expresses some surprise that the Dominican nuns of the Katharinenkloster in Nuremberg annotated the first, much longer preparatory scheme in their copy of the treatise, rather than the second, when the second was that which was 'surely' relevant to them: an interpretation thus which proceeds somewhat against the evidence.

More problematic is Willing's description of the sixth section of the *Eucharistietraktat* as a scheme of mystical ascent. She argues that the third scheme, for weekly reception, is a *via purgativa* that Marquard restricts to the *perfecti*. But were this third scheme a *via purgativa*, then it could not be restricted to those who are already perfected in the contemplative life: perfection would be its result, not its precondition. Willing does not take into account the flexibility that is inherent in Marquard's system, and infers from the adoption of material from Tauler or Eckhart that Marquard's resultant text is necessarily mystical. The heart of the matter is her interpretation of the fourth and final criterion in the third scheme (for weekly reception), which begins with Tauler and incorporates one sentence by Eckhart:

Das vierd ist, er sol sin ein tempel gottes.[154] Dz ist also ze verstande, das kein creatur statt habe in sinem hertzen. Mer er sol aller bilde als ledig stan, als er was, e er ie ward geborn.[155] Dar vmb sol got lúchten allein in sinem hertzen in einer vinster-nisse aller bilden vnd formen. Won sich selb vnd alles, dz got nit ist, sol er haben ze ruggen gestossen vnd bloss komen mit dem crútz vff sinem ruggen. Vnd denne so nim war, wie wúrket got so adellich in disen lúten; wes sind si trostes warten vnd heimlicheit von dem heilgen sacrament.[156]

[152] See, in the following, Willing, *Literatur und Ordensreform*, pp. 211–16.
[153] Ibid. 212.
[154] Cf. Johannes Tauler, *Predigt* 60f. (311. 17; repeated 312. 4–5).
[155] Cf. Eckhart, *Predigt* 2 (vol. 1: 25. 1–2).
[156] *Eucharistietraktat*, §6 (297. 30–298. 6).

(The fourth [criterion] is that he should be a temple of God. This is to be understood thus: namely, that no created thing should occupy a place in his heart. Instead he should be as free of all images as he was before he was ever born. Thereupon God alone shall illuminate his heart in a darkness of all images and forms, for he shall have turned his back on himself and on everything that is not God, and shall come nakedly with the cross upon his back. And so take note how nobly God works in these people: what consolation and intimacy they await from the holy sacrament!)

The sentence adapted from Eckhart (whose original read, with a much stronger Platonic overtone, 'dô er niht enwas' ('when he was nothing') rather than 'e er ie ward geborn' ('before he was ever born')), together with the following statement, full of Dionysian language, about God alone illuminating into the heart that is totally dark in its freedom from all images, does create the impression that the passage has mystical import. Yet there is a difference between using mystical language, and describing mystical experience. Here, the point is not mystical, but ethical: the person should have rejected all that is not God. There is no reference to union, eucharistic or otherwise, in the passage. Marquard speaks merely of God working nobly in such a person—and the passage continues thereafter with ethical import, concerning the need for proper introspection and caution against the danger of venial sin. Willing argues that this passage represents the culmination in union of a mystical scheme.[157] But there is no real discussion of union here, and certainly no mystical scheme. The idea that the three schemes of the sixth section represent a ladder of contemplative ascent is, as I have already argued, to impose an energetic model not present in the work itself.

The division of the preparatory schemes for reception according to the three stages of the religious life is, by contrast, clear and present in the final three sections of Matthaeus of Cracow's *Dialogus*.[158] These are short sections which outline the correct *dispositio* of the *incipientes*, the *proficientes*, and the *perfecti* respectively. As in the *Eucharistietraktat*, the implications for the frequency of communion are indirect. Unlike the *Eucharistietraktat*, Matthaeus' focus, judging by the respective length and detail of the sections, is on the central section—the *proficientes*. They should prepare to receive the sacrament more often, even frequently, by modifying their entire pattern of existence:

---

[157] Willing, *Literatur und Ordensreform*, pp. 229–30.
[158] Matthaeus of Cracow, *Dialogus*, §12–14, ll. 1174–264 (pp. 406–9).

Proficienti vero, qualis debet esse omnis, qui saepe aut frequenter communicare proponit, non sufficit haec predicta, sed tota vita sua debet esse praeparatio ad susceptionem tantae rei[.][159]

(For the *proficiens*, which category should include everyone who proposes to receive communion often or frequently, these aforesaid things are insufficient; rather, his entire life should be a preparation to receive something so great.)

The stipulations are partly normative, ethical features like flight from vice and avoiding the occasion of sin; but also partly contemplative, most notably so in the case of preparation 'by inserting the self into Christ's wounds' ('inserendo se vulneribus Jesu Christi'[160]), an idea originating with Bernard of Clairvaux. Matthaeus' Reason, for whom the final three sections of the *Dialogus* are monologues, then describes eucharistic union before setting out methods of spiritual exercise and producing an invective against hypocrites, more concerned with disciplining the outer than the inner person.

Matthaeus is clear in identifying the three *dispositiones* with the three stages of the religious life. He does not set out model frequencies in the same way that Marquard does. There is no indication or implication whatsoever that he would instruct the *perfecti* to receive more frequently than the *proficientes*. Nor is there any indication as to what those frequencies should be—'saepe aut frequenter' ('often or frequently') is, as we have seen, his rather general designation with regard to the *proficientes*. Where frequency of reception is concerned, the crucial point to note is that the issue was, paradoxically, not central either for Marquard or Matthaeus. Neither stipulate rigid restrictions; Matthaeus' scheme is vague and Marquard's is internally flexible. As far as Marquard is concerned, this is not surprising, because he was not part of the Bohemian debate, and the issue had no such pressing urgency in Germany. The contours of the Bohemian debate cannot be imposed onto the *Eucharistietraktat*, and so we cannot state—as Annelies Hofmann did—'daß [Marquard] für häufigen Sakramentsempfang eintritt'[161] ('that Marquard takes a stand in favour of frequent sacramental reception'). Instead, Marquard stands on this issue in a much older tradition of producing interpretable, malleable guidelines. We have seen this represented by the works of his Franciscan forebears,

[159] Matthaeus of Cracow, *Dialogus*, §13, ll. 1209–12 (p. 407).
[160] Ibid., l. 1218 (p. 407).
[161] Hofmann (ed.), *Der Eucharistie-Traktat*, p. 248.

David von Augsburg and Nicholas of Lyra. Marquard's permission of weekly reception for the most devout was by no means exceptional—Jean Gerson stated the same thing in his *Doctrinal aux simples gens* of 1387.[162]

Matthaeus of Cracow, however, is rather more interesting in this regard. The *Dialogus* was written in the Prague of 1388, at the height of the debate. Matthew of Janov incorporated part of it, heavily and tendentiously altered to support his own position, into a concatenation of authoritative texts which supposedly supported the idea that weekly lay reception had been solid ecclesiastical tradition since the primitive church, and which formed part of the *Regulae*.[163] So tendentious was Matthew's adaptation of his source material, however, that as Matthias Nuding has pointed out, we cannot draw any conclusions from his use of the *Dialogus* as to the real position of that work in the Bohemian debate.[164] Nuding concludes that the *Dialogus* was perhaps written as a response to the same synodal decision of 1388 that exercised Matthew of Janov to produce the *Regulae*, whilst admitting that Matthaeus of Cracow himself was not evidently concerned with numerical frequency.[165] Sven Grosse goes further, and sees the *Dialogus* as something of a partisan treatise in support of Matthew of Janov.[166]

All three—Grosse, Marin, and Nuding—only provide cursory considerations of the *Dialogus*, and consider it as part of the complex of Bohemian texts produced on the issue of the permissible frequency of sacramental reception. This is entirely logical, given the time and place of its composition. But all have some difficulty in assigning the work a place within that debate. In fact, it engages with a quite different set of issues. Matthaeus' reticence to specify appropriate frequencies of reception may even reflect a conscious decision to avoid engaging with that particular debate in the heated climate of 1388, and rather to produce a work that would address a much wider audience, and have (as it then did) a far greater readership. Matthaeus, like Marquard—and not like the other Bohemian writers—was concerned not with the nature of the ecclesiastical restrictions on sacramental reception, but with the kind of restrictions individuals imposed on themselves; restrictions imposed out of a tremendous and overwhelming sense of fear.

---

[162] See Caspers, *De eucharistische vroomheid*, pp. 199–201.
[163] Marin, *L'Archevêque, le maître et le dévot*, pp. 497–8, with an identification of the texts used at pp. 592–5.
[164] Nuding, *Matthäus von Krakau*, pp. 35–8.
[165] Ibid. 39–41.
[166] Grosse, *Heilsungewißheit und Scrupulositas*, p. 200.

Only in the fifteenth century did the frequent reception of the sacrament become more widely controversial outside of Bohemia, where the debate was rapidly subsumed into the much more ferocious utraquist controversy. The advocacy of more frequent reception that Browe notes in the sermons of Vincent Ferrer (d. 1419) and Bernardino of Siena (d. 1444) does not really exceed the frequency encouraged by the fourteenth-century intellectuals we have encountered. Events in Bohemia did not have a widespread, uniform impact.[167] Frequent reception was explicitly discouraged in the late medieval movement often compared to the Bohemian reform, the Dutch *Devotio Moderna*, because differing frequencies of reception promoted unhealthy rivalry within the institutions of a movement that laid especial emphasis on its communal character. This appears to have changed completely in the period after 1450—with the notable exception of the humanist Wessel Gansfort (d. 1489), whose belief in the efficacy of spiritual communion was so strong that he held sacramental communion to be unnecessary.[168] The *Imitatio Christi* of Thomas à Kempis, by contrast, was very much a representative of this late fifteenth-century Dutch emphasis on relatively frequent sacramental reception.[169] Frequent lay communion without the insistence on the kind of intensive preparation that authors such as Marquard regarded as necessary, however, was essentially a post-Tridentine phenomenon.

If the permissible frequency of sacramental reception was yet to become controversial when Marquard produced the *Eucharistietraktat*, then a whole series of theological issues were no longer controversial. Leaving aside the hornet's nest that John Wyclif was stirring up in Oxford, key aspects of sacramental theology, such as the nature of the real presence, were issues that had essentially been settled, and on which a basic community of agreed opinion had become established. Marquard's *Eucharistietraktat*, moreover, is neither a work of university theology nor a theoretical or programmatic tract like Wyclif's *De eucharistia*. In consequence, there is little point in demonstrating here how Marquard's position on all the central points of sacramental theology conformed to the orthodox position, and drew in particular on this or that canonical work; in any case, Willing offers a useful

---

[167] See Browe, *Die häufige Kommunion*, pp. 36–8.
[168] See Caspers, *De eucharistische vroomheid*, pp. 217–19; and id., '*Meum summum desiderium*', pp. 143–6.
[169] Goossens, 'Résonances eucharistiques', pp. 182–4.

and thorough study of this nature.[170] Instead, we should look at those areas where there is some difference, innovation, or unusual emphasis in the theology that Marquard explores in the *Eucharistietraktat*: areas where the interface of piety and theology is perceptible. We shall look at the perception of sweetness in the sacrament and then at eucharistic visions.

At the end of the second section of the *Eucharistietraktat*, Marquard makes a long statement about the imperceptibility of Christ's body in the consecrated host. The wider point is that belief in the real presence is a matter of faith, and is not to be proven empirically—a similar point to that which the example of St Louis, which we saw previously, demonstrated earlier in the treatise. The imperceptibility extends beyond the ocular. Marquard states firmly that those who claim to perceive palpable sensation and sweetness in reception of the host are in the wrong:

Du solt gedenken, das dz sacrament in den gelouben ist gesenkt. Dar vmb hat ouch got geordnet, das man sin wise in dem sacrament weder gesechen noch gehörren mag, noch des sacramentes lust in im selb nit enpfindent. [. . .] Dar vmb soltu wüssen, das die gar unrecht hand, die da wellent in dem sacrament bevintlichen lust und süssikeit haben. Won alles enpfinden aller hertzen sol hie verborgen sin, und alles, dz da ist, dz sol in der arch des heilgen geloubens stan.[171]

(You should consider that the sacrament is rooted in faith. Thus God also ordained it that no one can either see or hear his presence in the sacrament, nor feel the pleasure of the sacrament in himself. [. . .] Therefore you should know that those who wish to have tangible pleasure and sweetness in the sacrament are totally in the wrong. For all perception of this kind by the hearts of men shall be concealed here on earth; and everything that is present there [i.e. in the sacrament] shall be located in the ark of holy faith.)

This is clearly a problem of sufficient substance that Marquard addresses it again, and condemns those who ask to receive the sacrament so that they might feel this sensation:

Won du solt vmb kein ander sach zûgan, won in der meinung, das din krankheit gesterkt werd vnd der ewig gott in dir dester me gelobet werd vnd du gebessert. Dis sol din meinung sin vnd anders nicht. Du solt nit zûgan durch lust sûchendes willen oder des gelichen.[172]

---

[170] On Marquard's reception of scholastic theology in the *Eucharistietraktat* see Hofmann (ed.), *Der Eucharistie-Traktat*, pp. 230–2, and Willing, *Literatur und Ordens-reform*, pp. 181–201. A useful guide to the history of eucharistic theology in the medieval period is provided by Rubin, *Corpus Christi*, pp. 14–35; on the specific issue of the nature of Christ's presence and the alternatives to transubstantiation see Burr, *Eucharistic Presence*.

[171] *Eucharistietraktat*, §2 (267. 6–21).

[172] Ibid., §6 (290. 30–4).

(For you should not go to receive for any other reason except in the intention that your frailty may be strengthened, that the eternal God may be praised in you all the more, and that you may be improved. This should be your intention, and nothing else. You should not go to receive for the sake of seeking pleasure or anything like that.)

The actual effects of the sacrament on the recipient are, as Marquard sets out in the eleventh section, spiritual.[173] The ninth section of the treatise, on the other hand, details the six manners in which the eucharistic host can be received. Willing has compared these closely, and has confirmed that Marquard essentially follows the four categories of reception identified by Scotus: unsacramental reception of the sacrament (where the recipient has no knowledge that the host is a sacrament, or no faith in it), sacramental but not spiritual reception, sacramental and spiritual reception, and, finally, purely spiritual reception without ingestion of the consecrated host.[174] Yet Scotus has four categories, and Marquard has six. One of these extra categories is drawn from Albert the Great, and adds in those who consumed likenesses of the sacrament—by which Marquard understands Old Testament prefigurations.[175] The other extra category is gained by dividing the existing, normative category of sacramental and spiritual reception, the *manducatio sacramentalis et spiritualis*. This is divided into such reception with the perception of especial sweetness, and such reception without it:

Die vierd wise ist, so man das war sacrament enpfachet in gnad sacramentlich vnd geistlich mit einem enpfinden sundriger süssikeit, so vil das ein mentschen dunkt, er möcht bas an liplich spis sin denn ân das sacrament. Vnd dz beschicht ettlichen menschen, die da in luterkeit irs hertzen got alleine lebend vnd sich selb vnd alle dinge hand ze ruggen gestossen, die got nit sind.

Das fünfft stuke ist, so der mentsche das sacrament in gnad geistlich vnd sacramentlich enpfachet ân alles enpfinden sundriges lustes, mer sin hertz allein senket in den glouben mit warer demütikeit. Vnd dz ist gemein vil lüten vnd beschicht vil den liebsten

---

[173] Cf. ibid., §11 (312. 10–313. 12).

[174] See Willing, *Literatur und Ordensreform*, pp. 197–201, on *Eucharistietraktat*, §9 (308. 31–310. 10).

[175] *Eucharistietraktat*, §9 (309. 8–13). See Willing, pp. 197–8, who notes that Marquard introduces a novelty not to be found in Albert's work in stating that (309. 11–13): 'Vnd also essent noch etlich lút hút dis tages gesegnoti brot, nit als dz war sacrament, mer als ein gelichniss des waren sacraments' ('Similarly nowadays some people still eat consecrated bread not as the true sacrament, but as a similitude of the true sacrament'). It is difficult to be certain about whom Marquard refers here: I am grateful to Alexander Murray for the suggestion that he may mean the Austrian Waldensians.

fründen gottes. Won der ewig got wil jnen alle süssikeit in die ewige selikeit sparen. Vnd dar vmb zúcht der ewig got sinen trost vnd heimlicheit dik semlichen lúten vnder ir gebetten vnd ăndacht vnd in disem sacrament durch irs bessren willen.[176]

(The fourth manner is that the true sacrament is received in grace, both sacramentally and spiritually, with the perception of especial sweetness—so much so that an individual thinks that he would rather forgo bodily food than the sacrament. This happens to certain people who live for God alone in the purity of their hearts, and who have turned their backs on themselves and on everything that is not God.

The fifth manner is that the individual receives the sacrament in grace, spiritually and sacramentally, without any perception of especial pleasure, but instead just embeds his heart in faith with true humility. This is an experience common to many people and often happens to the dearest friends of God, because the eternal God wants to save all sweetness for them until the eternal blessedness. Thus the eternal God often withdraws his consolation and intimacy from such people in their prayers and devotions and in this sacrament, for the sake of their improvement.)

Here, there is no condemnation of the perception of sweetness upon reception; though, as Willing has also argued, there is a slight priority accorded to reception without, over reception with the perception of sweetness.[177] The same division recurs in Marquard's sermon 33, one of the two to deal with the eucharist:

Die frăg: Enpfindent sămlich edel menschen hie in zit die süssikeit des hailgen sacramentes?

Die antwúrt: Es beschiht wol ettlichen menschen, daz in die brôsemli vallend in ir luter gemût von dem richen tisch der ewikait. Aber es beschihet in nit allen, wan got der wil dik sin aller liebsten haben in ainer ellender frômder durrer wis in allem irem leben vnd behaltet in sin selbes süssikait bis in daz ewig leben, da er si des ellendes tusent valteklich ergeczet.[178]

(Question: Do all such noble people in this life perceive the sweetness of the holy sacrament?

Answer: It happens to some people that breadcrumbs fall into their pure minds from the rich table of eternity. But it does not happen to them all, because God often wants to keep his dearest ones in a piteous, distant, and arid state for their entire lives: he keeps his sweetness from them until the eternal life, where he compensates them a thousandfold for their misery.)

---

[176] *Eucharistietraktat*, §9 (309. 14–28); the central idea is repeated at §14 (321. 3–8).

[177] Willing, *Literatur und Ordensreform*, pp. 199–200. Her conclusion, that Marquard views both as ascending stages in a mystical *via purgativa*, is untenable. The six kinds of reception are placed in parallel, proceeding from the most corporeal to the most spiritual forms in the standard manner of contemporary sacramental theology. The individual is not required to progress through earlier stages, like reception without recognizing the sacrament to be a sacrament.

[178] *Predigt* 33, ll. 159–65 (pp. 235–6).

Perhaps the most significant aspect of all this is the interface that can be seen between scholastic theology and piety. A pragmatic issue of the religious life—perceiving sweetness in the sacrament—is of sufficient importance for Marquard to modify a series of established scholastic distinctions to incorporate it. At the same time, we are faced with an apparent contradiction amongst Marquard's different statements on this issue of sweetness. There is no simple resolution. It may well be that Marquard is referring to two different kinds of sweetness. The 'bevintlichen lust und süssikeit' ('tangible pleasure and sweetness') that he condemns may apply to enclosed women seeking psycho-sexual satisfaction in eucharistic reception, or who believed that they could discern consecrated from unconsecrated hosts from the sweetness of their taste. Here we should remember that Marquard's condemnation comes in a passage on the general imperceptibility of Christ in the consecrated host. Browe records a number of individuals reported to possess this alleged ability, including St Odilia of Liège (d. 1220) and the Franciscan tertiary St Margaret of Cortona (d. 1297).[179] Nor is the idea that Marquard might have been speaking of psycho-sexual responses an anachronistic speculation. As André Vauchez notes, the experience of sacramental reception of Marquard's German contemporary (and subsequent patroness of the Teutonic order), Dorothea von Montau (d. 1394), is described by her confessor Johannes Marienwerder as a 'copula [...] intime peracta'[180] ('an intimately consummated coupling'). David von Augsburg certainly referred directly to psycho-sexual experiences ('non solum amplexibus et osculis, sed etiam aliis indecentioribus gestibus et actibus [...] demulceri'; 'to be caressed not just with hugs and kisses, but also with other more indecent deeds and actions')—but in the context of visions of Christ or Mary, not reception of the eucharist.[181] He does not mention the eucharist in his discussion on sensations of sweetness.[182]

If the kind of sweetness that Marquard condemns can be associated, to use Bynum's apt phrase, with paramystical phenomena, then the kind that he does not condemn is rather harder to define. Concomitant sweetness

---

[179] Browe, *Die eucharistischen Wunder*, pp. 38–9 and 45–6; on the significance of Margaret of Cortona to the Franciscan order see Schlager, 'Foundresses of the Franciscan Life', pp. 157–66.

[180] Vauchez, *The Laity*, p. 238; see Johannes Marienwerder, *Septililium B. Dorotheae Montoviensis*, tractatus 3, c. 27 (vol. 3 (1884), pp. 446–8; here p. 447). On the connection between eucharistic reception and psycho-sexual sensation see further Bynum, *Fragmentation and Redemption*, pp. 125–34.

[181] David von Augsburg, *De compositione*, lib. 3, c. 66, §5 (pp. 359–60).

[182] Ibid., c. 68 (pp. 365–7).

with sacramental reception is a recurrent feature of late thirteenth- and fourteenth-century saints' lives, other *vitae*, and related records of individual experience.[183] This plethora of material is problematic from our perspective, as it becomes difficult to select relevant examples for comparison with Marquard. One possibility is to compare Marquard with himself.

Marquard's sermon 34 describes the sweetness of the eucharist as the gift of the experience of Christ's divinity:

vns ist hút gegeben daz wǎr honigsam aller gǒttlichen sǘssikait. Sich frǒwet hie vor Jonathas, des kúnges Saul sun, do er vand in der wildi ain honigsaim, vnd lesend wir, do er es ǎss, do wurdent sin ǒgen erlúhtet, vnd ward er gesterket so vast, daz er die vigend flúhtig machet. Nun ist vns hút nit allain daz honigsaim, mer der brunn aller sǘssikait gegeben, von dem die minnend sel sprichet: >Conmedi fauum meum cum melle. Ich hǎn daz hong húseli gessen mit dem hong.< [Cant. 5: 1] Das húseli ist die luter menschait vnsers herren, vnd daz sǘss honig ist sin vnmǎssigú sǘsse gotthait, die vns alle gancz vnd gar ist hút gegeben.[184]

(The true honeycomb of all divine sweetness has been given to us today. In earlier times Jonathan, the son of king Saul, rejoiced when he found a honeycomb in the wilderness; and we read that when he ate it, his eyes were illuminated and he was strengthened so greatly that he put the enemy to flight. Now today not just the honeycomb, but the source of all sweetness has been given to us, of which the loving soul says, 'Conmedi fauum meum cum melle. I have eaten the honeycomb together with the honey.' The honeycomb is the pure humanity of our Lord, and the sweet honey is his inconceivably sweet divinity, which today has been given completely to us all.)

Later in the same sermon, the same term 'sǘssikait'—sweetness—is used to describe the conversation of divinity within the hypostatic union, and to characterize the subsequent conversation of Christ with the recipient's soul—albeit a conversation that is usually imperceptible:

[. . .] in dem hailgen sacrament ist ain sprechen des ewigen vatters zǔ dem sun nǎch ainer vernúnftiger geburt, so sich der vatter in den sun sprichet, vnd daz sǘss gesprǎch lúhtet in die sel Jesu Cristi mit wunnberender sǘssikait. [. . .] da ist ain minnriches sǘsses sprechen der sel Jesu Christi zǔ der sel dez menschen, der daz sacrament enpfǎhet, wie daz daz gewonlich vnbevintlich sige.[185]

---

[183] See principally Browe, *Die eucharistischen Wunder*, pp. 44–7; also Vauchez, *The Laity*, p. 239 (on Catherine of Siena and Dorothea von Montau); Caspers, *De eucharistische vroomheid*, p. 147 (on *exempla* in Caesarius von Heisterbach's *Dialogus*); and Bynum, *Fragmentation and Redemption*, p. 119 (on Marie d'Oignies).

[184] *Predigt* 34, ll. 44–53 (p. 259).

[185] Ibid., ll. 105–8 and 112–14 (p. 241).

(In the holy sacrament the eternal Father speaks to the Son in the manner of an intellectual birth, by which the Father speaks himself into the Son, and the sweet conversation illumines into the soul of Jesus Christ with sweetness bringing forth joy. [. . .] There the soul of Jesus Christ speaks lovingly and sweetly to the soul of the individual who receives the sacrament, even though that is usually imperceptible.)

What Marquard describes as 'sweetness' is the divinity of Christ. Where Marquard speaks of eucharistic reception with or without the perception of sweetness in the *Eucharistietraktat*, he may well be speaking of the direct perception of Christ's divinity: that is, an essentially mystical experience. This interpretation cannot, however, be pressed too firmly. The relevant passages in sermon 34 do not speak explicitly of unitive or mystical experience; we can only read this implication into them. Furthermore, the sermon collection is a work that enjoys a particular status in Marquard's oeuvre. It is very different in character to the *Eucharistietraktat*. It engages directly with contemplative and mystical issues of the day, and with crucial texts of the late medieval mystical tradition, at an advanced level. We may legitimately use it to elucidate the *Eucharistietraktat*, but it provides us with a possibility for understanding the latter work rather than the definitive solution.

Fortunately, Marquard is not alone in dealing with the perception of sweetness in the sacrament. About half of Matthaeus of Cracow's *Dialogus*, rather surprisingly, is concerned with this very issue—far more attention than Marquard gives to it. If one remembers that David von Augsburg, writing more than a century earlier, did not mention the eucharist when discussing perceptions of sweetness, one can see quite clearly how much prominence the issue had acquired in the intervening period. The central problem that is addressed in the *Dialogus* is the perception or non-perception of sweetness prior to (thus as a signal for) and/or during reception of the sacrament. Of particular importance as a comparative aspect to Marquard is Reason's argument in the *Dialogus* that sweetness is inherent in the consecrated host, because God is present, and is therefore imparted to the communicant whether perceived or not. We see an early example of this in the second section, where Conscience complains that however hard the individual had tried, sweetness had never been perceived. Reason answers:

Non erat intentionis meae probare esse dulcedinem cordis tui, sed sacramenti. Si ergo dulcis et rectus est Dominus, immo ipsa dulcedo, quomodo potest sumi sine dulcedine[?][186]

[186] Matthaeus of Cracow, *Dialogus*, §2, ll. 281–4 (p. 376).

(It was not my intention to show that sweetness is in your heart, but in the sacrament. If, therefore, the Lord is sweet and just—nay, rather sweetness itself—how can he be consumed without sweetness?)

In the long concluding speech to this section, Reason locates sweetness alongside related items flowing to the recipient from Christ: devotion, virtue, and grace. These are all aspects of the sacramental quality of the eucharist:

Non dubites omnem huiusmodi veram dulcedinem, omnem devotionem, virtutem, aut gratiam a Christo capite nostro fluere. Cuius quidem corpus non solum est res hic sub speciebus contenta, sed etiam sacramentum.

(Do not doubt that every true sweetness of this kind, every act of devotion, virtue, and grace flows from the head of our Christ—whose body, in fact, is not just the essence here contained under the species, but also the sacrament.)

Reason defines sweetness more precisely, with reference to the institution of the sacrament at the Last Supper. Here, the sacrament conferred no grace: but Christ's presence constituted the conferred sweetness. It is this sweetness that elevates the eucharist above all the other sacraments, and it has an affective influence upon the communicant:

[Christus] desiderio desideravit hoc pascha manducare cum discipulis, sic sine dubio delectabiliter corpus suum et sacramentaliter sumpsit, nullam tamen gratiam inde consecutus. Quid enim iocundius, dulcius, delectabilius esse potest quam habere personaliter et corporaliter praesentem Dominum Jesum Christum, donum utique excellentissimum et totius spiritualis delectationis obiectum seu materiam, causam efficientem et finem. Et haec est dulcedo, quae huic sacramento singularis est, et ei numquam deest[, i]n qua etiam omnia alia transcendit sacramenta. Haec est enim, quae sola accendere desiderium, humilitatem ingerere, compunctionem inducere, praebere fiduciam, spem erigere, et amorem inflammare, infundere gaudium, excitare ad reverentiam, totam mentem liquefacere et oblectare deberet, et ad affectus dulcissimos provocare.[187]

(Christ desired ardently to eat this paschal meal with his disciples, and so without a doubt he consumed his body delightfully and sacramentally; yet no grace followed from it. For what can be more delightful, more sweet, and more delicious that to have the Lord Jesus Christ personally and bodily present, who is certainly the most excellent gift of all, and the object (or focus) and cause, both efficient and final, of all spiritual delight. This is the sweetness which is unique to this sacrament, which is never absent from it, and in which also it surpasses all of the other sacraments. For it is this which alone should kindle desire, impose humility, induce compunction, test faith, encourage hope, inflame love, pour in joy, excite to worship, liquefy and delight the whole mind, and provoke to the sweetest emotions.)

[187] Ibid., ll. 310–23 (p. 377).

Matthaeus, then, can be said to define sweetness—*dulcedo*—as the experience of the direct presence of Christ's divinity in the sacrament, whether that experience is sensibly perceived or not. Much of the rest of the discussion over sweetness in the *Dialogus* centres around the evidently germane question of whether a sensation of spiritual sweetness prior to reception could be interpreted as an affirmation of the individual's worthiness to receive the sacrament. As we might expect, Reason opposes the use of such signals as determinants of the decision to receive the sacrament.[188] Matthaeus deals at length with the issue of why sweetness is sometimes not perceived, and the related questions of the withdrawal of grace and of perceptible sweetness respectively from the contemplative.[189] Pertinent to the definition of sweetness is a complex passage in which Reason explains the relationship between the *affectus* that sweetness provokes in the recipient (that is, the spiritual *affectus* of sacramental reception: compunction of the heart, the shedding of tears, the stimulation of the love of God and so forth), and grace:

Ratio: Affectus huiusmodi aliquando veniunt omnino praeter gratiam, aliquando cum gratia, sed non ex gratia; quandoque vero ex gratia et speciali dono Dei. Nam cum gentiles in ritibus suis, Judaei in sacrificiis, haeretici in erroribus suis nonnunquam lacrimas fundant et cordialiter afficiantur, quis dubitet talia *praeter* gratiam omnino venire[,] et quandoque cooperante diabolo cum quadam dementatione vel deceptione creditur ab infidelibus resuscitare mortuum vel aliud facere, quod miraculosum vel divinum reputatur[. C]um gratia veniunt, non tamen semper ex gratia, dum quidam boni maxime simplices moventur, et promoventur ad dulces affectus ex cantu suavi et devoto vel organis; ex gratia vero sunt lacrimae sanctorum, quorum exemplis scriptura plena est.[190]

(Reason: Emotions (*affectus*) of this kind sometimes come wholly apart from grace, sometimes with grace, yet not from grace—but occasionally from grace and the special gift of God. For when the pagans in their rites, the Jews in their sacrifices, and the heretics in their errors sometimes shed tears and are affected in a heartfelt way, who doubts that such things come wholly apart from grace—and whenever, with the devil working with a certain madness or deception, he is believed by the infidels to resurrect the dead or do something else that is considered to be miraculous or divine. They [i.e. the *affectus*] come with grace, but nevertheless not always

---

[188] See ibid., §3, ll. 357–406 (pp. 378–80).

[189] On the withdrawal of grace, see ibid., ll. 475–524a (pp. 382–4); on the withdrawal of perceptible sweetness, see §4, ll. 530–55 (pp. 384–5); in summary, see further §6, ll. 700–6 (p. 390). The whole issue of this economy of grace and sweetness in the *Dialogus* is discussed in comparison with Jean Gerson's *De signis bonis et malis* by Grosse, *Heilsungewißheit und Scrupulositas*, pp. 91–3.

[190] Matthaeus of Cracow, *Dialogus*, §4, ll. 580–93 (p. 386).

from grace, most of all when certain good simpletons are influenced and drawn
onwards to sweet emotions by pleasant and holy song, or by musical instruments.
The tears of the saints are truly from grace, of which Scripture is full of examples.)

The entire fifth section is then spent on discussing these *affectus* in more
detail, the reasons for their presence or absence, and the superiority of signs
of interior grace over corporeal *affectus*.[191] The section is basically a treatise
on the discretion of spirits, an emergent genre in the 1380s and one which,
in this period, is concerned much more with the examination of internal
sensations than the identification of diabolical inspirations.

The sixth section, and the last to address the issue of *dulcedo*, deals with
the signs of interior grace. These might best be described as the inclination
to the central aspects of the religious life: hatred of sin and of injustice,
desire of heaven, contempt of vanities and the consolations of the world
feature strongly among them.[192] These interior signs of grace are not
sweetness, just as grace itself was not identical to sweetness; but sweetness
is bestowed to assist their maintenance, in proportion to bestowed grace:

Haec et his similia numquam possunt haberi constanter sine divina dulcedine, quia,
ut ait Augustinus VI Musicae, numquam expugnaretur amor temporalium, nisi
aliqua suavitas esset aeternorum. [...] Haec est consolatio, haec est dulcedo[,]
quam boni semper habent habitualiter et quilibet secundum gradum gratiae sibi
datae.[193]

(These, and that which is similar to them, can never be held constantly without
divine sweetness; for, as Augustine says in the sixth book of *De musica*, the love of
the temporal would never be overcome unless there were some sweetness of the
eternal. [...] This is consolation, this is sweetness, which the good always have
habitually and each one according to the degree of the grace given to him.)

The sweetness assists in perseverance, rather than functioning as a reward; it
is much more efficacious than the kind of sweetness that is sensibly
perceived. Unlike perceptible sweetness, the imperceptible kind that assists
the maintenance of religious disciplines may be legitimately sought—
though only within certain limits. The reception of sweetness must be
dealt with rationally, and not welcomed with overt weeping and other
displays; any perceptible sweetness is to be treated as a supererogatory
reward.[194]

---

[191] Ibid., §5 (pp. 386–9); esp. Reason's closing speech at ll. 644a–659a (pp. 388–9).
[192] See ibid., §6, ll. 662–70 (p. 389).
[193] Ibid., ll. 670–8 (p. 389).
[194] Ibid., ll. 678–710 (pp. 389–90).

Through a series of convoluted discussions, Matthaeus tries to define the different forms of sweetness. On the one hand, he is concerned to establish rules for handling these different forms, and to explode certain myths about the relationship between perception of sweetness and worthiness to receive the sacrament. On the other hand, he engages in a sophisticated attempt to define the different kinds of sweetness and their relationship to grace. Here, he is engaged in an exploration of the relationship between a field of experience and the established theological categories of grace. We can see here the interface between, put simply, piety and university theology. Marquard's primary responsibilities evidently lay in the *cura animarum*. So, he drew on scholastic theology and modified its distinctions in categorising the experience of piety that he witnessed. Matthaeus worked from the opposite perspective, that of a university theologian at Prague (and then at Heidelberg). So, he sought to work out in this treatise how contemporary experience could be positioned within the established framework of scholastic theology. This is the real, historical significance of a superficially somewhat obtuse issue: the attempt to relate the existing theological framework for the forms of reception and the nature of grace to an issue of new prominence in late fourteenth century piety, the perception of sweetness in the sacrament. The exploration of this interface is part of a wider contemporary development, being intimately connected to the emergent genre of treatises on the *discretio spirituum*: the application of theological categories to the understanding of inner experience.

The second notable feature of the eucharistic theology in the *Eucharistietraktat* is more significant: Marquard's attitude towards miracles and visions. This will allow us to look at a broad spectrum of related issues, drawing together a number of themes and establishing a series of competitive traditions in the attitude to eucharistic miracles in the later Middle Ages. Our starting point in the *Eucharistietraktat* is in the fourth section, where Marquard explains how Christ is present in the sacrament. He begins by setting out how Christ is present in the sacrament not as he was during his life, but as he is, glorified in heaven:

Du solt wússen zů dem ersten, das der lieb Ihesus Cristus in der gesegneten oflaten nit ist in dem schin als er mit den jungren vor sinem tod vff ertrich wonet. Mer er ist dar jn mit aller der clarheit vnd gezierd, so er in dem himel hat. Dar vmb ist er nu czierlicher in der gesegneten oflaten, denn er was, do er vff ertrich in dem armen schin wonet vnd denn er wz, do er sich den jungren an dem grůnen donstag gab. Won er gab sich do den jungren, als ouch da der lib was, vnd wan sin lib denocht

lidberlich was vnd nit clarificiert, dar vmb gab er sich jnen in semlicher vnclarifi-
cierter wise. Won aber nu sin lib clarheit der lesten vrstendi hat, dar vmb git er sich
nu in der selben clarheit.[195]

(First you should know that the beloved Jesus Christ is not in the consecrated host in
the same form that he had when he dwelt on earth with the disciples prior to his death.
Rather, he is present there with all the clarity and splendour that he has in heaven. Thus
he is now more splendid in the consecrated host than he was when he lived on earth in
the form of a poor man, and also than he was when he gave himself to the disciples on
Maundy Thursday. For he gave himself then to the apostles with his [human] body
also present, and because his body at that time was still passible and not clarified, so he
gave himself to them in that same unclarified manner. Since however his body now has
the clarity of the last resurrection, so he gives himself now in this same clarity.)

This glorified state in heaven—this clarity—is literally clarity. The clarified
body of Christ cannot be perceived in the sacrament with corporeal eyes:

Der Junger sprach: Mich wundret, sider er da ist mit so grosser klarheit, das es nit
ettwz mag gebrüfet werden.
Der Meister sprach: Ich han dir vorgeseit, dz die wirdig spise stat in dem gelouben vnd
nit in dem sechen oder brüfen. War vmb wundert denn dich? Du solt gedenken, dz
got in allen stetten in himel vnd uff erden ist, vnd in allen dingen vnd mit aller siner
clarheit, vnd doch so sichest du sin schöni nit noch kanst si nit gebrüfen, wie
gegenwürtig si ist dinen ougen vnd dinem hertzen. Sus wie ouch das die gross clarheit
in der gesegnoten offloten sig, so mag si doch nit gebrüfet werden.[196]

(The pupil said: It surprises me that given he is there with such great clarity, that it
cannot be perceived even a little.
The master said: I have already told you that the noble food rests on faith and not on
sight or perception. Why, then, are you surprised? You should consider that God is
in every place on earth and in heaven, and in everything and with all of his clarity—
and yet you neither see his beauty, nor can you perceive it, however present it is to
your eyes and your heart. Likewise, however much this great clarity may be in the
consecrated host, it can still not be perceived.)

Marquard then talks about the manner in which Christ would be seen in
the sacrament, if that were possible: not as a judge or magnate, but as a
loving father, prepared to embrace all who will receive him. This is very
much an element of Marquard's overarching strategy in the work to
encourage love and reduce fear of the sacrament. This passage then serves
as the launchpad for an extremely important linked question:

[195] *Eucharistietraktat*, §4 (281. 1–11).
[196] Ibid. (281. 12–21).

Der Junger sprach: Nu sprechent doch etlich menschen, si sechend da got in eines kindlis wise, dar vmb so sag mir, wie ich davon halten sôlle.

Der Meister sprach: Ich sag dir, dz nie kein mentsch Cristum gesach mit liplichen ougen in der gesegnoten oflaten, als er da ist. Vnd wie dz sig, das wir lesen, das sanctus Gregorius seche fleisch vnd blût in der ofloten, vnd etlich lút sechend in ir andacht ein kindelin in der ofloten oder in dem kelch, doch soltú wússen, das es nit der war lib Cristi ist, als hoch lerer sprechent. Es ist allein ein gelicheit sines libes. Dar vmb so da ein kindelin gesechen wirt, so ist es nit der fronlicham Ihesu Cristi in sacramentlicher wise, es ist allein sin gelicheit. Vnd die lat got in dem heiligen sacrament sechen durch andechtiger hertzen willen. Doch mag sich got ouch wol zôigen in der ofloten in eines kindlis wise, das es warer Cristus sig. Aber wie das ein mentsch in da also seche, so sol er jnn niemer in der wise anbetten denn mit geding, also: „Bistu Cristus, so bett ich dich an."[197]

(The pupil said: Now certain people say that they see God there [i.e. in the sacrament] in the form of a child; so tell me what I ought to think of that.

The master said: I say to you that no one has ever seen Christ in the consecrated host with their bodily eyes in the manner in which he is there. Though it may be that we read that St Gregory saw flesh and blood in the host, and certain people see a small child in the host or in the chalice as they pray, you should know that it is not the true body of Christ, as the great teachers say. It is merely a similitude of his body. Therefore if a small child is seen there, it is not the physical body of Jesus Christ in sacramental form, but merely his similitude. God allows this to be seen in the holy sacrament for the sake of devout hearts. Yet God can also show himself in the host in the form of a child, such that it may be truly Christ. But should an individual see him there in this way, then he should never worship him in that form except conditionally, like this: 'If you are Christ, then I will worship you.')

We shall return presently to the theological issue of the perceptibility of Christ's body in the sacrament and its clarified nature, and will begin with this final section, in which Marquard tackles the question of eucharistic visions. He repeats his statement that Christ cannot now be seen with corporeal eyes. He refers to Gregory having seen the host transform into flesh and blood, and speaks of people seeing a child in the host or the chalice, before stating that this is not Christ in his sacramental presence: it is but a similitude of Christ. That argument, as Willing has identified, is an adaptation from Aquinas.[198] What is definitely not from Aquinas is the final, critical statement of this kind of visions: a eucharistic vision is not to be welcomed, but to be regarded with the utmost scepticism. Here, Marquard touches on the possibility of diabolical inspiration, and casts

---

[197] *Eucharistietraktat*, §6 (281. 32–282. 10).
[198] Willing, *Literatur und Ordensreform*, p. 195.

thereby a very dark shadow over the validity of such visions. We are faced with a whole series of different, yet interlinked points, each of which has its own particular tradition, and must adopt a tripartite strategy. First, we must identify what Marquard is referring to, and on what contemporary issues his asseverations touch. Second, we must position Marquard relative to the dominant trend of contemporary piety on each of these issues. Third, we must construct a wider tradition of thought similar to Marquard's position on these issues, if there is evidence to do so.

Marquard's brief discussion of visions begins with the aforementioned reference to Gregory.[199] At this stage, it may seem that his argument is purely theoretical, drawing on an ancient example. Then, however, he refers to people seeing the Christ-child in the sacrament. This is by no means purely theoretical, but instead engages directly with a remarkable proliferation in fourteenth-century Germany of exactly this kind of vision. Browe persuasively relates the emergence of different types of eucharistic vision to developments in contemporary religious practice. The vision of the Christ-child in the sacrament is, aside from an isolated ninth-century incident, a development that appears in the late eleventh and twelfth centuries and became the dominant form of eucharistic vision in the thirteenth and, above all, fourteenth centuries. Browe sees the development as related to the new practices of elevation and exposition, and the idea of purely spiritual communion. Initially recorded in Cistercian convents and the associated women's communities in Brabant, these Christ-child visions reached the height of their popularity among female Dominican convents in south-west Germany in the fourteenth century.[200] Browe found fewer such recorded incidents in the Franciscan Order: 'Den Franziskanerinnen wurden zwar viele Wunder und alle möglichen Visionen nachgerühmt, aber gerade diese eucharistischen waren verhältnismäßig selten'[201] ('The Franciscan women were acclaimed for many miracles and every possible vision, but precisely these eucharistic ones were relatively rare'). Nonetheless, a little group of famous Franciscan women were held to have received this type

---

[199] See Browe, *Die eucharistischen Wunder*, pp. 113–15: the association of this vision with Gregory (d. 604) appears to be 9th-cent. tradition. This exact host had allegedly been preserved in Rome before being taken to Bamberg by Benedict VIII in 1020 and transferred to the Bavarian convent of Andechs in 1182, where it was buried in the early 13th cent. It was 'rediscovered' in 1388 (towards the end of Marquard's life) and, alongside two other miraculous hosts, made Andechs into a major centre of pilgrimage.

[200] See ibid. 42, 93, and 101–11; for additional examples, see Bynum, 'The Blood of Christ', pp. 688–90, and Rode, *Studien zu den mittelalterlichen Kind-Jesu-Visionen*, pp. 49–54; on the iconographical consequences, see Rubin, *Corpus Christi*, pp. 137–9.

[201] Browe, *Die eucharistischen Wunder*, p. 104.

of eucharistic vision: Margaret of Cortona (d. 1297), Angela of Foligno (d. 1309), and, perhaps most importantly of all, Clare of Assisi (d. 1253).[202] It is, further, inconceivable that no contact existed between Franciscan and Dominican convents in fourteenth-century Germany: Marquard would undoubtedly have been aware of the proliferation of reports of these Christ-child visions in female Dominican convents. It is also legitimate to question whether the apparent 'Dominican' concentration of this kind of vision is illusory, a result of the production and survival of particular written sources, rather than a reflection of the actual pattern of visionary experience in fourteenth-century German convents. Caroline Bynum holds this position, and regards Christ-child visions in the thirteenth and fourteenth centuries as a feature characteristic more generally of contemporary female religiosity.[203]

That Christ-child visions proliferated in south-west Germany in the fourteenth century is without doubt. Literary and artistic works propagated the memory of earlier visions in Franciscan as well as Dominican circles, and provided this kind of vision a particular status. A set of retable paintings made around 1360 for the Klarissenkloster in Nuremberg—one of the most important Franciscan female convents in Germany—depicts Clare's vision of the Christ-child in the eucharist.[204] The four paintings, arranged in a square, have an unusually complex iconography. The incarnation of Christ, depicted with Joseph recognizing Mary's pregnancy, is paralleled to its right by the coronation of Mary by Christ in heaven, and paralleled in the lower register by Francis receiving the stigmata from a six-winged seraph in the form of a crucified Christ. The association of the incarnation of Christ and the stigmatization of Francis presents the latter as the *alter Christus*, the second Christ. The coronation of Mary in the top-right panel is then paralleled in the final, lower-right panel by the mystical coronation of Clare by an angel at the moment of her vision of Christ in the eucharistic host. Clare commends her sisters to Christ (and receives his approbation) in a further parallel to Mary's coronation in the upper panel, symbolically interpreted as the marriage of Christ to the church.

---

[202] See ibid. 104–5.

[203] Bynum, *Fragmentation and Redemption*, pp. 121–5.

[204] The four panels of this altar are in separate collections: see the complete description and reproductions in *Krone und Schleier*, pp. 511–14 [Cat. no. 459 a–d]. They are the earliest example of the Flemish style in Southern Germany, and are thus of particular art-historical significance. A second altarpiece from the Klarissenkloster, depicting the Life of St Clare, also incorporates the Christ-child vision: see *Krone und Schleier*, pp. 509–12 [Cat. no. 458 a–e].

Clare's vision of Christ in the host is therefore positioned as the moment in her life that matches St Francis's stigmatization. The contemporary significance attached to this vision is all the more striking because it is not included in Clare's official Life, the *Legenda S. Clarae virginis*, written (probably by Thomas of Celano) shortly after her canonization in 1254. The *Legenda* draws on a larger body of material collected in the acts of the canonization process. These acts record a number of visions, not all of which are taken up into the *Legenda*; amongst these is that of the Christ-child in the host. This is the source of the memory of the vision: surprisingly so, given that the acts are extant in just one manuscript of an Italian translation.[205] An incident in Clare's life that did not appear significant enough to her thirteenth-century hagiographer to include in her official *vita* had, a century later, been elevated to represent the defining point in her life, associated with mystical coronation and comparable with Francis's stigmatization. These retable paintings were produced during Marquard's lifetime, and he may well have seen them—he held a provincial chapter in Nuremberg in 1390, and it is without doubt that he would have visited the church of the main Poor Clare convent in that city. The altarpiece is a powerful testimony to the status that this type of Christ-child vision held in Franciscan circles in late fourteenth-century Germany.

Marquard states categorically that no one sees Christ, in the way in which he is present in the sacrament, with corporeal eyes. This addition of 'mit liplichen ougen' ('with bodily eyes') refers to Augustine's tripartite categorization of visions into intellective, spiritual or imaginative, and corporeal visions.[206] Only the last category—visions of things which became corporeally present—could be seen with corporeal eyes. Aquinas had taught that Christ could not fall into this category, because he, or rather the extrinsic accidents pertaining to his spatially constrained body, was in heaven (an argument that, he is careful to note, does not apply to the conversion of the host into the species of his body).[207] Intellective or imaginative visions of Christ were acceptable, on the other hand, because they involved a change in the beholder's mind, rather than anything actually present. Yet crucially, as Elliott has shown, this doctrine was not

---

[205] *Acts of the Process of Canonization of St Clare*, witness 9, §10, pp. 473–4 (ed. Lazzeri); p. 2489 (ed. Brufani and Menestò); pp. 167–8 (trans. Armstrong).

[206] See Haas, 'Traum und Traumvision', pp. 30–1, with all further references.

[207] Cf. Aquinas, *Summa theologiae*, pars 3, q. 76, a. 5, esp. ad 3 (vol. 4, p. 510). The accidents intrinsic to Christ's species are in the sacrament, but his extrinsic accidents—those applying to his body as a body subject to spatial constraints—are not, because that body is in heaven. See Bynum, 'The Blood of Christ', pp. 696–7, and Browe, *Die eucharistischen Wunder*, pp. 48–9.

the last word on the issue. In the later fourteenth century, prominent claims
were made that Christ had been seen with corporeal eyes. Alphonse of
Pecha, bishop of Jaén (d. 1388), claimed this about Birgitta of Sweden in
his defence of her visions. In Germany, albeit after Marquard's death, the
Prussian theologian Johannes Marienwerder (d. 1417) claimed that Christ
in the host had spoken to Dorothea von Montau (d. 1394) through her
corporeal ears.[208] Marquard's unusually emphatic 'Ich sag dir, dz nie kein
mentsch Cristum gesach mit liplichen ougen in der gesegnoten oflaten, als
er da ist' ('I say to you that no one has ever seen Christ in the consecrated
host with their bodily eyes in the manner in which he is there') may thus
reflect the emergence of notable claims for this very ability.

As mentioned earlier, Willing has shown that Marquard was also drawing on Aquinas in stating that corporeally perceptible visions of Christ in
the eucharist were not actually of Christ at all, but of a similitude of him.
A change in the extrinsic accidents of the bread or wine had taken place:

Et ideo dicendum quod, manentibus dimensionibus quae prius fuerunt, fit miraculose quaedam immutatio circa alia accidentia, puta figuram et colorem et alia
huiusmodi ut videatur caro vel sanguis, aut etiam puer.[209]

(Therefore it is to be said that, with the dimensions remaining the same as they were
beforehand, a certain transmutation miraculously takes place with regard to the
other accidents—shape and colour, for instance, and the others of that kind—so
that flesh or blood may be seen, or even a boy.)

Aquinas continues with his wider point, however, which was to demonstrate that this involved no deception of the onlooker. Such miraculous
transformations served as a divinely ordained confirmation of the reality of
Christ's presence:

Et, sicut prius dictum est, hoc non est deceptio: quia fit in figuram cuiusdam
veritatis, scilicet ad ostendendum per hanc miraculosam apparitionem quod in
hoc sacramento est vere corpus Christi et sanguis.[210]

(Just as was said beforehand, this is no deception, because it takes place in the
representation of a certain truth—namely, to demonstrate by this miraculous
apparition that the body and blood of Christ are truly in this sacrament.)

---

[208] On all the above see Elliott, 'True Presence/False Christ', pp. 244–53.
[209] Aquinas, *Summa theologiae*, pars 3, q. 76, a. 8, in corp. (vol. 4, pp. 513–14); see
Willing, *Literatur und Ordensreform*, p. 195.
[210] Aquinas, *Summa theologiae*, pars 3, q. 76, a. 8, in corp. (vol. 4, p. 514); see further
Caspers, *De eucharistische vroomheid*, pp. 239–42.

Marquard, as we might expect, does not adopt this argument that such miracles are there to prove the real presence. Visions are seen in the sacrament only 'durch andechtiger hertzen willen' ('for the sake of devout hearts'), a reason similar to that which David von Augsburg had given.[211] He follows this with an astonishing injunction that casts doubt on the entire validity of these eucharistic visions, whatever their nature may be: 'Aber wie das ein mentsch in da also seche, so sol er jnn niemer in der wise anbetten denn mit geding, also: "Bistu Cristus, so bett ich dich an"' ('But should an individual see him there in this way, then he should never worship him in that form except conditionally, like this: "If you are Christ, then I will worship you"').

With this one statement, Marquard expresses a profound scepticism concerning all kinds of vision seen in the eucharist, whether similitudes of Christ or otherwise, and wherever they may be located in the Augustinian classification. If the Christ-figure seen is not Christ or a divinely generated similitude, then it is either a self-deception or a diabolical manifestation. There was, of course, a patristic tradition of healthy scepticism towards apparitions of Christ.[212] Yet it is precisely in the last quarter of the fourteenth century that treatises on the *discretio spirituum*, the discernment of spirits, emerged. With the notable exception of the *De quatuor instinctibus* of Heinrich von Friemar (d. 1340), the pioneer in its field, no such work pre-dates 1380. Heinrich von Langenstein's *De discretione spirituum* was written in 1383; Pierre d'Ailly's *De falsis prophetis* around 1410–15; and a whole series of influential *discretio* treatises flowed from the pen of Jean Gerson, beginning with the *De distinctione verarum*

---

[211] See David von Augsburg, *De compositione*, lib. 3, c. 66 (itself a useful statement of the Augustinian classification of visions), here in §4 (p. 359): 'Credimus, Christum glorificatum corporaliter esse in caelo nec ultra[,] secundum substantiae suae veritatem nasci de Virgine, lactari vel pati, vel alia, quae evangelica docet historia eum fecisse, cum corporaliter cum hominibus in terra conversabatur; et tamen sic saepe refertur aliquibus Sanctis et devotis apparuisse in visione, vel nascens, vel matris gremio contentus, vel extensus in cruce, non quod ita secundum veritatem fuerit, sed quod illis propter aliquam singularem consolationem et devotionis excitationem, vel propter aliquam spiritualem significationem sic appareret' ('We believe that the glorified Christ is bodily in heaven, and not outside it, in accordance with the truth of his substance born of the Virgin, suckled, suffered, and having done all the other things that the Gospel account teaches that he had done when he kept company with mankind bodily on earth. And yet he is often said by some saints and devout people to have appeared in this way in a vision— either being born, or content in his mother's lap, or stretched upon the cross—not because this is in accordance with the truth, but because he appeared to them on account of some unique consolation and stimulation of devotion, or on account of some spiritual signification').

[212] See Elliott, 'True Presence/False Christ', pp. 254–8.

revelationum a falsis in 1401.[213] By the fifteenth century, the debate over
eucharistic visions was regularly informed by the concern for diabolical
origins, as Caspers has explored with the example of the prominent Dutch
visionary, Lidwina van Schiedam (d. 1433).[214] Jan Hus's influential treatise
De sanguine Christi, written in 1405 following his investigation of the
miraculous hosts of Wilsnack by order of the archbishop of Prague, deals
at length with the role of the devil in the generation of eucharistic 'miracles', but without any specific reference to visions of Christ.[215] Marquard's
statement has two implications. First, it illuminates his awareness of the
emergent concern for the sceptical discernment of the origin of visions.
Second, it places Marquard in opposition to the dominant fascination with
eucharistic visions in the convents of fourteenth-century Germany. Following Marquard, the Clare of Assisi of the Nuremberg altarpiece should not
have commended her sisters to Christ's care when she saw him in the host,
but should have deliberated as to the vision's potentially diabolical origin.

What, then, are we to make of Marquard's repeated insistence on the
clarity of Christ's body in heaven and in the sacrament? It is not obvious
that this is central to, or even an aspect of, sacramental theology. Yet the
issue of the clarity, and the perceptibility, of Christ's body and blood was
extremely significant in the later Middle Ages, and particularly in Germany. It was pertinent to the debate surrounding all the different types of
eucharistic miracle with which late medieval Germany abounded. And to
say that late medieval Germany abounded with eucharistic miracles, miraculous hosts, relics of the holy blood, and sites of worship and pilgrimage
erected to them all is no understatement.[216] Many of these attracted what
we might term 'practical' criticism: criticism from elsewhere in the ecclesiastical hierarchy or the local polity on the grounds that the miraculous host

---

[213] See the useful conspectus in id., 'Seeing Double', pp. 28–31. Elliott holds
Gerson responsible for the 'misogynization' of the discretion of spirits ('Seeing Double',
pp. 32–8); cf. Newman, *God and the Goddesses*, pp. 288–9, on the internal development
of Gerson's treatises in this direction.

[214] Caspers, *De eucharistische vroomheid*, pp. 244–8.

[215] See Jan Hus, *De sanguine Christi*, §11–13 (pp. 28–32).

[216] On miracle hosts of all kinds, see the seminal Browe, *Die eucharistischen Wunder*,
pp. 117–28, 139–46 (with a conspectus of known miracle hosts venerated in Germany)
and 166–8 (on the origins of the famous hosts at Wilsnack). For a statistical analysis of
Sakramentskapellen, chapels dedicated to miraculous hosts, see Sprandel, 'Der Sakramentskult', pp. 300–1. An excellent overview of miracle hosts in the Low Countries is
provided by Caspers, *De eucharistische vroomheid*, pp. 99–100 and 232–4. On the
prominence of miracle hosts and blood cults in Germany compared to the rest
of Europe, see Rubin, *Corpus Christi*, p. 314, and now Bynum, *Wonderful Blood*,
pp. 49–68, with important criticisms of the statistical methodology employed by Browe.

was a fabrication, or the shrine a moneymaking machine. There was nothing exceptional about this, though it is hard to call it a 'tradition' because the set of allegations depended so heavily on local circumstance.[217] Alongside this 'practical' criticism stood theological criticism of the validity of the relic or miraculous host, a subject with which Caroline Bynum has dealt in her recent *Wonderful Blood*. The nature of the theological arguments applied depended on the nature of the miracle claimed. Four main categories can be identified. First, hosts that had proven resistant to fire. These appear to have been exempt from theological criticism, as there was no claim involved that blood or some other part of Christ had manifested itself. Second, relics of the Holy Blood from Christ's Passion. Third, miraculous hosts that had apparently bled and had turned red. Fourth, hosts in which a vision had been seen or which had undergone some kind of miraculous transformation.

The validity of blood relics that had allegedly been preserved from the Passion depended ultimately on the principle that blood, like fingernails or hair, was not integral to the body—to use the technical term, did not form part of the 'veritas humanae naturae' ('the truth of human nature')—and did not need to have ascended to heaven at the Ascension. This principle had already been a matter of debate for the scholastic theologians of the thirteenth century.[218] The influential voice of Thomas Aquinas had opposed it, on the grounds that Christ's blood belonged to the 'veritas humanae naturae', and so must all have ascended. Alleged blood relics, so Aquinas, had miraculously appeared out of maltreated images of Christ (and would have been, as we saw earlier, a similitude of Christ's blood and not his blood itself).[219] In the course of the fourteenth and fifteenth

---

[217] For some examples, see Sprandel, 'Der Sakramentskult', pp. 302–10, and Browe, *Die eucharistischen Wunder*, pp. 152–63; Wyclif criticized eucharistic miracles similarly, on which see Phillips, 'John Wyclif', p. 571.

[218] See Bynum, *Wonderful Blood*, pp. 96–108.

[219] Ibid. 101–2; see Aquinas, *Summa theologiae*, pars 3, q. 54, a. 3 (vol. 3, pp. 337–8), esp. ad 3: '[…] dicendum quod totus sanguis qui de corpore Christi fluxit, cum ad veritatem humanae naturae pertineat, in Christi corpore resurrexit. Et eadem ratio est de omnibus particulis ad veritatem et integritatem humanae naturae pertinentibus. Sanguis autem ille qui in quibusdam ecclesiis pro reliquiis observatur, non fluxit de latere Christi: sed miraculose dicitur effluxisse de quadam imagine Christi percussa' ('it is to be said that all the blood that flowed out of Christ's body, since it pertains to the truth of human nature, was resurrected in the body of Christ. And the same reason applies to all the constituent parts that pertain to the truth and integrity of human nature. That blood, however, which is honoured in certain churches in place of relics, did not flow from Christ's side; but is said to have flowed forth miraculously out of a certain image of Christ that had been struck hard').

centuries, a small number of fierce controversies would arise concerning the validity of particular blood relics remaining from the Passion. The foremost of these broke out in Barcelona in 1350–1 and in Italy in 1462–4, and Bynum's recent study has shed much light on these affairs.

The earlier controversy at Barcelona is the more interesting here, because of its much closer temporal proximity to Marquard. The immediate cause was Lenten sermons delivered 'clero et populo' in the vernacular by Francis Baiuli, then warden of the Franciscan convent in the city. Baiuli had evidently taught in these sermons that the blood Christ had shed in the Passion was separated from his divinity upon his death, and therefore was not to be venerated as the blood of the Son of God. Even so, that did of course imply that such relics could exist. Dominican inquisitors charged Baiuli with heresy; his Franciscan colleagues laid countercharges; but ultimately Baiuli was required to recant in a formal notarized document, and revoke his statements publicly in the vernacular.[220] In this controversy, a clear division is evident between the two main mendicant orders, and as Bynum notes, the underlying theology was important to both parties. Baiuli's Franciscan supporters agreed that he should stop his additional speculations on what would have happened had Christ died of old age, but came firmly to his defence on the principal charges concerning relics of the holy blood.[221]

This was very much a local affair, which did not gain much wider attention. Only one manuscript (London, British Library, MS Add. 22795) contains material pertaining to it, and it is that manuscript that forms the basis of Michelle Garceau's unpublished study on which Bynum relies. None of the papal correspondence that may have existed survives. The affair was known to the Dominican inquisitor Nicholas Eymeric (d. 1399), who mentioned it extremely briefly in his *Directorium inquisitorum* of 1376.[222] It was also known independently to the Irish Franciscan chronicler Luke Wadding (d. 1657), who associated it with the more famous controversy involving James of the March in 1462–4.[223]

---

[220] Bynum, *Wonderful Blood*, pp. 113–14.
[221] Ibid. 114–15.
[222] Nicholas Eymeric, *Directorium inquisitorum*, pars 2, q. 10, §1 (Rome 1578, p. 196; Venice 1607, p. 262); also contained in the extracts from the *Directorium* published under the title *Summa utilissima errorum et haeresum* by Stanislaus Polonus, c. 1500 (copy consulted: Oxford, Bodleian Library, Inc. e. 54. 1; *Bod-inc* E-090).
[223] Wadding, *Annales minorum*, to 1351, §13 (vol. 8, pp. 68–9); on the events of 1462–4, see §14–21 (vol. 8, pp. 69–73).

It is nonetheless important, because it is actually the key piece of evidence that has supported the idea of a more widespread division between the two mendicant orders regarding the status of this kind of blood relic remaining from the Passion in the period prior to 1400. Charles Zika postulates such a division, and relies on an article published by Livarius Oliger in 1918; Oliger in turn relies solely on the testimony of Nicholas Eymeric regarding the Barcelona controversy.[224] Bynum also argues for such a division, and it is certainly true that in the controversy of 1462–4—a far more significant affair than that of 1350–1, involving senior intellectual figures of European standing like Nikolaus von Kues (Nicholas Cusanus) and a much broader range of theological and philosophical questions—a polarization between the two orders is evident.[225] But the evidence for a long-standing polarization of this nature is, aside from the Barcelona controversy, very limited. The scholastic theologians of the thirteenth century gave very little attention indeed to the issue. Aquinas's position against the potential existence of blood relics surviving from the Passion, which we mentioned above, was not met by directly opposed positions taken by Franciscan scholars. Both Robert Grosseteste, a theologian close to the early Franciscans, and Bonaventura himself broadly supported the possibility of the existence of such relics; but did so in a complex and (especially in Bonaventura's case) tentative manner that was in agreement with Aquinas on blood having been an integral part of the 'veritas humanae naturae'.[226] The most powerful defence of such blood relics, and one of only a couple of thirteenth-century works specifically dedicated to the issue, was written by a Dominican: the *Tractatus de sacratissimo sanguine Domini* of Gerhard von Köln, written in 1280 at the request of abbot Hermann von Weingarten to defend the Weingarten relics against criticism.[227]

In 1350–1, Francis Baiuli was actually only able to refer to just one theologian to support his position: Francis of Meyronnes (d. 1328). Francis had developed a very complex theology on the nature of the death of Christ that, by implication, supported the existence of blood relics. In this he was heavily influenced (as was all his work) by the philosophy of Scotus, and we need not elaborate this here.[228] But

---

[224] Zika, 'Hosts, Processions, and Pilgrimages', p. 52 n. 85; Oliger, 'Johannes Kannemann', p. 46.

[225] See Bynum, *Wonderful Blood*, pp. 120–8.

[226] See ibid. 98–101.

[227] Ead., 'The Blood of Christ', pp. 699–704; and, *Wonderful Blood*, pp. 106–8.

[228] Ead., *Wonderful Blood*, pp. 115–16.

he was well aware of the controversial implications of applying his ideas to relics of blood remaining from the Passion, as he makes clear at the end of the relevant section in his commentary on the Sentences:

[D]ifficultas: Si post resurrectionem aliquid de sanguine remansit in terra. Dicunt aliqui quod non[; i]mmo est periculosum dicere quod remansit; et ita de reliquijs qui dicuntur esse de sanguine christi, non est tutum. Sed dico, quod non est necessarium de quicumque parte sanguinis quod ipsam resumpserit, sicut nec lachrymas; quia non fuit necessarium tantum de sanguine in corpore glorioso, sicut in corpore mortali quid indiget ipso pro alimento corporis. Vnde potest dici, quod non totum resumpsit.[229]

(Difficulty: Whether some of [Christ's] blood remained on earth after his resurrection. Some say no: rather, it is dangerous to say that blood remained, and so there is no certainty about the relics that are said to be from the blood of Christ. But I say that it is not necessary that he took back each and every particle of blood, just as it is not so with his tears; because such an amount of blood was not necessary in his glorious body as what in his mortal body he needed for himself for the digestion of food. Wherefore it can be said that he did not take it all back.)

Francis of Meyronnes was, of course, a Franciscan. Yet what we see here is not the staunch, partisan defence of blood relics against a concerted Dominican theological opposition, but an awareness of the logical consequences of his positions on the nature of Christ's death and the integrity of the human body—consequences that could still be imprudent to assert.

A somewhat different, though related theology governed both of the final two categories of miraculous host: those which have apparently bled, and those in which a vision, seen by many and therefore requiring a change in the accidents of the host (i.e. a corporeal, and not just an imaginative or intellectual vision), has occurred. For simplicity's sake, we shall use the term 'manifestation' in the following to refer to both types. The primary theological issue at stake is whether the accidents pertinent to the spatially constrained body or blood of Christ, in the form that it has in heaven, can be present on earth. Though the *Summa Halensis* addresses the question of whether these manifestations are of Christ himself, in a rather general manner (its author stated a cautious yes),[230] it was Aquinas who dealt first with the theological detail. As we have seen, his position was that Christ's body and blood could not become visible in this way. What appeared was some kind of similitude, because the multiple local presence

[229] Francis of Meyronnes, *In IV Sententiarum*, lib. 4, d. 8, a. 1 (Venice 1520, fol. 184[rb–va]).
[230] See Browe, *Die eucharistischen Wunder*, p. 185.

of the right kind of accidents was not possible.[231] For Scotus, concerned to demonstrate that a deception (which he understood the 'similitude' idea to be) was not taking place, this was less problematic. His complex doctrine of the *respectus extrinsecus adveniens* permitted the multiple local presence of the divine body, and did so entirely independently of any words of consecration.[232] Both positions were influential, and not all adherents of the broadly Scotist position were Franciscans—the infamous Dominican Heinrich Institoris (d. 1505) was among them.[233] These core positions underlie the subsequent theological argument over such manifestations of the fifteenth century, most crucially in the debates in the middle decades of that century on the bleeding hosts of Wilsnack. The large number of interested parties, and the interplay of political alongside purely theological concerns, means that affiliation to a particular order is an unreliable guide to the stance individual theologians took—although a certain preponderance of Franciscan Conventuals amongst the supporters can be detected.[234]

The reader may reasonably question what any of this has to do with Marquard's statements about the imperceptibility of Christ's glorified body. The answer can be found by turning to the work that forms the 'missing link' between the scholastic theology of the universities and the mid-fifteenth century debate that developed from the Wilsnack controversy. This work drew on the thirteenth- and early fourteenth-century theological tradition, and was used as a kind of textbook by the opponents of the

---

[231] See in addition Bynum, *Wonderful Blood*, pp. 88–9; for an example of local clergy applying Aquinas' solution to a bleeding host (here, in the Netherlands in 1422), see Caspers, *De eucharistische vroomheid*, pp. 253–4.

[232] For the *respectus extrinsecus adveniens* see Burr, *Eucharistic Presence*, pp. 78–87, and Cross, *Duns Scotus*, pp. 139–42; on the underlying metaphysics, see Cross, *The Physics of Duns Scotus*, pp. 193–202.

[233] See Browe, *Die eucharistischen Wunder*, pp. 186–93. Caspers and Bynum both regard Scotus' position as closer in nature to the currents of contemporary devotion: see Caspers, *De eucharistische vroomheid*, p. 242, and Bynum, *Wonderful Blood*, p. 89. For Heinrich Institoris' defences of miraculous hosts, see Zika, 'Hosts, Processions and Pilgrimages', pp. 27–8.

[234] There is a massive literature on Wilsnack. For the events, see summatively Bynum, *Wonderful Blood*, pp. 25–9; on the theological arguments see pp. 29–41; Zika, 'Hosts, Processions, and Pilgrimages', pp. 51–6; and Brückner, 'Liturgie und Legende', pp. 148–55. A useful case-study of the relationship between theological and political motivations is provided in Albert, 'Matthias Döring', pp. 62–72. Though both were Franciscans who defended the Wilsnack hosts, the Conventual Matthias Döring was eventually excommunicated for his litigious opposition to the Observant John of Capistrano and the introduction of the Observance into Germany. A solid overview of his life and works is provided by Colberg, 'Döring'; see now Weigel, *Ordensreform und Konziliarismus*.

Wilsnack hosts in the mid-fifteenth century (principally Heinrich Tocke, the theology faculty of Erfurt university, and Nikolaus von Kues). It is Jan Hus's *De sanguine Christi*, written in 1405 following Hus's investigation of the Wilsnack hosts at the behest of the archbishop of Prague.[235] This work has previously attracted scholarly attention insofar as it was drawn upon by Nikolaus von Kues fifty years after its composition. It is, however, an important witness to the piety of its own age, and deserves a more comprehensive presentation than that which can be provided here. The circumstances of the Wilsnack incident are relegated to the background; in the foreground are the underlying theological issues. Hus sets out his conclusions in a short *quaestio* which preceeds their full exposition in the lengthy treatise that follows.

Hus spends much of the time arguing that the blood which Christ shed during his life on earth had to have been entirely reintegrated into and glorified with him.[236] In part, of course, this concerns blood relics remaining from the Passion. As regards miraculous effusions of blood (and, by implication, corporeal visions of the corporeal Christ), he follows the general direction of the Thomist position in arguing that Christ is locally present only in heaven. But that argument had not gone entirely unopposed (not least by Scotus), and Hus was evidently not concerned to produce a defence of Aquinas. Instead he introduced a distinctive novelty: the argument that Christ's body and blood, in their glorified state, can no longer be manifest on earth in a non-glorified form. An initial statement of this is found in the conclusions to the *quaestio*:

Nullus sangwis Christi nec aliquis crinis Christi est hodie super terram sine glorificacione extra corpus Christi. [. . .] Vnde patet vlterius, quod nullus sangwis vel crinis Christi est nostris temporibus localiter et visibiliter super terram, quia corpus Christi cum omnibus partibus suis solum in celo est localiter et dimensiue, licet in sacramento altaris sit realiter et vere.[237]

(None of Christ's blood nor any of Christ's hair is on earth nowadays, external to the body of Christ and without having been glorified. [. . .] Wherefore it is further evident that in our times none of Christ's blood or hair is on earth in a visible and locally present way, because the body of Christ with all its constituent parts is solely in heaven in a locally present and dimensional way; though he is really and truly in the sacrament of the altar.)

---

[235] Hilsch, *Johannes Hus*, pp. 70–1; Bynum, *Wonderful Blood*, pp. 36–7; and Zika, 'Hosts, Processions, and Pilgrimages', pp. 50–1.

[236] See Hus, *De sanguine Christi*, quaestio (pp. 3–8); §1 (pp. 9–10), and §2 (pp. 10–11). §6 (pp. 15–17) and §7 (pp. 17–20) discuss the mechanics of the reconstitution of a resurrected body, enabling Hus to explain his crucial concept of the restitution of blood into a glorified body *in proporcione armonica*.

[237] Ibid., quaestio, conclusio 2, corellarium 3 (p. 7).

Hus argues that, with all Christ's blood having been assumed and reintegrated harmoniously into his body, it is now all glorified in heaven. He is unable to argue categorically that it would not be possible for some of this glorified blood to become manifest on earth in a non-glorified (and therefore visible) form, as God might act *de potentia absoluta*.[238] His tactic is thus to exclude the possibility entirely that Christ would, in any way, want any of his glorified blood to become manifest in non-glorified form.[239] He produces a series of powerful arguments to this end, which he summarizes in his concluding castigation of their opponent:

Sed quod hoc facit iam, ostendat adversarius scriptura, racione, revelacione spiritus sancti et habebit propositum, quod Christus sangwinem suum glorificatum ostendit sub natura inglorificationis.[240]

(But because he [i.e. the opponent] now makes this [argument], let him show himself opposed to Scripture, to reason, and to the revelation of the Holy Spirit, and he will hold the proposition that Christ manifests his glorified blood under an unglorified nature.)

Hus's argumentation is several orders of theological sophistication, and many pages of detail, above Marquard's short statements on the imperceptibility of Christ's glorified body on earth. It also has an explicit practical reference-point—the miraculous hosts of Wilsnack—that Marquard's statements do not. Yet there is still a significant community of ideas. From the perspective of Hus scholarship, it is important to know that his insistence on Christ's body or blood not being perceptible on earth in their present, glorified form *because they were imperceptible* (and not because they could not be locally present) is not entirely original, but is the full theological exposition of an idea whose seed was already present. From Marquard's perspective, his close association of the imperceptibility of Christ in the sacrament (implicitly referring to visions and to the related manifestation of blood) as a consequence of the sacrament being rooted in faith places him in intellectual community with Hus, for whom this idea forms a central pillar of *De sanguine Christi*. It is a key component of Hus's argument that Christ does not want to manifest his glorified blood in non-glorified, perceptible form, occupying the treatise's entire third section. This culminates in statements identical to Marquard's, such as:

---

[238] Ibid., §5 (pp. 14–15).
[239] See ibid., §3 (pp. 11–13); and §4 (pp. 13–14).
[240] Ibid., §5, solucio (p. 15).

Vnde infallibiliter est credendum, quod si melius fuisset nobis Christum corporaliter conversari et suum sangwinem visibiliter bibere vel videre sensu corporeo, ipse
hec fecisset. Sed quia fides non haberet meritum, cum sic humanus sensus haberet
experimentum: ideo voluit remunerator fidei pro nostro maiori merito cum suo
sangwine sic abscondi.[241]

(Wherefore it is infallibly to be believed that if it had been better for us to be
accompanied by Christ in a bodily manner, and to drink his blood in a visible manner
or to see it with our bodily senses, he would have made it so. But because faith would
have no merit, were the human senses to have such experience, so he who rewards
faith wanted to be hidden thus with his blood for our greater reward.)

This is not just an argumentative strategy. Hus restates the dichotomy
between inner faith and external, miraculous signs again and again. In this
crucial respect, which opposed the preponderant forms of the eucharistic
cult, Marquard and Hus tread the same path. Marquard provides his
example of Louis IX, who would refuse to look at Christ if he stood before
him to maintain the purity and quality of his faith; his asseverations and
exposition that the sacrament is rooted in faith; his deep suspicion of
eucharistic visions; and his refusal to use *exempla* to 'prove' the tenets of
sacramental theology. Hus sets out the same opposition between faith and
the desire for visible proofs and the miraculous. He does not confine his
attention to miraculous hosts, but treats these as one symptom of a wider,
problematic preoccupation with outward signs that is not merely current
among the laity, but is being actively propagated by clergy.[242] As a general
principle, he maintains 'quod vere credentes signis non indigent, et quod
sunt maioris meriti aput Deum, qui credunt firmiter sine miraculis, quam
qui miraculis conuertuntur'[243] ('that the true believers are not without
signs, and that those who believe firmly without miracles are of greater
worth in the sight of God than those who are converted by miracles'). It is
hard to overstate exactly how much space Hus spends repetitiously making
this point.

Amongst all this, the work's penultimate section is illuminative. It sets
out fifteen consequences that Hus fears will arise from the entire complex of
problems he saw before him, and places especial emphasis on the condition
of belief.[244] This can be seen, for example, in the eighth consequence:

---

[241] Hus, *De sanguine Christi*, §3 (pp. 11–13, here p. 12).
[242] See ibid., §8 (pp. 20–6); §11 (pp. 28–9), on the misguided or nefarious activity of
clergy; similarly §14a (pp. 32–3). The edition is misnumbered: there is no section 9, and
two sections 14, which I label 14a and 14b.
[243] Ibid., § 8 (p. 22).
[244] Ibid., §14b (pp. 33–6), esp. mala 3, 4, 5, 8, and 14.

8°, quod de fide, constituta a Christo, qui sangwinem suum voluit et constituit esse occultum, ut maius exinde fideles sui haberent premium, tales increduli non sunt contenti[.][245]

(Eighth: that such unbelievers are not content with the faith established by Christ, who wanted his blood to be concealed and made it so, so that the faithful might thereby have greater reward of him.)

Nor was Hus unaware of the main problem with which the *Eucharistie-traktat* and Matthaeus of Cracow's *Dialogus* dealt, the generation of a climate of fear around the Eucharist. The focus should be on reception of the sacrament, not on its excessive veneration:

Et quarto decimo: cum Christus sacramentum venerabile, in quo est corpus suum et sangwis suus, dedit ad comedendum et bibendum in sui memoriam, dicens: »Accipite et comedite« similiter »accipite et bibite« et non dixit 'accipite et ser-uate'—qua intencione et temeritate, si non lucri gracia temporalis, seruant et non comedunt, si est illud, quod ostenditur, venerabile sacramentum, cum digne man-ducare illud sit melius quam seruare? Nam si seruant presbiteri in ecclesiis sacra-mentum, tunc semper finaliter fit propter manducare, ut infirmi in casu non valentes altare accedere, manducent salubriter conseruatum[.][246]

(Fourteenth: When Christ gave the venerable sacrament, in which is his body and his blood, to be eaten and drunk in memory of him, saying 'Take this and eat it' and likewise 'Take this and drink it', he did not say 'Take this and conserve it'. With what intention and audacity, if it is not on account of temporal riches, do they conserve it and not eat it—if that, which is displayed, really is the venerable sacrament—since it is better to eat it worthily than to conserve it? For if priests conserve the sacrament in their churches, then it is always done in order finally to be eaten, so that the infirm, in the event that they are unable to go to receive from the altar, may eat beneficially the conserved sacrament.)

What we see in Hus and Marquard is a concern for immutability and invisibility. The effect on the condition of faith is the central concern for both. At the same time we can see what Caroline Bynum identifies as a discourse on the understanding of soteriology and redemption, in which attitudes to blood relics remaining from the Passion, emanations of blood in eucharistic hosts, and transformations of the host into an apparition of Christ are all interlinked. Dominican theologians, she argues, held a 'higher' theology that saw Christ (and especially his blood) as invisible and immutable, whether in relic or vision, and so problematized the supposed manifestations of Christ's presence. Franciscans on the other hand stressed Christ's humanity and the accessibility of it on a 'lower'

---

[245] Ibid., malum 8 (p. 35).
[246] Ibid., malum 14 (pp. 35–6).

level, where such manifestations served as 'a promise of glory'; relics and
eucharistic visions reminded the devout of Christ's death, and pointed
beyond it to redemption.[247] I have cast doubt on the gravity of that split
between the two main mendicant orders prior to 1400 as far as blood relics
remaining from the Passion are concerned. Certainly by the mid-fifteenth
centuries the waters were substantially muddied in various ways—whether
by the involvement of political factors, as at Wilsnack, or by the intertwine-
ment of the different theological debates, as at La Rochelle in 1448, where
the type of blood relic concerned was not certain.[248] What is clear is that, as
far as 'new' emanations of blood in eucharistic hosts, and transformations
of the host into apparitions of Christ are both concerned, one underlying
theology applied, and similar objections were raised against both. These
were, in part, purely theological objections, which rested on the belief that
Christ, with all his blood, was glorified in heaven and so imperceptible on
earth. This emphasis on glorification is itself new, and occupies a prominent place in the discussions of the issues presented by both Marquard and
Hus. The presence of this discourse in Marquard's oeuvre is especially
significant, in that it indicates its existence prior to the theological controversy generated by the Wilsnack debates, which is generally understood as
its motor, and prior to Hus's *De sanguine Christi*. Hus, then, is not the
originator of this discourse, but nor is he dependent on Marquard. Rather,
he gave a full, formal, and highly influential theological elaboration to a
current of thought that was already in the ascendancy, and of which
Marquard is representative. Driving these objections was a profound concern for the condition of faith; a concern that appears to transcend the
boundaries drawn on other issues between the principal mendicant orders.

This ideological community formed by Marquard's *Eucharistietraktat*
and Hus's *De sanguine Christi* with regard to eucharistic miracles, and their
effect on the condition of belief, can be extended. Peter Browe lists two
works critical of eucharistic visions.[249] One has already been encountered,
David von Augsburg's *De compositione*, and it can be discounted here. The
section to which Browe refers, entitled 'Quatuor sunt genera revelationum
et visionum'[250] ('There are four kinds of revelations and visions'), offers a
classification of visions. David is sceptical about visions, because in them
'quidam de veritate aliquando erudiuntur, et plurimi deluduntur'[251] ('some

[247] Bynum, *Wonderful Blood*, pp. 112–13, 128–31, and 138–41.
[248] See ibid., pp. 109–10.
[249] Browe, *Die eucharistischen Wunder*, pp. 108–11.
[250] David von Augsburg, *De compositione*, lib. 3, c. 66 (pp. 355–60).
[251] Ibid., §1 (p. 356).

people are sometimes instructed about something true, and most people are deluded'), but eucharistic visions are not specifically mentioned, and David says nothing on the relationship between visions (or other miracles) and belief. The second work is more promising, but something of an odd fish: the anonymous German treatise *Schwester Katrei*. The last word has yet to be written on this work from around 1320, associated with the reception of Eckhart's works and with the so-called Heresy of the Free Spirit.[252] Although it pre-dates Marquard's activity by at least a generation, it does indeed take a highly critical stance towards visions, particularly those seen in the eucharistic host. Those who seek such visions are targeted for particular criticism, because they are too preoccupied with external forms and insufficiently disciplined inwardly, where God is actually to be perceived. They lack faith, and place their trust in external proofs, which are deceptive because visions of Christ are actually diabolical:

Die [...] lutt, von den wir da vor gerett hand,[253] die gott hie wenent sechen mitt vssern ogen, das sind vnglöbig lütt. Hie bestattet jn der tüffel iren vngloben, vff das sÿ ewanklich mitt jm bliben, vnd nimet an sich jn dem luffte von den elementen ein forme, wie er wil, vnd erschinet den lütten, wenn er wil vnd wa er wil: vnder wilen als ein kind jn der oflatten mitt krussem har; er erschinet jn ze dem andern mal als ein zwelffjärig jungling, er erschinet jn als ein frome man von drissig jaren, kurcz gerett: Er erschinet jn als der vatter vnd der sun, er erschinet jn, wie sÿ begerent oder wie sÿ wellend, vnd redet mitt jn vnd bescheidet sÿ vnderscheit, wie sÿ wellent, als verre als er icht weis—vnd wissent: Er seit jn dicke war, vff das er si bestetige in dem vngloben. Wissent, das dis das verflüchtest folck ist, das ie geborn wart[.][254]

(The people of whom we have previously spoken, who believe that they see God here with their exterior eyes, are unbelievers. The devil confirms them in their unbelief so that they will remain with him eternally. From the elements in the air he takes upon himself whatever form he wants, and appears to people when and where he wants: sometimes as a child in the host with curly hair; then again he appears to them as a twelve-year-old boy, or he appears to them as a respectable man of thirty years of age. In short, he appears to them as the Father and the Son; he appears to them however they desire or however they want, speaks with them, and teaches them with whatever sort of instruction they want, as far as he knows something of it—and know that he often tells them the truth, so that he may confirm them in their unbelief. Know that this is the most accursed people that has ever been born.)

252 See Schweitzer, 'Schwester Katrei'.
253 This refers to those who beseech visions, first described at 357. 10–26.
254 *Schwester Katrei*, 358. 2–21; cf. 358. 21–41 on the superiority of inner disciplines over outer works.

down in corporeal things, makes them err a great deal, to such an extent that they reckon that they see in a real way God crucified or under another corporeal form, either in the elevation of the body of Christ or in some other deliberation of theirs; others think that they hear voices like that of Christ or those of his saints.)

Gerson's target is not the general criticism of visions: his next statement refers to the great difficulty of distinguishing true from false revelations, and of identifying their origins. His treatises on the *discretio spirituum* deal with these issues, indicating Gerson's concern to distinguish the true from the false, rather than to reject wholesale. His target, rather, is the 'profundata phantasiatio circa corporalia'—the mental preoccupation with external images, primarily visions, which retards the progress of the soul, leads the person into error, and gets in the way of the spiritual truth. Setting aside *Schwester Katrei*, which has very particular, theologically radical motivations for the assertions it makes, the direction of Marquard's *Eucharistietraktat* with regard to the nexus of external miracles, eucharistic visions, contemplation—and more crucially, faith—points clearly away from the tendencies of the eucharistic cult in the later fourteenth century, and towards a position characteristic of the 'new brooms' that were at work in the early fifteenth-century church.

The relationship between the *Eucharistietraktat* and mysticism was first raised as an issue by Annelies Hofmann, who addressed the question: 'Der Eucharistie-Traktat, ein Werk der Mystik?'[264] ('Is the *Eucharistietraktat* a mystical work?'). Willing's more recent examination of the work deals implicitly with the same question. She concludes in the affirmative. But there are reasons to be cautious about this conclusion. Marquard's use of terminology coined by earlier writers of mystical texts—'mystical language'—and his unacknowledged quotation from the works of Eckhart, Tauler, and Ruusbroec does not necessarily make the *Eucharistietraktat* into a mystical work, not least because much of that quotation itself has no mystical import. Much of the text that Willing views as having such mystical import, furthermore, need not be read in this way. For example, let us examine the following statement from the seventh section of Marquard's treatise:

---

[264] Hofmann (ed.), *Der Eucharistie-Traktat*, p. 226, with her answer pp. 233–45.

Nim war der grossen liebi Ihesu Cristi, wie das were, das er in disem zit nie ân bitter liden gestûnd, doch so wolt er sin grundlosen minn von dem menschen nit scheiden. Er wolt sich in das sacrament verbergen, das er echt in dem mentschen beliben möcht vnd im helfen, das er bestan möcht in allen sinen striken wider all sin vyend.[265]

(Take note of the great love of Jesus Christ! Although he was never without bitter suffering in his earthly life, he did not want to detach his bottomless love from mankind. He wanted to conceal himself in the sacrament in order that he could truly remain in an individual and assist him, so that he might endure in all his entanglements and against all his enemies.)

Willing comments on this passage that '[w]eiter sei der im Sakrament real gegenwärtige Christus dem Menschen eine dauernde und gegenwärtige Hilfe gegen die Verstrickung der Welt, für das Erreichen der *abegescheidenheit* und Gelassenheit'[266] ('Further, Christ, who is really present in the sacrament, is an enduring and present aid for the individual against the entanglements of the world and for the attainment of spiritual detachment and passivity'). The first part of this is clear. But the second idea, namely that the sacrament aids a person not just to resist the entanglements of the world, but to do so as a means of achieving a state of passivity and total detachment from all that is created (*abegescheidenheit*), is evident neither in this passage of the *Eucharistietraktat* nor in its surrounding context. I have similarly argued earlier against the imposition of an energetic model of mystical progress onto the sixth section of the work; that is to say, against the view that it represents a programme of mystical ascent in which the *via purgativa* is opened to the *perfecti*, and that Marquard 'den mystischen Stufenweg verstanden wissen will als adequäte Vorbereitung auf die tägliche Kommunion'[267] ('wants the mystical path of ascent to be understood as sufficient preparation for daily communion').

Willing concludes by presenting an interpretation of the work as a vehicle for the transmission of Eckhart's mysticism in new clothing:

Marquard bindet im Eucharistietraktat die mystische Lehre Eckharts in eine Katechese ein; mystische Lehre ist hier verbunden mit der Vermittlung des Wissens, das zu ihrem rechtgläubigen Verständnis dient [. . .] Denn in Marquards Eucharistietraktat steht Eckharts Lehre gleichberechtigt neben theologischer Unterweisung und praktischer Anleitung, neben Katechese und Pastoration.[268]

---

[265] *Eucharistietraktat*, §7 (302. 1–6).
[266] Willing, *Literatur und Ordensreform*, p. 223.
[267] Ibid. 214.
[268] Ibid. 232.

(In the *Eucharistietraktat*, Marquard integrates Eckhart's mystical doctrine into a catechesis. Mystical doctrine is connected here to the transmission of knowledge that aids its orthodox understanding. [...] For in Marquard's *Eucharistietraktat* Eckhart's doctrine stands equal alongside theological instruction and practical guidance; alongside catechesis and pastoral counsel.)

Yet there is barely a handful of lines of quotation or adaptation from Eckhart in the seventy-five pages of the entire edited work. We have already seen one of these rare adaptations, and observed that the quotation is realigned to substantiate an ethical, rather than a mystical, point. Another is an allegory that has no mystical implication at all.[269]

In examining the presence of mysticism in the *Eucharistietraktat* we have to distinguish between mystical ideas, contemplative ideas, and 'mystical language'—the German terms with specific meanings in the works normally associated with the tradition known as the 'Deutsche Mystik'. Marquard's German works are full of this language used in contexts that dissociate it from its original meaning. For the purpose of examining the place of mystical thought in the *Eucharistietraktat*, we may disregard it here. Further, the genuinely mystical has to be distinguished from the more broadly contemplative. As far as the eucharist is concerned, the conceptions of mystical union associated with the 'Deutsche Mystik' ought to be distinguished from conceptions of eucharistic union. Willing refers to this distinction, though does not uphold it in her analysis. That is not without reason: the eucharistic union is, by its very nature, mystical. Even a work as pragmatic as Matthaeus of Cracow's *Dialogus* makes mention of the eucharistic union—of the recipient becoming part of Christ's mystical body—as here, in the section on the correct disposition of the *proficientes*:

Nam, cum constet hoc sacramentum institutum esse in memoriam dominicae passionis et mortis, in pignus amoris, in medium unionis et incorporationis et transformationis in Christum, quilibet tanto magis dispositus est, quanto plenius mundi concupiscentiis et delectationibus carnis moritur aut mori conatur et communicando Christi passionibus consepelitur in morte, ut summe desideret unum esse cum Christo et sibi ipsi mori, ut vivat Christus in eo, quatenus possit dicere cum Apostolo: Vivo autem iam non ego, vivit vero in me Christus. [Gal. 2: 20][270]

---

[269] See *Eucharistietraktat*, §1 (260. 21–4); cf. Hofmann (ed.), *Der Eucharistie-Traktat*, p. 234, identifying the parallel in Eckhart, *Predigt* 20a (vol. 1: 328. 5–6).

[270] Matthaeus of Cracow, *Dialogus*, §13, ll. 1221–30 (p. 408). A brief discussion of eucharistic union expressed in 13th-cent. works is provided by Rubin, *Corpus Christi*, pp. 27–8.

(For, since it is known that this sacrament has been instituted in memory of the Lord's suffering and death, as an assurance of love, and as a means of union—both of incorporation and of transformation—in Christ; then the more well-disposed someone is [i.e. to receive the sacrament], the more fully he dies or endeavours to die to the lusts of the world and the delights of the flesh. By participating in the sufferings of Christ he is buried with him in death, so that he might desire in the highest to be one with Christ and to die to himself, so that Christ may live in him, in order than he can say with the Apostle, 'I, however, am not alive; rather Christ lives in me.')

Eucharistic union is implicitly mystical. The reverse is not true, which must be borne in mind when examining mysticism in the *Eucharistietraktat*—as must the distinction between different types of mystical union. Eckhart's conception is, to take an obvious example, radically different from the much more traditional, Pauline conception held by Matthaeus of Cracow.

Many elements that might be considered to have 'mystical' content in the *Eucharistietraktat* have a somewhat inchoate quality. An allusion to a mystical aspect is presented without subsequently being fully developed and informing the pertinent section of the treatise. The opening of the work has precisely this quality. Marquard interprets the scriptural text by elaborating the idea of the divine speaking into the pure mind of the individual, but then develops this interpretation no further, and does not make it thereafter the focus of attention:

Also spricht der edel kúng Dauid in dem salter: hôr, tochter, und sich vnd neig din ore hie zů, won der kúng hat diner schôni begert [Ps. 44: 11–12]. Ach ewige wissheit, wie sind din zúge so minneriche, wie ist din jnsprechen so sûsse vnd so heimlich, wie ist din hertz so milt vnd so senftmútig, das du begerest in alle jnwendikeit ze sprechen, da du geneiget oren vnd ein lutern grund vindest. Ach herre, wie ist die creatur so selig, der schôni du begerest, die du zů dinem gemachel haben wilt vnd ir die kúnglichen kronen vff setzen wilt!²⁷¹

(Thus speaks the noble king David in the Psalter: 'Listen, daughter, see, and incline your ear to this, because the king has desired your beauty.' Oh, eternal wisdom, how are your raptures so full of love; how is your speech within me so sweet and so intimate; how is your heart so merciful and so gentle, that you desire to speak into every innermost being where you find an inclined ear and a pure foundation. Oh, Lord, how is the creature so blessed, whose beauty you desire, whom you want to have as your bride, and on whom you want to place the royal crown!)

---

²⁷¹ *Eucharistietraktat*, prologue (254. 15–23).

This is a characteristic phenomenon of Marquard's German works, and we need not work through all such passages in the entire treatise here.[272]

Expressions of eucharistic union of the more traditional kind are to be found, starting at the end of the first section. Here sacramental reception is presented as a means to integration in Christ's mystical body:

Dar zů soltu wissen, sid das brot vnd der win allen menschen wachsent ze nutz vnd ze sterki, vnd ouch von vil kornen ein brot wirt gemacht, vnd von vil truben win ze samen flůsset [. . .]: hierumb, sider das wirdig sacrament als das brot und der win gemeinlich allen menschen geben ist, vnd ouch alle menschen sôllent in im gesterket werden vnd alle gelider vnd alle menschen sollent ein in Cristo werden in diser spise, als von vil kornen ein brot wirt.[273]

(Regarding this, you should know that as the bread and the wine grow to be useful for and to strengthen mankind, and that a loaf of bread is made from many grains, and wine flows together from many grapes [. . .]: so, given that the worthy sacrament is given as bread and wine to all mankind universally, all mankind should be strengthened in him, and all the limbs—all the individual people—should become one in Christ in this food, as one loaf of bread is made from many grains.)

We may legitimately describe this as traditional, because this passage, as Hofmann noted, has a close parallel in Aquinas' *Summa theologiae*.[274] Aquinas, in turn, draws explicitly on the *Glossa ordinaria*. It is followed, somewhat later in the same passage, by another short passage of similar import:

Wie ist denn so billich, das du von Egipto der begird aller creaturen varest mit allem dinem gemůte zů diser wirdigen spise jn der du nit allein die wissheit des rechten Salomonem hôrrest, mer in wesenlich und liplich enpfachest vnd ein geist mit im wirst in warer ewikeit.[275]

(How very fitting, then, is this: namely that you should journey with your whole mind from the Egypt of desire of all the created to this worthy food, in which you do not just hear the wisdom of the just Solomon, but rather receive him essentially and bodily and become one spirit with him in true eternity.)

---

[272] For other examples, see the post-reception prayer, ibid., §6 (294. 22–295. 7); the sixth reason for the individual to seek sacramental reception at §13 (317. 12–20); and the twelfth fruit of the eucharist at §14 (321. 9–13).

[273] Ibid., §1 (260. 31–261. 5).

[274] Hofmann (ed.), *Der Eucharistie-Traktat*, p. 231; see Aquinas, *Summa theologiae*, q. 74 a. 1 in resp. 4 (vol. 4, p. 487^b). The related point of the eucharist as spiritual food, remaining in the soul after the bread has been digested, likewise has a parallel in the *Summa theologiae*: see *Eucharistietraktat*, §2 (266. 31–267. 2); Aquinas, *Summa theologiae*, q. 77 a. 6 ad 1 (vol. 4, p. 521^a); and Willing, *Literatur und Ordensreform*, p. 193 n. 96.

[275] *Eucharistietraktat*, §1 (261. 16–20).

The term *wesenlich* ('essentially') was, however, incorporated into the printed text by Hofmann from a second manuscript.[276] But even if we accept its presence, it is not necessary to consider it as a mystical term indicating essential union in the Eckhartian sense. It may simply refer to the consumption of the *res* of Christ's body, the *essentia*, in the sacrament.

In fact, much of the work is devoid of mystical import, which is not to be found even where it might be expected. So, in the *Meßauslegung*, the moment at which transubstantiation takes place is not interpreted allegorically as the individual's mystical conversion into the divine (an association which had attracted censure for Eckhart in the bull *In agro dominico*),[277] but is interpreted in an entirely ethical sense:

> Das sechste stuk ist die wandlung, in der die natur des brotes in warheit verwandlet wirt jn den fronlicham Ihesu Cristi vnd der win in sin heiliges blůt. Vnd betůt, dz der sůnder von vngerechtikeit in die gerechtikeit wirt verwandlet, vnd dz in der ewig got von nicht ze icht hat geschaffen, vnd dz die schuld gŏtliches flůches in gŏtlich minne wirt verkert.[278]

(The sixth element is the transformation, in which the nature of the bread is truly transformed into the body of Jesus Christ and the wine into his holy blood. It signifies that the sinner is transformed from an unjustified to a justified state; that the eternal God has created him from nothing into being; and that the blame of the divine curse is switched to divine love.)

It is then reception of the sacrament that is associated with union: spiritual, eucharistic union that explicitly excludes essential transformation and points, in the accompanying prayer, towards the traditional idea of incorporation into Christ's mystical body, the community of the faithful:

> Das vierd stuk ist die heilig niessung vnd betůtet, als die liplich spise wirt verwandlet in vnser blůt vnd fleisch, also wirt der mentsch geistlich, nit wesentlich, verwandlet in das heilig sacrament vnd wirt eins mit got. Dem soltu denn nach gedenken und sprechen: "O minnenklicher got, sider du alle verirret wider samnest vnd in ewikeit alle zerspreiten dinge tribest, so gib mir, herre, das ich

---

[276] Hofmann's principal manuscript (A) was Wolfenbüttel, Herzog-August-Bibliothek, Cod. Guelf. 29. 9; she does not explictly indicate in her note from which manuscript she derived the addition, but it was probably her manuscript B, namely Schaffhausen, Stadtbibliothek, Ms. Gen. 20.

[277] See Sturlese (ed.), *Acta Echardiana*, in Eckhart, *Die lateinischen Werke*, vol. 5, pp. 149–617, here no. 65: John XXII, *In agro dominico* [27 Mar. 1329] (pp. 596–600), §10, ll. 43–6 (p. 598).

[278] *Eucharistietraktat*, §3 (275. 5–10). The accompanying prayer (275. 11–16) works over the same ideas.

vergangner mentsch wider zů dir gesamnet werd in ware ewikeit. Gib mir, herre, das ich vereint werd mit allen gelidern der heilgen kilchen. Gib mir, herre, das min verirrekeit in din luter einikeit gezogen werd. Kum, her got, in min hertz vnd mach es eins mit dir. Owe her got, ich bin aber nit wirdig, dz du komest in min hus.["][279]

(The fourth element is the holy reception. It signifies that as the bodily food is transformed into our flesh and blood, so the individual is spiritually, not essentially, transformed into the holy sacrament and becomes one with God. You should then reflect on this and say, 'O God, full of love, as you gather together all that has gone astray, and bring all the disparate together in eternity; so grant it to me, Lord, that I, a fallen man, may be brought together with you again in true eternity. Grant it to me, Lord, that I may be unified with all the limbs of holy church. Grant it to me, Lord, that my disunity may be drawn into your pure unity. Come, mighty God, into my heart and make it one with you. But alas, mighty God, I am not worthy that you should come into my house.')

But the central component in Willing's argument strongly in favour of the *Eucharistietraktat* as a mystical work is Marquard's adaptation of material from Eckhart. The implications of one of the two key passages has already been considered, in examining Marquard's instructions for preparing to receive the sacrament. There, the import of the original phrase is nullified by its adaptation within a passage making a primarily ethical point. The second key passage forms the sixth and final point in the seventh section. It details the love by which the sacrament overcomes man's failings, and the issue in question is man's great distance from and dissimilarity to God. Marquard begins by showing how God counters this by giving himself lovingly in the sacrament, so as to draw the individual closer to him and so reduce the distance. He follows this with a statement that is both drawn from Eckhart's sermon 20a, where it likewise concerns the eucharist, and deals with union:

Won nim war, als die liplich spis gewandlet wirt in dem lib des mentschen, dz ein winkelin in der natur des mentschen nit enist, die spise werd da vereint, sider ein krafft ist in der natur, die scheidet ab das grobeste von der spise vnd wirffet es vs, vnd dz edlest tringet sich in daz marck, das nienent so vil ist als ein nadel spitz in dem lib es werd da mit vereinet.[280] Sus durch warer einung zwúschent got vnd dem mentschen so hat sich der wirdig kúng zů einer spise geben in dem heilgen sacrament, das er eines in im werde, wie doch das der mentsch wesentlich in got

[279] Ibid. (278. 10–22).
[280] Cf. Eckhart, *Predigt* 20a (vol. 1: 328. 6–10); for the identification see Hofmann, *Der Eucharistie-Traktat*, p. 235.

niemer ein in einem wirt. Vnd dar vmb sprach ouch Cristus: „Qui manducat meam
carnem, etc", dz spricht: Wer isset min lib vnd trinkt min blůt, der belibt in mir vnd
ich in im. [John 6: 56][281]

(Take note that when the bodily food is transformed into the body of the individual,
such that there is not even a tiny particle of the individual's nature into which the
food is not transformed. This is because there is a power in the nature that separates
the basest part of the food out and casts it aside, so that the noblest part penetrates
into the very marrow; and thus there is nowhere in the body, even a pinprick's
worth, that is not unified with it. So, for the sake of true union between God and
man the worthy king has given himself as food in the holy sacrament, so that God
may become one in him [i.e. in the individual], although the individual never
becomes one in one in God essentially. Therefore Christ said also, 'Qui manducat
meam carnem, etc.', which means, 'Whoever eats my body and drinks my blood
will dwell in me, and I in him'.)

Willing rightly points out that Eckhart, in his statement comparing the
process of union between God and man and the process of digestion,
operates within a relatively conventional tradition of similar comparisons,
also found in Augustine and the sermons of Bernard of Clairvaux.[282]
Marquard has adopted and adapted a descriptive comparison, not Eckhart's
formulation of the mystical union, as is clear from the following statement
on the impossibility of unindividuated and essential (*wesentlich*) union. In
fact, the defining character to this long, sixth point of the seventh section is
given not by Eckhart's comparison of union with the digestive process, but
by Augustinian quotations on eucharistic union. The passage continues:

Hier vmb so sprach ouch sanctus Agustinus: Wz ist das, das ein mentsch den
fronlicham Cristi enpfachet, denn dz der mensch in Cristo belibet vnd den liplich
in im hab. Won wer in Cristo nit belibet, der enpfachet geistlich den fronlicham
Cristi nit, wie dz ist, dz er in mit sinem mund liplich in warheit des sacramentes
enpfachet. Es sprach ouch sanctus Agustinus in der person gottes: „Manducabis
me". Dz spricht: du issest mich vnd ich wirt nicht verwandlet in dich, mer du wirst
verwandlet in mich. By disem spruch merkest du wol, das der mensch eins wirt mit
Cristo, der dise spise enpfachet, vnd dz alle verheit des menschen wirt in der einung
genechet. Won si got in den jnwendigen grund zúchet in einikeit sin selbs vnd gottes
vss aller manigvaltikeit, wo man si wirdenklichen nússet.[283]

(On this topic St Augustine said likewise, 'What is it that an individual receives the
body of Christ, save that the individual dwells in Christ and has him bodily within
him?' For whoever does not dwell in Christ does not receive the body of Christ

[281] *Eucharistietraktat*, §7 (304. 20–32).
[282] See Willing, *Literatur und Ordensreform*, pp. 226–9.
[283] *Eucharistietraktat*, §7 (304. 32–305, 12).

spiritually, however much it may be that he received it bodily in his mouth in the truth of the sacrament. Speaking in the person of God, St Augustine also said, 'Manducabis me', which means: 'You will eat me, and I will not be transformed into you; but rather you will be transformed into me'. From this statement you can clearly see that the individual who receives this food becomes one with Christ, and that the individual's distance from God is turned into proximity with him in the union. For the sacramental food, when one consumes it worthily, draws God into the innermost foundation, in unity of himself [i.e. the individual] and God aside from all multiplicity.)

The import of this passage is then further relativized by the lengthy conclusion to the seventh section. This deals with the necessity of interior devotion to God, rather than external works of piety—which, adds Marquard, obscure the absence of any interior devotion in many people.[284]

It is fair to say that the quotations from Eckhart's sermons are reclothed by Marquard in the *Eucharistietraktat*. But those quotations do not contain formulations of Eckhart's conception of the mystical union. Marquard deploys them in passages that reflect a much more traditional, Pauline conception of the eucharistic union—the mysticism that the reception of the eucharist inevitably implies. It is not possible to agree with Willing that a specifically Eckhartian mystagogy forms any aspect, let alone the definitive aspect, of the *Eucharistietraktat*. Mystagogy does play a central role, however, in the eighth section of the work. The first part of this sets out how an individual is purified (*bekleret*) by the sacrament, and is able to respond with love to the love manifested within it. It is in this section, and in this section alone, that the *Eucharistietraktat* espouses a mysticism that goes beyond the conventional interpretations of eucharistic union. Marquard adapts almost the entire passage from Ruusbroec's *Geestelijke brulocht*. This is well known, and so we need not repeat the precise relationship between the respective passages here.[285]

The relevant section is divided into three groups of three distinctions. The first group sets out the three manners in which Christ gives himself in the sacrament: in body, in soul, and (though this is not entirely clear) in divinity.[286] It is in describing the last of these that the mystical union is first mentioned: 'Zů dem dritten mal git er ŭns sin personlicheit mit gŏtlicher klarheit, die erhebt sinen geist vnd allen verklerten menschen geist in die

[284] See ibid. (305. 13–306. 9).

[285] See Hofmann, *Der Eucharistie-Traktat*, pp. 237–41; Eichler, *Jan van Ruusbroecs 'Brulocht'*, pp. 41–5; and Willing, *Literatur und Ordensreform*, pp. 203–8. I have indicated above that Willing's extension of these parallels cannot be maintained.

[286] *Eucharistietraktat*, §8 (306. 16–26).

hohe gebrúchlich einikeit'[287] ('Third, he gives us his person with divine
clarity, which raises his spirit and the spirit of every purified individual into
the supreme participatory unity'). The second group then expands on the
distinctions of the first.[288] Where Christ's soul is concerned, it is just
possible that Marquard is still speaking of the conventional understanding
of eucharistic union. This is not the case with the gift of divinity. The
individual is drawn up, via (and not in) the reception of Christ's body and
soul in the sacrament, into union with God at a higher level:

Er git vns ouch sinen gerichten geist in allen gaben vnd tugenden vnd in allen
wundren. Vnd hiemit werden wir beklert vnd geziert in einikeit vnsers geistes vnd
mit dem jnwonen Cristi werden wir gezogen ettwz in die obresten krefft siner sele
mit aller siner richheit. Er git ouch sin personlicheit in vnbegriffenlicher clarheit,
vnd hie mit werden wir vereinet vnd vbergefúrt zu dem vatter, vnd der vatter
enpfachet sin vserkorne kind mit sinem natúrlichen sun. Vnd also komen wir in
dem sacrament zu vnserm erbe, der gotheit.[289]

(He also gives us his elevated spirit in every gift, virtue, and miracle, and by this we
are purified and made splendid in the unity of our spirit. With the in-dwelling of
Christ we are drawn somewhat into the upper powers of his soul with all his majesty.
He gives his person as well in inconceivable clarity, and by this we are united and
translated to the Father, and the Father receives his chosen child with his natural
Son. And so in the sacrament we come to our inheritance, the divinity.)

In the final group, Marquard changes direction and explains (still adapting
Ruusbroec) how the individual should respond to meet these three levels of
body, soul, and divinity.[290] Imaginative recreation of the Passion takes care
of the bodily aspect, in accordance with the scriptural institution of the
eucharist as a remembrance of the Passion. Focusing the self in the soul and
'flowing' out with love towards heaven and earth meets Christ's gift of his
soul: 'Wir sond [. . .] inwonent sin in einikeit vnsers geistes vnd vsfliessen
mit wider minn in himel vnd ertrich mit clarer bescheidenheit'[291] ('We
should dwell within [him] in the unity of our spirit, and flow out with
reciprocal love into heaven and earth with clear understanding'). Finally,
the individual must transcend himself with the outpouring of love, passing
through Christ's humanity to achieve mystical rest in God:

[287] *Eucharistietraktat*, §8 (306. 23–5).
[288] Ibid. (306. 25–307. 8).
[289] Ibid. (306. 32–307. 8).
[290] Ibid. (307. 9–29).
[291] Ibid. (307. 19–23).

Wir sond ŏch zŭ dem dritten mal mit der personlicheit Cristi mit einfaltiger meinung vnd mit gebruchliger minn v́berfaren v́ns selb vnd durch Cristi geschaff-enheit vnd rasten in v́nserm erb, das ist das gŏtlich wesen. Das wil v́ns Cristus alles geistlich geben, so wir in enpfachent.[292]

(Third, with the person of Christ, with simple intention and with participatory love, we should transcend ourselves, pass through Christ's created form, and rest in our inheritance, which is the divine being. Christ wants to give us all of that spiritually, when we receive him.)

The emphasis on love in effecting the mystical union reflects the common dependence of both Ruusbroec and Marquard on the Victorine tradition of contemplation, inherited and propagated definitively in the Franciscan sphere by Bonaventura.

It is here, and here alone, that Marquard goes beyond the inevitable mysticism of eucharistic union into a higher plane. Reception of the sacrament provides the starting point for this mystical ascent, rather than its culmination. Ruusbroec's terminology is distinctive, and it is his (not Eckhart's, or Tauler's) formulation of the mystical union which Marquard adopts. Nonetheless, this new mystical scheme is described very briefly. The second half of the eighth section, which follows it, deals (as we saw earlier) with the pragmatic issue of whether abstinence out of humility, or recep-tion out of love, is superior. The mystical plays no role whatsoever here, and its absence relativizes the significance of its presence in the first half of the section. Rather than view this eighth section as the centrepiece of the treatise purely because of its mystical content, as Willing does, it should be seen as a mystagogy that Marquard lays open to the contemplative: but which is neither the apex of the treatise, nor enforced upon the recipient of the eucharist. One might even argue that its presence results primarily from its emphasis on meeting love with love, rather than because of the mystical aspect. It is, after all, the answer provided to the pupil's opening question, 'wie der mensch bekleret wurd von dem sacrament vnd wie er der minne Ihesu Cristi wider gnŭg were als es die minne Ihesu Cristi vordret'[293] ('how the individual is purified by the sacrament, and how he might sufficiently return Jesus Christ's love for him, as the love of Jesus Christ demands').

If that overstates the case, it is nonetheless true that, this section aside, the mystical does not occupy a prominent position in the work as a whole. Marquard was familiar with genuinely mystical and mystagogical works, and drew heavily on Tauler's eucharistic sermons in the *Eucharistietraktat*—

---

[292] Ibid. (307. 24–8).
[293] Ibid. (306. 13–15).

but for moral and ethical elements, not for their mysticism.[294] We have to approach 'mysticism' in the *Eucharistietraktat* by trying to forget what is known of the origin of certain passages in the works of earlier intellectuals. Instead, we should examine the import of the 'mystical' passages as they stand, in the context of their presentation in the *Eucharistietraktat*. That work seeks to redirect attitudes towards the eucharist, to replace fear with love in the context of a wider crisis in the eucharistic cult across northern Europe in the later fourteenth century. The incorporation of a short mystagogy that fits those aims, appropriate for a particular group of contemplatives who fell within Marquard's target audience, but by no means exclusively constituted it, is secondary.

---

[294] On Marquard's use of Tauler, see summatively Willing, *Literatur und Ordensreform*, pp. 208–11 and 216–21; on Tauler's eucharistic sermons themselves, see pp. 136–63. An alternative (not to say idiosyncratic) perspective on Tauler is offered by Browe, *Die häufige Kommunion*, p. 31.

3

The Virgin Mary

We should begin by recalling just one, perhaps the key, aspect of the manifold significance of Mary in the Middle Ages: namely, that Mary presented a potent model for identification and imitation to the individual. She may only be infrequently present in the Gospels, but she participates in all the most significant episodes, from the incarnation through the wedding at Cana to the Passion itself. The image of Mary, *mater dolorosa*, standing beneath the crucified Christ is, with the exception of the crucified Christ himself, perhaps the most ubiquitous of all medieval images. It is no surprise, then, that Marquard deals with this image at length.

There is an enormous body of scholarship on the genesis of particular Mariological dogmas. It would be relatively unrewarding here to show how each of Marquard's theological positions corresponded to this or that contemporary Mariological view, because the positions he holds are conventional. He believed in the immaculate conception, Mary's virginity post-partum and her corporeal assumption. On the tricky subject of co-redemption, Mary's active participation in Christ's work of salvation in the crucifixion, he says nothing. His argumentation, by contrast, was by no means as conventional as this set of positions is for a Franciscan of the later fourteenth century. His use of the Islamic justification of the immaculate conception, otherwise hardly known in medieval Europe, is a distinctive case in point.[1] Two further central aspects of the late medieval devotion to Mary may be set aside: her role as the *dispensatrix* or *mediatrix* of grace, and her position as heavenly intercessor with her son on mankind's behalf. Marquard mentions both of these issues in his works without ever calling particular attention to them.

---

[1] See Mossman, 'The Western Understanding'.

Nonetheless, Marquard was a significant contributor to the Marian cult in late medieval Germany. Leaving aside a handful of minor issues considered in his Latin works, no less than five out of his collection of forty-one German sermons are devoted to Marian feasts. His principal Marian work is the *Dekalogerklärung*. This was his largest and most widely circulated work, and one of the great best-sellers (if not, indeed, the best-seller) of the German language before the Reformation. It is as much about Mary as about the ethical issues arising from the Ten Commandments, and it is correspondingly this work that we shall prioritize. Marquard presents Mary as a prayerful contemplative, and so we will first examine this general presentation, its context, and the tradition on which it draws, identifying in the process some of Marquard's principal sources for his depiction of Mary's manner of life. We shall mention a crucial component of this depiction, namely Mary standing beneath the cross. Marquard elaborates at length on this image, but does so in explicit and direct opposition to its normative presentation in contemporary literature and art. We will then consider Marquard's specific presentation of Mary as a mystical contemplative who enjoyed the beatific vision in this life, and who forms thereby a model for imitation. In part, Marquard draws here on the German-language mysticism of Meister Eckhart and Johannes Tauler. But this is more than simply the integration of the terminology and ideas of the Rhenish mystics into a pre-existent depiction of a prayerful, contemplative Mary. In reality, the *Dekalogerklärung* represents the culmination of what I shall argue is a largely unrecognized medieval tradition of presenting Mary as a 'mystic', the development of which can be shown to have been particularly prevalent in the thirteenth and fourteenth centuries. Understanding this tradition, which will take us well away from Marquard himself, has important implications—not merely for the historical presentation of the medieval Marian tradition, but for the consequent understanding of writings that have been the focus of much recent scholarship, and that bear relation to the imitation of Mary: sermons, hagiographies, contemplatives' writings, and the accounts of nuns' lives in the *Schwestern-bücher*. We must begin by looking more closely at the *Dekalogerklärung*.

The date of composition for the *Dekalogerklärung* is unknown. The oldest manuscript identified thus far dates from 1391 (Stuttgart, Landesbibliothek, cod. theol. et philos. 4° 54, discussed in Chapter 2 on the *Euchar-istietraktat*), only one year before Marquard died. It is probable that a shortened version of the *Dekalogerklärung* was produced for integration halfway through the *Auszug*, but it is not certain that this was Marquard's own undertaking. Even if this could be proven, it would not demonstrate that the *Dekalogerklärung* was written before or after the *Auszug*. These two treatises are not otherwise linked thematically. Although the 1391 manuscript provides the date *ante quem*, the date *post quem* can be made no more specific—as with most of Marquard's works—than *c*.1370.

The transmission of the *Dekalogerklärung* is equally problematic. Mayr's classification of the main recensions, dependent on just thirty-five manuscripts and three printed versions, is nearly eighty years old and—covering only ten pages—does not fulfil the requirements of modern scholarship.[2] What is clear is that the recensions differ greatly. The C[3] recension, incorporating extensive interpolations from the *Buch von geistlicher Armut* and other material, is perhaps twice the length of the A[1] recension, which represents the base text from which all other recensions diverge. Exactly how many recensions can be attributed to Marquard is uncertain. Assuming that Marquard was responsible for the abridged version incorporated into the *Auszug* (which is not widely transmitted without it), we can presume at least two. Without a more detailed analysis, anything further is speculation, and so this study proceeds from the A[1] text alone.[3] It is perhaps worth noting that the 'interpolated' material in the longer recensions does not generally affect the Marian components of the work, beyond reducing its relative extent within the treatise.

The Ten Commandments provide the framework for the *Dekalogerklärung*, but the resultant treatise, written as a master–pupil dialogue,[4] is not a strict commentary. Each of the ten sections follows a tripartite structure. First, ethical direction and guidance is provided, largely formulated as sets of prohibitions, and drawing heavily on the Augustinian Heinrich von Friemar's *De decem preceptis*.[5] It is this dependence on Heinrich von Friemar that helps to explain some of the unusual features of the ethical guidance, such as the presence of a discussion on almsgiving in the midst of the fifth commandment, ostensibly concerning homicide.[6] Second, Mary is presented as the model of perfection in the fulfilment of

---

[2] Mayr, 'Zur handschriftlichen Ueberlieferung', pp. 70–80; see further Palmer, 'Marquard von Lindau', cols. 85–90. For a full conspectus of the manuscripts, see id., 'Latein, Volkssprache, Mischsprache', pp. 105–10; with additions in id., 'Marquard von Lindau', cols. 85–6.
[3] I cite from Basel, Universitätsbibliothek, cod. A. X. 138, fols. 127[r]–225[v], and provide parallel references to the facsimile editions by van Maren (as ed. 1516 [recension C[1]] and ed. 1483 [recension C[3]]).
[4] On the nature of the dialogue, see Störmer-Caysa, *Gewissen und Buch*, pp. 315–24.
[5] Identified by Palmer, 'Marquard von Lindau', col. 90.
[6] Compare the *Dekalogerklärung*, fols. 179[v]–180[v] (cf. ed. 1516, pp. 60[b]–61[a]; ed. 1483, 80. 8–81. 4), with Heinrich von Friemar, *De decem preceptis*, V. 253–436 (pp. 102–11).

the given commandment, with only occasional references back to the
material presented in the first section—Mary is not simply the flip side of
the coin, but a positive model for identification and emulation. As Mary is
(for Marquard) unsurpassed in perfection, the third section presents a
second positive model: the *amici Dei*, 'friends of God', who have most
perfectly emulated Mary. We need not discuss the nature of these first and
third sections further here. I have considered the *amici Dei* elsewhere,[7] and
two exemplary studies have recently presented detailed discussions of the
structure of the *Dekalogerklärung*.[8]

It is difficult to provide a general characterization of the *Dekalogerklärung*. To describe it as 'catechetical' finds its adherents: van Maren presents
the work as 'ein katechetischer Traktat' ('a catechetical treatise') in the very
title of his facsimile edition of 1980; and Christoph Burger speaks of
Marquard himself as 'der Katechet'.[9] But 'catechesis' is a problematic
term, not least because it reduces our expectations of the work's content.
Burger compares Marquard negatively to the Viennese theologian Ulrich
von Pottenstein (d. 1417/18), whose truly massive treatise on the Ten
Commandments transmits the most modern conclusions in scholastic
and monastic theology to his German-speaking audience.[10] This comparison, however, misses the object of Marquard's work, which is less
concerned with the transmission of information than with guidance on
pragmatic issues of the Christian life. Störmer-Caysa is definitely right to
maintain that it is not an encyclopedic reference work on moral conduct,
but rather a treatise that proceeds in an associative manner to draw the
reader through to its conclusion, and instruct him underway.[11] Yet Störmer-Caysa's verdict, conditioned by her primary interest in Marquard in
terms of his attitude to moral conscience, is somewhat reductive. It neglects
the equally substantial devotional and contemplative aspect of the work:
Mary (and the *amici Dei*) are not merely models of normative moral
conduct, but exemplars of religious devotion and the contemplative life.
Amongst all Marquard's German treatises, it is surprisingly the *Dekalogerklärung* which has perhaps the closest affinity to the sermon collection, with
its strongly pseudo-Dionysian undercurrents. The treatise has an indefinite
implied audience: or perhaps better, a plurality of implied audiences, who

[7] See Mossman, 'Zu Marquard von Lindau', pp. 257–62.
[8] Störmer-Caysa, *Gewissen und Buch*, pp. 298–315; van Dijk, 'De wil op God afstemmen', pp. 93–7.
[9] Burger, 'Theologie und Laienfrömmigkeit', p. 408.
[10] Ibid., esp. pp. 408–9.
[11] Störmer-Caysa, *Gewissen und Buch*, pp. 324–5.

could—and undoubtedly did—read the work in different ways. Störmer-Caysa's approach to reading the *Dekalogerklärung* is, on this basis, just as valid as the approach that this study will take. To see that the work was commonly read primarily for its Marian content, one need only look at the series of fifteenth-century works on Mary known to be dependent— in some cases, probably exclusively—on the *Dekalogerklärung* for their content.[12]

Marquard presents Mary as a quiet contemplative. I do not propose to renarrate the *Dekalogerklärung* in order to demonstrate this; the material is simply too extensive, and we will focus in close detail on the 'mystical' aspect subsequently. The following overview of the presentation of Mary, in which I shall point only to the key aspects, is intended simply as a preliminary guide.

Marquard does not provide a chronological life of Mary. He offers instead a series of snapshots, which are taken primarily from the period of her life after Christ's ascension, augmented by a small number of other images: her childhood as a temple virgin, the annunciation, and the crucifixion of Christ. His approach is accumulative rather than systematic. In the first commandment, setting the tone for the Marian presentation in the rest of the treatise, Marquard deals solely with the nature of Mary's prayer, exemplifying her relationship with God. In the second, his focus is on the manner of her speech; and his approach to this subject is illuminating. He begins by noting that Mary is only known from Scripture to have spoken seven times. A strict, systematic commentary—of which there are many examples—would then proceed with an exegesis of each of those seven speeches in order. Marquard's subsequent interest, by contrast, is in the general tenor of Mary's speech. All that the scriptural attestation of seven speeches means is that Mary did not talk very much:

Du solt wússen, daz wir nút lesen jn der geschrift daz vnser frow je geretti denne ze siben malen. Doch meinet es anders nút, denne daz ir rede lútzel was, wie doch daz si dick[er] gerett hab denne ze siben malen.[13]

(You should know that we do not read in Scripture that our Lady ever spoke, except on seven occasions. Yet this means nothing more than that her speech was not extensive, however much she may have spoken more than on just seven occasions.)

---

[12] See Palmer, 'Marquard von Lindau', col. 96; and Hilg (ed.), *Das >Marienleben<*, pp. 410 and 432.
[13] *Dekalogerklärung*, fol. 141ᵛ (cf. ed. 1516, p. 20ᵃ; ed. 1483, 21. 23–5).

A recurring theme is Mary's poverty, and her poverty of spirit (principally in the seventh and ninth commandments). But it is the third commandment that considers Mary at greatest length. It details the concrete pattern of Mary's daily life, organizing her life according to the canonical hours. At midnight she awoke and prayed until dawn; Marquard elaborates on the content of her prayer, the manner of her mental preparation before prayer, and her attitude in prayer. From dawn until prime she engaged in contemplation, the six principal objects of which are then enumerated, with particular attention paid to the three ways in which she contemplated the sixth, namely Christ's suffering. At prime she walked to the temple, contemplating further until midday, tucked away in a corner and (at the appropriate time) listening attentively to the temple service. On feast days she would then go to hear the reading of Scripture—or if it was not being read, she would read silently or speak of God with those around her; and on all other days she would return home and sew,[14] frequently visited by an angel bringing food. From vespers to compline she would sing the psalms and pray, and from compline to nightfall she would contemplate Christ's life and teaching before ordering her sleep in God, sleeping then without dreaming and surrounded by guardian angels.

I have skipped over the important statements that Marquard makes on the nature of her contemplation, which form the content of much of this presentation, in order to discuss the significance of this depiction of Mary as contemplative more generally. The presentation of Mary either sewing, reading from a psalter, or praying at the moment of the annunciation has ancient roots, and has been studied closely by Schreiner. He argues, inter alia, that the change in the eleventh and twelfth centuries from the portrayal of Mary sewing to her reading in a book, and then simply praying, reflects the changing conception of the ideal form of female aristocratic life.[15] The apocryphal text known as the Protoevangelium of James, one of a series of similar infancy narratives, is the origin of the idea that Mary spent her childhood as a temple virgin in Jerusalem, where she displayed particular facility at sewing with fine threads;[16] a theme elaborated by the ninth-century Greek life of Mary by the Constantinopolitan monk Epiphanius

---

[14] A conspectus of assertions that Mary provided for herself by sewing from the key patristic and medieval texts is provided by Schreiner, 'Marienverehrung', p. 316; see further Schreiner, *Maria*, pp. 300–2.

[15] Schreiner, 'Marienverehrung', pp. 318–48; note pp. 329–30 on Marquard; see also Schreiner, 'Konnte Maria lesen?'

[16] Schmolinsky, 'Imaginationen vorbildlicher Weiblichkeit', pp. 81–3; Schreiner, *Maria*, pp. 24–5.

(a work translated into Latin by Paschalis Romanus in the twelfth century),[17] and which remained current throughout the Middle Ages—including, not least, for Marquard.[18] Equally, the presentation of Mary as the paragon of all virtues is entirely conventional.[19] It is the *Vita beatae virginis Mariae et salvatoris rhythmica* (hereinafter the *Vita rhythmica*) which provides the first complete life of Mary, and the first account of Mary's life after Christ's ascension.[20]

The *Vita rhythmica* is a long text in rhyming prose, which dates to the central years of the thirteenth century, probably before 1250. Fifty-four manuscripts of the full text, two of a secondary prose version, and twenty-nine containing excerpts attest to its popularity.[21] Mlinarič's analysis of the manuscript transmission demonstrates that over one-third derive from southern Germany, with the best manuscripts (and the oldest, namely Munich, Bayerische Staatsbibliothek, Clm 12518, from the Cistercian abbey of Raitenhaslach) from Bavaria. It is therefore probably of Bavarian, and of Cistercian or Benedictine origin.[22] The work enjoyed its widest circulation in the fourteenth century.[23] It presents Mary as contemplative at a number of points: during her childhood in the temple (vv. 591–6 and 819–32); immediately following her betrothal to Joseph (vv. 1432–7); after Pentecost (vv. 6480–99); and thereafter whilst living with John (vv. 6600–6).[24] The description of Mary's life at vv. 6480–99 mirrors exactly that of her childhood in the temple: prayer, contemplation, reading Scripture, living a pure and chaste life full of virtue, grace, and beneficial speech: with the addition of propagating the faith of her son by her words. Amongst all the details that then follow of her life after Christ's ascension, by far the most important is the so-called *Regula Mariae* (vv. 6612–741).

---

[17] Schreiner, *Maria*, p. 118. There are many misleading or confused references concerning Epiphanius in the scholarly literature; see definitively Longo, 'Epiphanios'.

[18] See *Dekalogerklärung*, fol. 167^{r-v} (cf. ed. 1516, p. 49^a; ed. 1483, 54. 27–40). For some comments on the persistence of this idea in the later Middle Ages, see Ellington, *From Sacred Body*, pp. 143–6.

[19] For some comparable examples from medieval German works, see Górecka, *Das Bild Mariens*, pp. 450–4.

[20] Schmolinsky, 'Imaginationen vorbildlicher Weiblichkeit', pp. 84–5. A good summary of the *Vita rhythmica* is provided by Hoffmann, '»Vita beate virginis Marie«'.

[21] See Gärtner, 'Vita beatae virginis Mariae', cols. 437–8; on the dating see further Mlinarič, *Srednjeveški latinski epos "Vita Mariae metrica"*, pp. 191–5.

[22] See Mlinarič, *Srednjeveški latinski epos "Vita Mariae metrica"*, pp. 196–200; in summary in Mlinarič, 'Das Epos "Vita Mariae metrica"', p. 34.

[23] Mlinarič, 'Das Epos "Vita Mariae metrica"', p. 35.

[24] At the annunciation, Mary is taking a break from sewing and is reading in the Psalms (vv. 1526–33).

Marked as a separate section, it begins by stating that Mary devised a rule for her life, becoming by implication thereby the foundress of monasticism: 'Maria sibi regulam statuit vivendi | Et sub quodam ordine deo serviendi' ('Mary established for herself a rule of living and of serving God under a certain order'; vv. 6612–13). This is ordered according to the canonical hours, and presents Mary dividing up her day into periods of prayer and contemplation, manual activity (sewing), and attendance at the temple. It is evidently the inspiration for Marquard's depiction of Mary's daily life, and enjoyed an independent popularity, transmitted in at least twenty-three manuscripts as an excerpt.[25]

The *Vita rhythmica* enjoyed a number of translations into German, most of which had only a very limited transmission and must be regarded as epigonal.[26] One translation, the early fourteenth-century *Marienleben* by the Carthusian Philipp von Seitz, conversely enjoyed a transmission even greater than that of the *Vita rhythmica* itself, with 102 manuscripts of the verse text and 22 of a secondary prose version extant; it became the most widely transmitted medieval German text in rhyming couplets.[27] Gärtner has compared the *Regula Mariae* in the *Vita rhythmica* with the version in Philipp's *Marienleben*, examining the substantial changes that Philipp made. Three are of especial note here. First, the more rigorous application of the structure of the canonical hours to Mary's day, introducing a distinction between the actual prayers said for the hours, and the meditations that followed them.[28] Second, the subject of the meditation after matins: Philipp reduces the *Vita rhythmica* presentation of Mary considering the entirety of Christ's life to a massive recollection of the Passion alone (*Marienleben*, vv. 8508–657), with attention drawn to the continual renewal of Mary's suffering that it represents. Third, the expanded description of the subject of Mary's contemplation between prime and terce.[29] The *Vita rhythmica* mentioned her contemplation of the joys of heaven in just two lines: 'Ab hinc [i.e. prime] usque tertiam contemplationi | Vacabat et celestium delectationi' ('From then [i.e. prime] until terce she devoted herself to contemplation and to delight in the heavenly beings'; vv. 6638–9). Philipp, by contrast, provides a long description of the joys of the saints in heaven, about which Mary thought (*Marienleben*,

[25] See the conspectus in Gärtner, 'Vita beatae virginis Mariae', col. 437.
[26] See ibid., cols. 441–2; Mlinarič, *Srednjeveški latinski epos "Vita Mariae metrica"*, pp. 351–62.
[27] Gärtner, 'Bruder Philipp', cols. 588–93.
[28] Gärtner, 'Regulierter Tageslauf', esp. pp. 59–60.
[29] See ibid. 50–5.

vv. 8674–727), preceded by a description of her elevation of her mind
to contemplate the joys of heaven and Christ in the Trinity (*Marienleben*,
vv. 8664–73):

> der selben andâht[30] was alsô
> daz sî iren geist ûf zô
> mit gedanc ze himelrîch
> dâ die sêle vreuwent sich[.]
> wie grôz der heiligen vreude ist
> dâ sî den süezen Jêsum Christ
> schouwent an der driveltekeit
> dâ drî persône und ein gotheit
> menschlîch natûre êwiclîch
> habent genomen gar an sich.

(It was a feature of these meditations that she drew up her spirit by her thoughts to
heaven, where the souls rejoice. How great is the joy of the saints where they see the
sweet Jesus Christ in the Trinity, where three persons and one Godhead have taken
human nature eternally and completely upon themselves!)

Philipp's adaptation of the so-called *Regula Mariae* provides a particularly widespread and therefore important example of the redirection of
the depiction; the modification of the ideal thereby presented to those
living a religious life. Given that Mary was a widow and not living in
a formal convent, this is not exclusive to nuns, an assertion supported
by the attention given to Mary's attitude when walking to the temple,
or when conversing with others outside. Whether Philipp's adaptation
represents peculiarly Carthusian preoccupations has not yet been addressed.

For our purposes, it provides a useful comparative example to Marquard's adaptation. Unlike Philipp, Marquard pays little attention to
making the structure of the day more rigorous—there is certainly
no indication in the *Dekalogerklärung* that Mary read specific lessons, or
recited particular prayers, according to the canonical hours. Like Philipp,
Marquard's Mary no longer considers the entirety of Christ's life between
matins and prime, but focuses on his Passion—albeit, as mentioned earlier,
as one of six objects of her contemplation during this time of day. Rather
than provide a graphic narrative of the Passion as Philipp does, Marquard's
focus is instead on the manner of that contemplation, with particular
reference to Mary's compassion and imitative suffering. Indeed, he refers

---

[30] *andâht* is Philipp's term for the meditations that follow the prayers for the
canonical hours.

the reader to other works in order to avoid having to provide a Passion narrative here: 'Zů dem sechsten betrachtet si daz liden jrs kindes, wie gar grosß vnd manigfaltig daz was, als du vindest jn den bůchern geschriben daz leben Ihesu Christi'[31] ('Sixth, she considered how very great and manifold was the suffering of her child, as you find the life of Jesus Christ described in books'). Both Philipp and Marquard attest here to the explosion in devotion to the Passion characteristic of the later thirteenth century onwards, a climate which was not yet constitutive for the author of the *Vita rhythmica*. Most importantly, Marquard—again like Philipp, but to a far greater extent—elaborates on Mary's contemplation of heaven and the mechanics of her mental ascent. It is this which is the most important feature of Marquard's version of the *Regula Mariae*, and which shifts the contemplation of heaven from being one aspect of Mary's day to the predominant, enduring feature of her existence; and which is not confined (as it is for Philipp) to the elevation of her mind to enumerate the joys of the saints in heaven, but becomes a genuinely mystical experience. It is precisely this presentation that we will examine in more detail subsequently.

---

[31] *Dekalogerklärung*, fol. 150ᵛ (cf. ed. 1516, p. 30ᵃ; ed. 1483, 30. 35–8). Another reference to a similar work is given in the seventh commandment, on the subject of Mary's poverty. Marquard writes: 'Wiltu aber me von jr armůt hồren, so lis jn dem vordren gebott, vnd ouch jn dem bůchlin des lidens Ihesu Christi; do vindest du etwaz geschriben von jr armůt' ('If, however, you wish to hear more of her poverty, then read the previous commandment, and also in the little book of the suffering of Jesus Christ. There you will find something written of her poverty') (fol. 202ᵛ; omitted in both printed versions). It is not clear to which work (if any) this refers. Certain variant manuscripts of Heinrich von St Gallen's *Extendit manum* Passion treatise also refer to a 'buch von dem leiden Cristi' by one 'Jacobus' (the principal manuscript, by contrast, speaks of a 'buch[ ] von dem leben Cristi' by one 'Josephus'): see Heinrich von St Gallen, *Extendit manum*, 4. 11–12; with the variants p. 78. Ruh's conjecture that this referred to a lost life of Christ by Jacques de Vitry (see the footnote to 4. 11–12; and Ruh, 'Studien über Heinrich von St Gallen', pp. 252–5) has been cast into doubt by Baier, who has established further that Heinrich's work is dependent on the Augustinian Michael de Massa's *Extendit manum* and *Angeli pacis* Passion treatises, and has taken these references over from these Latin works (see Baier, 'Untersuchungen zu den Passionsbetrachtungen', pp. 341–3). As Michael refers to a *vita Christi* by this elusive Josephus (who is not Flavius Josephus), the manuscripts referring to a 'buch von dem leiden Cristi' by 'Jacobus' are evidently secondary. Whether they have been consciously altered to refer to a different work, specifically on Christ's sufferings, and whether this is the same work to which Marquard refers here, is impossible to say. On the identity of 'Josephus' *vita Christi'* in the works of Michael de Massa, see now Kemper, *Die Kreuzigung Christi*, pp. 113–14.

It is evident and unsurprising that Marquard had a number of apocryphal texts on Mary at his disposal in producing the *Dekalogerklärung*. The *Vita rhythmica* narrative, however, appears to have had a particular prominence. A whole series of small details in the *Dekalogerklärung* accord precisely with the *Vita rhythmica*, and are not found in exactly the same form elsewhere. This applies in particular to Mary's childhood in the temple (especially vv. 557–630), including such details as her being called 'queen' because she sewed the purple cloth (vv. 881–900).[32] Similarly, Marquard follows the *Vita rhythmica* in giving the precise composition of Mary's household after Joseph's death as comprising three virgins and two widows (vv. 6688–91).[33] Of particular interest is a letter that Marquard reproduces in the fourth commandment, ostensibly written from Ignatius to John the Evangelist. This is one of a group of four letters that presents a correspondence between Ignatius, John, and Mary, and which have been regarded as apocryphal since the sixteenth century. Although they were the first Ignatian letters to be printed (in 1495), their Latin manuscript tradition begins in the mid-thirteenth century, and there are no manuscripts in Greek or any other oriental language. Some evidence points to their composition in 1245. Thomson argued that Robert Grosseteste had translated them from a now-lost Greek manuscript, but there has been no comprehensive study of the transmission.[34] Their circulation was substantial—Diekamp's and Thomson's lists (counting the manuscripts in both lists only once) produce a combined total of sixty manuscripts, and even a preliminary survey adds a further twenty.[35] They are also incorporated fully

[32] Cf. *Dekalogerklärung*, fol. 167ᵛ (cf. ed. 1516, p. 49ᵃ; ed. 1483, 54. 32–40).
[33] Cf. ibid., fol. 156ʳ⁻ᵛ (cf. ed. 1516, p. 34ᵃ⁻ᵇ; ed. 1483, 35. 6–13). On the purported origins of this primitive Christian community, see *Vita rhythmica*, vv. 6565–71.
[34] A number of older editions exist. By far the best is that of Funk and Diekamp, *Patres Apostolici*, vol. 2, pp. 319–22. See further their superb commentary, pp. lxi–lxiv; Zahn, *Ignatius von Antiochien*, pp. 80–2; and Thomson, *The Writings of Robert Grosseteste*, pp. 58–62. All further literature is derivative.
[35] See Funk and Diekamp, *Patres Apostolici*, vol. 2, pp. lxiii–lxiv; and Thomson, *The Writings of Robert Grosseteste*, pp. 61–2. Further manuscripts: Admont, Stiftsbibliothek, Cod. 240, 8ʳff. (13th cent.) and Cod. 614, 33ᵛ–34ʳ (14th cent.); Aschaffenburg, Hofbibliothek, Ms. 17, 636ᵛ–637ᵛ (mid-13th cent.); Berlin, Staatsbibliothek zu Berlin— Preußischer Kulturbesitz, Ms. Ham. 631, 44ʳ–45ʳ (14th cent.), and Ms. theol. lat. qu. 321, 34ʳ–35ʳ (1523); Cologne, Historisches Archiv, GB 8° 76, 93ᵛ–94ᵛ (*c*.1412); Cracow, Biblioteka Jagiellońska, cod. 1211, 557ʳ⁻ᵛ (1462); Hildesheim, Dombibliothek, Ps 3, 186ʳ⁻ᵛ (third quarter of 15th cent.); Klosterneuburg, Stiftsbibliothek, Cod. 573, 198ʳ⁻ᵛ (14th cent.); Koblenz, Landeshauptarchiv, Best. 701 Nr. 124, 233ᵛᵃ–234ʳᵇ (first half of 14th cent.), and Best. 701 Nr. 151, 172ᵛ–174ʳ (*c*.1475); Kremsmünster, Stiftsbibliothek, CC 280, 387ᵛᵃ–388ʳᵃ (first quarter of 14th cent.), and CC 334, 206ᵛᵃ⁻ᵛᵇ (early 14th cent.); Mainz, Stadtbibliothek, Hs. I 232, 41ʳ⁻ᵛ (early 15th cent.); Melk, Stiftsbibliothek,

254 *The Virgin Mary*

into the prose glosses that accompany some of the earliest manuscripts of the *Vita rhythmica*. It is not clear whether the author of the *Vita rhythmica* is also responsible for the glosses; leaving aside those secondary glosses obviously of fourteenth- and fifteenth-century origin in later manuscripts, Mlinarič's examination indicates that no one extant manuscript (of those known to him) preserves the 'original' set of glosses in its entirety.[36] The author of the *Vita rhythmica* certainly had access to the texts, however, as versified versions of two of the four letters are incorporated into the main text itself (vv. 7022–59 and 7060–81). It is also important to note that these four letters form part of the treatise *De gratiis et virtutibus beatae et gloriosae semper virginis Mariae* (hereinafter *De gratiis et virtutibus Mariae*) by the Benedictine Engelbert von Admont (d. 1331).[37] It is, of course, quite possible that Marquard knew these pseudo-Ignatian letters independently or through Engelbert's treatise; but given the cumulative body of evidence, it is most likely that Marquard had a glossed manuscript of the *Vita rhythmica* at his disposal. Marquard translates the letter from Ignatius to John in full, but changes its internal order so that it begins with a statement on Mary's attitude to suffering, matching the topic to which Marquard attaches it.[38]

It is not without purpose to establish that Marquard drew on the *Vita rhythmica* as a model for his presentation of Mary's life after Christ's ascension. Other works, equally widely circulated, present a very different account. The *Legenda aurea*, for example, only briefly mentions Mary's life during this period: Mary is said to have lived in a house near Mount Zion, and to have revisited all the sites associated with Christ's life 'with earnest devotion':

Cod. 1092 (olim 241), 136^{r-v} (15th cent.); Munich, Bayerische Staatsbibliothek, Clm 14081, 199rb (late 15th cent.), and Clm 14089, 286^r (1502); Uppsala, Universitetsbibliotek, C 228, 294^v–295^r (*c*.1300), and C 523, 3^{r-v} (first half of 14th cent.); Würzburg, Universitätsbibliothek, M. p. th. q. 75, 17^r–18^r (1390).

[36] See Mlinarič, *Srednjeveški latinski epos "Vita Mariae metrica"*, pp. 128–38, with a full edition of the glosses and identification of their sources pp. 139–81. A less comprehensive, but more accessible edition is provided by Päpke, *Das Marienleben*, pp. 121–51. The pseudo-Ignatian letters are (following Mlinarič's numeration) glosses 123–26 (pp. 172–5; cf. Päpke, 144. 16–146. 29). They offer evidence that no one manuscript contains the full set of glosses, as the first three letters (but not the fourth) are found in (and edited from) Karlsruhe, Badische Landesbibliothek, HB 252, with the fourth found on its own in Munich, Bayerische Staatsbibliothek, Clm 12518. The *Vita rhythmica* versifies the first and the third letters (see Mlinarič, *Srednjeveški latinski epos "Vita Mariae metrica"*, p. 134); Marquard translates the second.

[37] Engelbert von Admont, *De gratiis et virtutibus Mariae*, pars 2, c. 4–7 (pp. 571–3) [Copy consulted: Oxford, Bodleian Library, S. 7. 1 Th.].

[38] *Dekalogerklärung*, fols. 169^v and 172^r [fols. 170^r–171^v are misbound, and belong after fol. 147^v] (cf. ed. 1516, p. 51^{a-b}; ed. 1483, 56. 38–57. 18).

Apostolis namque ob predicationis gratiam diuersas mundi subeuntibus regiones, uirgo beata in domo iuxta montem Syon posita dicitur remansisse omniaque loca filii sui, scilicet locum baptismi, ieiunii, passionis, sepulture, resurrectionis et ascensionis quoad uixit deuotione sedula uisitabat.[39]

(For with the apostles going out into the various parts of the earth by virtue of the gift of preaching, the blessed Virgin is said to have remained stationed in her house next to Mount Zion, and visited all the places of her son—namely the places of his baptism, fasting, Passion, burial, resurrection, and ascension—with zealous devotion as long as she lived.)

It is probably this statement in the *Legenda aurea* that informs the much longer account of Mary's life after Christ's ascension in the *Speculum humanae salvationis*. This work, probably written in Italy in 1324, is preserved in over three hundred manuscripts. It found an adoptive home in the German-speaking world, and at least fifty-five manuscripts in German translation exist, alongside a series of translations into other European vernaculars.[40] It may legitimately be regarded as a Marian text, and section 35 presents Mary after Christ's ascension (to be precise, after Pentecost). Mary lives in Jerusalem, but circulates around Palestine, kissing the places where Christ had been and venerating them with genuflections and prayers, and crying in memory of his presence:

> Post ascensionem Domini beata Virgo in Jerusalem habitavit,
> Omnia loca Filii sui, quae attingere potuit, devote visitavit
> Et prae dulcedine amoris singula osculabatur,
> Cum genuflexionibus et orationibus venerabatur.
> Multa lacrimarum effusione ipsa loca irrigabat,
> Quando mellifluam praesentiam Filii sui recogitabat.[41]

(After the ascension of the Lord the blessed Virgin dwelt in Jerusalem, and devoutly visited all the places of her son that she was able to reach. She kissed each one of them because of the sweetness of her love, and venerated them with genuflections and prayers. She watered these places with the outpouring of many tears when she remembered the mellifluous presence of her son.)

---

[39] Jacobus de Voragine, *Legenda aurea*, sermo 115 (*De assvmptione beate virginis Marie*), §2 (vol. 2, p. 779); see further the even briefer description of Mary when an angel arrives to inform her of her imminent assumption: sermo 115, §6 (vol. 2, pp. 779–80).

[40] See Stork and Wachinger, 'Speculum humanae salvationis', cols. 52–8 on the Latin text.

[41] *Speculum humanae salvationis*, c. 35, 3–8 (vol. 1, p. 72).

Mary's pilgrimage tour of the sites of Christ's life, culminating in what is essentially a set of Stations of the Cross, is then described.[42] The author restates that Mary's tears were shed at Christ's absence:

> Omnia haec loca et plura alia cum lacrimis visitavit
> Et absentiam Filii sui lamentabiliter deploravit;
> Lugere et dolere quam gaudere ipsa maluit,
> Quamdiu melliflua praesentia Filii sui caruit.[43]

(She visited all these places and many others besides, and with tears dolefully bewailed the absence of her son. She preferred rather to mourn and grieve than to rejoice as long as she was without the mellifluous presence of her son.)

Mary's search, we are reminded, was for Christ's corporeal presence, which she found again when she herself was assumed into heaven.[44] As Christ's life provides a good example, the reader is exhorted to the spiritual imitation of Mary's 'pilgrimage' and therein not just to meditate on Christ's life, but to bewail—*deplorare*—his Passion:

> Praedicta ergo loca debemus exemplo ejus perambulare
> Et passionem Christi recolendo ferventer deplorare;
> Quod si nequimus ea perambulare corporaliter,
> Perambulemus saltem ea devoto corde spiritualiter.[45]

(Therefore we should travel through the aforesaid places with her example, and ardently bewail Christ's Passion in calling it to mind again. And if we are unable to travel through them in body, then let us at least travel through them with devout hearts in spirit.)

There is no mention, here or in the subsequent sections of the work on Mary, of any deeper contemplation in this period of her life.[46] The ideal that is presented for emulation by the *Speculum humanae salvationis* is very different to that presented by the *Vita rhythmica*, Philipp's *Marienleben*, and (especially) Marquard. The emphasis is on Christ's physical presence, not on the heavenly or on any aspect of the interior life. The reader is exhorted to mental peregrination, instead of a fixed and stable perspective, and in considering the Passion, is encouraged here to little more than tears at Christ's resultant absence, rather than anything more subtle. Of course,

---

[42] *Speculum humanae salvationis*, c. 35, 9–34 (vol. 1, p. 72).
[43] Ibid., c. 35, 35–8 (vol. 1, p. 72).
[44] Ibid., c. 35, 65–8 (vol. 1, p. 73).
[45] Ibid., c. 35, 73–6 (vol. 1, p. 73).
[46] Contemplation is, nonetheless, a feature of her childhood in the temple: see c. 5, 54–64 and 91–6 (vol. 1, pp. 13–14).

this neglects the wider context of the Passion texts elsewhere in the treatise, but the picture there is not substantively different. The different accounts of Mary's life after Christ's ascension, circulating in equally widespread, equally authoritative texts, present different principal models for imitation, and different ideals of the religious life, writ large. In following the *Vita rhythmica*, we might even say that Marquard was making a conscious decision to reject one model, and thereby one ideal, in favour of another; to present Mary the quiet contemplative, and not Mary the lachrymose pilgrim.

This is both substantiated and taken further by Marquard's presentation of Mary under the cross, in the *Dekalogerklärung* and in sermon 21. He presents a figure who suffered internally, but who neither wept nor otherwise displayed excessive emotion. He is fully aware of his opposition to the dominant contemporary tradition, and explains that earlier writers presented a different image of the suffering Mary in order to stimulate compassion in the beholder, illustrating what Mary might have said and done—but, in reality, had not.[47] We do not have the room here to set out Marquard's theological justification for stating that Mary behaved in this sober and outwardly impassive manner, nor to present the intellectual tradition in which he stood in opposing the emotive depiction of Mary under the cross (principally involving Ambrose of Milan and Meister Eckhart). In recasting this image, it is probable that Marquard was motivated less by an intellectual interest in the theory that justified the presentation of Mary as a deeply emotive figure, than by the aim of realigning the nature of contemporary religious devotion, particularly among women, by radically changing the ideal presented for imitation. The image of Mary lamenting under the cross was not a minor invention, but was perhaps the centrepiece of the medieval representation of Mary: an image that was, quite literally, iconic. No one, not even Eckhart, took as radical a position as did Marquard—in the Middle Ages, at least, for his intellectual companions on this issue are to be found amongst the theologians of the Counter-Reformation, not least François de Sales.[48]

[47] See *Dekalogerklärung*, fols. 167ᵛ–168ʳ (cf. ed. 1516, p. 49ᵇ–50ᵇ; ed. 1483, 55. 1–26), and *Predigt* 21, ll. 134–68 (pp. 141–2); for a full analysis see Mossman, 'Kritik der Tradition' [in press].
[48] See Ellington, 'Impassioned Mother', pp. 245–6.

We must now turn to Marquard's depiction of Mary as a contemplative who enjoyed mystical union with God, the central aspect of her presentation in the *Dekalogerklärung*. As Marquard presents such extensive material on this theme, we shall look in detail at the first commandment, and augment this with the relevant sections from the remainder of the treatise.

Marquard begins the ethical section of the first commandment by identifying the three fitting modes of prayer according to Augustine: with faith, with confident hope, and with complete love. In fact, Marquard has taken this over from Heinrich von Friemar.[49] Marquard then structures the Marian section according to this tripartite division, an unusually tight association between the ethical and Marian sections within a commandment. The theme is Mary's manner of prayer, and Marquard starts by considering its quality of faith. He emphasizes her humility—in fact, her conscious self-humiliation—desiring to know no more of God than was revealed to her, and considering herself even unworthy to know that she was party to such revelation. She directed all her natural knowledge and all her mental powers into the light of faith, and in such great humility, that the light of faith illuminated her with the uncreated light:

[S]o wissest, das si [i.e. Mary] jren einigen got mit dryerhand wise also an bettet. Ze dem ersten, mit worem glouben, mit leben erfüllet. Nim war, si satzte ir bekantnisse in also tieffe demütikeit, daz si [nit mer] begerte von der verborgenheit gottes ze wissende denne jr geoffenbaret ward. Zum andren mal, so dunkte si sich selben nit wirdig ze wissent, daz ir geoffenbart ward. Zem dritten so waz si gar snell vnd bereit ze allen werken cristenlicher gesetzte, als ob si tugent nie geübet hette. Vnd befalch als jr natúrlich wissen so gar dem liecht des gloubens, vnd satzt aller jr kraft jn daz liecht, so gar jn tieffer demütikeit, das von not daz liecht des glouben jr fúrbasser jn luchte daz vngeworden oder vngeschaffen liecht. Sust merkest du wol, wie gar s[i] mit gantzem glouben jren einigen got an bettet.[50]

(So you should know that Mary prayed to her one God in three ways. First, filled with life and with true faith. Take note that she grounded her cognition in such profound humility that she desired to know no more of the hidden secrets of God than was revealed to her. Second, she thought herself to be unworthy to know what was revealed to her. Third, she was very quick and ready to perform each and every work of Christian law, as if she had never practised virtue before. She entrusted all her natural knowledge so completely to the light of faith, and placed all her [mental]

---

[49] Compare the *Dekalogerklärung*, fol. 131^r (cf. ed. 1516, pp. 8^b–9^a; ed. 1483, 11. 13–26) with Heinrich von Friemar, *De decem preceptis*, I. 9–13 (p. 20).
[50] *Dekalogerklärung*, fol. 135^{r-v} (cf. ed. 1516, p. 12^b; ed. 1483, 14. 38–15. 7). I have emended the meaningless 'mit jm' to 'nit mer' in the manuscript text, following the sense (though not the letter) of the incunable texts, themselves badly corrupt in this passage.

powers into that light in such profound humility, so that the light of faith was impelled further to illuminate her with the unbegotten or uncreated light. Thus you can clearly see how fully she prayed to her one God with complete faith.)

This is a brief description of mystical union in prayer: the humiliation of the self, followed by the illumination of the mind (the light of faith) by God, the uncreated light. Turning next to the aspect of confident hope, Marquard adds little of importance, except to state that Mary submitted her will to God in humble passivity:

Si bettet jn ŏch an mit worer zůuersicht, wanne si het missetrúwen nie an der gůti gottes alles des si jn bat. Si getrúwet jm jn allen dingen, daz er daz aller beste tet. Si befalch siner gůti alles jr gebet, daz er es richteti nach allem sinem liepsten willen, vnd gab iren gantzen willen jn demůtig gelassenheit. Darzů hat si ŏch jren einigen got mit gantzer zůuersicht, wanne si [bat] allein vmb ir teglich brot den himelschen vatter; in den so warf si alle ir sorg. Dem befalch si alles ir tůn in gantzem zůuersicht.[51]

(She prayed to him with true confidence, because she never doubted God's goodness in respect of everything about which she prayed to him. She trusted that he would do the very best in all things. She commended all her prayers to his goodness, that he might order it according to his most beloved will, and gave up her entire will in humble passivity. Further, she had complete confidence in her one God, because she prayed even for her daily bread to the heavenly Father, in whom she thus cast all her concerns. She commended all her actions to him in complete confidence.)

Finally, Marquard turns to the aspect of love. Mary's love for God was total; it was not mediated by any image, and so she loved all things in God with eternal love:

Si bettet jn ŏch an mit gantzer minne; wanne du salt wissen, daz si vsser got creatur nie geminte. Es viel ŏch kein bild in ir hertz nie, daz ir minne gegen got vermitlete. Si hat ein vngeteilt minne mit got, vnd minnte alle ding jn jm mit ewiger minne.[52]

(She prayed to him further with total love: for you should know that she never loved any creature outwith God. Nor did any image ever fall into her heart that mediated her love for God. She had an undivided love with God and loved everything in him with eternal love.)

Then follows a renewed description of her mystical union with God. Mary withdrew all her powers inwards, to her innermost fundament (the *grund*) where the divine image is located. The foundation of her soul is described as Godlike, *deiformis*, with God dwelling therein and emanating the Son and the Holy Spirit essentially:

---

[51] Ibid., fol. 135^v (cf. ed. 1516, p. 12^b; ed. 1483, 15. 7–14).
[52] Ibid. (cf. ed. 1516, pp. 12^b–13^a; ed. 1483, 15. 14–18).

Si kerte ouch sich mit jren kreften jn jren jnwendigen grund, do daz gôtliche bild jnne verborgen lit in dem jnwendigen tempel. Sich, do wonet si, vnd kerte sich mit aller kreften do jn; vnd bettet do an jrem einigen got jn dem geist vnd der worheit. [...] Jr grund der jnwendikeit w[a]z so gût vnd so gotfôrmig, wer jn jr hertz het gesehen, er het got gesehen vnd geschowet jn aller siner klarheit, vnd het do gesehen vsgeflossen sun vnd heiligen geist jn jr wesentlichen wisen.[53]

(Further she directed herself with her mental faculties into her innermost fundament, where the divine image lies hidden in the innermost temple. See, there she dwelt, and directed herself with all her mental faculties therein. There she prayed to her one God in the spirit and the truth. [...] The fundament of her innermost self was so good and Godlike that someone who looked into her heart would have seen God; he would have looked upon him in all of his clarity, and would have seen the Son and the Holy Spirit emanated there in their essential forms.)

Marquard concludes that a person would be willing to suffer from the creation of the world until the Last Judgement, if he could see Mary's heart, as he would thus have seen God:

Sich, wer ein mônsch von angengi der welt jn allem liden vnd pin gesin, vnd wer jm denne darnach geben, daz er allein ein ougenblick môchte jn daz gôtlich, minnrich hertz vnser frowen gesehen han, jm wer wol gedanket aller siner pin vnd leid—het er joch vntz an den jungsten tag geluten alle arbeit vnd alles leid, wenne er het die ewige klarheit geschowet, vnd gesehen got jn aller siner klarheit grûnen vnd blûgen jn allem sinen adel, der mir vnd mengem mônschen verborgen ist.[54]

(See, if a person were to have been in total suffering and pain from the beginning of the created world, and were then to be granted even one moment's sight into the divine, loving heart of our Lady, then he would have been well repaid for all his pain and suffering—even if he had then suffered every travail and every form of suffering until the Last Judgement, because he had looked upon God in all his clarity, budding and blossoming in all his nobility, which is hidden to me and to many people.)

This idea is derived from Eckhart's sermon 2:

Haete ein mensche ein ganzez künicrîche oder allez daz guot von ertrîche und lieze daz lûterlîche durch got und würde der ermesten menschen einer, der ûf ertrîche iener lebet, und gaebe im denne got alsô vil ze lîdenne, als er ie menschen gegap, und lite er allez diz unz an sînen tôt und gaebe im denne got einen blik ze einem mâle ze schouwenne, wie er in dirre kraft ist: sîn vröude würde alsô grôz, daz alles diss lîdens und armüetes waere nochdenne ze kleine. Jâ, engaebe

---

[53] *Dekalogerklärung*, fol. 136ʳ (cf. ed. 1516, p. 13ª; ed. 1483, 15. 18–27).
[54] Ibid. (cf. ed. 1516, p. 13ª⁻ᵇ; ed. 1483, 15. 27–35).

im joch got her nâch niemer mê himelrîches, er haete nochdenne alze grôzen lôn enpfangen umbe allez, daz er ie geleit; wan got ist in dirre kraft als in dem êwigen nû.[55]

(If a person were to possess an entire kingdom, or all the earth's treasure, and were to leave it completely for God's sake and become one of the poorest people who ever lived on earth; and God were then to give him as much to suffer as he ever gave to anyone, and he were to suffer all of this until his death; then if God were just once to give him a single glance to look upon him as he is in this power, his joy would be so great that all of that suffering and poverty would have been simply all too insignificant. Indeed, if God never gave him anything more of heaven after that again, he would nevertheless have received all too great a reward for everything that he had ever suffered, because God is in this power as he is in the eternal now.)

Eckhart repeats the same argument later in the sermon.[56] Clearly, Marquard has not taken over the intellectual import of Eckhart's text, which deals with the operation of God in the intellect. He has, instead, transposed the argumentation to apply to the perception of God operating in Mary. The metaphor of 'grünen vnd blügen' ('budding and blossoming') for the operation of God is also found twice in this same Eckhart sermon.[57] In this case, the adoption of Eckhartian material is of no real significance for Marquard's presentation of Mary; but it does indicate that Marquard is constructing his image of Mary as mystical contemplative against the background of German-language mystical works.

A more interesting adoption of Eckhartian material occurs in the third commandment, in the *regula Mariae*. Marquard describes six features of Mary's prayer between midnight and prime. The first three are not relevant here. In the fourth, she is described as a bride talking to the bridegroom, and is said to see the bottomless essence of God immediately—that is, she experiences the beatific vision without constraint:

Zů dem vierden, so ret si mit got jn jrem gebett als ein kint zů sinem vatter, oder ein geminetes lieb zů dem andren tůt. Jn dem reden jr gõtlichen ougen jr dick wurdent vf geton, daz si daz grundloß wesen schowet on mittel jn aller clarheit vnd lieplicheit, vnd [got] gat mit jr rede als mit siner liepsten erwelten gemachel.[58]

[55] Eckhart, *Predigt* 2 (vol. 1: 32. 8–34. 2).
[56] Ibid. (vol. 1: 36. 3–7).
[57] Ibid. (vol. 1: 32. 3 and 40. 5).
[58] *Dekalogerklärung*, fol 149^{r–v} (cf. ed. 1516, pp. 28^b–29^a; ed. 1483, 29. 29–34).

(Fourth, she spoke with God in her prayer as a child to its father, or a cherished lover to his partner. In this conversation her godly eyes were opened frequently to her, so that she gazed upon the bottomless being without any mediate instance in all clarity and the fullness of love, and God speaks with her as with his most beloved chosen bride.)

The fifth and sixth pick up the theme of the first commandment: Mary praises God, but recognizes that she cannot do so worthily, and so God (in Mary) praises himself:

Zum fúnften fieng si denne an jn jrem gebette, got ze lobent mit lebendigem lobe, daz vß einem gőtlichen, blůgenden grund gien[g], der von gott do zů getriben wart. Ach, daz lob was so sůsß vnd so luter, daz es got lustlicher was, denne do er himel vnd erden geschůff! Zum sechsten sanck si do nider jn jrem gebett, vnd bekant, daz si dem hochen gott nút kond angebetten nach siner ere, vnd begerte denne von jm, daz er sich selber jn jr lobte; vnd liess denne alle kreft sinken jn jren jnnigosten grunde, vß dem der ewig vatter daz liepst lob vnd gebet allein enpfahet.[59]

(Fifth, she then began her prayer by praising God with living praise, which rose from a divine, blossoming fundament that was impelled by God to do so. Ah, that praise was so sweet and so pure that it was more delightful to God than his creation of heaven and earth! Sixth, she sank down in her prayer and acknowledged that she could not pray to the high God with the honour that he was due. Thus she desired of him that he would praise himself in her; and then allowed all her powers to sink into her innermost fundament, out of which alone the eternal Father receives the most loving praise and prayers.)

The idea that Mary's praise was more pleasing to God than his creation of heaven and earth is another adoption of an Eckhartian phrase, this time from sermon 106:

Dar umbe hât got die sêle geschaffen, daz er sînen eingebornen sun in sie gebere. Dô disiu geburt geschach geistlîche in unser vrouwen, daz was gote lustlîcher, dan dô er lîplîche von ir geborn wart. Dô disiu geburt geschiht noch hiute dises tages in einer gotminnender sêle, daz ist gote lustlîcher, dan dô er himel und erde geschuof.[60]

(God has created the soul for this reason: namely, that he might give birth to his only begotten Son into it. It was more delightful to God when this birth took place spiritually in our Lady than when he was born from her corporeally. It is more delightful to God when this birth takes place nowadays in a soul that loves God than when he created heaven and earth.)

---

[59] *Dekalogerklärung*, fol. 149ᵛ (cf. ed. 1516, p. 29ᵃ; ed. 1483, 29. 34–42).

[60] Eckhart, *Predigt* 106 [Recension A], ll. 31–40 (vol. 4/2, p. 686). The identification is given by van Maren, *Marquard von Lindau. Die zehe Gebot (Straßburg 1516 und 1520)*, p. 30; cf. Löser, 'Rezeption als Revision', p. 430.

Here, Eckhart is discussing his famous conception of the birth of God in the soul: it is this which is more pleasing to God than his creation of heaven and earth. Mary's spiritual birth of God, and beyond that her physical birth of Christ, implicitly stand lower on the scale (a statement that Eckhart makes clearly elsewhere). Marquard takes this 'highest' level of being pleasing to God, and attaches it not to the individual soul, but to Mary. That he does so indicates the different position Mary occupies for Eckhart and Marquard, a theme to which we will return.

A passage important for its terminology is encountered when Mary's manner of contemplation in the temple between prime and midday is described. It is clear again that she enjoys the beatific vision. The three powers of the soul—memory, intellect, and will—are all illumined, and the will is inflamed in silent love into an unrestricted ascent above all creation. Here she rests in God (that is, she finds the mystical *quies*), and losing herself in the embrace of bottomless love in the darkness of God, she is unified immediately with God. The passage is distinctive for its description of Mary's mystical experience using more precise philosophical-theological concepts than we have seen thus far:

[Mary] was jn dem tempel vntz gegen mittem tag, vnd mit vfgespannen gemûte jn ewikeit betrachtet si die gebot vnd die rede jrs kindes. Sich, jr hertz ward jn schowen gesetzet ob aller vernunft. Si wart jn jrem gemût verkleret in allen kreften. Jr ge-húgnisse stûnd jn einfaltigem liechte erhaben, vber alle sinnikliche jnvelle gesetz[t], vnd bestetiget jn ewikeit des geistes. Jr vernunft wart vberstúrtzet mit klarheit, jn der si verstûnd vnd bekant alle tugent vnd wise vnd vbung vnd heilikeite der geschrift mit vnderscheid. Der wille was mit jngebrúnstiger hitz enzúndet jn stiller minne, jn einer vberfart vber alle geschaffenheit. [In diser] erhebung was si ob wúrken vnd ob bescheidenheit. Hie jn diser wise enpfienge si daz gôtlich gerrûme jn einer stillen wise, vnd wart jr geist durch flossen vnd durch gossen mit dem vberwesentlichen brunnen ob aller wirdikeit eigener kraft. Hie rastet si jn got ob allen dingen, vnd verlor do sich selber jn einem vmb fang der grundlosen minne jn der wilden vinsternisß der gotheit; vnd also vereiniget sunder mittel eines mit dem geist gotz. Dis was ob allen gaben vnd aller geschafner gnaden vnd liecht.[61]

(Mary stayed in the temple until around midday. She contemplated the command-ments and the words of her child with her mind opened out in eternity. See, her heart was placed in revelation above all reason. She was clarified in all the powers of her mind. Her memory stood elevated in flawless light, placed above all sensory input, and secured in the eternity of the spirit. Her intellect was overwhelmed with clarity in which she recognized and understood every virtue, manner, discipline, and holiness of Scripture with discretion. Her will was inflamed with burning heat in

---

[61] *Dekalogerklärung*, fols. 151^v–152^r (cf. ed. 1516, pp. 30^b–31^a; ed. 1483, 31. 24–38). I have emended 'jrdescher' to 'In diser', following the incunable editions.

silent love, transcendent above all the created. In this elevation she was beyond action and beyond understanding. Here in this state she received the divine susurration in a silent way, and her spirit was deluged and inundated by the superessential spring beyond all splendour of an individual's own power. Here she rested in God above everything else, and lost herself there in an embrace of the bottomless love in the wild darkness of the Godhead. Thus she was unified as one with the spirit of God without any mediate instance. This was beyond all gifts and any created grace or light.)

Marquard follows this with a statement on the three necessary components of proper contemplation ('rechte schowunge'), a passage long known to have been taken from Ruusbroec's *Geestelijke brulocht*: total inner freedom from the external; loving adherence to God with burning desire; and the total loss of the created self in the abyss of darkness.[62] After a brief excursus on this darkness, which Marquard compares to the cloud in which Moses encountered God, he returns to Mary, stating that her beatific vision ('schowen') was superior to that of any other creature save the soul of Christ. He then provides a description of the nature of Mary's vision, focusing on the perception of light in the darkness. This description, on closer examination, reveals itself also to be dependent on Ruusbroec's *Brulocht* (corresponding passages in bold):

Nu wil ich dir öch sagen was si schowet jn der andacht. Du solt wissen, wenne die wirdige mûter gottes jn der schowung stůnd, der dunkli vnd der vinsternisse, daz si do nút anders schöwet denne **ein einualtig liecht, jn dem si sach klarheit, die got selber ist.**[63] **Si sach got jn allen dingen sunder vnderscheid, jn einem einualtigen sehen:**[64] **daz liecht mit dem liecht vnd jn dem liecht.**[65] **Vnd dis offenbarung dis ewigen liechtes ernúwert sich on vnderlasß**[66] jn jr, jn dem jnwendigosten jrs grundes, **jn der hôchsten edelkeit des geistes.**[67] Dis was all zit jn vnmessigem lust, wanne si hat hie jn jrem enpfinden der kúnftigen selikeit, vnd minnet hie jnne got

---

[62] *Dekalogerklärung*, fol. 152ᵛ (cf. ed. 1516, pp. 31ᵃ⁻ᵇ; ed. 1483, 31. 42–32. 13); see Ruusbroec, *Geestelijke brulocht*, III: 52–64 (ed. Eichler, pp. 219–20); c53–c67 (ed. Alaerts, pp. 579–81); for the identification see Eichler, *Jan van Ruusbroecs 'Brulocht'*, pp. 44–5.

[63] Cf. Ruusbroec, *Geestelijke brulocht*, III: 67–8 (ed. Eichler, p. 220); c71–c73 (ed. Alaerts, p. 581): ... dis gôtteliche lieht wurt gegeben in dem einfaltigen sehende des geistes, do der geist die clarheit, die got selber ist, enpfahet ...

[64] Cf. ibid. 173–4 (ed. Eichler, p. 224); c183–c184 (ed. Alaerts, p. 593): ... vnd beschowent got vnd alle ding sunder vnderscheit in einem einfaltigen sehende ...

[65] Cf. ibid. 91 (ed. Eichler, p. 221); c95–c96 (ed. Alaerts, pp. 583–5): ... ein ewig schowen vnd staren daz lieht mit dem liehte vnd in dem liehte.

[66] Cf. ibid. 87–8 (ed. Eichler, p. 221); c90–c91 (ed. Alaerts, p. 583): ... her vmb wurt die offenbarunge des ewigen liehtes sunder vnderlaz ernuwet ...

[67] Cf. ibid. 90 (ed. Eichler, p. 221); c94 (ed. Alaerts, p. 583): ... in der hôhesten edelkeit des geistes.

mit ewigen gaben; vnd alle creaturen mûsten hie jn dirre wise beliben, vnd alle creatúrlich werk ûben. Darumb so ward si hie jnne geformiert mit der gôtlichen klarheit ob allen bilden vnd vernúnftikeit, waz daz waz als hie verswunden vnd vergangen. Si **wart hie eins mit dem liecht vnd eruolget hie jr ewige bilde.**[68, 69]

(Now I shall also tell you what she saw in her meditation. You should know that when the worthy mother of God stood in this state of vision, in the blackness and the darkness, she saw nothing else there save a flawless light, in which she saw the clarity that is God himself. She saw God in everything, without distinction, in a flawless sight: the light with light and in light. This revelation of eternal light was renewed without remission in her, in the innermost part of her fundament, and in the highest nobility of the spirit. Her spirit was always in incalculable delight, because here she had something of the future blessedness in her perception, and loved God here with eternal gifts. As all created things must remain down here and perform the tasks appropriate to their nature, so she was transformed with the divine clarity beyond all images and reason, because all of that was totally gone and lost to sight here. Here she became one with the light and here pursued her eternal image.)

Here again Marquard has taken a general description (or rather, parts of one) and applied it to Mary, in a similar way to his adoption of Eckhartian material noted above.

A more direct adoption of earlier material is found in the Marian section of the fourth commandment, in which Marquard elaborates the manners of Mary's thankfulness. The third of these ways involves the returning of any gift to God, its eternal origin. This provides the opportunity for a brief excursus on Mary's own journey into God, finding *quies* there alone, in a passage adopted from Johannes Tauler:[70]

Die dritte wise jr danckberkeit waz, daz si keiner flússe von oben, noch keinen vsser gabe nie an gesach mit rast vnd benûglicheit; me ze hand so schielt si es wider vf in g[o]t, von dem es ouch komen ist, vnd nam allein do jr rast vnd benûglicheit. Vnd darumb sprach si: **'Jn allen han ich rûwe gesûchet, vnd bin beliben wonend in dem erb mines herren.'**[71] Daz soltu also verston, daz die edel magt **fúr mit jr vernunft vber die himel, jn daz abgrunde der helle vnd daz tieff mer [vnd] jn**

---

[68] Cf. ibid. 170–2 (ed. Eichler, p. 224); c181–c183 (ed. Alaerts, p. 593): . . . so werdent sú vber formet vnd ein mit dem selben liehte, do sú mitte sehent vnd daz sú sehent. Vnd also eruolgent die sch(ôwende menschen ir ewigen bilde . . .

[69] *Dekalogerklärung*, fol. 153ʳ⁻ᵛ (cf. ed. 1516, 31ᵇ–32ᵃ; ed. 1483, 32. 19–34).

[70] For the identification see Clark, 'Marquard von Lindau and his "Dekalogerklärung"?', p. 76; Steer, 'Der Armutsgedanke', p. 290 n. 11; and van Maren, *Marquard von Lindau. Die zehe Gebot (Straßburg 1516 und 1520)*, p. 33.

[71] Cf. Johannes Tauler, *Predigt* 46 (201. 21–2): 'in allen dingen han ich rûwe gesûcht und bin bliben wonende in dem erbe mins herren'.

dem vmb kreise des ertrichs, vnd si vand nie rŭw.[72] **Dis waz grosß wunder,**[73] **daz si jr kint, daz si bekant on zwifel got vnd mŏnsch, bi jr hatte wie si wolt; vnd ouch jn allem jr hertz, jrem leben, nie ein blick do vf entg[eraste] mit ge[nŭgde] an siner mŏnscheit, denne das jr gemŭte on vnderlos vf gieng vnd vbergieng jn daz gŏtlich abgrŭnd, jn dem alle[i]n waz jr rŭw.**[74, 75]

(The third aspect to her thankfulness was that she never looked upon any outpouring from above, nor any external gift, with repose and contentment. Rather, she immediately redirected it back upwards into God, from whom it also came, and only there [i.e. in God] took her repose and contentment. Therefore she said, 'I have sought repose in all things, and have remained dwelling in the inheritance of my lord.' You should understand that in this way: namely, that the noble maiden journeyed with her intellect beyond the heavens, into the abyss of hell, the deep sea, and the whole compass of the globe, and she never found repose. It was a great miracle that she had her child, whom she knew without a doubt to be God and man, with her as she wanted. In all her heart and her life her glance never tarried with fulfilment on his humanity, since her mind ascended without intermission and passed over into the divine abyss, in which alone was her repose.)

Here the text already applied to Mary in Tauler's sermon, and Marquard has made no real changes, other than to abbreviate the content. There is, in fact, little more in this sermon on Mary than this passage, and so Marquard can be seen to have integrated a 'Marian fragment' into his much more extensive presentation of Mary.

This passage is also of use in considering the relationship between the Marian sections of the *Dekalogerklärung* and Marquard's Marian sermons. Sermon 11, on Mary's nativity, lists in its third section six nobilities ('edelkaiten') that distinguish Mary from the rest of mankind. The fourth is clearly related to this passage based on Tauler in the *Dekalogerklärung*. It maintains that Mary was only satisfied by God, and only considered Christ's humanity as a means to the divinity of God:

---

[72] Cf. ibid. (201. 23–5): . . . si fŭr mit ir vernunft úber die himel in das abgrúnde der helle und in das tieffe mer und in den umbekreis des ertrichs, und sie envant nie rŭwe.

[73] Cf. ibid. (202. 3–4): . . . Was wunders was das . . .

[74] Cf. ibid. (202. 6 10): . . . und was des sicher das er ir Got was, und mochte mit im gebaren wie si wolte, und er wandelte mit ir als ir kint, das ir herze in allem irem lebende nie ein ögenblick do uffe engeraste mit genŭgde, denne das ir gemŭte ane underlos uf gieng und úber gieng in das gŏtlich abgrúnde; in dem allein was ir rŭwe . . .

[75] *Dekalogerklärung*, fol. 172^{r–v} (cf. ed. 1516, pp. 51^b–52^a; ed. 1483, 57. 17–30). I amend 'gemŭt' to 'genŭgde', following the incunable editions and the source of the passage in Tauler.

Die vierd edelkait waz, daz si lust noch benúglichait nie gewan von kainer creatur
denn allain von irem got vnd schŏpfer, noch nie vff der minneklichen menschait ires
kindes gestŭnd denn als vff ainem weg in die lutren blŏssen gothait.[76]

(The fourth nobility was that she never received delight nor contentment from any
created being, save from her God and creator. Nor did she ever dwell on the lovable
humanity of her child, save as a path into the pure and naked Godhead.)

Likewise, the third item in the same list is clearly related to the presentation
of Mary's heart as *deiformis* in the first commandment of the *Dekalogerklärung*:

Die dritt waz, daz alles ir leben von der stund, vnd ir edel sel geschaffen waz, beclåret
waz mit dem ewigen lieht in wisshait vnd in vŏlli dez hailgen gaistz, vnd lucht in der
hŏhsten luterkait inrlich vnd vsserlich. Hier vmb wer in ir sel gesehen hett, er hett da
all zit geschŏwet die geburt dez ewigen wortes in allem lust, vnd ain hercz vnd
gemút, in daz nie viel vnordenlich bild noch gedank, mer die hŏh driualtikait schain
in ir in allem adel vnd luterkait.[77]

(The third was that from the moment when her noble soul was created, her whole
life was clarified with the eternal light in wisdom and in the plenitude of the Holy
Spirit, and was illumined in the highest purity inwardly and outwardly. Therefore
someone who looked into her soul would have seen the birth of the eternal word
there at all times, and a heart and mind into which no disordered image or thought
ever fell. Rather, the high Trinity shone in her in all nobility and purity.)

The presentation of Mary as a mystical contemplative in the sermons is
remarkably coherent with the *Dekalogerklärung*, with several further similar
parallels—not to mention the consistent depiction of Mary under the cross,
which we examined earlier. This is surprising, given the particular status
that the sermons (together with the Latin commentary on John) occupy
within Marquard's oeuvre, as we have seen in earlier chapters, and the
otherwise ethical-normative content of much of the *Dekalogerklärung*. In
other respects, the sermons do represent an advance on the 'mystical'
content of the *Dekalogerklärung*—particularly with regard to the integration of pseudo-Dionysian ideas, and the close attention paid to the mechanics of the mystical union itself (union taking place in the *apex
affectionis* and so forth). Though some of the Marian sermons do contain
this kind of more elevated material, it is not transposed into the presentation that the sermons offer of Mary herself as mystical contemplative.

---

[76] *Predigt* 11, ll. 112–15 (p. 103).
[77] Ibid., ll. 105–11 (p. 103).

We could continue and search out all the remaining, less interesting passages in the *Dekalogerklärung* and the sermons that detail Mary's mystical contemplation. But these would refine our impression little further. So far, moreover, we have only examined Marquard's presentation of Mary as mystical contemplative as it is dependent on its direct sources. In fact, Marquard stands at the zenith of a long medieval tradition of presenting Mary as a mystical contemplative, which until now has scarcely been recognized as such. Aside from a couple of (admittedly, enormously valuable) pages on the origins of the idea in the eleventh and twelfth centuries by Jean Leclercq, this tradition has received almost no scholarly attention. It attracted the eye, upon occasion, of the Jesuit scholar Johannes Beumer, and of the Catholic writer Hilda Graef—but only insofar as both (especially Graef) disapproved of the idea, which meant that neither gave it any particular attention. Marzena Górecka does not examine the Latin works after 1200 in which the tradition develops, and consequently does not highlight the idea when it appears in the German works she considers. We cannot hope here to have found every work in which this presentation of Mary occurs; nor to have defined every contour of the tradition precisely. But we can look at all the major Marian works of the thirteenth and fourteenth centuries, and at least some of the minor ones, and present as clear a picture of the intellectual history of this tradition as possible.

Leclercq noted that Mary is presented as the model of both active and contemplative lives in texts from the eleventh century onwards. The origin is liturgical. The Gospel reading for the feast of Mary's assumption is Luke 10: 38–42, which tells of Jesus' entry into the house of Martha and her sister Mary. Martha and Mary, of course, were understood allegorically as the active and contemplative lives, with priority accorded to the contemplative life because, in Christ's words, 'Maria optimam partem elegit' ('Mary chose the best part'; Lk. 10: 42). By way of the liturgical coincidence, Mary (the virgin) is then understood as the perfect exemplar of both Martha and this other Mary; that is, of the active and contemplative lives. This association becomes reasonably popular amongst twelfth-century authors.[78] Another contributory impulse during the same period was undoubtedly the understanding of Mary as *sapientia*, at which Ingrid Roitner has recently looked. This interpretation is essentially Christological: with Christ, understood as wisdom, dwelling in Mary, so Mary herself becomes the seat of wisdom (the *sedes sapientiae*), the throne of Solomon,

[78] Leclercq, *Études sur le vocabulaire monastique*, pp. 150–1.

and so forth, and is ultimately associated with wisdom herself.[79] The production of the first Marian commentaries on the Song of Songs in the later twelfth century, beginning with the Augustinian canon William of Newburgh, had—as Rachel Fulton has shown—an important role to play in this process by which traditionally Christological attributes were increasingly associated with Mary; and this was surely also the case for wisdom, for knowledge of the divine.[80]

Leclercq edited a sermon on Luke 10: 38–42 by Odo of Canterbury (d. 1200) as a text representative of the developments he had identified in the eleventh and twelfth centuries. Mary, says Odo, is said to be the wisdom of Christians. This is not just because Christians seeking wisdom should 'study' in her (i.e. learn from her example), but because Mary herself contemplated the divinity of Christ:

Dicta est Maria a quodam sapiente «christianorum philosophia», quod interpretatur «studium sapientiae», non solum, secundum quod supra dictum est, quia ad inueniendam ueram sapientiam studere in Maria debeant christiani, uerum etiam quia in Christo, qui est christianorum sapientia[ ] supra omnes homines[,] tam eius humanitati ministrando quam diuinitatem contemplando, ipsa semper studuit.[81]

(Mary was called 'philosophy of the Christians' by a certain wise man, which means by interpretation 'the study of wisdom'—not just in accordance with what was said above, namely because Christians should study in Mary to discover true wisdom; but also because she herself always studied in Christ, who is the wisdom of the Christians beyond all men, both in her ministrations to his human form and in her contemplation of his divinity.)

Mary (the Virgin) surpassed Martha in the active life, because she had nourished Christ in her womb and looked after him throughout his childhood. But she also surpassed the other Mary in the contemplative life, because Christ, the wisdom of God, had been present in her womb:

Qualis enim in contemplatione fuit, quae ipsam diuinitatem, suae carni in persona filii Dei unitam, in utero habuit? Ipsum Verbum Dei, quod in principio apud Deum erat, et Deus erat [cf. John 1: 1], hoc in utero suo Maria habebat, hoc audiebat, cum hoc loquebatur, cum hoc contemplabatur et delectabatur. 'Christus est Dei uirtus et Dei sapientia' [1 Cor. 1: 24]; Christus autem in Maria; igitur in Maria Dei uirtus et Dei sapientia.[82]

---

[79] Roitner, «*Mater misericordiae*», pp. 659–77.
[80] See Fulton, *From Judgment to Passion*, pp. 429–64; see further Górecka, *Das Bild Mariens*, pp. 248–81; and Ellington, *From Sacred Body*, pp. 61–5.
[81] Odo of Canterbury, *Sermo* to Lk. 10: 38–42 (p. 152). The 'wise man' in question is, in fact, Pythagoras.
[82] Ibid. (p. 153).

(For in what way was she in contemplation—she, who had divinity itself united to her flesh in the person of the Son of God in her womb? The Word of God itself, which was with God in the beginning, and which was God: this Mary had in her womb; this she heard; with this she spoke, contemplated, and was delighted. 'Christ is the strength of God and the wisdom of God'; Christ, further, was in Mary; therefore the strength of God and the wisdom of God was in Mary.)

By a similar process of association, Mary is replete with divinity, and the whole Trinity dwells in her—providing her with unsurpassed contemplative possibilities:

'Omnis plenitudo diuinitatis corporaliter' [Col. 2: 9] in Christo; Christus autem in Maria: omnis igitur plenitudo diuinitatis in Maria. Quod si plenitudo diuinitatis in Maria, igitur Pater in Maria, igitur Filius in Maria, igitur Spiritus Sanctus in Maria. Qualis igitur contemplatiua Maria, quae in utero Dei Unigeniti, de sua carne genito, totius Trinitatis contemplabatur gloriam![83]

('All the plenitude of divinity was bodily' in Christ; Christ, further, was in Mary; therefore all the plenitude of divinity was in Mary. And if the plenitude of divinity was in Mary, therefore the Father was in Mary, the Son was in Mary, and the Holy Spirit was in Mary. Of what kind a contemplative therefore was Mary, who contemplated the glory of the only-begotten God, begotten of her flesh in her womb, and of all the Trinity!)

Odo continues with similar associative chains to establish that the glory of divinity was revealed to Mary in contemplation more fittingly than to any other person, on account of her purity of heart; and thus, her contemplation of God by the presence of Christ within her exceeds that of all others.

Odo's sermon is associative in structure and unspecific in content, and as such is typical of the late eleventh- and twelfth-century sermons that present Mary as contemplative. There is no mention of the nature of Mary's contemplation, nor of the temporal duration of this contemplation across Mary's life; any unitive (that is, mystical) aspect to this contemplation, or the sight of the beatific vision, is not specified. Walter Delius noted that the new attention to Mary in this period, and the development of new Marian themes, generated new questions that were treated as new theological issues, worked through and defined in the scholastic environment of the thirteenth century.[84] The presentation of Mary as a (mystical) contemplative fits well into this overall pattern. But we find that even in the twelfth

---

[83] Odo of Canterbury, *Sermo* to Lk. 10: 38–42 (p. 153).
[84] Delius, *Geschichte der Marienverehrung*, pp. 158–60.

century, certain intellectuals were beginning to deal with these new issues, and were beginning to locate the nature of Mary's contemplation more precisely.

Hugh of St Victor (d. 1141) had clearly dwelt on these issues before writing his relatively short, but difficult commentary on the Magnificat, the *Explanatio in canticum beatae Mariae.*[85] Hugh begins by narrating the annunciation. With Mary's fiat, Christ is conceived, and Mary must have received the extraordinary and inexpressible sweetness of the joys of heaven and the eternal delight (i.e. God) when the eternal light descended into her:

Statim ergo adveniente Spiritu sancto in Virginem, et omnium gratia virtutum sacrosanctum habitaculum in adventu Filii Dei replente, dubium non est quin coelestium gaudiorum, et aeternae dulcedinis miram atque inenarrabilem suavitatem Virgo ipsa conceperit, quando illud aeternum lumen cum toto majestatis suae fulgore in eam descendit: et quod non capit mundus, totam se intra viscera virginis collocavit.[86]

(Immediately, thus, when the Holy Spirit came into the Virgin, and when the most holy dwelling place was filled with the grace of all the virtues in the advent of the Son of God, there is no doubt that the Virgin herself received the marvellous and ineffable sweetness (*suavitas*) of the heavenly joys and the eternal sweetness (*dulcedo*) when this eternal light descended into her with all the majesty of its splendour: and what the world cannot contain took its residence within the Virgin's womb.)

Hugh explores the nature of Mary's experience. He asks what Mary was able to say of what she saw and felt, having such a plenitude of divinity within her. But Mary does not say very much at the annunciation, and so he states that she was unable to express what she bore within her, because the Holy Spirit had limited the extent of her knowledge. Had this not been so, then Mary would not have been unable to speak of such miraculous things as she knew:

Tali ergo, ac tanta divinitatis praesentia plena, quid viderit, aut quid senserit quis dicere potest? Audacter pronuntio, quod nec ipsa plene explicare potuit, quod capere potuit. In tantis ergo mirabilibus quomodo lingua humana tacere potuisset, nisi idem ipse Spiritus, qui virginem repleverat[,] torrentem suae affluentiae impetum[ ] suavissimo moderaretur amplexu?[87]

---

[85] An examination of this work is given by Górecka, *Das Bild Mariens*, pp. 243–6, but without comment on the graduated distinctions Hugh makes on Mary's mystical experience. Graef dismisses all Victorine works on Mary in less than a page, deciding that they 'contributed very little to our subject': see Graef, *Mary*, vol. 1, pp. 253–4.

[86] Hugh of St Victor, *Explanatio in canticum*, col. 415.

[87] Ibid.

(Who can say what she saw or felt in such a—and such a replete—presence of divinity? Boldly I declare that she herself was unable to express fully what she was able to grasp. How, therefore, could the human tongue have stayed silent in such miracles, unless the same spirit who suffused the Virgin were to tame the roaring current of his plenty with his sweetest embrace?)

Proceeding from John 3: 8, Hugh asserts—now addressing Mary directly— that she accepted the Holy Spirit into her without knowing its origin: that is, without knowing God. Mary cannot 'investigate' the origin: in other words, she feels the effects of the infusion of the Spirit (sweetness, and so on), but she does not enjoy the beatific vision, and does not contemplate God directly at this point:

Clamavit eminus jam, tunc sapientia Dei in illa beata anima: 'Spiritus ubi vult spirat, et vocem ejus audis: sed nescis unde veniat, aut quo vadat.' [John 3: 8] Tu enim, inquit, ingredientem in te Spiritum sanctum subito accepisti: nec scientia tua adventum ejus praevenisti, ut aut venturum quaereres, aut venientem diligeres, aut ingredienti aperires. Subito tibi illapsus est, gratis se obtulit, non quaesitus venit, improvisus se infundit. Infusionem percipis: sed ad fontem immensitatis ejus te non extendis. Et ideo nescis unde veniat, quia quantum tibi datum est, sentire potes, sed ex quanto datum sit, investigare non potes.[88]

(Now the wisdom of God called out from afar, as then in that blessed soul, 'The Spirit breathes where he will, and you hear his voice; but you do not know whence he came, or whither he may go.' For you, he says, have accepted the Holy Spirit suddenly entering into you. Your knowledge did not precede his arrival, so that you might enquire of the one who was about to come, or might love the one who was coming, or might open yourself to the one who was entering. Suddenly he flowed into you, freely he showed himself; unsought he comes, unexpectedly he streams in. You feel the influx, but you cannot stretch yourself to the fount of his immensity. And therefore you do not know whence he came; because you are able to sense how much has been given to you, but are unable to discover out of how much it may have been given.)

God, continues Hugh, determines the time and manner at and by which he will reveal his secrets, and to whom he will reveal them; Mary, tempered by such considerations, prudently kept silent and submitted to God's will. But because Mary must be silent of what she knew (and what had not yet been revealed to her), so it was celebrated alternatively: the exultation of John in Elizabeth's womb at the visitation, and Mary's response to Elizabeth—the Magnificat. From this point Hugh's interpretation of the Magnificat then proceeds.

---

[88] Hugh of St Victor, *Explanatio in canticum,* cols. 415–16.

This interpretation is difficult and sometimes unclear. As we have seen, Hugh held that Mary did not, and could not enjoy the beatific vision at the incarnation. It now becomes clear that Hugh believed that a superior state of knowledge of God, a superior level of contemplation, had been revealed to Mary at, and was manifest in, the Magnificat. Hugh indicates this initially by using the language of bridal mysticism to express Mary's new relationship to God; further, in interpreting 'et exsultavit spiritus meus in Deo salutari meo' ('and my spirit has rejoiced in God, my saviour'; Lk. 1: 47), he states not only that Mary expressed the memory of the abundance of divine sweetness that she had perceived, but that she had actually seen the majesty of God:

Vere dilecta, et unica, et in illam cellam vinariam a rege sponso tuo introducta [cf. Cant. 1: 4 and 2: 4], ab ubertate domus ejus inebriata, et fonte vitae (qui apud ipsum est) potata [cf. Ps. 36: 9–10] memoriam abundantiae suavitatis ejus eructasti, et in justitia ejus exsultasti. Vidisti, et gustasti; vidisti majestatem, gustasti suavitatem. Ideoque quod intus hauseras, foras propinasti.[89]

(Truly beloved, and unique, when you were brought into that wine cellar by the king, your bridegroom; when you were intoxicated from the plenty of his house, and having drunk from the fountain of life (which is with him), you have proclaimed [literally, 'belched forth'] the memory of the abundance of his sweetness, and have rejoiced in his justice. You have seen, and you have tasted; you have seen his majesty, and you have tasted his sweetness. And thus what you had drunk in to yourself, you have yielded forth.)

Hugh continues with an exposition on the fitting division of labour between Mary's soul, magnifying ('anima'—'magnificare') and her spirit, exalting ('spiritus'—'exaltare'). Soon he turns to the question of why two distinct terms are used, and why they occur in this specific order. He justifies this question (which, one assumes, might otherwise appear based on a meaningless distinction) by stating that the terms, in this order, derived from the summit of truth in which Mary's mind inhered. She spoke, moreover, not from the vagaries of her own thought, but resident in the sole source of wisdom (i.e. God) through mental contemplation:

Primum discernamus quare distincte posuit, magnificat et exsultat; vel quare prius magnificat, postea exsultat. Nihil enim ratione caret; quia omne, quod dictum est ab illa intima summae veritatis luce cui mens virginis excellenter inhaeserat emanavit.

---

[89] Ibid., col. 416. On this particular constellation of scriptural texts, which together present a kind of mystical union as a state of intoxication, see Jean Châtillon's excellent note to Achard of St Victor, *Sermo* 8, §2 (pp. 94–5 n. 17), with all further references.

Nec potuit aliud dicere, quae meditando locuta non est, sed gustando: quam non docuit per varia discurrens cogitatio, sed uni inhaerens fonti sapientiae per contemplationem mentis devotio.[90]

(Let us first distinguish why she articulated 'magnify' and 'exalt' discretely; or rather, why 'magnify' came first, and 'exalt' afterwards. For this is not without reason, because everything that was said emanated from that most profound light of the supreme truth in which the Virgin's mind had sublimely inhered. She could not say anything different; for she spoke not from meditation, but from tasting [i.e, tasting the sweetness of the divine], and was not taught by thought, running about through various things, but rather by her devotion, being inherent in the unique fount of wisdom through mental contemplation.)

Hugh then implicitly confirms the impression formed by these passages: Mary has indeed been elevated by God to a higher state of knowledge, and to a closer mystical union. He explains first that the angels and saints see two things: the incomprehensible majesty of God and his ineffable goodness. The first generates fear and the second, love; accordingly, they revere and love God, and do so simultaneously. God is sweetness itself, which is enjoyed more perfectly as they love more ardently; and so they desire to see God more closely (and so perceive greater sweetness), and are not petrified by fear into immobile rigidity. Crucially, states Hugh, the saints and angels always look at God above them: they never perfectly comprehend him. It is to this level of contemplation that Mary was raised as she uttered the opening words of the Magnificat:

Ad hanc ergo contemplationis lucem mens Mariae sublevata fuerat, quae coelestis patriae dulcedinem in verbis suis tam mirabiliter expressit, quam ineffabiliter comprehendit. Nam cum se Dominum magnificare perhibuit, venerandam illam reverendamque universis aeterni numinis majestatem interna visione contueri se manifeste declaravit. Cum vero se in suo salutari exsultare asseruit, gustum se internae dulcedinis percepisse ostendit.[91]

(Thus Mary's mind had been raised up to this light of contemplation, who expressed the sweetness of the heavenly kingdom in her words as miraculously as she understood it ineffably. For when she stated that she was magnifying the Lord, she declared openly that with inner sight she beheld that majesty of the one eternal God, which majesty is to be honoured and revered. When, indeed, she asserted that she exulted in her saviour, she disclosed that she had perceived the taste of inner sweetness.)

---

[90] Hugh of St Victor, *Explanatio in canticum*, col. 417.
[91] Ibid., cols. 417–18.

From Mary's words (or lack of them) at the incarnation and, in the Magnificat, at the visitation of Elizabeth, Hugh thus laboriously extracts an understanding of Mary's contemplation of God as bipartite: restricted at the incarnation, and more fully revealed at the visitation. In this second level, Mary is raised in contemplation to the vision of God, to a level equal to that of the saints and angels in heaven. It is the Holy Spirit alone who is active; Mary is humble and submissive, and awaits revelation patiently without mental action on her own part. Most importantly, it is with Hugh that we find the transposition of the very general presentation of Mary as contemplative in sermons on the Assumption, as represented by the (albeit later) Odo of Canterbury, onto specific instances in Mary's life and with far greater precision as to the nature of that mystical experience.

The twelfth-century canons of St Victor appear to have played an important role in this definition of Mary's contemplative experience, and its functionalization to become an imitable instance. Richard of St Victor (d. 1173) took the opposite line to Hugh in his *De differentia sacrificii Abrahae a sacrificio beatae Mariae virginis*, an allegorical treatise that proceeds from a comparison of the offerings made by Abraham and Mary to comment on the nature of contemplative experience. Mary, says Richard, loved Christ above all others, and out of this love desired most ardently to die, that she might enjoy the sweetness of union with the divine—a sweetness, and so a union, that she did not have in this life because of the restrictions that corporeal existence place on mystical experience. From the terminology of the central denial it is probable that Richard had been reading Hugh's *Explanatio in canticum*:

Quis unquam ex omnibus Christi dilectoribus libentius mori vellet, ut ejus divinitatem videre posset, ut majestati illius immensitatique perpetua contemplatione inhaereret? Quis unquam hujusmodi desiderii fervore ardentius aestuavit? Quanto certe prae caeteris dilexit, tanto prae caeteris divinae visionis dulcedinem, dulcedinisque sempiternitatem ardentius desideravit. Audenter dico quod nec illa quae prae caeteris dilexit huic dulcedini inseparabiliter inhaerere, vel hanc solam et sine interpolatione haurire potuit, quandiu in hac vita fuit, et corpus corrruptibile portavit. Corpus enim quod corrumpitur aggravat animam, et terrena inhabitatio deprimit sensum multa cogitantem. Quia igitur illam plenitudinem gratiae et gloriae in hac vita obtinere non potuit, quam in sua assumptione accepit, quid mirum si acceptionis illius horam ardenter desideravit, quam nullus cadendi vel patiendi timor ad mortis desiderium impellere potuit?[92]

---

[92] Richard of St Victor, *De differentia sacrificii*, col. 1048.

(Whoever, of all those who love Christ, might want more willingly to die, so that he might see his divinity and be inherent in his majesty and immensity in uninterrupted contemplation? Whoever burned more ardently with the fervour of this kind of desire? For sure, the more she loved him above all else, the more she more ardently desired the sweetness of the divine vision and an eternity of that sweetness above all else. Boldly I state that she, who loved him above all else, was neither inseparably inherent in this sweetness, nor was able to partake of it alone and without intermission, as long as she was in this life and bore a corruptible body. For a body which decays oppresses the soul, and dwelling on earth weighs down the [cognitive] sense as it considers many things. Thus because she was unable in this life to obtain that plenitude of grace and glory which she received in her assumption, what wonder is it if she, whom no fear of suffering or being killed could drive to desire death, ardently desired the hour of that reception?)

If Richard was sceptical, his contemporary Achard of St Victor (d. 1170/1) was less so.[93] Achard refers to Mary as the perfect exemplar of both active and contemplative lives in sermon 8 (on Mary's nativity), though not very clearly—it is difficult to tell if he is speaking of Mary during her earthly existence, or glorified in heaven.[94] Sermon 14 is structured around the liturgical office for All Saints, specifically the nine responses at matins calling for aid, that begin with God and descend through the heavenly hierarchy. Achard inverts this order, presenting eight imitable models for different aspects of the enclosed life, arranged in approximately increasing level of difficulty (and not primarily as a scheme of contemplative ascent). Mary is initially functionalized in the first division (on virgins) as the exemplar of chastity.[95] The seventh division is on Mary qua herself, and she is understood as the perfection of purity, insofar as this is attainable in this life. With her purity of heart, she was able to contemplate God in himself: that is, to enjoy the beatific vision. The references to this (earthly) life, and to Mary giving birth to Christ, indicate that Achard is speaking of Mary as she was on earth, not as she is in heaven:

Hic itaque ei occurrit virginum Virgo, munditia munditiarum, puritas puritatum, id est munditia et puritas cordis secundum hujus vite possibilitatem consummata atque perfecta. Hec est et mater Dei; hec parit Filium Dei, sapientiam Dei,

[93] Górecka mentions Achard's sermons very briefly (see *Das Bild Mariens*, p. 246), with the sole and wholly erroneous reference to *Patrologia Latina*, vol. 196, which contains only two short letters by Achard (cols. 1381–2). Her references to Richard's sermons are equally erroneous: they are located in vol. 177 (cols. 899–1210), under Hugh's name, and not in either vols. 196 (Richard's treatises) or 202 (i.a. Peter of Celle).

[94] Achard of St Victor, *Sermo* 8, §3–4 (p. 96).

[95] Ibid., *Sermo* 14, §2–3 (pp. 173–6).

contemplationem Dei; hec enim facit videre 'regem in decore suo' [Is. 33: 17], Deum contemplari in seipso. 'Beati' namque 'mundo corde, quoniam ipsi Deum videbunt' [Matt. 5: 8].[96]

(And so here she came to meet him; she, the Virgin of virgins, cleanliness of all cleanliness, purity of all purity—that is, cleanliness and purity perfected and consummated insofar as is possible in this life. This is the mother of God; she bears the Son of God, the wisdom of God, and the contemplation of God; for she is meet to see the king in his beauty, to contemplate God in himself. For 'blessed are the clean in heart, because they will see God'.)

Divine grace, continues Achard, is necessary alongside purity of heart in order to attain this level of contemplative, indeed avowedly mystical, experience; an experience in which the soul is elevated by the action of the Holy Spirit, and which Achard describes as the spiritual conception, pregnancy, and birth of Christ. The real significance of Achard's sermon here is this explicit functionalization of Mary's mystical contemplation of God as a direct model for imitation, which goes beyond the subsequent use of Mary's actual conception, pregnancy, and birth of Christ as a metaphor to describe the soul's passage into God:

Non tamen ad hanc visionem sufficit quantalibet cordis munditia, absque Dei gratia. Oportet siquidem ut ex Spiritu Dei concipiat Filium Dei. Tunc autem ex Spiritu sancto mens munda fecundatur ut ab ea vere et fructuose Filius Dei concipiatur, cum ad eum in seipso contemplandum non presumptione spiritus sui, sed instinctu divini Spiritus, instigatur atque provocatur, cum ad faciem Dei videndam estu ineffabili amoris divini tota inflammatur et, quasi mole deposita carnis, vi caritatis et attractu interne dulcedinis tota raptatur, dilatatur atque sublevatur. Parturit vero quotiens, sic concepto spirituali desiderio quasi in lumine contemplationis posita, tota nititur in contemplationem ipsam erumpere et quasi in Deum tota transire. Parit autem cum id consequitur ad quod nititur, cum pulsanti aperitur, cum in abscondito faciei divine absconditur, cum, Paulum consequens, in tertium celum rapitur.[97]

(As much purity of the heart as you want is still insufficient to receive this vision without the grace of God. It is necessary insofar that one may conceive the Son of God from the Spirit of God. At that point, further, the pure mind is made fertile through the Holy Spirit so that the Son of God may truly and fruitfully be conceived by it. When it is stimulated and incited to contemplate him in himself, not by the presumption of its spirit, but by the incitement of the divine Spirit; when it is wholly inflamed by the ineffable fire of divine love to see the face of God; then, as if with the weight of the flesh set aside, it is wholly enraptured, enlarged, and

[96] Ibid., §22 (pp. 193–4).
[97] Ibid. (p. 194).

raised up by the power of love and the attraction of the inner sweetness. Whenever it is pregnant, in fact, it has been placed thus by a spiritually conceived desire as if it were in the light of contemplation; it strives wholeheartedly to burst forth into contemplation and, as it were, to pass over wholly into God. It gives birth, however, when it attains that for which it strives, when it opens the door to the one who knocks upon it, when it is concealed in the concealment of the divine face: when, following Paul, it is enraptured into the third heaven.)

Achard is not alone in this kind of functionalization of Mary's mystical experience towards the end of the twelfth century. Górecka discusses the *Meditationes* of the Carthusian prior Guigo II (d. 1193), in which Mary functions as the type of the mystical soul. Guigo II maintains that she reached the highest (seventh) level of the contemplative life, the state of *quies*, through her receipt of the seven gifts of the Spirit.[98] Bernard of Clairvaux, incidentally (and contrary to expectation), does not play a part in the development of this tradition. His sermons on the Assumption do not present Mary as the exemplar of both lives, and he does not otherwise portray Mary as a contemplative.[99] Bernard's presentation of the incarnation in his third homily *super 'Missus est'* is more traditional: the corporeal union of God to Mary followed from the union of wills, predicated on Mary's submissive consent to the divine will. The implication for the

---

[98] See Górecka, *Das Bild Mariens*, pp. 246–7. Górecka notes (p. 247 n. 61) the role of Mary in later Carthusian contemplative writing, with reference to the *De contemplatione* of Guigo du Pont (d. 1297): 'Maria ist für ihn das Modell der christozentrischen Betrachtung: Sie habe als erste die *meditatio* Christi verwirklicht und gelebt. Der Betrachter solle sich darum in der *Imitatio Mariae* in die Gegenwart des Heilsgeschehens versetzen und die wichtigsten Heilsmysterien im Gedächtnis festhalten, Maria dienen und wie Maria Christus' ('For him, Mary is the model of Christocentric contemplation, because she first realized and lived the *meditatio Christi*. The contemplative, therefore, should place himself in the *imitatio Mariae* in the presence of the events of man's salvation, preserve the most important mysteries of salvation firmly in the memory, serve Mary, and like Mary, Christ'). This overstates the Marian aspect to Guigo's point: he declares the contemplative life to have been the life of the apostles, of Mary, and now of the saints in heaven: as they meditated on Christ as he stood before them alive (and for the saints, as he stands before them), so the contemplative now should meditate and recollect the life of Christ: see Guigo du Pont, *De contemplatione*, lib. 2, c. 4 (vol. 1, pp. 192–7). There is no indication that Guigo means anything much more than that the apostles and Mary learned from Christ's example; his concern is with contemporary experience, not with defining the nature of Mary's contemplative experience. There is certainly no question (nor does Górecka claim there is) of any mystical aspect to this meditation.

[99] See Leclercq, *Études sur le vocabulaire monastique*, p. 151. A thorough study of the role of Mary in Bernard's works is given by Górecka, *Das Bild Mariens*, pp. 299–334.

contemplative is principally ethical; there is no clear indication that Bernard understands the union of wills as a mystical union, let alone as the beatific vision.[100]

In such a brief glance across the twelfth century, we cannot hope to have identified all the definitive texts in which the tradition of Mary as mystical contemplative began, and which shaped its development most decisively thereafter. But what we have seen is that the idea had arisen, and approximately how; such that towards the later twelfth century, it could be functionalized as a directly imitable model, and had begun to constitute a theological issue open to debate. The thirteenth century sees these trends amplified. Moreover, the thirteenth century sees the production of the great Marian summae, which allow a much clearer sight of the tradition. It is with the first of these that we should begin: Richard of St Laurent's *De laudibus beate Marie virginis*.

Richard's *De laudibus* was probably written in the 1240s, making this first *summa Mariana* exactly contemporary with the first complete medieval life of Mary, the *Vita rhythmica*. Richard is attested 1239–45 as a deacon of the metropolitan chapter of Rouen; though he was not a Cistercian, the *De laudibus* (as Beumer has shown) is a product from a Cistercian milieu. Notwithstanding, an important source (and one which Richard does not name directly) was Dominican: the Postilla on Luke by Hugh of St Cher (d. 1263), whom Richard knew personally.[101] Richard presented Mary under the cross as a quiet and submissive figure, and—like Marquard—Mary's calm deportment and quiet introversion is repeatedly stressed in the *De laudibus*.[102] The work is predominantly exegetical. Its Mariology is not underpinned by any one guiding principle, but through the application of scriptural and liturgical texts usually applied to Christ, and indeed to God the Father, the work offers what Beumer has termed 'eine Angleichung Mariens an Christus'[103] ('an assimilation of Mary to Christ'). One passage in the fourth book sheds light on the significance of this exegetical method for Richard. He holds that Mary had an unparalleled knowledge of Scripture and of interpretative method, and became the tutor of the apostles.

---

[100] See Bernard of Clairvaux, *Homilia super 'Missus est'*, 3. 38. 9–18.

[101] See Beumer, 'Die Mariologie Richards', pp. 20–5; see further pp. 26–37 for an overview of the content and character of the *De laudibus*, and (with comprehensive bibliography) Roten, 'Richard v. St. Laurentius'. Graef, *Mary*, pp. 266–70, is derivative of Beumer.

[102] In particular see (interpreting Mary's speech) lib. 2, c. 6, §8 (p. 130^b), and lib. 4, c. 31, §12–21 (pp. 260^b–266^b).

[103] Beumer, 'Die Mariologie Richards', pp. 27–8 (here p. 28).

Thus she is responsible for the content of the Gospels; covered over by the text, wisdom—identified with Mary—has progressed in the light of the spiritual understanding of Scripture:

Item, Job, XXVIII, 11: 'Profunda quoque fluviorum', id est, sacrorum librorum, scilicet quatuor Evangeliorum quae sunt quatuor flumina paradisi, scrutatur beata Virgo, id est, facit scrutari. De quibus dicit, Eccli. XXIV, 40: 'Ego sapientia effudi flumina[', e]t abscondita sub velamine litterae produxit in lucem spiritualis intelligentiae.[104]

(Job 28: 11, 'also the depths of the rivers', that is, of the holy books, namely the four Gospels, which are the four rivers of Paradise, the blessed Virgin examines; that is, is meet to examine. Of which Ecclesiasticus 24: 40 says, 'I, wisdom, have poured out rivers', and hidden under the veil of letters, have advanced in the light of spiritual understanding.)

Extended across the entirety of the Bible, this allows almost all of Scripture to be interpreted with regard to Mary—an approach taken to its extreme by another massive thirteenth-century work, the *Biblia Mariana*.

Under the chapter heading *De sapientia Maria*, Richard establishes Mary's knowledge of Scripture. Her wisdom derives from study and meditation on the scriptural texts,[105] and is augmented by Christ's explication of 'incerta et occulta sapientiae suae' ('uncertain and concealed aspects of his wisdom') after the incarnation, during Mary's pregnancy and her life with Christ thereafter.[106] This augmentation of her natural wisdom allows Mary to penetrate the mysteries of the interpretation of Scripture. Richard begins each of the several explanations of this with constellations of scriptural texts from which a mystical interpretation would more commonly be expected to proceed. The following example stands as representative, which I select as we will recognize the underlying constellation of scriptural texts from Hugh of St Victor:

Item, Quia Filius ejus revelaverat incerta et occulta sapientiae suae, ideo dicit ipsa, Cantic. I, 3: 'Introduxit me rex', id est, Christus, 'in cellaria sua', id est, manifestavit mihi secreta Scripturarum sanctarum, quae dicuntur 'cellaria', quia ibi est panis fortium, lac puerorum, vinum devotorum, et omnia necessaria animae, sicut in cellario necessaria corpori. Bene autem dicit, quod 'introduxit eam rex', id est, intus duxit, scilicet usque ad medullam sensus spiritualis.[107]

---

[104] Richard of St Laurent, *De laudibus*, lib. 4, c. 31, §11 (p. 260[b]).
[105] See ibid., §2–6 (pp. 256[a]–259[a]).
[106] See ibid., §7–11 (pp. 259[a]–260[b]).
[107] Ibid., §11 (p. 260[a]).

(Because her son had revealed uncertain and concealed aspects of his wisdom, so she says in the Song of Songs 1: 3, that 'the king', i.e. Christ, 'brought me into his wine cellars'; that is, 'he made known the secrets of the sacred Scriptures to me'. These are called 'wine cellars' because here is the bread of the strong, the milk of the children, the wine of the devout, and every necessity of the soul, just as the necessities of the body are in a wine cellar. It is also well said that 'the king brought her' (*introduco*), that is, led her inside (*intus duco*), namely right to the heart of the spiritual sense.)

Thus in the next chapter, *De taciturnitate Mariae*, it is from Mary's meditation on Scripture, combined with the revelation of complex meanings to her by Christ, that she knows of Christ's divinity and promulgates this knowledge after his death.[108] But in this same chapter, Mary is also described as a contemplative, a theme then developed in the following chapters. In *De actione Mariae*, Christ is said to have dwelt in Mary 'in corpore novem mensibus, ab anima numquam recessurus'[109] ('for nine months in her body, but never going to depart from her soul'); and she is the seat of the Trinity, the *triclinium Trinitatis*.[110] All of this points towards a more intimate, contemplative relationship between Mary and God, and this is precisely what we find in the next chapter, *De actione et contemplatione Mariae*.

Richard begins this chapter by establishing Mary as a contemplative whose vision of God in this life exceeded that of the saints:

Ratione actionis et contemplationis dictum est ab Angelo Mariae: 'Ave, gratia plena', gratia scilicet coelestium donorum: quia virtute contemplandi quodammodo patriam donata est. Unde de ea dictum est, Sapient. XVIII, 16: 'Coelum attingebat stans in terra.' Et ipsa dicit cum Filio: 'Providebam Dominum in conspectu meo semper' [Ps. 15: 8]. Quantum enim distat inter odorem et gustum aromaticae speciei, tanta inter contemplationem Mariae et aliorum sanctorum distantia est.[111]

(By reason of both action and contemplation 'Hail, full of grace' was said by the angel to Mary; grace, namely, of the gifts of heaven, because heaven was given to her in a certain way by virtue of contemplating. Wherefore it was said of her in Wisdom 18: 16, 'standing on the earth she reached heaven'; and with the Son she herself says, 'I saw the Lord from afar always in my sight'. For there is as much difference between the smell and the taste of an aromatic spice as there is a distance between Mary's contemplation and that of the other saints.)

[108] See ibid., c. 32 (pp. 267ᵃ–268ᵇ); cf. further lib. 5, c. 1, §2, under 'species columbae' (pp. 276ᵇ–277ᵃ).
[109] Ibid., lib. 4, c. 34, §1 (p. 269ᵃ).
[110] Ibid. (p. 269ᵇ); cf. further lib. 10, c. 10–11 (pp. 489ᵃ–491ᵇ).
[111] Ibid., c. 35, §1 (p. 271ᵃ).

As Mary was able to enjoy Christ's humanity in activity, through her ministration to him as a child, so—says Richard cautiously—she received something of the sweetness of his divinity in contemplation. Thus Gabriel was able to say 'Dominus tecum' ('The Lord is with you'). Richard is unwilling to commit one way or the other to the opinion, asserted by certain *viri magni*, that Mary in this life *fruebatur*:

Sicut enim singularem activam a Christo accepit, videlicet ejus humanam naturam portare, lactare, pannis involvere, balneare, fovere, nutrire, pascere, potare, lenire, amplecti, et osculari, caeteraque humilitatis obsequia exhibere: sic, ut dicam quod ministrat cordis mei devotio, etiam dulcedidem [*sic*] suae divinitatis matri singulariter experiendam indulsit. Unde plenitudini gratiae subjunxit Angelus: 'Dominus tecum'. Ideo de matre senserunt viri magni et adhuc sentiunt, quod viatrix fruebatur, quod nec asserimus, nec negamus.[112]

(For just as she received an exceptional active life from Christ, namely to bear his human nature, to suckle him, to wrap him in swaddling-clothes, to bathe him, to keep him warm, to nourish him, to feed him, to quench his thirst, to soothe him, to embrace him, to kiss him, and to proffer to him the other obedient acts of humility; so too, to say what my heartfelt devotion proposes, he also granted it to his mother exceptionally to experience the sweetness of his divinity. Wherefore the angel added to his statement on the plenitude of grace, 'the Lord is with you'. Thus great men have believed, and even now believe, about the mother that when she was in this life she delighted in heaven (*fruor*), which we can neither confirm nor deny.)

This deponent verb *frui* is a *terminus technicus* that usually indicates the direct and unmediated enjoyment of the beatific vision. Richard's equivocation on this central issue has also caught Beumer's eye, who comments:

Es wird demnach für Maria in ihrem Erdenleben eine tiefere Erkenntnis der Gottheit ihres Sohnes gefordert, aber von deren näheren Bestimmung, etwa im Sinne eines ‚frui', bewußt abgesehen; mit dem letzten Ausdruck kann nicht gut die ‚visio beatifica' einschließlich all ihrer Wirkungen gemeint sein, weil eine solche bei einer ‚viatrix' überhaupt nicht in Betracht kommt und wohl auch kaum jemals von ‚viri magni' aufgestellt worden ist, sondern eher nur die unmittelbare Gottesschau für sich allein genommen.[113]

(He claims accordingly a deeper cognition of the divinity of her son for Mary in her earthly life, but consciously refrains from defining it more closely—for instance, in the meaning of a 'frui'. With this last expression he can hardly mean the 'visio beatifica', together with all of its effects, because such an experience cannot possibly

---

[112] Richard of St Laurent, *De laudibus*, lib. 4, c. 35, §1 (p. 271ᵃ).
[113] Beumer, 'Die Mariologie Richards', p. 32.

come into consideration with regard to a 'viatrix'—and more likely than not was never put forward by 'viri magni'—rather just the unmediated vision of God on its own.)

Beumer is clearly right initially: Richard does propose that Mary had a close cognition of Christ's divinity (by contemplation), and is unwilling to define its nature more precisely. But his distinction between the *visio beatifica* and 'die unmittelbare Gotteschau' ('the unmediated vision of God') does not, I think, hold—except in temporal terms, in that saints in heaven enjoy the eternal vision of God, rather than brief glimpses. Moreover, we only need to remember Hugh of St Victor's *Explanatio in canticum* to think of a *vir magnus* who had indeed proposed that Mary's mystical experience of God in this life had been equivalent to that of the saints in heaven.

Richard is not totally unwilling to define further the nature of Mary's contemplation, even if he is uncertain on the precise relationship with God. Mary is the perfect exemplar of both lives, but she cannot be compared to either Martha or Mary (or Rachel or Leah), because she did not 'switch' between action and contemplation. Instead, she remained constantly in contemplation of the divine whilst active: 'beata Virgo [. . .] sic omnia activae opera Filio exhibebat, quod interim a divina contemplatione nullatenus recedebat'[114] ('the blessed Virgin offered all the works of the active life to the Son such that she did not withdraw meanwhile in any way from divine contemplation'). Mary's access to God is permitted because of her love of the divine, not fear of suffering or pecuniary desire for reward: she receives all the graces of contemplation and is inebriated by their enjoyment, Richard deploying the *ebrietas* texts again, though quite differently:

Item, Ratione suae contemplationis dicit ipsa, Cantic. II, 4: 'Introduxit me rex in cellam vinariam', id est, in cogitationem gaudiorum coelestium. 'Rex', non servus, id est, timor poenae, qui quandoque facit [me] coelestia cogitare. Non amicus, id est, desiderium praemii, sed ipse rex, id est, amor sponsi, qui facit me in coelestia meditari. Innuens igitur, quod non timore supplicii ut serva, nec amore tantum praemii ut mercenaria, sed sola dilectione et charitate patris ut filia, in cellam vinariam est introducta, quae est meditatio spiritualium, non in aquarium, quae est cognitio temporalium: et sic ei collata est gratia spiritualis. Dicit ergo: 'Introduxit me rex in cellam vinariam', id est, omnium bonorum spiritualium mihi contulit affluentiam. Vel, haec cella vinaria, contemplationis gratia, quae multiplicia continet pocula. Primum, puritas mentis. Secundum, requies mentis. Tertium, securitas mentis. Quartum, gaudium in Spiritu sancto. Est ergo sensus: 'Introduxit me rex in cellam vinariam', id est, contulit mihi gratiam contemplationis, cujus poculis me multipliciter inebriavit.[115]

(By reason of her contemplation she herself said in the Song of Songs 2: 4, 'The king brought me into his wine cellar'; i.e. into consideration of the heavenly delights. 'The king'; not a servant, i.e. the fear of punishment, which from time to time causes me to consider the heavens; nor a friend, i.e. the desire of reward; but the king, i.e. the love of the bridegroom, which causes me to meditate in the heavens. Thus she indicates that neither from the fear of punishment like a servant, nor from the love of reward like a mercenary, but from the love and affection for the father like a daughter was she brought into the wine cellar, which is meditation on spiritual matters; and not into the water cistern, which is consideration of temporal matters. In this way spiritual grace was bestowed upon her. Therefore she says, 'The king brought me into his wine cellar'; i.e. he bestowed an abundance of every spiritual good upon me. Alternatively: this wine cellar, the grace of contemplation, contains many different drinks. First, mental purity; second, mental peace; third, mental security; and fourth, joy in the Holy Spirit. The sense is therefore this: 'The king brought me into his wine cellar', i.e. 'he bestowed the grace of contemplation upon me, with whose drinks he intoxicated me in many ways'.)

In the first chapter of the next book, Mary's soul is even described as deified, transformed into God, by the incarnation:

Sicut enim ferrum ab igne extractum, non solum ignitum, imo totum est ignis [. . .]: sic anima Mariae Spiritu sancto repleta, et maxime luce illa coelesti, id est, Filio Dei in eam descendente, non solum luminosa est jam effecta, sed tota est deificata.[116]

(For as iron that has been extracted from fire is not just fiery, but rather is wholly fire, so when Mary's soul was filled with the Holy Spirit—and most of all when that light of heaven, i.e. the Son of God, descended into her—she was now not just made full of light, but was wholly deified.)

Richard explores this deification at length, considering differing contemporary interpretations of 'dilectus meus mihi, et ego illi' ('my beloved is mine, and I am his'; Cant. 2: 16) with reference to it; he asserts that Mary was deified through her unity of love and grace with God in a bipartite process, mirroring her duple sanctification at her conception and at the incarnation.[117]

---

[115] Richard of St Laurent, *De laudibus*, lib. 4, c. 35, §4 (p. 272^{a-b}).

[116] Ibid., lib. 5, c. 1, §1 (p. 275^{b}); cf. also lib. 4, c. 18, §3 (p. 223^{a-b}). On the *lux–ignis* metaphor in the Marian context see Kern, *Trinität, Maria, Inkarnation*, pp. 96–100.

[117] See Richard of St Laurent, *De laudibus*, lib. 5, c. 1, §1 (pp. 275^{b}–276^{a}); cf. lib. 1, c. 3, §1 (pp. 17^{b}–18^{a}).

The second of the great Marian summae was Franciscan in origin: the *Speculum beatae Mariae virginis* of the German Franciscan Konrad von Sachsen (d. 1279). Written within the approximate period 1264–70, it is probably thirty years younger than Richard's *De laudibus*, on which it silently drew.[118] It is distinguished by its enormous transmission: de Alcantara Martinez counted 247 extant manuscripts in 1975, of which seven-eighths are of Germanic origin.[119] It is structured as a commentary on the 'Ave Maria', and like the *De laudibus* before it, is primarily exegetical in its approach.[120] Unlike Richard, Konrad also frequently deploys rhetorical questions instead of scriptural exegesis to establish details on Mary.[121]

On the issues in which we are interested, Konrad is considerably more reticent and much less definite than even Richard of St Laurent. Much of his exposition on Mary's spiritual birth of Christ is ethical, not mystical, interpreted as the birth of virtues against the vices.[122] When Konrad discusses God's specific relationship to Mary, he describes her as the *aula* of God in soul as well as in body, and proceeds to explore the relationship of Mary as daughter, mother, bride, and handmaid of the persons of the Trinity: but does so in a very conventional, dogmatic exposition without any implication of a mystical union or similar intrinsic connection.[123] Girotto comments: 'Maria, con la divina maternità, è divenuta, immediamente dopo Cristo, la glorificatrice suprema di Dio, uno e trino, la sua pienezza, il suo compimento, non in senso sostanziale od intrinseco, ma accidentale ed estrinseco'[124] ('Mary, as the mother of God, became—directly after Christ—the supreme glorifier of God, one and triune, his plenitude and his fulfilment; not in a substantial or intrinsic, but an accidental and extrinsic sense'). Konrad is clearly not keen to develop the mystical aspects that were open to him in the themes he addresses, and

[118] See de Alcantara Martinez (ed.), *Conradus de Saxonia O. F. M., Speculum*, pp. 57–66 (on the dating of Konrad's works) and 77–85 (on the sources of the *Speculum Mariae*); on Konrad and his works see more recently Stamm, 'Konrad von Sachsen'.

[119] See de Alcantara Martinez (ed.), *Conradus de Saxonia O. F. M., Speculum*, pp. 95–133 for a full conspectus.

[120] See further (including a summary of its content) Girotto, *Corrado di Sassonia*, pp. 132–47.

[121] A good example is Konrad's use of this method to establish that Mary, assumed into heaven, bears the gifts bestowed on souls in heaven more than any other such soul: see Konrad von Sachsen, *Speculum Mariae*, c. 6, §4 (259. 11–260. 3).

[122] See ibid., c. 14, §2 (447. 10–17); cf. c. 5, §4 (230. 10–231. 10); c. 7, §2–3 (271. 6–275. 18), and (with Mary as the type of the *fidelis anima*) c. 15 (461. 1–464. 6).

[123] See ibid., c. 8, §3 (309. 17–324. 20); see Girotto, *Corrado di Sassonia*, pp. 150–4.

[124] Girotto, *Corrado di Sassonia*, p. 149.

Girotto notes that it is characteristic of Konrad's works as a whole to show little interest in mystical theology and the speculative aspects of contemplation.[125]

Konrad may be reticent, but he is not silent. The prerequisites for imputing an intrinsic contemplative relationship between Mary and God are present in the *Speculum Mariae*. Konrad follows Richard of St Laurent in imputing a duple process of sanctification to Mary, in her own conception and in the incarnation, which bestowed on Mary the complete plenitude of all grace so that she became *superplena gratia*.[126] He states that Mary was illuminated by the light of wisdom and truth from the eternal sun,[127] and is the wisest of all, because God, who is the wisest of the wise, was with her ('Dominus tecum');[128] by the indwelling of God in her mind after the incarnation, she is the 'solium excelsum [. . .] in intellectu, elevatum in affectu; excelsum [. . .] super homines, elevatum super angelos'[129] ('the throne elevated in the intellect and raised up in the will (*affectus*); elevated above men, raised up above the angels'). Discussing Mary as 'plena [. . .] respersione odoriferae famae'[130] ('full with the besprinkling of fragrant renown'), he alludes to her perfection in action and in contemplation:

De isto odore [the 'suavissimus odor [. . .] spiritibus angelicis'] ipsa sancte gloriando dicere potest: 'Sicut cinnamomum et balsamum aromatizans odorem dedi, quasi myrrha electa dedi suavitatem odoris' [Eccl. 24: 20]. Odor Mariae fuit sicut cinnamomum exterius in cortice conversationis; sicut balsamum interius in unctione devotionis; sicut myrrha inferius in amaritudine castificationis. Fuit quoque odor Mariae sicut cinnamomum in actione, sicut balsamum in contemplatione, sicut myrrha in passione.[131]

(Of this aroma [the 'sweetest aroma of the angelic spirits'] she is able to say, boasting piously, 'I exuded a perfumed aroma like cinnamon and balsam; I exuded a sweetness of aroma like the chosen myrrh.' Mary's aroma was outwardly like cinnamon in the shell of her daily life; inwardly like balsam in the anointing of

---

[125] See Girotto, *Corrado di Sassonia*, pp. 109–11.
[126] See Konrad von Sachsen, *Speculum Mariae*, c. 7, prologue (266. 1–267. 16), and c. 11, §4 (385. 6 17). In virtue, Mary progresses from perfection to perfection throughout her life; see Girotto, *Corrado di Sassonia*, pp. 158–60.
[127] Ibid., c. 7, §1 (267. 17–271. 5); cf. c. 7, §8 (284. 10–286. 15).
[128] Ibid., c. 8, §1 (293. 17–295. 2).
[129] Ibid., c. 7, §5 (278. 5–280. 6; here 278. 15–17).
[130] Ibid., § 7 (282. 8–284. 9; here 282. 9–10).
[131] Ibid. (283. 4–14).

her devotion; and subsequently like myrrh in the bitterness of purification. Mary's aroma was also like cinnamon in her action, like balsam in her contemplation, and like myrrh in her suffering.)

The ascended Mary in heaven is the particular aid and *consolatrix* of the contemplative *perfectus*, shocked by the inaccessible clarity of the divine glory or the terrible severity of divine justice—a theme that Konrad sets out at length.[132]

We find only the slightest of hints as to the nature of Mary's contemplative experience in the *Speculum Mariae*. In the ninth section, Konrad discusses Mary's spiritual conception of Christ and begins by making a general point: without peace of mind (such as Mary had), speculative contemplation in the divine and the indwelling of God in the mind is not possible:

Dico quod primus locus, quo Maria Dominum suscepit spiritualiter, est mens Mariae pacificata et quieta, secundum quod in Psalmo dicitur: 'Factus est in pace locus eius et habitatio eius in Sion' [Ps. 75: 3], quod interpretatur «speculum» vel «speculatio». Ecce, quicumque Deum in mente sua habitare, quicumque Deum mente speculari desiderat[,] oportet[ ] ut ei in pace mentis locum faciat, nam sine pace mentis nemo venit ad speculationem contemplationis. Unde Apostolus ad Hebr. 12, 14: 'Pacem sequimini cum omnibus et sanctimoniam, sine qua nemo videbit Deum.'[133]

(I maintain that the first place in which Mary conceived the Lord spiritually was the mind of Mary at peace and at rest, in accordance with what is said in the psalm: 'His place was made in peace, and his dwelling in Sion', which means 'mirror' (*speculum*) or 'speculative contemplation' (*speculatio*). See, it is necessary that whoever desires God to dwell in his mind, or to contemplate God speculatively in the mind, should make a place for him in the peace of his mind, for without peace of the mind no one comes to speculative contemplation. Wherefore the Apostle said in his letter to the Hebrews 12: 14, 'Follow peace with everyone and with holiness, without which no one will see God.')

Turning back to Mary, Konrad states by way of a rhetorical question that the object of Mary's own speculative contemplation lies beyond the knowledge of man, with the divine mysteries having been made better known to her than to any other mortal:

---

[132] Ibid., c. 10, §1 (356. 5–358. 5); on the different synonyms Konrad uses for those at different stages in the contemplative life, which can make sections like this confusing to follow, see Girotto, *Corrado di Sassonia*, pp. 104–5.

[133] Konrad von Sachsen, *Speculum Mariae*, c. 9, §4 (337. 11–338. 6). The interpretation of 'Sion' as *speculum* or *speculatio* is (p. 337 n. 21) from Jerome's *Liber interpretationum hebraicorum nominum*.

O quis enarrare vel etiam cogitare sufficiat, in qualibet quotidie speculationibus
sancta illa Sion, sancta illa mens Mariae fuerit, dum omnia illa mysteria, prae
omnibus mortalibus sibi nota, ferventissima mente revolvit?[134]

(Who would be proficient to explain—or even to consider—any one of the states of
speculative contemplation in which that holy Sion, that holy mind of Mary was
daily, whilst she, with the most fervent mind, thought over all those mysteries that
had been made known to her before all other mortals?)

Only at one point does Konrad provide any further definition. In the sixth
section, he describes Mary, by way of the incarnation, as recipient of the
grace of truth. Through the gift of wisdom, this grace ordered Mary's soul
in truth, including 'above' her in the most joyful contemplation of the
delights of heaven. For these Konrad uses the key term *fruenda*; subsequently he refers to the ascended Mary being 'plena [...] fruitione laetitiae
aeternae'[135] ('full with the enjoyment of eternal delight'):

Gratia veritatis ordinavit Mariam in veritate supra se et infra se, intra se et extra se.
Gratia, inquam, veritatis ordinavit Mariam in veritate supra se per donum sapientiae; infra se per donum consilii; intra se per donum intellectus; extra se per donum
scientiae. Gratia utique veritatis ordinavit animam Mariae in veritate: supra se, in
sapidissima fruendorum contemplatione; infra se, in consultissima fugiendorum
provisione; intra se, in certissima credendorum cognitione; extra se, in rationabil-
issima agendorum discretione.[136]

(The grace of truth appointed Mary in truth above herself and below herself, within
herself and outwith herself. The grace of truth, I state, appointed Mary in truth
above herself through the gift of wisdom; below herself through the gift of counsel;
within herself through the gift of understanding; outwith herself through the gift of
knowledge. The grace of truth especially appointed Mary's soul in truth: above
itself, in the most delicious contemplation of those things that are to be enjoyed
(the *fruenda*); below itself, in the most well-considered foresight of those things that
are to be fled; within itself, in the most certain knowledge of those things that are to
be believed; outwith itself, in the most rational understanding of those things that
are to be done.)

Konrad's reticence represents a marked reluctance by comparison with
Richard of St Laurent, himself equivocatory, to present Mary as a contemplative who enjoyed an intrinsically unitive relationship—a mystical relationship—with God. This may represent a more generalized contemporary
Franciscan reluctance to assert this of Mary, for Konrad's near-exact con-

---

[134] Konrad von Sachsen, *Speculum Mariae*, c. 9, §4 (338. 7–11).
[135] Cf. ibid., c. 7, §9 (286. 17).
[136] Ibid., c. 6, §1 (240. 5–16); on Mary's receipt of the gifts of the Spirit see Girotto,
Corrado di Sassonia, pp. 160–2.

temporary Bonaventura (d. 1274: Konrad, as minister provincial of the Saxon province 1247–62 and 1272–9, must have known him personally) offers compatible theological assessments of the subject. We must turn first to his commentary on the Sentences, and then to his Marian sermons.[137]

Bonaventura is clear that Mary's comprehension of God was of a lesser quality than that of the heavenly host, specifically of Gabriel; it was not the direct beatific vision. In a passage discussing the order of events at the annunciation, he states:

[. . .] beata Virgo erat in statu viatricis, sed Angelus in statu comprehensoris; et ideo voluntatem Domini clarius pro illo tempore agnoscebat, quia Deum videbat Angelus 'facie ad faciem', beata Virgo 'per speculum in aenigmate' [cf. 1 Cor. 13: 12].[138]

(The blessed Virgin was in the position of one who journeys through this earthly life (a *viatrix*), but the angel was in the position of one who knows the heavenly life (a *comprehensor*), and therefore he recognized the Lord's will more clearly for that time—because the angel saw God 'face to face', and the blessed Virgin saw him 'through a glass (*speculum*) in a dark manner'.)

Yet earlier in the same discussion, he had introduced a statement that God, by grace, was closer to Mary's heart than to angels' minds:

Item, Deus vicinior erat beatae Virginis cordi per gratiam quam angelicae menti— unde Bernardus: «Virgo creditur exaltata super omnes ordines Angelorum»[139]

(God was nearer to the blessed Virgin's heart by grace than to the angel's mind; as Bernard says, 'The Virgin is believed to have been exalted above all the hierarchies of the angels')

He removes this objection with the assertion that this is true of election, but not of comprehension (of God):

Ad illud quod obiicitur, quod proximior erat Virgo Maria Deo quam Angelus; dicendum, quod verum est quantum ad gratiam electionis, sed non quantum ad gratiam comprehensionis.[140]

(To the objection that the Virgin Mary was closer to God than the angel was, it is to be said that this is true as far as the grace of being chosen is concerned, but not true in respect of the grace of [heavenly] understanding.)

---

[137] A conspectus of Bonaventura's writings on Mary is given by Beumer, 'Eine dem hl. Bonaventura . . .', p. 14 (repeated in Graef, *Mary*, pp. 281–8); see further Beumer, 'Die Predigten des heiligen Bonaventura', pp. 458–60.

[138] Bonaventura, *In III Sent.*, d. 2, dubia 4 (vol. 3, pp. 57a–58b; here p. 57b).

[139] Ibid. (vol. 3, p. 57a).

[140] Ibid. (vol. 3, p. 58a).

But Mary did have a closer knowledge of God—if not in the sense of an intrinsic or mystical relationship—that began with the incarnation. Like both Richard and Konrad before him, Bonaventura maintains a duple sanctification of Mary. With the incarnation came the extinction of concupiscence in Mary,[141] and through the conjunction of word with flesh Mary was assisted to the sight ('contuitus') of God. The context here is a discussion of 'et virtus altissimi obumbrabit tibi' ('and the power of the most high will overshadow you'; Lk. 1: 35), wherein Bonaventura asks why *obumbrare* and not *illuminare* is used, given that Christ is the 'candor lucis aeternae' ('the brightness of eternal light'; Wis. 7: 26):

'Virtus Altissimi' Virginem potius dicitur 'obumbrare' quam 'illuminare'. Obumbratio enim visum adiuvat et calorem refrigerat, et in adventu Filii Dei Virgo Maria refrigerata fuit fomitis exstinctione; fuit etiam ad Dei contuitum adiuta per carnis coniunctionem cum Verbo, ut quae non poterat Deum sentire in se propter suae lucis immensitatem, sentiret et cognosceret intra se per assumtam carnis humilitatem.[142]

('The power of the most high' is better said 'to overshadow' than 'to illuminate' the Virgin. For overshadowing aids sight and cools heat. In the coming of the Son of God the Virgin Mary was cooled in the extinction of sin, and she was also aided to behold God through the union of her flesh with the Word; so that she, who had been unable to perceive God in herself because of the immensity of his light, might perceive and discern him within herself through the humility of the flesh that he had assumed.)

Related references are further to be found in Bonaventura's sermons on Mary being inebriated with grace, filled with inner joy and exultation in the incarnation.[143]

A crucial passage is contained in a discussion on whether faith can coexist with the *visio sensibilis* of God. There are four propositions: the first on Thomas, the next two on the apostles collectively, and the fourth on Mary. Mary knew that she had conceived of the Spirit by sensible perception (not by revelation, or anything similar), but this did not diminish her faith—it helps to remember that faith is meant to be blind:

---

[141] See Bonaventura, *In III Sent.*, d. 3, p. 1, a. 2, q. 3 (vol. 3, pp. 76ᵃ–78ᵇ).

[142] Ibid., dubia 2 (vol. 3, p. 79ᵃ⁻ᵇ). Regarding why *obumbratio* aids the sight of God, Bonaventura is probably thinking of Moses on Mount Sinai, who went into a dense cloud to see God (Ex. 19: 9 and 16–20)—one of the two scriptural *loci classici* (along with Paul's rapture) of direct visions of God.

[143] See (e.g.) id., *Sermo 11 in vigilia nativitatis Domini* (vol. 9, pp. 97ᵇ–99ᵇ, at p. 98ᵇ); cf. *Sermo 3 de annuntiatione b. virginis Mariae* (vol. 9, pp. 667ᵃ–671ᵇ, at p. 669ᵇ).

Item, beata Virgo sensibili experimento novit, se concepisse de Spiritu sancto absque virili semine; sed constans est, quod propter conceptionem Filii Dei nihil demptum est fidei suae: ergo simul stabant in ea cognitio fidei et cognitio sensibilis experimenti.[144]

(The blessed Virgin knew by sensory experience that she had conceived of the Holy Spirit without the seed of man. But it is certain that nothing was taken away from her faith on account of her conception of the Son of God, and therefore the knowledge of her faith and the knowledge of her sensory experience were present in her at the same time.)

Bonaventura resolves the issue by stating that the vision of Christ's humanity must still be accompanied by faith (and so does not diminish faith), because his divinity—in which one must believe—is not made visible. This also applies to Mary, who knows that she has conceived without the seed of man by sensible experience, but knows that she has conceived the person of the word only by her faith:

Et sicut de Thoma dicitur, ita etiam de ceteris Apostolis et de beata Virgine, quae, quamvis certitudinali experientia sciverit, se concepisse sine virili semine; tamen se concepisse personam Verbi novit mediante fide.[145]

(And just as it is said of Thomas, so too of the other apostles and of the blessed Virgin—who, although she knew by certain experience that she had conceived without the seed of man, nevertheless knew by means of faith that she had conceived the person of the Word.)

Thus in order to have the necessary quality of faith, Mary cannot know directly that she bears the Son of God within her; all she knows from her sensory experience is that she has conceived without sexual intercourse. By implication, this rules out the direct transmission of the knowledge of Christ's divinity by divine inspiration, intrinsic connection of some kind, or mystical relationship with God (including the beatific vision). This might have diminished Mary's faith.[146] Moreover, Bonaventura states directly that Mary knew of Christ's divinity solely *mediante fide*. For the first time, we have a theological reason given that excludes—for this stage in her life, anyway—Mary enjoying a mystical relationship with God. This problem of faith should not be forgotten: it is of particular significance for

---

[144] Id., *In III Sent.*, d. 24, a. 2, q. 1 (vol. 3, pp. 517ª–519ᵇ, at pp. 517ᵇ–518ª).

[145] Ibid. (vol. 3, p. 518ᵇ).

[146] Corroboratively see further Chiettini, *Mariologia S. Bonaventurae*, pp. 159–61. Chiettini's problem in reconciling this position with the *Sermo 6 de assumptione Mariae* is not actually a problem at all, because this *sermo* (as noted below) is inauthentic.

the proposition of the opposite position to Bonaventura in another *summa Mariana*, the *Mariale* of the pseudo-Albert the Great, to which we shall turn shortly.

Bonaventura's sermons basically follow the line taken in his commentary on the Sentences. The older scholarship propounds the opposite on the basis of the *Sermo 6 de assumtione Mariae*; but Beumer has conclusively shown it to be inauthentic, and we shall refer to it subsequently at its correct chronological position.[147] In the authentic sermons, there are occasional, general references to Mary as a contemplative. Thus, for example, Mary practises virtue 'ut paratam viam [cf. Is. 62: 10] haberet ad continuam contemplationem et planam et mitem haberet conversationem'[148] ('so that she might have a ready path to continual contemplation and a gentle and well-balanced way of life'). In the now-traditional manner, she is the perfect exemplar of both active and contemplative lives, focused solely on the divine and full of divine light—'repleta luminibus deificis, circa divina tota intenta' ('filled with divine lights and attending wholly to the divine')—her perfection in action and contemplation the results of her perfect love.[149] Similarly, in another sermon the perfection of her thought is set out, with Mary thinking always of the heavenly: 'et Virgo semper supercaelestia cogitabat, secundum illud primae ad Corinthios septimo: "Mulier innupta et virgo cogitat quae Domini sunt, ut sit sancta corpore et spiritu" [1 Cor. 7: 34]'[150] ('and the Virgin always thought on the super-celestial beings, according to the statement in the seventh chapter of the first letter to the Corinthians: "The woman who is unmarried and a virgin thinks on the things of the Lord, so that she may be holy in body and spirit"'). In this same sermon, divine wisdom is said to have descended into Mary's mind—and into her body, in the incarnation—with Mary becoming a *speculum* of the divine radiance (reflecting Bonaventura's designation of her comprehension of God compared to that of angels in his Sentences commentary). The quotation from Bernard used in support here, whilst referring to Mary's penetration of divine mysteries, firmly excludes a unitive relationship with God:

[147] The inauthenticity of this text is established by Beumer, 'Eine dem hl. Bonaventura...'; and defended, over the confused objections of Kolping, 'Das Verhältnis', in Beumer, 'Die literarischen Beziehungen'.
[148] Bonaventura, *Sermo* 11 *de Dominica I. Adventus* (vol. 9, pp. 35ᵇ–36ᵇ, at p. 36ᵃ).
[149] Id., *Sermo* 1 *de purificatione b. virginis Mariae* (vol. 9, pp. 633ᵃ–640ᵇ, at p. 638ᵃ⁻ᵇ); cf. *Sermo* 3 *de purificatione b. virginis Mariae* (vol. 9, pp. 648ᵃ–649ᵇ, at pp. 648ᵇ–649ᵃ).
[150] Id., *Sermo* 5 *de assumtione b. virginis Mariae* (vol. 9, pp. 699ᵃ–700ᵇ, at p. 699ᵃ).

Candor autem sapientiae Virginis designatur in candore lucis; de qua, Sapientiae septimo: 'Candor est lucis aeternae et speculum sine macula Dei maiestatis' [Wis. 7: 26]; quia enim mens Virginis fuit sine macula, hinc est, quod fuit speculum idoneum ad recipiendum irradiationem divinam. Unde in tanta copia descendit in eam sapientia, ut non tantum inhabitaret in eius mente, immo et habitaculum formaret ex eius carne. [...] Unde Bernardus: «Beata Maria profundissimam divinae sapientiae, ultro quam credi valeat, penetravit abyssum, ut, quantum sine personali unione creaturae conditio patitur, illi luci inaccessibili videatur immersa».[151]

(The brightness of the Virgin's wisdom, furthermore, is represented in the brightness of light; of which it is said in the seventh chapter of the book of Wisdom that 'She is the brightness of eternal light, and the flawless mirror of God's majesty.' For because the Virgin's mind was flawless, it was consequently a fitting mirror to receive divine radiance. Wherefore wisdom descended in such abundance into her, that it not only dwelt in her mind, but rather formed a dwelling place from her flesh. Bernard writes on this: 'Blessed Mary penetrated the deepest abyss of divine wisdom, beyond what we may be able to believe, such that she seems to have been immersed in that inaccessible light—as far as this status is permitted to a created being without a personal union [to God].')

None of these references is particularly instructive, and simply reflects contemporary Marian phraseology rather than any deeper meaning.[152] Elsewhere, much of the interpretation of scriptural texts and other phrases that one would expect to concern contemplation is instead ethical—most surprisingly when Mary is said to be 'purgatrix, illuminatrix, et perfectrix'[153] ('she who purifies, illuminates, and perfects').

Only in one sermon is anything more pointed found; the *Sermo 5 de nativitate b. virginis Mariae*. Structured around a complex allegory of the ark of the covenant, Mary is said to have had a plenitude of wisdom (signified by the two cherubim of Exodus 25: 18). A different version of the same Bernard quotation that we have just seen is deployed, which excludes a unitive relationship much less strictly, and Mary is said to have indeed known secrets of the divine wisdom:

Quarto fuit arca testamenti, quia desuper continens Cherubim per plenitudinem sapientiae; secundi Paralipomenon quinto: 'Cherubim expandebant alas suas super locum, in quo posita erat arca' [2 Chr. 5: 8]. Cherubim interpretatur plenitudo scientiae, quae super arcam erant, quia Maria Virgo hac sapientia fuit plena,

---

[151] Ibid. (vol. 9, p. 699[b]).

[152] Beumer takes the same opinion; see 'Eine dem hl. Bonaventura . . .', pp. 18–19.

[153] See Bonaventura, *Sermo 1 de purificatione b.virginis Mariae* (vol. 9, pp. 635[b]–636[b]); similarly *Sermo 26 in nativitate Domini* (vol. 9, pp. 124[b]–126[a]), with an ethical interpretation of Mary understood as the tabernacle in which God dwells.

secundum quod dicit Bernardus: «Maria profundissimam divinae sapientiae penetravit abyssum, ut, quantum de creatura credi fas est, illi luci inaccessibili videatur
immersa». Et quia arcana et secreta divinae sapientiae in se continebat, merito
dicitur et est arca testamenti, quia in se continuit carnem Christi, in quo 'sunt
omnes thesauri sapientiae et scientiae absconditi' [Col. 2: 3].[154]

(The fourth was the ark of the covenant, because it holds cherubim from above
through the plenitude of wisdom—as in the fifth chapter of the second book of
Chronicles, 'the cherubim spread out his wings over the place in which the ark was
located'. The cherubim that had been above the ark is interpreted to mean 'the
plenitude of knowledge', because the Virgin Mary was full with this wisdom,
according to what Bernard says: 'Mary penetrated the deepest abyss of divine
wisdom such that she seemed immersed in that inaccessible light, as far as it is
licit to be believed of a created being.' And because she held the mysteries and secrets
of divine wisdom in herself, it is justly said that she is the ark of the covenant,
because she held the flesh of Christ in her, in whom 'were hidden all the treasures of
wisdom and knowledge'.)

On the one hand, this phrase 'arcana et secreta divinae sapientiae' ('the
mysteries and secrets of divine wisdom') may simply be a synonym for
Christ, being carried in Mary's womb. But it is strongly reminiscent of
Richard of St Laurent's statement, seen earlier, of the revelation of 'incerta
et occulta sapientiae [divinae]' ('uncertain and concealed aspects of divine
wisdom') to Mary through Christ's presence within her. In fact, Beumer
has indicated further parallels to the *De laudibus* in this sermon: added to
the transmission of this text in just one manuscript (Munich, Bayerische
Staatsbibliothek, Clm 7776, fols. 209[v]ff.) without ascription to Bonaventura, he regards it as probably inauthentic, and our brief examination here
adds weight to that conclusion.[155]

Notwithstanding Bonaventura's objections, it is clear that exactly this
kind of idea was being popularized in the thirteenth-century lives of Mary
(though not, it should be said, in the *Legenda aurea*). The *Vita rhythmica*
refers to Mary as a child in the temple contemplating the secrets of heaven
and delighting in joy—'[s]ecretaque celestia vel contemplabatur, | [v]el in
iubilatione deliciabatur'[156] ('and she either contemplated the heavenly
secrets, or delighted in jubilation'). It uses a similar phrase, this time
referring to Mary's spirit being carried upwards in jubilation, on her
contemplation after Christ's ascension: '[s]ecretaque celestia vel contem-
plabatur, | [v]el spiritus in iubilo sursum ferebatur'[157] ('and she either

[154] Id., *Sermo 5 de nativitate b. virginis Mariae* (vol. 9, pp. 715[a]–719[a], at p. 717[b]).
[155] See Beumer, 'Die Predigten des heiligen Bonaventura', p. 455.
[156] *Vita rhythmica*, vv. 825–6.
[157] Ibid., vv. 6604–5.

contemplated the heavenly secrets, or her spirit was carried upwards in
joy'); and repeats this in the *regula Mariae*, to describe Mary's contemplation after compline:

> Postea dulciflue se devotioni
> Dedit et celestium contemplationi,
> Secretaque celestia corde meditando,
> Ac elevato spiritu iocunde iubilando.[158]

(Afterwards she gave herself over sweetly to devotion and to contemplation of the
heavenly beings by meditating in her heart on the heavenly secrets, and by rejoicing
delightfully with her spirit raised up.)

Likewise the *Speculum humanae salvationis*, though a much later work,
states (by way of a strange typological association with the hanging gardens
of Babylon seen by Nebuchadnezzar's wife) that Mary ascended to contemplate the heavenly fatherland in her childhood contemplation: 'patriam
coelestem semper contemplari nitebatur'[159] ('she ascended always to contemplate the heavenly kingdom'). Considering the circumstances of Mary's
pregnancy, Joseph subsequently asserts that Mary '[t]antummodo in rebus
divinis et coelestibus delectabatur'[160] ('only took delight in divine and
heavenly things').

   This, however, is a minor aside; we must now turn to another *summa
Mariana*, perhaps the central work for the issues that we are looking at here:
the *Mariale*, or *Laus virginis*, by the pseudo-Albert the Great. The inauthenticity of this text was not established until the 1950s,[161] Albert's
purported authorship having given the work a theological authority that
had endured into the twentieth century. Adolf Kolping's textual and
codicological analysis established that the *Mariale* is a later thirteenth-
century work that drew on Richard of St Laurent's *De laudibus*. It originated in Austria or Bavaria, probably in a Cistercian or Benedictine
convent, though with a strong Dominican influence upon its author.
Very soon (before 1300) the work was available in Cologne and in Paris;
these later, 'western' manuscripts bear the attribution to *frater* Albert,
suggesting that the ascription to Albert the Great was of Dominican
origin.[162] Though indebted to the exegetical tradition through Richard's *De
laudibus*, the *Mariale* is a very different work. It is an enormous series

[158] Ibid., vv. 6684–7; cf. vv. 6738–41.
[159] *Speculum humanae salvationis*, c. 5, 54–64 (vol. 1, p. 13), here v. 60; cf. vv. 95–6: Mary's
eyes were always downcast, but her heart was borne upwards in heaven.
[160] Ibid., c. 7, 22 (vol. 1, p. 16).
[161] For a summary of the debate, see Graef, *Mary*, pp. 270–1.
[162] See Kolping, 'Zur Frage der Textgeschichte', pp. 288–318.

of *quaestiones* which establish, in formal scholastic manner and on a principally philosophical-theological basis, the different prerogatives and attributes
of Mary.[163] Concerning Mary's contemplation, its position is genuinely
radical and highly influential.

The *Mariale* collects together *quaestiones* 44–61 and provides the *responsiones* to all of them in one block thereafter. In between, we are
presented with an excursus on contemplation that forms a prolegomenon
to the *responsiones*.[164] Much of this excursus is a compendium of different
schemes set out by earlier intellectuals on the contemplative ascent. Towards the end, the author considers the different ways of categorizing the
different levels reached by souls ascending towards God. The third way is
according to the state of the subject being elevated—'secundum diversitatem status subjecti quod elevatur, et diversitatem medii per quod elevatur'[165] ('according to the different states of the subject that is raised up, and
the different ways by which it is raised up'). There are four such evident
states: 'alii sunt statu viae, alii praeter statum viae, alii supra statum viae et
juxta statum patriae, alii in statu patriae'[166] ('some are in the state of the
journey [i.e. through this life to God]; others are beyond the state of
the journey; some are above the state of the journey and near to the state
of the heavenly kingdom; others are in the state of the heavenly kingdom').
The fourth and last of these, obviously, are the saints and angels in heaven.
But the first, those 'in statu viae' ('in the state of the journey through this
life'), are those who see 'per speculum in aenigmate' ('through a mirror,
darkly'). This is how Bonaventura classifies Mary's comprehension of God,
and indeed amongst those listed in the *Mariale* who know God in this way,
we find 'by faith':

Illi qui elevantur per modum viae, vident 'per speculum in aenigmate' [1 Cor. 13:
12], et faciunt quinque gradus. Primus gradus est videre per vestigium in creaturis.
Secundus, per imaginem in anima. Tertius, fide informi. Quartus, fide formata.
Quintus est gradus contemplantium.[167]

---

[163] Brief overviews of the principal interests of the *Mariale* are given by Graef, *Mary*,
pp. 271–3; and Beissel, *Geschichte der Verehrung*, pp. 217–20. A good example of how
the *Mariale* operates on an individual issue is given by Schreiner, 'Marienverehrung',
pp. 338–9, concerning what Mary was doing when Gabriel appeared at the annunciation
(she was contemplating: see ps.-Albert, *Mariale*, q. 12 (pp. 29–31)).

[164] ps.-Albert, *Mariale, praemittenda* to qq. 44–61 (pp. 104^b–111^a).

[165] Ibid., §5 (pp. 109^b–111^a).

[166] Ibid. (p. 110^a).

[167] Ibid.

(Those who are raised up by way of the journey through this life see 'through a glass, in a dark manner', and achieve five degrees. The first degree is to see by traces in created things. The second, by an image in the soul; the third, by unformed faith; the fourth, by formed faith; and the fifth is the degree of the contemplatives.)

Had Bonaventura been writing, this is where we would find Mary. But we do not; nor do we find Mary amongst the second group, those who are 'praeter statum viae' ('beyond the state of the journey'), and who see 'per speculum in lumine' ('through a glass, in a clear manner')—this includes the visions of prophets, of Moses (in Ex. 33: 11), and so on. The third group, the last before saints in heaven, are those who see 'supra modum viae' ('above the way of the journey'); they have a direct vision of God, 'sine speculo in lumine' ('without a mirror, in a clear manner'), and are sub-divided into three ascending categories. The first is Adam in ecstatic sleep; the second, *raptus*, such as that experienced by Paul or by John in the Apocalypse; and the third is Mary's contemplation of God in her earthly existence. Her perfect purity, unquantifiable plenitude of grace, and unsur-passed love from God combined to provide Mary with the highest possible mystical contemplation of God in this life ever achieved:

Tertius gradus est in via cognitio beatae Virginis, quae omnes praedictas cognitiones tribus gradibus supergreditur. Primus est elevata puritas, qua excellit omnem viatorem. Secundus est medii improportionabilis quantitas, videlicet gratiae pleni-tudo, quae in ea tanta fuit, quod in pura creatura aequalis esse non potuit. Tertius est elevantis charitas, scilicet Dei, qui eam super omnem creaturam dilexit, et improportionabili charitate eam sibi sociavit: et ideo haec visio ejus super omnem visionem viae fuit propinquissima visioni patriae, et tamen citra quantum ad actum.[168]

(The third degree is the blessed Virgin's form of cognition in her journey through this life, which surpasses all the aforesaid forms of cognition by three degrees. The first is the uplifted purity in which she exceeds everyone else who passes through this life. The second is the disproportionate quantity of the means, namely the plenitude of grace that was in her to an extent that cannot be equalled in a pure created being. The third is the love of the one who raises her up, namely God, who loved her above all other created beings, and by disproportionate love united her to him. Thus her manner of sight was above every other manner of sight of the journey through this life, and the closest of all to the manner of sight of the heavenly kingdom—but still short of it as far as the act is concerned in itself.)

In a subsequent *quaestio*, concerning the manner in which the gift of understanding was given to Mary, this position is further refined. Between the living ('viatores') and the dead in heaven ('comprehensores'), a middle category is created of the living who see 'in lumine creato sine imagine'[169] ('in created light, but without images'). Mary is the sole occupant of this middle category; her *lumen creatum*—possibly a synonym for the *intellectus agens*[170]—is a means for the unification of the seeing to the seen, of Mary's mind to God:

> Sed cognitio media pertinet ad statum medium: status autem medius pertinet ad beatissimam Virginem: ergo cognitio beatissimae Virginis erit talis, quod cognoscet lumen increatum, non quidem per speciem et imaginem, sed per lumen creatum. Et sic cognoscit increatum per creatum, et illud lumen non erit medium sicut speculum et vestigium vel imago, vel sicut signum est medium inter apprehensivum et signatum, sed sicut lumen solis est medium conjungens visibile ad visum.[171]

(But the middle form of cognition pertains to the middle state, and the middle state pertains to the most blessed Virgin. Therefore the most blessed Virgin's form of cognition was such that she will perceive the uncreated light not, in fact, by forms and images, but by created light. In this way she perceives the uncreated through the created; and that light was neither a medium like a mirror, a trace, or an image; nor as a sign is a medium between the apprehending individual and the signified; but as the light of the sun is a medium that binds the visible object to sight.)

The author confirms in the *responsio* to this group of *quaestiones* on the gifts of the Spirit that Mary received them all in this middle state, and defines the nature of Mary's reception of the gifts more precisely with regard to the *status viae et patriae*.[172]

It is not without significance that the prolegomena to the *responsiones* for qq. 44–61 are primarily directed towards the solution of *quaestio* 44: whether Mary had faith. That she must have had faith, of course, was Bonaventura's reason for denying Mary any higher intrinsic or mystical relationship with God. *Quaestio* 44 contains nothing other than eleven oppositions to the notion of Mary having had faith, on the principal grounds that her cognition of the divine was the greatest possible, and so exceeded the way of faith. The author uses different methods to build his sequence of oppositions. The third, for example, relies on a process of logical extension:

---

[169] ps.-Albert, *Mariale*, q. 64 (pp. 120ᵃ–121ᵇ; here p. 120ᵃ⁻ᵇ).
[170] See Kolping, 'Zur Frage der Textgeschichte', p. 286 n. 13.
[171] ps.-Albert, *Mariale*, q. 64 (p. 121ᵇ).
[172] Ibid., *responsiones* to qq. 62–9 (pp. 125ᵇ–126ᵇ, esp. pp. 125ᵇ–126ᵃ).

Munditia cordis est ad videndum Deum dispositio, juxta illud: 'Beati mundo corde' etc. [Matt. 5: 8]. Ergo ubi major munditia, ibi major visio: sed nulla umquam creatura habuit tantam munditiam, quantam illa quae ea puritate nitebat qua sub Deo nulla major nequit intelligi: ergo numquam aliqua creatura habuit tam altam cognitionem: ergo ejus cognitio fuit supra raptum: ergo supra fidem. Quod enim superius est superiore, superius est inferiore.[173]

(Cleanliness of the heart is the proper disposition to see God, as per the statement: 'Blessed are the clean in heart', and so forth. Thus where there is greater cleanliness, there is greater sight. But no created being has ever had such cleanliness as she who shone in her purity so great that no greater can be understood below God himself. Thus no other created being has had such a lofty form of cognition; thus her form of cognition was above rapture; thus it was above faith. For what is higher than the higher, is higher than the lower.)

By contrast the ninth draws on the exegetical tradition, establishing Mary's totality of wisdom not merely by the interpretation of individual sapiential quotations, but by the Marian interpretation of the entire biblical book:

Quod beatissima Virgo fuit sapientior omni creatura, signatur per hoc quod liber qui intitulatur de Sapientia, de beatissima Virgine specialiter exponitur: et quae de sapientia Domini dicuntur, quasi de ipsa dicuntur, Ecclesia interpretatur, ut patet in epistolis quae de ipsa leguntur: in sapientia autem nihil est de stultitia vel ignorantia: ergo beatissima Virgo plena fuit sapientia: sed in fide non est plena sapientia, sed ex parte, juxta illud: 'Ex parte cognoscimus, ex parte prophetamus' [1 Cor. 13: 9]: ergo beatissima Virgo non habuit fidem, sed plenam cognitionem.[174]

(That the most blessed Virgin was more wise than all other created beings is indicated by this; namely, that the book which is entitled 'Wisdom' is expounded specifically of the most blessed Virgin. The church interprets what is said of the Lord's wisdom as if it is said of her, as is evident in the epistles which are read of her. In wisdom, moreover, there is no stupidity or ignorance, and therefore the most blessed Virgin was full of wisdom. But in faith, wisdom is not complete, but only partial, as per the statement: 'In part we know; in part we prophesy'. Therefore the most blessed Virgin did not have faith, but complete knowledge.)

In the *responsio* to *quaestio* 44, the author states that Mary enjoyed this highest of all contemplation from the incarnation to her assumption, and continually so ('semper et continuo', 'always and continuously'). Her mystical experience was illuminative, comparable to the transfiguration of Christ, and not effected through abstraction of the mind, removal from her senses ('stupor', like Paul), ecstasy, or sleep (like Peter). Mary's intellect was deified—made *deiformis*—proportional to the unbounded influx of light.

---

[173] Ibid., q. 44 (pp. 87ª–89ᵇ, here p. 88ª).
[174] Ibid. (p. 89ª).

This implies, logically, the total deification of the mind.[175] The reconcilia-tion of the problem of faith is introduced almost as an afterthought, and is not very convincing. It amounts to little more than a concession that Mary did have faith, followed by a statement that there is always some obscurity for an individual with this *habitus fidei*; he cannot be purified (and deified) to the same extent as the saints in heaven:

Concedimus igitur, quod in beatissima Virgine fuit habitus fidei. Et possunt duo habitus esse simul: unus ad minus perfectum actum, alter ad magis perfectum: sicut et actus qui est in raptu, potest esse cum habitu fidei, sed non e converso fidei actus cum habitu raptus. Unde quamdiu est in potentia habitus fidei, tamdiu est aliquid de obscuritate, et non ita plene depurata sicut in statu comp[re]hensorum, est tamen illi depurationi simillima quae est in patria quando potentia omnino erit deiformis.[176]

(We concede, therefore, that the habit of faith was in the most blessed Virgin. Two habits are able to coexist: one pertaining to the less perfect act, and the other to the more perfect one. And so the act which is in rapture can exist with the habit of faith, but the act of faith cannot, on the contrary, exist with the habit of rapture. Thus as long as the habit of faith is in the mental powers, so there are things which are unknown, and which are not made so evidently clear as in the state of those who know the heavenly life (*comprehensores*). Nevertheless, when the mental powers have been wholly deified, there is something most similar to that clarification which is in the heavenly kingdom.)

This concession does not count for very much. It does not prevent the author from maintaining later that Mary had a perfect cognition of every-thing, including the divine, using similar reasoning to that which we have seen here and explored at length.[177] Basically, the *Mariale* author ignores the problem of faith that had been quite so significant for Bonaventura, which laid the way open for such claims to be made of Mary's mystical contemplation and knowledge of God. The authority that the subsequent attribution to Albert the Great gave to this work should not be understated, as subsequent to the *Mariale* we find none of the reticence that character-ized the earlier works.

This influence is nowhere more striking than in the Marian sermons of the Franciscan cardinal Matthew of Aquasparta (d. 1302). Matthew had stud-ied under Bonaventura and himself held the office of minister general (1287–9); he taught in Paris, Bologna, and Rome, and is an intellectual

---

[175] ps.-Albert, *Mariale, responsio* to q. 44 (pp. 111[b]–112[a]).
[176] Ibid. (p. 112[a]).
[177] See ibid., q. 111 (pp. 166[a]–168[b]).

of great importance for the philosophical theology of the later thirteenth century, specifically with regard to the issue of cognition.[178] His commentaries on the Sentences, which would add much to our understanding of Matthew's contribution to our present concerns, remain unedited. Matthew is often considered to be Bonaventura's greatest heir, and indeed certain of his Marian sermons are clearly indebted to their Bonaventuran counterparts on the issue of Mary's contemplation. *Sermo 6 de assumptione b. v. Mariae*, for example, presents Mary in the now-traditional manner as the perfect exemplar of both active and contemplative lives. This is followed by a triple interpretation of the name 'Maria', then mapped on to the categories of the 'triplex via', so that Mary is understood as having been 'purgatrix, illuminatrix, et perfectrix' ('she who purifies, illuminates, and perfects'), which is then interpreted ethically.[179] Even a brief comparison reveals all of this to be directly dependent on Bonaventura's *Sermo 1 de purificatione b. virginis Mariae*, mentioned earlier.[180] Yet we find here a tantalizing mention of Mary as 'lumine sapientiae repleta'[181] ('filled with the light of wisdom'), which is certainly not in Bonaventura's text.

It is equally clear that Matthew's Marian sermons are also very early witnesses to the influence of the *Mariale*. The justification of the Marian interpretation of the entire biblical book of Wisdom, which we saw in the *Mariale*, is adopted and expanded by Matthew in his *Sermo 2 de nativitate b. v. Mariae*, allowing him to describe Mary as 'mater sapientiae' ('mother of wisdom')—an appellation that is elevated into the status of a mariological principle.[182] More significant is the *Sermo 1 de nativitate b. v. Mariae*, in which Matthew considers the seven gifts bestowed on Mary at the incarnation (Matthew, like Bonaventura, holds a duple purification for Mary).[183] In discussing *caritas*, Matthew's use of the *Mariale* is clear. Mary is wholly united to and transformed into God, by her love reaching 'ad intima

<hr>

[178] See the comprehensive bibliography on the Franciscan Authors' Website, at <http://users.bart.nl/~roestb/franciscan/franautm.htm#_Toc409561361> [accessed 17 July 2008].
[179] Matthew of Aquasparta, *Sermo 6 de assumptione b. v. Mariae* (pp. 252–75). Mary is again the exemplar of both lives in the *Sermo 2 de nativitate b. v. Mariae* (pp. 20–34), at 22. 6–23. 13; see Simoncioli, 'La mariologia del Card. Matteo', pp. 328 and 351.
[180] See Bonaventura, *Sermo 1 de purificatione b. virginis Mariae* (vol. 9, pp. 633ᵃ–640ᵇ).
[181] Matthew of Aquasparta, *Sermo 6 de assumptione b. v. Mariae*, 266. 15–16.
[182] See id., *Sermo 2 de nativitate b. v. Mariae*, 20. 3–21. 3.
[183] On the principle of divine maternity underpinning Mary's prerogatives, see Simoncioli, 'La mariologia del Card. Matteo', pp. 327–8; on the resultant beatific vision, see p. 335. Beumer, 'Die literarischen Beziehungen', p. 460 n. 24, had also noticed that Matthew presents Mary enjoying the beatific vision in this life.

divinitatis' ('to the innermost of his divinity'), and can be described with
the verb *frui*; her cognition of the divine exceeds—following the schema of
the *Mariale*—the rapture of Paul. Two adjustments are of particular
significance for understanding Matthew's position. First, the emphasis on
the caritative impulse as the motor of Mary's mystical ascent into union
with God, an idea present in the *Mariale* but given a new priority by
Matthew that reflects his strict voluntarism elsewhere.[184] Second, the use of
pseudo-Dionysius to understand the mechanics of the mystical union:

[Caritas] est enim forma et perfectio omnium virtutum, omnes complens, omnes in
finem movens, dirigens et perducens; et ideo sine hac omnes informes sunt et cassae,
iuxta quod dicit Apostolus, I Cor 13, 1–3: 'Si linguis hominum loquar et angelorum', et cetera quae enumerat, 'caritatem autem non habeam, nihil mihi prodest,
nihil sum.' Maria autem ardentissima caritate et perfectissime ac simplicissimo
amore consummata, omnino Deo unita, Dei mater effecta, tota in Deum transfor-
mata et ultra omnes creaturas filio assimilata, omnino transivit in Deum. Hic enim
amor mobile habet fervidum et acutum,[185] penetrans usque ad intima divinitatis;
«est enim vita copulans amantem cum amato» secundum Augustinum; est et «virtus
unitiva» secundum Dionysium;[186] et «transformat amantem in amatum», secundum Hugonem, *De arrha sponsae*. Et ideo, licet scriptum non sit, tamen sicut
Paulus, immo amplius quam Paulus, isto amore exstatico a se deficiens, in Deum
transiens, rapiebatur in Deum, ipsum 'facie ad faciem' [1 Cor. 13: 12] contemplans,
ipsoque fruens.[187]

(For charity is the form and the perfection of every virtue, crowning them all,
moving, directing and leading them all to their end. Without it thus they are all
formless and useless, as the Apostle says in the first letter to the Corinthians 13: 1–3,
'If I should speak in the tongues of men and of angels', and the other things which
he enumerates, 'and would not have charity, it is all useless to me, and I am
nothing'. Mary, however, who was perfected with the most ardent charity and the
most perfect and most sincere love, wholly united to God, made mother of God,
wholly transformed into God and assimilated to the Son above all other created
beings, passed over entirely into God. For here love has a burning and acute motion,
penetrating to the innermost of the divinity; 'for it is a life binding the lover with the
beloved', according to Augustine; it is 'a unitive power', according to Dionysius,
and 'transforms the lover into the beloved', according to Hugh [of St Victor] in *De
arrha animae*. And therefore, although it is not written, nevertheless just like Paul—

---

[184] See Trottmann, 'La Vision béatifique', pp. 135-7; see more widely pp. 122–42 on
Matthew's understanding of the beatific vision, without mention of the Marian sermons
(or of Mary).

[185] cf. ps.-Dionysius, *De caelestia hierarchia*, c. 7, §63 (vol. 2, p. 838).

[186] cf. id., *De divinis nominibus*, c. 4, §19 (vol. 1, p. 225).

[187] Matthew of Aquasparta, *Sermo* 1 *de nativitate b. v. Mariae* (pp. 1–19), at 16.
5–17. 10.

nay, rather more than Paul—she, abandoning herself in this ecstatic love and passing over into God, was enraptured into God, contemplating him 'face to face' and delighting in him.)

This conception is further found in additional sermons. In the *Sermo* 1 *de annuntiatione b. v. Mariae*, Mary's elevation in continual mystical contemplation and deification by love is designated as the tenth of Mary's twelve prerogative virtues.[188] Matthew explains how Mary's mystical experience was unconstrained because of her total purification,[189] before setting out once again the mechanics of her mystical union. A crucial aspect to this, expressed in more detail than in the *Sermo* 1 *de nativitate b. v. Mariae*, is the loss of the self through the ecstatic love that deifies Mary. Loss of the self in mystical union is a characteristic feature of negative theology, evidently transmitted here through pseudo-Dionysius, and which points towards the German mystics of the coming generation:

Denique per exstaticum amorem a semetipsa deficientem, totam super dilectum innixam et prae amoris dulcedine se sustinere non valentem et sic ascendentem, ideo sancti angeli admirantur ipsam, Cant. 8, 5: 'Quae est ista quae ascendit de deserto, deliciis affluens, innixa super dilectum suum?'[190]

(Finally she abandons herself through the ecstatic love, and, leant entirely upon her beloved, she is incapable of sustaining herself because of the sweetness of the love. Thus she ascends, wherefore the holy angels admire her, as in the Song of Songs 8: 5: 'Who is this who ascends out of the desert, abounding with delights, leant upon her beloved?')

Immediately after this, Matthew uses a vocative exhortation to the reader to imitate Mary directly along the 'triplex via' into mystical union with God—an important signal that these considerations on the nature of Mary's contemplation were not merely academic speculations, but changed the nature of the Marian model presented for contemporary imitation.

But Bonaventura's inheritance was not so lightly rejected by all. Surprisingly it is Ubertino da Casale who represents a retrograde step over Matthew in the development of the tradition. We have encountered Ubertino's *Arbor vitae crucifixae*, written in 1305, in an earlier chapter, and should note here that Ubertino did in fact draw on several Bonaventuran works in its composition: notably the *Lignum vitae*, the *Brevilo-*

---

[188] Id., *Sermo* 1 *de annuntiatione b. v. Mariae* (pp. 48–75), at 69. 16–70. 1.

[189] Ibid., 70. 9–18; see likewise *Sermo* 1 *de assumptione b. v. Mariae* (pp. 146–86), 159. 1–10; 162. 18–22; and culminating in Mary's knowledge of all things, 169. 8–170. 5.

[190] Id., *Sermo* 1 *de annuntiatione b. v. Mariae*, 70. 23–71. 4.

quium, the *Apologia pauperum,* and the *Legenda maior s. Francisci.*[191]
Ubertino is typically forthright on the issues with which we are concerned,
and he first addresses the subject whilst describing the annunciation. He
comments on how it was most suitable ('conueniens') that the annunciation should be performed by an angel. His first reason is that Mary's mind
would be elevated into God on account of such a messenger, inflamed with
fervent love, and conceive Christ spiritually before the corporeal conception. To this Ubertino adduces the Augustinian dicta on Mary's spiritual
birth that every medieval writer knew. With this emphasis on the caritative
impulse and on Mary's mental elevation into God ('ut [. . .] eleuaretur
mens eius in deum'; 'so that her mind might be raised up into God'), he
goes beyond their import to suggest a closer cognitive relationship between
Mary and God.[192]

Subsequently Ubertino discusses the words of the angelic salutation,
establishing thereby in the conventional manner a duple purification of
Mary. Turning to 'Spiritus Sanctus superveniet in te, et virtus Altissimi
obumbrabit tibi' ('the Holy Spirit will come upon you, and the power of
the most high will overshadow you'; Lk. 1: 35), he looks at the implications
for Mary's cognition of God. By the total purification and descent of the
divine light, Mary's cognition of God reaches such a level that all other
cognition is but a shadow of it. But knowledge of this cognition is
shadowed from us, says Ubertino, a mystery comparable to the virgin
birth itself. From this he proceeds to a thorough excoriation of all those
who seek to define Mary's mental perfection:

[. . .] et ipsi uirgini nota quod etiam aliter dicat: 'Tu habebis plenitudinem
diuinitatis corporaliter in te', cui omnis alia cognitio comparata potest merito
umbra dici. In hoc etiam uerbo ostendit, quod spiritus sanctus umbram refrigerantis
concupiscentie et totalis eradicationis fomitis fecit purissime uirgini. In hoc etiam
ostendit, quod ineffabile lumen diuinitatis quasi umbram sibi condescendit, et se
capabile pro modo uirginis tribuit. In hoc etiam ostendit, quod ad tantam nobili-
tatem matrem uirginem substulit, quod nulla creatura plene et comprehendere et
cogita[r]e sufficit, sicut illud quod est obumbratum et aliis occ[ul]tum. Dicitur
autem obumbratum incertum, quia non solum uirginis fecunditas propter suam
incomprehensibilitatem obumbratur a nobis; sed ipsa uirgo in omni sua uirtute
circumquaque nobis est incomprehensibilis et inexpressibilis, quia in isto actu
omnes uirtutes fuerunt ad tantam perfectionem adducte, quod omnibus aliis sunt

[191] See Knoth, *Ubertino von Casale,* pp. 14–19, with an overview of the *Arbor vitae*
pp. 9–14; a conspectus of the central Marian portions is provided by Damiata, *Pietà
e storia,* pp. 66–9.
[192] See Ubertino da Casale, *Arbor vitae crucifixae,* lib. 1, c. 7 (22^b–26^a, at p. 23^b).

incognite; et ideo obumbrate. Propter quod sunt bene fatui, qui perfectiones mentis uirginis et ineffabiles status sibi datos ex tunc uolunt secundum suam miserabilem mensuram taxare; et quibusdam friuolis et stultissimis cauillare rationibus.[193]

(Note that in another way he also says to the Virgin, 'You will have a plenitude of divinity bodily in you', compared with which every other form of cognition can justly be called a shadow. In this speech he also made it known that the Holy Spirit created a shadow to cool concupiscence and to eradicate all sin for the most pure Virgin. In this he also made it known that the ineffable light of divinity descended from heaven like a shadow, and gave itself tangibly by means of the Virgin. In this he also made known that he raised the Virgin mother up to a nobility so great that no created being is capable of understanding and comprehending it fully, as that which was overshadowed and so hidden to others. 'Overshadowed', however, is also called 'uncertainty', because it is not just the Virgin's fertility that is overshadowed [i.e. hidden] from us because of its incomprehensibility, but the Virgin herself in every one of her virtues is everywhere incomprehensible and inexpressible to us, because in that act [i.e. the incarnation] all her virtues had been drawn up to a perfection so great that they were unknown to anyone else, and therefore 'over-shadowed'. Because of this, those individuals are extremely foolish who want to estimate the perfections of the Virgin's mind and the ineffable states given to her from that point onwards in accordance with their miserable capacities, and to put forward their silly cases with certain frivolous and most stupid reasons.)

This is not the end of Ubertino's disquisition on Mary's interior relationship to God. The following chapter of the *Arbor vitae* considers four soteriological aspects of the incarnation, and within this—as indeed Graef noted[194]—Ubertino states that Mary's infusion with virtue at the incarnation was the most complete possible for a person in this life without (crucially) personal union with God:

[. . .] et tanta uirtutum omnium consumatio fuerit beatissime uirgini matri Dei in illo concepto data, quanta potest recipere uiatrix creatura sine unione personali.[195]

(and as great a consummation of every virtue was given to the most blessed Virgin and mother of God in that conception as a created being who journeys through this life can receive without personal union [with God].)

Mary, continues Ubertino, had the most consummate perfection in all things, active and contemplative. After the incarnation, her mind was held in a stable, elevated position of contemplation, superior to that of any other

[193] Ibid. (p. 25ᵃ⁻ᵇ).
[194] Graef, *Mary*, p. 293; on Ubertino more generally see pp. 292–4.
[195] Ubertino da Casale, *Arbor vitae crucifixae*, lib. 1, c. 8 (pp. 26ᵃ–33ᵇ, at p. 31ᵇ).

person—but, again crucially, stopping short of the beatific vision. Ubertino sails rather close to the wind in the light of his vituperative comments in the previous chapter:

Opinor autem pie erigendo mentem ad uirginis matris excellentiam, quod ex tunc mens eius taliter fuit stabilita, quod sine aliqua interruptione fuerit summe in contemplationis actu et gustu; et hoc supra omnem modum alterius creature, citra tamen beatificam uisionem.[196]

(I am of the opinion, however, by raising up my mind piously to the excellence of the Virgin mother, that from that point onwards her mind was made steadfast to such a degree that she was in the highest contemplation in act and taste without any interruption; and this more loftily above every other way of created beings, but still short of the beatific vision.)

Taking up a standard theme, he explains that Mary's total purification at the incarnation, and her 'plenissimus habitus sapientie' ('most abundant habit of wisdom') infused thereupon by the Spirit, meant that no external impulses from her senses, nor exterior activity, impeded her contemplation.[197] Even sleep, which Ubertino reckons as a consequence of original sin, did not impede her contemplation, described now as the soul's inclination into God ('anima sua [. . .] tendebat in deum'; 'her soul inclined into God').[198]

In considering Mary's superiority over the *primi parentes* before the Fall on account of her divine maternity, Ubertino establishes a transfer mechanism by which aspects of Christ, such as (in this example) the plenitude of grace within him, pertained also to Mary. But a distinction is retained, and Mary is not deified thereby:

Dicit enim H[i]eronymus, in sermone assumptionis domine, quod totius gratie plenitudo, que est in Christo, in Mariam uenit quamquam aliter. Aliter, inquam, ut mihi uidetur, quia in Christo sicut in homine personaliter deificato, et in Maria sicut in templo ipsi uerbo singulariter dedicato.[199]

(For Jerome says in a sermon on the Lord's ascension that the plenitude of every grace, which is in Christ, came into Mary, however, in a different way. It seems to me, I say, to be 'in a different way' because it was in Christ as in a man personally deified, and in Mary as in a temple uniquely dedicated to the Word.)

---

[196] Ubertino da Casale, *Arbor vitae crucifixae*, lib. 1, c. 8 (p. 31^b).
[197] Ibid.
[198] Ibid. (p. 32^{a-b}).
[199] Ibid. (p. 32^b).

Finally we discover the underlying reason for Ubertino's rejection of Mary having enjoyed the beatific vision in her earthly life, in his expansion on this principle. He distinguishes between Christ's perfections pertaining to his earthly life, which were transferred to Mary, and those pertaining to his personal union with the Word, which were not; and this applies particularly to the beatific vision. Thus Mary did not *frui* in this life:

Si ergo tota plenitudo gratie, que in Christo est, uenit in Mariam, ergo ille plenitudines superius dicte, et alie multe maiores et ineffabiles nobis. Nec ualet instantia si diceres, quod in Christo fuerit beatifica uisio ab instanti sue conceptionis; nec ista prerogatiua fuit tunc data uirgini: igitur similiter nec iste alie; non enim est simile. Gratia enim uisionis beate omnino competit Christi humanitati, et est decens ex unione personali uerbi. Non enim est decens, ut uniatur uerbo ut supposito, et non fruatur ipso. Sed perfectiones, que competunt Christo secundum perfectionem uie, debent diffundi in sua beatissima matre. Vnde puto, quod omnes gratie substantialiter mentem perficiunt, et que non repugnant statui creature et qui sunt citra beatitudinem patrie, debent sibi communicari.[200]

(But if, therefore, the total plenitude of grace that is in Christ comes into Mary, then the same is true of those plenitudes mentioned above, and many others that are greater and ineffable for us. This objection does not hold if you were to say that the beatific vision was in Christ from the moment of his conception. This prerogative was not given to the Virgin at that point, and consequently nor were the others likewise, for it is not similar. For the grace of the beatific vision is entirely appropriate to the humanity of Christ, and is seemly on account of his personal union to the Word. For it is not seemly that he should be united to the Word, as I assume, and should not delight in it. But the perfections that are appropriate to Christ according to the perfection of his earthly journey ought to be diffused into his most blessed mother. Wherefore I believe that all the graces [which] perfect the mind substantially, which are not inconsistent with the status of a created being, and are short of the blessedness of the heavenly kingdom, ought to be communicated to her.)

These conclusions are not forgotten in the rest of the work. By a complex set of associations, Ubertino states much later that, as Mary received the *influxus* of the Spirit as fully as possible for a creature not united to God, and as the suffering of Christ's heart and body is the root of all grace and reward, so among all creatures Mary participated most fully in Christ's suffering.[201]

---

[200] Ibid. (pp. 32^b–33^a).
[201] See ibid., lib. 4, c. 15 (pp. 321^b–25^b, here pp. 323^b–324^a); cf. lib. 4, c. 25 (pp. 336^a–337^a, at p. 336^a); see further Colasanti, 'I SS. cuori di Gesù e di Maria', pp. 57–64; on Mary's compassion in the *Arbor vitae* see Colasanti, 'Maria SS. nella vita di Cristo', pp. 362–75.

Ubertino's contemporary, Meister Eckhart, has not traditionally been regarded as a particular Marian exponent. Several of his most well-studied German sermons are written for Marian feasts, with lemmata that conventionally bear a Marian interpretation, but do not mention Mary at all.[202] Górecka, in line with prior scholarship, adopts this rather negative assessment of Eckhart's stance towards Mary.[203] The approach is perfectly valid, and rests heavily on Eckhart's repeated revalorisation of the relative importance of Mary's birth of Christ and the spiritual birth of God in the mind of the contemporary individual. The following example, from *Predigt* 22, is probably the most famous. Initially Eckhart repeats the Augustinian notion of the priority of Mary's spiritual birth of Christ, before interpreting Christ's words to an unnamed woman in Luke 11: 27–8 to locate the spiritual birth of God in the soul of a contemporary above Mary's corporeal birth of Christ:

Ich spriche: und haete Mariâ niht von êrste got geistlîche geborn, er enwaere nie lîplîche von ir geborn worden. Ein vrouwe sprach ze unserm herren: 'saelic ist der lîp, der dich truoc'. Dô sprach unser herre: niht enist der lîp aleine saelic, der mich getragen hât; 'saelic sint, die daz wort gotes hoerent und daz behaltent'. Daz ist gote werder, daz er geistlîche geborn werde von einer ieglîchen juncvrouwen oder von einer ieglîchen guoten sêle, dan daz er von Mariâ lîplîche geborn wart.[204]

(I say: Had Mary not first given birth to God spiritually, she would never have given birth to him bodily. A woman said to our Lord, 'Blessed is the body that bore you. ' At this our Lord said, 'It is not just the body which bore me that is blessed; blessed are they, who hear the word of God and keep it.' It is of greater worth in God's eyes that an individual maiden or an individual good soul should give birth to him spiritually, than that Mary gave birth to him bodily.)

The significance of this understanding for our purposes lies in the relative demotion of Mary. Mary, from this sermon and its counterparts, is no longer presented as the single imitable instance, whose birth of Christ inculcated the salvation of mankind and thereby opened the mystical potential for the direct encounter with God. Mary's spiritual birth of God is placed on a par with that of all subsequent imitators, and her pre-eminence in this respect is lost. Eckhart reveals himself to be simultaneously

---

[202] Notably *Predigten* 2 (vol. 1: 21–45), for Mary's assumption; 38 (vol. 2: 227–45), for the annunciation; and 44 (vol. 2: 331–51), for Candlemas.

[203] See Górecka, *Das Bild Mariens*, pp. 386–7 and 527–9.

[204] Eckhart, *Predigt* 22 (vol. 1: 375. 10–376. 5); cf. *Predigt* 49 (vol. 2: 427. 1–428. 7 and 432. 1–8); expanded commentaries on the Augustinian dictum are given in *Predigten* 78 (vol. 3: 351. 5–352. 3) and 110, ll. 11–17 (vol. 4/2, pp. 781–2). See further Górecka, *Das Bild Mariens*, pp. 387–8 and 428–34.

profoundly radical and profoundly conservative: radical in the novelty of the doctrine, conservative in that he strips the understanding of Mary's contemplation thereby of the merits and eminence that had been incrementally accorded to it over the previous generations.

Freimut Löser has recently commented that the image of Eckhart as having shown little interest in Mary is partly predicated on the circumstances of the modern edition. It is precisely those German sermons dealing with Mary that have either only recently, or not yet, been published in the critical edition, but whose authenticity may now be regarded as certain.[205] In these texts Eckhart presents much richer material, which takes a different approach towards the understanding of Mary. Let us start with *Predigt* 93, a sermon from the *Paradisus anime intelligentis* collection that deals with Mary's nativity. In remaining on this subject throughout, the approach is much more conventional than in other sermons specifically for Marian feasts. Eckhart compares Mary to the *aurora consurgens* of Canticles 6: 9 (which forms the lemma), and notes that the dawn contains both light and dark. This demonstrates, says Eckhart, that Mary was conceived in original sin and then purified by the Spirit. In Mary's nativity, God's perfect love was manifest, as he produced no purer creature than Mary, and yet did not make her so perfect that a soul might desire to be, and be, unified with her. God does not want the soul to have anything more beloved than him, for he has created the soul for union with him alone:

Dâ mite ist bewîset diu geburt unser vrouwen, alsô daz diz morgenrôt beide lieht und vinster an sich hât. Dâ mite ist bewîset, daz unser vrouwe in den sünden wart enpfangen und ir lîp und ir sêle vereinet in der erbesünde, und dar nâch mit der vart wart si von dem heiligen geiste gereiniget und wart heilic geborn. Und dar umbe begât man ir geburt. Dar ane ist uns bewîset volkomene liebe unsers herren, wan er nie lûterer crêatûre geschuof, diu alsô edel waere, und enwolte sie doch sô volkomen niht machen, daz diu sêle mit liebe in ir vereinet waere oder möhte gesîn. Got wil wol, daz diu sêle sehe und hoere, daz got niht enist, er enwil aber niht, daz si iht liebers habe dan in, wan er hât sie ze sîner einunge geschaffen.[206]

(Our Lady's birth is indicated thereby, as this roseate dawn has both light and dark aspects. By this it is indicated that our Lady was conceived in sin, her body and soul united in original sin, and that she was then purified by the Holy Spirit in due course and so born holy. Because of this her birth is celebrated. In this our Lord's perfect love is made known to us, because he never created a more pure created being, who was as noble as this; and yet did not want to make her so perfect that the

---

[205] Löser, 'Maria im Mittelpunkt', p. 273.
[206] Eckhart, *Predigt* 93, ll. 24–32 (vol. 4/1, pp. 126–7).

soul was, or could have been, united with love in her. God wants that the soul should well see and hear that which is not God; but he does not want the soul to have anything more beloved than him, because he has created the soul to be unified with him.)

Eckhart extends the same argument then to apply to truth and to goodness. God created nothing as true or as good as himself, so that the truth-seeking and/or loving soul could not be unified with such a creation, nor would desire to be so.[207] Nonetheless, God did bestow upon Mary all the perfection that could be given to a creature: 'Alsô ist ez umbe unser vrouwen: alle die volkomenheit, die got ie gelegen mohte an keine crêatûre, die hât si enpfangen'[208] ('It is similarly of our Lady: she received all the perfections that God ever bestowed upon any created being'). Likewise, Eckhart can apply individual sapiential texts to Mary, but not the absolute concept of perfect wisdom (implied by the *Mariale* and Matthew of Aquasparta). Christ, by implication not Mary, is the wisdom of God, a point we see in the Latin *Sermo 2 super Ecclesiastici*:

'Spiritus meus' [Eccl. 24: 27] etc. Expositis supra his verbis de sapientia dei patris nunc exponenda restant de matre ipsius verbi, quod virtus et sapientia dei patris, Cor. [cf. 1 Cor. 1: 24].[209]

('My spirit', etc. As these words have been expounded above of the wisdom of God the Father, they remain now to be expounded of the mother of the Word itself, which [Word] is 'the power and the wisdom of God' the Father, as per Corinthians.)

And so, as all virtues were in Mary in as perfect a way as possible, so too was perfect detachment from the self, *abegescheidenheit*—a point Eckhart explores with reference to the annunciation in the treatise *Von abegescheidenheit*.[210]

Recently Erik Panzig has provided a comprehensive and clear exposition on the meaning of *abegescheidenheit*,[211] and so in place of a detailed exposition, it will suffice to cite one illuminative and representative definition from the treatise. This feature of *abegescheidenheit*, according to Eckhart, is that which brings man to the closest similitude with God:

---

[207] Eckhart, *Predigt* 93, ll. 33–58 (vol. 4/1, pp. 127–31).

[208] Ibid. ll. 96–8 (vol. 4/1, pp. 134–5); cf. *Predigt* 110, ll. 8–10 (vol. 4/2, p. 781).

[209] Eckhart, *Sermo 2 super Ecclesiastici*, §39 (vol. 2: 266. 8–10).

[210] See Eckhart, *Von abegescheidenheit* (vol. 5: 406. 9–409. 6); see further Górecka, *Das Bild Mariens*, pp. 476–81.

[211] Panzig, '*gelâzenheit* und *abegescheidenheit*', pp. 344–9; see pp. 349–55 on the relationship to passivity (*gelâzenheit*).

Hie solt dû wizzen, daz rehtiu abegescheidenheit niht anders enist, wan daz der geist alsô unbewegelich stande gegen allen zuovellen liebes und leides, êren, schanden und lasters als ein blîgîn berc unbewegelich ist gegen einem kleinen winde. Disiu unbewegelîchiu abegescheidenheit bringet den menschen in die groeste glicheit mit gote. Wan daz got ist got, daz hât er von sîner unbewegelîchen abegescheidenheit, und von der abegescheidenheit hât er sîne lûterkeit und sîne einvalticheit und sîne unwandelbaerkeit. Und dâ von, sol der mensche gote glîch werden, als verre als ein crêatûre glîcheit mit gote gehaben mac, daz muoz geschehen mit abegescheidenheit.[212]

(Here you should know that true detachment is nothing other than the Spirit standing as immovable in the face of every exigency—of love and of sorrow, of honour, and of shame and scorn—as a leaden mountain is immovable in the face of a gentle breeze. This immovable detachment brings the individual into the greatest similitude with God. For God is God on account of his immovable detachment, and from this detachment he derives his purity, his simplicity, and his immutability. Therefore if the individual is to become similar to God, to the furthest extent that a created being may have similitude with God, this must take place through detachment.)

Górecka has remarked that in *Von abegescheidenheit*, Mary is presented as an imitable model in her attainment of perfect *abegescheidenheit*, culminating in her spiritual birth of Christ. Eckhart uses Mary as an example of *abegescheidenheit*, but he proceeds from the concept to the example, not vice versa. That is, Mary was not the *institutrix*—she cannot be, for Eckhart, the author of some kind of *regula Mariae*—but is nonetheless a useful model for contemporaries, able to attain the same level of *abegescheidenheit*, the same level of contemplative distinction, as Mary.[213]

Other texts provide further illustration of Eckhart's use of Mary as a model. An (authentic) annunciation sermon is comparable to *Predigt 93* in its Marian focus, and presents Mary as the exemplar of the principles Eckhart sets out for the individual. So, for example, the idea that the perfection of virtues enables God to work freely in the individual is exemplified by Mary after her union, by grace, with Christ in the incarnation:

Wan swer gote alsô stat in sîme herzen gêbe mit allen tugenden, in dem têtе got alsô würken, daz er ledic und lôz aller bildnisse würde. Wan in solher mâze was Marîâ alsô ledic, daz got alwege volle stat in ir ze würken hete nâch allem sînen willen.[214]

---

[212] Eckhart, *Von abegescheidenheit* (vol. 5: 411. 12–412. 8).

[213] See Górecka, *Das Bild Mariens*, pp. 480–1.

[214] Eckhart, *Predigt* CVI (ed. Pfeiffer, pp. 343–7), 344. 18–22. I use Roman numerals for (authentic) German sermons as yet available only in Pfeiffer's edition, to distinguish them from different sermons with the same number in the critical edition.

(For God will work in whomsoever gives God a place in his heart, with every virtue, in such a way that he will become free and quit of every image. For Mary was free to this extent, such that God always had the place to himself to work in her according to his every wish.)

Mary's exemplarity, used in this way, structures the whole sermon, culminating in a statement of her *deiformitas*—a similitude to, and unification in, God that is as open to the contemporary individual as it is to Mary. The context here is an interpretation of the word 'ave':

[...] daz wort âvê bediutet stêtikeit, unde stêtikeit bediutet einen man. Der ist ein man, der in sînem muote niht gewandelt noch beweget wirt. Dar umbe, swenne ein wîp in ir muote nicht gewandelt würde, sô wêre si ein man unde niht ein wîp. Die beide hâte Marîâ. Si was ein wîp nâch dem nidersten teil irs ûzern menschen und ist got in got mit got nâch dem obersten teil irs geistes. Und in dem sinne mügent alle menschen Marîâ sîn alsô, daz daz wort âvê zuo uns allen in der wârheit mac gesprochen werden.[215]

(The word 'ave' means 'constancy', and 'constancy' means 'a man'. He is a man who is neither mutable nor movable in his mind. Therefore should a woman be immutable in her mind, then she would be a man and not a woman. Mary was both. She was a woman according to the lowest aspect of her exterior person, and is God in God with God according to the highest aspect of her spirit. In this sense all people may be Mary, such that the word 'ave' may be spoken to us all in truth.)

A third sermon with a pronounced Marian focus is a Candlemas sermon, which uses various conventional appellations of Mary ('Maria illuminata', 'Maria hierosolymitana', and so on) to present Mary as the example of the soul seeking union with God. Here, Mary is understood less as a person, than as a set of attributes: in the following example, as virgin, spiritual person, and bearer of God:

Marîâ was ein juncfrouwe und ein geistlîcher mensche und ein gebererin gotes. Si was ein juncfrouwe, wan kein crêatûre hete ruowe in ir sêle denne got alleine. Si was ein geistlîcher mensche, wan alliu ir werc, diu si zwischen ir unt gote worhte, diu vollebrâhte si nâch den aller edelsten tugenden, die si verstuont under dar zuo si von gote vermant wart. Si was ouch ein gebererin gotes, wan si gotes in ir sêle mit tegelîcher gnade nie vermissete. Dar umbe, swer Marîen der juncfrouwen welle nâch volgen und ir leben êren unde zuo ir lobe komen wil, der muoz ein juncfrouwe sîn, daz ist, er muoz sîn selbes und aller dinge ledic sîn, sô er sich in der crêatûre mêr vindet dan in gote. Unde swer ouch Marîâ rehte êren wil, der muoz ein geistlîch mensche sîn, daz ist, er muoz durch gotes willen alle zît diu dinc lieber lâzen, diu er

---

[215] Eckhart, *Predigt* CVI (ed. Pfeiffer), 346. 9–17.

von eigem willen lieber behielte. Ouch swer ein gebererin gotes welle sîn, der muoz der minne gotes in sîme herzen niemer âne sîn, alsô daz er sich schame, sô im ein ander in tugenden vor gêt.[216]

(Mary was a virgin, a spiritual person, and a bearer of God. She was a virgin because no created being found rest in her soul save God alone. She was a spiritual person because she completed all her acts, which she worked between her and God, according to the most noble virtues of which she had comprehension, and to which she was exhorted by God. She was also a bearer of God, because she was never without God in her soul with daily grace. Therefore whoever wishes to imitate the Virgin Mary, to honour her life and to come to her praise must be a virgin: that is, he must be free of himself and of all things when he finds himself more engaged in created beings than in God. Whoever wishes to honour Mary properly must be a spiritual person: that is, he must prefer always, following God's will, to leave aside the things that he would prefer to retain, following his own will. Whoever wishes to be a bearer of God must never be without the love of God in his heart, such that he would be ashamed of himself if another individual should outdo him in virtue.)

There is no space to treat the rest of this sermon in detail; Eckhart's strategy should by now be clear. To this group of German Marian sermons (centrally *Predigten* 93, CV, and CVI) and a substantial portion of the Latin *Sermo 2 super Ecclesiastici*[217] can be added the alternative version to *Predigt* 2, with a central Marian focus in which the themes we have just seen are also elaborated. Löser has made a compelling case for this alternative version potentially to be considered as a version closer to Eckhart's original text, with the version in the modern edition representing a later, inauthentic redaction of the text that was regarded as particularly incriminating in the inquisitorial process, and which Eckhart disavowed.[218]

From these texts we can construct a rather different picture of Eckhart's Marian interests, for which I have given here only a brief overview. The upshot of this, for our purposes, is twofold. First, we can see Eckhart's position in the tradition of presenting Mary as a mystical contemplative. Second, we can see quite how different Marquard really is to Eckhart with regard to Mary. Marquard may have adopted Eckhartian dicta on Mary, and 'Marianized' Eckhartian conceptions in the presentation of Mary in the *Dekalogerklärung*, but he does not adopt the central imports of Eckhart's

---

[216] Id., *Predigt* CV (ed. Pfeiffer, pp. 340–3), 340. 35–341. 15.

[217] See id., *Sermo 2 super Ecclesiastici*, §39–40 (vol. 2: 266. 8–268. 13).

[218] See Löser, 'Maria im Mittelpunkt', pp. 241–9 and 253–72. The edition in Löser, *Meister Eckhart in Melk*, pp. 537–49 supersedes the diplomatic transcription printed in Löser, 'Maria im Mittelpunkt', pp. 249–53.

broader view of Mary. Marquard's release from the implicit charge of epigonality to Eckhart should be as evident here as it was in the previous chapter on the eucharist.

A contemporary of both Eckhart and Ubertino da Casale, the Benedictine abbot Engelbert von Admont (d. 1331) was the author of the last great Latin *summa Mariana* of our period, the *De gratiis et virtutibus beatae et gloriosae semper virginis Mariae tractatus* (hereinafter *De gratiis*). Engelbert was something of a polymath, being *inter alia* a noted music theorist, and had studied at the Dominican *studium* in Padua. He had read the *Mariale* closely, and his personal copy (Admont, Stiftsbibliothek, Cod. 272) is heavily annotated.[219] It is thus little surprise that the *De gratiis*, probably written in the later 1320s, is the apogee of the Latin tradition presenting Mary as a mystical contemplative. Its circulation was moderate: Fowler counted slightly more than a dozen manuscripts in 1947, and its transmission was limited to the south-eastern Germanic region.[220]

The *De gratiis* is Engelbert's principal work on contemplation,[221] and Ubl has shown that Engelbert uses the work in part to set out a clear rejection of the possibilities of purely philosophical speculation without the assistance of divine grace. The immediate cognition of God, according to Engelbert, can be approached thereby but never reached, as a consequence of original sin. This implicitly rejects a theory of the intellect propounded by Albert the Great, who had drawn on Averroes to formulate a conception of the intellect's potential to connect of itself with separated substances—and so with God *per essentiam*. Engelbert's rejection sharpened arguments already formulated by Aquinas: philosophical contemplation could not prefigure eternal blessedness in any way, not even (as Aquinas had held) by speculation—and certainly not by connection to separated substances, which exceeds the capacity of the soul in and of itself.[222] The relevance of this to our concerns is manifold. Mary, for Engelbert, is the ultimate embodiment of theological contemplation—the opposite of the philosophical speculation that he excoriates as pointless.[223] As the individual most replete with divine grace, upon which for Engelbert all higher cognition depends,

---

[219] See Ubl, *Engelbert von Admont*, p. 24; on Engelbert's life, library, and wider interests, see pp. 12–21. The relationship between the *Mariale* and Engelbert's *De gratiis* was first established by Albert Fries, albeit with the wrong conclusion as to the direction of the dependence: see Fries, *Die unter dem Namen des Albertus Magnus . . .* , pp. 53–66.

[220] See Fowler, *Intellectual Interests*, pp. 193–4.

[221] See ibid., pp. 118–19.

[222] Ubl, *Engelbert von Admont*, pp. 44–7.

[223] See Engelbert von Admont, *De gratiis et virtutibus Mariae*, pars 3, c. 11 (pp. 614–15).

Mary was the ultimate contemplative, whose experience of mystical union
with God was most perfect in this life. Furthermore, Engelbert approaches
Mary primarily from the perspective of providing guidance on the contemplative life, and as such—though there are clear differences in the conception
of Mary—the *De gratiis* is the Latin work most similar to Marquard's
Dekalogerklärung. Unlike the other *summae Marianae,* Engelbert does not
seek to elaborate every Marian aspect.

Like Marquard, Engelbert pays notable attention to Mary's life between
Christ's ascension and her own assumption.[224] Following convention, he
presents Mary as the perfect exemplar of both active and contemplative
lives,[225] and justifies her perfection in the contemplative life by her repletion with all conceivable graces and virtues.[226] But at the end of this windy
justification, Engelbert makes an important statement that sharpens the
position taken by the *Mariale* on Mary's status. He maintains that her
repletion with grace and virtue was so great that she enjoyed the beatific
vision in the manner of the saints in heaven; though a *viatrix,* she was, as
Graef noted,[227] simultaneously a *comprehensatrix* 'secundum quid' (that is,
in terms of the perfection of her contemplation), occupying a middle state
between living men and saints:

Unde notandum, quod predictas virtutes et dona, et deinceps fructus et beatitudines
differenter habeant viatores et comprehensores, sive quantum ad habitum et actum,
sive quantum ad actum tantum: quia viatores habeant eas cum actuum imperfectione sub merendi conditione; comprehensores vero cum actuum perfectione sine
merendi conditione. Ut igitur ista materia de excellenti perfectione beatae virginis,
ipsam disponente et praeparante in hac vita ad summum gradum contemplationis,
et intimae degustationis aeternae beatitudinis, generaliter concludatur: hoc de b.
virgine sentiendum et tenendum est; quod in plenitudine gratiae, quam ei angelus
annuntiavit, omnes gratias sacramentales et praedictas virtutes et dona, et fructus et
beatitudines statum viae perficientes, ex eo, quod ipsa fuerit viator simpliciter et
comprehensor secundum quid, medio et meliori modo habuerit inter viatores
et comprehensores: quia cessante actuum imperfectione habuit eas sub merendi
conditione; et cum actuum perfectione cum excellentia super omnes.[228]

(Wherefore it is to be noted that those who journey through this life (the *viatores*)
and those who know the heavenly life (the *comprehensores*) have the aforesaid virtues
and gifts, and thereafter the fruits and beatitudes, in different ways; either as far as
the habit and the act are concerned, or as far as the act alone is concerned. This is

---

[224] See ibid., pars 2, c. 3–7 (pp. 569–73); and pars 3, c. 45–7 (pp. 686–91).
[225] See ibid., pars 2, c. 8 (pp. 573–4).
[226] See ibid., pars 3, c. 4–7 (pp. 599–608).
[227] See Graef, *Mary,* pp. 294–6.
[228] Engelbert von Admont, *De gratiis et virtutibus,* pars 3, c. 7 (pp. 607^d–608^b).

because those who journey through this life have these things with the imperfection of acts in the state of gaining reward, whilst those who know the heavenly life have them with perfection of acts outwith the state of gaining reward. In order, therefore, that this subject of the blessed Virgin's pre-eminent perfection, with her ordering and preparing herself to the highest degree of contemplation and of the innermost enjoyment of eternal blessedness in this life, may be brought to a general conclusion, the following is to be understood and held of the blessed Virgin: that in the plenitude of grace that the angel announced to her, she had all the sacramental graces, the aforesaid virtues and gifts, and the fruits and beatitudes that perfect the state of the journey through this life in a way that is both better than, and in-between that of those who journey through this life (the *viatores*) and those who know the heavenly life (the *comprehensores*). This was because she was one of the former (a *viatrix*) in an unqualified way, and one of the latter (a *comprehensor*) in a qualified way; because with the cessation of the imperfection of acts, she had those things in the state of gaining reward; and with the perfection of her acts, so with her pre-eminence above all others.)

Engelbert goes further in the next chapter, and holds that this intermediate state that Mary occupied was (astonishingly) by nature as well as by grace:

[...] cum b. virgo inter Christum Deum et hominem, et inter puros homines caeteros, non solum secundum plenitudinem gratiae, sed etiam secundum perfectionem naturae, medium statum habuerit.[229]

(Because the blessed Virgin had an intermediate state between Christ, who is God and man, on the one hand, and the other pure humans on the other, not just in accordance with her plenitude of grace, but also in accordance with the perfection of her nature.)

The following justification reveals that this is not as daring as it looks, because ultimately grace underpins this natural perfection. Christ, says Engelbert, was able by virtue of the hypostatic union of his soul with God to permit no impediment on the part of his lower faculties, or his body, to his higher faculties. Thus, in the Passion, he was able to perceive the greatest joy alongside the greatest suffering, as the latter did not interfere with the former. This much is standard. Engelbert then transfers this argument onto Mary: by plenitude of grace, her inferior faculties did not impinge on her superior faculties, and so her action did not impede her contemplation.[230] This is an argument also used by Ubertino, but with the caveat that her contemplation did not encompass the beatific vision, and without the extravagant corollary that Mary was (albeit by grace) thereby elevated above the status of mankind in her nature.

---

[229] Engelbert von Admont, *De gratiis et virtutibus*, pars 3, c. 8 (p. 608^c).
[230] Ibid. (p. 609^b).

Mary was, according to Engelbert, continually and wholly united to the
divine in contemplation, chained to Christ in perfect love: 'mundae et
sanae et sanctae cogitationi et meditationi ac contemplationi semper innixa
et infixa, et vinculo summae charitatis Filio affixa'[231] ('[she was] always inclined
towards and firmly fixed upon pure, healthy, and holy consideration, meditation, and contemplation, and bound to the Son with the chain of the highest
charity'). Engelbert dwells on this caritative impulse, which had numerous
objects; with voluntarist overtones he expresses its import in the ignition of
the *ignis amoris* of the direct, mystical union with God, generating a state
of spiritual inebriation[232]—a motif we recognize from Hugh of St Victor.
This indication in Hugh's direction is not idle, because very shortly Engelbert
presents a commentary on the Magnificat in twenty chapters, and—like
(perhaps following) Hugh—understands the Magnificat as the expression and
product of Mary's contemplation. We see this, for example, in the following
statement from the beginning of the commentary proper:

Merito igitur beata virgo, suae humilitatis donum et meritum ac praemium contemplando, et in jubilo sui cordis in vocem et canticum erumpendo, memoriam
abundantiae divinae suavitatis erga se eructavit dicens: 'Magnificat anima mea
dominum' etc.[233]

(Therefore the blessed Virgin, in her contemplation of the gift, merit, and reward of
her humility, and in her paroxysms of speech and song in the delight of her heart,
justly poured out the memory of the abundance of divine sweetness towards herself,
saying, 'Let my soul magnify the Lord', and so forth.)

Engelbert is then able to describe Mary's exultation of spirit in terms of a
contemplative ascent.[234] As regards what Mary contemplated, he twice
specifies the three different categories of divine work (of creation and the
present condition, of salvation, and of glorification),[235] providing him with
the opportunity to elaborate on each; she also meditated on Christ's life and
crucifixion.[236]

Whilst her contemplation of all of these gave her insight into the divine
mysteries, Engelbert spends by far the most time considering her knowledge of the *opera glorificationis*, those things 'quae pertinent ad meditatio-

[231] Ibid., c. 11 (p. 614[a]).
[232] Ibid. (p. 614[a–b]).
[233] Ibid., c. 21 [Magnificat commentary, c. 8] (p. 632[d]); cf. c. 27 [Magnificat
commentary, c. 14] (p. 642[c]).
[234] See ibid., c. 23 [Magnificat commentary, c. 10] (pp. 634[d]–635[b]).
[235] See ibid., c. 11–12 (pp. 614–18); and c. 34 (pp. 667–8).
[236] See ibid., c. 35 (pp. 668–71).

nem et visionem status gloriae et glorificatorum secundum dispositionem et
ordinem triumphantis Ecclesiae et coelestis Hierarchiae'[237] ('which pertain to
the meditation and vision of the state of glory and of the glorified beings,
according to the order and disposition of the church triumphant and the
heavenly host'). It is here that Engelbert introduces his scholastic disquisition
on the cognition of God *per essentiam* that Ubl has examined.[238] Only after
this does he further define Mary's intermediate state, with the assertion that
it excepted her from the normal state of mankind subject to the cognitive
limitations he has just established. The underlying justificatory principle is
again her plenitude of grace.[239] He follows the *Mariale* in maintaining that
Mary's contemplation was above inspiration in dreams, rapture, and so on;[240]
drawing on the motif of spiritual inebriation, he continues his dependence on
the *Mariale* to assert that Mary saw God by her own created light in the
uncreated light:

Cum etiam fuerit quantum ad gratiam in contemplatione sua elevata nullo depri-
mente, et liberata nullo retinente, vel retrahente, sed adjuta Deo descendente et
manu ducente: juxta illud Cant. I[: 3] 'Introduxit me rex in cellam vinariam'[, u]bi
fuit inebriata ab ubertate domus Dei, et torrente voluptatis divinae potata: propter
hoc in sua contemplatione non vidit per speculum in aenigmate; sed per speculum
in lumine et lumen in lumine.[241]

(When, furthermore, she was raised up in her contemplation, as far as grace permits,
with nothing weighing her down, and was set free with nothing restraining her or
holding her back, she was aided by God coming down and leading her by the hand.
As it says in the Song of Songs, 'The king brought me into his wine cellar', where she
was intoxicated from the plenty of the house of God, and was drunk in the torrent
of divine delight: on account of which she saw in her contemplation not through a
glass in a dark manner, but through a glass in a clear manner, and through a light in
a clear [literally, 'light'] manner.)

The following chapter then elaborates eight different modes of perception
in contemplation, and shows for each that Mary saw that which pertains to
the *patria* more perfectly than any *viator*.[242] This all represents a huge
expansion of the treatment of these issues over the *Mariale*, indicating the
importance that Engelbert attached to them. With reference to the discourse on intellectual cognition, one should note that in the third of these

[237] Engelbert von Admont, *De gratiis et virtutibus*, pars, 3, c. 36 (p. 671[b]).
[238] See ibid., c. 36–42 (pp. 671–82).
[239] See ibid., c. 43 (pp. 682[a]–683[b]).
[240] See ibid. (p. 683[c–d]).
[241] Ibid. (pp. 683[d]–684[a]).
[242] See ibid., c. 44 (pp. 684–6).

eight modes, Mary is said to have been capable of seeing angels and her own soul 'per speciem propriam'—that is, as separated substances—'et hoc per naturam in summo purificatam, et per gratiam consummatam'[243] ('and this by nature, purified in the highest, and by perfected grace').

The fourth part of Engelbert's treatise incorporates a lengthy series of chapters that enumerate twelve aspects of Mary in her earthly life, that she possessed more perfectly than all other saints.[244] The ninth of these is particularly instructive, entitled 'De Divina amicitia et familiaritate' ('On divine friendship and familiarity'). John the Baptist, says Engelbert, was sanctified in the womb and so is termed 'amicus Christi' ('the friend of Christ'; cf. John 3: 29). John the Evangelist was termed 'dilectus' ('the beloved'; cf. John 21: 7) on account of his chastity. But *divina amicitia* was most perfectly in Mary: she was mother as well as friend, and her proximity to God was by grace and (albeit itself by grace) by nature. It is this proximity, this *divina amicitia* which is the principal amongst all Mary's perfections:

Istud donum proprie et excellentissime fuit in b. virgine. Major enim et propinquior est conjunctio, quae causatur ex natura et gratia, et quae fit corpore et mente, quam quae causatur a gratia sola, et fit mente tantum. Conjunctio autem et amor b. virginis ad Christum facta est per naturam et gratiam et corpore et mente, tanquam matris ad filium; et non solum tanquam familiaris et amici ad familiarem et amicum. Ergo istud donum et bonum conjunctionis et amicitiae ad Deum beata virgo consecuta est in ultimo propinquitatis et summo gradu. Unde nonum et summum ipsius privilegium, quasi prima et praecipua stella corona[e] ipsius [cf. Rev. 12: 1], a qua omnes aliae stellae coronae ipsius causam habent et ortum, est summus ille titulus, quod ipsa est et dicitur mater Dei, summa et immediata propinquitate habens se secundum naturam et gratiam ad Deum.[245]

(This gift was especially and most excellently in the blessed Virgin. For the bond which has both nature and grace as its cause, and which occurs in both body and mind, is greater and more intimate than that which has grace alone as its cause, and occurs only in the mind. The bond with, and the blessed Virgin's love for, Christ, moreover, was effected by nature and grace and in body and mind, as that of a mother for her son—and not just as that of a friend and companion for a friend and companion. Therefore the blessed Virgin obtained this gift and benefit of bonding and friendship to God in the ultimate intimacy and the highest degree. Wherefore the ninth and highest of her privileges—like the first and principal star in her crown, from which all the other stars of her crown have their cause and origin—is that

---

[243] Ibid. (p. 685[b]).
[244] See ibid., pars 4, prooemium (pp. 695–7) and c. 35–46 (pp. 749–57).
[245] Ibid., c. 43 (p. 755[b–c]).

highest title, namely that she is, and is called, the mother of God; being in the highest unmediated intimacy with God possible according both to nature and to grace.)

Mary is raised into inimitability; Engelbert's conception of her position could hardly be more different to Eckhart's. Perhaps the more important contrast is with the *Dekalogerklärung*. Engelbert restricts the perfect friendship with God to Mary alone: whilst others may be friends, Mary is elevated to such a level that her value as an imitable model is substantially reduced, and it is noteworthy that Engelbert is uniquely unconcerned with the issue of imitation. His intellectual preoccupations with Mary are rather more those excoriated by Ubertino. Though Marquard elevates Mary to a level of ethical and contemplative perfection above all others, he does not ascribe to her a 'medius status' and has particular concern to demonstrate her imitability. The important *amicitia Dei* for Marquard is not Mary's, which is self-evident, but that of the contemporary imitators, the *amici Dei* whose conduct and contemplative example Marquard considers after the Marian section in each commandment of the *Dekalogerklärung*.

With Engelbert the identifiable influence of the *Mariale* is not exhausted. The existence of a Latin sermon on Mary's assumption, printed under Bonaventura's name, was mentioned earlier,[246] as was Beumer's demonstration of its inauthenticity. As this is such a small and relatively poor text, there is no need to examine it in close detail, beyond stating that it draws on Richard of St Laurent's *De laudibus* and on the *Mariale* to present a sermon on Mary's supernatural wisdom and cognition.[247] The importance of the sermon is in its geographical origin. It was known to the editors in Quaracchi from just one fourteenth-century manuscript (Münster, Bibliotheca Paulina, Cod. 610, fols. 232–6), which otherwise contained no further Bonaventuran texts, but works by Aquinas. Its adoption in the Bonaventura edition rested on the probably secondary ascription to Bonaventura in the upper margin of fol. 232ʳ, and the editors speak of the 'sermo tamen [. . .] imperfecte reportatus, et codex non raro vitiose scriptus'[248] ('the sermon, nevertheless, is imperfectly recorded, and the manuscript is not infrequently defective'). The manuscript was lost during the war and so Beumer was unable to perform a codicological examination and determine its origin. In fact, the sermon survives in a second copy, in Koblenz, Landeshauptarchiv, Best. 701 Nr. 123, fols. 173ʳᵇ–178ᵛᵃ, as one

---

[246] Edited as Bonaventura, *Sermo 6 de assumptione Mariae* (vol. 9, pp. 701ᵃ–706ᵇ).

[247] See Beumer, 'Eine dem hl. Bonaventura . . .', pp. 5–13 and 17–18.

[248] See Bonaventura, *Opera omnia*, vol. 9, p. 700 n. 8; cf. Beumer, 'Eine dem hl. Bonaventura . . .', pp. 2–5.

of 199 discrete texts, principally sermons (and including some German items) in a manuscript from the Dominican convent in Koblenz. A palaeographical dating points to the mid-fourteenth century; but most crucially the binding points towards the Cologne workshop of Henricus Walram.[249] The sermon evidently originates in a Rhenish Dominican convent, probably Cologne, where the *Mariale* is known to have been available from around 1300 (though Cologne was not an important centre for its transmission).[250] The sermon proves that the *Mariale* was being used for Marian preaching, as well as for intellectual tracts like Engelbert's *De gratiis*; and more importantly, that it was being used in this way by at least one Rhenish Dominican in the first half of the fourteenth century, perhaps even during Eckhart's lifetime—one should not forget that Cologne was arguably Eckhart's principal centre of activity and influence.

Johannes Tauler (d. 1361) was another Rhenish Dominican of the generation after Eckhart, and an intellectual and author of comparable stature to Marquard. A small number of Tauler's German sermons consider Mary, and we have already seen Marquard's utilization of passages from them in the *Dekalogerklärung*. Marzena Górecka has considered these sermons in depth, and in the following we will draw largely on her conclusions. It is first worth noting that, like Eckhart, several sermons on Marian feasts and/or themes make little or no mention of Mary. With Tauler this can become patently incongruous. *Predigt* 80 examines the attributes of being a bride of Christ, and Mary would surely have been a better example to illustrate the principle of the spiritual parturition of God by contemplation of the divine than Tauler's actual example, drawn from Albert the Great, that hens give birth to sparrowhawk-shaped chicks if they have been nesting next to sparrowhawks.[251]

Tauler's Christmas Day sermon (*Predigt* 1) is undoubtedly the text with greatest Marian significance. The Eckhartian echo is clear in the first half of the sermon, in which Tauler stresses the eternal birth of the Word by God as the example for the contemporary to give birth to God spiritually.[252] The second half of the sermon addresses Mary's birth of Christ—naturally

---

[249] See Meckelnborg, *Die nichtarchivischen Handschriften*, pp. 161–4. A full register of the contents, not provided by Meckelnborg, is accessible at <http://www.manuscripta-mediaevalia.de> [accessed 19 Sept. 2006]: input 'Best. 701 Nr. 123' into search field 'Signatur'.

[250] See Kolping, 'Zur Frage der Textgeschichte', pp. 295–311.

[251] See Tauler, *Predigt* 80 (426. 23–427. 1).

[252] See id., *Predigt* 1 (7. 12–11. 1).

following the Augustinian dicta to prioritize the spiritual birth—and, like Eckhart, reduces Mary to the embodiment of a set of abstract principles (notably purity, detachment, introversion, and obedience) to be followed by the contemporary contemplative.[253] Unlike Eckhart, there is no revalorization of the corporeal birth of Christ beneath his spiritual birth by the contemporary. It is by this corporeal birth that Christ was born, by whose redemptive work the possibility of the spiritual birth of God in the soul was opened to all mankind: a point Tauler makes in the Marian opening to *Predigt* 49.[254] Notwithstanding, it is Mary's conduct at the annunciation that Tauler interprets with relevance to mystical contemplation; Mary's contemplation itself is only very weakly functionalized as a model for direct imitation.

This is not the case in two other sermons, albeit works which treat Mary only briefly. The opening to *Predigt* 46 describes, with clear pseudo-Dionysian influence, the continual elevation of Mary's mind into the divine abyss, the sole place in which she found rest. This is appended to an exhortation to praise and serve Mary, that she might assist the contemplative to Christ; only then does it become a model for proper *quies*, the mystical rest in God, to which Tauler immediately turns his attention.[255] The passage is familiar; as we saw earlier, Marquard drew on it in the fourth commandment of the *Dekalogerklärung*:

'In omnibus requiem quesivi'. Dis wort sprach der wise man und liset man es von unser fröwen, und sprach: 'in allen dingen han ich rûwe gesûcht und bin bliben wonende in dem erbe mins herren' [Eccl. 24: 11]. Dis wort mag man von unser fröwen aller eigenlichest nemen, wan si für mit ir vernunft úber die himel in das abgrúnde der helle und in das tieffe mer und in den umbekreis des ertrichs, und sie envant nie rûwe. Kinder, nieman ensol in disem lebende so hoch fliegen an úbungen, er ensúlle ie ein stunde dar zû tûn, das er diser minneklichen fröwen ie ein sunderlich wunneklich lob und dienst erbiete, und si minneklichen bitten das si uns fûre und ziehe und helfe zû irem geminten kinde. Kinder, ir wirdikeit die gat úber alle wise und mosse. Was wunders was das, das si iren Got und iren schöpfer hatte in irre schosse und an iren armen und in den aller begerlichesten lustlichesten wisen, die úber alle sinne woren, und enzwivelte ein har nút, und was des sicher das er ir Got was, und mochte mit im gebaren wie si wolte, und er wandelte mit ir als ir

[253] See id., *Predigt* 1 (11. 1– 2. 15); see Górecka, *Das Bild Mariens*, pp. 383–5 and 423–4. A similar approach is implicit in *Predigt* 49; see Górecka, *Das Bild Mariens*, pp. 505–6. For Mary as a model of obedience, cf. *Predigt* 49 (223. 31–224. 3); on which see Górecka, *Das Bild Mariens*, pp. 485–6.
[254] See Tauler, *Predigt* 49 (219. 20–220. 10); see Górecka, *Das Bild Mariens*, pp. 424–6.
[255] See Górecka, *Das Bild Mariens*, pp. 426–8 and 525–7.

kint, das ir herze in allem irem lebende nie ein ǒgenblik do uffe engeraste mit genûgde, denne das ir gemûte ane underlos uf gieng und úber gieng in das gǒtlich abgrúnde; in dem allein was ir rûwe; do was ir erbe und ir raste, ir wonende stat.²⁵⁶ ('In omnibus requiem quesivi.' These words were spoken by the wise man, and they are read in respect of our Lady. They mean, 'I have sought repose in all things, and have remained dwelling in the inheritance of my Lord.' These words can be taken to refer most particularly to our Lady, because she journeyed with her intellect beyond the heavens into the abyss of hell, into the deep sea, and throughout the whole compass of the globe; and she never found repose. My children, in this life no one should soar so high in spiritual exercises without always giving a moment to offer an especial instance of delightful praise and service to this loving lady, and to ask her most lovingly that she might lead, draw, and assist us to her beloved child. My children, her worthiness exceeds all measures and means. How miraculous it was that she had her God and her creator in her lap, in her arms, and in all the most desirable, most joyful ways that were beyond all sensory perception; that she did not doubt for a second that he was her God, being entirely sure of that; that she could conduct her life with him as she wanted, and he lived with her as her child, in such a way that her heart never tarried even for a moment with satisfaction on his physical presence without her mind ascending without intermission and passing over into the divine abyss, in which alone was her repose. There was her inheritance, her rest, her dwelling place.)

In *Predigt* 52 Tauler functionalizes Mary's humility—her self-humiliation—at the annunciation as an exemplification of the mystical descent into the abyss, though only very indirectly imputing such a mystical descent to Mary. The cognition of God by way of such humiliation of the self stands in contrast to the limited potential of purely philosophical speculation. The context here is the comprehension of the dimensions of God, following Ephesians 3: 18:

Kinder, dis ze begriffende das ist unmúgelich; aber es ist mit minne und mit luter meinunge dran ze hangende; do sol dis gemûte uf swimmen in die hǒhi der úber weselicheit und über klimmen alle nidere sinneliche ding an an sehen das Got, der alle ding vermag, vermochte des nút das er ein creature so edel machen mochte, das der hochen weselicheit sins wesens mit irem natúrlichen verstentnisse iergent nach gelangen mochte oder bekennen mochte; denne die tieffe des gǒtlichen abgrúndes das ist unervǒlgig allen vernúnften. Aber der tieffe sol man volgen mit einer vertieffeter demûtkeit. Dar umbe unser frǒwe verswig alles des grossen gûtz das

²⁵⁶ Tauler, *Predigt* 46 (201. 19–202. 11). For further statements of Mary's inexpressible eminence, see *Predigten* 50 (224. 9–17), linked to a prayer for assistance, and 52 (234. 28–31).

Got in si gegossen hatte, und sprach von ir grundeloser demûtkeit, daz si dar umbe solten selig sagen alle geslechte, wan der herre het die alleine an gesehen [cf. Lk. 1: 48].[257]

(My children, it is impossible to comprehend this; but with love and pure intention one can affix oneself to it. There the mind should swim upwards into the heights of the superessential, transcend all lower things perceptible with the senses, and perceive that God, who is capable of all things, was unable to make a created being so noble that it could ever attain or know the high essentiality of his being with its natural faculties of understanding, for the depths of the divine abyss are unattainable to any intellect. But one should fathom this depth with a more profound humility. Therefore our Lady kept silent about all the great gifts that God had poured into her, and spoke instead of her bottomless humility, in order that all generations should call her blessed because of it, for the Lord regarded it alone.)

Marquard excerpted Tauler's *Predigt* 52 a number of times in his works. He did not adopt this Marian passage into his presentation of Mary in the *Dekalogerklärung*, but incorporated an abridged version of it into a set of instructions for the friends of God in the relevant section of the third commandment.[258] He makes the same point about Mary in the normative-ethical section of the sixth commandment, using a quotation attributed to Bernard of Clairvaux. There he enumerates six things that contaminate the virtue of purity, of which the sixth is pride, and Mary's silence about her purity at the annunciation is considered a demonstration of her humility. The import—in total contrast to Tauler's sermon—is wholly ethical.[259]

From *Predigt* 46 in particular, Tauler clearly does hold that Mary enjoyed a mystical contemplation in God. But these indications are few and far between, and it is Tauler, not Eckhart, to whom the charge of having little to say about Mary more pertinently applies. Whilst the underlying tenor of Tauler's conception and functionalization of Mary is closer to that of Marquard than is Eckhart's—as evidenced by Marquard's quotation of the critical passage from *Predigt* 46—the extent of Tauler's writing on Mary, let alone on Mary's contemplation, is so small that it is difficult to establish any more satisfying connection. It is certainly clear that Marquard's presentation of Mary cannot be regarded as epigonal to Tauler, even more so than to Eckhart.

---

[257] Id., *Predigt* 52 (238. 34–239. 8); see Górecka, *Das Bild Mariens*, pp. 481–2.
[258] See *Dekalogerklärung*, fol. 160ʳ (cf. ed. 1516, p. 36ᵇ; ed. 1483, 37. 15–23); for the identifications see Steer, 'Der Armutsgedanke', p. 290; and van Maren (ed.), *Marquard von Lindau. Die zehe Gebot (Straßburg 1516 und 1520)*, p. 33.
[259] See *Dekalogerklärung*, fol. 190ʳ⁻ᵛ (cf. ed. 1516, p. 72ᵃ⁻ᵇ; ed. 1483, 90. 29–43).

Birgitta of Sweden (d. 1373) belonged to the same generation as Tauler, and her extensive corpus of writing must be considered as one of the major contributions to the Marian literature of the later Middle Ages, despite its very different character from the works discussed thus far.[260] Indeed, a compendium of the Marian components of her work, the *Celeste viridarium*, was produced in the 1380s by her confessor Alfonso of Jaén.[261] Birgitta's principal Marian work (on which the *Celeste viridarium* drew heavily) is the *Sermo angelicus*, probably written in 1354, and which presents itself as a set of lections concerning Mary for the Birgittine nuns, ordered by Christ and dictated to Birgitta by an angel.[262] Many aspects of the tradition with which we are concerned are asserted by Birgitta. Mary is replete with all the gifts of the Spirit, so much so that she knew she would be inseparable from Christ even after his birth;[263] the gifts bestowed on her exceeded those bestowed upon angels,[264] and her virtues exceeded those bestowed upon the entire world, such that God delighted more in Mary than in that world.[265] Her knowledge (by faith, that is) of God in her childhood was precocious, and Birgitta uses the language of contemplative ascent to describe this early knowledge: 'sensus et intellectus virginis in celorem celsitudinem frequenter ascendens Deum constanter per fidem apprehendebat, cuius dulcissima caritate suauiter amplexata in se ipsam redibat'[266] ('as the Virgin's sense and intellect ascended frequently into the height of the heavens, by faith she steadfastly perceived God; sweetly embraced in his sweetest love, she returned to herself'). Even at this early age, Mary desired an intimate relationship with God,[267] and—as we saw earlier—having foreknowledge of the incarnation from Scripture, was

---

[260] For surveys of Birgitta's Marian material see Rossing, *Studier*, pp. 160–74; and Sahlin, *Birgitta of Sweden*, pp. 78–82.

[261] See Eklund (ed.), *Sermo angelicvs*, pp. 13, 20, and 42.

[262] See Birgitta of Sweden, *Sermo angelicus*, prologue (pp. 75–8); on the dating see Eklund (ed.), *Sermo angelicvs*, pp. 18–19. For surveys of the *Sermo angelicus*, see Piltz, '*Nostram naturam sublimaverat*', pp. 256–67; Morris, *St Birgitta of Sweden*, pp. 105–9; and Børresen, 'Birgitta's Godlanguage', pp. 51–3.

[263] See Birgitta of Sweden, *Sermo angelicus*, c. 2, §15–17 (p. 83); on Mary's repletion with the Spirit from her infancy cf. *Revelationes*, lib. 3, c. 8, §2 (p. 107).

[264] See ead., *Sermo angelicus*, c. 4, §13–19 (p. 88).

[265] See ibid., c. 5, §15–17 (pp. 90–1).

[266] Ibid., c. 13, §2–6, here §5 (pp. 110–11); cf. *Revelationes*, lib. 1, c. 51, §10–11 (pp. 403–4).

[267] See ead., *Sermo angelicus*, c. 14, §14 (pp. 114–15); cf. *Revelationes*, lib. 1, c. 51, §18–19 (p. 405).

inflamed with love at the prospect of Christ's physical presence within her.[268] Birgitta's conception of the contemplative ascent, one should note, is strongly voluntarist.[269]

Birgitta repeatedly states that Mary was replete with divine wisdom, both in general terms and with specific reference to the incarnation.[270] It is not totally clear what Birgitta understands by Mary's 'divina sapientia' ('divine wisdom'). She defines it twice as the total submission of Mary's own will to that of God,[271] and once as an ability Mary had not only to understand the words of religious intellectuals, but to discern whether those words proceeded from the genuine love of God or only from their literary skill.[272] A further definition of 'divina sapientia', now without Marian reference, is the living of a virtuous life and carrying out of good works.[273] Exactly how far this wisdom extends is not made clear. As regards the specific question of mystical union, there is somewhat more evidence. Birgitta presents, if at times somewhat hazily, both the incarnation and the nativity of Christ as moments of mystical union between Mary and God: as, for example, here in the first book of the *Revelationes*:

Ad quod verbum [i.e. Mary's 'fiat'] illico concipiebatur filius meus in utero meo cum ineffabili exultacione anime mee et omnium membrorum. [. . .] Quando vero peperi eum, sine dolore et peccato peperi eum, sicut et concepi, cum tanta anime et corporis exultacione, quod pedes mei pre exultacione non senciebant terram, ubi stabant. Et sicut in omnia membra mea cum gaudio tocius anime mee intrauit, sic cum gaudio omnium membrorum exultante anima ineffabili gaudio sine lesione virginitatis mee exiuit.[274]

(At that word [i.e. 'fiat'] my son was instantly conceived in my womb with an ineffable exultation of my soul and of all the limbs of my body. When indeed I gave birth to him, I gave birth to him with neither suffering nor sin; but rather as I conceived him, with such an exultation of body and soul that my feet did not feel

---

[268] See Birgitta of Sweden, *Sermo angelicus*, c. 15, §17–18 (p. 118).

[269] See ibid., c. 13, § 18 (p. 112); *Revelationes*, lib. 1, c. 1, §11–12 (pp. 243–4), and lib. 5, rev. 4, § 8 (p. 122).

[270] See ead., *Revelationes*, lib. 1, c. 31, §8 (p. 330); lib. 1, c. 51, § 9 (p. 403); and (at the incarnation) lib. 1, c. 50, § 7–10 (p. 399). See further Sahlin, *Birgitta of Sweden*, pp. 96–8; Morris, *St Birgitta of Sweden*, pp. 108–9; and Koch, 'Lignelses-, Symbol- og Billedsprog', pp. 478–86.

[271] See Birgitta of Sweden, *Revelationes*, lib. 2, c. 22, §18–20 (p. 99); and *Revelationes extravagantes*, c. 3, §3–5 (pp. 116–17); the latter passage is the *locus classicus* for Birgitta's expression of Mary's co-redemption of mankind.

[272] See ead., *Revelationes*, lib. 3, c. 8, § 7 (p. 108).

[273] See ibid., lib. 2, c. 25, §31–43 (pp. 108–9).

[274] Ibid., lib. 1, c. 10, §11–12 (p. 265).

the earth where they stood on account of the exultation. And just as he entered with joy in all my limbs and of all my soul, so he left me with joy in all my limbs, with my soul exulting in ineffable joy, and without harm to my virginity.)

This reception of joy and sweetness at the incarnation and nativity is repeated elsewhere.[275] A crucial passage is located in the fifth book of the *Revelationes*. Here, in a vision (or rather, an audition) dictated by Christ, we find an interpretation of all the parts of Mary's body, each of which illuminates a particular virtue. In considering her mouth, 'Christ' refers to Mary's words drawing his divinity into her—probably an oblique reference to Mary's 'fiat'—but only to a certain extent, only *quodammodo*. Birgitta (or potentially her then confessor, translating her Swedish text into Latin) may well be guarding here against reading the influx of the divine into Mary as a deification:

Os tuum fuit quasi lampas, intus ardens et lucens abextra, quia verba et affecciones tue anime fuerunt ardentes interius diuina intelligencia et exterius splendentes ex disposicione laudabili tuorum motuum corporalium et concordancia pulcherrima tuarum virtutum. Vere, mater carissima, verbum oris tui traxit quodammodo deitatem meam in te, et feruor diuine dulcedinis tue nunquam separabat me a te, quia verba tua dulcia sunt super mel et fauum [cf. Ps. 18: 11].[276]

(Your mouth was like a lantern, burning within and beaming forth, because the words and inclinations of your soul were burning inwardly with divine intelligence, and shining outwardly from the praiseworthy disposition of your bodily movements and the most beautiful unity of your virtues. Truly, dearest mother, the word of your mouth drew—to a certain extent—my Godhead into you, and the fervour of your divine sweetness never separated me from you, because your words are sweet beyond honey and honeycomb.)

Whether the intimate union of Mary's heart with that of Christ could, furthermore, be seen as a mystical union is a matter of debate that we cannot develop here. It is certainly not made explicit.[277] Rather more explicit, however, is the *locus classicus* of Birgitta's presentation of Mary as mystically united with Christ: her vision of the nativity whilst on pilgrim-

---

[275] For the incarnation, see ibid., c. 51, §20–2 (p. 405), and lib. 6, c. 59, §1–3 (pp. 202–3); for the nativity, see lib. 6, c. 88, §5 (pp. 247–8); on Mary's repletion with divine sweetness in heaven, see lib. 1, c. 31, §11 (pp. 330–1).

[276] Ibid., lib. 5, rev. 4, §12–13 (pp. 122–3); on Mary as 'speculum divinitatis' ('mirror of divinity') in heaven, in which the Trinity can be seen, see lib. 1, c. 42, §5–9 (pp. 369–70).

[277] On the importance of the heart for Birgitta as 'the principal locus for human encounters with God', see Sahlin, *Birgitta of Sweden*, p. 91.

age in the Holy Land. Mary gives birth whilst in prayer, suspended in contemplative ecstasy and intoxicated with divine sweetness. At the actual moment of birth she is surrounded by divine light:

Cumque hec omnia sic parata essent, tunc virgo genuflexa est cum magna reuerencia, ponens se ad oracionem, et dorsum versus presepe tenebat, faciem vero ad celum leuatam versus orientem. Erectis igitur manibus et oculis in celum intentis stabat quasi in extasi contemplacionis suspensa, inebriata diuina dulcedine. Et sic ea in oracione stante vidi tunc ego mouere iacentem in vtero eius, et illico in momentu et ictu oculi peperit filium, a quo tanta lux ineffabilis et splendor exibat, quod sol non esset ei comparabilis. Neque candela illa, quam posuerat senex, quoquomodo lumen reddebat, quia splendor ille diuinus splendorem materialem candele totaliter annichilauerat.[278]

(And when all these things were made ready in this way, the Virgin then knelt down with great reverence, positioning herself to pray; she kept her back towards the manger, and her face lifted up to heaven and looking towards the east. With her hands then raised up and her eyes focused on heaven, she remained as if she was suspended in the ecstasy of contemplation and intoxicated with divine sweetness. And as she stood in prayer in this way, I saw at that point the one who lay in her womb move; and instantly, in the momentary blink of an eye, she gave birth to the Son, from whom ineffable light and radiance shone forth to which even the sun could not compare. Nor did that candle, which the old man [i.e. Joseph] had set down, give out light in any way, because this divine radiance totally annihilated the material radiance of the candle.)

This, of course, is the passage in Birgitta's *Revelationes* that had such a powerful iconographical significance. As early as the 1370s, immediately after Birgitta's death but before her canonization, Florentine painting began to depict this version of the nativity, with Mary kneeling in prayer and surrounded by a bright light, in place of the older depictions of Mary in bed with the Christ-child in her arms or in the manger. This pictorial representation spread rapidly—several Southern German examples date from the very beginning of the fifteenth century—and entirely supplanted the earlier, more naturalistic iconography.[279]

---

[278] Birgitta of Sweden, *Revelationes*, lib. 7, c. 21, §6–9 (p. 188). On the related issue of Birgitta's own mystical pregnancy (and its relationship to her understanding of her prophetic vocation as parturition), see Sahlin, *Birgitta of Sweden*, pp. 82–4; more fully in Sahlin, '"A Marvelous and Great Exultation"', and (examining Birgitta's subsequent influence) Sahlin, 'The Virgin Mary'.

[279] The seminal study is that of Cornell, *The Iconography of the Nativity*, pp. 1–44; which should be read in conjunction with the thorough revision by Svanberg, 'De allra äldsta bilderna'. See now, summatively, Aili and Svanberg, *Imagines Sanctae Birgittae*, vol. 1, pp. 93–101, and vol. 2, pp. 106–23 (plates 65a–71). All further literature is

Birgitta, of course, was not a systematist and expressed her ideas very differently to the other intellectuals whose work we have considered. But the striking cast she gave to the nativity had, as we shall now see, a direct influence on the works of the subsequent generation—Marquard's generation. Our focus turns now to Germany, and first to the *Marienleben* of Heinrich von St Gallen. The *Marienleben* is a very long work that can only be approximately dated to the first quarter of the fifteenth century, but had a reasonable transmission: thirty-four manuscripts, from across the Southern Germanic region, are extant.[280] It shares a common author, probably Heinrich, with a German commentary on the Magnificat (hereinafter the *Magnifikat-Auslegung*), but whether the same author is also responsible for the German *Extendit manum* Passion treatise—and certain other German works—is not clear from the known evidence.[281] Both the *Marienleben* and the *Magnifikat-Auslegung* mix short narrative passages with curious quasi-scholastic questions, in which question, argument, and solution are all attributed to mostly fictitious authorities—notably Simon of Cassia—in whose works the relevant passage is rarely to be found. One important exception to this in the *Marienleben* is Birgitta of Sweden. Heinrich's quotations from Birgitta's works are verifiable, and silently he drew more widely on those works.[282]

The second chapter of the *Marienleben* discusses Mary's repletion with the seven gifts of the Spirit. The sixth of these is given as the cognition of the divine. Mary is said to have deduced the power of the Father, the wisdom of the Son, and the goodness of the Spirit by a process of philosophical abstraction from natural phenomena, thus identifying the persons of the Trinity according to their principal qualities.[283] But her cognition went further: she perceived the divinity of God by supernatural means, more clearly than any other human in this life:

derivative, although some examples from the Low Countries are given by de Kreek, 'Bene veneris deus meus'. More comprehensive analyses of the texts here are given by Morris, *St Birgitta of Sweden*, pp. 135–9, and Lindgren, 'Birgitta och bilderna', pp. 244–5.

[280] See Hilg, *Das >Marienleben<*, pp. 69 and 118–19, with details of 31 manuscripts; augmented now by the relevant entry in the 'Marburger Repertorium', at <http://cgi-host.uni-marburg.de/~mrep/liste_inhalt.php?id=1061> [accessed 2 Feb. 2007].

[281] On the dating and authorship of the *Marienleben*, see Hilg, *Das >Marienleben<*, pp. 373–90.

[282] On the structure and manner of quotation, see ibid. 367–73.

[283] See Heinrich von St Gallen, *Marienleben*, c. 2, ll. 72–93 (pp. 135–6).

Daß hat Maria die schon wol bekant (die macht deß himelischen vaterß) nach
naturlichen lauffen; aber vber naturlich hat sie bekant sein heilige ware gothait
klerlicher, wan kain creatur ye getet, dye ain lauter creatur haist, oder ymmer
erkennen mag ewiglichen.[284]

(Mary already knew well the power of the heavenly Father according to the natural
course of things; but supernaturally she knew his true, holy divinity more clearly
than any other created being, even a pure created being, ever did, or may ever
perceive in all time.)

In the *Magnifikat-Auslegung*, this clearest possible cognition of God is then
predicated on Mary's deepest possible humility.[285] Further, Mary is said
(before the annunciation) to have woken at midnight to contemplate the
heavenly in prayer, to which activity Heinrich refers with the term 'daß
schewlich leben' ('the visionary life'), indicating mystical experience.[286] But
it is at the nativity that Heinrich's presentation of Mary's mystical experience becomes most clear, a section in which he draws explicitly on Birgitta's
Revelationes, and implicitly on the pseudo-Albert's *Mariale*.[287] Mary was
engaged in her usual contemplation, in which she perceived the abyss of
God's divinity more clearly than any other, when at the moment of sharpest
cognition—of closest union—she gave birth supernaturally to Christ.
However Birgitta may have understood the nativity, it is clear that Heinrich
recognizes and heightens the mystical aspect:

Do die hochwirdig himelschawerin also knyet vnd contemplirt vnd yczund nyes-
send waß deß abgrunds der heiligen waren gotheyt klerlicher vnd lewterlicher, dan
kein creatur ye geprauecht het, do wart der vinster stal durchleucht mit einem
vbernaturlichen, feynen vnd claren liecht. Vnd do sie also yczund waß yn dem
allerhochsten bekantnuß vnd freuden vnd sussikeit, dar yn sie bekant vnd sach got
den vater irs suns vnd den behenden werckmeister den heiligen geist vnd iren sun,
der wesenlich eins mit in waß vnd ye waß vnd ymer ist an end, vnd alß hymelisch
her, daz do gegenwurtig waz, vnd do hort daz gesanckt der heiligen engel, die do
lobten die heiligen drivaltigkeit—yn dem zug gepar die awßerwelt zart schon vnd
miniclich iungfraw Maria iren eingeporen lieben sun.[288]

(When the reverend visionary of heaven thus kneeled, contemplated, and now
delighted in the abyss of the true, holy divinity more clearly and purely than any
created being ever enjoyed, the dark stable was illuminated with a supernatural, fine,
and clear light. At that moment when she was in the highest cognition, joy, and

---

[284] See Heinrich von St Gallen, *Marienleben*, ll. 93–7 (pp. 136–7).
[285] See id., *Magnifikat-Auslegung*, ll. 366–9 (p. 40).
[286] See id., *Marienleben*, c. 4, ll. 147–52 (p. 153), here l. 151.
[287] See Hilg's notes to c. 6 (Hilg, *Das>Marienleben<*, pp. 337–40).
[288] Heinrich von St Gallen, *Marienleben*, c. 6, ll. 64–74 (p. 183); cf. ll. 75–82
(pp. 183–4).

sweetness of all, in which she perceived and saw God, the father of her son; the subtle architect, namely the Holy Spirit; her son, who was essentially one with them, always was so and ever will be so without end; and all the heavenly host that was present there; when she heard the song of the holy angels there, who praised the Holy Trinity: in this rapture the chosen, tender, beautiful, and loving Virgin Mary gave birth to her only-begotten, beloved son.)

The same terminology is deployed by Heinrich in a long, strongly voluntarist digression on contemplation in the eleventh chapter. Therein he asserts the primacy of contemplation over pilgrimage, on the grounds that the rewards of contemplation (the cognition of God) outweigh the rewards of pilgrimage (indulgence remitting time in purgatory).[289] He describes the rewards of contemplation thus: 'Wann alß vil sich der mensch hie kert zu got, alß vil sicht er klerlicher yn den spigel der heiligen ewigen gotheit vnd alß uil neust er dieffer deß abgrundes gotlicher bekantnuß'[290] ('For the more an individual turns to God here, the more clearly he will see into the looking glass of the holy, eternal Godhead, and the more deeply he will enjoy the abyss of divine cognition'). Finally, he repeats much of this terminology to describe Mary's contemplative life after Christ's ascension,[291] concluding with a definitive statement that Mary was frequently drawn into contemplative ecstasy:

Also lebt die zart rein fraw nach der auffart irs liben kindes, alß etlich lerer halten, biß yn daz dreyzehent iar, in den sie offt an allen zweifel gezogen ist worden in daz lustig paradeiß vnd in daß ewig leben in ein geistlichen zug, piß daz die zeit kom, daz sie ir liber sun wolt beruffen von diser werlt zu im yn daz ewig leben.[292]

(In this way the tender, pure lady lived after the ascension of her beloved son, as some authorities claim, for thirteen years. In this time she was without doubt often drawn into the delightful paradise and into the eternal life in spiritual rapture, until the time came that her beloved son wanted to call her from this world to him, into eternal life.)

The ideas that were only intimated in the *Vita rhythmica* have, several generations later, become explicit in and firm constituents of Heinrich's narrative, as a direct product of the tradition we have outlined. The same development can be seen if we turn to a second major German work, the *Nürnberger Marienbuch*. This incorporates a series of non-narrative

---

[289] See ibid., c. 11, ll. 106–217 (pp. 222–8); cf. the *Magnifikat-Auslegung*, ll. 1167–79 (pp. 65–6).
[290] Id., *Marienleben*, c. 11, ll. 128–30 (p. 223); for Mary as the *speculum divinitatis*, see the *Magnifikat-Auslegung*, ll. 544–55 (p. 46).
[291] See id., *Marienleben*, c. 18, ll. 57–94 (pp. 309–11).
[292] Ibid., ll. 90–4 (p. 311).

sources—sermons, hymns, exegetical works, and accounts of miracles—into a *vita Mariae*, becoming thereby a *libellus* rather than a purely narrative *vita*.[293] It drew on an extremely wide range of sources, both Latin and German (including Birgitta of Sweden), and probably originated in the Dominican convent in Nuremberg around or shortly after 1410.[294] Though itself preserved in just one manuscript, its particular importance lies in its having been the sole source for the Marian sections of the *Heiligen Leben*, the most successful German narrative prose text of the entire Middle Ages.[295]

The *Nürnberger Marienbuch*, like Heinrich's *Marienleben*, demonstrates similar fruits of the tradition presenting Mary as a mystical contemplative. Thus in a passage translated from a sermon by the Polish Dominican Peregrine of Opole (d. after 1335), Mary is said to have experienced the beatific vision daily.[296] The description of the nativity follows Birgitta's account, and more closely so than in Heinrich's *Marienleben*. Here, Mary's soul is drawn into God's divinity—'ir geist enzuket wer in die gothait' ('her spirit was enraptured into divinity')—at the parturition (as for Birgitta); she was not in a pre-existent, normal state of mystical contemplation (as for Heinrich).[297] Another section, interpolated between two passages drawn from the *Vita rhythmica* on Mary's life after Christ's ascension, defines Mary's contemplative ecstasy and explains that Mary was not left senseless (as one might normally expect) during these experiences.[298] The author adapts the *regula Mariae* from the *Vita rhythmica*, and extends those passages dealing with Mary's contemplation of heaven.[299] Most extensively, a long section drawn principally from an assumption sermon attributed to the German Cistercian Konrad von Brundelsheim (d. 1321), expanded with passages from Bernard of Clairvaux and (again) Peregrine of Opole, examines Mary's contemplation in the context of a discussion on her grace and virtues.[300] Her mystical experience exceeds that of all other saints:

[293] See Jung (ed.), *Das Nürnberger Marienbuch*, pp. 8*–14*.
[294] See ibid., 15*–40*.
[295] On the manuscript, see ibid. 3*–7*; on the reception in the *Heiligen Leben*, see pp. 40*–55*, and on the further reception in the *Magnet unserer lieben Frau*, the most compendious Marian treatise in German, see pp. 55*–64*.
[296] See *Nürnberger Marienbuch*, 11. 24–8.
[297] See ibid. 32. 16–25.
[298] See ibid. 70.14–23.
[299] See ibid. 70. 23–73. 17; esp. 72. 13–15; 72. 22–6; and 73. 13–17.
[300] The full section is ibid. 86. 8–93. 3, with the part on contemplation at 89. 20–90. 35.

Dy ander genad, dy der junckfraw Maria mit getailt ist worden, ist dy, das sy ist gewest dy aller andehtigist in empsigen contempliren. Es sprechen ir andehtig fronpoten, das sy stetiglichen sey gewest in der begir der andaht, zv der dy aller grosten heiligen in einem verzucken vnd in einem augenplick einer stund dannoch gar selten zu kumen sein.[301]

(The second grace that was bestowed on the Virgin Mary is that she was the most devout of all in eager contemplation. Those who are in a position to make judgements devoutly about her say that she continually desired the meditative state to which the greatest of all the saints came in rapture but very rarely indeed for even an instant of a single moment.)

Mary is then said to have been accorded, 'alls guticklich zu gelauben ist' ('as is graciously to be believed'), the highest contemplative grace as described by means of a quote integral to Konrad's original sermon and attributed to Bernard, in which the loss of self in almost unindividuated union with God is expressed.[302] After this, a very long passage in which the author interpolates Konrad's text with genuine material from Bernard's *Homilia 4 super 'Missus est'* returns to the issue of how Mary was not left senseless and in a trance-like state, despite enjoying such great and constant mystical union with God.[303]

We have named here two further fourteenth-century intellectuals, Konrad von Brundelsheim and Peregrine of Opole, who occupy a position in the tradition that we have set out. Both are distinguished by the exceptionally wide transmission of their (Latin) sermons; both are contemporaries of Ubertino da Casale, Meister Eckhart, and Engelbert von Admont. We cannot examine their works here; but they belong to this tradition nonetheless, and provide an important attestation of the breadth of its dissemination. The presentation of Mary as mystical contemplative is not an abstract matter, confined to a limited academic audience; and there is no greater testimony to this than the *Dekalogerklärung*. With this work, Marquard did not produce a *vita Mariae* like Heinrich von St Gallen; nor a compendium like the *Nürnberger Marienbuch*. His focus was narrower, broadly on Mary's manner of life and particularly on her contemplative experience. As a Marian work, the *Dekalogerklärung* is much closer to the long Latin texts of earlier generations; along with the *Nürnberger Marienbuch*, it forms a precursor to the generation of vernacular *summae Marianae* (like the *Magnet unserer lieben Frau*) in the fifteenth century. It is undoubtedly the first German text to deal comprehensively and originally

[301] Ibid. 89. 20–5.
[302] See ibid. 89. 25–90. 1.
[303] See ibid. 90. 1–35.

with the subject of Mary's contemplation, at an intellectual level comparable with that of its Latin predecessors—most notably, given their common
focus, with the *De gratiis et virtutibus* of Engelbert von Admont. Unlike
Engelbert, Marquard vocalized the imitability of Mary much more strongly, rather than elevating her experience out of reach to the ordinary
contemplative. His use of existing descriptions of the process of contemplative ascent and mystical union, without reference to Mary in their
original locations (notably in Ruusbroec's *Geestelijke brulocht*), to apply
to Mary demonstrates in itself his intention to position Mary as the first to
tread a particular path; as the individual to have trodden that path most
perfectly; but not as essentially distinct from those who followed her along
it. His mechanism of showing how the *amici Dei* imitate Mary in the
contemplative life makes this explicit. It is, finally, hard to find a work
mentioned whose circulation and influence exceeded that of the *Dekalogerklärung*: it may validly be regarded as the apogee of the tradition, a
tradition that stretched across Europe (though with a notable concentration
of works from the Germanic regions) and across the religious orders.

Conclusion

The Introduction to this book suggested that there was such a thing as a 'Marquard ethos'. With Marquard's contribution to the piety, generally speaking, of the later Middle Ages now examined across a range of central issues, it is pertinent to question that initial statement and ask in what such an ethos may have consisted.

Marquard presented models for imitation that constituted radical alternatives to the predominant forms of the later fourteenth century. The Christ of *De anima Christi* is a Christ who suffered inwardly for the entire duration of his life, from the moment of his conception until his final breath, and for whom the corporeal afflictions of the Passion in his final hours were of distinctly secondary importance. The Mary of the *Dekalogerklärung* is a quiet contemplative who has achieved mystical union with God in this life, and lives out her earthly existence in a manner that defines the future shape of the monastic life. As she stood under the cross, she stood calm in her bearing and avoided the excessive display of emotion or weeping. Marquard's works represent in this way a decisive break in the iconographical tradition, just as his treatise on the eucharist marks a decisive break with the dominant patterns of theological instruction on the nature of the sacrament and the conventional insistence on the individual's worthiness to receive it.

Too little is known of the historical Marquard to present any kind of convincing explanation for this manifest trend in his works that relies on knowledge of his personal circumstances and personal sensibilities. In some cases, such as his understanding of Christ's Passion, Marquard is seen to favour one intellectual tradition over another—in that case, involving the highly unusual decision to base his presentation on that of Petrus Johannis Olivi—just as his mystical theology charts an independent path between competing models and competing authorities. But those decisions are not merely academic decisions to prefer, for reasons that now remain inscrutable, the tenets of one of his intellectual predecessors over another. They are surely motivated by Marquard's understanding of and engagement with his audience. His presentation of imitable models strikingly different to the contemporary norm reflects a desire to change the nature of contemporary devotional practice and religious life amongst the 'laity' writ large: a practice that he regarded as overtly fixated on the bodily, the external, the sensory, and the sensational, and insufficiently concerned with the inner condition of the mind and the nature of the individual's actual being.

This concern for the interior can be seen more widely in Marquard's oeuvre. It is most easily visible in his presentation of Mary as a contemplative who enjoyed the mystical union. The Marian material of the *Dekalog-erklärung* was not somehow intended to be read separately to the ethical-normative sections of the work, even if it has been isolated in that heuristic way for the purposes of this study. It provided instead an exemplification of the ethical principles that structure the entire work put into in action. The reader is guided thereby not to fulfil a set of specific formal criteria that can be judged externally, but to redirect his inner self in accordance with the path Marquard sets out through his presentation of Mary. The individual who seeks to live in accordance with the Ten Commandments does not—or rather, not just—have to respect a particular set of statutory requirements, but must reshape his life around the pattern offered to him in the figure of Mary, and actualized in the contemporary world by the friends of God. Marquard's allegorical works, which have not formed part of this study so far, offer another example of this concern for the interior. They are broadly exegetical treatises that present contemplative schemata. But their focus is not so much on contemplation itself as on the way in which the contemplative should bear interior, mental suffering. The issues that underpin these works are not the ascetic discipline of the body or the endurance of physical illness or corporeal weakness, but loneliness, isolation, temptation, and depression. In addition, Marquard's rationalization in those works of the purpose—indeed, the necessity—of such suffering is highly distinctive in that it is not Christological. It does not, that is, rest on the assumption that the individual's suffering is imitative of the suffering of Christ, and so is beneficial in that it offers the securest path to salvation. Rather, it rests on a more complex theological justification of the innate value of suffering, which secures heavenly reward, and on the necessity of mental suffering in the cultivation of the mind in the process of the contemplative ascent to God. The link to the graphic and bodily suffering of Christ is broken again.

Similarly, Marquard opposed the conventional ways in which central aspects of the faith were approached, communicated, and taught. The clearest example of this is the *Eucharistietraktat*. There Marquard sought to take a new direction in the instruction of eucharistic theology, and in the approach to the sacrament to which the individual was guided. This was no abstract consideration of best practice, but a treatise intended for widespread consumption that shows Marquard to be attuned to the problems and difficulties of contemporary individuals on an intimate, mental level—their hopes and fears—as they were confronted with the supernatural in the most concrete form. Instead of the incalculable might of God's judicial authority, he emphasized the love that God had manifested in the sacrament for the individual. That love was to be met by the individual's reciprocal love for God, rather than the fulfilment of an arduous set of criteria to prove the individual's worthiness in the sight of God and so allow him to receive the sacrament without incurring divine wrath. This emollient aspect to Marquard's writing means that he is very different to the now more famous Franciscans of earlier generations who had preached the formidable *sermones ad status*, not least Berthold von Regensburg. Yet reading the *Eucharistietraktat* in the light of its historical context reveals that Marquard sought to change established patterns of thought in his audience just as decisively as Berthold did, though in a less direct way.

This, then, is the 'Marquard ethos'. But Marquard's significance is not merely a question of tone and approach. The positions he took on central issues were often markedly different from those of his contemporaries, and set new trajectories in late medieval German thought. One example, which has been alluded to above, stands out above all others: the insistence that the individual must come to acknowledge his own unworthiness and his inability to make himself worthy—to be justified in the sight of God—without divine grace; grace that was accessed by simple faith in God's mercy and a heartfelt desire to improve oneself in future. This principle underpins Marquard's instruction on the preconditions for eucharistic reception, and there are indications in the *Dialogus rationis et conscientiae* that his contemporary Matthaeus of Cracow held and communicated similar ideas. There is a long and winding road between this and the idea of justification by faith and faith alone that is associated with Martin Luther. Marquard sought a strategy to tackle a pragmatic issue—the fear of eucharistic reception—and showed no interest in the elaboration of a general principle about the nature of man's justification in the eyes of God that held in all situations, not just the specific circumstances of eucharistic reception. But that road, however winding, is nonetheless there. The way of thinking about the relationship between man and God that produces the theology on which justification by faith alone rests—that is, the intellectual climate within which such a doctrine could arise—is a development of the later fourteenth century and one for which Marquard (and Matthaeus of Cracow) is responsible.

In instances such as this, the perspective of the *longue durée* of intellectual history in pre-Reformation Germany enables an argument to be constructed that Marquard's works, not least on account of the remarkable extent of their manuscript transmission, were responsible for changing the trajectory of thought on particular issues. It would be extremely incautious to assert anything more. Nor should too much be claimed for Marquard, who was no voice in the wilderness. Other intellectuals of his and later generations—some well known, like Jean Gerson, and others rather less so, like Matthaeus of Cracow—made powerful contributions to the very issues that Marquard addressed. But what Marquard has in common with both Matthaeus and with Gerson, and which raises him above the parapet, is the extremely broad spectrum of his works and their massive circulation. Some of the writers who have been mentioned in the course of this study, no less important in terms of the content of their works, nonetheless had a much more limited sphere of influence. Novel ideas and engaging approaches may well be identified in the oeuvres of a Johannes Hiltalingen von Basel or an Engelbert von Admont, but the transmission of Hiltalingen's works is tiny, and that of Engelbert is confined to a very specific geographical region (Austria and Bavaria). The more theoretical tone and scholastic form of their works further differentiates their works from an appeal to the kind of audience that Marquard's pragmatic works, at least, sought to address.

His works were certainly read by the Observants of all orders in the fifteenth century. There is no German author aside from Heinrich Seuse whose works were copied and distributed as comprehensively within the reformed convents. This is not just a question of literary taste, though the tone of Marquard's works and their treatment of issues on a pragmatic level must have struck a chord with the Observants to have attained such a level of popularity. It is also the case that many of the distinctive positions commonly associated with the Observants are also characteristic of Marquard's writing. This is evident, for example, in his profound scepticism towards eucharistic visions of the Christ-child, and his cautious and differentiated approach to the perception of sweetness in the sacrament. Now Marquard had simply too little to say on either of these issues for him to be credited with a position of any tangible influence in their respective intellectual histories. But they are sufficient to indicate that Marquard must be accorded a position in those histories. In so doing, the intellectual genesis of the literary works of the German Observants can be placed within a longer and broader historical context, to be seen less as an immediate rupture in the religious practice of the early fifteenth century, and more as a substantive development of a broad approach that had rather longer roots. On this issue, there is much more work to be done.

It is the focus of much of Marquard's oeuvre on pragmatic issues of the Christian life, a factor that helps to explain the popularity of his works with the Observants, which makes it—to recall Berndt Hamm's term—undoubtedly 'Frömmigkeitstheologie'. To view Marquard's oeuvre as catechesis is to view it outside of its historical context, and to miss its point. The *Eucharistietraktat* shows that most clearly. Catechetical instruction on certain aspects of eucharistic theology is certainly offered, but is not the point of the work. The point, rather, is primarily to adjust the way in which individuals conceived of, and approached the sacrament, and so to effect a change in the minds of the work's readers; and secondarily to counter the effects of certain prevailing tendencies that Marquard regarded as negative and harmful to the condition of belief, and provide a limited amount of catechetical instruction on difficult points. This pragmatic direction of the work also conditions its form. It is not an encompassing catechetical work that presents a comprehensive exposition of every aspect of eucharistic theology. Only those points are extracted that prove necessary in one way or another for its particular focus, or which evidently presented certain difficulties of comprehension to Marquard's intended audience. The *Eucharistietraktat* is a new kind of work which marks the beginning of the process of 'normative Zentrierung'—to draw on Hamm's terminology again—that characterizes applied theological writing in pre-Reformation Germany. The process is by no means complete, but it has undoubtedly begun, and the further development of subsequent works influenced by the direction that Marquard had set can be traced from this point.

Marquard's pragmatic works form just one part of his contribution to the literary history of late medieval Germany. He was similarly innovative in other fields. His long allegorical treatises—notably the *Auszug der Kinder Israel*, which enjoyed an extremely wide circulation, but also *De Nabuchodonosor* and the Latin *De archa Noe*—may not have formed part of this present study, but are important works on contemplation whose structure is determined by Victorine models of scriptural exegesis. They bear very close comparison to certain works by Marquard's older Dutch contemporary, especially *Van den gheestelijken tabernakel*. Taken together, Ruusbroec and Marquard represent a rebirth of Victorine exegesis without compare in the later Middle Ages, and which lose nothing in their complexity from their composition in the vernacular. Marquard, indeed, wrote such works in the same style, in the same genre, and at the same level in both Latin and German. In addition, his oeuvre played a major and hitherto overlooked role in the generation of a German vocabulary capable of expressing the complex ideas of scholastic thought—and, furthermore, of becoming a language fully capable for the independent generation of sophisticated, even academic, writing. The position of Marquard's oeuvre in this development is not entirely Marquard's responsibility. It is above all the translations of his two longest Latin works, *De reparatione hominis* and the *Johannes-Auslegung*, which are remarkable for their precise, fluent, and competent handling of the specialized Latin vocabulary that Marquard had used. The very fact that German translations of these extremely substantial works were produced is testimony to the interest that existed in making Marquard's oeuvre accessible, and the importance that it was accorded after he himself had died.

Marquard's period of activity stands on an important boundary in the history of late medieval Germany. In his survey of Christianity in the later Middle Ages the importance of Germany did not escape Alexander Murray's eye:

[T]he council of Constance in 1415, which healed the Schism, was also called to 'reform' the church, a mission its successor at Basle, fifteen years later, sought to continue. But most of the reforms were designed to slim down the papacy, and once the conciliarists had gone home there was no one to enforce the reforms except secular princes. By a judicious use of the red pencil, they sanctioned reforms which strengthened their own churches. That, thought conservative Italians, is what happens when councils meet in Switzerland, not in the Lateran. When the council of Constance deposed the Italian antipope John XXIII, in 1415, a historically-minded German curialist compared the act to Otto the Great's deposition of John XII in 963. Power, in a word, had moved back north.[1]

Marquard's works, on the one hand, look backwards. They address issues inherited from the past, such as Eckhart's conception of the mystical union or his theories concerning the eternity of the world. On the other hand, they look forward. They point towards the issues that were about to preoccupy the theologians of the fifteenth century; they condition the approaches that many would then take; and they represent the beginning of a new, German tradition of intellectual history that would culminate in the Reformation. Power really was moving north. The wave of new universities, in many cases founded in close cooperation with the centres of mendicant learning—sometimes even inside them—took place in Marquard's latter years. It would be centres like Vienna and Heidelberg (where Matthaeus of Cracow became professor of theology in 1389, whilst the university was still housed in the Franciscan convent) that would drive this tradition forward in the fifteenth century, together with the impetus offered by the luminaries of the Observant reforms, not least the Dominican

---

[1] Murray, 'The Later Middle Ages', p. 125.

Johannes Nider. Marquard's works, meanwhile, were the best-sellers of
the fifteenth century, and they evidently retained their relevance long
thereafter. In the early sixteenth century, Johann Geiler von Kaysersberg
revised the now outdated language of Marquard's *Auszug der Kinder Israel*
and included it as one of the major components of his *Granatapfel*, which
he then had printed in substantial editions. Amongst Marquard's other
works, *De fide* rather surprisingly went into print; less surprisingly, so did
the *Dekalogerklärung*, which had already received its first printing as an
incunable in 1483 in Venice. A separate recension of the text was published
in a very large edition at Strasbourg in 1516 and again, with the Reformation now well underway, in 1520—equipped with a set of illustrative
woodcuts specially commissioned for the *Dekalogerklärung* by the Strasbourg printer Johann Grüninger from no less a figure than Hans Baldung
Grien.[2]

[2] Oldenbourg, *Die Buchholzschnitte*, nos. 329–8, pp. 96–105 and 152.

Bibliography

ABBREVIATIONS

CCCM   Corpus Christianorum: Continuatio Mediaevalis
CCSL   Corpus Christianorum: Series Latina
ISTC   Incunabula Short-Title Catalogue
PBB   Beiträge zur Geschichte der deutschen Sprache und Literatur (Paul und Braune's Beiträge)
VL   Verfasserlexikon

MANUSCRIPTS

Augsburg, Staatsarchiv
    Reichsstadt Lindau Urkunden 147/1
Basel, Universitätsbibliothek
    Cod. A. X. 138, fols. 127^r–225^v [= Marquard von Lindau, *Dekalogerklärung*]
Konstanz, Heinrich-Suso-Gymnasium
    Cod. 36, fols. 8^r–42^v [= Marquard von Lindau, *Johannes-Auslegung* (Latin)]
Mainz, Stadtbibliothek
    Hs. I 51, fols. 4ra–13ra [= Marquard von Lindau, *De corpore Christi*]
    Hs. I 51, fols. 104ra–153va [= Johannes von Zazenhausen, Passion treatise (German)]
Manchester, John Rylands University Library
    MS. lat. 70, 141^r–184^v [= Marquard von Lindau, *Johannes-Auslegung* (Latin)]
Nuremberg, Stadtbibliothek
    Cent. VI 54, fols. 211^r–302^v [= Johannes von Zazenhausen, Passion treatise (German)]
    Oxford, New College Library MS. 49 [= Petrus Iohannis Olivi, *Lectura super Matthaeum*]
Paris, Bibliothèque Nationale de la France
    Ms. lat. 9074–83
    Ms. all. 214–18
Strasbourg, Archives de la Ville et de la Communauté Urbaine
    AST HE I–II and V
    AST 1066 – 90
Stuttgart, Württembergische Landesbibliothek
    Cod. theol. et philos. 4° 54, fols. 125^v–183^r [= Marquard von Lindau, *Eucharistietraktat*]

CITED WORKS OF MARQUARD VON LINDAU

Marquard von Lindau. *Der Eucharistie-Traktat Marquards von Lindau*, ed. Annelies Julia Hofmann, Hermaea N.F. 7 (Tübingen, 1960).
——*Der Traktat De paupertate von Marquard von Lindau*, ed. Josef Hartinger, (doctoral dissertation, Würzburg, 1965).
——*De anima Christi*, in Josef Hartinger (ed.), *Der Traktat De paupertate von Marquard von Lindau* (doctoral dissertation, Würzburg, 1965), 180–229.
——*Der Hiob-Traktat des Marquard von Lindau. Überlieferung, Untersuchung und kritische Textausgabe*, ed. Eckart Greifenstein, Münchener Texte und Untersuchungen 68 (Munich, 1973).
——*De reparatione hominis. Einführung und Textedition*, ed. Hermann-Josef May, Regensburger Studien zur Theologie 5 (Frankfurt a. M. etc., 1977).
——*De perfectione humanitatis Christi*, in Hermann-Josef May (ed.), *Marquard von Lindau OFM. De reparatione hominis. Einführung und Textedition*, Regensburger Studien zur Theologie 5 (Frankfurt a. M. etc., 1977), 154–61.
——*Die zehe Gebot (Straßburg 1516 und 1520). Ein katechetischer Traktat. Textausgabe mit Einleitung und sprachlichen Beobachtungen*, ed. Jacobus Willem van Maren, Quellen und Forschungen zur Erbauungsliteratur des späten Mittelalters und der frühen Neuzeit 14 (Amsterdam, 1980).
——*Das Buch der zehn Gebote (Venedig 1483). Textausgabe mit Einleitung und Glossar*, ed. Jacobus Willem van Maren, Quellen und Forschungen zur Erbauungsliteratur des späten Mittelalters und der frühen Neuzeit 7 (Amsterdam, 1984).
——*De fide*, in Kurt Ruh (ed.), *Franziskanisches Schrifttum im deutschen Mittelalter*, vol. 2. *Texte*, Münchener Texte und Untersuchungen 86 (Munich, 1985), 290–322.
——*Deutsche Predigten. Untersuchungen und Edition*, ed. Rüdiger Blumrich, Texte und Textgeschichte 34 (Tübingen, 1994).

PRIMARY SOURCES

Acts of the Process of Canonization of St Clare of Assisi (1253), in Zeffirino Lazzeri, 'Il processo di canonizzazione di S. Chiara d'Assisi', *Archivum Franciscanum Historicum* 13 (1920), 403–507; repr. in Stefano Brufani and Enrico Menestò (eds.), *Fontes Franciscani* (Assisi, 1995), 2453–507.
Acts of the Process of Canonization of St Clare of Assisi (1253), in Regis J. Armstrong (trans.), *Clare of Assisi. Early Documents* (St Bonaventure, NY, 1993), 132–85.
Achard of St Victor, *Sermons inédits*, ed. Jean Châtillon, Textes philosophiques du Moyen Âge 17 (Paris, 1970).
ps.-Albert the Great, *Mariale sive Quaestiones super evangelium, Missus est Gabriel [Lk. 1, 26] etc.*, ed. Auguste and Émile Borgnet, B. Alberti Magni, Ratisbonensis episcopi, ordinis praedicatorum opera omnia 37 (Paris, 1898).

Angela da Foligno. *Il libro della beata Angela da Foligno (Edizione critica)*, ed. Ludger Thier and Abele Calufetti, Spicilegium Bonaventurianum 25 (Grottaferrata, ²1985).

Aquinas, Thomas, *Summa theologiae* [...] *cum textu ex recensione Leonina*, ed. Petrus Caramello, 4 vols (Turin and Rome, 1948).

——*Scriptum super sententiis magistri Petri Lombardi*, ed. R. P. Mandonnet [vols. 1–2] and Maria Fabianus Moos [vols. 3–4], 4 vols. (Paris, 1929–47).

Augustine. *Sancti Avrelii Avgvstini epistvlae I–LV*, ed. Kl. D. Daur, Avrelii Avgvstini opera 3/1. CCSL 31 (Turnhout, 2004).

Bernard of Clairvaux, *Homiliae super 'Missus est'*, in Jean Leclercq and Henri M. Rochais (eds.), *Sancti Bernardi opera*, vol. 4 (Paris, 1966), 1–58.

Biblia latina cum glossa ordinaria. Facsimile Reprint of the Editio Princeps. Adolph Rusch of Strassburg 1480/81, introd. Karlfried Froehlich and Margaret T. Gibson, 4 vols. (Turnhout, 1992).

Biblia Sacra iuxta vulgatam versionem, ed. Robert Weber (Stuttgart, ⁴1994).

Birgitta of Sweden. *Sancta Birgitta. Revelaciones. Book I with Magister Mathias' Prologue*, ed. Carl-Gustaf Undhagen (Stockholm, 1977).

——*Sancta Birgitta. Revelaciones. Book II*, ed. Carl-Gustaf Undhagen and Birger Bergh (Stockholm, 2001).

——*Sancta Birgitta. Revelaciones. Book III*, ed. Ann-Mari Jönsson (Stockholm, 1998).

——*Sancta Birgitta. Revelaciones. Book IV*, ed. Hans Aili (Stockholm, 1992).

——*Sancta Birgitta. Revelaciones. Book V*, ed. Birger Bergh (Uppsala, 1971).

——*Sancta Birgitta. Revelaciones. Book VI*, ed. Birger Bergh (Stockholm, 1991).

——*Den heliga Birgittas Revelaciones. Book VII*, ed. Birger Bergh (Uppsala, 1967).

——*Sancta Birgitta. Revelaciones. Book VIII*, ed. Hans Aili (Stockholm, 2002).

——*Sancta Birgitta. Opera minora II. Sermo angelicus*, ed. Sten Eklund (Uppsala, 1972).

——*Den heliga Birgittas Reuelaciones extrauagantes*, ed. Lennart Hollman, Samlingar utgivna av Svenska Fornskriftsällskapet Ser. 2. Latinska skrifter 5 (Uppsala, 1956).

Bonaventura. *Doctoris seraphici s. Bonaventurae S. R. E. episcopi cardinalis opera omnia*, ed. PP. collegii a S. Bonaventura, 10 vols. (Quaracchi, 1882–1902).

——*Sancti Bonaventurae sermones dominicales*, ed. J. G. Bougerol, Bibliotheca Franciscana scholastica medii aevi 27 (Grottaferrata, 1977).

Bullarium franciscanum sive Romanorum pontificum constitutiones, epistolae, diplomata tribus ordinibus minorum, clarissarum, poenitentium a seraphico patriarcha sancto Francisco institutus [...], ed. Conrad Eubel, vol. 7 (Rome, 1904).

Caesarius von Heisterbach. *Caesarii Heisterbacensis monachi ordinis cisterciensis Dialogus miraculorum*, ed. Joseph Strange, 2 vols. (Cologne etc., 1851; repr. Ridgewood, NJ, 1966).

Christi Leiden in einer Vision geschaut (A German Mystic Text of the Fourteenth Century). A critical account of the published and unpublished manuscripts, with an edition based on the text of MS. Bernkastel-Cues 115, ed. F. P. Pickering (Manchester, 1952).

Corpus iuris canonici, ed. Aemilius Ludouicus Richter and Aemilius Friedberg, 2 vols. (Leipzig, ²1869–81).

David von Augsburg. *David ab Augusta O.F.M. De exterioris et interioris hominis compositione secundum triplicem statum incipientium, proficientium et perfectorum libri tres*, ed. PP. collegii S. Bonaventurae (Quaracchi, 1899).

ps.-Dionysius. *Dionysiaca. Recueil donnant l'ensemble des traductions latines des ouvrages attribués au Denys de l'Aréopage*, ed. Philippe Chevalier, 2 vols. (Paris, 1937).

Eckhart, *Deutsche Predigten*, in Franz Pfeiffer (ed.), *Deutsche Mystiker des vierzehnten Jahrhunderts*, vol. 2. *Meister Eckhart* (Leipzig, 1857), 1–370.

——*Die deutschen und lateinischen Werke. Die deutschen Werke*, ed. Josef Quint [vols. 1–3] and Georg Steer, with Wolfgang Klimanek and Freimut Löser [vols. 4/1–4/2 (fascicules 1–2)] (Stuttgart, 1958–2003; first fascicule 1936).

——*Die deutschen und lateinischen Werke. Die lateinischen Werke*, ed. Konrad Weiss, Josef Koch, Loris Sturlese et al., 5 vols. (Stuttgart, 1956–2006; first fascicule 1936).

Engelbert von Admont, *De gratiis et virtutibus beatae et gloriosae semper virginis Mariae tractatus*, in Bernard Pez (ed.), *Thesaurus anecdotorum novissimus*, vol. 1/1 (Augsburg, 1721), 503–762.

Francis of Meyronnes. *Franciscus de Mayronis. In libros Sententiarum, Quodlibeta, Tractatus Formalitatum, De Primo Principio, Terminorum Theologicalium Declarationes, De Univocatione* (Venice, 1520; repr. Frankfurt a. M., 1966).

Gerson, Jean, *De meditatione cordis*, in Palémon Glorieux (ed.), *Œuvres complètes*, vol. 8 (Paris, 1971), 78–84.

——*De simplificatione cordis*, in Palémon Glorieux (ed.), *Œuvres complètes*, vol. 8 (Paris, 1971), 85–97.

Glaßberger, Nikolaus. *Chronica fratris Nicolai Glassberger ordinis minorum observantium*, ed. PP. collegii S. Bonaventurae, Analecta franciscana 2 (Quaracchi, 1877).

Guigo du Pont. *Guigues du Pont. Traité sur la contemplation. Introduction, texte critique, traduction française et notes*, ed. Philippe Dupont, Analecta Cartusiana 72, 2 vols. (Salzburg, 1985).

Heinrich von Friemar, *De decem preceptis*, ed. Bertrand-G. Guyot, with an introduction by Loris Sturlese (Pisa, 2005).

Heinrich von St Gallen. *Der Passionstraktat des Heinrich von St. Gallen*, ed. Kurt Ruh (Thayngen, 1940).

——*Die Magnifikat-Auslegung*, ed. Wolfram Legner, Kleine deutsche Prosadenkmäler des Mittelalters 11 (Munich, 1973).

——*Das >Marienleben< des Heinrich von St. Gallen. Text und Untersuchung. Mit einem Verzeichnis deutschsprachiger Prosamarienleben bis etwa 1520*, ed. Hardo Hilg, Münchener Texte und Untersuchungen 75 (Munich, 1981).

346   *Bibliography*

Hueber, Fortunatus, *Dreyfache Cronickh von dem dreyfachen Orden deß grossen H. Seraphinischen Ordens-Stifters Francisci, so weith er sich in Ober: vnd Nider Teutschland* [...] *erstrecket* [...] (Munich, 1686).

Hugh of St Victor, *Explanatio in canticum beatae Mariae*, in J.-P. Migne (ed.), *Patrologia Latina*, vol. 175 (Paris, 1854), 413–32.

——*De quatuor voluntatibus in Christo libellus*, in J.-P. Migne (ed.), *Patrologia Latina*, vol. 176 (Paris, 1854), 841–6.

Hus, Jan. *Mag. Joannis Hus De sanguine Christi*, ed. Wenzel Flajšhans, Mag. Jo. Hus opera omnia 1/3 (Prague, 1903; repr. Osnabrück, 1966).

Jacobus de Voragine. *Iacopo da Varazze. Legenda aurea*, ed. Giovanni Paolo Maggioni, Millennio Medievale 6. Testi 3, 2 vols. (Tavernuzze near Florence, ²2000).

Jerome. *S. Hieronymi presbyteri commentariorum in Matheum libri IV*, ed. D. Hurst and M. Adriaen, S. Hieronymi presbyteri opera pars 1. Opera exegetica 7. CCSL 77 (Turnhout, 1969).

Johannes de Caulibus, *Meditaciones vite Christi olim S. Bonauenturo attributae*, ed. M. Stallings-Taney, CCCM 153 (Turnhout, 1997).

Johannes von Paltz, *Coelifodina*, in Christoph Burger et al. (eds.), *Johannes von Paltz. Werke*, vol. 1, Spätmittelalter und Reformation. Texte und Untersuchungen 2 (Berlin and New York, 1983).

Konrad von Sachsen. *Conradus de Saxonia O. F. M., Speculum seu salutatio Beatae Mariae Virginis ac sermones Mariani*, ed. Petrus de Alcantara Martinez, Bibliotheca Franciscana ascetica medii aevi 11 (Grottaferrata, 1975).

Lipmann Mühlhausen, Yom-Tov, *Sefer ha-Nizzahon. R. Lipmanni Disputatio Adversus Christianos ad Esaiae & XII. minorum Prophetarum libros instituta* [...], trans. Sebaldus Snellius (Altdorf, 1644).

——*R. Lipmanni Disputatio Adversus Christianos ad Jeremiae, Ezechielis, Psalmorum & Danielis libros instituta* [...], trans. Sebaldus Snellius (Altdorf, 1645).

——*R. Lipmanni Disputatio Adversus Christianos ad Josuae[,] Judicum, Samuelis, Regum, Ruthae, Hiobi, Proverbiorum, Ecclesiastis, Cantici Canticorum, Threnorum, Estheris, Esrae, Paralipomenon libros, unà cum Appendice adversus Petrum quendam, qui à Judaeis desciverat* [...] trans. Sebaldus Snellius (Altdorf, 1645).

Ludolf von Sachsen. *Vita Jesu Christi e quatuor evangeliis et scriptoribus orthodoxis concinnata per Ludolphum de Saxonia ex ordine Carthusianorum* [...], ed. A.-C. Bolard, L.-M. Rigollot, and J. Carnandet (Paris and Rome, 1865).

——*Vita Jesu Christi ex evangelio et approbatis ab ecclesia catholica doctoribus sedule collecta*, ed. L.-M. Rigollot, 4 vols. (Paris and Rome, 1870).

Marienwerder, Johannes. *Septililium B. Dorotheae Montoviensis auctore Joanne Marienwerder*, ed. Franciscus Hipler, *Analecta Bollandiana* 2 (1883), 381–472; 3 (1884), 113–40 and 408–48; 4 (1885), 207–51.

Martí, Ramon. *Pugio fidei Raymundi Martini ordinis praedicatorum adversus mauros, et iudaeos* [...] *cum observationibus Domini Iosephi de Voisin* [...] (Paris, 1651).

——*Raymundi Martini Ordinis Praedicatorum Pugio Fidei adversus Mauros et Judaeos, cum observationibus Josephi de Voisin, et introductione Jo.* Benedicti Carpzovi, *Qui simul appendicis loco Hermanni Judaei opusculum de sua conversione* [. . .] *recensuit* (Leipzig, 1687).

Matthew of Aquasparta. *Matthaei ab Aquasparta O. F. M., S. R. E. cardinalis sermones de Beata Maria Virgine*, ed. Caelestinus Piana, Bibliotheca franciscana ascetica medii aevi 9 (Quaracchi, 1962).

Matthaeus of Cracow, *Dialogus rationis et conscientiae de crebra communione*, in Władysław Selko and Adam Ludwik Szafrański (eds.), *Mateusza z Krakowa. Opuscula theologica dotyczące spowiedzi i komunii*, Textus et studia historiam theologiae in Polonia excultae spectantia 2/1 (Warsaw, 1974), 354–409.

Michael de Massa, *Vita Ihesu Christi* [printed as *Vita ihesu a venerabili viro fratre ludolpho carthusiensis edita*] (Cologne: Arnold ther Hoernen, 1472) [Copinger 3662, ISTC i100336500].

Müller, Berard. *Chronica de ortu et progressu almae provinciae Argentinensis sive superioris Germaniae* [. . .] *composita a F. Berardo Müller 1703* [partes I and II], ed. Meinrad Sehi (unpublished typescript, Würzburg, 1957).

——*P. Berardus Müller (d. 1704) und P. Victor Tschan (d. 1754), Chronica de ortu et progressu Almae Provinciae Argentinensis sive superioris Germaniae* [. . .] [pars II only], ed. Meinrad Sehi, Alemania Franciscana Antiqua 12 (Landshut, 1964).

Nicholas Eymeric. *Nicolaus Eymericus. Summa utilissima errorum et haeresum* (Seville: Stanislaus Polonus, c.1500) [Copinger 5687; ISTC le00186000].

—— *Directorivm inquisitorvm R. P. F. Nicolai Eymerici Ord. Praed. S. Theol. Mag. Inquisitoris haereticae prauitatis in Regnis Regis Aragonum* [. . .], ed. Franciscus Pegña (Rome, 1578).

——*Directorivm inqvisitorum P. Nicolai Eymerici Ordinis Praedicatorum* [. . .], ed. Franciscus Pegña (Venice, 1607).

Nicholas of Lyra, *Dicta de sacramento* (*De sacramento eucharistiae*) (Cologne: printer of Augustine, 'De fide', 1473) [Hain/Copinger 1374; ISTC it00291000].

Das Nürnberger Marienbuch. Untersuchungen und Edition, ed. Bettina Jung, Texte und Textgeschichte 55 (Tübingen, 2004).

Odo of Canterbury, *Sermo* on Luke 10: 38–42 ('Intravit Jesus in quoddam castellum'), in Jean Leclercq, *Études sur le vocabulaire monastique du Moyen Âge*, Studia Anselmiana 48 (Rome, 1961), 152–4.

Philipp von Seitz, *Bruder Philipps des Carthäusers Marienleben*, ed. Heinrich Rückert, Bibliothek der deutschen National-Literatur 34 (Quedlinburg, 1853; repr. Amsterdam, 1966).

Richard of St Laurent, *De laudibus Beatae Mariae Virginis libri duodecim*, ed. Auguste and Emile Borgnet, B. Alberti Magni, Ratisbonensis episcopi, ordinis praedicatorum opera omnia 36 (Paris, 1898).

Richard of St Victor, *De differentia sacrificii Abrahae a sacrificio beatae Mariae virginis*, in J.-P. Migne (ed.), *Patrologia Latina*, vol. 196 (Paris, 1855), 1043–60.

Ripelin von Straßburg, Hugo, *Compendium theologicae veritatis*, ed. Augustus Borgnet, B. Alberti Magni, Ratisbonensis episcopi, ordinis praedicatorum opera omnia 34 (Paris, 1895), 1–306.

van Ruusbroec, Jan. *Jan van Ruusbroecs 'Brulocht' in oberdeutscher Überlieferung. Untersuchungen und kritische Textausgabe*, ed. Wolfgang Eichler, Münchener Texte und Untersuchungen 22 (Munich, 1969).

——*Die geestelike brulocht*, ed. J. Alaerts, Jan van Ruusbroec. Opera omnia 3, Studiën en Tekstuitgaven van Ons Geestelijk Erf 20/3 (Turnhout, 1988).

Schwester Katrei, in Franz-Josef Schweitzer, *Der Freiheitsbegriff der deutschen Mystik. Seine Beziehung zur Ketzerei der »Brüder und Schwestern vom Freien Geist«, mit besonderer Rücksicht auf den pseudoeckhartschen Traktat »Schwester Katrei« (Edition)*, Arbeiten zur mittleren deutschen Literatur und Sprache 10 (Frankfurt a. M. and Bern, 1981), 322–70.

Seuse, Heinrich, *Deutsche Schriften*, ed. Karl Bihlmeyer (Stuttgart, 1907).

——*Heinrich Senses Horologium sapientiae. Erste kritische Ausgabe unter Benützung der Vorarbeiten von Dominikus Planzer OP*, ed. Pius Künzle, Spicilegium Friburgense 23 (Fribourg, 1977).

Speculum humanae salvationis. Texte critique. Traduction inédite de Jean Miélot (1448). Les Sources et l'influence iconographique principalement sur l'art alsacien du XIV* siècle, ed. J. Lutz and P. Perdrizet, 2 vols. (Leipzig, 1907–9).

Stimulus amoris, in *S. R. E. Cardinalis s. Bonaventurae ex ordine minorum, episcopi Albanensis, doctoris ecclesiae seraphici opera omnia* [. . .], ed. A. C. Peltier, vol. 12 (Paris, 1868), 631–703.

——*Schriften Johanns von Neumarkt. 3. Teil. Stachel der Liebe. Übersetzung des Liber, qui dicitur Stimulus amoris*, ed. Joseph Klapper, Vom Mittelalter zur Reformation. Forschungen zur Geschichte der deutschen Bildung 6/3 (Berlin, 1939).

Supplementum ad bullarium franciscanum continens litteras Romanorum pontificum annorum 1378–1484 pro tribus ordinibus S. P. N. Francisci ulterius obtenta [. . .], vol. 1. *1378–1471*, ed. Caesar Cenci (Grottaferrata, 2002).

Tauler, Johannes. *Die Predigten Taulers aus der Engelberger und der Freiburger Handschrift sowie aus Schmidts Abschriften der ehemaligen Straßburger Handschriften*, ed. Ferdinand Vetter, Deutsche Texte des Mittelalters 11 (Berlin, 1910).

Thomas of Ireland. *Thomas de Hibernia, Manipulus florum* (Piacenza: Jacobus de Tyela, 1483) [Copinger 8542*; ISTC ih00149000].

Tschamser, Malachias, *Annales oder Jahrs-Geschichten der Baarfüseren oder Minderen Brüdern S. Franc. ord. insgemein Conventualen genannt, zu Thann (1724)*, with an introduction by A. Merklen, 2 vols. (Colmar, 1864).

Twinger von Königshofen, Jakob. *Chronik des Jacob Twinger von Königshofen. 1400 (1415)*, in C. Hegel (ed.), *Die Chroniken der oberrheinischen Städte. Straßburg, Die Chroniken der deutschen Städte vom 14. bis ins 16. Jahrhundert 8–9*, 2 vols. (Leipzig, 1870–1), 153–917.

Ubertino da Casale, *Ubertinus da Casali, Arbor vitae crucifixae Jesu*, with an introduction and bibliography by Charles T. Davis, Monumenta politica et philosophica rariora series 1/4 (Turin, 1961).

Urkundenbuch der Stadt Strassburg, vol. 5/2. Politische Urkunden von 1365 bis 1380, ed. Hans Witte and Georg Wolfram (Strasbourg, 1896).

Urkundenbuch der Stadt Strassburg, vol. 7. *Privatrechtliche Urkunden und Rathslisten von 1332 bis 1400*, ed. Hans Witte (Strasbourg, 1900).
Vita Beate Virginis Marie et salvatoris rhythmica, ed. Adolf Vögtlin, Bibliothek des litterarischen Vereins in Stuttgart 180 (Tübingen, 1888).
Wadding, Luke. *Annales minorum seu trium ordinum a S. Francisco institutorum auctore A. R. P. Luca Waddingo Hiberno*, ed. Joseph Maria Fonseca, 25 vols. (Quaracchi, ³1931–5).

SECONDARY LITERATURE

Aili, Hans, and Svanberg, Jan, *Imagines Sanctae Birgittae: The Earliest Illuminated Manuscripts and Panel Paintings Related to the Revelations of St. Birgitta of Sweden*, 2 vols. (Stockholm, 2003).
Albert, P., *Matthias Döring, ein deutscher Minorit des 15. Jahrhunderts* (Stuttgart, 1892).
Angenendt, Arnold, 'Seuses Lehre vom Ablaß', in Remigius Bäumer (ed.), *Reformatio ecclesiae. Beiträge zu kirchlichen Reformbemühungen von der Alten Kirche bis zur Neuzeit. Festgabe für Erwin Iserloh* (Paderborn etc., 1980), 143–54.
Auerbach, Erich, *Literatursprache und Publikum in der lateinischen Spätantike und im Mittelalter* (Bern, 1958).
Bacher, Rahel, 'Mgf 1030 Berlin—eine frühe deutsche Historienbibel? Untersuchungen einer spätmittelalterlichen Kompilation', *PBB* 128 (2006), 70–92.
Baier, Walter, *Untersuchungen zu den Passionsbetrachtungen in der Vita Christi des Ludolf von Sachsen. Ein quellenkritischer Beitrag zu Leben und Werk Ludolfs und zur Geschichte der Passionstheologie*, Analecta Cartusiana 44 (Salzburg, 1977).
Barth, Médard, 'Fronleichnamsfest und Fronleichnamsbräuche im mittelalterlichen Strassburg', *Archives de l'Église d'Alsace* 25 [NS 9] (1958), 233–5.
Beifuss, Helmut, 'Matthäus von Krakau. Edition der deutschen Übersetzung(en) des *Dialogus rationis et conscientiae de communione sive de celebratione missae*', in Hans-Gert Roloff (ed.), *Editionsdesiderate der frühen Neuzeit. Beiträge zur Tagung der Kommission für die Edition von Texten der frühen Neuzeit*, Chloe. Beihefte zum Daphnis 25 (Amsterdam, 1997), 983–94.
——'Ein frühneuhochdeutsches Erbauungsbuch aus Bayern: "Hdschr. 242" der Staatsbibliothek Preußischer Kulturbesitz Berlin', *Mediaevistik* 12 (1999), 7–40.
Beissel, Stephan, *Geschichte der Verehrung Marias in Deutschland während des Mittelalters* (Freiburg, 1909).
Bestul, Thomas H., *Texts of the Passion: Latin Devotional Literature and Medieval Society* (Philadelphia, 1996).
Beumer, Johannes, 'Die Mariologie Richards von Saint-Laurent', *Franziskanische Studien* 41 (1959), 19–40.
——'Eine dem hl. Bonaventura zu Unrecht zugeschriebene Marienpredigt? Literarkritische Untersuchung des Sermo VI De assumtione B. Virginis Mariae (ed. Quaracchi IX, 700b–706b)', *Franziskanische Studien* 42 (1960), 1–26.

Beumer, Johannes, 'Die literarischen Beziehungen zwischen dem Sermo VI De Assumtione BMV (Pseudo-Bonaventura) und dem Mariale oder Laus Virginis (Pseudo-Albertus)', *Franziskanische Studien* 44 (1962), 455–60.

——'Die Predigten des heiligen Bonaventura. Ihre Authentizität und ihr theologischer Gehalt', in *S. Bonaventura 1274–1974. Volumen commemorativum anni septies centenarii a morte S. Bonaventurae Doctoris Seraphici cura et studio commissionis internationalis Bonaventurianae*, vol. 2. *Studia de vita, mente, fontibus et operibus sancti Bonaventurae* (Grottaferrata, 1973), 447–67.

Blumrich, Rüdiger, 'Feuer der Liebe. Franziskanische Theologie in den deutschen Predigten Marquards von Lindau', *Wissenschaft und Weisheit* 54 (1991), 44–55.

——'Die *gemeinú ler* des >Büchleins der ewigen Weisheit<. Quellen und Konzept', in id. and Philipp Kaiser (eds.), *Heinrich Seuses Philosophia spiritualis. Quellen, Konzept, Formen und Rezeption. Tagung Eichstätt 2.–4. Oktober 1991*, Wissensliteratur im Mittelalter 17 (Wiesbaden, 1994), 49–70.

——'Die deutschen Predigten Marquards von Lindau. Ein franziskanischer Beitrag zur *Theologia mystica*', in Maarten J. F. M. Hoenen and Alain de Libera (eds.), *Albertus Magnus und der Albertinismus. Deutsche Philosophische Kultur des Mittelalters*, Studien und Texte zur Geistesgeschichte des Mittelalters 48 (Leiden etc., 1995), 155–72.

Bonmann, Ottokar, 'Marquard von Lindau und sein literarischer Nachlaß', *Franziskanische Studien* 21 (1934), 315–43.

——'Ein franziskanischer Literarkatalog des XV. Jahrhunderts', *Franziskanische Studien* 23 (1936), 113–49.

Børresen, Kari Elisabeth, 'Birgitta's Godlanguage: Exemplary Intention, Inapplicable Content', in Tore Nyberg (ed.), *Birgitta, hendes værk og hendes klostre i Norden*, Odense University Studies in History and Social Sciences 150 (Odense, 1991), 21–72.

Breuer, Mordechai et al. (eds.), *Germania Judaica*, vol. 3. *1350–1519*, pt. 2. *Ortschaftsartikel Mährisch-Budwitz—Zwolle* (Tübingen, 1995).

Browe, Peter, *Die eucharistischen Wunder des Mittelalters*, Breslauer Studien zur historischen Theologie NF 4 (Wrocław, 1938).

——*Die häufige Kommunion im Mittelalter* (Münster, 1938).

Brückner, Wolfgang, 'Liturgie und Legende. Zur theologischen Theorienbildung und zum historischen Verständnis von Eucharistie-Mirakeln', *Jahrbuch für Volkskunde* NF 19 (1996), 139–68.

Burger, Christoph, 'Theologie und Laienfrömmigkeit. Transformationsversuche im Spätmittelalter', in Hartmut Boockmann et al. (eds.), *Lebenslehren und Weltentwürfe im Übergang vom Mittelalter zur Neuzeit. Politik—Bildung—Naturkunde—Theologie. Bericht über Kolloquien der Kommission zur Erforschung der Kultur des Spätmittelalters 1983 bis 1987*, Abhandlungen der Akademie der Wissenschaften in Göttingen. Philologisch-historische Klasse. Dritte Folge 179 (Göttingen, 1989), 400–20.

——'Transformation theologischer Ergebnisse für Laien im späten Mittelalter und bei Martin Luther', in Hans-Jörg Nieden and Marcel Nieden (eds.), *Praxis Pietatis. Beiträge zu Theologie und Frömmigkeit in der Frühen Neuzeit. Wolfgang Sommer zum 60. Geburtstag* (Stuttgart etc., 1999), 47–64.

——'Direkte Zuwendung zu den ,Laien' und Rückgriff auf Vermittler in spätmittelalterlicher katechetischer Literatur', in Berndt Hamm and Thomas Lentes (eds.), *Spätmittelalterliche Frömmigkeit zwischen Ideal und Praxis*, Spätmittelalter und Reformation. Neue Reihe 15 (Tübingen, 2001), 85–109.

Burr, David, *Eucharistic Presence and Conversion in Late Thirteenth-Century Franciscan Thought*, Transactions of the American Philosophical Society 74/3 (Philadelphia, 1984).

——*Olivi and Franciscan Poverty: The Origins of the* Usus Pauper *Controversy* (Philadelphia, 1989).

——*The Spiritual Franciscans: From Protest to Persecution in the Century After Saint Francis* (University Park, Pa., 2001).

Bynum, Caroline Walker, *Fragmentation and Redemption: Essays on Gender and the Human Body in Medieval Religion* (New York, 1992).

——'The Blood of Christ in the Later Middle Ages', *Church History* 71 (2002), 685–714.

——*Wonderful Blood: Theology and Practice in Late Medieval Northern Germany and Beyond* (Philadelphia, 2007).

Caspers, Charles M. A., *De eucharistische vroomheid en het feest van sacramentsdag in de Nederlanden tijdens de late middeleeuwen*, Miscellanea Neerlandica 5 (Leuven, 1992).

——'The Western Church during the Late Middle Ages: *Augenkommunion* or Popular Mysticism?', in Charles M. A. Caspers, Gerard Lukken, and Gerard Rouwhorst (eds.), *Bread of Heaven: Customs and Practices surrounding Holy Communion: Essays in the History of Liturgy and Culture*, Liturgia condenda 3 (Kampen, 1995), 83–97.

——'*Meum summum desiderium est te habere*. L'Eucharistie comme sacrement de la rencontre avec Dieu pour tous les croyants (ca. 1200–ca. 1500)', in André Haquin (ed.), *Fête-Dieu (1246–1996)*, vol. 1. *Actes du Colloque de Liège, 12–14 Septembre 1996*, Université Catholique de Louvain. Publications de l'Institut d'Études Médiévales. Textes, Études, Congrès 19/1 (Louvain-la-Neuve, 1999), 127–51.

Catto, Jeremy I., 'John Wyclif and the Cult of the Eucharist', in Katherine Walsh and Diana Wood (eds.), *The Bible in the Medieval World: Essays in Memory of Beryl Smalley*, Studies in Church History. Subsidia 4 (Oxford, 1985), 269–86.

Chiettini, Emmanuel, *Mariologia S. Bonaventurae*, Bibliotheca mariana medii aevi 3 (Šibenik and Rome, 1941).

Ciceri, Antonio, *Petri Iohannis Olivi. Opera. Censimentio dei manoscritti*, Collectio Oliviana 1 (Grottaferrata, 1999).

Clark, James M., 'Marquard von Lindau and his "Dekalogerklärung"', *Modern Language Review* 34 (1939), 72–8.

Coates, Alan, et al., *A Catalogue of Books Printed in the Fifteenth Century now in the Bodleian Library*, 6 vols. (Oxford, 2005) [Cited as *Bod-inc*].

Colasanti, Giovanni, 'I SS. cuori di Gesù e di Maria nell' «Arbor vitae» (1305) di Ubertino da Casale, O. Min.', *Miscellanea Francescana* 59 (1959), 30–69.

——'Maria SS. nella vita di Cristo secondo «l'arbor vitae» (1305) di Ubertino da Casale, O. Min.', *Marianum* 24 (1962), 349–80.

Colberg, Katharina, 'Döring, Matthias', [2]*VL*, vol. 2 (1980), 207–10.

Constable, Giles, *Three Studies in Medieval Religious and Social Thought* (Cambridge, 1995).

Cornell, Henrik, *The Iconography of the Nativity of Christ*, Uppsala Universitets Årsskrift. Filosofi, språkvetenskap och historiska vetenskaper 3 (Uppsala, 1924).

Courtenay, William J., 'The Franciscan Studia in Southern Germany in the Fourteenth Century', in Ferdinand Seibt (ed.), *Gesellschaftsgeschichte. Festschrift für Karl Bosl zum 80. Geburtstag* (Munich, 1988), 2: 81–90.

Cross, Richard, *The Physics of Duns Scotus. The Scientific Context of a Theological Vision* (Oxford, 1998).

——*Duns Scotus* (New York and Oxford, 1999).

Cullen, Christopher M., *Bonaventure* (Oxford, 2006).

D'Alverny, Marie-Thérèse, 'Un adversaire de Saint Thomas: Petrus Iohannis Olivi', in Armand A. Maurer et al. (eds.), *St. Thomas Aquinas 1274–1974: Commemorative Studies*, 2 vols. (Toronto, 1974), 2: 179–218.

D'Avray, David, *The Preaching of the Friars: Sermons diffused from Paris before 1300* (Oxford, 1985).

Damiata, Marino, *Pietà e storia nell'Arbor vitae di Ubertino da Casale*, Biblioteca di studi Francescani 19 (Florence, 1988).

Delhaye, Philippe, 'La Charité, «premier commandement» chrétien chez S. Bonaventure', in *S. Bonaventura 1274–1974. Volumen commemorativum anni septies centenarii a morte S. Bonaventurae doctoris seraphici cura et studio commissionis internationalis Bonaventurianae*, vol. 4. *Theologica* (Grottaferrata, 1974), 503–21.

Delius, Walter, *Geschichte der Marienverehrung* (Munich and Basel, 1963).

Deschamps, Jan, and Mulder, Herman, *Inventaris van de Middelnederlandse handschriften van de Koninklijke Bibliotheek van België (voorlopige uitgave)*, 8 vols. (Brussels, 1998–2006).

van Dijk, Mathilde, 'De wil op God afstemmen. De *Decaloog* van Marquard van Lindau in een gemeenschap van moderne devoten', *Ons Geestelijk Erf* 78 (2004), 83–98.

Dinzelbacher, Peter, and Ruh, Kurt, 'Magdalena von Freiburg (M. Beutlerin; auch Beitlerin, Buttelerin, Büttlerin; M. von Kenzingen)', [2]*VL*, vols. 5 (1985), 1117–21 and 11 (2004), 944.

Douie, Decima L., 'Olivi's "Postilla super Matthaeum" (MS. New College B. 49)', *Franciscan Studies* 35 (1975), 66–92.

Duffy, Eamon, *The Stripping of the Altars: Traditional Religion in England 1400–1580* (New Haven and London, 1992).

Eisermann, Falk, >*Stimulus amoris*<. *Inhalt, lateinische Überlieferung, deutsche Übersetzungen, Rezeption*, Münchener Texte und Untersuchungen 118 (Tübingen, 2001).

Ellington, Donna Spivey, 'Impassioned Mother or Passive Icon: The Virgin's Role in Late Medieval and Early Modern Passion Sermons', *Renaissance Quarterly* 48 (1995), 227–61.

——*From Sacred Body to Angelic Soul: Understanding Mary in Late Medieval and Early Modern Europe* (Washington, 2001).

Elliott, Dyan, 'True Presence/False Christ: The Antinomies of Embodiment in Medieval Spirituality', *Medieval Studies* 64 (2002), 241–65.

——'Seeing Double: John Gerson, the Discernment of Spirits, and Joan of Arc', *American Historical Review* 107 (2002), 26–54.

Elze, Martin, 'Das Verständnis der Passion Jesu im ausgehenden Mittelalter und bei Luther', in Heinz Liebing and Klaus Scholder (eds.), *Geist und Geschichte der Reformation. Festgabe Hanns Rückert zum 65. Geburtstag*, Arbeiten zur Kirchengeschichte 38 (Berlin, 1966), 127–51.

Ennis, Hyacinth J., 'The Place of Love in the Theological System of St. Bonaventure in General', in *S. Bonaventura 1274–1974. Volumen commemorativum anni septies centenarii a morte S. Bonaventurae doctoris seraphici cura et studio commissionis internationalis Bonaventurianae*, vol. 4. *Theologica* (Grottaferrata, 1974), 129–45.

Ertl, Thomas, *Religion und Disziplin. Selbstdeutung und Weltordnung im frühen deutschen Franziskanertum*, Arbeiten zur Kirchengeschichte 96 (Berlin and New York, 2006).

Fowler, George Bingham, *Intellectual Interests of Engelbert of Admont*, Studies in History, Economics and Public Law 530 (New York, 1947).

Freed, John B., *The Friars and German Society in the Thirteenth Century*, Mediaeval Academy of America Publication 86 (Cambridge, Mass., 1977).

Fries, Albert, *Die unter dem Namen des Albertus Magnus überlieferten mariologischen Schriften*, Beiträge zur Geschichte der Philosophie und Theologie des Mittelalters 37/4 (Münster, 1954).

Fulton, Rachel, *From Judgment to Passion: Devotion to Christ and the Virgin Mary, 800–1200* (New York, 2002).

Funk, Franz Xaver, and Diekamp, Franz (eds.), *Patres Apostolici*, vol. 2. *Clementis Romani Epistulae de virginitate eiusdemque martyrium. epistulae pseudoignatii. Ignatii martyria. fragmenta polycarpiana. Polycarpi vita* (Tübingen, ³1913).

Gärtner, Kurt, 'Regulierter Tageslauf im 'Marienleben' Philipps von Seitz', in James Hogg (ed.), *Kartäuserregel und Kartäuserleben. Internationaler Kongress vom 30. Mai bis 3. Juni 1984, Stift Heiligenkreuz*, Analecta Cartusiana 113/1 (Salzburg 1984), 47–60.

——'Bruder Philipp OCart', ²*VL*, vols. 7 (1989), 588–97, and 11 (2003), 1234.

——'Vita beatae virginis Mariae et salvatoris rhythmica', ²*VL*, vol. 10 (1999), 436–43.

Gatz, Johannes, 'Valduna/Vorarlberg', in id. (ed.), *Alemania Franciscana Antiqua*, vol. 18 (Landshut, 1973), 46–98.

Gebele, Eduard, 'Markwart von Lindau', in Götz Freiherr von Pölnitz (ed.), *Lebensbilder aus dem Bayerischen Schwaben*, vol. 7, Schwäbische Forschungsgemeinschaft bei der Kommission für bayerische Landesgeschichte Veröffentlichungen Reihe 3/7 (Munich, 1959), 81–124.

Geith, Karl-Ernst, 'Lateinische und deutschsprachige Leben Jesu-Texte. Bilanz und Perspektiven der Forschung,' *Jahrbuch der Oswald von Wolkenstein Gesellschaft* 12 (2000), 273–89.

Girotto, Samuele, *Corrado di Sassonia. Predicatore e mariologo del sec. XIII*, Biblioteca di studi Francescani 3 (Florence, 1952).

Gonzalez, Justo L., 'The Work of Christ in Saint Bonaventure's Systematic Works', in *S. Bonaventura 1274–1974. Volumen commemorativum anni septies centenarii a morte S. Bonaventurae Doctoris Seraphici cura et studio commissionis internationalis Bonaventurianae*, vol. 4. *Theologica* (Grottaferrata, 1973), 371–85.

Goossens, André, 'Résonances eucharistiques à la fin du Moyen Âge', in André Haquin (ed.), *Fête-Dieu (1246–1996)*, vol. 1. *Actes du Colloque de Liège, 12–14 Septembre 1996*, Université Catholique de Louvain. Publications de l'Institut d'Études Médiévales. Textes, Études, Congrès 19/1 (Louvain-la-Neuve, 1999), 173–91.

Górecka, Marzena, *Das Bild Mariens in der Deutschen Mystik des Mittelalters*, Deutsche Literatur von den Anfängen bis 1700 29 (Bern etc., 1999).

Gössi, Anton, *Das Archiv der oberdeutschen Minoritenprovinz im Staatsarchiv Luzern*, Luzerner Historische Veröffentlichungen. Archivinventare 2 (Luzern and Munich, 1979).

Graef, Hilda, *Mary: A History of Doctrine and Devotion*, 2 vols. (London, 1963–5).

Groebner, Valentin, *Ungestalten. Die visuelle Kultur der Gewalt im Mittelalter* (Munich and Vienna, 2003).

Grosse, Sven, *Heilsungewißheit und Scrupulositas im späten Mittelalter. Studien zu Johannes Gerson und Gattungen der Frömmigkeitstheologie seiner Zeit*, Beiträge zur historischen Theologie 85 (Tübingen, 1994).

Haas, Alois M., 'Traum und Traumvision in der Deutschen Mystik', in James Hogg (ed.), *Spätmittelalterliche geistliche Literatur in der Nationalsprache*, vol. 1, Analecta Cartusiana 106/1 (Salzburg, 1983), 22–55.

——'»Trage Leiden geduldiglich«: Die Einstellung der deutschen Mystik zum Leiden', in id. (ed.), *Gottleiden—Gottlieben. Zur volkssprachlichen Mystik im Mittelalter* (Frankfurt a. M., 1989), 127–52.

——'Sinn und Tragweite von Heinrich Seuses Passionsmystik', in Walter Haug and Burghart Wachinger (eds.), *Die Passion Christi in Literatur und Kunst des Spätmittelalters*, Fortuna vitrea 12 (Tübingen, 1993), 94–112.

Hamm, Berndt, *Promissio, pactum, ordinatio. Freiheit und Selbstbindung Gottes in der scholastischen Gnadenlehre*, Beiträge zur historischen Theologie 54 (Tübingen, 1977).

——'Das Gewicht von Religion, Glaube, Frömmigkeit und Theologie innerhalb der Verdichtungsvorgänge des ausgehenden Mittelalters und der frühen Neuzeit', in Monika Hagenmaier and Sabine Holtz (eds.), *Krisenbewußtsein und Krisenbewältigung in der Frühen Neuzeit—Crisis in Early Modern Europe. Festschrift für Hans-Christoph Rublack* (Frankfurt a. M. etc., 1992), 163–96.

Bibliography 355

——'Was ist Frömmigkeitstheologie? Überlegungen zum 14. bis 16. Jahrhundert', in Hans-Jörg Nieden and Marcel Nieden (eds.), *Praxis Pietatis. Beiträge zu Theologie und Frömmigkeit in der Frühen Neuzeit. Wolfgang Sommer zum 60. Geburtstag* (Stuttgart etc., 1999), 9–45.

——'Normative Zentrierung im 15. und 16. Jahrhundert. Beobachtungen zu Religiosität, Theologie und Ikonologie', *Zeitschrift für Historische Forschung* 26 (1999), 163–202.

——'Die »nahe Gnade"—innovative Züge der spätmittelalterlichen Theologie und Frömmigkeit', in Jan A. Aertsen and Martin Pickavé (eds.), *»Herbst des Mittelalters"? Fragen zur Bewertung des 14. und 15. Jahrhunderts*, Miscellanea Mediaevalia 31 (Berlin and New York, 2004), 541–57.

Hessel, Alfred, *Elsässische Urkunden, vornehmlich des 13. Jahrhunderts*, Schriften der Wissenschaftlichen Gesellschaft in Straßburg 23 (Strasbourg, 1915).

Hilsch, Peter, *Johannes Hus (um 1370–1415). Prediger Gottes und Ketzer* (Regensburg, 1999).

Hoffmann, W. J., '»Vita beate virginis Marie et Salvatoris rhythmica«', *Marienlexikon* 6 (St Ottilien, 1994), 644–6.

Holeton, David R., 'The Bohemian Eucharistic Movement in its European Context', in David R. Holeton (ed.), *The Bohemian Reformation and Religious Practice*, vol. 1. *Papers from the XVIIth World Congress of the Czechoslovak Society of Arts and Sciences, Prague 1994* (Prague, 1996), 23–47.

Illing, Kurt, *Alberts des Großen >Super Missam<-Traktat in mittelhochdeutschen Übertragungen. Untersuchungen und Texte*, Münchener Texte und Untersuchungen 53 (Munich, 1975).

Isenmann, Eberhard, *Die deutsche Stadt im Spätmittelalter 1250–1500. Stadtgestalt, Recht, Stadtregiment, Kirche, Gesellschaft, Wirtschaft* (Stuttgart, 1988).

Janota, Johannes, *Geschichte der deutschen Literatur von den Anfängen bis zum Beginn der Neuzeit 3. Vom späten Mittelalter zum Beginn der Neuzeit 1: Orientierung durch volkssprachige Schriftlichkeit (1280/90–1380/90)* (Tübingen, 2004).

Jaspert, Bernd, 'Leid und Trost bei Heinrich Seuse und Dag Hammarskjöld', in id. (ed.), *Leiden und Weisheit in der Mystik* (Paderborn, 1992), 167–205.

Kadlec, Jaroslav, 'Milíč, Jan, von Kremsier (Kroměříž)', [2]*VL*, vol. 6 (1987), 522–7.

Kaiser, Philipp, 'Die Christozentrik der *philosophia spiritualis* Heinrich Seuses', in Rüdiger Blumrich and Philipp Kaiser (eds.), *Heinrich Seuses Philosophia spiritualis. Quellen, Konzept, Formen und Rezeption. Tagung Eichstätt 2.–4. Oktober 1991*, Wissensliteratur im Mittelalter 17 (Wiesbaden, 1994), 109–23.

Kemper, Tobias A., *Die Kreuzigung Christi. Motivgeschichtliche Studien zu lateinischen und deutschen Passionstraktaten des Spätmittelalters*, Münchener Texte und Untersuchungen 131 (Tübingen, 2006).

Kern, Peter, *Trinität, Maria, Inkarnation. Studien zur Thematik der deutschen Dichtung des späteren Mittelalters*, Philologische Studien und Quellen 55 (Berlin, 1971).

Kieckhefer, Richard, *Unquiet Souls: Fourteenth-century Saints and Their Religious Milieu* (Chicago and London, 1984).

356 _Bibliography_

Knoth, Ernst, _Ubertino von Casale. Ein Beitrag zur Geschichte der Franziskaner an der Wende des 13. und 14. Jahrhunderts_ (Marburg, 1903).

Knuuttila, Simo, _Emotions in Ancient and Medieval Philosophy_ (Oxford, 2004).

Koch, Helga, 'Lignelses-, symbol- og billedsprog hos Birgitta. Visdommens efterfølgelse som imitatio Christi et Mariae', in Tore Nyberg (ed.), _Birgitta, hendes værk og hendes klostre i Norden_, Odense University Studies in History and Social Sciences 150 (Odense, 1991), 21–72.

Kolping, A[dolf], 'Zur Frage der Textgeschichte, Herkunft und Entstehungszeit der anonymen «Laus Virginis» (bisher _Mariale_ Alberts des Grossen)', _Recherches de théologie ancienne et médiévale_ 25 (1958), 285–329.

——'Das Verhältnis des ps.-Bonaventurianischen Sermo VI de Assumtione BMV zu dem ps.-Albertinischen Mariale »Laus Virginis«', _Zeitschrift für katholische Theologie_ 83 (1961), 190–207.

Köpf, Ulrich, 'Die Passion Christi in der lateinischen religiösen und theologischen Literatur des Spätmittelalters', in Walter Haug and Burghart Wachinger (eds.), _Die Passion Christi in Literatur und Kunst des Spätmittelalters_, Fortuna Vitrea 12 (Tübingen, 1993).

——'Passionsfrömmigkeit', _Theologische Realenzyklopädie_, vol. 27 (Berlin and New York, 1997), 722–64.

——'Produktive Christusfrömmigkeit', in Hans-Joachim Eckstein et al. (eds.), _Jesus Christus als die Mitte der Schrift. Studien zur Hermeneutik des Evangeliums_, Beihefte zur Zeitschrift für die neutestamentliche Wissenschaft und die Kunde der älteren Kirche 86 (Berlin and New York, 1997), 823–74.

Krämer, Sigrid, _Mittelalterliche Bibliothekskataloge Deutschlands und der Schweiz_, Ergänzungsband 1. _Handschriftenerbe des deutschen Mittelalters_, pt. 2. _Köln–Zyfflich_ (Munich, 1989).

de Kreek, M. L., '"Bene veneris deus meus, dominus meus..." Een middeleeuws geboortevisioen nader bekeken', in L. C. B. M. van Liebergen (ed.), _Birgitta van Zweden 1303–1373. 600 jaar kunst en cultuur van haar kloosterorde. Tentoonstelling Museum voor Religieuze Kunst, Uden, 22 maart t/m 25 mei 1986_ (Uden, 1986), 31–41.

Krone und Schleier. Kunst aus mittelalterlichen Frauenklöstern, exhibition catalogue of the Ruhrlandmuseum, Essen, and the Kunst- und Ausstellungshalle der Bundesrepublik Deutschland, Bonn (Munich, 2005).

Labrosse, Henri, 'Oeuvres de Nicolas de Lyre', _Études franciscaines_ 19 (1908), 41–52, 153–75, 368–79; 35 (1923), 171–87 and 400–32.

Lamy, Marielle, _L'Immaculée conception: Étapes et enjeux d'une controverse au Moyen-Âge (XIIᵉ–XVᵉ siècles)_, Collection des Études augustiniennes. Série Moyen Âge et Temps modernes 35 (Paris, 2000).

Langer, Otto, 'Passio und compassio. Zur Bedeutung der Passionsmystik bei Bernhard von Clairvaux', in Gottfried Fuchs (ed.), _Die dunkle Nacht der Sinne. Leiderfahrung und christliche Mystik_ (Düsseldorf, 1989), 41–62.

——'Memoria passionis: spirituelle Praktiken und ihre Grenzen. Zu Heinrich Seuses Passionsmystik reiner Innerlichkeit', in Wolfgang Braungart et al. (eds.), _Wahrnehmen und Handeln. Perspektiven einer Literaturanthropologie_, Bielefelder Schriften zu Linguistik und Literaturwissenschaft 20 (Bielefeld, 2004), 57–74.

Largier, Niklaus, 'Das Glück des Menschen. Diskussionen über *beatitudo* und Vernunft in volkssprachlichen Texten des 14. Jahrhunderts', in Jan A. Aertsen et al. (eds.), *Nach der Verurteilung von 1277. Philosophie und Theologie an der Universität von Paris im letzten Viertel des 13. Jahrhunderts. Studien und Texte*, Miscellanea Mediaevalia 28 (Berlin and New York, 2001), 827–55.

Leclercq, Jean, *Études sur le vocabulaire monastique du Moyen Âge*, Studia Anselmiana 48 (Rome, 1961).

Lentes, Thomas, '>Andacht< und >Gebärde<. Das religiöse Ausdrucksverhalten', in Bernhard Jussen and Craig Koslofsky (eds.), *Kulturelle Reformation. Sinnformationen im Umbruch 1400–1600*, Veröffentlichungen des Max-Planck-Instituts für Geschichte 145 (Göttingen, 1999), 29–67.

Lievens, Robrecht, 'Alijt Bake van Utrecht', *Nederlands Archief voor Kerkgeschiedenis*, NS 42 (1958), 127–51.

Limor, Ora, and Yuval, Israel Jacob, 'Skepticism and Conversion: Jews, Christians, and Doubters in *Sefer ha-Nizzahon*', in Allison P. Coudert and Jeffrey S. Shoulson (eds.), *Hebraica Veritas? Christian Hebraists and the Study of Judaism in Early Modern Europe* (Philadelphia, 2004), 159–80.

Lindgren, Mereth, 'Birgitta och bilderna', in Alf Härdelin and Mereth Lindgren (eds.), *Heliga Birgitta—budskapet och förebilden. Föredrag vid jubileumssymposiet i Vadstena 3–7 oktober 1991*, Kungl. vitterhets historie och antikvitets akademien. Konferenser 28 (Stockholm, 1993), 231–51.

List, Gerhard, and Powitz, Gerhardt, *Die Handschriften der Stadtbibliothek Mainz*, vol. 1, *Hs I 1–Hs I 150* (Wiesbaden, 1990).

Longo, Augusta Acconcia, 'Epiphanios', in Walter Kasper et al. (eds.), ³*Lexikon für Theologie und Kirche* 3 (Freiburg etc., 1995), 722–3.

Löser, Freimut, 'Rezeption als Revision: Marquard von Lindau und Meister Eckhart', *PBB* 119 (1997), 425–58.

——'Maria im Mittelpunkt. Eine Zweitfassung von Meister Eckharts >Bürglein-Predigt< (DW I Nr. 2)', in Claudia Brinker-von der Heyde and Niklaus Largier (eds.), *Homo Medietas. Aufsätze zu Religiosität, Literatur und Denkformen des Menschen vom Mittelalter bis in die Neuzeit. Festschrift für Alois Maria Haas zum 65. Geburtstag* (Bern etc., 1999), 241–73.

——*Meister Eckhart in Melk. Studien zum Redaktor Lienhart Peuger. Mit einer Edition des Traktats >Von der sel wirdichait vnd aigenschaffi<*, Texte und Textgeschichte 48 (Tübingen, 1999).

——'Jan Milíč in europäischer Tradition. Die Magdalenen-Predigt des Pseudo-Origenes', in Dominique Fliegler and Václav Bok (eds.), *Deutsche Literatur des Mittelalters in Böhmen und über Böhmen. Vorträge der internationalen Tagung, veranstaltet vom Institut für Germanistik der Pädagogischen Fakultät der Südböhmischen Universität České Budjovice, 8. bis 11. September 1999* (Vienna, 2001), 225–45.

Ludewig, Anton, *Das ehemalige Klarissenkloster in Valduna* (Valduna, 1922).

McGinn, Bernard, *The Presence of God. A History of Western Christian Mysticism*, vol. 3. *The Flowering of Mysticism. Men and Women in the New Mysticism (1200–1350)* (New York, 1998).

——*The Presence of God. A History of Western Christian Mysticism*, vol. 4. *The Harvest of Mysticism in Medieval Germany (1300–1500)* (New York, 2005).

Macy, Gary, *Treasures from the Storeroom: Medieval Religion and the Eucharist* (Collegeville, Minn., 1999).

Madigan, Kevin, *Olivi and the Interpretation of Matthew in the High Middle Ages* (Notre Dame, Ind., 2003).

——*The Passions of Christ in High-Medieval Thought: An Essay on Christological Development* (Oxford, 2007).

van Maren, J. W., 'Zitate deutscher Mystiker bei Marquard von Lindau', in M. A. van den Broek and G. J. Jaspers (eds.), *In diutscher diute. Festschrift für Anthonÿ van der Lee zum sechzigsten Geburtstag* [*Amsterdamer Beiträge zur älteren Germanistik* 20] (Amsterdam, 1983), 74–85.

van Maren, Jaap, 'Receptie en reductie van het decaloogtractaat van Marquard von Lindau in de Nederlanden', in Maurice Vliegen and Jaap van Maren (eds.), *'Uten schatschrine des herten.' Vriendenboek voor Henk Meijering bij zijn afscheid* (Amsterdam, 1998), 103–10.

Marin, Olivier, *L'Archevêque, le maître et le dévot: Genèses du mouvement réformateur pragois, années 1360–1419*, Études d'histoire médiévale 9 (Paris, 2005).

Marini, Alfonso, 'Ubertino e Angela: L'«Arbor vitae» e il «Liber»', in Giulia Barone and Jacques Dalarun (eds.), *Angèle de Foligno. Le Dossier*, Collection de l'école française de Rome 255 (Rome, 1999), 319–44.

Marrow, James H., *Passion Iconography in Northern European Art of the Late Middle Ages and Early Renaissance: A Study of the Transformation of Sacred Metaphor into Descriptive Narrative*, Ars Neerlandica 1 (Kortrijk, 1979).

Martínez Ruiz, Carlos Mateo, 'Ubertino de Casale, autor de dos versiones del *Arbor vitae*', *Archivum Franciscanum Historicum* 89 (1996), 447–68.

——'Il processo redazionale dell'*Arbor uite crucifixe Iesu* di Ubertino da Casale', in Alvaro Cacciotti and Barbara Faes de Mottoni (eds.), *Editori di Quaracchi. 100 Anni dopo bilancio e prospettive. Atti del colloquio internazionale, Roma 29–30 Maggio 1995, Scuola superiore di studi medievali e francescani Pontificio Ateneo Antonianum*, Medioevo 3 (Rome, 1997), 275–8.

——*De la dramatizacion de los acontecimientos de la pascua a la cristologia. El cuarto libro del* Arbor vitae crucifixae Iesu *de Ubertino de Casale*, Studia Antoniana 41 (Rome, 2000).

Mayr, Anton, 'Zur handschriftlichen Ueberlieferung der Dekalogerklärung Marquards von Lindau', in Eugen Abele (ed.), *Hundert Jahre humanistisches Gymnasium Freising. Fest-Schrift zum hundertjährigen Jubiläum 1828–1928* (Freising, 1928), 69–86.

Meckelnborg, Christina, *Die nichtarchivischen Handschriften der Signaturengruppe Best. 701 Nr. 1–190, ergänzt durch die im Görres-Gymnasium Koblenz aufbewahrten Handschriften A, B und C*, Mittelalterliche Handschriften im Landeshauptarchiv Koblenz 1 (Wiesbaden, 1998).

Mlinarič, Jože, *Srednjeveški latinski epos "Vita Mariae metrica". Tekstnokritična-historiografska in literarna analiza* (unpublished doctoral dissertation, University of Ljubljana, 1977).

——'Das Epos "Vita Mariae metrica" als Unterlage für das Marienlied des Karthäusers Philipp von Seitz', in James Hogg (ed.), *Kartäuserliturgie und Kartäuserschrifttum*. *Internationaler Kongreß vom 2. bis 5. September 1987*, vol. 2, Analecta Cartusiana 116/2 (Salzburg, 1988), 29–39.

Morée, Peter C. A., *Preaching in Fourteenth-Century Bohemia. The Life and Ideas of Milicius de Chremsir († 1374) and his Significance in the Historiography of Bohemia* (Heršpice near Slavkov, 1999).

Morris, Bridget, *St Birgitta of Sweden*, Studies in Medieval Mysticism 1 (Woodbridge, 1999).

Moser, Oskar, 'Die fünfzehn geheimen Leiden Christi. Nach einer mündlichen Überlieferung aus Kärnten', *Österreichische Zeitschrift für Volkskunde* 95 [NS 46] (1992), 483–94.

Mossman, Stephen, 'The Western Understanding of Islamic Theology in the Later Middle Ages. Mendicant Responses to Islam from Riccoldo da Monte di Croce to Marquard von Lindau', *Recherches de théologie et philosophie médiévales* 74 (2007), 169–224.

——'Die Konzeptualisierung des inneren Menschen im Traktat *De horto paradisi* Marquards von Lindau und in der *Theologia deutsch*. Mit einer Textedition', in Burkhard Hasebrink et al. (eds.), *Innenräume in der Literatur des deutschen Mittelalters*. *XIX. Anglo-German Colloquium* (Tübingen, 2008), 327–54.

——'Zu Marquard von Lindau, Konrad von Braunsberg, den Gottesfreunden und dem Gottesfreundschaftsbegriff', *Oxford German Studies* 36 (2007), 247–67.

——'Ubertino da Casale and the *Devotio Moderna*', *Ons Geestelijk Erf* [in press].

——'Kritik der Tradition. Bildlichkeit und Vorbildlichkeit in den deutschen Predigten Marquards von Lindau und die Umdeutung der *mater dolorosa*', in René Wetzel (ed.), *Die Predigt im Mittelalter zwischen Mündlichkeit, Bildlichkeit und Schriftlichkeit* [in press].

Mückshoff, Meinolf, 'Der Einfluss des hl. Bonaventura auf die deutsche Theologie mit besonderer Berücksichtigung der Theologie und Mystik des seligen Heinrich Seuses', in *S. Bonaventura 1274–1974*. *Volumen commemorativum anni septies centenarii a morte S. Bonaventurae doctoris seraphici cura et studio commissionis internationalis Bonaventurianae*, vol. 2, *Studia de vita, mente, fontibus et operibus sancti Bonaventurae* (Grottaferrata, 1973), 225–77.

Murray, Alexander, 'The Later Middle Ages', in Richard Harries and Henry Mayr-Harting (eds.), *Christianity: Two Thousand Years* (Oxford, 2001), 96–131.

Newman, Barbara, *God and the Goddesses. Vision, Poetry, and Belief in the Middle Ages* (Philadelphia, 2003).

Nuding, Matthias, *Matthäus von Krakau. Theologe, Politiker, Kirchenreformer in Krakau, Prag und Heidelberg zur Zeit des Großen Abendländischen Schismas*, Spätmittelalter und Reformation. Neue Reihe 38 (Tübingen, 2007).

Oberman, Heiko Augustinus, *The Harvest of Medieval Theology: Gabriel Biel and Late Medieval Nominalism* (Cambridge, Mass., 1963).

Oldenbourg, M. Consuelo, *Die Buchholzschnitte des Hans Baldung Grien. Ein bibliographisches Verzeichnis ihrer Verwendungen*, Studien zur deutschen Kunstgeschichte 335 (Baden-Baden and Strasbourg, 1962).

Oliger, Livarius, 'Johannes Kannemann, ein deutscher Franziskaner aus dem 15. Jahrhundert', *Franziskanische Studien* 5 (1918), 39–67.

——'Die deutsche Passion des Johannes von Zazenhausen O. F. M. Weihbischofs von Trier († c.1380)', *Franziskanische Studien* 15 (1928), 245–51.

Paciocco, Robert, 'Miracles and Canonised Sanctity in the "First Life of St Francis"', *Greyfriars Review* 5 (1991), 251–74.

Palmer, Nigel F., 'Latein, Volkssprache, Mischsprache. Zum Sprachproblem bei Marquard von Lindau, mit einem Handschriftenverzeichnis der 'Dekalogerklärung' und des 'Auszugs der Kinder Israel'', in James Hogg (ed.), *Spätmittelalterliche geistliche Literatur in der Nationalsprache*, vol. 1, Analecta Cartusiana 106/1 (Salzburg, 1983), 70–110.

——'Marquard von Lindau OFM', ^2VL, vol. 6 (1987), 81–126.

——*Bibelübersetzung und Heilsgeschichte. Studien zur Freiburger Perikopenhandschrift von 1462 und zu den deutschsprachigen Lektionaren des 15. Jahrhunderts. Mit einem Anhang: Deutschsprachige Handschriften, Inkunabeln und Frühdrucke aus Freiburger Bibliotheksbesitz bis ca. 1600*, Wolfgang Stammler Gastprofessur 9 (Berlin and New York, 2007).

Panzig, Erik Alexander, '*gelâzenheit* und *abegescheidenheit*—zur Verwurzelung beider Theoreme im theologischen Denken Meister Eckharts', in Andreas Speer and Lydia Wegener (eds.), *Meister Eckhart in Erfurt*, Miscellanea Mediaevalia 32 (Berlin and New York, 2005), 335–55.

Päpke, Max, *Das Marienleben des Schweizers Wernher. Mit Nachträgen zu Vögtlins Ausgabe der Vita Marie Rhythmica*, Palaestra 81 (Berlin, 1913).

Pelikan, Jaroslav, *The Christian Tradition. A History of the Development of Doctrine*, vol. 3. *The Growth of Medieval Theology (600–1300)* (Chicago and London, 1978).

Penn, Stephen, 'Wyclif and the Sacraments', in Ian Christopher Levy (ed.), *A Companion to John Wyclif: Late Medieval Theologian*, Brill's Companions to the Christian Tradition 4 (Leiden and Boston, 2006), 241–91.

Phillips, Heather, 'John Wyclif and the Religion of the People', in Jacqueline Brown and William P. Stoneman (eds.), *A Distinct Voice: Medieval Studies in Honor of Leonard E. Boyle, O. P.* (Notre Dame, Ill., 1997), 561–90.

Piltz, Anders, '*Nostram naturam sublimaverat.* Den liturgiska och teologiska bakgrunden till det birgittinska mariaofficiet', in Sven-Erik Brodd and Alf Härdelin (eds.), *Maria i Sverige under tusen år. Föredrag vid symposiet i Vadstena 6–10 oktober 1994* (Skellefteå, 1996), vol. 1, 255–87.

Poppi, Angelico, 'La passione di Gesù nelle opere di S. Bonaventura', in *Teologia e filosofia nel pensiero di S. Bonaventura. Contributi per una nuova interpretazione* (Brescia, 1974), 67–122.

Rapp, Francis, *Réformes et Réformation à Strasbourg. Église et société dans le diocèse de Strasbourg (1450–1525)*, Associations des publications près les universités de Strasbourg. Collection de l'Institut des hautes études alsaciennes 23 (Paris, [1975(?)]).

Bibliography 361

Rauch, Winthir, *Das Buch Gottes. Eine systematische Untersuchung des Buchbegriffes bei Bonaventura,* Münchener Theologische Studien. II. Systematische Abteilung 20 (Munich, 1961).

Reynaert, J., *Catalogus van de Middelnederlandse handschriften in de Bibliotheek van de Universiteit te Gent,* vol. 2/1. *De handschriften verworven na 1852 (deel 1)* (Gent, 1996).

Rode, Rosemarie, *Studien zu den mittelalterlichen Kind-Jesu-Visionen* (unpublished doctoral dissertation, University of Frankfurt am Main, 1957).

Roest, Bert, *A History of Franciscan Education (c.1210–1517),* Education and Society in the Middle Ages and Renaissance 11 (Leiden etc., 2000).

Roitner, Ingrid, «*Mater misericordiae*». *Das Marienbild des Hochmittelalters, dargestellt anhand der Marienpredigten Gottfrieds von Admont (1138–65) vor dem Hintergrund der religiösen Laien- und Frauenbewegung* (unpublished doctoral dissertation, University of Vienna, 2002).

Rossing, Anna Jane, *Studier i den heliga Birgittas spiritualitet* (Stockholm, 1986).

Roten, J., 'Richard von St. Laurentius', *Marienlexikon* 5 (St Ottilien, 1993), 486–8.

Rouse, Richard H., and Rouse, Mary A., *Preachers, Florilegia and Sermons: Studies on the Manipulus florum of Thomas of Ireland,* Studies and Texts 47 (Toronto, 1979).

Rubin, Miri, *Corpus Christi: The Eucharist in Late Medieval Culture* (Cambridge, 1991).

——'The Eucharist and the Construction of Medieval Identities', in David Aers (ed.), *Culture and History 1350–1600: Essays on English Communities, Identities and Writing* (Hemel Hempstead, 1992), 43–63.

Ruh, Kurt, 'Zur Theologie des mittelalterlichen Passionstraktats', *Theologische Zeitschrift* 6 (1950), 17–39.

——'Studien über Heinrich von St. Gallen und den «Extendit manum» - Passionstraktat', *Zeitschrift für schweizerische Kirchengeschichte* 47 (1953), 210–30 and 241–78.

——*Bonaventura deutsch. Ein Beitrag zur deutschen Franziskaner-Mystik und - Scholastik,* Bibliotheca Germanica 7 (Bern, 1956).

——Review of Annelies Julia Hofmann, *Der Eucharistie-Traktat Marquards von Lindau, Anzeiger für deutsches Altertum* 73 (1961), 13–24.

——and Wachinger, Burghart (eds.), *Die deutsche Literatur des Mittelalters. Verfasserlexikon,* founded by Wolfgang Stammler and continued by Karl Langosch, 13 vols. (Berlin and New York, [2]1977–2007).

——'Bernhardin von Siena', [2]*VL,* vol. 1 (1978), 789–93.

——'De Heimelike Passie ons Heeren Ihesu Christi', [2]*VL,* vol. 3 (1981), 642–4.

——'Hubertinus von Casale', [2]*VL,* vol. 4 (1983), 211–19.

——*Geschichte der abendländischen Mystik,* vol. 2. *Frauenmystik und Franziskanische Mystik der Frühzeit* (Munich, 1993).

——*Geschichte der abendländischen Mystik,* vol. 3. *Die Mystik des deutschen Predigerordens und ihre Grundlegung durch die Hochscholastik* (Munich, 1996).

Rüther, Andreas, *Bettelorden in Stadt und Land. Die Straßburger Mendikantenkonvente und das Elsaß im Spätmittelalter*, Berliner historische Studien 26. Ordensstudien 11 (Berlin, 1997).

Saak, Eric L., *High Way to Heaven: The Augustinian Platform between Reform and Reformation, 1292–1524*, Studies in Medieval and Reformation Thought 89 (Leiden etc., 2002).

Sahlin, Claire L., '"A Marvelous and Great Exultation of the Heart": Mystical Pregnancy and Marian Devotion in Bridget of Sweden's *Revelations*', in James Hogg (ed.), *Studies in St. Birgitta and the Brigittine Order*, vol. 1, Analecta Cartusiana 35: Spiritualität Heute und Gestern 19 (Salzburg, 1993), 108–28.

——'The Virgin Mary and Birgitta of Sweden's Prophetic Vocation' in Sven-Erik Brodd and Alf Härdelin (eds.), *Maria i Sverige under tusen år. Föredrag vid symposiet i Vadstena 6–10 oktober 1994* (Skellefteå, 1996), vol. 1, 227–54.

——*Birgitta of Sweden and the Voice of Prophecy*, Studies in Medieval Mysticism 3 (Woodbridge, 2001).

Satzinger, Georg, and Ziegeler, Hans-Joachim, 'Marienklagen und Pieta', in Walter Haug and Burghart Wachinger (eds.), *Die Passion Christi in Literatur und Kunst des Spätmittelalters*, Fortuna Vitrea 12 (Tübingen, 1993), 241–76.

Scheepsma, Wybren, *Deemoed en devotie. De koorvrouwen van Windesheim en hun geschriften* (Amsterdam, 1997).

Schiewer, Hans-Jochen, 'Auditionen und Visionen einer Begine. Die >Selige Schererin<, Johannes Mulberg und der Basler Beginenstreit. Mit einem Textabdruck', in Timothy R. Jackson et al. (eds.), *Die Vermittlung geistlicher Inhalte im deutschen Mittelalter. Internationales Symposium, Roscrea 1994* (Tübingen, 1996), 289–317.

Schilling, Heinz, 'Die Reformation—ein revolutionärer Umbruch oder Hauptetappe eines langfristigen reformierenden Wandels?', in Winfried Spietkamp and Hans-Peter Ullmann (eds.), *Konflikt und Reform. Festschrift für Helmut Berding* (Göttingen, 1995), 26–40.

——'Reformation—Umbruch oder Gipfelpunkt eines Temps des Réformes?', in Bernd Moeller, with Stephen E. Buckwalter (eds.), *Die frühe Reformation in Deutschland als Umbruch. Wissenschaftliches Symposion des Vereins für Reformationsgeschichte 1996*, Schriften des Vereins für Reformationsgeschichte 199 (Gütersloh, 1998), 13–34.

Schlager, Bernard, 'Foundresses of the Franciscan Life: Umiliana Cerchi and Margaret of Cortona', *Viator* 29 (1998), 141–66.

Schlosser, Marianne, *Cognitio et amor. Zum kognitiven und voluntativen Grund der Gotteserfahrung nach Bonaventura*, Veröffentlichungen des Grabmann-Institutes N. F. 35 (Paderborn etc., 1990).

Schmid, Josef, 'Kettenbücher mit besonderer Berücksichtigung der Kettenbücherei des Franziskanerklosters in der Au in Luzern', *Innerschweizerisches Jahrbuch für Heimatkunde* 1 (1936), 48–65.

Schmidt, Charles, *Histoire du chapitre de Saint-Thomas de Strasbourg pendant le moyen âge suivie d'un recueil de chartes* (Strasbourg, 1860).

Bibliography

Schmidt, Leopold, 'Das geheime Leiden Christi', *Volk und Volkstum* 3 (1938), 370–1.

Schmidtke, Dietrich, 'Pastoraltheologische Texte des Matthäus von Krakau', in Fritz Peter Knapp et al. (eds.), *Schriften im Umkreis mitteleuropäischer Universitäten um 1400. Lateinische und volkssprachige Texte aus Prag, Wien und Heidelberg: Unterschiede, Gemeinsamkeiten, Wechselbeziehungen*, Education and Society in the Middle Ages and Renaissance 20 (Leiden and Boston, 2004), 178–96.

Schmitt, Clément, 'Le Parti clémentiste dans la province franciscaine de Strasbourg: Notes et documents', *Archivum Franciscanum Historicum* 55 (1962), 82–102.

——'Documents sur la province franciscaine de Strasbourg aux XIV–XVᵉ siècles d'après un formulaire de Lucerne', *Archivum Franciscanum Historicum* 59 (1966), 209–300.

Schmolinsky, Sabine, 'Imaginationen vorbildlicher Weiblichkeit. Zur Konstitution einer exemplarischen Biographie in mittelalterlichen lateinischen und deutschen Marienleben', in Claudia Opitz et al. (eds.), *Maria in der Welt. Marienverehrung im Kontext der Sozialgeschichte 10.–18. Jahrhundert*, Clio Lucernensis 2 (Zürich, 1993), 81–93.

Schneider, Karin, *Die deutschen Handschriften der Bayerischen Staatsbibliothek München. Die mittelalterlichen Handschriften aus Cgm 888–4000* (Wiesbaden, 1991).

Schreiner, Klaus, 'Marienverehrung, Lesekultur, Schriftlichkeit. Bildungs- und frömmigkeitsgeschichtliche Studien zur Auslegung und Darstellung von "Mariä Verkündigung"', *Frühmittelalterliche Studien* 24 (1990), 314–68.

——'Konnte Maria lesen? Von der Magd des Herrn zur Symbolgestalt mittelalterlicher Frauenbildung', *Merkur. Deutsche Zeitschrift für europäisches Denken* 44 (1990), 82–8.

——'Laienfrömmigkeit—Frömmigkeit von Eliten oder Frömmigkeit des Volkes? Zur sozialen Verfaßtheit laikaler Frömmigkeitspraxis im späten Mittelalter', in Klaus Schreiner (ed.), with Elisabeth Müller-Luckner, *Laienfrömmigkeit im späten Mittelalter. Formen, Funktionen, politisch-soziale Zusammenhänge*, Schriften des Historischen Kollegs. Kolloquien 20 (Munich, 1992), 1–78.

——*Maria. Jungfrau, Mutter, Herrscherin* (Munich, ²1996).

Schuppisser, Fritz Oskar, 'Schauen mit den Augen des Herzens. Zur Methodik der spätmittelalterlichen Passionsmeditation, besonders in der Devotio Moderna und bei den Augustinern', in Walter Haug and Burghart Wachinger (eds.), *Die Passion Christi in Literatur und Kunst des Spätmittelalters*, Fortuna Vitrea 12 (Tübingen, 1993), 169–210.

Schweitzer, Franz Josef, 'Schwester Katrei', ²*VL*, vol. 8 (1992), 947–50.

Scott, Tom, and Scribner, Bob, 'Urban Networks', in Bob Scribner (ed.), *Germany: A New Social and Economic History*, vol. 1. *1450–1630* (London, 1996), 113–43.

Seegets, Petra, *Passionstheologie und Passionsfrömmigkeit im ausgehenden Mittelalter. Der Nürnberger Franziskaner Stephan Fridolin (gest. 1498) zwischen Kloster und Stadt*, Spätmittelalter und Reformation. Neue Reihe 10 (Tübingen, 1998).

Semler, Alfons, 'Die historischen Handschriften der Leopold-Sophien-Bibliothek in Überlingen', *Zeitschrift für die Geschichte des Oberrheins* 80 [N.F. 41] (1928), 117–31.

Shaffern, Robert W., 'The Medieval Theology of Indulgences', in R. N. Swanson (ed.), *Promissory Notes on the Treasury of Merits. Indulgences in Late Medieval Europe*, Brill's Companions to the Christian Tradition 5 (Leiden and Boston, 2006), 11–36.

Simoncioli, Feliciano, 'La mariologia del Card. Matteo d'Acquasparta, O. F. M.', *Divus Thomas* [Piacenza] 65 (1962), 321–52.

Snoek, Godefridus J. C., *Medieval Piety from Relics to the Eucharist: A Process of Mutual Interaction*, Studies in the History of Christian Thought 63 (Leiden etc., 1995).

Sprandel, Rolf, 'Der Sakramentskult des Spätmittelalters im Spiegel der zeitgenössischen Chronistik', in Joachim Kuolt, Harald Kleinschmidt, and Peter Dinzelbacher (eds.), *Das Mittelalter—Unsere fremde Vergangenheit. Beiträge der Stuttgarter Tagung vom 17. bis 19. September 1987*, Flugschriften der Volkshochschule Stuttgart N.F. 6 (Stuttgart, 1990), 299–314.

Staber, Josef, 'Die Bildhaftigkeit der spätmittelalterlichen Eucharistiepredigt', in A. W. Ziegler (ed.), *Eucharistische Frömmigkeit in Bayern. Zweite, ergänzte und vermehrte Auflage der "Festgabe des Vereins für Diözesangeschichte von München und Freising zum Münchener Eucharistischen Weltkongreß 1960"*, Beiträge zur altbayerischen Kirchengeschichte 23/2 (Munich, 1963), 109–22.

Stamm, Gerhard, 'Konrad von Sachsen (Holtnicker, Konrad)', [2]*VL*, vol. 5 (1985), 247–51.

Steer, Georg, *Scholastische Gnadenlehre in mittelhochdeutscher Sprache*, Münchener Texte und Untersuchungen 14 (Munich, 1966).

——'Der Armutsgedanke der deutschen Mystiker bei Marquard von Lindau', *Franziskanische Studien* 60 (1978), 289–300.

——*Hugo Ripelin von Straßburg. Zur Rezeptions- und Wirkungsgeschichte des >Compendium theologicae veritatis< im deutschen Spätmittelalter*, Texte und Textgeschichte 2 (Tübingen, 1981).

——'Die Stellung des >Laien< im Schrifttum des Straßburger Gottesfreundes Rulman Merswin und der deutschen Dominikanermystiker des 14. Jahrhunderts', in Ludger Grenzmann and Karl Stackmann (eds.), *Literatur und Laienbildung im Spätmittelalter und in der Reformationszeit. Symposion Wolfenbüttel 1981*, Germanistische Symposien Berichtsbände 5 (Stuttgart, 1984), 643–60.

——'Mönch von Heilsbronn OCist', [2]*VL*, vol. 6 (1987), 649–54.

Stettner, Thomas, 'Marquard von Lindau, ein deutscher Mystiker', in K[arl] Wolfart (ed.), *Geschichte der Stadt Lindau im Bodensee*, vol. 2 (Lindau, 1909), 41–51 and 233.

Stork, Hans-Walter, and Wachinger, Burghart, 'Speculum humanae salvationis', [2]*VL*, vols. 9 (1995), 52–65, and 11 (2004), 1442.

Störmer-Caysa, Uta, *Gewissen und Buch. Über den Weg eines Begriffes in die deutsche Literatur des Mittelalters*, Quellen und Forschungen zur Literatur- und Kulturgeschichte 14 (Berlin and New York, 1998).

Strack, Bonifatius, 'Das Leiden Christi im Denken des hl. Bonaventura', *Franziskanische Studien* 41 (1959), 129–62.

——*Christusleid im Christenleben. Ein Beitrag zur Theologie des christlichen Lebens nach dem heiligen Bonaventura*, Franziskanische Forschungen 13 (Werl, 1960).

Stracke, D. A., 'Een brokstuk uit de Passie des Heeren', *Ons Geestelijk Erf* 11 (1937), 121–90.

Sturlese, Loris, 'Über Marquard von Lindau und Meister Eckhart', in Albert Franz (ed.), *Glauben, Wissen, Handeln. Beiträge aus Theologie, Philosophie und Naturwissenschaft zu Grundfragen christlicher Existenz. Festschrift für Philipp Kaiser, Eichstätt, zum 65. Geburtstag* (Würzburg, 1994), 277–89.

Svanberg, Jan, 'De allra äldsta bilderna av den heliga Birgitta och hennes vision av Jesu födelse', Kungl. vitterhets historie och antikvitets akademiens årsbok (1997), 132–46.

Swanson, R. N., 'Passion and Practice: The Social and Ecclesiastical Implications of Passion Devotion in the Late Middle Ages,' in A. A. MacDonald, H. N. B. Ridderbos, and R. M. Schlusemann (eds.), *The Broken Body: Passion Devotion in Late-Medieval Culture*, Medievalia Groningana 21 (Groningen, 1998), 1–30.

Thomson, S. Harrison, *The Writings of Robert Grosseteste, Bishop of Lincoln 1235–1253* (Cambridge, 1940).

Tönsing, Michael, *Johannes Malkaw aus Preussen (ca. 1360–1416). Ein Kleriker im Spannungsfeld von Kanzel, Ketzerprozess und Kirchenspaltung*, Studien zu den Luxemburgern und ihrer Zeit 10 (Warendorf, 2004).

Torsy, Jakob, 'Eucharistische Frömmigkeit im späten Mittelalter', *Archiv für Mittelrheinische Kirchengeschichte* 23 (1971), 89–102.

Trottmann, Christian, 'La Vision béatifique dans la seconde école franciscaine: De Matthieu d'Aquasparta à Duns Scot', *Collectanea Franciscana* 64 (1994), 121–80.

Turck, Sandrine, *Les Dominicains à Strasbourg entre prêche, prière et mendicité (1224–1420)*, Publications de la société savante d'Alsace. Collection 'Recherches et documents' 68 (Strasbourg, 2002).

Ubbink, Rijkert Alex, *De receptie van Meister Eckhart in de Nederlanden gedurende de middeleeuwen* (Amsterdam, 1978).

Ubl, Karl, *Engelbert von Admont. Ein Gelehrter im Spannungsfeld von Aristotelismus und christlicher Überlieferung*, Mitteilungen des Instituts für Österreichische Geschichtsforschung. Ergänzungsband 37 (Vienna and Munich, 2000).

Ulrich, Peter, 'Zur Bedeutung des Leidens in der Konzeption der *philosophia spiritualis* Heinrich Seuses', in Rüdiger Blumrich and Philipp Kaiser (eds.), *Heinrich Seuses Philosophia spiritualis. Quellen, Konzept, Formen und Rezeption. Tagung Eichstätt 2.–4. Oktober 1991*, Wissensliteratur im Mittelalter 17 (Wiesbaden, 1994), 49–70.

——*Imitatio et configuratio. Die philosophia spiritualis Heinrich Seuses als Theologie der Nachfolge des Christus passus*, Eichstätter Studien N. F. 36 (Regensburg, 1995).

Vauchez, André, *The Laity in the Middle Ages. Religious Beliefs and Devotional Practices* (Notre Dame and London, 1993).

Völker, Paul-Gerhard, *Die deutschen Schriften des Franziskaners Konrad Bömlin. Teil I. Überlieferung und Untersuchung*, Münchener Texte und Untersuchungen 8 (Munich, 1964).

Weigel, Petra, *Ordensreform und Konziliarismus. Der Franziskanerprovinzial Matthias Döring (1427–1461)*, Jenaer Beiträge zur Geschichte 7 (Frankfurt a. M. etc., 2007).

Weiske, Brigitte, 'Bilder und Gebete vom Leben und Leiden Christi. Zu einem Zyklus im Gebetbuch des Johannes von Indersdorf für Frau Elisabeth Ebran,' in Walter Haug and Burghart Wachinger (eds.), *Die Passion Christi in Literatur und Kunst des Spätmittelalters*, Fortuna Vitrea 12 (Tübingen, 1993), 113–68.

Willing, Antje, *Literatur und Ordensreform im 15. Jahrhundert. Deutsche Abendmahlsschriften im Nürnberger Katharinenkloster*, Studien und Texte zum Mittelalter und zur frühen Neuzeit 4 (Münster etc., 2004).

Witte, Karl Heinz, *Der Meister des Lehrgesprächs und sein >In-principio-Dialog<. Ein deutschsprachiger Theologe der Augustinerschule des 14. Jahrhunderts aus dem Kreise deutscher Mystik und Scholastik. Untersuchung und Edition*, Münchener Texte und Untersuchungen 95 (Munich, 1989).

——'Der 'Traktat von der Minne', der Meister des Lehrgesprächs und Johannes Hiltalingen von Basel. Ein Beitrag zur Geschichte der Meister-Eckhart-Rezeption in der Augustinerschule des 14. Jahrhunderts', *Zeitschrift für deutsches Altertum* 131 (2002), 454–87.

——'Die Rezeption der Lehre Meister Eckharts durch Johannes Hiltalingen von Basel. Untersuchung und Textausgabe', *Recherches de théologie et philosophie médiévales* 71 (2004), 305–71.

Worstbrock, F. J., 'Matthäus von Krakau (Matheus de Cracovia)', ^2VL, vol. 6 (1987), 172–82.

Zahn, Theodor, *Ignatius von Antiochien* (Gotha, 1873).

Zika, Charles, 'Hosts, Processions, and Pilgrimages: Controlling the Sacred in Fifteenth-Century Germany', *Past and Present* 118 (1988), 25–64.

Zinn, Grover A., Jr., 'Book and Word. The Victorine Background of Bonaventure's Use of Symbols', in *S. Bonaventura 1274–1974. Volumen commemorativum anni septies centenarii a morte S. Bonaventurae doctoris seraphici cura et studio commissionis internationalis Bonaventurianae*, vol. 2. *Studia de vita, mente, fontibus et operibus sancti Bonaventurae* (Grottaferrata, 1973), 143–69.

Zoepfl, Friedrich, 'Das unbekannte Leiden Christi in der Frömmigkeit und Kunst des Volkes', *Volk und Volkstum* 2 (1937), 317–36.

Index